Enterprise Networks: Infrastructure & Security

Thomas Case

Georgia Southern University

Prospect Press

Founded in 2014, Prospect Press serves the academic discipline of Information Systems by publishing essential and innovative textbooks across the curriculum including introductory, emerging, and upper-level courses. Based in Burlington, Vermont, Prospect Press distributes titles worldwide. We welcome new authors to send proposals or inquiries to Beth.golub@prospectpressvt.com.

Editor: Beth Lang Golub
Associate Editor: Dave Williams
Production Management: Peter Holm, Sterling Hill Productions
Copyeditor: Carl Quesnel, Assurance Editorial
Cover Design and Illustrations: Annie Clark

eTextbook:
ISBN: 978-1-958303-09-2
Available from Redshelf, VitalSource, and Perusall

Printed Paperback:
ISBN: 978-1-958303-10-8
Available from Redshelf

For more information, visit https://www.prospectpressvt.com/textbooks/case-enterprise-networks

To my wife Carol for her patience and loving support throughout this project and to our grandchildren Audrey and Arlo who entered our lives while it was underway.

BRIEF CONTENTS

CONTENTS

Preface

Enterprise Networks: Infrastructure & Security provides a realistic description of today's business networks. It provides an overview of the networking and communication technologies that enable data transfers between endpoints and the security technologies that protect them. It enables students to develop a reasonably comprehensive understanding of the technologies included in today's business networks, how they are interrelated, how they work, and how they are evolving.

Enterprise networks support business applications. Cloud-based business applications are increasingly being used to support both employees in business facilities and those who work remotely. Hence, enterprise networks do more than interconnect business facilities, they extend to the cloud and employee homes.

Target Audience

This book is designed for undergraduate and graduate data communications and networking courses. Because enterprise networks are business-centric, the book is well suited for networking courses in business and information systems degree programs. However, it has sufficient breadth and depth for use in introductory networking courses in information technology and computer science curricula.

It assumes that most readers will have limited or no prior knowledge of networking and attempts to describe networking concepts from the ground up. Fundamental concepts are introduced in a simplified manner and are used as building blocks for understanding more complicated topics.

Balancing practical and technical orientations is a challenge for data communications and networking books, courses, and instructors. This book tries to strike a balance between both perspectives. It provides the business rationale for enterprise network technologies and describes them in technically accurate ways without excessive detail.

The book's content enables it to be used in a range of courses. For example:

- Its business focus makes it appropriate for one-semester data communications and networking undergraduate courses in business and information systems (IS) degree programs.
- Its focus on networking technologies, protocols, and security aligns with the goals of undergraduate networking courses in information technology (IT) or computer science (CS) curricula.
- Its relatively comprehensive coverage of enterprise networks enables it to be used in required graduate-level communication and networking courses in IS, IT, or CS programs (e.g., MSIS, MSIT, MSCS).
- Because security is addressed in every chapter, the book may also be used in introductory network security and information assurance courses.

The book is designed to be a resource that instructors can rely on to ensure coverage of networking topics that are challenging to fully address in limited classroom interactions with students. It is also designed to be a resource that provides a reasonably comprehensive depiction of enterprise network infrastructure and security that can be used to brush up on networking fundamentals after students have launched their professional careers.

Key Features of the Book

Business and Applications Focus

Enterprise networks exist to support business applications, especially mission-critical applications. Computing, networking, and security technologies in enterprise networks are configured to support, manage, optimize, and protect mission-critical applications such as enterprise systems.

Enterprise systems (ERP, CRM, SCM, etc.) are centerpieces of the computing architectures of many businesses and typically include interorganizational links with business partners. Enterprise systems receive special attention in several chapters, especially those that focus on business applications, network performance management, and application security. As priorities in business networks, they exemplify the centrality of business applications in enterprise networks.

Layered Descriptions

Layered models, including the OSI and TCP/IP models, are used to facilitate understanding of data transfers between network endpoints. They make complex end-to-end communications more digestible and understandable by focusing on communications between corresponding layers at endpoints.

The upper layers of the OSI and TCP/IP models promote understanding of how applications are supported in networks and how the Internet works. They are featured in the book's opening chapters. The lower layers of these models facilitate understanding of communications in local networks and are featured across the book's middle chapters.

Other layered models are used in the book's closing chapters to promote understanding of the deployments of networking equipment and security defenses. Mapping networking and security technologies to the layers of these models enriches understanding of the functions the technologies perform.

Contextualized Discussions

Students can be overwhelmed by the volume of concepts and the level of detail in networking textbooks. This can make it challenging to correctly associate related concepts and to "connect the dots." To promote better appreciation of how and where concepts come together, this book separates some of the concepts that have been traditionally bundled in networking textbooks to provide a clearer understanding of contexts in which they intersect.

For example, whereas other textbooks often lump digital symbol/signal generation in one chapter and local area networks in another, this book considers the symbols/signals and technologies used in wired LANs in one chapter and the symbols/signals used in wireless LANs in a separate chapter. This helps students better associate digital symbols/signals and line encoding schemes used on physical cables and switches with wired LANs while also helping them appreciate that analog symbols/signals from modulation schemes are most closely associated with wireless LANs and technologies such as access points. Considering communications in wired and wireless LANs in separate chapters also promotes better understanding of their associated media access protocols, security requirements, and evolving standards.

Contextualized discussion of security technologies is also provided. Security technologies are introduced across chapters to help students understand where they are commonly used. They are described in greater detail within the context of layered security defenses in the final two chapters of the book.

The Cloud

When "enterprise network infrastructure" is used as a search term, the results reveal that the cloud is an important enterprise network domain. Cloud applications and infrastructure are widely used by businesses to enable communications among devices, users, and applications regardless of their location; these are important parts of today's business networks that challenge/blur traditional perspectives about network boundaries. Because it is untenable to argue that the cloud is external to business computing landscapes, the Internet and the cloud are considered essential enterprise network components, and cloud apps, services, storage, infrastructure, and security are discussed in context across chapters. Surging IoT deployments across industries reflect how enterprise networks and the cloud are increasingly intertwined and are a primary reason why this book includes a chapter on the IoT.

Transformative Technologies

Traditional networking and security technologies continue to evolve, but the digital transformation of business and the changing landscape of enterprise networks is most closely tied to technologies that are transforming how business applications are supported, managed, and secured. 5G radio access networks (RANs) are becoming more common in business facilities and the connection preferences for IoT deployments. Software-defined networking (SDN) is reshaping how business application performance is optimized and managed. And secure access service edge (SASE) and zero trust architectures provide frameworks for protecting enterprise network users, devices, applications, and services regardless of their location. These and other transformative technologies, including AI, are featured in the book to provide a clearer picture of future enterprise networks.

Security

Security is an important topic for all enterprise network domains and components. It is too important to be relegated to a catch-all chapter or two as in traditional networking textbooks. To promote better understanding of why, where, and how security technologies are deployed, each chapter includes one or more sections that pinpoint topically relevant security issues, remedies, and technologies. These contextualized introductions provide the foundation for more detailed descriptions of security architectures and infrastructure in the book's concluding chapters.

Chapter Elements

The beginning of each chapter includes:

- *Learning Objectives*: A list of the student learning objectives for the chapter
- An *Introduction*: An introductory section that connects the chapter's contents to an overall understanding of enterprise networks and sets the stage for what students will encounter

Sections and their major subsections are numbered to enable quick links for e-book users. Definitional descriptions of key terms/concepts are highlighted in boldface. Italics are used to identify other important concepts.

The end of each chapter includes:

- A *Summary*: A recap of the chapter's major topics and concepts
- *Key Terms*: A summary of the key concepts described across the chapter's various sections
- *Review Questions*: Approximately 30 questions to assist students in zeroing in on the most important topics and concepts in each chapter

- *Problems and Exercises*: Five or more items designed to promote additional understanding and exposure to chapter-relevant topics
    - Most are *scenario-based* to promote practical understanding of chapter concepts.
    - *Hands-on* exercises are included in most chapters. These include Wireshark activities, Wi-Fi router configuration exercises, network diagram creation, data transfer calculations, and the application of network administration protocols and tools.
- *Chapter References*: A summary of the major sources consulted to construct the chapter

The following are also included:

- *Chapter Minicase*: Each chapter includes a minicase that focuses on one or more especially important chapter-relevant topics. These cases provide an opportunity to dive more deeply into the practical application of topics addressed in the chapters.
- *Chapter Appendices*: Except for the first and last chapters, each chapter includes multiple appendices. Some appendices are included to provide a stronger business focus for specific topics. Others provide more comprehensive or in-depth technical descriptions of specific networking or security technologies. Appendices are included with the e-book version; those who have the print version of the book can access them online.

Overview of Chapters

The book is divided into three major sections:

1. Enterprise network overview
2. Enterprise network components
3. Enterprise network design, management, and security

The first section includes four chapters that provide an overview of enterprise networks, the business applications that are supported, the types of data that they transfer and store, and endpoint-to-endpoint communications. Students learn that enterprise networks are business-centric, have multiple components, and are continually evolving. They learn that a wide range of applications, including enterprise systems and other mission-critical applications, with various client-server deployments are supported. They also learn that enterprise network applications process, generate, store, and transfer a wide range of data, as well as how the various types of data are digitized. In the fourth chapter, end-to-end communications between enterprise network endpoints is explained by identifying the major communication functions performed by corresponding OSI and TCP/IP layers in senders and receivers.

The second section of the book focuses on the various types of networks that enterprise networks interconnect: the Internet LANs, WANs, and IoT networks. Widespread business use of cloud services and infrastructure and VPNs makes it impossible to separate enterprise networks and the Internet. Internet architecture and services and the major protocols used at the upper layers of the OSI and TCP/IP communication models are described in the first chapter in this part.

The second and third chapters in the second section consider how the lower layers of the OSI and TCP/IP models are deployed in wired and wireless networks in business facilities. Ethernet is featured in the wired network chapter, and backbone networks are described. Wi-Fi is the dominant topic in the wireless networks chapter, but cellular RANs in business facilities are also introduced.

Business WANs are the focus of the fourth chapter in this section. Dedicated circuit connections are described, but more attention is focused on packet switching services for business location interconnections, including MPLS, Carrier Ethernet, VPNs, and software-defined WANs. The final chapter in this section focuses on IoT deployments in businesses, especially Industrial

IoT applications. The IoT is an important part of the digital transformation of businesses, and IoT architectures, platforms, protocols, and security technologies are reshaping enterprise networks.

The third section considers enterprise network design, management, and security. Business and technical design goals and tradeoffs are considered in the first chapter in this section, along with network management architectures, systems, and protocols. The second chapter in this section provides an overview of network vulnerabilities, common attacks, and security goals. It also discusses network security plans, policies, procedures, and architectures, including zero trust architecture. This chapter also considers physical, cloud, perimeter, and internal network defenses. The final chapter in this section, and the book, focuses on protecting network endpoints, applications, and data.

Instructor and Student Resources

Instructor Resources include:

- PowerPoint slides for each chapter
- An image library with images of all figures and tables in the chapter
- A test bank
- Recommended grading rubrics for problems, exercises, and minicases
- Additional problems and exercises for each chapter
- An Instructor's Guide with answers to review questions

To access the Instructor Resources: https://www.prospectpressvt.com/textbooks/case-enterprise-networks

Student Resources include:

- Key concepts overview PowerPoint presentation
- Chapter learning tips: Tips for mastering chapter concepts
- Problems and exercises tips: Tips for succeeding on assigned problems and exercises
- Links to supplemental videos and readings on chapter-relevant topics

To access the Student Resources: https://www.prospectpressvt.com/textbooks/case-enterprise-networks

Acknowledgments

Many colleagues and former students have contributed to the shape and content of the networking courses I have taught, and ultimately the context of this book. I am especially grateful to the coauthors of my previous networking textbooks, especially William Stallings and David Stamper, for demonstrating the importance of coupling technical accuracy with a clear writing style in data communications and networking books. The authors of textbooks that I have used in my courses across the years have also been influential in determining what a good networking book should include and effective ways to approach particular topics.

I also want to thank the many friends and colleagues who have shared student exercises, course materials, and instructional advice over the past four decades. Your generosity and determination to help students master networking concepts has been beneficial to both my students and me. I am especially thankful for my professional friendship with Art Gowan and for the support and encouragement of John Overton and Wade Berzett in crafting workable network design learning modules for U.S. Army Signal Corp Officers. They have helped me appreciate the importance of practical relevance and realism in networking courses.

Numerous former students have contributed to this book by challenging my understanding and presentation of networking concepts and inspiring me to continually search for better ways to introduce and explain them. Scott Burns, Joey Reeves, Mark Pierce, Jason Williams, and others with genuine concerns about how to best engage students with networking concepts have been especially influential in ensuring that my courses and this book include practical realism.

The teams at Prospect Press, Assurance Editorial, and Sterling Hill Productions have made immeasurable contributions to the development and refinement of this book. I am especially thankful to Carl Quesnel for his remarkable work and attention to detail as copyeditor, and to Annie Clark for the countless hours she devoted to creating and tweaking the book's figures. I would also like to acknowledge Beth Golub for her advice, support, and guidance in the development of this book.

Last, but certainly not least, I would like to thank my wife, Carol, for her patience and loving support throughout the development of this book.

Finally, I would like to thank the following reviewers for their valuable feedback on the manuscript:

Tosan Atele-Williams, Ontario Tech University
Dr. Dmytro Babik, James Madison University
Robert Boardman, Professor, Durham College of Applied Arts & Technology
Rohit Dua, PhD, Missouri University of Science & Technology
Mostafa El-Said, Grand Valley State University
Dr. Biswadip Ghosh, Metropolitan State University of Denver
C. Matt Graham, PhD, University of Maine—Maine Business School
Ricky Green, University of South Alabama
Jun He, PhD, Associate Professor of ISM at University of Michigan-Dearborn
Ahmed Ezzeldin Khaled, Northeastern Illinois University
Jelena Mirkovic, USC Information Sciences Institute
Mark Monnin, University of Southern Maine, Department of Technology
René Moquin, PhD, Northeastern State University
Wilfred Mutale, Duquesne University, School of Business, Information Systems, and Technology
Dr. Uchenna Peters, New Mexico State University
Al Pilcher, Algonquin College
Abdelmounaam Rezgui, Illinois State University
Dr. Andrew Schwarz, Louisiana State University
Dr. Lou Thompson, University of Texas at Dallas
Shouhong Wang, University of Massachusetts Dartmouth
Dr. Harris Wu, Old Dominion University
Jiao (Aimee) Wu, Northern Illinois University
Yanwei Wu, UW-Platteville

About the Author

Thomas (Tom) Case is an Emeritus Professor of Information Systems at Georgia Southern University's Parker College of Business who has taught data communications and networking courses for more than three decades and is very familiar with the challenges that these courses present to both students and instructors. He is coauthor of three previous networking textbooks, and this book is his first as a solo author. He is also coauthor of two MIS textbooks.

Tom is a charter member of the Association of Information Systems and was one of the founders of the Southern Association of Information Systems. Across his career, Tom has served in numerous leadership roles in professional organizations and on the editorial boards of respected journals. He also served as the chair of his academic department at Georgia Southern and is a recipient of the university's Excellence in Contributions to Instruction and Excellence in Service awards.

In addition to writing textbooks, Tom continues to be active in scholarly pursuits, including journal publications, reviewing, part-time instruction, and service on advisory boards.

Chapter 1

Enterprise Networks: An Introduction

LEARNING OBJECTIVES

After reading and studying this chapter, you should be able to:

- Describe the characteristics of enterprise networks.
- Explain why layered frameworks are valuable in understanding enterprise networks.
- Identify and briefly describe each of the components of enterprise architecture (EA).
- Briefly describe the differences among LANs, BNs, WANs, and cloud infrastructure.
- Explain how EA contributes to understanding enterprise networks.
- Identify and briefly describe how businesses leverage enterprise networks.
- Briefly describe the differences among e-commerce, e-business, and digital business.
- Explain the importance of standards in communication networks.
- Identify and briefly describe several technologies that are shaping the evolution of enterprise networks.

1.0 INTRODUCTION

Computer networking was one of the most important technological breakthroughs of the twentieth century. Long before the Internet, scientists and engineers worked to enable computers to connect and communicate. Their work laid the foundation for the networks that we use today.

The history of modern computer networking technology is usually traced back to 1969, when ARPANET (Advanced Research Projects Agency Network) connected computers at UCLA and Stanford, soon thereafter expanding the network to include computers at UCSB and the University of Utah. The first data transmission between UCLA and Stanford is often considered the birth of the Internet.

The development of ARPANET began earlier in the 1960s under the auspices of the U.S. Department of Defense's Advanced Research Projects Agency (ARPA). The goal of ARPANET was to build a resilient network capable of keeping lines of communication open in the event of a nuclear exchange between the United States and the Soviet Union.

ARPANET revolutionized communications by using packet switching instead of direct connections. In packet switching, data is formatted into packets, and each packet includes the address of its intended destination. After packets are created, they are transmitted over communication circuits in the network. Packaging data in this manner enables the packets to reach their intended destination even when no direct connection exists between the sender and receiver.

ARPANET relied on phone lines for connecting its early sites. These were also used in early business networks, including the SABRE (semi-automatic business research environment) network that IBM developed for American Airlines to support the first electronic airline reservation

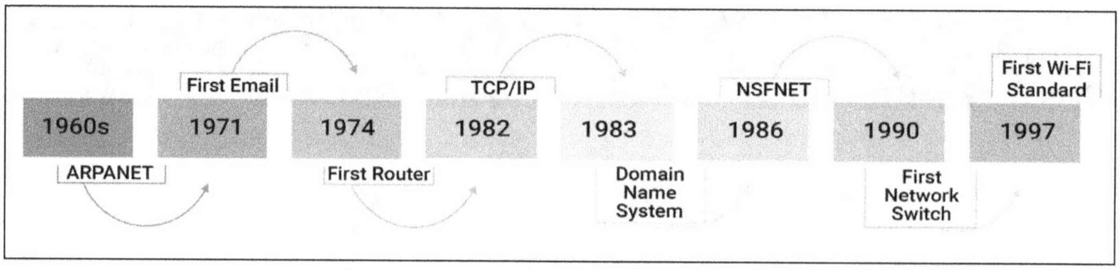

Figure 1-1: Some of the notable milestones in the evolution of computer networks in the twentieth century.

system. That reservation system is considered to be the first strategic use of information and communication technology (ICT). The 1960s also saw the deployment of the first electronic data interchange (EDI) systems. These systems used telephone lines to enable the computer systems in two businesses to exchange documents such as purchase orders and invoices. While a lot has changed between the launch of ARPANET and now, the basic ideas that enabled communication among ARPANET's computers are still with us today.

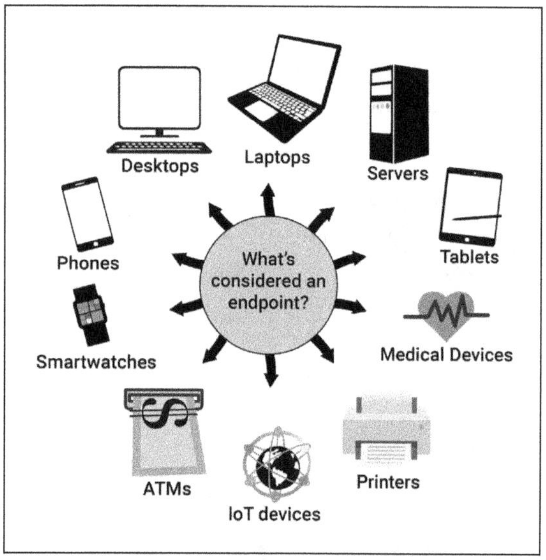

Figure 1-2: Network endpoint examples.

Since the advent of these systems, an increasingly diverse range of user devices and networking technologies has been added to business networks, as shown in Figure 1-1. By 2022, the number of new Internet users worldwide was increasing at an annual rate of nearly 4%. This translates to the addition of about half a million new users each day and about 180 million new users each year. Citizens in developed nations take the Internet for granted, but in 2022, more than one-third of the world's population did not use the Internet.

The number of devices connected to the Internet is also increasing. Industry experts contend that nearly 30 billion devices will be connected to the Internet by the start of 2024. Today, Internet of Things (IoT) devices and mobile devices (e.g., smartphones and wearables) account for most of the growth. In 2022, more than 125 new IoT devices were added to the Internet every second.

Today, it is useful to differentiate between the technologies used to connect to networks, called network endpoints, and technologies used to relay messages, data, and information between network-attached devices. IoT devices and mobile devices are considered endpoints. Other examples of network endpoints are included in Figure 1-2.

Examples of equipment used to move data among endpoints connected to networks are illustrated in Figure 1-3. Networking equipment includes Wi-Fi access points, switches, and routers. Network adapters that enable endpoints to connect to local networks and modems are other examples of networking equipment. As you make your way through the chapters in this book, you will gain a broader understanding of networking equipment and endpoints.

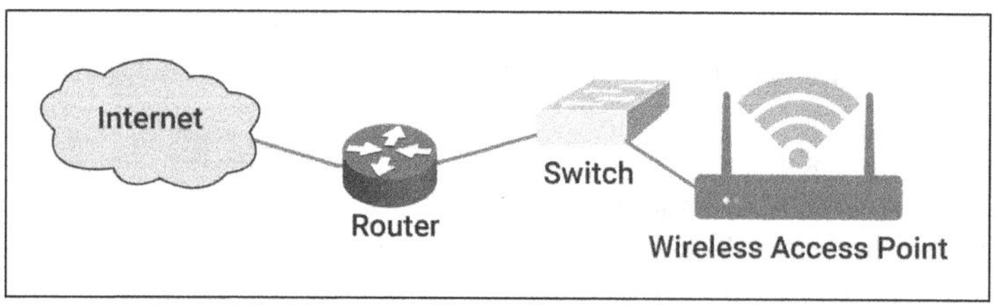

Figure 1-3: Examples of networking equipment.

Network endpoints connect to network equipment by physical or wireless communication media. Ethernet and fiber optic cables are examples of physical media. Wi-Fi, cellular, and satellite Internet connections are examples of wireless media. Communication media and networking equipment collectively constitute much of today's network infrastructure.

Security technologies are also important parts of networks, especially business networks. Firewalls are examples of security technologies and are deployed as software in routers and other networking equipment or included in specialized devices. They play a significant role in how networks function.

In this book, networks are discussed against the backdrop of business. However, the topics and concepts described also apply to networks in other types of organizations. It is possible to tune out the business examples and allusions and still gain a solid understanding of how networks are deployed and function.

Businesses deploy computer networks to support processes that enable them to achieve their objectives. They are usually purposeful in choosing and investing in network technologies that support their everyday operations. They do not add new things to their networks just because they are new and shiny; they add them because it makes business sense to do so.

This book covers a lot of ground. Much of what is discussed is likely to be new territory for many readers, but all of it is important for appreciating the reality of today's business networks. Business networks are ever-evolving entities with many moving parts. Important and exciting changes are continually in the offing, and this book provides glimpses of what lies ahead. The trek begins with a high-level depiction of enterprise networks.

1.1 WHAT ARE ENTERPRISE NETWORKS?

An **enterprise network** is the hardware and software infrastructure that connects a business's computers, servers, and other devices. It is sometimes called a *corporate network* because it serves as the foundation and chief support of communications in a business. For some, the term *enterprise network* is reserved for the computer networks of larger businesses. However, it is not always clear how big an organization needs to be or how many different locations it needs to connect before it is considered to have an enterprise network.

1.1.1 Enterprise Networks Are Business-Centric

If a *network* is a group of connected computers, an enterprise network can be considered a group of connected computers that serves the needs of a business. Because computer networks are interwoven with almost all business activities, an enterprise network is often the organization's communications backbone.

A key purpose of an enterprise network is to integrate an organization's users, business units, and workgroups. Ideally, an enterprise network enables all systems used by a business to communicate with, provide data and information to, and retrieve data and information from one another. The applications that enterprise networks support should be available, be secure, and have adequate and reliable performance levels.

Holistically, an enterprise network should facilitate organization-wide communications and system integration. System integration is often achieved by combining and using a wide range of applications, devices, and communication protocols.

It is sometimes useful to think of an enterprise network as a focused internet, or private intranet, that helps an organization's employees and machines communicate, share data and information, access applications, and drive business operations. Typically, an enterprise network is configured to provide secure and efficient communication channels among a limited number of individuals, applications, and systems. It is not a general-purpose network like the public Internet.

An enterprise network and its components are architected, designed, implemented, configured, and optimized to perform specific business and technical tasks. It is woven into the fabric of what the business is and what it does and should be evaluated within the context of the business it supports.

1.1.2 Enterprise Networks Have Multiple Components

An enterprise network often includes both local and wide area networks (LANs and WANs). Backbone networks (BNs) often interconnect LANs in different buildings on a campus, and the local networks at different locations are interconnected by WANs.

Employees use a wide range of devices with different operating systems to connect to enterprise networks, and the servers that support business applications run a variety of additional operating systems. Multiple communication and routing protocols are typically involved in transferring data among the network's diverse array of devices.

So, an enterprise network has many parts/facets:

- Endpoints (servers, mobile devices, desktop computers, printers, IoT devices, etc.)
- Network devices (routers, switches, access points, etc.)
- Local area networks
- Backbone networks
- Wide area networks
- Data centers (on premises and/or cloud based)
- Cloud infrastructure and services
- Security technologies (firewalls, etc.)
- Business applications
- Communication protocols

Cloud data centers and infrastructure are included in the list because, today, an organization's IT environment often includes a combination of on-premises and off-site computing and networking infrastructure. Business data and applications may be hosted in private or public cloud data centers accessed via secure communication channels over the public Internet. Here, the cloud is an extension of a business's on-premises network infrastructure. This arrangement is illustrated in Figure 1-4.

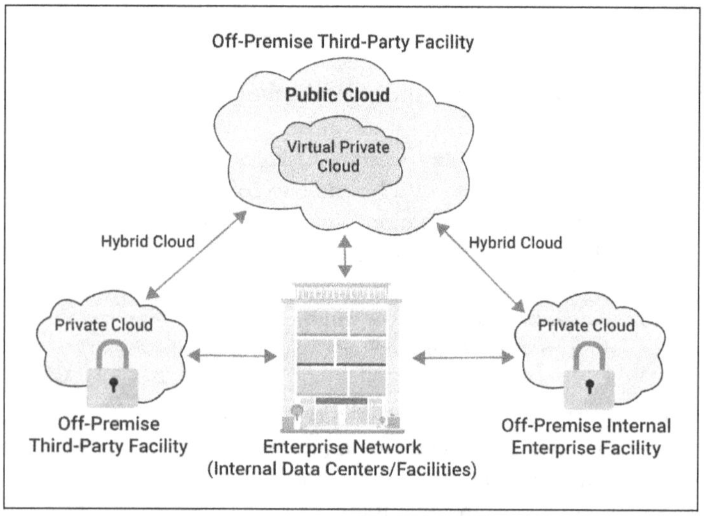

Figure 1-4: Cloud services, both private and public, are common in today's enterprise networks.

There continues to be a tendency to view enterprise networks as private networks whose resources are available only to authorized users. However, increasing reliance on cloud services and infrastructure, especially public cloud services, is challenging traditional notions of enterprise network boundaries.

Also, since the COVID-19 pandemic, large numbers of enterprise network users work remotely some or all of the time. Many businesses give employees the option of working from home one or more days each week, and most remote workers use VPN (virtual private network) tunnels through the public Internet to connect to the corporate network. When employees exercise their work-at-home options, the enterprise network extends to the networks in employees' homes.

In addition to connecting to cloud providers and residential networks, enterprise networks also include connections to branch offices. Many also include connections to business partners (see Figure 1-5). A sense of privacy remains in how enterprise networks are viewed, but today, much of the privacy comes from secure communications among the network's numerous components.

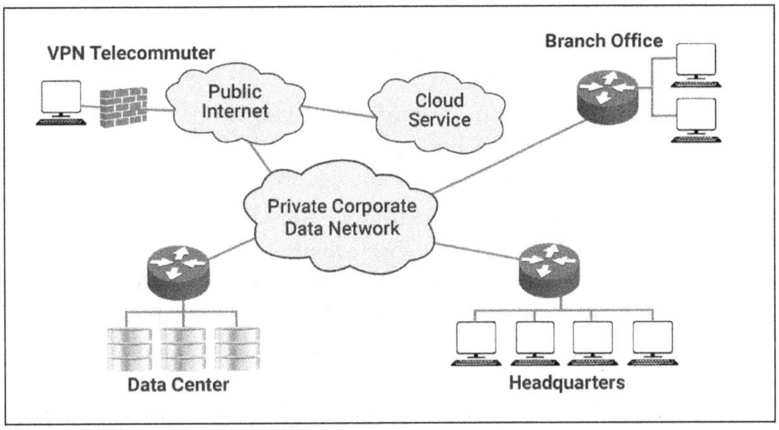

Figure 1-5: High-level depiction of enterprise network architecture.

Private clouds (e.g., data centers that are dedicated to the exclusive use of a single business) are attractive to businesses that value the privacy traditionally provided by their enterprise networks. However, today, businesses routinely subscribe to public cloud services owned and operated by third-party companies, and when they do, they are sharing the provider's facilities and infrastructure with other subscribers. Some public cloud services provide virtual public cloud services that are like private cloud services but are housed in shared rather than dedicated data center facilities.

These and other enterprise network components will be described more fully in subsequent chapters. For now, it is important for you to get a sense that there are many different pieces and more are likely to be added. The exact makeup of an enterprise network is a function of the business processes and operations that the organization needs to support. A business typically has options for deploying, integrating, and securing the components of its enterprise network, and the deployment decisions that it makes are driven by its business needs.

It can be challenging to make sense of how all the pieces hang together and work. It can be tempting to try to look at the components separately (for example, by focusing on LANs, WANs, cloud infrastructure, and security technologies) as distinct rather than intertwined entities. It may also be tempting to look outside of the context of the organizations in which the different components are deployed. Losing sight of the contextual factors responsible for the collection of components in an enterprise network can make it harder to understand how/why they are there and how they interact, so this book strives to maintain a bigger picture perspective.

Numerous networking textbooks include technically accurate descriptions of enterprise network components and how they work. These are useful from a technical perspective. However, businesses rarely invest in technology for technology's sake, and most IT and networking investment decisions are driven by business considerations. Ignoring this is ignoring why some technologies are attractive to businesses and others struggle to gain traction.

Business investment in cloud infrastructure is a good example. While an organization could persist in expanding on-premises data storage and processing infrastructure, today it is more likely to subscribe to cloud services for additional storage and processing capabilities. Such services are usually less expensive than the costs associated with in-house expansion and often provide on-demand scalability. Easier scaling at less cost can be a compelling business rationale for choosing the cloud over on-premises data storage when more storage or processing capability is needed.

1.1.3 Enterprise Networks Are Continually Evolving

In addition to being business-centric and made up of many parts, enterprise networks continue to evolve. As they evolve:

- Their resources and services are becoming more distributed.
- The number of services and resources located outside traditional network boundaries is growing.
- The number of remote users they support is increasing.
- An increasing number and variety of IoT systems are being incorporated.
- Security technologies are adapting to increasing security threats.

Enterprise networks are not static entities, and it is folly to think otherwise.

Enterprise network evolution manifests in various ways, such as new generations of network components being added to enterprise networks. For example, Wi-Fi 7 technologies are beginning to supplant Wi-Fi 6 technologies in some business networks, and Cat 8 Ethernet cabling is often recommended for new business and data center facilities because of its ability to provide better transmission speeds and performance than Cat 6 or 7 cabling. Operating systems (e.g., Windows 11 vs. Windows 10), processors (e.g., i7 vs. i5), and cellular services (e.g., 5G vs. 4G) also are generational.

The communication and security protocols also evolve in response to standard revisions, with the publication and formal adoption of the revisions serving as the next generation of the protocols. Typically, upgrading to the newest generation of its various components enables superior enterprise network performance or capabilities. Hence, there is an incentive to continually evolve.

In this book, descriptions of enterprise network components tend to focus on their newer generations. Doing this facilitates appreciation of how the different technologies are evolving and what is likely to come next. Section 1.6 introduces some of the technologies that are significantly affecting the current trajectories of enterprise networks.

1.2 LAYERED MODELS FACILITATE UNDERSTANDING

In the following chapters, you will be exposed to multiple layered communication and networking models. Collectively, these models make it easier to understand how communication takes place in an enterprise network, how its networking equipment is deployed, and how it is secured.

Layered models also contribute to this book's organization. For example, enterprise architecture (EA), introduced in section 1.3, is why enterprise network applications (Chapter 2) and data (Chapter 3) are discussed before the book's attention turns toward network infrastructure in Chapters 4 through 9.

The layered TCP/IP model accounts for the sequence of topics in Chapters 5 through 8. And the layered defense in depth (DiD) model is used to organize Chapters 11 and 12. Layered models are also used to promote understanding of the IoT in Chapter 9 and network design and management in Chapter 10.

This section provides a very brief introduction to some of the more important layered models and how they facilitate understanding of enterprise networks.

1.2.1 Layered Communication Models

Figure 1-6 identifies the layers of the Open Systems Interconnection (OSI) and Transmission Control Protocol/Internet Protocol (TCP/IP) models. Both models describe how communication between two networked devices can be broken down into a layered set of smaller and more understandable functions.

In both models, the layers provide modularity, and there is independence between layers. Also, the layers are numbered from the bottom up (as in Figure 1-7). For any given layer, communication services can be provided without having to know how the services provided at the layers beneath or above are implemented. Each layer can pass its work down (or up) to the next layer, and anything done at that layer will not affect the work done at the layer beneath or above. Each layer can provide communication services without having to reveal the details of how the services are implemented to other layers.

Protocols enable a sender to let a receiver know what it should do with received data at each layer of the model. Protocols enable communication between the corresponding layers of senders and receivers (see Figure 1-7). They define the communication rules used at each layer, rules that primarily concern the contents and order of the packets that are exchanged. Packet senders add a header at each layer that identifies how packet receivers should handle the packet at that level. When the receiver reads the header information, it knows what it should do with the data.

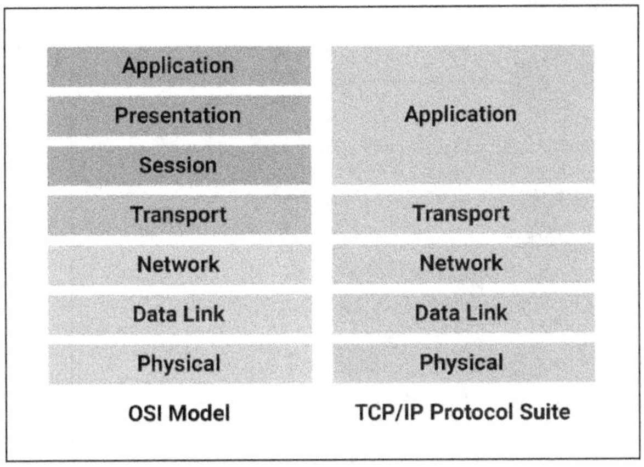

Figure 1-6: Layers in the OSI and TCP/IP models.

Some of the protocols associated with specific layers are well known. For example, Internet Protocol (IP) is used at the Network layer (Layer 3) of both the OSI and TCP/IP models.

With layered communications, data is *not* directly transferred from a layer on one device to the corresponding layer on the other device. Instead, each layer sends the packet and its data to the layer immediately below it until the lowest layer is reached. The physical communication medium that the network uses is located at the lowest layer in the model (Layer 1).

Dividing network communication functions into layers helps to reduce the overall complexity of the process to make it more manageable and understandable. Layered communication models also make it easier for hardware and software designers to concentrate on the functions that need to be performed at a given layer without having to worry about what must happen at other layers.

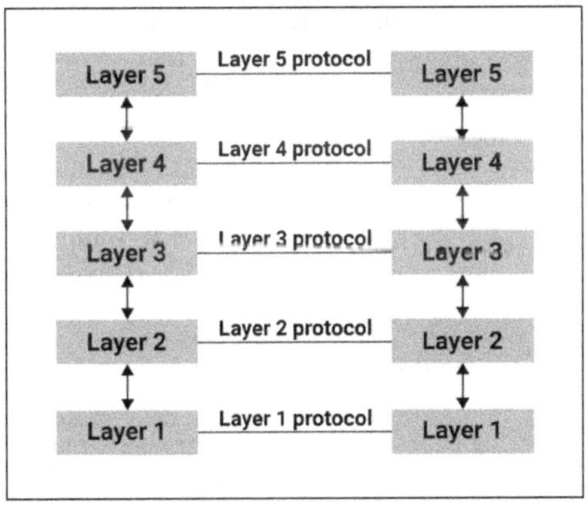

Figure 1-7: Protocols enable packet handling communications between corresponding layers of senders and receivers.

Networking technologies, both hardware and software, are mapped to specific layers of the TCP/IP and OSI models. Routers, for example, are identified as Network layer (Layer 3) devices in both models. When router manufacturers can concentrate only on Network layer functions that routers perform, they are positioned to manufacture good routers to sell at competitive prices.

The independence of layers is also beneficial. When better ways to perform the functions at a layer are identified, they can replace the existing status quo without affecting other layers. For example, protocols can be revised at one layer without requiring revisions to the protocols used at other layers.

The layers of OSI and TCP/IP models are described more fully in Chapter 4. Protocols at the different layers of the TCP/IP model are identified and described in Chapters 5, 6, and 7.

1.2.2 Layered Network Design and Equipment Deployment

Another layered model that you will encounter in Chapters 6 and 10 is the *three-layer hierarchical model*. First championed by Cisco, this model is widely considered a network design and equipment deployment best practice.

In this model, user devices, servers, printers, and other endpoints connect to Access layer

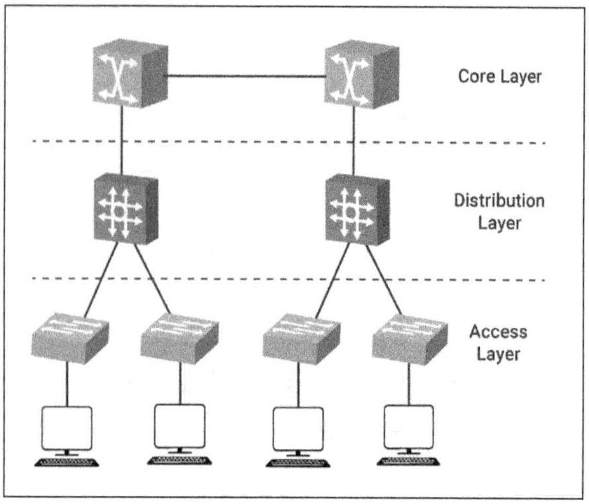

Figure 1-8: The three-layer hierarchical model.

technologies (see Figure 1-8), such as Ethernet switches and Wi-Fi access points. Rather than connecting directly to one another, Access layer networks interconnect at the Distribution layer via routers or Layer 3 switches. Distribution layer networking equipment interconnects via Core layer technologies, which are usually very high performance routers and switches. High-bandwidth (and high-speed) communication media, such as fiber optic cabling, is used to interconnect Core layer technologies but is also widely used to interconnect Distribution and Access layer networking equipment.

This deployment of networking technologies provides a separation of duties among the layers as well as a modular blueprint for network expansion and scalability. It outlines how a network can expand to accommodate more users, devices, or networks and how/where increased transfer speeds and bandwidth can be realized. Hence, this model helps businesses visualize how their networking equipment can be optimally deployed and where existing infrastructure can be upgraded to improve overall network performance.

This model also facilitates appreciation of how/where redundant devices or connections might be added to increase network resilience or availability. For example, in Figure 1-8, each Access layer switch might have a second link to another Distribution layer device in case the one it is currently linked to fails or is taken offline for maintenance. The model is also valuable for visualizing security technology deployments.

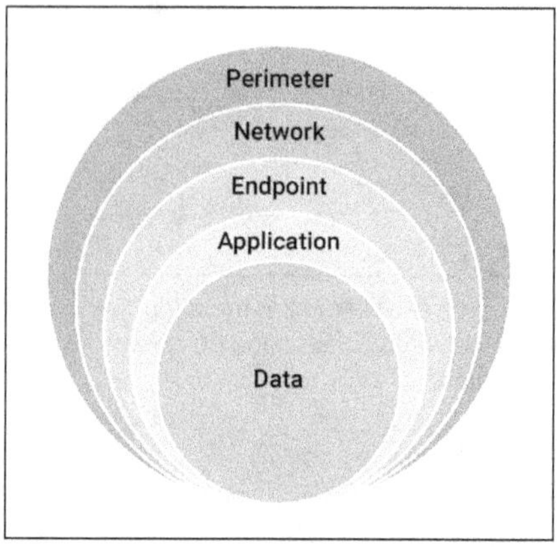

Figure 1-9: A traditional depiction of layered security and defense in depth (DiD).

1.2.3 Layered Security Defenses

Layered security models, such as defense in depth (DiD), illustrated in Figure 1-9, are also useful. Systematic layering of network defenses can improve the overall security of a network. Data is located at the innermost layer of DiD because it is the ultimate target of most network attacks. It makes sense to force attackers to thwart defenses at other DiD layers before they can get to an enterprise network's sensitive/valuable data.

The DiD model is used to structure the discussion of security defenses in Chapters 11 and 12. It serves as a convenient vehicle for identifying some of the major security mechanisms associated with each DiD layer and for understanding how they individually and collectively contribute to overall enterprise network security.

1.3 ENTERPRISE ARCHITECTURE

Enterprise architecture (EA) is another layered framework/model that is useful for understanding enterprise networks. It provides insights into the connections between business objectives and enterprise network components.

Today's businesses require powerful, reliable, scalable, and secure networks that contribute to profitability and business success. Although invisible to most users, network infrastructure is the platform that supports the organization's core business and its most important applications.

In the context of enterprise networks, EA is a strategic planning approach that helps ensure that a business's applications, data, and networks are appropriately aligned with business requirements. EA applies architectural principles and practices to help businesses identify the processes, data and information, applications, and technologies needed to execute their strategies. It provides a vehicle for connecting data, applications, and technologies to the business functions they support.

In practice, EA involves documenting, analyzing, designing, and deploying an organization's IT and network assets. It helps business managers and IT practitioners view their computing and networking infrastructure from a holistic perspective.

EA can be used to align technology with strategy in a single subunit or across the entire organization. It can also be applied to a collection of organizations with shared goals, such as a supply chain.

Business and IT alignment is a key goal of EA, but applying EA's architectural principles and practices also can help an organization to do the following:

- Make beneficial modifications to its structure or operations
- Standardize or integrate business processes
- Improve the quality and timeliness of data and information
- Identify innovative uses of its information technologies and network assets

Better alignment of strategy and computing and network infrastructure often enables the business to provide greater value to its customers.

EA is often depicted as consisting of four domains:

- Business architecture
- Data/information architecture
- Application architecture
- Technology architecture

These components are frequently illustrated as a pyramid (see Figure 1-10a). However, a fifth domain that provides protection to each of the other domains, security architecture, is often identified (see Figure 1-10b). Brief descriptions of each EA domain are provided in the following subsections.

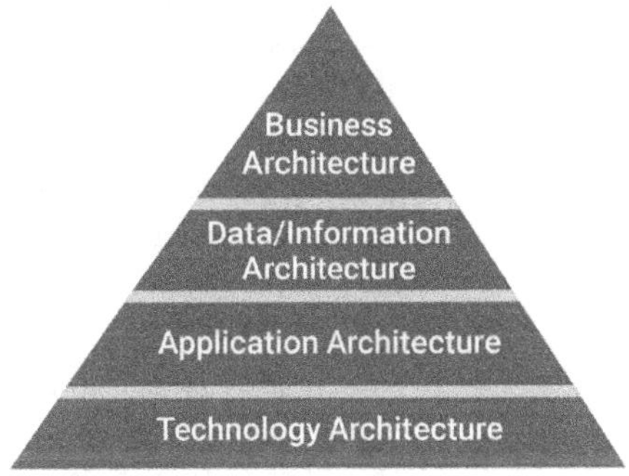

Figure 1-10a: Enterprise architecture (EA) domains.

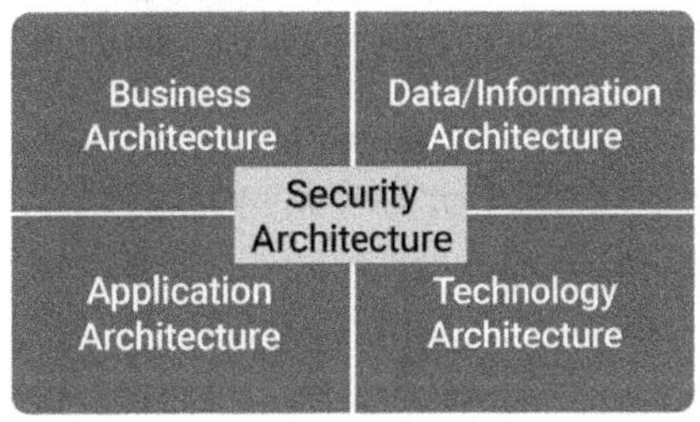

Figure 1-10b: EA security architecture.

1.3.1 Business Architecture

Business architecture is EA's business domain. It encompasses the business's organizational structure (e.g., its divisions, departments, subunits, functional areas, etc.) and how the different areas interact. EA principles and practices are applied to this domain to identify what the business wants to do, what it does, how it is organized, how it creates value, and how it realizes revenue. In a nutshell, business architecture focuses on the organization's mission/vision, structure, and critical success factors (CSFs).

Mission/vision identifies the business's stated role within its environment and its evolutionary intentions. Organizational structure identifies how work and reporting relationships are distributed within the organization. CSFs identify what the organization must do to survive or thrive in its environment.

Other important business architecture considerations include business processes, application requirements, and configuration rules for crucial applications such as enterprise systems (ESs).

1.3.2 Data/Information Architecture

EA's data/information domain includes the data and information that the business architecture requires. It is often separated into two subdomains: data architecture and information architecture:

- *Data architecture* consists of the standards, policies, models, and rules that govern the data collected by the organization; how it is collected and stored; and how it is arranged, integrated, and used by the business. It documents all major types and sources of data, the organization's physical and logical data assets, and the resources used to manage data.
- *Information architecture* describes how the organization's data is structured, maintained, and shared from both a business and technical (IT) perspective. It includes blueprints for physically and semantically integrating data assets via data models and data flows. It illustrates the connections between business strategy and the organization's data and information assets, as well as how these assets are structured, classified, associated, and used by the business. And it helps the organization prescribe application architecture and technical architecture requirements.

Data quality is an important data/information architecture consideration. Data governance and data management are also important. The organization's use of data analytics, business intelligence (BI), and reporting tools is included in this domain.

Considering the data/information domain from an architectural perspective can help a business identify gaps in what data and information it has and what it needs. This may direct it toward collecting data from additional sources or doing a better job of leveraging what it already has in data warehouses, data lakes, and other data repositories. Sometimes, expertise or appropriate processing/analytics platforms are the only missing ingredients.

Big Data

Big Data is increasingly addressed in data/information architecture and is a driver of enterprise network evolution. **Big Data** refers to large, diverse sets of information that are growing at ever-increasing rates. This is illustrated in Figure 1-11. (A zettabyte [ZB] is one billion terabytes.)

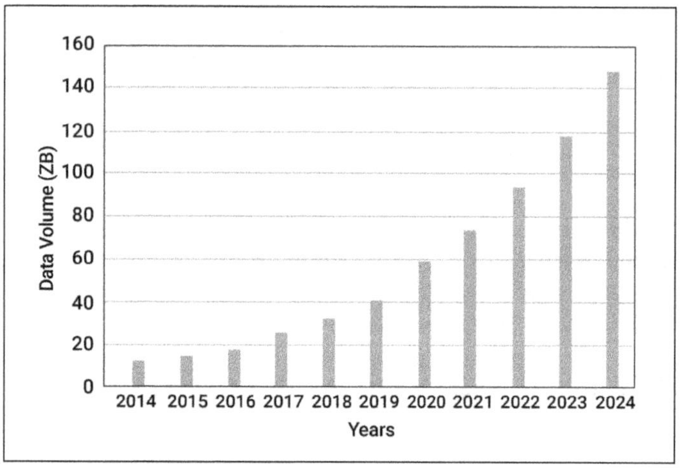

Figure 1-11: Big Data worldwide 2010 to 2024. Sources: IEEE Computer Society and Statista.

Many businesses amass vast quantities of both *structured data* (which is often numeric data that can be easily formatted and stored) and *unstructured data* (data that is more free-form and less quantifiable). Structured data includes information that can be organized and managed by databases and spreadsheets. Unstructured data is more challenging to organize and manage because it does not fit predetermined models or formats.

Big Data results from businesses capturing and storing data from social media, web browsing, chatbots, wearables, sensors, IoT devices, digital assistants, and other inputs from smart devices, in addition to that generated by enterprise system (ES) applications, customer transactions, product purchases, and daily business operations.

As noted in Chapter 3, Big Data is stored in computer databases, data warehouses, and data lakes that are usually located in cloud data centers capable of handling the continually growing data volumes. Some of the differences between data warehouses and data lakes are identified in

Table 1-1: Some of the major differences between data lakes and data warehouses.

	Data Lake	Data Warehouse
Data Scope	Broad, raw data	Select, cleaned
Prior Processing	None to light	Moderate to high
Analysis Limitations	Limited by nature of input sources and amount of preprocessing	Limited by data extraction, cleaning, and transformation choices
Ease of Navigation/Search	Hard	Moderate

Table 1-1. Both are described more fully in Chapter 3, along with business intelligence (BI) applications and Big Data analytics and processing.

Big Data analytics and other software specifically designed to handle large, complex data sets are used to analyze Big Data. Today, numerous cloud service providers specialize in managing Big Data for businesses.

The presence of Big Data in today's businesses contributes to the increasing volumes of data traffic on enterprise networks and the Internet. It also has important implications for the evolution of network infrastructure. Big Data is here and will only get bigger. Enterprise networks have no choice but to adapt to these realities.

1.3.3 Application Architecture

This EA domain focuses on the programs, applications, and tools that the business uses to process data into the information needed for strategically relevant decisions and choices. It also considers how applications are integrated and how data processing is coordinated to ensure that decision-makers have what they need to monitor and manage business processes and performance.

Software services from cloud providers, ES software, and commercial off-the-shelf (COTS) software that the organization uses are documented in the application architecture. Custom applications that serve specialized data processing or information requirements are also documented; so are legacy systems.

The key question for the application architecture is whether the business has the apps and processing capabilities that it needs. If there are gaps, they should be filled. Options for acquiring needed applications and integrating them with existing applications should be identified.

Often, businesses do not know or take full advantage of the features and capabilities of the software they already use. For example, at universities, students are frequently exposed to an extensive range of features and capabilities of Microsoft Excel, but most realize that they are only scratching the surface of the full range of capabilities available in the spreadsheet software.

Also, when existing software is augmented by other apps, its processing capabilities can be leveraged more fully. For example, proficient Excel users are often amazed how Tableau can transform Excel worksheets into powerful sources of data for data visualization and data mining.

E-commerce applications are essential aspects of business computing architecture in many organizations. And IoT applications are expanding at accelerating rates in many businesses and are increasingly important to efficient business operations.

The relative importance of apps in an organization's application architecture is an important consideration of this EA domain. Data traffic in enterprise networks is typically prioritized to align with the relative importance of the applications that they support. Highly important applications usually have higher priority than less important apps.

Applications that are crucial to business success are considered mission-critical. A **mission-critical application** is a software program (or set of programs) that must function continuously for the organization to be successful. Hence, special efforts are devoted to ensuring that mission-critical applications are continuously available on enterprise networks and perform adequately.

Enterprise Systems

Enterprise systems (ESs) are large, complex software packages that handle large volumes of data and enable organizations to integrate and coordinate their business processes. Such systems are typically centerpieces of the computing infrastructures of organizations and are considered mission-critical. They ensure information sharing across functional levels and management levels. They enable companies to integrate information across operations on an enterprise-wide basis, address enterprise-wide problems, improve data integration, and generate valuable data for decision-making.

ESs include enterprise resource planning (ERP), customer relationship management (CRM), and supply chain management (SCM). One or all of these may be included in an organization's portfolio of business applications.

Enterprise systems applications often link an organization's computing infrastructure to those of business partners, such as suppliers and customers (see Figure 1-12). The boundary-spanning nature of ESs means that they serve as electronic links that bind organizations to their partners and facilitate data/information exchanges that enable mutually beneficial coordination of operations. As such, they are e-commerce enablers that help businesses procure the materials they need to produce and deliver products to their customers.

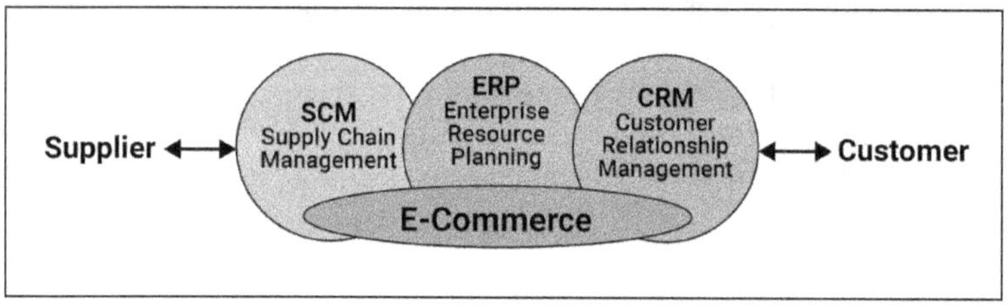

Figure 1-12: SCM, ERP, and CRM systems are examples of enterprise systems.

Prior to the 2000s, ES software was usually supported on in-house computing and networking infrastructure. Since then, organizations have transitioned to supporting ES applications with cloud infrastructure, in part or in whole. Numerous experts predict that, in the future, hosted, cloud-based ESs will be the most common.

Because ESs are mission critical, special attention is devoted to their availability and security. Keeping them running and performing at optimal levels—and secure—positions the organization to achieve its business objectives.

This book assumes that ESs are an important part of the application architecture and a driver of enterprise network configuration and management. Enterprise networks exist to support business applications, especially those most closely tied to a company's daily operations and success.

1.3.4 Technology Architecture

The technical domain of EA includes the computers, networks, storage technologies, operating systems (OSs), middleware, and database management systems (DBMSs) needed to support the organization's application architecture. It encompasses the computing and networking infrastructure that supports the programs, applications, and tools that the organization uses to turn data into information that is operationally and strategically valuable.

EA's technology architecture documents the telecommunication equipment, such as routers, switches, circuits, and servers, used in the organization's wide area network (WAN) to interconnect geographically dispersed locations. It also documents the organization's user devices (desktop systems, laptops, tablets, smartphones, etc.) and the servers (application servers, database servers, email servers, web servers, etc.) in the organization's local area networks (LANs) and backbone networks (BNs) at its different locations. As noted in section 1.1.2, all of these are components of enterprise networks.

Enterprise Networks

Enterprise networks are a major part of the technical architecture of many businesses. Enterprise network architecture diagrams like Figure 1-13 provide a high-level depiction of network modules. Modules including enterprise campus, enterprise edge, enterprise branches, enterprise data center, and enterprise telework depict major sources and destinations of network traffic. Interconnections among the modules may also be illustrated.

Network architecture diagrams like Figure 1-13 facilitate more detailed consideration of the individual modules without losing sight of their contributions to the overall network. For example, LANs and BNs may exist at corporate headquarters (the enterprise campus) and at branch locations, and remote workers (enterprise teleworkers) often have Wi-Fi LANs in their homes. In short, they convey that an enterprise network is a "network of networks" while also enabling designers to concentrate on improving/optimizing individual modules.

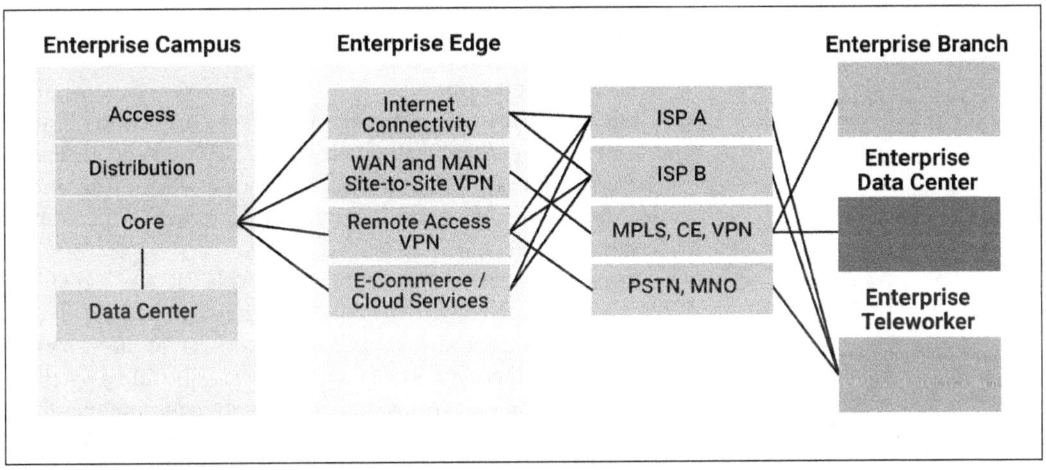

Figure 1-13: An example of an enterprise network architecture diagram.

Local Area Networks

Both wired and wireless LANs are common in business facilities. A **local area network (LAN)** is a collection of connected devices located in a single physical location, such as a home, office, or building.

In wired LANs, physical cables connect user devices to switches (see Figure 1-14). Typically, Ethernet cables connect to Ethernet switches, but fiber optic cables may be used for some or all connections. The cables provide physical pathways that carry data transmissions between devices in the local network. Network adapters in user devices create and receive transmitted signals. Almost all LANs also include a router that provides a means for exchanging data with devices in other networks.

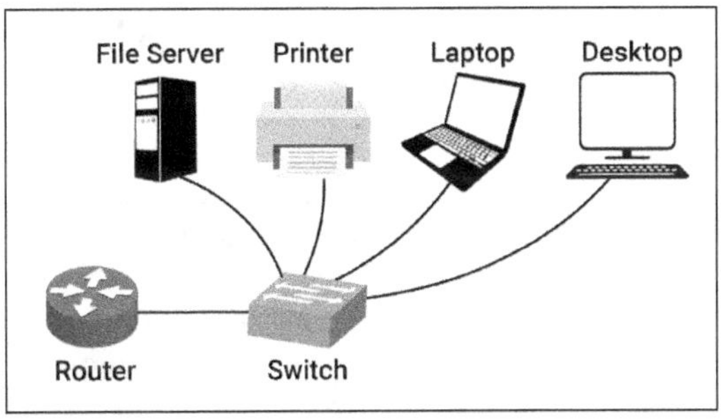

Figure 1-14: Examples of user and networking devices in a wired LAN.

Wi-Fi networks are the most common wireless LANs in today's enterprise networks. They enable mobile devices (e.g., smartphones, tablets, and laptops) to connect wirelessly to the LAN via access points (see Figure 1-15). Access points connect to wired network switches or specialized switches called Wi-Fi controllers via physical cables, typically Ethernet cables. This arrangement enables mobile devices to communicate with devices connected to wired LANs.

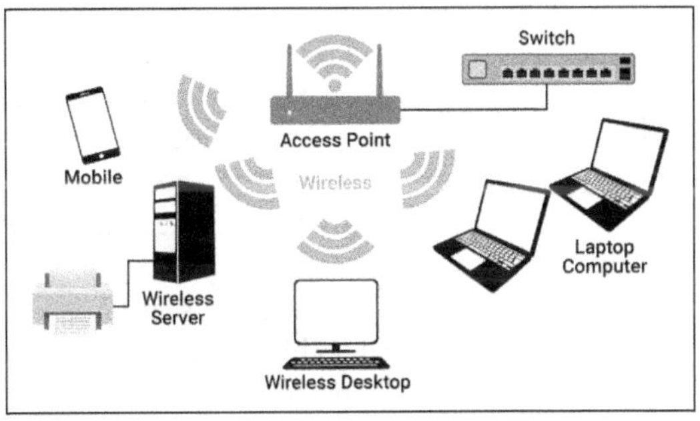

Figure 1-15: Example of a Wi-Fi LAN.

Wired and wireless networks in business facilities are described in Chapters 6 and 7.

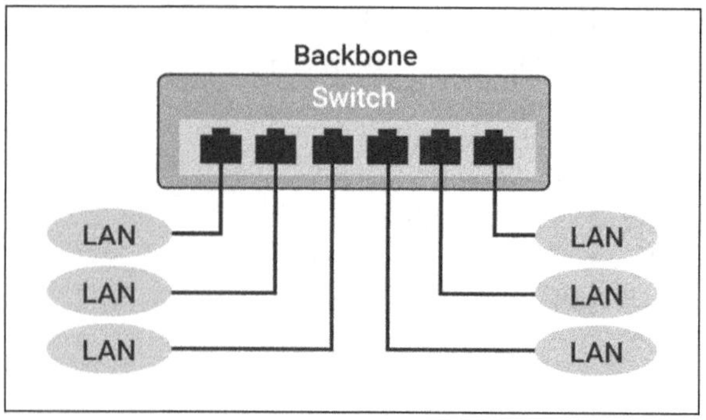

Figure 1-16: Some backbones interconnect multiple LANs.

Backbone Networks

A **backbone** is network infrastructure that connects multiple networks and provides a conduit for data to flow between them. A backbone switch, like that in Figure 1-16, is considered a distribution layer technology in the three-layer hierarchical model introduced in section 1.2.2. LAN switches map to the access layer of the three-layer model.

Today, fiber optic cables are often used to connect LAN and backbone switches; however, copper Ethernet cables are sometimes used. When fiber optic cables are used, the BN may be called a fiber optic backbone.

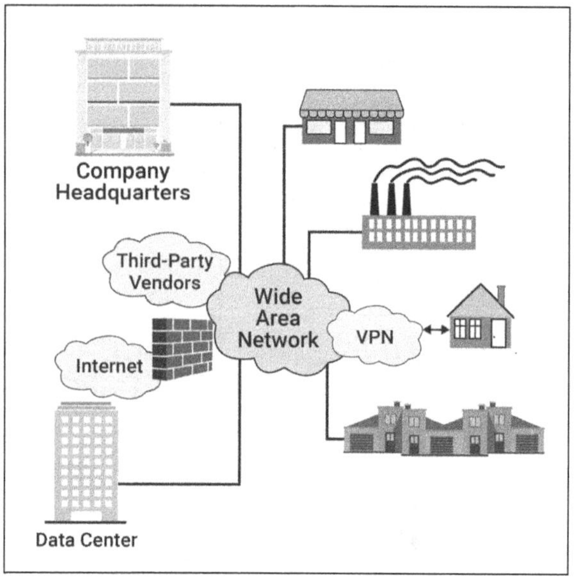

Figure 1-17: An example of a business WAN.

Wide Area Networks

Basically, a **wide area network (WAN)** is a collection of interconnected, geographically distributed LANs. Like an enterprise network, a WAN is essentially a network of networks. WANs vary in geographic scope; the Internet is the world's largest WAN.

Business WANs interconnect LANs at an organization's geographically distributed locations (branches). Today, such WANs typically support connections to networks in employee homes, and most support links to business partners, third-party organizations such as network equipment and ES software vendors, and cloud services (see Figure 1-17). Often, there is not much distinction between a business WAN and an enterprise network.

Cloud Infrastructure

Cloud computing and cloud infrastructure are common parts of a business's technology architecture. Essentially, **cloud computing** is the delivery of computing services, including data storage, servers, software, analytics, and other resources, over the Internet.

Cloud computing is attractive to businesses because it provides resource flexibility and economies of scale. With cloud computing, a business pays only for the resources that it uses (which can contribute to lower IT costs) while also having the ability to scale in response to changing business needs. Some of the common drivers of business adoption and use of cloud services are identified in Table 1-2.

Most businesses subscribe to cloud services for increased processing capabilities (more servers) and storage capacity (cloud storage). Many also use cloud services for applications (e.g., software as a service [SaaS]), for virtual desktop capabilities, or as platforms for deploying specialized software applications.

The IoT is another major reason why cloud infrastructure is increasingly prevalent in enterprise networks. Business adoption and use of IoT devices and applications is accelerating, and most of them are supported by cloud-based IoT platforms like that illustrated in Figure 1-18.

As noted in section 1.1.3, technologies included in enterprise networks and a business's technical architecture continue to evolve. Current standards for LANs and communication protocols are superseded by those for the next generation when the standards are revised.

Table 1-2: Common drivers of business adoption of cloud services.

Adoption Driver	Description
Cost	Cloud computing reduces the capital expenses associated with buying the hardware, software, and expertise needed to set up, run, and maintain on-site data centers.
Speed	Most cloud computing services are provided on a self-service and on-demand basis and enable vast amounts of computing resources to be provisioned in minutes if needed. This provides flexibility and eases the burden of capacity planning.
Scalability	Elastic scalability enables cloud services to deliver on demand needed amounts of computing resources (processing power, storage, bandwidth) to business locations that need them.
Performance	Big cloud computing services (e.g., AWS [Amazon Web Services] and Microsoft Azure) include worldwide networks of data centers that are regularly upgraded to the latest generation of computing hardware. This rarely happens in on-premises data centers. Such regular upgrades typically translate into improved performance and reduced latency (response times) for applications.
Reliability	Cloud computing makes data backup, disaster recovery, and business continuity easier and less expensive; data can be mirrored at multiple redundant sites in the cloud provider's network of data centers.

Cloud services are also evolving. New services targeting business subscribers come at a dizzying rate. Such continual and rapid technological advancements create new opportunities, and businesses should regularly assess their technical architectures and consider what is likely to come next. This also means that aligning technical architecture with EAs' business, data/information, and application architectures is an ongoing challenge.

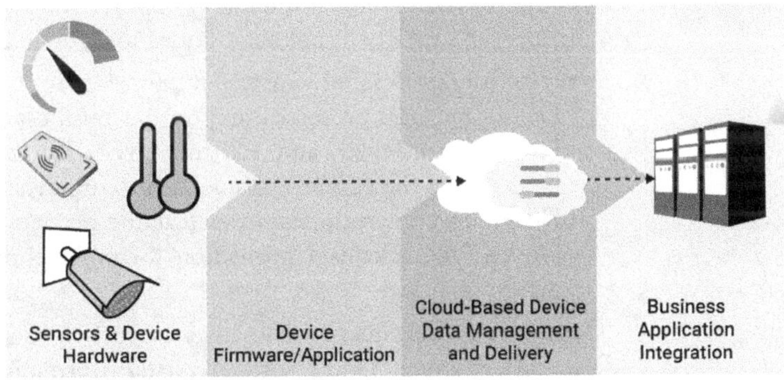

Figure 1-18: IoT applications contribute to increasing business reliance on cloud infrastructure.

1.3.5 Security Architecture

Today's organizations understand that business risk is inherently tied to the security of their data, applications, and data processing technologies. Information security is a crucial business issue, and EA's security architecture seeks to align business goals with adequate protection for the organization's data, information, data processing, and network infrastructure.

An organization's security architecture strives to provide *information assurance (IA)* by protecting the organization's data, applications, devices, and networks. It strives to ensure the integrity of business processes, the systems that support them, and the information that they generate, especially the resources most critical to the achievement of strategic goals.

Enterprise network security focuses on ensuring the confidentiality, integrity, and availability of data and other network assets. It strives to provide an interlocking set of security policies, procedures, and security defenses that collectively provide unified and cohesive protection of the organization's data and network assets.

Today, it is impossible to overemphasize the importance of enterprise network security. It is a major consideration for all enterprise network components. While this book devotes its final two chapters to security, it also includes contextualized discussion of security threats and defenses for the various parts of enterprise networks throughout the book.

Layered Protection

As noted in section 1.2.3, the DiD model (Figure 1-9) is used to structure the discussion of security in Chapters 11 and 12. Layered security makes sense when focusing on an individual device or a whole network.

Individuals often protect their personal devices with two-factor authentication, such as a fingerprint scan and a passcode. Cloud services, likewise, often require more than a user ID and password to access apps; many also send one-time security codes via text or email, while others require correct answers to one or more security questions. This is sometimes annoying, but each layer of authentication represents an additional layer of protection for the device or user.

Rapid and continual advances in the technical components of enterprise networks require an organization to constantly revisit its security posture. Each new application or component can have vulnerabilities that increase the network's *attack surface* (possible entry points for attackers), and attackers are constantly looking for vulnerabilities that they can exploit.

1.3.6 Business and Enterprise Network Alignment

EA seeks to help organizations achieve their strategic objectives by enabling them to assess their business, data/information, application, technical, and security architectures from a holistic perspective. EA makes it easier to identify opportunities for better alignment. It enables an organization to answer a variety of important questions, including:

- Is our organizational structure appropriate for our business strategy?
- Do our business processes support our business strategy?
- Do we have the data and information needed to achieve our strategic objectives?
- Do we have the applications needed to produce strategically relevant information?
- Do we have the technical infrastructure needed to support our applications?
- Do we have adequate protection for our technical infrastructure, applications, and data?

Confronting such questions enables executives to see where gaps exist and to identify where additional investments in IT, software, data/information, and security may be needed.

Business strategy is foremost in EA. When strategy or technology changes, EA provides a mechanism for identifying changes that should be made in each of the other domains to align with the new strategy or technology. When EA components are appropriately aligned, the business is better positioned to execute its strategy. When EA components are inadequately aligned, the organization's performance may be constrained.

EA fits with the business-centric nature of enterprise networks and their continually evolving components. EA provides a business-first perspective for considering IT and network infrastructure. It also influences how this book is structured and how its various topics are described.

1.4 LEVERAGING ENTERPRISE NETWORKS

Enterprise networks exist to serve business needs. In addition to supporting business applications, they are used in numerous other ways. Three common usage categories are e-commerce, e-business, and digital business.

1.4.1 E-commerce

E-commerce includes selling, buying, and sometimes exchanging products and services over online channels. Completing sales transactions usually involves the transfer of money between buyers and sellers. Today, the Internet is involved in most e-commerce transactions, but other networks are sometimes used.

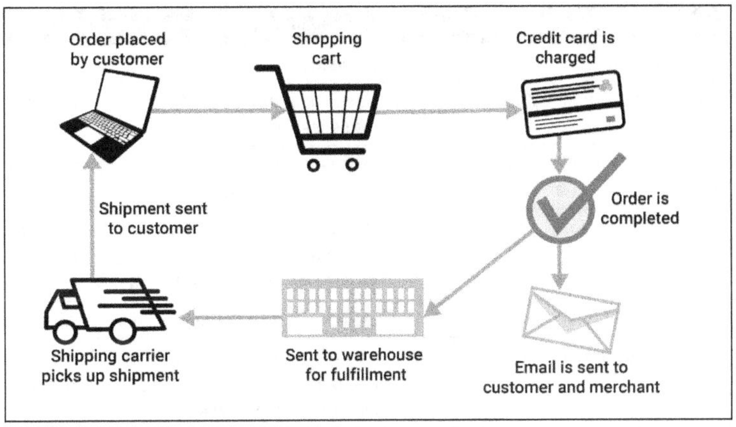

Figure 1-19: Example of a B2C e-commerce transaction.

Business-to-consumer (B2C) and business-to-business (B2B) are commonly supported by enterprise networks. Figure 1-19 illustrates a typical B2C transaction. Here, a shopper visits the company's e-commerce website, places one or more items in their shopping cart, provides their payment and shipping information, and places their order. Upon order receipt, the company typically sends the shopper an order confirmation email and simultaneously sends the order information to its warehouse to fulfill the order and ship the ordered items to the customer.

The e-commerce servers that buyers use to place orders communicate with back-end servers in the enterprise network, such as ERP servers, and are responsible for order fulfillment and shipping processes.

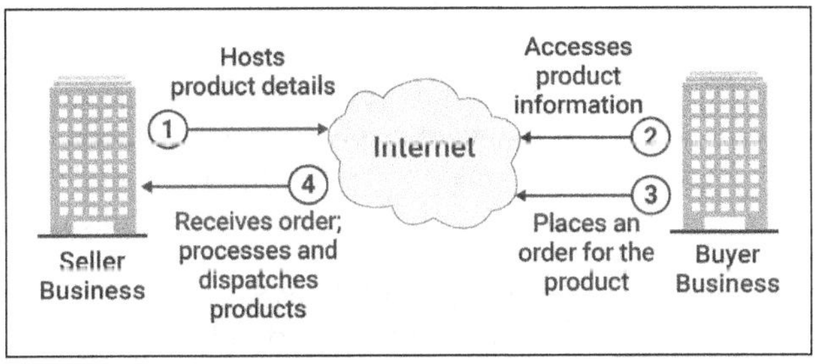

Figure 1-20: A high-level depiction of B2B e-commerce.

B2B e-commerce is similar, but here, both buyers and sellers are businesses (see Figure 1-20). Sellers provide product details online, typically using product web pages like those used for B2C e-commerce. Buyers place orders, which are received and fulfilled by sellers. Back-end systems, such as ERP systems, in buyer and seller enterprise networks may be involved in order transmittal and receipt. And businesses may use *electronic data interchange (EDI)* document formats for their online transactions. EDI is described in section 2.2.5 in Chapter 2.

For B2B transactions, ordered items may be shipped from the seller's warehouse directly to the buyer's warehouse. Buyer payments may involve immediate bank-to-bank transfers, or some buyers may have a line of credit with a seller that enables them to defer payment to a later date.

There are other types of e-commerce, including consumer-to-consumer (C2C), that may or may not involve enterprise networks. E-procurement and *vendor managed inventory (VMI)* partnerships usually involve ES applications supported on buyer and seller enterprise networks.

1.4.2 E-Business

Electronic business (e-business) refers to the use of the Internet, intranets, extranets, or some combination of them to support business operations. E-business includes e-commerce but extends beyond it to a wide range of activities that companies engage in to operate efficiently (see Table 1-3). E-business, for example, includes search engine optimization (SEO), digital marketing, internal and external collaboration systems, e-signature systems, and electronic workflow systems —just about anything that electronically enables businesses and their teams to coordinate operations and activities.

As Table 1-3 indicates, e-business leverages enterprise networks more extensively than e-commerce. For example, videoconferencing has become a standard format for business team meetings, and during the COVID-19 pandemic, the use of Zoom meetings and other videoconferencing platforms surged to facilitate the interactions of remote workers with fellow employees, clients, and business partners.

Table 1-3: Some of the differences between e-commerce and e-business.

E-Commerce	E-Business
Involves sales transactions over the Internet	Uses the Internet, intranets, extranets, and other networks to support a wide range of business processes and activities
Focuses on buying and selling products and services online	Includes more than online sales transactions, such as e-sourcing and e-procurement, presales, and post-sales activities
Is externally focused on customers	Is both internally and externally focused: internally, e-business helps individual employees and teams perform their work tasks; externally, e-business enables organizations to create and maintain strong relationships with customers, suppliers, business partners, and other stakeholders
Is limited to monetary transactions	Includes a wide range of business transactions
Has a scope limited to online transactions	Has a broader scope that also includes market monitoring and research, business intelligence (BI) and data mining, customer education, supply chain and logistics coordination, crowdsourcing, and electronic workflows
Focuses on business–customer communication	Also involves communication with online communities and the use of collaboration technologies for internal and external communication

Business adoption and use of e-signature and electronic workflow systems also surged during the pandemic and became entrenched on numerous enterprise networks. Digital marketing (e.g., email marketing, social media marketing, search engine marketing, and content marketing) is another important e-business application supported on business networks.

1.4.3 Digital Business

Digital business is considered a step beyond e-business in that it enables new business models and generates new revenue streams using new combinations of people, things, and business. It represents the convergence of digital and physical worlds and uses technology to create new value in traditional business models, new customer experiences, innovations, and new capabilities.

Digital business is often described as an offshoot of *digital transformation*—the adoption and use of digital technologies to replace manual or nondigital processes with digital processes. Today, this often involves replacing older digital technologies with newer ones but is also considered a departure from traditional mind-sets to a culture that continually experiments with digital technologies, challenges the status quo, and encourages both intrapreneurial and entrepreneurial thinking about the deployment of digital technologies.

Digital twins (virtual replicas of physical entities) are examples of digital business applications. For example, attaching IoT sensors to a wind turbine and creating a digital twin enables engineers to simulate how the wind turbine is likely to perform in extreme conditions, identify shortcomings in its current design, and generate data needed to create next generation turbines. The digital twin may also be used to develop artificial intelligence (AI) algorithms that can be used to optimize real turbines' electrical generation in changing environmental conditions.

Tying wearable technologies, such as fitness monitors, to e-commerce systems is considered another digital business frontier. Cloud-based AI algorithms tracking fitness data might decide that someone is more likely to achieve their fitness goals by purchasing new running shoes and automatically place a pair in an online shopping basket.

The IoT devices that businesses are deploying are frequently cited as digital business applications. For example, sensors in refrigerated shipping containers are being used to track perishable goods in transit and to ensure that products are maintained at appropriate temperatures. These same containers may be equipped with GPS trackers to monitor their location while in transit and with radio frequency identification (RFID) tags to make them instantly findable at storage locations.

In some networks, sensors that monitor the performance of Wi-Fi access points and AI algorithms perform "beam shaping" to minimize signal interference and improve overall performance. Here, digital business applications are benefiting the networks that support them.

Digital business applications enable the communication capabilities of enterprise networks to be utilized more fully. However, sometimes using networks in nontraditional ways can create unanticipated security and network management challenges.

1.5 NETWORK STANDARDS

Multiple standard setting organizations are involved in creating, maintaining, and revising data communication and networking standards. After completing this book, you may find yourself agreeing with a long-standing attempt at networking humor that states, "If you like standards, you'll love data communications because there are so many of them."

Basically, *standards* are the sets of rules that govern data exchanges between network devices. They make it possible for network devices to communicate. They also help ensure that networking hardware and software can work together.

Standards also enable different vendors to make network components that will interoperate with components made by other vendors. Today, many networking components are commodities, and numerous companies compete to sell their products to businesses. Ethernet switches, for example, are manufactured and marketed by numerous vendors, and specifications for the switches frequently include a lengthy list of the networking standards they support. These specifications inform buyers of a switch's capabilities and the extent to which it will fit with the buyer's network infrastructure.

Like it or not, it is impossible to cleanly separate the discussion of network infrastructure and security from standards. Standards, including security standards, are meaningful and enrich the information associated with network hardware and software.

Networking standards can be categorized in one of two ways: formal and de facto (informal).

Formal standards result from deliberations of standards-issuing organizations. *De facto* means "by tradition" or "by facts." These standards emerge from market processes and historical developments rather than formal planning or deliberation by industry groups. A de facto standard often achieves its status through dominance of the market in which it applies. The QWERTY keyboard layout is an example of a de facto standard.

Formal standards are developed and/or officially recognized by standard setting organizations (SSOs). These are also known as *de jure* standards. The primary activities of SSOs include developing, revising, amending, and interpreting technical standards. Table 1-4 identifies some of the SSOs for networking.

Table 1-4: Examples of standard setting organizations (SSOs) for networking standards.

SSO Acronym	SSO Name
ANSI	American National Standards Institute
EIA	Electronic Industries Alliance
TIA	Telecommunications Industry Association
IEEE	Institute of Electrical and Electronics Engineers
ISO	International Organization for Standardization
ITU-T	International Telecommunication Union—Telecommunications Sector

Most standards are essentially voluntary in nature. They are offered/recommended for adoption without being mandated by law. Some standards, however, become mandatory when they are adopted by regulators as legal requirements for specific industries or domains.

The development and issuing of formal standards often involves a multiyear process. Frequently, technology advances that occur while a standard is being developed or revised limit the standard's shelf life or usefulness. However, revisions and amendments to prevailing standards provide insights into trends for the capabilities of the technologies to which they apply and offer glimpses of what the future may hold.

The *Internet Engineering Task Force (IETF)* is often considered to be an SSO because it governs standards for communication protocols used on the Internet. However, the IETF is different from the SSOs identified in Table 1-4 in that it does not have an official membership. Anyone can participate in the development of the standards that the IETF oversees. The transparency and openness of the process is reflected in the *RFC (request for comment)* phases of its standards development and revision processes.

As you will see in subsequent chapters, a networking standard often maps to a single layer in the OSI or TCP/IP model. IEEE Ethernet and Wi-Fi standards, for example, primarily map to the Data Link layer of these models.

1.6 TECHNOLOGIES SHAPING THE EVOLUTION OF ENTERPRISE NETWORKS

Amendments/revisions to networking standards are often triggered by technology advances. Hardware and software vendors compete via continual product improvement encouraged by receptive markets that are ready to adopt technologies that conform to the latest standards or revisions to protocols. Hence, standard revisions/amendments and technology advances go hand in hand. Next generation standards spawn product upgrades that contribute to the ongoing evolution of enterprise networks.

Cloud computing and Big Data are reshaping enterprise networks, but several other technologies are also having an effect. These include the IoT, 5G, artificial intelligence (AI), software-defined networking (SDN), secure access service edge (SASE), and blockchain.

1.6.1 The IoT

The **Internet of Things (IoT)** refers to the network of physical objects ("things") that are embedded with sensors, software, processing ability, and other technologies that enable them to connect to and exchange data with other devices and/or applications. Basically, the IoT provides an interface between the physical world and the digital world.

The IoT is one of the most important and disruptive technologies of the twenty-first century. It enables physical things to collect and share data with minimal human intervention, and it enables digital systems to monitor, record, and adjust to interactions among connected things.

IoT devices are used in all types of industries and consumer markets. In 2020, consumers were responsible for about 60% of all IoT connected devices, and this percentage is predicted to remain relatively stable through 2030. However, more than 100 million IoT devices have been deployed in each of multiple industries, including electrical utilities, retail and wholesale companies, manufacturers, and transportation and warehouse companies. By 2030, each of these and several other industries are expected to have more than one billion IoT connected devices.

IoT devices are being added to the Internet at a dizzying rate. By 2025, experts predict that more than 150,000 new devices will be added to the IOT each minute, and by 2030, experts expect IoT devices to generate more than 73 zettabytes of data traffic.

The cloud provides inexpensive storage for IoT data, and IoT data is one of the drivers of Big Data's continuous expansion. Deployment of IoT systems and applications in manufacturing and warehousing facilities, called the Industrial Internet of Things (IIoT), contributes to process automation and improved energy management, especially when they are combined with AI algorithms. In manufacturing facilities, AI-fueled IoT systems are ushering in predictive and preventive maintenance processing that identifies and addresses maintenance issues before equipment failures occur. Different aspects of the IIoT are illustrated in Figure 1-21.

Business deployment of IoT systems and applications means increasing volumes of IoT data traffic on enterprise networks. Often, for both security and performance reasons, IoT traffic is seg-

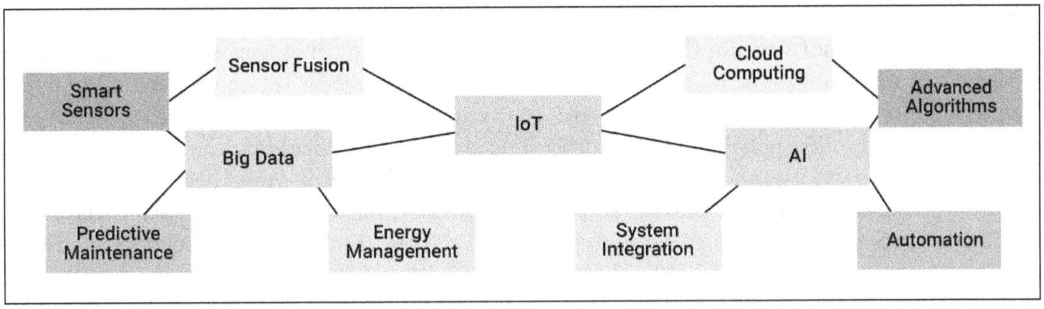

Figure 1-21: Examples of IIoT technologies and applications.

mented from other enterprise network data traffic. IIoT technologies, platforms, and applications are described in Chapter 9.

1.6.2 5G

It is impossible to avoid 5G advertising from cellular service providers. 5G is their latest and greatest thing and will remain so until they begin touting 6G, which is already on the horizon. Relative to 4G (including 4G LTE), 5G supports faster data services and connection speeds for mobile devices such as smartphones and tablets.

Certainly, employees are using consumer-oriented cellular services in important ways, but 5G is making inroads into businesses and affecting enterprise networks in other ways. For example, as you will learn in Chapters 7 and 8, private 5G microcells and radio access networks (RANs) are increasingly being used in manufacturing facilities and warehouses to support machine-to-machine (M2M) communications and other IIoT applications.

Numerous experts predict that most new IIoT device connections will be 5G, and some contend that private RANs may replace Wi-Fi networks in business facilities. Since RANs can connect to external 5G services, they can provide alternative links to cloud services and be used in wireless WANs to supplement or replace traditional WAN connections.

1.6.3 AI

Artificial intelligence (AI) and machine learning (ML) algorithms are increasingly being used for network monitoring and management, optimizing network performance, and strengthening network security. They can detect, isolate, and resolve problems, often without the intervention of network managers.

AI can be used to identify correlations among network events and for root cause analysis. AI is also used to configure, deploy, and troubleshoot networking equipment.

AI can quickly detect and isolate problems by correlating historical and real-time data from network devices. It frees network personnel from time- and resource-intensive activities associated with addressing current problems and enables them to focus their attention on more strategic and high-value tasks.

AI is being used for risk profiling and for providing deep network visibility that enables security policy enforcement in network endpoints. Threat-aware enterprise networks are more important than ever, and AI capabilities are increasingly utilized in network security technologies. For example, AI is being used to quickly identify and react to compromised devices. It is also being used to identify potential phishing attacks and malicious user behaviors. Using AI to persistently monitor applications and user behaviors enables anomalous and potentially malicious activity to be flagged.

This is a small sampling of the ways AI is being used to improve and transform enterprise networks. Thanks to AI, in the years ahead, enterprise networks will increasingly be self-monitoring, self-healing, and self-managing.

1.6.4 SDN

Software-defined networking (SDN) is a networking approach that uses software-based controllers that communicate with underlying hardware infrastructure (routers and switches) to direct data traffic on a network. Traditionally, software installed on network devices (e.g., switches and routers) has controlled network traffic; forwarding decisions are made by the devices that also forward/transmit the packets to their destinations. SDN enables forwarding decisions to move to a software-based control plane, and the control plane tells the devices how to forward packets. The devices (routers and switches) continue to perform the actual transmittal, but network managers have centralized control of data traffic through the network.

Table 1-5: SDN benefits.

SDN Benefit	Description
Increased control and flexibility	Instead of manually programming multiple hardware devices, network managers can control the flow of traffic through a network by programming a software-based controller. Networking administrators have more flexibility in choosing networking equipment and can use a single protocol to communicate with the hardware devices.
Customizable provisioning of network infrastructure	With SDN, administrators can configure network services and make changes to the network infrastructure in real time. They can optimize the flow of data through the network and prioritize applications that require continuous availability.
Robust security	A software-defined network makes the entire network more visible and provides a holistic view of security threats. Network operators can create separate zones (segments) for devices that require different levels of security; they can also quarantine compromised devices before they infect the rest of the network.

SDN provides a new way of controlling the routing of data packets within the physical network by way of a centralized software-based server. Several SDN benefits are identified in Table 1-5.

Collectively, SDN improves the agility and scalability of enterprise networks. It enables enterprise networks to quickly adjust to new applications, services, business requirements, or changing circumstances.

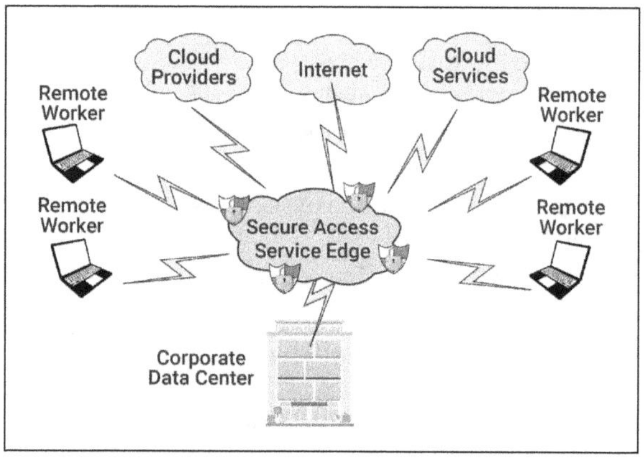

Figure 1-22: SASE is a security response to increasing reliance on cloud services and remote workers.

1.6.5 SASE

Secure access service edge (SASE), pronounced "sassy," is an emerging cybersecurity approach first described by Gartner in its 2019 report *The Future of Network Security*. It is based on the reality that employees require immediate, uninterrupted access to their employers' enterprise networks no matter where they are located.

With increased numbers of remote users, increased use of cloud applications and services, increased data movement between on-premises and cloud data centers, and increased data transfers between branch offices and cloud providers, cloud-oriented security solutions are needed for enterprise networks. Figure 1-22 provides a high-level depiction of SASE.

SASE represents a convergence of WAN and several cloud-oriented security defenses into a single security model. Like this book, SASE is grounded in the assumption that the cloud and remote workers are fundamental components of enterprise networks. SASE strives to ensure that organizations have a systematic and comprehensive approach for securing the entirety of the enterprise network, including its remote users and cloud components.

1.6.6 Blockchain

Blockchain databases and applications are increasingly common in today's businesses and enterprise networks. Like cloud services, they are often viewed as logical extensions of enterprise network infrastructure because much of what happens in them takes place outside of traditional enterprise network boundaries.

A **blockchain** is a type of shared database that stores data in blocks that are linked together via cryptography. New data to be added to the database is entered into a new block, and once the block is filled with data, it is chained onto the previous block through a cryptographic hash code. The cryptographic process used to chain blocks to one another is described at the end of Chapter 12. Data is chained together in chronological order and is distributed and visible to all entities in the network.

While different types of information can be stored in a blockchain database, transaction data is most common. Decentralized blockchains are immutable, which means that once data is added, it is irreversible; transactions are permanently recorded and viewable by everyone in the network.

Figure 1-23 identifies some of the reasons why blockchain applications are attractive to today's businesses. Blockchain applications are being used to track materials/goods movements in supply chains. They are also becoming more common in security trading and financial services. More information about blockchain databases is provided in Chapter 3.

Blockchain, SASE, SDN, 5G, AI, the IoT, and other technologies that are shaping the evolution of enterprise networks are also converging and leveraging each other's capabilities. The interactions and innovations that result from this convergence are likely to affect enterprise networks in ways that are difficult to foresee.

Today, it is impossible to view business networks as static entities. Just as businesses evolve in response to changing circumstances, so do enterprise networks. Technology advances and changing business needs and desires ripple through enterprise networks and cause them to adapt and evolve in interesting ways. What is in place today will change in response to new standards, services, applications, devices, business models, and opportunities.

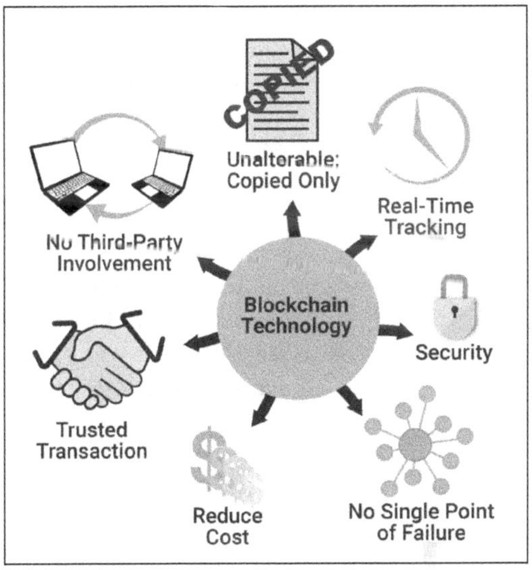

Figure 1-23: Some of the characteristics of blockchain applications that are attractive to businesses.

1.7 OVERVIEW OF THE BOOK

This book provides an overview of enterprise networks and their major components. It describes many different pieces of the networking puzzle, and collectively they provide a reasonably complete and accurate picture of today's business networks.

It may be challenging to wrap your head around everything that you are learning in this book. Even if you have relevant prior knowledge and experience, many of the concepts and descriptions are likely to be new, and many students consider networking courses among the most technical and challenging courses that they take.

But guess what? When there is a lot of new stuff to learn, a lot of learning can occur. As you make your way through this book, including its more technical sections, you might sometimes feel overwhelmed. But when you give yourself enough time to read carefully and engage with the concepts, you can understand them.

If you find yourself tripping over details, step back to consider the bigger picture. This may mean revisiting the book's Table of Contents to see how a chapter and its topics are structured.

Sometimes, revisiting a previous section is key to understanding the concepts that you are currently trying to master.

1.7.1 Applications and Data

Chapters 2 and 3 consider enterprise network applications and data, focusing on serving the needs of businesses and considering the business applications that enterprise networks support to emphasize that enterprise networks are "business-centric" networks.

Chapter 2 provides brief descriptions of some of the major types of applications that enterprise networks support. The list includes commercial off-the-shelf (COTS), horizontal market, vertical market, and open-source software, as well as mobile apps. This chapter also provides brief descriptions of enterprise system (ES) applications (CRM, ERP, SCM, etc.) and the reasons why such applications are usually considered mission-critical. It also describes how ES applications are configured as distributed client-server applications.

Cloud services, of course, are also being used to support an ever-widening range of business applications, so the chapter discusses cloud infrastructure and how it is interwoven with enterprise networks. Chapter 2 also introduces several important security issues for business applications and some of the major approaches for securing them.

Chapter 3 considers the different types of data being captured, stored, and processed on enterprise networks. It describes how different types of data (including text, images, video, and audio data) are digitized and represented by binary code (0s and 1s), the format needed to represent them as symbols/signals on network communication media.

Chapter 3 provides brief summaries of traditional logical data repositories (such as databases and data warehouses) and the reasons why burgeoning volumes of unstructured and semistructured data have increased business reliance on No-SQL databases, data lakes, cloud storage, and Big Data processing platforms, such as Hadoop clusters. Data storage technologies, data governance, and data security are other important topics in Chapter 3.

1.7.2 The Internet

In Chapters 4 and 5, attention turns to layered communication models and the Internet. Chapter 4 begins with a closer look at the OSI and TCP/IP layered communication models and their similarities and differences. The rest of the chapter provides a layer-by-layer discussion of the major communication functions performed at each of the layers of the TCP/IP model. Some of the networking and security technologies associated with each layer are also introduced.

Chapter 5 provides an overview of some of the most important components of the Internet architecture, including autonomous systems, Internet service providers (ISPs), and Internet domains. This chapter considers the communication protocols used at the Application, Transport, and Network layers of the TCP/IP model.

Special attention is devoted to Transport layer and Network layer communication functions and protocols because they are key to understanding how the Internet works. Transmission Control Protocol (TCP) and how it contributes to reliable data transfers receives special attention. IP addressing, both IPv4 and IPv6, and routing are other important Network layer topics. Because they leverage Internet technologies and protocols, intranets and extranets are also introduced in Chapter 5.

1.7.3 LANs and Backbone Networks

Chapters 6 and 7 focus on wired and wireless networks in business facilities. It is here that the Data Link and Physical layers of the TCP/IP model are most fully described.

Chapter 6 considers wired LANs and BNs. Line encoding, the manner in which 0s and 1s are represented on twisted-pair wire and fiber optic cables, is described here along with the characteristics of the physical cables. Structured cabling standards that govern the deployment of cabling and networking equipment in business facilities are introduced, and important Data Link and Physical layer technologies, including network adapters and switches, are described.

The widespread Ethernet network architecture and deployment are described in Chapter 6. The format of Ethernet frames is identified and is used to explain Ethernet media access control, error detection, and virtual local area network (VLAN) support. Power over Ethernet (PoE) is also introduced in Chapter 6.

Chapter 6 also describes wired BNs, both switched and routed. The deployment of switches and cabling in wired backbones is described, along with the importance of ensuring the physical security of wired infrastructure.

Chapter 7 focuses on wireless networks in business facilities, especially Wi-Fi networks and RANs. The characteristics of radio waves are described along with how these characteristics are changed (modulated) to represent data. The challenges associated with media access and error control in wireless networks are also discussed.

Wi-Fi network architectural components (e.g., BSSs [basic service sets], ESSs [extended service Sets], and distribution systems) are described to provide an accurate understanding of Wi-Fi network deployments in business facilities and how they differ from residential Wi-Fi networks. CSMA/CA (the Wi-Fi protocol) is described.

The evolution of Wi-Fi standards is briefly described in Chapter 7. Special attention is paid to the communication capabilities associated with Wi-Fi 6 and those anticipated for Wi-Fi 7. Wi-Fi frequency bands (e.g., 2.4, 5, and 6 GHz) and channels are discussed to clarify the differences between their characteristics and capabilities. Orthogonal frequency-division multiplexing (OFDM) and its importance in Wi-Fi connectivity and performance are also discussed.

Chapter 7 also considers Wi-Fi security vulnerabilities and how malicious actors may exploit them. That section also addresses Wi-Fi security controls and best practices.

Chapter 7 concludes by introducing radio access networks (RANs) and the reasons why RANs are becoming more common in business facilities.

1.7.4 Business WANs

Chapter 8 considers WAN connection options for interconnecting distributed, geographically dispersed business locations. Point-to-point T-carrier and Synchronous Optical Network (SONET) circuits/services may be leased to connect pairs of business locations. Business WANs built using dedicated circuits can have different physical topologies, including hub-and-spoke, ring, and partial mesh.

Multiprotocol label switching (MPLS) services' application-centric features and ability to prioritize different types of network traffic have made them popular in business WANs. Today, Carrier Ethernet, virtual private network (VPN), or software-defined WAN (SD-WAN) services have replaced MPLS in many business WANs.

Some enterprise networks also include wireless WAN links/services, such as terrestrial microwave, satellite, fixed wireless, and cellular services. More businesses are leveraging mobile network operator (MNO) networks to provide wireless links among their different branches, especially those deploying RANs in their facilities.

SD-WAN solutions enable businesses to improve the overall performance of their WANs in an application-centric manner by controlling and optimizing data traffic on their WANs' links/connections centrally and dynamically.

Chapter 8 concludes by considering WAN vulnerabilities and security issues. SD-WAN, security information and event management (SIEM), and SASE technologies are identified as WAN security solutions.

1.7.5 IoT and IIoT

Chapter 9 focuses on IoT systems and applications in enterprise networks and the increasing volume of IoT data traffic. Some of this traffic is device-to-device (M2M) communication and some is device-to-cloud or device-to-IoT platform.

Chapter 9 pays special attention to Industrial Internet of Things (IIoT) systems and applications. IIoT systems and applications contribute to smart manufacturing and Industry 4.0, smart logistics and supply chains, Warehouse 4.0, and other applications that illustrate the transition from e-business to digital business.

Chapter 9 discusses IoT architectures and platforms. IoT technologies, protocols, and security controls are best understood by mapping them to specific layers in IoT architectures. **IoT platforms** monitor and manage/control IoT devices under the guidance of IoT applications.

Adding IoT devices and applications to enterprise networks introduces a wide range of potentially exploitable vulnerabilities that merit specialized vigilance and defenses. Deploying IoT and IIoT systems in today's businesses is a driver of business adoption of SD-WAN and SASE.

1.7.6 Network Design and Management

Chapter 10 describes the processes that businesses use to design and manage their enterprise networks. These processes are easier to grasp after the technologies and protocols described in Chapters 2 through 9 are understood.

The ongoing evolution of businesses and networking technologies encourages network designers to reconsider the current composition and deployment of enterprise network components. Factors influencing network design decisions include current and future business needs and evolving networking technologies, protocols, applications, and services.

Network life cycle models, enterprise network architectures, and hierarchical network architectures enable designers to proceed systematically and in a modular fashion. Designers consider input from business managers and IT managers when determining business and technical requirements for the redesigned network.

ESs and mission-critical applications are important network design considerations. Often, networks are designed and configured to ensure that these applications are available, perform adequately, and are secure. After the new design is implemented, network personnel monitor, modify, update, manage, and maintain the network.

Network management (NM) encompasses activities used to configure, monitor, control, and coordinate network resources. NM software, architectures, and standards support NM activities.

NM architectures include managed devices, software agents in managed devices, and network management system (NMS) software. NMSs collect data from network devices that is used to identify and troubleshoot performance issues and monitor security.

Common NM functions include fault management, configuration management, accounting management, performance management, and security management (FCAPS). These functions, along with network and network security audits, are briefly described in Chapter 10. The roles of SDN and unified endpoint management (UEM) are also described.

1.7.7 Layered Security

Chapters 11 and 12 focus on layered security in enterprise networks. Chapter 11 begins by considering network vulnerabilities and attack surfaces. It identifies common types of network attacks and the processes, procedures, and tools used to respond to security incidents.

Chapter 11 identifies the most important enterprise network security goals (confidentiality, integrity, availability, business continuity) as well as risk assessment and management activity. It explains the rationale for layered security defenses and how/why security plans, policies, procedures, and architectures contribute to protecting enterprise networks. Special attention is devoted to zero trust architectures.

Several layers of the DiD model are described in Chapter 11. It focuses on security threats, defenses, and best practices for the layers of DiD. Several cloud-oriented defenses used in today's enterprise networks are identified.

An extensive section on perimeter defenses is included in Chapter 11. This provides a broader understanding of network perimeter vulnerabilities and the array of defenses used to protect enterprise network perimeters. Special attention is devoted to the contributions of demilitarized zone (DMZ) networks, intrusion detection systems (IDSs), and intrusion prevention systems (IPSs). Perimeter defense best practices are also described.

Insider threats and advanced persistent threats (APTs) are among the more important internal network threats. Lateral movement monitoring tools (e.g., user behavior analysis) and controls (such as least privilege access and network segmentation) are used to detect and deter APTs. Cryptography and using symmetric and asymmetric encryption for data in motion are also discussed as internal network security mechanisms.

Chapter 12 addresses the security threats and mechanisms associated with the innermost layers of the DiD model—the endpoint, application, and data layers.

Malware, including zero-day and fileless malware, is identified as an endpoint threat, and a wide range of endpoint security defenses are identified, including browser isolation, sandboxing, endpoint protection platform (EPP), endpoint detection and response (EDR), and extended detection and response (XDR) tools. Endpoint security best practices are also identified.

Chapter 12 describes fundamental application controls. It identifies ES characteristics that add complexity to these applications and make them challenging to secure. It also describes several specialized ES security mechanisms, such as role- and attribute-based access controls and other security defenses, including zero trust.

Secure coding practices, and best practice recommendations, are briefly described in Chapter 12 as vehicles for ensuring that security is not overlooked by application developers.

Data threats, including data exfiltration, modification, or destruction and data in use (DIU) threats, are described in Chapter 12. Data security controls described in Chapter 12 include encrypting data at rest, enterprise data rights management (EDRM), data masking, and database access controls.

Chapters 11 and 12 afford an opportunity to dive deeper into security controls identified in previous chapters by considering them within the context of DiD. These chapters also provide a bigger picture of how various defenses are deployed and orchestrated to protect business networks.

1.7.8 Learning Aids

When you reach the end of the final chapter, you should have a broader and deeper understanding of enterprise networks and their roles in today's businesses. There are many places to plug in and get started, but having a better understanding of the big picture is an important beginning.

The book includes multiple learning aids to help you wrap your head around the networking concepts and technologies that are discussed. Each chapter begins by identifying its major learning objectives and concludes with a summary of its contents. A list of key terms is included after the summary, followed by review questions intended to sharpen your focus on especially important parts of the chapter's contents. Problems, exercises, and a minicase are included at the end of each chapter to help you better understand the applicability of specific concepts. A list of references is also included for further study and to identify some of the major sources used to write the chapter.

Most chapters have appendices that provide a more complete, business-focused, or technically detailed examination of some of the topics discussed in the chapters. You are encouraged to explore them, especially if you seek a stronger business understanding of enterprise systems or desire a more in-depth technical focus.

SUMMARY

An enterprise network is a hardware, software, and security infrastructure that serves the needs of a business. Enterprise networks include a wide range of endpoints interconnected by network devices in LANs, BNs, WANs, and data centers and utilize a range of communication protocols to transfer data. Cloud infrastructure and security technologies are other important parts of enterprise networks.

Layered models facilitate understanding of enterprise network communications, network equipment deployment, and security. Enterprise Architecture (EA) is a layered framework that enables businesses to systematically assess the extent to which their data; applications; and information, networking, and security technologies align with their business objectives. EA promotes a business-first orientation to IT and network infrastructure.

E-commerce is commonly supported on enterprise networks. Selling products and services to customers (B2C e-commerce) is common; transactions with other businesses (B2B e-commerce) are also common.

E-business leverages enterprise networks more extensively than e-commerce and includes a wide range of applications and services that automate business processes and improve both internal and external communication and collaboration. Digital business is considered a step beyond e-business that produces new revenue streams and business models by combining people, things, and business.

Standards provide the rules needed for exchanging data among network devices. They help ensure that hardware and software from different vendors can work together, as well as helping promote competition to hold down prices on the products and services vendors bring to market. Several standard setting organizations (SSOs) are involved in creating and updating networking standards.

Standards are revised or amended in response to technology advances and fuel upgraded and continually improving networking technologies. Numerous advancing technologies are influencing the evolution of enterprise networks, including the IoT, 5G, AI, SDN, SASE, and blockchain.

This book strives to provide an accurate description of today's enterprise networks, their components, and their security. Completing the book provides readers with a broader and deeper understanding of enterprise networks, their roles in today's businesses, and how they are evolving in response to technological advances and business needs.

KEY TERMS

Backbone
Big Data
Blockchain
Cloud computing
Enterprise Architecture (EA)
E-commerce
Enterprise network
Enterprise system
Internet of Things (IoT)
IoT platform
Local area network (LAN)
Mission-critical application
Network management (NM)
Software-defined networking (SDN)
Wide area network (WAN)

REVIEW QUESTIONS

1. What are the differences between network endpoints, network equipment, and security technologies?
2. What is an enterprise network? How/why are enterprise networks business-centric?
3. Identify the different types of networks included in enterprise networks. Briefly explain how/why cloud infrastructure is considered an enterprise network component.
4. Identify several examples of enterprise network evolution.
5. Briefly describe how/why layered communication models are valuable.
6. Briefly describe the usefulness of the three-layer hierarchical model.
7. How/why do layered security defenses enhance the security of enterprise network data?

8. What is Enterprise Architecture (EA), and how can it be beneficial to organizations?
9. What does EA's business architecture encompass?
10. How does data architecture differ from information architecture? Why is it useful to consider an organization's data and information from an architectural perspective?
11. What is Big Data, and why is it an issue in today's businesses? How is Big Data affecting enterprise networks?
12. What does EA's application architecture encompass? What is a mission-critical application?
13. What are enterprise systems? What are examples of enterprise systems? Why do enterprise systems receive special treatment in enterprise networks?
14. What does EA's technology architecture encompass?
15. Identify several modules included in network architecture diagrams.
16. What is a local area network (LAN)? What types of LANs are found in business facilities?
17. What is a backbone? Identify examples of backbone network infrastructure.
18. What is a wide area network (WAN)? What are the characteristics of business WANs?
19. What is cloud computing? Identify several reasons why businesses are adopting cloud services and infrastructure.
20. What does EA's security architecture encompass? Why is layered protection common?
21. How does EA contribute to business and enterprise network alignment?
22. What is e-commerce? How does B2C e-commerce differ from B2B e-commerce?
23. How does e-business differ from e-commerce? What are examples of e-business technologies and applications?
24. What is digital business? How does it differ from digital transformation? Identify examples of digital business applications.
25. What are standards, and how/why are they important for enterprise networks? What are the differences between formal and de facto standards?
26. Identify several SSOs that develop and maintain network standards.
27. Briefly explain how the IoT is shaping the evolution of enterprise systems. What are IoT platforms?
28. How is 5G being used in business facilities, and how is it shaping the evolution of enterprise networks?
29. How is AI being used in enterprise networks?
30. What is SDN? How does it differ from traditional networking?
31. What is SASE? Why is it increasingly common in enterprise networks?
32. What is a blockchain? How are blockchains related to enterprise networks?
33. What does network management encompass?

PROBLEMS AND EXERCISES

Exercise 1-1 "5G" is used in reference to both Wi-Fi networks and cellular services. Do some online research on what 5G means in the context of Wi-Fi networks and how this differs from 5G services from mobile network operators (MNOs) such as Verizon and T-Mobile. Create a professionally formatted Word document that clearly explains the difference between Wi-Fi 5G and 5G cellular services. Your document should be a minimum of 500 words in length and should include at least two online sources as references.

Exercise 1-2 Do some online research comparing the specifications for the Wi-Fi 6 standard to what is expected to be included in the Wi-Fi 7 standard. Identify and briefly describe how/why Wi-Fi 7 technologies will improve Wi-Fi network performance and provide a better Wi-Fi user experience. Summarize what you learn in a professionally formatted Word document of at least 750 words or a PowerPoint presentation with at least five slides. At least two online sources should be included as references in your research summary.

Exercise 1-3 Section 1.5 identifies some of the major SSOs for networking standards. Do some online research to identify the type(s) of networking standards that each of these organizations is responsible for creating and revising and the types of technologies affected by their standards. Summarize your findings in a three-column table in a Word document or PowerPoint slide that identifies the SSO in the left column, lists examples of standards created/revised by the organization in the middle column, and identifies examples of affected networking standards in the right column.

Exercise 1-4 If you had to rank the technologies identified in Section 1.6 in terms of overall importance to the evolution of enterprise networks, what would your rankings look like? Provide justification for them. Summarize your rankings and justifications in a two-column table in a Word document or PowerPoint slide.

Exercise 1-5 If you were to add another technology to Section 1.6, what technology would you add? Briefly explain why your selected technology should be included in the list of technologies that are shaping the evolution of enterprise networks.

CHAPTER REFERENCES

Chartio. (n.d.). The Data Storage Hierarchy: Lakes, Warehouses, and Marts. Retrieved from: https://chartio.com/learn/data-warehouses/the-data-storage-hierarchy-lakes-warehouses-and-marts/

Chauhan, P., & Sood, M. (2021). Big Data: Present and Future. *Computer*, 54, pp. 59–65. Retrieved from: https://www.computer.org/csdl/magazine/co/2021/04/09399951/1sF3Fj2mlMY

Cisco Systems. (n.d.). What Is an Enterprise Network? Retrieved from: https://www.cisco.com/c/en/us/solutions/enterprise-networks/what-is-an-enterprise-network.html

Cloudflare. (n.d.). What Is Enterprise Networking? Retrieved from: https://www.cloudflare.com/learning/network-layer/enterprise-networking/

Cox, K. (n.d.). A Brief History of Networking Technology. trueCABLE. Retrieved from: https://www.truecable.com/blogs/cable-academy/a-brief-history-of-network-technology

Gao, Y. (2015). The Evolution and Revolution of Business Networks. *Forbes*. Retrieved from: https://www.forbes.com/sites/sap/2015/09/02/the-evolution-and-revolution-of-business-networks/?sh=37b20f087c8e

Info-Tech Research Group. (n.d.). Enterprise Network Design Considerations. Retrieved from: https://www.infotech.com/research/ss/enterprise-network-design-considerations

Jame, A. (2018). 5 Brilliant Ways to Use AI in Networking. DataCaptive. Retrieved from: https://blog.datacaptive.com/5-brilliant-ways-to-use-ai-in-networking/#:~:text=By%20using%20AI%20in%20networking%2C%20it%20would%20be,topologies%20and%20software%20we%20can%20revolutionize%20the%20networks

javaTpoint. (n.d.). Computer Network Models. Retrieved from: https://www.javatpoint.com/computer-network-models

Juniper Networks. (n.d.). What Is Artificial Intelligence for Networking? Retrieved from: https://www.juniper.net/us/en/research-topics/what-is-ai-for-networking.html

MacDonald, N., Lerner, A., & Watts, J. (2022). 2022 Strategic Roadmap for SASE Convergence. Gartner. Retrieved from: https://www.forcepoint.com/resources/industry-analyst-reports/gartner-2022-strategic-roadmap-sase-convergence

Microsoft. (n.d.). What Is Cloud Computing? A Beginners Guide. Retrieved from: https://azure.microsoft.com/en-us/resources/cloud-computing-dictionary/what-is-cloud-computing/#cloud-deployment-types

Palo Alto Networks. (n.d.). What Is SASE? Retrieved from: https://www.paloaltonetworks.com/cyberpedia/what-is-sase

Raza, M. (2021). Enterprise Networking Explained: Types, Concepts & Trends. *IT Operations Blog*. BMC Software. Retrieved from: https://www.bmc.com/blogs/enterprise-networking/

Segal, T. (2022). What Is Big Data? Definition, How It Works, and Uses. Investopedia. Retrieved from: https://www.investopedia.com/terms/b/big-data.asp

Solarwinds. (n.d.). What Is an Enterprise Network? Retrieved from: https://www.solarwinds.com/resources/it-glossary/enterprise-network

VMware. (n.d.). What Is Software-Defined Networking (SDN)? Retrieved from: https://www.vmware.com/topics/glossary/content/software-defined-networking.html

MINICASE: Business Network Evolution and Revolution

Some of the major changes that have occurred in manufacturing industries since the seventeenth century are summarized in Table 1-6. Across time, technology advances have affected how work gets done, especially manufacturing work. Along the way, a new world economy has been created.

As they transitioned to the *IT Revolution* during the second third of the twentieth century, businesses benefited from significant improvements in automation, productivity, and data-driven decision-making. This was followed by the *Internet Revolution* during the 1990s and early 2000s, which produced an explosion of data and information, and what is now being called the *Network Revolution*.

In today's Network Revolution, businesses and markets are becoming increasingly interconnected and digital. This change is transforming how people conduct business. Companies that understand this, actively participate in their business networks, and are willing to trailblaze the path to becoming digital businesses are more likely to benefit from disruptive transformation than to just be disrupted.

Numerous changes have also taken place in how companies relate to one another. Prior to the Industrial Revolution, companies were usually self-interested loners in the marketplace and often only interacted with a few other businesses. Today, a business is often a partner in multiple supply chains and markets, both physical and electronic. This has meant that a business's computing network, its enterprise network, is increasingly linked and interwoven with those of other businesses. A business's network is often a component of numerous business networks, different collections, and constellations of the networks of individual businesses.

Platforms that enable and support an organization's participation in business networks should help the organization capitalize on the combined strength of its business network memberships and data. Such platforms should combine the vir-

Table 1-6: Characteristics of the first through fourth industrial revolutions.				
	1st Industrial Revolution	2nd Industrial Revolution	3rd Industrial Revolution	4th Industrial Revolution
Theme	Mechanization	Electrification	Automation	Digitalization
Occurrence	Occurred during the 17th and 18th centuries, mainly in Europe and North America	From the late 1800s to the start of World War I	1940s through 1990s	Start of the 21st century
Key Drivers	Steam engines replacing horse and human power	Production of steel, electricity, and combustion engines	Computers, networks, and the Internet	AI, robotics, IoT, and blockchain
Examples	Introduction of mechanical production facilities driven by water and steam power	Division of labor and mass production, enabled by electricity	Automation of production through electronic and IT systems	Robotics, artificial intelligence, machine learning, augmented reality, virtual reality

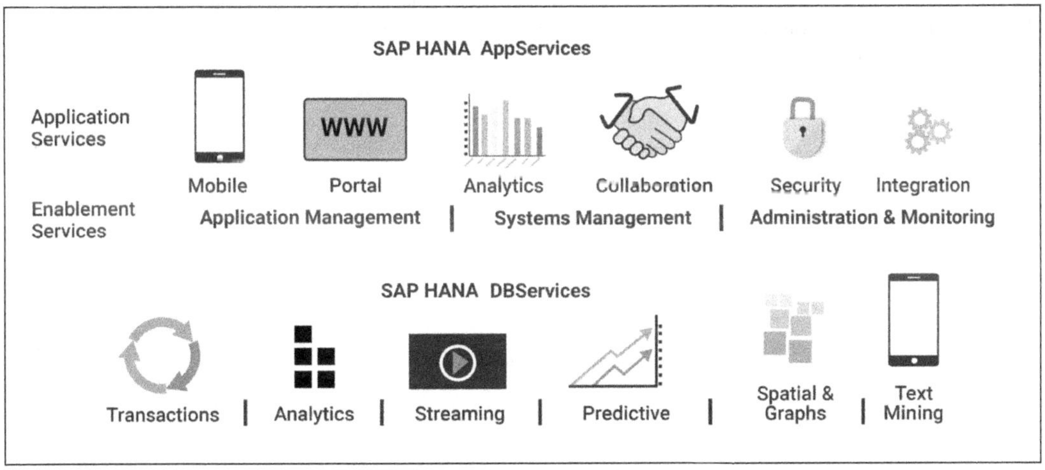

Figure 1-24: Some of the key features of the SAP HANA Cloud Platform.

tual platforms that businesses currently depend on (e.g., Internet search, e-commerce, digital payments, communication, collaboration, social media, etc.) but should also extend beyond them.

SAP touts its SAP HANA Cloud Platform as an example of a platform designed to help businesses navigate the Network Revolution. It uses the cloud to help companies link applications, Big Data, analytics, and network services to other business network members. This facilitates collaborative and mutually beneficial relationships with other businesses.

Some of the key characteristics of this platform are illustrated in Figure 1-24. Its enablement services can be especially valuable for business network participation. Whether this platform can live up to its billing as a business network enabler remains to be seen.

Minicase Questions

1. Chapter 1 describes the differences between e-commerce, e-business, and digital business. Which industrial revolution stage(s) in Table 1-6 is/are the best fit for each of these types of business? Briefly explain and justify your choices.
2. Sharing data and information with other businesses has increased as businesses have evolved from being largely independent with few trading partners, to being participants in supply chains, to being parts of numerous supply chains and business networks. Do you think that this increased sharing of data and information with other organizations is related to the elevated importance of Big Data in today's organizations? Why or why not?
3. Cloud computing applications, services, and infrastructure are increasingly important parts of enterprise networks. Do you think that this has caused the emergence of business networks, or is it the other way around, with growing reliance on cloud computing applications, services, and infrastructure being the result of the emergence of business networks? Explain your reasoning.

4. Enterprise systems (ESs) are mission-critical applications in many businesses. Often, ES applications are boundary-spanning and include links to business partners. Do you think that businesses with ESs may be more receptive to participating in business networks than businesses without ESs? Why or why not?
5. How/why has the emergence of business networks created new security challenges for enterprise networks? Do you think it is possible to develop security solutions to protect business network participants? Why or why not?
6. The SAP HANA Cloud Platform (Figure 1-24) is an example of a platform designed to help businesses navigate the Network Revolution. What would you add to this platform to help businesses identify and capitalize on new opportunities for business network membership? Explain your reasoning.

Minicase References

Gao, Y. (2015). The Evolution and Revolution of Business Networks. *Forbes*. Retrieved from: https://www.forbes.com/sites/sap/2015/09/02/the-evolution-and-revolution-of-business-networks/?sh=37b20f087c8e

SAP. (2015). Business Networks: The Evolution and Revolution. Retrieved from: https://blogs.sap.com/2015/09/01/business-networks-the-evolution-and-revolution/

Chapter 2

Enterprise Network Applications

LEARNING OBJECTIVES

After reading and studying this chapter, you should be able to:

- Identify and briefly describe the major types of applications that enterprise networks support.
- Identify and briefly describe several ESs commonly found in enterprise networks.
- Identify and briefly describe how application processing work is distributed among clients and servers in client-server (C/S) applications.
- Explain how ES software architectures align with C/S computing.
- Explain how cloud computing aligns with C/S computing.
- Briefly describe the differences among public, private, and hybrid clouds.
- Identify and briefly describe the major types of cloud provider services.
- Briefly describe the characteristics of e-commerce website architecture and infrastructure.
- Identify and briefly describe enterprise network application vulnerabilities and security threats.
- Identify and briefly describe how enterprise network applications can be protected and secured.

2.0 INTRODUCTION

As noted in Chapter 1, application architecture is the EA domain that includes the applications, programs, services, and software tools used to process data and create the information needed to make strategic decisions.

Application architecture describes the behavior and interaction of application software, databases, and middleware systems used in a business. It focuses on how applications interact with one another on business networks and how they are used and experienced. It also focuses on the data that applications consume and produce. Application architecture strives to ensure that the collection of applications that a business uses is reliable, available, manageable, and scalable.

Application portfolio management maps applications to business processes and functions and considers their costs and their functional and technical quality when assessing their value. It also helps identify integration problems, gaps in functional coverage, systems near the end of their life cycles, and systems that have inherent technological risks or the potential to disrupt the business should they fail or be compromised.

This EA domain considers how applications are integrated and coordinated to enable decision-makers to monitor and manage business processes and business performance. Software services from cloud providers, enterprise systems software, commercial off-the-shelf (COTS) software, and open-source software used by the organization are documented in EA's application architecture.

Custom applications written in-house or acquired through outsourcing to serve specialized data processing requirements are also documented.

Most business applications are designed to run on networks and to be shared by network users. Software applications enable enterprise network users to perform their jobs, and mission-critical applications are especially important drivers of business performance. Dozens, if not hundreds, of applications may be formally supported in enterprise networks.

Enterprise system (ES) software is often used organization-wide to integrate and support business processes. ES applications are among the more important applications that enterprise networks support and are often considered mission-critical. ES software architectures include tiers that conform to client-server (C/S) computing models and that enable them to be deployed in various ways. Fully hosted ES applications from software as a service (SaaS) cloud providers are increasingly common in today's businesses, but some businesses prefer infrastructure as a service (IaaS) cloud services for their ESs.

Business websites are another important part of enterprise networks, especially when they support e-commerce transactions. Like ES and other applications that are critical to business operations and performance, business websites should be protected and secured. Application vulnerabilities are frequently targeted by attackers, so it is important to ensure that safeguards are in place to protect applications, especially those that are mission-critical.

2.1 ENTERPRISE NETWORK APPLICATIONS

An **application** is a computer software program that performs a specific function for an end user or another application. Applications are sometimes called application programs or application software. An application may be self-contained and have a limited set of capabilities, or it may be part of a group of application programs with a wide range of features and capabilities.

Software that enables users to play games, surf the web, or listen to music is another example of application software. Application software for mobile devices or virtual desktops is usually called an *app*.

Application software enables business employees to process sales transactions, create documents and spreadsheets, update databases, and analyze data stored in data warehouses. ES software (enterprise resources planning [ERP], customer relationship management [CRM], supply chain management [SCM], etc.) and database management systems (DBMSs) are other important examples of application software. Software that businesses use can be categorized in various ways, and some of the more important categories are briefly described in this section.

2.1.1 Commercial Off-the-Shelf (COTS) Software

Most of the application software supported on today's enterprise networks consists of purchased application software products. *Commercial off-the-shelf (COTS)* software is ready-made application software created by a third party that is available for sale. Microsoft Office is an example of a COTS software package that has been adopted by a wide range of organizations. Some COTS products can be used "out of the box"; however, it is common for organizations to configure COTS products to improve their integration with other applications or how they perform on an enterprise network.

2.1.2 Custom Software

Custom software is application software developed to meet the specialized needs of a specific organization or user. Unlike COTS software, which is designed for use by a wide range of organizations, custom software is created for a single organization (customer) and is designed to accommodate the customer's unique needs, expectations, and preferences.

Businesses use custom software to fill gaps in existing software or provide functionality not included in COTS software. Some companies prefer custom over COTS software to support their critical functions or their specialized inventory management or HR needs. Although an organization may develop custom software in-house, today it is more common for custom software development to be outsourced to contract programming firms.

2.1.3 Horizontal Market Software

Horizontal market software refers to applications that are useful to organizations in a wide range of industries. Many COTS products, such as Word, Excel, PowerPoint, and other Microsoft Office applications; Google G Suite applications; and general-purpose bookkeeping software (such as QuickBooks), are examples of horizontal market software. Because it is designed for general use, horizontal market software generally does not include customer- or market-specific customizations; however, some organizations may reconfigure it to ensure effective performance on their enterprise networks.

2.1.4 Vertical Market Software

Often contrasted with horizontal market software, *vertical market software* is developed and customized to meet the needs of businesses within a *vertical market* (a specific industry or market). Because it is industry-specific, vertical market software is developed to help a limited group of customers serve their customers or clients. Major ERP software vendors, including SAP, have developed vertical market versions of their ERP software products. These versions are configured to meet the specialized business and information processing requirements of organizations in that vertical market.

2.1.5 Open-Source Software

COTS, horizontal market, and vertical market software products are licensed software whose licenses specify the legal use and distribution of the software. In the United States, licensed software is protected by federal and state copyright laws that specify that the software's source code is owned by its creator, who is the only legal entity entitled to profit from its use. Because of such protections, licensed software is often called *proprietary software*.

The source code of open-source software, in contrast, is not owned by anyone, and it can be inspected and modified by anyone. Because it is publicly available, modifications and improvements to open-source software can be, and usually are, shared among its users. Development and maintenance of the software is "community" in nature, rather than a closely guarded activity of the owner of proprietary software.

Open-source software "licenses" give users permission to use the software as they wish but stipulate that when they modify the application's source code, the modifications must be shared with its community of developers and users. The community nature of open-source software development and use promotes collaborative efforts to continuously improve the application.

Open-source software projects have produced a wide range of applications that are widely used in enterprise networks. Open-source collaboration has produced web browsers (e.g., Firefox), web server software (e.g., Apache), operating systems (e.g., Linux and Ubuntu), database management systems (e.g., Cassandra), learning management systems (e.g., Moodle), content management systems (e.g., WordPress), general-purpose office suites (e.g., Open Office), and generative AI tools (e.g., GPT-4).

2.1.6 Mobile Apps

Mobile apps are applications designed to run on mobile devices such as tablets and smartphones. Thousands of mobile apps have been developed to help business users perform their jobs. Business software vendors have adapted their applications for use on mobile devices, and mobile interfaces to enterprise systems (e.g., CRM and ERP) are common, especially for cloud-based versions of these systems.

2.1.7 Virtual Desktops

Virtual desktops look and act like applications on physical devices, but they are actually remote versions of applications running on virtual devices. The virtual desktop environment is separate from the physical devices used to access it. Users access virtual desktops remotely over enterprise network connections, the Internet, or other networks. Users typically have personalized desktops like those on their physical devices and use virtual desktops to work from remote locations, upload and download files, and save on virtual drives the work that they complete.

The virtual servers that support virtual desktops are usually cloud based, and virtual desktops are typically considered cloud services. *Desktop as a service (DaaS)* is a cloud-based service that delivers virtual desktops to subscribers over the Internet. Increasing business adoption of virtual desktops has convinced some industry pundits to speculate that they will become the dominant mode of deploying business software in the years ahead.

2.1.8 Database Management Systems (DBMSs)

A *database management system (DBMS)* is software that manages data stored in a database. Although often viewed as a type of system software, a DBMS is actually application software that does not operate at the same level as an operating system or other types of system software. DBMS software is installed as an application on servers (called database servers) that interact with operating systems to enable users to add, modify, and retrieve data that is physically stored on network storage devices.

An enterprise network may formally support dozens or hundreds of applications, and an organization's employees may use hundreds or thousands of other applications that add traffic to network circuits. Because they are used organization-wide or by major subunits, ESs are especially important business applications that warrant and receive specialized treatment.

2.2 ENTERPRISE SYSTEMS AND ENTERPRISE NETWORKS

Enterprise systems (ESs) are large-scale application software packages that enable organizations to track and control their business operations. They support business processes and are often adopted to streamline and integrate business processes to conform to industry best practices. They have centralized databases that facilitate data and process visibility, information flows, and reporting. Today, most ESs include advanced data analytics capabilities. Essentially, ESs serve as central command systems for automating business operations and facilitating reporting and decision-making.

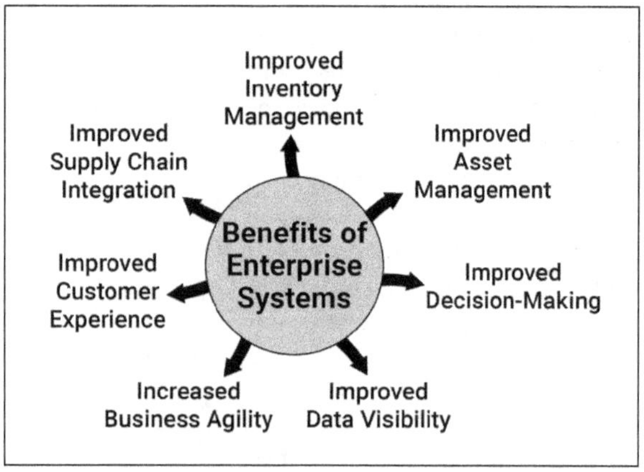

Figure 2-1: Examples of enterprise systems benefits for businesses.

When successfully implemented, ESs provide a wide range of potential benefits, including those identified in Figure 2-1. Organizations adopt ESs to replace legacy systems, integrate systems across locations, improve performance and competitiveness in their industry, and position themselves for growth. Businesses are attracted by ESs' potential to increase process efficiencies and reduce costs. Cost savings may be realized from more efficient supply chains, reduced inventory levels, and process automation and integration. ES adopters often experience improved decision-making because of better data/information visibility, transparency, and flow. Data-driven decision-making and better informed decisions are facilitated by real-time access to ES data and information.

Enterprise resource planning (ERP), customer relationship management (CRM), and supplier relationship management (SRM) are examples of ESs that are widely supported on enterprise networks.

2.2.1 Enterprise Resource Planning (ERP) Systems

Businesses use **enterprise resource planning (ERP)** to manage and integrate the most important parts of their day-to-day operations. This often includes their purchasing, inventory management, manufacturing, sales, and human resources activities. When these activities are appropriately automated, real-time management of integrated business processes is possible.

ERP software is adopted and used by businesses to link processes and systems across the enterprise. It is used to streamline workflow, facilitate information sharing among functional areas, and provide sufficient data/information about business operations to enable data-driven decision-making. Instead of having separate databases to support different functions (e.g., sales, purchasing, and manufacturing), an ERP system stores data in a single database that provides real-time, organization-wide access to its data/information.

Figure 2-2: Examples of the functions and activities supported by ERP systems.

Figure 2-2 illustrates an ERP system's ability to integrate business functions, processes, and systems. To be considered a full-fledged ERP system, an ERP software product must be able to support accounting and finance, human resource management, inventory management, manufacturing, purchasing, and sales. It must also be capable of being integrated with other ESs used by the organization (e.g., CRM and SRM systems). Because it often serves as the interconnection point among other ESs, an ERP system is typically viewed as the central component of an organization's constellation of ESs.

2.2.2 Customer Relationship Management (CRM) Systems

Customer relationship management (CRM) focuses on managing the various aspects of an organization's relationship with its customers. This includes a business's presales contacts with prospective customers and post-sales service, sales, and support activities focused on ensuring that customers are satisfied with their purchases and/or are getting the most out of the products or services they bought (see Figure 2-3). CRM strives to promote profitable customer relationships and to increase customer loyalty and retention and the likelihood of repeat sales. It assumes that organizations with superior customer understanding are best positioned for developing

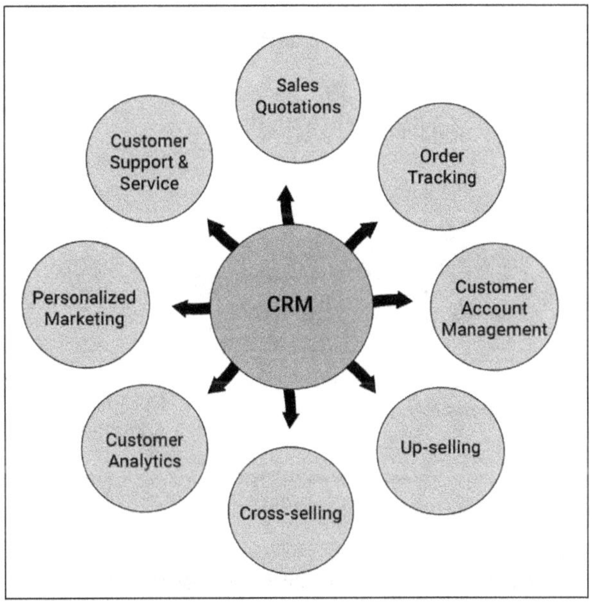

Figure 2-3: Customer relationship management (CRM) software capabilities.

appropriate strategies for sustainable competitive advantage. Today, such understanding is often derived from applying advanced analytics to CRM databases.

Three major aspects of CRM are commonly identified. One focuses on supporting and automating the activities of sales personnel (sales force automation). Customer support/service is a second major aspect of CRM. The third aspect of CRM focuses on marketing to current and previous customers. This may include marketing to prospective customers who are leaning toward placing an order (and becoming a "customer") or marketing to entice repeat sales to current or previous customers. Such marketing is distinct from generic marketing aimed at attracting interest from the general population. The software capabilities for each aspect are as follows:

- Sales force automation uses software to automate presales and sales activities. Presales includes identifying/contacting prospective customers and responding to prospective customer inquiries or requests for quotations (RFQs). Sales activities include receiving and tracking customer orders through fulfillment processes. Both activities involve capturing and updating prospect/customer information and monitoring product inventories.
- Customer support/service management uses software to coordinate the various facets of an organization's customer service and ongoing support activities.
- Marketing automation uses software to market to prospective, current, and previous customers. Today, this involves various forms of digital marketing, including personalized email and social media marketing. It also involves coordinating and analyzing marketing and branding efforts across sales channels.

2.2.3 Supplier Relationship Management (SRM) Systems

Supplier relationship management (SRM) focuses on managing an organization's engagement with vendors that supply needed materials/supplies and services. It strives to streamline and improve the efficiency of the activities, tasks, and processes that connect an organization to its suppliers. SRM includes procurement and purchasing activities as well as strategic sourcing activities, such as forging long-term partnerships and assessing supplier performance.

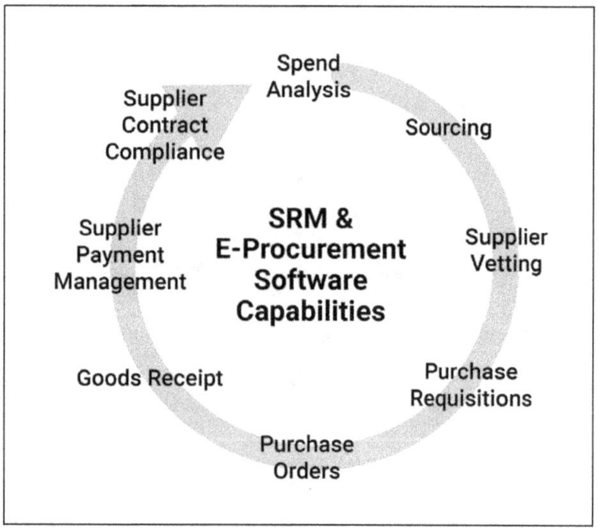

Figure 2-4: SRM software enables businesses to conduct procurement and purchasing activities over communication networks.

SRM software provides digital tools to manage relationships with suppliers and service contractors. It provides an electronic means for carrying out the activities depicted in Figure 2-4.

Procurement and sourcing managers use SRM software for requisitioning activities, such as the creation, approval, and electronic transmittal (tendering) of requests for proposals (RFPs) or requests for quotations (RFQs). SRM software's competitive bidding capabilities help organizations evaluate vendor responses to RFPs and RFQs (tenders) and select the best vendor for specific materials/products or services. This enables organizations to evaluate bids on a combination of factors, including price and delivery history. SRM contracting tools assist organizations in appropriately structuring purchase contracts and finalizing arrangements with successful bidders.

Most SRM software products are web based and provide real-time interfaces between organizations and suppliers. After purchase contracts are finalized, SRM software automates the creation and electronic transmission of purchase orders (POs) and enables buyers to check the status of POs and scheduled deliveries. It also automates the electronic receipt, processing, and payment of vendor invoices to ensure compliance with purchase contracts.

SRM software includes sourcing, supplier management, electronic purchasing, operational procurement, and spend and performance analysis capabilities.

- Sourcing capabilities help in identifying, evaluating, and engaging suppliers.
- Supplier management capabilities help to centrally manage supplier engagements and to minimize associated risks.
- Electronic procurement capabilities enable organizations to aggregate suppliers' web catalogs. They also facilitate purchasing, invoicing, and payment activities.
- Operational procurement capabilities facilitate the creation, verification, approval, transmission, and confirmation of POs. They also support goods receipt and inventory monitoring activities.
- Spend and performance analysis capabilities are used to analyze procurement spending data, identify potential cost saving opportunities, and monitor purchase contract compliance.

2.2.4 Supply Chain Management (SCM) Systems

A **supply chain** includes the entities (organizations) directly or indirectly involved in the procurement and distribution of materials/supplies or products. A supply chain consists of the steps needed to get a product or service to the customer. This may include transforming raw materials into finished products, transporting products, and distributing products to end users. As Figure 2-5 illustrates, supply chain entities may include raw material suppliers, manufacturers, distributors, and firms that sell products to customers, such as retailers. A supply chain often includes warehouses, transportation companies, and distribution centers.

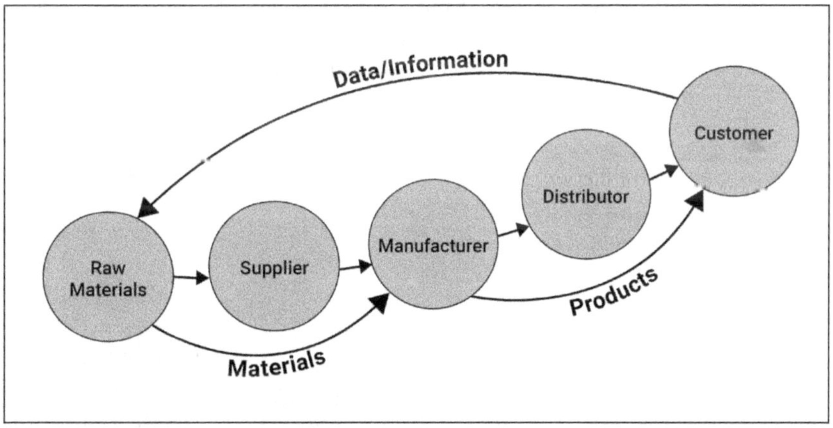

Figure 2-5: Examples of supply chain entities.

Supply chain management (SCM) focuses on efficient movement of materials and products among supply chain entities to maximize their individual and collective profitability. When a supply chain is efficient and well managed, it can lower an entity's costs and increase its profitability. Effective SCM involves managing the information needed to coordinate the operations of supply chain entities.

SCM software includes ESs and other software products that include capabilities for executing supply chain transactions, managing supplier relationships, and coordinating the procurement and fulfillment processes of supply chain entities. Examples of SCM software capabilities include demand planning, supply chain planning (SCP), and supply chain execution (SCE):

- Demand planning capabilities include statistical modeling and forecasting tools for generating product and material demand forecasts.
- SCP capabilities include sophisticated mathematical algorithms for identifying opportunities to improve material and product flows within the supply chain and to increase overall supply chain efficiency.
- SCE capabilities support/automate materials and product handoffs among supply chain entities.

Other types of software used for SCM include electronic document interchange (EDI), vendor managed inventory (VMI) systems, warehouse management system (WMS), inventory management systems, transportation planning software, and distribution management software. These may be stand-alone systems or additional capabilities included in SCM ES software products.

2.2.5 Enterprise Systems and Interorganizational Linkages

SCM systems rely on electronic connections among supply chain entities. When each supply chain entity has its own enterprise network, a supply chain can be viewed as a set of interconnected enterprise networks that exchange information relevant to the procurement and distribution of materials and products. SCM systems are also examples of boundary-spanning **interorganizational systems (IOSs)**—information and communication technology (ICT) systems that enable organizations to electronically share data/information and conduct business with business partners.

Other ESs, including ERP, CRM, and SRM, also have electronic connections to suppliers and/or customers. Like SCM, they effectively extend an organization's enterprise network to the networks and computing systems of other organizations. They span organizational boundaries and function as IOSs. While these applications primarily serve the purposes and interests of their adopters, some of the business benefits of ESs stem from their links to business partners (e.g., suppliers, distributors, and customers).

Figure 2-6 illustrates how ESs link an organization's enterprise network to those of upstream and downstream supply chain entities. It also illustrates some of the common internal linkages among ES applications.

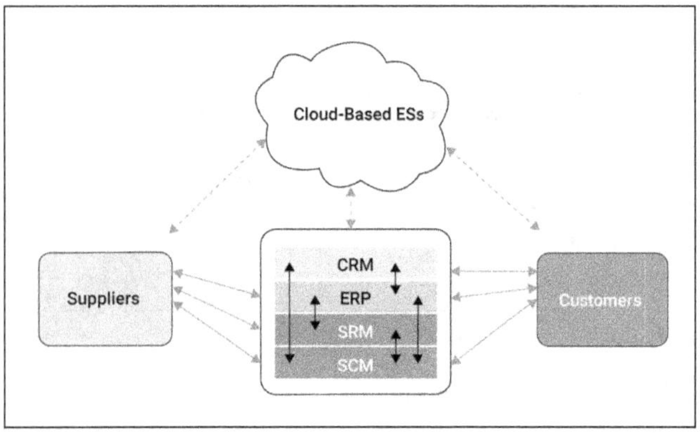

Figure 2-6: ES applications interconnect the enterprise networks of supply chain entities.

Because ERP systems usually support both procurement and fulfillment processes within an organization, they have links to both suppliers and customers. CRM systems have links to customers, and SRM systems enable e-procurement via electronic links to suppliers. Because they focus on materials movement among supply chain entities, like ERP systems, SCM systems have both upstream and downstream links.

Figure 2-6 also illustrates that an organization's ES applications may be cloud based. In such instances, the cloud essentially serves as a communication intermediary among supply chain partners.

Electronic Data Interchange (EDI)

Electronic data interchange (EDI) is the electronic interchange of business documents with standardized formats between trading partners. In EDI transactions, data/information moves directly from an application in one organization to an application in another organization over communication circuits (see Figure 2-7). Because of this, EDI is often considered to be an IOS.

Today, trading partners in a wide range of industries use EDI to exchange a variety of business documents, including RFQs, purchase orders, invoices, shipping notices, and inventory status reports. EDI frequently provides electronic links in supply chains and business-to-business (B2B) networks.

Historically, EDI was one of the first mechanisms used to electronically exchange business documents among the computer systems of trading partners. Because of this, EDI is often described as the first B2B e-commerce system.

Figure 2-7 illustrates EDI in its basic form. In supply chains, commonly exchanged documents include:

- Purchase orders (EDI 850 documents)
- Order receipts—purchase order acknowledgments (EDI 855 documents)
- Invoices (EDI 810 documents)
- Advance shipping notices [ASNs] (EDI 856 documents)
- Payments (EDI 820 documents)—EDI-facilitated payments typically involve ACH (Automated Clearing House) transfers between buyer and seller bank accounts.

Traditionally, there have been two basic types of EDI connections:

- Point-to-point (direct) connections: Two computers or systems directly connect with no intermediary (such as the Internet). These connections may employ leased communication circuits, such as those discussed in Chapter 8, and secure communication protocols.
- Value-added networks (VANs): These third-party communication networks manage secure EDI data transmission among their subscribers using logical, rather than physical, point-to-point connections.

Today, EDI documents are also exchanged via the public Internet using VPN tunnels, which provide a logical equivalent to point-to-point (direct) circuits and are less expensive. *Cloud-based EDI* (a.k.a. *cloud EDI* or *web-based EDI*) services enable EDI documents to be exchanged among trading partners via browser interfaces on a pay-per-use basis. These services enable small and medium-sized businesses to utilize EDI without having to invest in the infrastructure required for traditional EDI connections.

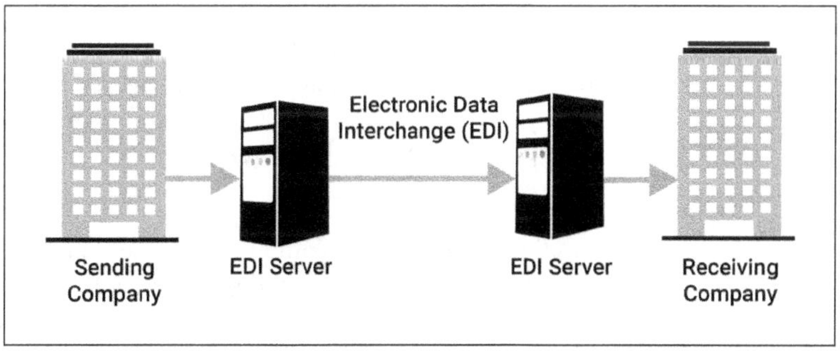

Figure 2-7: EDI continues to provide electronic links among business partners.

SCM and other ESs may leverage EDI for document exchanges between business partners. Whether or not EDI is involved, because of their central role in business operations, ESs are typically considered to be mission-critical applications. As such, they warrant special attention and treatment by network administrators. For example, ES data traffic is given priority on network circuits, and SD-WAN or specialized routing may be used to ensure that ES applications perform at adequate levels. ESs also receive special security considerations.

ES software has a three-tier architecture that maps easily to a three-tier client-server (see Figure 2-11 in section 2.3.3) and/or cloud deployment.

2.3 CLIENT-SERVER COMPUTING APPLICATIONS

Client-server computing is a type of distributed computing in which a client application requests resources or services from another program (a server). Typically, client applications and server resources/services are on different computers, so essentially client-server computing involves two (or more) computers working together over a network. In most instances, servers are faster and more powerful than client devices and are used to manage databases, extract data from storage devices, and run large and/or complex application programs such as ESs. Interfaces are provided on client devices that enable users to request server services and display and/or interpret results

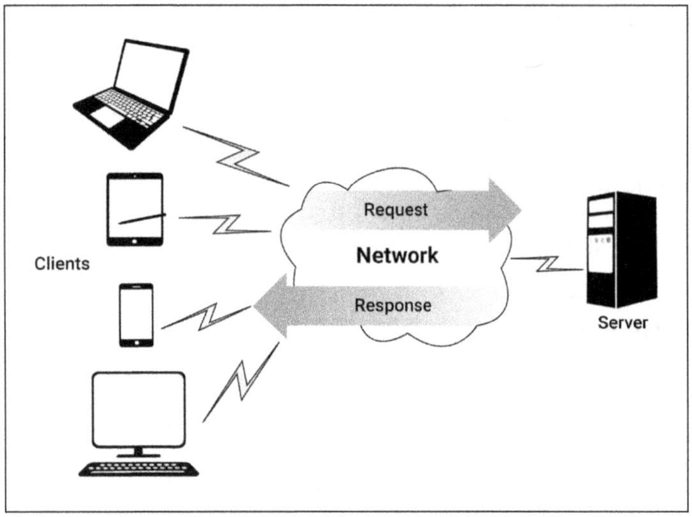

Figure 2-8: In client-server computing, applications running on client devices request services or resources from servers.

returned by servers. Clients and servers use communication software and protocols to interact over network circuits.

A generic depiction of client-server computing is illustrated in Figure 2-8. A server can usually simultaneously serve multiple clients. Each client, however, connects and interacts with a single server for each application that it uses. When running multiple applications at the same time, a client device is connected and interacting with multiple servers.

Clients and servers use a request–response messaging pattern to interact. The client sends a request, and the server returns a response. To communicate, clients and servers need a common language and set of communication rules so that they each know what to expect. These are defined in communications protocols that determine the dialog pattern for the application.

2.3.1 Clients

Relative to servers, clients typically have less robust computing configurations, and most are user-facing computing devices. Essentially, a client is a computer or computer-controlled device that provides network access and runs software applications that send requests to servers and interpret or display server responses.

Client Devices

A **client device** is any computing device that connects to and uses the resources and services of remote servers. Resources and services requested by client devices include files, data/information, intranet or Internet access, external processing, and storage. When applications are processed, the processing work that clients perform is called "client-side" and that performed by servers is "server-side."

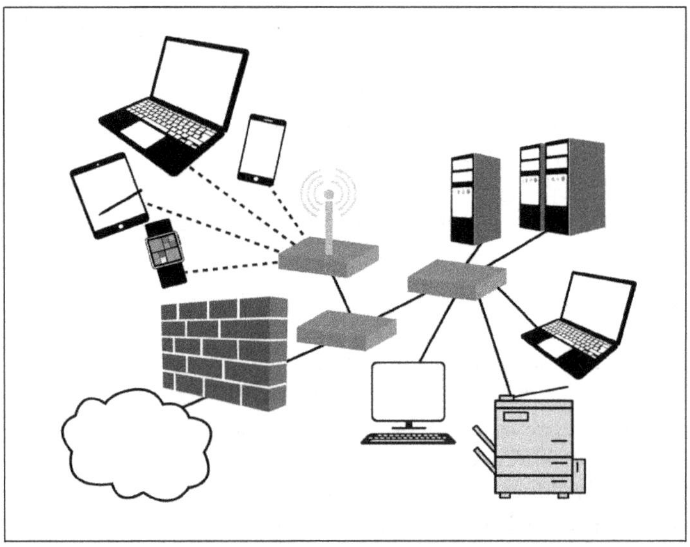

Figure 2-9: Examples of client devices and connections in business environments. Source: mathisworks/iStock. Stock illustration ID:636224940

Client devices do not always have to be continuously powered, but some are. When they are turned on, they provide network access (connections to communication networks) and can interact with servers.

As Figure 2-9 illustrates, there are a wide variety of common client devices in businesses with wireless or wired network connections, including desktop computers, laptops, tablets, smartphones, wearables, and office copier systems. These interact with servers located in the local network or the cloud.

Some clients are specialized hardware devices dedicated to specific functions. One example would be cameras installed on stoplights or toll roads that capture photos of vehicles and license plates to enforce compliance with traffic laws. Many IoT devices also function as specialized clients that connect to cloud and IoT applications that cause IoT devices to take specific actions.

Client Software

Client software is a software program that a client device uses to connect to and interact with a server. It is the program that sends requests to another program (a server) to perform actions. Everyday examples of client software include web browsers, email clients, and instant messaging chat clients. In IoT devices, IoT client software establishes connections with cloud services.

Basically, *mobile apps* are client software programs that turn smartphones, tablets, wearables, and other mobile devices into clients that can send requests to servers to do processing on their behalf. When an app is downloaded and installed, the mobile device is equipped with client software that communicates and interacts with the servers that perform the bulk of the app's processing work.

To interact with device hardware, client software relies on the device's operating system. It works with the device's operating system to take advantage of the device's cameras, microphone, speakers, display, and/or data storage.

Client software has two primary components: client application modules and communication software. Client application modules determine client-side application processing activities. Communication software enables clients and servers to interact; it provides network access, enables the client to create/send requests, and interprets and displays server responses.

Client devices used in businesses differ in physical size, display dimensions, storage capabilities, processors, network connections, and operating systems (see Table 2-1). Underlying differences in client devices are the reason why a mobile app often has different versions designed to work with specific operating systems (e.g., iOS versus Android) and hardware configurations (e.g., iPhone versus iPad).

Table 2-1: Examples of operating systems for client devices and servers.

Laptops and PCs	Smartphones/Tablets	Servers
Chrome OS	iOS	Linux
macOS	Android	UNIX
Windows	Samsung	Windows Server

2.3.2 Servers

Servers are typically faster and more powerful than the client devices that access them, and their operating systems are usually different (see Figure 2-13 in section 2.3.4). They are usually equipped with faster processors and faster input-output (I/O) data access and often have multiple processors to enable them to simultaneously process and respond to requests from multiple clients.

Relative to client LANs, server LANs typically have faster switches and data transmission speeds. Today, servers are commonly connected to switches via high-speed fiber optic circuits. Servers are frequently rack mounted, housed in data centers, and configured for specific functions.

To enable clients to have 24/7 access to their resources and services, servers are usually continuously powered and connected to the communication network. Most are dedicated to performing single functions but can be configured to perform multiple functions. For example, a small business might use a single machine as both a file and print server. Examples of servers used in business networks are identified in Table 2-2.

Servers are the controlling entities in client-server interactions. A client cannot force a server to respond to its requests. Some servers will respond to any client request because their data is designed to be openly accessible. However, if a server's data is commercially valuable or sensitive, it should only respond to requests from legitimate sources.

For security, a server often requires client authentication before responding to its request. If the client cannot provide authentication, its request is ignored or rejected. Doing otherwise could expose the data and the enterprise network to unauthorized or malicious actors.

Table 2-2: Examples of servers used in enterprise networks.

Server Type/Name	Major Functions
Application	Provides business logic and processing for application programs
Content/cache	Provides access to the content of Internet documents, such as web pages and articles
Database	Provides database access, data manipulation, and/or data storage
Domain Name System (DNS)	Translates URLs into IP (Internet Protocol) addresses to enable clients to connect to servers
E-commerce	Functions as an online storefront, with product displays, shopping carts, and payment processing
Email	Directs email to intended recipients and filters spam
File	Provides files to clients
Load balancer	Distributes client requests across a pool of servers; functions as a traffic cop by routing client requests across servers in a way that minimizes response time and maximizes server capacity utilization
Media	Provides access to digital media or media streaming services
Print	Connects clients to printers, directs client print jobs to specific printers, and queues print jobs when they arrive more rapidly than a printer can handle
Proxy	Functions as a relay/intermediary between clients and servers; can be used to mask client identities for privacy or anonymity; may also be used for load balancing, user authentication, encryption/decryption, and content caching
Storage	Stores, accesses, secures, and manages digital data, files, and services over a shared network or through the Internet
Web	Provides web pages in response to client requests

A business may have private servers that are only available for employees or are used for internal communications such as videoconferencing. However, the trend is decidedly away from investing in physical machines and on-premises infrastructure. Server virtualization and increased use of rented servers in cloud datacenters exemplify this trend.

Server Virtualization

Server virtualization is common in both private networks and the cloud. **Server virtualization** uses *virtualization software* to partition a physical server into multiple virtual servers (see Figure 2-10). Each virtual server has its own operating system and runs applications that behave like those running on different physical servers.

The server virtualization process transforms a physical server into a "cloud" of virtual servers. Because it reduces the number of physical servers needed by an enterprise or cloud provider to satisfy its processing requirements, virtualization is considered a *green computing* solution. It also reduces the costs associated with managing and running physical servers.

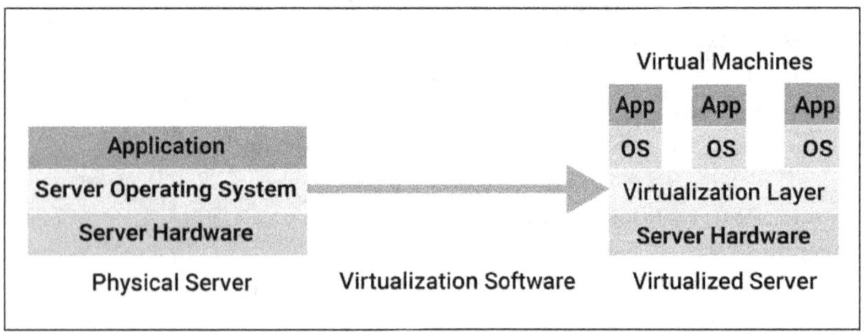

Figure 2-10: Virtualization software enables a single physical server to function as multiple virtual servers.

Resource-intensive applications (such as video editing, computer-aided design [CAD], 3D modeling, cryptography, data compression/decompression) often perform better when server virtualization is used. Virtualizing database servers typically improves their ability to quickly respond to client requests.

2.3.3 Client-Server Software Architecture

Software engineers usually consider client-server applications as *multi-tier* (or *n-tier*) software architectures that facilitate the development of flexible and reusable applications. When an application has distinct tiers or layers, developers can modify the software code at one layer without having to rework the entire application. This also enables independent updating of tiers in response to changing technology or business requirements.

Multi-tier (n-tier) software architectures are the de facto model for enterprise-level client-server applications. They enable separation of client-side and server-side processing activities. The most common client-server software architecture is a three-tier architecture that separates an application into presentation, application logic, and data tiers (see Figure 2-11) that can be distributed across client devices, servers, and data storage technologies. However, because tiers are logical, all three may be colocated in a single device.

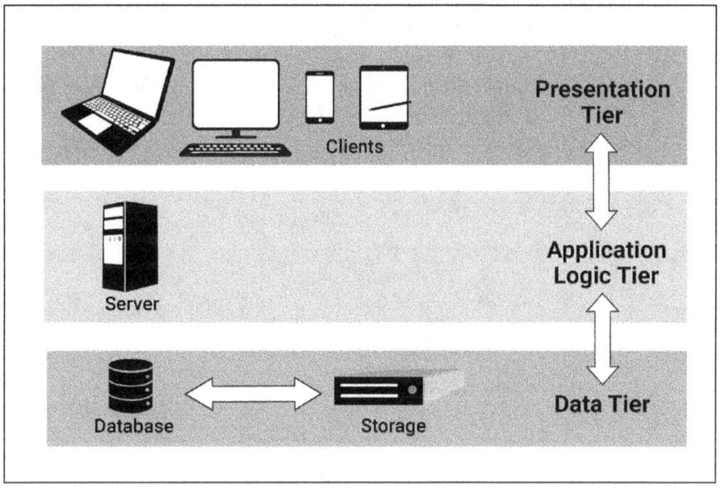

Figure 2-11: Conceptual depiction of the distribution of client-server software tiers across devices in an enterprise network.

The ability to distribute client-server processing activities among devices and network locations increases application fault tolerance, scalability, availability, and security. Additional servers, server virtualization, and storage capacity at server locations enable increasing numbers of clients to be accommodated. And when an application is supported at multiple locations, rather than a single one, its availability is improved by ensuring continued access when a disruption occurs at one of its locations. Uninterrupted access contributes to business continuity by enabling persistent availability of important software.

When multi-tier client-server applications are distributed across network locations, messages are passed among the distributed devices to coordinate and communicate their actions. This enables the application to be perceived by users as a single system even though it is supported by a collection of systems situated at different locations.

A closer look at the differences among tiers is provided in Table 2-3. This summarizes the major functions performed at each tier.

Table 2-3: Summary of the roles among tiers in three-tier client-server software applications.

Client-Server Tier	Description
Presentation Logic	This topmost tier of the application is sometimes called the *UI layer* because it includes user interface (UI) programming. It usually resides on client devices. It communicates with the other tiers and displays the results they return. This tier's primary function is to translate tasks and results into a user understandable form.
Application Logic	The application's functionality is controlled at this layer. It coordinates the processing of the application and performs detailed processing tasks such as interpreting commands/requests, performing calculations, and making logical evaluations and decisions. It communicates with both the presentation and data tiers and relays data requests and responses. It is sometimes called the Business Logic tier or Logic tier.
Data Logic	This tier is responsible for storing and retrieving data in a database or file system. Database management and data access management are performed at this tier. It responds to data requests from the presentation layer that are relayed by the application logic layer and passes requested data to the application logic layer for processing.

Most ESs have software architectures that map to the tiers identified in Figure 2-11. Today's ESs have UIs or apps for mobile devices. Application servers typically perform the bulk of the processing work and process or generate data stored in their centralized databases. ES software architectures and how they map to client-server computing, client-server networks, and cloud-computing are described in Appendix 2-1.

Distributing Application Processing Work Among Clients and Servers

There are various ways to divide the processing of client-server applications between clients and servers. The distribution used for a particular application usually depends on the nature of the

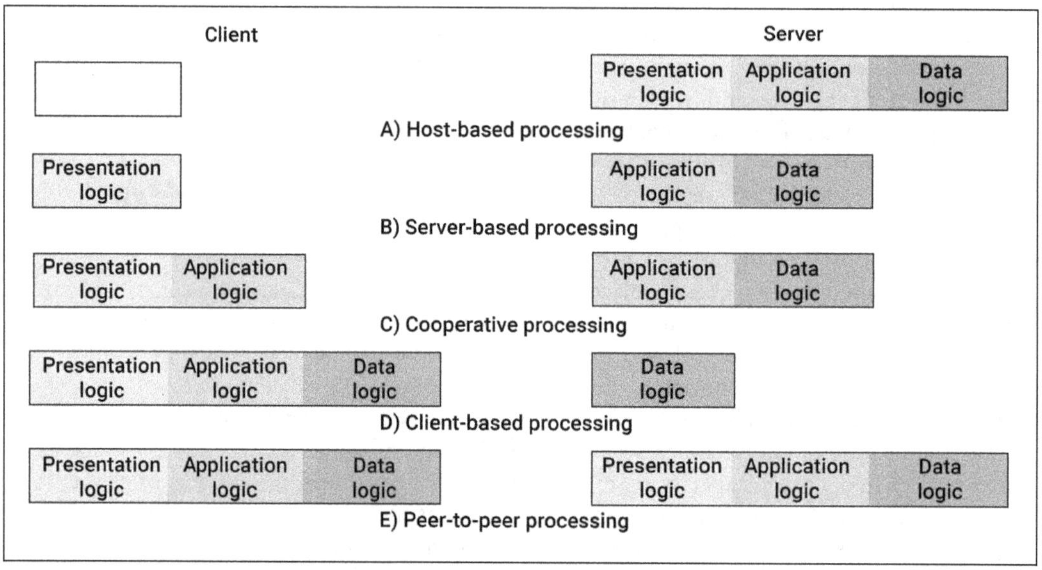

Figure 2-12: Examples of processing work division in client-server applications.

Table 2-4: An overview of various divisions of application processing work between clients and servers.

Name	Other Name(s)	Description
Host-based processing	Zero client; ultra-thin client	Virtually all processing is done by servers. Clients are essentially display devices, and client dialog with servers is server-driven rather than client-side. This is used with client devices (such as IoT devices) that have little or no memory, storage, or processing capabilities. Virtual desktops may be deployed on zero-client devices. In theory, zero clients have few attack surfaces and can contribute to increased network security, but this is not always the case.
Server-based processing	Thin client; fat server	The client is principally responsible for providing a user-friendly interface, and all important or major processing is done by servers. Servers may cause clients to display dialog boxes, windows, or menus that enable users to structure requests or display responses. Mobile apps often turn user devices into thin clients.
Cooperative processing		Clients and servers share application processing work. Processing tasks are distributed to leverage the respective strengths of server and client hardware configurations and how data is distributed among network locations. This is arguably the most complex and challenging client-server processing option to implement and maintain but has the potential to increase user productivity and network efficiency.
Client-based processing	Thick client	Most of the application processing work is performed by the client, with limited involvement/contribution of servers. Servers primarily process client requests for data, and requested data is returned to clients for processing. This application processing approach is better suited for the hardware configurations and computing capabilities of desktop and laptop computers than for mobile devices.
Peer-to-peer (P2P) processing		In P2P networks and applications, all computers can be both a client and a server; no devices are designated to solely serve or receive services or data. All devices may have equal permissions and processing responsibilities. File/folder and printer sharing in home networks are examples of P2P applications. Some P2P applications facilitate file sharing over the Internet; BitTorrent is an example.

application and the functions it performs. It affects the amounts of messages and data passed between clients and servers over the network.

Several common distribution approaches are illustrated in Figure 2-12, and each approach is briefly described in Table 2-4. At one extreme, servers do all or most of the processing, and as you near the other, clients do most of the work. *Cooperative processing* lies between these extremes. Here, application logic is split between clients and servers in ways that capitalize on the strengths of each device. In *peer-to-peer (P2P) processing*, no devices are strictly designated as clients or servers, and all are capable of being both a server and a client.

The division of processing responsibilities affects network traffic and application performance. These are important considerations, especially for ES and other mission-critical applications whose performance is dependent on rapid server responses to client requests.

2.3.4 Client-Server Networks

Client-server computing is a de facto norm in today's networks, and networks configured to facilitate the processing of client-server applications are often called *client-server networks*. Some applications require clients to establish a connection with the server before sending requests for server resources or services, but others do not.

Essentially, a client-server network is a network that includes dedicated servers. Clients and servers communicate over network (LAN and/or WAN) circuits. For connection-oriented applications, after the server has fulfilled a client's request, the connection is terminated to free the server to respond to a request from a different client. If the client requires additional resources or services from the server, another connection is established before the client sends another request.

Because multiple clients share the services/resources of servers in client-server networks, a server may include a program, called a *daemon* (or *daemon server*), that receives and queues incoming client requests while it is busy responding to a specific request. A daemon is like a staffed reception or check-in desk at a health clinic that verifies patient arrivals and provides a waiting area until the health professional is available.

Client-server networks are usually classified as being two-tier or multi-tier. Figure 2-13 depicts an example of a two-tier client-server network. Figures 2-14 and 2-15 provide examples of multi-tier client-server networks.

In each figure, the client connects to and interacts with a single server. Servers that communicate directly with clients are considered *front-end* (or *front-side*) *servers*, while the others involved in processing the application are called *back-end servers* because they do not have direct communications with clients.

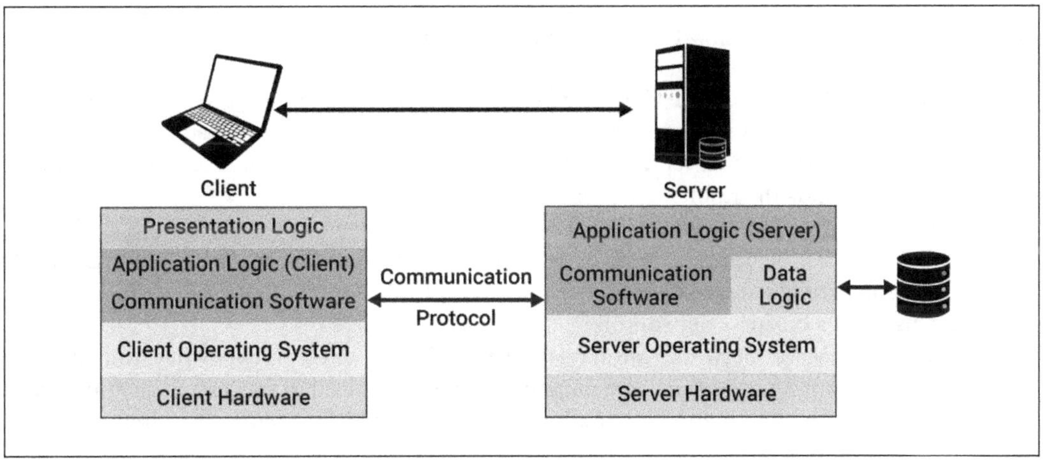

Figure 2-13: An example of a two-tier client-server network.

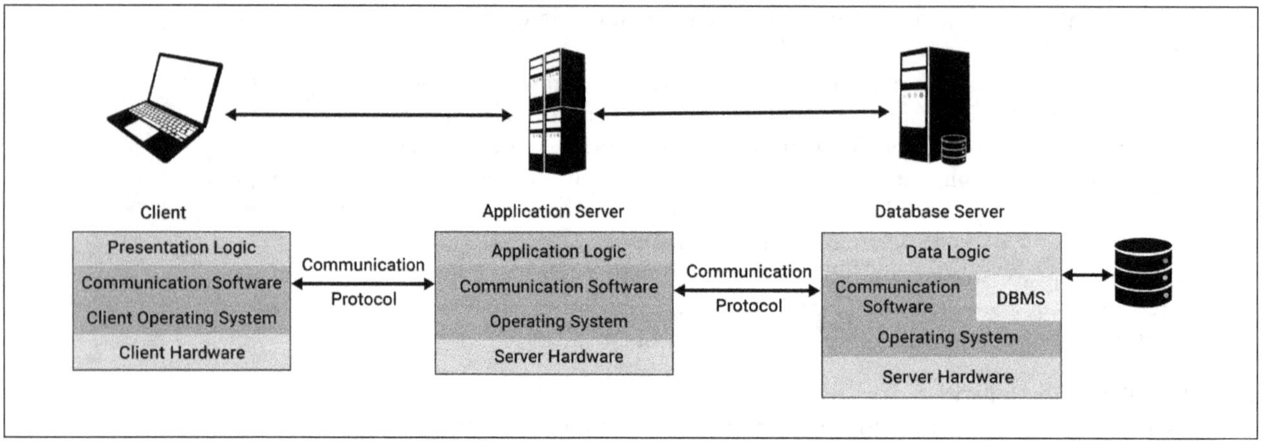

Figure 2-14: An example of a three-tier (multi-tier) client-server network.

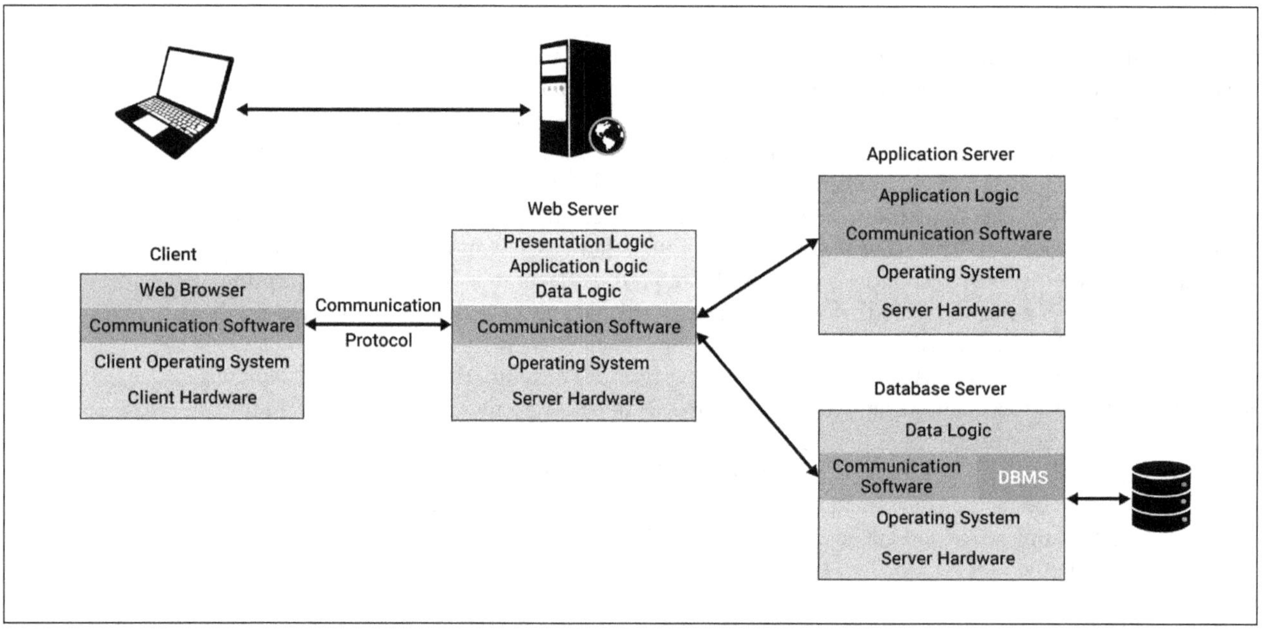

Figure 2-15: An example of a multi-tier client-server network in which clients interact with a web server.

For example, in Figure 2-14, the client sends data processing requests to the application server, which is the front-end server. The application server then sends data requests to the database server, which is the back-end server. When the application server processes data received from the database server, it sends the results to the client.

When clients connect to a web server, all other servers involved in processing the application are back-end servers. Today, the volume of server-to-server communication in networks usually exceeds the volume of client-to-server communication. This is especially true when the cloud is a logical extension of a business network.

Multi-tier client-server networks can have alternate physical deployments while still adhering to client-server computing practices. The number of servers involved in processing an application, their physical locations, and their configurations should be driven by business requirements.

Client-Server Communication Protocols

TCP/IP (Transmission Control Protocol/Internet Protocol) provides a standardized set of rules that allows computers to communicate over the Internet and other networks. It is the most common form of communication between clients and servers. Because it is used on the public Internet, TCP/IP is often labeled the "Internet protocol," but it is also used in private networks, including intranets and extranets. Technically, TCP and IP are separate protocols that work together to support client-server communications; both are described in more detail in other chapters, beginning with Chapter 4.

The three layers at the top of the TCP/IP protocol suite are most relevant to client-server computing. Usually, the "communication software" depicted in figures 2-13 to 2-15 is the set of communication protocols in the topmost layers of the TCP/IP protocol suite (see Table 2-5).

Application layer protocols rely on transport layer protocols such as TCP to pass messages between clients and servers. TCP is a connection-oriented protocol that helps ensure reliable message exchanges between clients and servers. It establishes and maintains a communication session between a client and server and terminates the connection after the server completes its response to a client request.

Table 2-5: Examples of communication protocols at the top three layers of the TCP/IP model.

TCP/IP Layer	Primary Communication Functions	Protocol Examples
Application	Enables use of browsers, email, file uploading and downloading, and other applications	HTTPS (Hypertext Transfer Protocol Secure) SMTP (Simple Mail Transfer Protocol) SNMP (Simple Network Management Protocol)
Transport	Provides connection-oriented and connectionless message transfers between clients and servers	TCP (Transmission Control Protocol) UDP (User Datagram Protocol)
Network	Provides end-to-end connections between clients and servers in different networks via routing, logical addressing, and internetworking	IPv4 (Internet Protocol version 4) IPv6 (Internet Protocol version 6) IPsec (Internet Protocol Security) ICMP (Internet Control Message Protocol) ARP (Address Resolution Protocol) NAT (Network Address Translation)

2.3.5 Middleware and Service-Oriented Architecture (SOA)

Middleware is software that enables communication and data management in distributed applications through standardized protocols and interfaces. It provides services to applications beyond those provided by operating systems and is often depicted as a software layer on either side of a distributed computing system that links applications and operating systems.

Middleware provides services above the transport layer in the TCP/IP protocol stack but below applications and application programming interfaces (APIs). An API is program code that enables data transfer between one software product and another; it is a software intermediary that allows two programs to talk to each other. When creating new programs, developers use APIs to allow the new programs to communicate with existing ones. Figure 2-16 illustrates middleware's location relative to the other elements in client-server applications and networks.

Middleware facilitates the deployment of an application to a variety of client devices and server platforms. It enables developers to provide a common look and feel on different types of client devices and consistent provision of server resources and services to clients regardless of differences in operating systems and hardware configurations. Because middleware enables various servers to communicate with various clients, it is sometimes called "software glue" or the hyphen in "client-server."

Service-oriented architecture (SOA) is a type of software design where an application's components provide services to other components via communication protocols. Technically, this makes SOA a type of client-server software architecture.

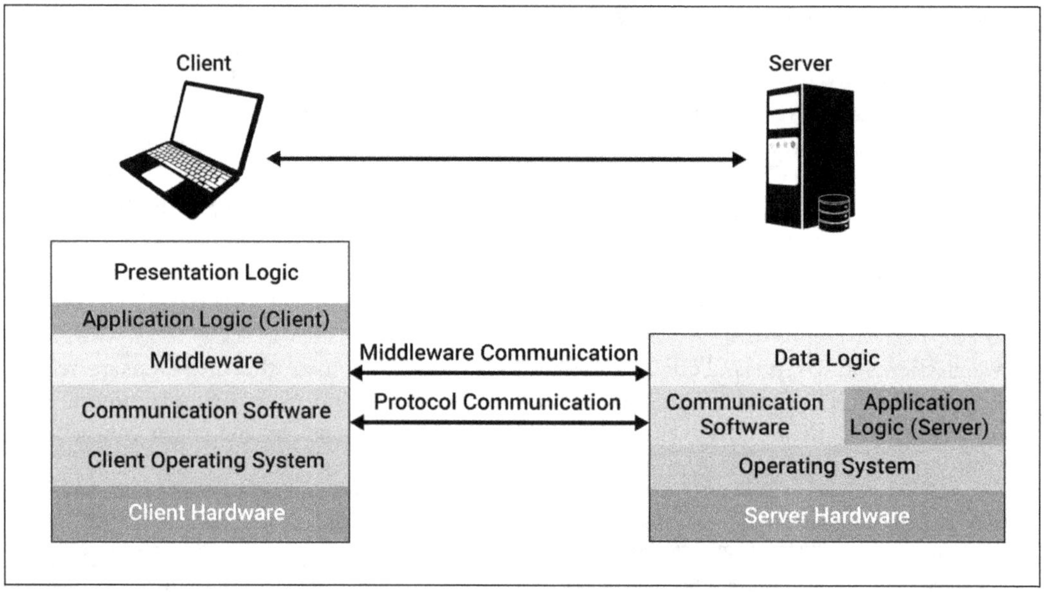

Figure 2-16: Conceptual depiction of middleware in client-server computing and networking.

In SOA, services are used to create/deploy business applications. A *service* is a self-contained, logical representation of a repeatable business activity. Services mirror real-world business activities, operations, and processes and have names that reflect the activities or processes that they represent. Examples include "check customer account balance," "check inventory level," "create purchase requisition," "create invoice," and "make payment."

In SOA, services communicate with one another via an enterprise service bus (ESB). Messages are passed between services over the ESB to enable them to communicate and collaborate. Basically, an ESB is a message-exchanging system that enables services to collaborate and is often considered middleware.

Middleware is described in more detail in Appendix 2-2. SOA is discussed more fully in Appendix 2-3. Appendix 2-3 also introduces microservices, which are widely used to develop cloud services.

2.4 CLOUD COMPUTING ARCHITECTURES AND APPLICATIONS

The National Institute for Standards and Technology (NIST) defines **cloud computing** as

> a model for enabling ubiquitous, convenient, on-demand network access to a shared pool of configurable computing resources (e.g., networks, servers, storage, applications, and services) that can be rapidly provisioned and released with minimal management effort or service provider interaction.

Cloud computing gets its name from data/information being accessed from a remote virtual space ("the cloud"), and because the Internet is commonly used for remote access, the Internet itself is sometimes called "the cloud." However, as noted in section 2.3.2, server virtualization can be described as transforming a physical server into a "cloud" of virtual servers regardless of the server's physical location, so virtualization processes are consistent with NIST's definition.

Cloud computing has benefits for both individuals and businesses. Cloud storage, for example, enables individuals and organizations to save files and data to remote storage devices, rather than on local storage devices, and to use the Internet or another network to access data and/or the applications that process it. This can free employees from having to be at specific locations to access data or do their work.

Cloud computing includes the provision and delivery of a wide range of computing resources, services, and applications. Data storage, servers, networks, software, databases, analytics, and business intelligence tools are among the computing resources and services that business subscribers most widely consume.

Today, the cloud is a logical extension of most business networks. In 2020, more than 90% of U.S. businesses subscribed to at least one cloud service, and most subscribed to multiple services. Cloud storage is the most common service used by businesses, but the use of cloud applications to support business operations is rapidly increasing.

Cloud computing is attractive to businesses for multiple reasons, including cost savings, reliability, flexibility and scalability, resilience, and security. Convenient on-demand access to computing resources and opportunities to reduce IT costs by offloading the acquisition, operation, and maintenance of IT infrastructure to cloud providers are important drivers. These and other factors fueling business adoption of cloud services are explored more fully in Appendix 2-4.

Fundamental knowledge of virtualization, client-server applications, client-server networks, and services is needed to understand and appreciate cloud computing. However, experts differ on whether cloud computing is an extension of client-server computing or should be considered different and distinct. Compelling arguments have been made on both sides, and it is likely to be awhile before a consensus is reached.

2.4.1 Client-Server Computing and the Cloud

Cloud computing is often used as a blanket term that encompasses all types of client-server computing models and purposely abstracts the various servers (e.g., application, database, and web servers) and client-server infrastructure details, such as hardware, location, ownership, and topology. Users interact with the Internet or "the cloud" rather than specific servers in specific locations (see Figure 2-17).

Abstracting architecture and infrastructure details behind a single endpoint is beneficial to cloud service providers. This arrangement enables them to change machines, topologies, data

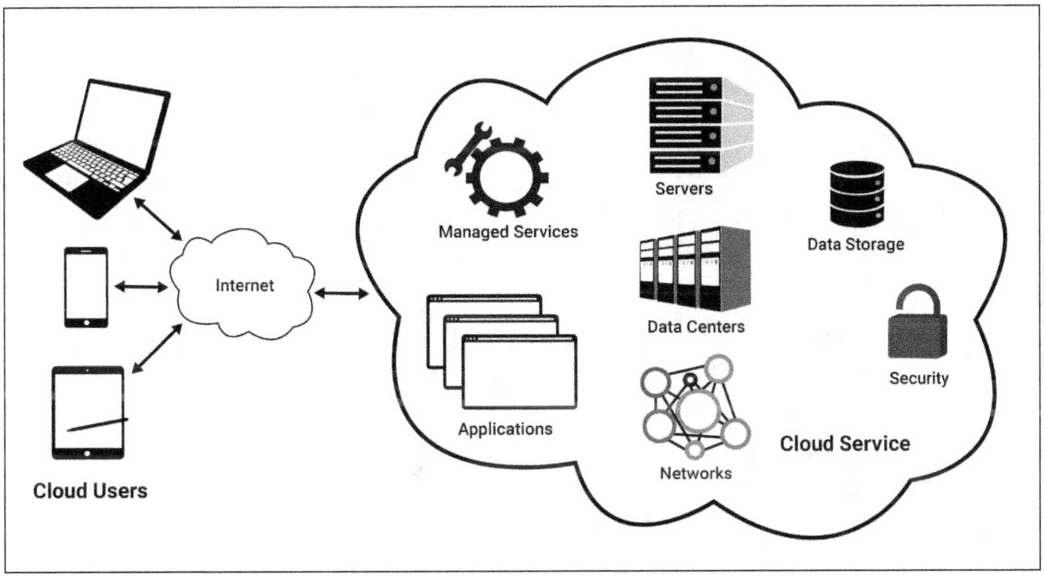

Figure 2-17: For users, the cloud abstracts infrastructure details behind a single endpoint.

center locations, software versions, and other infrastructure details without changing how users experience applications. This arrangement also enables cloud providers to scale by adding hardware and data centers and by virtualizing servers and assets that are already in place.

Cloud application users typically do not have to follow a regimented login process. Cloud access often relies on login credentials stored on user devices that provide user authentication. Often, users can "launch and go" and only need to provide additional authentication when the cloud service is unable to find the credentials on their device.

Usually, a user's credentials are stored on their device when they download and install an app. When device users log into an app store to acquire an app, their app store credentials can be stored with the app and used for cloud service authentication. Some apps enable users to authenticate using credentials for other apps; for example, users may be prompted to "continue" or log into the app using their Google or Facebook credentials for authentication.

As many users can attest, using a different device to access an app may trigger additional authentication steps, such as one-time codes being sent to a known phone number or email address. Many cloud services include "remember me" and "remember this device" options to facilitate future authentication attempts, but these options may not guarantee foolproof access to the app in the future.

2.4.2 Network Virtualization

Virtualization is another hallmark of cloud computing. Historically, some of the first deployments of virtualized servers were called "cloud servers," and this term continues to be used.

Virtualization enables cloud providers to create virtual versions of their computing hardware and provide subscribers with the appearance of unlimited resources. Virtualizing hundreds or thousands of physical servers enables cloud providers to effortlessly provide their subscribers with on-demand scalability for the computing resources they need.

Network virtualization abstracts network resources traditionally delivered as hardware to software. For example, this enables the creation of virtual adapters for virtual servers. It also enables the creation of virtual switches and virtual circuits that provide communication paths between virtual servers and real devices in real networks (see Figure 2-18).

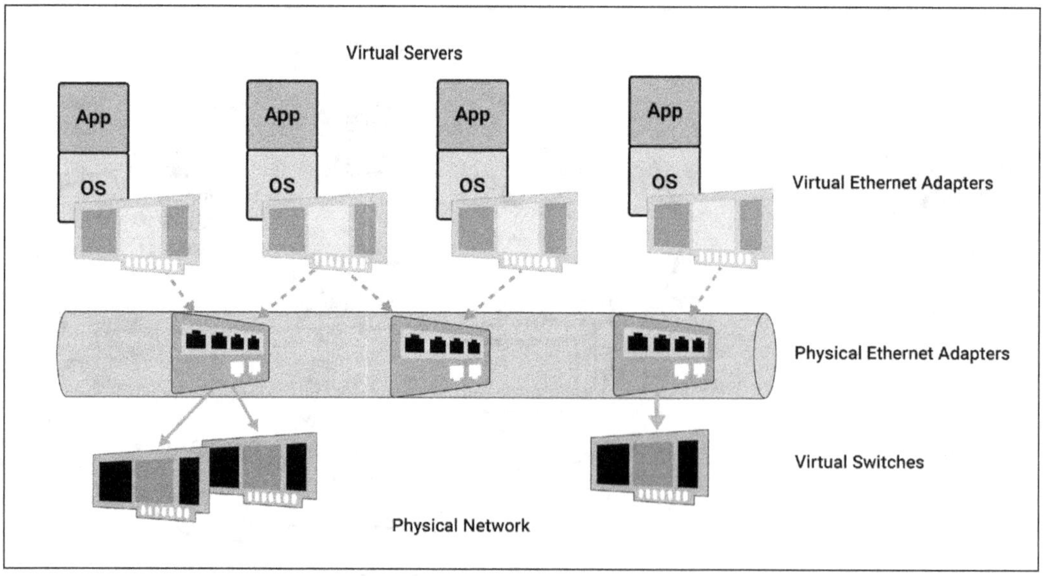

Figure 2-18: Conceptual depiction of network virtualization.

The term *network virtualization* is also used to describe the process of partitioning a single physical network (e.g., a network in a data center) into multiple separate and independent virtual networks. Mobile network operators (MNOs) use network virtualization to provide "private" 5G networks to business subscribers. Basically, network virtualization enables providers to move virtual hardware across different subscriber domains without having to reconfigure their physical networks.

On the other hand, in SDN (introduced in Chapter 1), *network virtualization* can refer to the process of combining multiple physical networks into a single software-based network. It is important to recognize the context in which the term is being used to appropriately understand its meaning.

In sum, some view cloud computing as being different from client-server computing or as a type of client-server computing that insulates users from the physical aspects of its implementation. Experts generally agree that, in the future, all client-server computing will look and act more like the cloud than traditional client-server networks. However, the degree to which this is true is likely to depend on the cloud type (e.g., private versus public) and who owns/controls it.

2.4.3 Private, Public, Hybrid, and Virtual Private Clouds

Businesses use several types of clouds to support their computing needs, including private, public, and hybrid clouds. They may also use community and virtual private clouds.

A **private cloud** consists of cloud computing resources that are dedicated to the sole use of a single organization. These resources may be virtualized in an on-premises or off-site data center. Sometimes, a third-party organization owns and operates the single-tenant data center. Users typically access private cloud resources over a private internal network or corporate VPN (see Figure 2-19a).

Private clouds facilitate the customization of cloud resources to meet the specific needs of the organization and how it wants these resources secured. Government agencies, financial institutions, and mid- and large-size enterprises that want enhanced control over their computing resources often prefer private clouds.

Public clouds are the most common type of cloud computing deployment that businesses use. In a **public cloud**, a third-party provider owns and operates computing resources and delivers them to subscribers over the public Internet or another network (see Figure 2-19b). The provider owns, maintains, and manages all infrastructure (hardware, software, storage, etc.). Business subscribers, called *tenants*, share the provider's computing resources, and few resources, if any, are dedicated to the exclusive use of a specific tenant. For subscribers, the level of infrastructure abstraction is typically higher for public than for private or hybrid clouds.

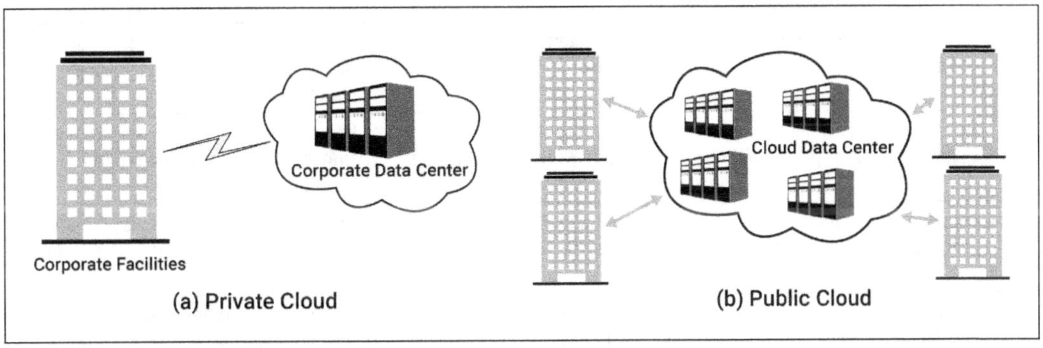

Figure 2-19: Conceptual depictions of a private cloud and a public cloud.

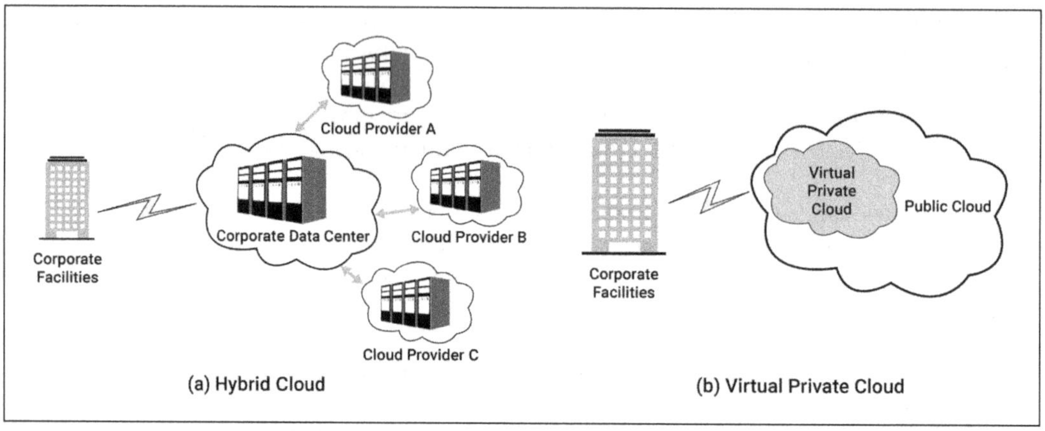

Figure 2-20: Conceptual depictions of a hybrid cloud and a virtual private cloud (VPC).

A **hybrid cloud** combines a private cloud with one or more public clouds and enables apps and data to move between the different clouds (see Figure 2-20a). Users access cloud resources over a private network or corporate VPN, but communication links between the private cloud and public cloud services enable the private cloud to include public cloud resources. This arrangement offers scalability beyond the limitations of private clouds while also providing greater customization than is typically available in public clouds. Some organizations choose hybrid clouds to meet regulatory or data sovereignty requirements, but others choose them to leverage previous investments in on-premises infrastructure or private clouds.

Some public cloud providers offer virtual private cloud services. A **virtual private cloud (VPC)** is a secure, isolated private cloud that is hosted within a public cloud (see Figure 2-20b). Technically, this may be considered a hybrid cloud. This arrangement enables VPC customers to run applications, store data, host websites, and so on, as they would in a private cloud while avoiding many of the disadvantages of owning and operating a private cloud. An overview of the characteristics of and differences among private, public, and hybrid clouds is provided in Table 2-6.

Table 2-6: Some of the characteristics of and differences between private, public, and hybrid clouds.

Dimension	Private Cloud	Public Cloud	Hybrid Cloud
Environment	Single-tenant environment	Multi-tenant environment	Combination of private and public cloud environments
Access	Access limited to tenant and/or tenant's partner network	Access by subscription	Dedicated access is provided to tenant using a subscription model
Control	Business controls architecture and configuration	Provider determines architecture and configuration	Business controls private cloud architecture and configuration but not the public cloud component
Ownership	Infrastructure is owned and managed by a single organization	Infrastructure is owned and managed by third-party service provider	Has a flexible infrastructure created from both private and third-party components
Resource Location	Computing resources remain behind organization's firewall	Computing resources are accessed via the public Internet	Provides a mixed services environment that uses both private access and public cloud services
Investment Requirements	Capital investment in infrastructure can be sizable	Avoids capital investment in infrastructure	The mixed environment often limits the capital investment needed for the private cloud component

Table 2-6, Continued.

Dimension	Private Cloud	Public Cloud	Hybrid Cloud
Operating Costs	Operating costs can be sizable	Operating costs are borne by provider; tenants are billed on a pay-per-use basis	More cost-effective than private cloud
Security	Can be highly secure because resources are not shared with others	Security is provided by third-party provider	Typically considered to be more secure than public cloud because sensitive data and computing assets are stored in the private cloud component
Customizability	Fully customizable	Limited or no customizability	Customizable, but compatibility issues for private and public cloud components can limit the amount of customization
Scalability	Scalability comes with added infrastructure cost	Unlimited scalability	High scalability
Common Users	Most common in large enterprises and government agencies	Most common for start-ups and SMEs	Most common in large enterprises and government agencies

NIST identifies community clouds as a fourth cloud deployment option. In a **community cloud**, cloud infrastructure is shared by several organizations and supports the specific needs of that community of organizations. For example, supply chain partners may create a community cloud to facilitate data and information sharing to coordinate the supply chain's operations. Their community cloud is private in the sense of only serving the supply chain partners, but by sharing resources, such a cloud has some of the characteristics of a multi-tenant public cloud.

2.4.4 Cloud Services

Businesses subscribe to various types of public cloud services to access needed computing resources. Three of the most common services are *software as a service (SaaS)*, *platform as a service (PaaS)*, and *infrastructure as a service (IaaS)*. However, the evolution of cloud services has spawned a variety of specialized services and resources that are attractive to businesses. Several of them are described in Appendix 2-5.

SaaS, PaaS, and IaaS

SaaS enables a business to add applications to its enterprise network without having to add the hardware and system software needed to run them. PaaS provides software platforms (operating systems, tools, middleware) as well as the hardware and networking infrastructure required to build and support business applications. And IaaS provides the operating system(s) and hardware/networking infrastructure needed to move applications from on-premises data centers to the cloud. Some of the major differences between these services and traditional on-premises deployment are summarized in Table 2-7.

In Table 2-7, the shaded infrastructure components for IaaS, PaaS, and SaaS are provided and managed by the cloud service and unshaded components are the responsibility of subscribers. With SaaS, all infrastructure components are provided and managed by the cloud service; with on-premises computing, the business is responsible for acquiring and managing all infrastructure components.

SaaS is a centrally hosted software licensing and delivery model in which application software is licensed on a subscription basis. Users typically access the application via a web browser. The SaaS provider owns, operates, and maintains the hardware, networking, and system software infrastructure that runs the application. A business subscriber is one of many tenants that use the

Table 2-7: Comparison of on-premises computing to IaaS, PaaS, and SaaS.

On Premises Computing	IaaS	PaaS	SaaS
Application	Application	Application	Application
Data	Data	Data	Data
Middleware	Middleware	Middleware	Middleware
OS	OS	OS	OS
Virtualization	Virtualization	Virtualization	Virtualization
Network	Network	Network	Network
Servers	Servers	Servers	Servers
Storage	Storage	Storage	Storage
☐ Managed by Business	☐ Managed by Cloud Service		

application. Salesforce, the widely used CRM, is delivered via the SaaS model. GoTo Meeting, Office 365, Gmail, and Google Docs are other widely used examples.

PaaS provides a software and hardware platform (system software, networking, servers, storage) that enable subscribers to develop, run, and manage applications. In this cloud services deployment model, the subscriber "owns" the applications and the data/information that is processed, while the service provider owns, operates, and maintains the equipment and system software that support subscriber applications. PaaS provides a fast and relatively inexpensive way to develop and deploy custom or highly customized applications. Apprenda, AWS Elastic Beanstalk, and Google App Engine are examples.

IaaS is a cloud service model that provides the hardware infrastructure used to support subscriber applications and is sometimes called *hardware as a service (HaaS)*. Typically, IaaS providers own, operate, and maintain the hardware components (storage, servers, networks) and data center space that subscribers use to run their applications. Relative to on-premises deployment, the burden of buying, managing, and maintaining hardware infrastructure shifts from the subscriber to the IaaS provider, but subscribers continue to be responsible for acquiring and maintaining the OSs, DBMSs, data, and application software that they use. AWS Elastic Compute, Microsoft Azure, and Google Compute Engine (GCE) are examples of IaaS services.

As Table 2-7 illustrates, SaaS has the highest level of abstraction by essentially hiding everything involved with running applications, whereas IaaS has a lower level of abstraction that only hides hardware and network infrastructure behind the cloud interface. The availability and affordability of cloud services challenges most businesses to consider which, if any, applications to support on premises and what makes sense to move to the cloud.

Pizza as a Service

"Pizza as a service" provides an everyday analogy for comparing the various cloud services to traditional on-premises computing, using pizza as a substitute for applications (see Table 2-8). Like SaaS, the cost of everything is included in the check when you dine in at the pizza shop; the shop provides the services, infrastructure, and ingredients. Making a pizza at home from scratch is like on-premises computing because you are responsible for providing and paying for everything. "Take and bake" pizza is analogous to IaaS because you are responsible for providing the infrastructure needed to bake the pizza, and getting a pizza delivered is like PaaS, because you get to choose the pizza type and/or its toppings, but you don't have to provide the oven or do the baking. An edible pizza results from each option, but there are differences in the level of involvement of pizza consumers and pizza vendors in the pizza-making process as well as who is responsible for providing and paying for what.

Table 2-8: Pizza as a service analogy.

Pizza Option:	Homemade	Take & Bake	Delivered	Dine at Pizza Shop
Is like:	On Premises Computing	IaaS	PaaS	SaaS
Major Components	Table	Table	Table	Table
	Drinks	Drinks	Drinks	Drinks
	Energy	Energy	Energy	Energy
	Oven	Oven	Oven	Oven
	Kitchen	Kitchen	Kitchen	Kitchen
	Pizza Dough	Pizza Dough	Pizza Dough	Pizza Dough
	Tomato Sauce	Tomato Sauce	Tomato Sauce	Tomato Sauce
	Toppings	Toppings	Toppings	Toppings
	Cheese	Cheese	Cheese	Cheese

☐ You Provide ▨ Vendor Provides

Other Cloud Services

Other types of cloud services have gained traction among business subscribers. These include *container as a service (CaaS)* and *function as a service (FaaS)*, which are variations or blends of SaaS, PaaS, and IaaS. They also include *business intelligence as a service (BIaaS)*, *Big Data as a service (BDaaS)*, and *data analytics as a service (DAaaS)* to help businesses analyze and manage their data. These services are described in Appendix 2-5.

2.5 WEBSITE ARCHITECTURE AND INFRASTRUCTURE

E-commerce and business websites exemplify the intersection of business needs and client-server computing. These customer-facing applications serve as the online face of the business and have important roles in business operations. They are logically part of an enterprise network, even when hosted or supported by cloud services.

2.5.1 Enterprise Network Zones

For security and manageability, zones are common parts of enterprise network architectures (see Figure 2-21). E-commerce and other public-facing services are typically located in an enterprise network's *public zone*, and visitors typically interact with front-end servers via browser interfaces. Firewalls separate public zone servers and computing resources in other enterprise network zones, including the *demilitarized zone (DMZ)* network and the *private zone*, which includes the internal corporate network. Back-end application and databases servers involved in e-commerce transactions are often located in the private zone (see Figure 2-22).

DMZs may include email servers to enable email messages to be scanned for malware before delivering them to employees to avoid compromising their devices or the corporate network. DMZs are described in Chapter 11.

Computing resources in the private zone are often used to create intranets to serve the needs of the business and its employees. This zone also includes mission-critical resources that support boundary-spanning applications, such as ES and inventory databases. A limited number of authorized external users may be permitted to pass through the DMZ or remote access zone to access specific private zone resources.

Remote access zones are common in enterprise networks to support remote work and enable intranet access. Remote access or VPN servers are commonly used to authenticate users and provide secure, encrypted communication via private "tunnels" through the public Internet. Network

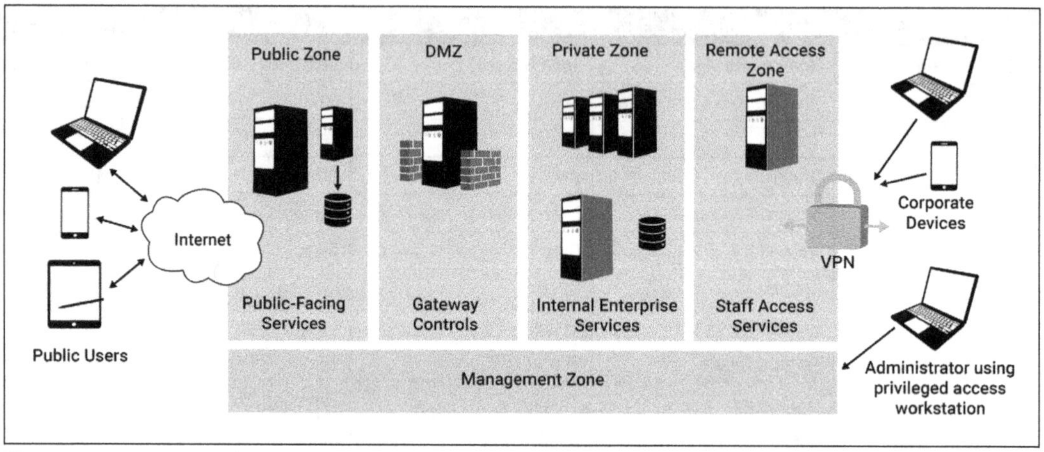

Figure 2-21: Supporting business and e-commerce websites in enterprise networks.

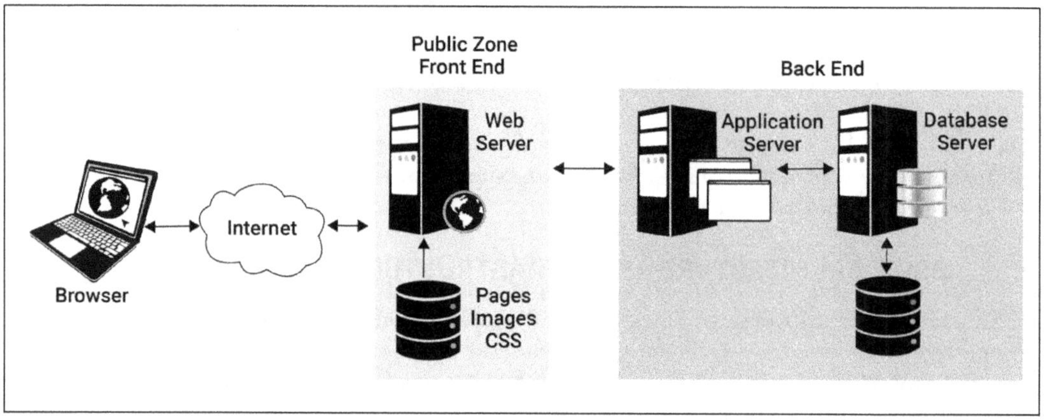

Figure 2-22: Website front-end and back-end infrastructure.

administrators typically have remote access rights that enable them to remotely monitor and control computing infrastructure in all zones.

Because of their importance to business operations, it is important to take a closer look at e-commerce architecture and infrastructure.

2.5.2 E-commerce Architecture and Infrastructure

Today, most e-commerce and business websites rely on HTTPS rather than HTTP to ensure secure connections with shoppers. Most browsers flag websites that only support HTTP, to warn visitors of the risks, and do not support connections with insecure websites. E-commerce servers typically require HTTPS (or another secure protocol) to ensure the security of encrypted communications and transactions.

Figure 2-23 provides a logical overview of traditional e-commerce infrastructure. To facilitate future/repeat purchasing and communication with shoppers, many businesses encourage their online customers to create accounts, but most allow shoppers to make purchases as a guest without creating an account. Customers with accounts are encouraged to log in before they shop or as they begin the checkout process to avoid having to input shipping and billing details or to take advantage of special offers.

Product pages associated with product details in the product database are used to populate the browser interface as visitors shop and navigate the website. Additional product data/information

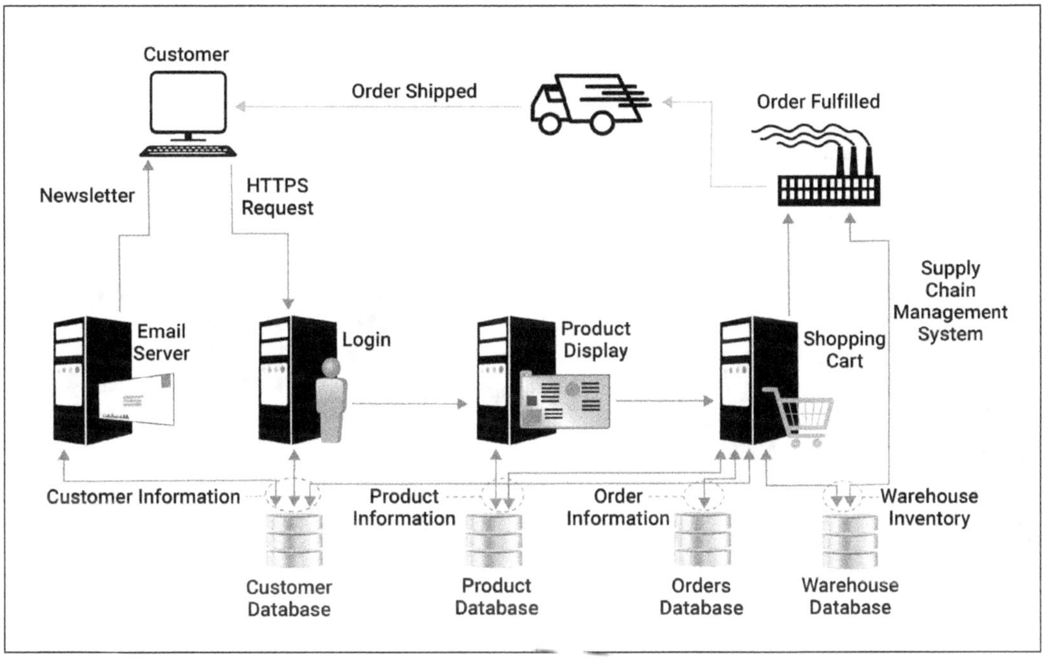

Figure 2-23: E-commerce website infrastructure.

from the product database may be transferred to the e-commerce server when an order is placed. Order details are recorded in an orders database and are passed to a warehouse database to enable warehouse personnel to pick, pack, and ship ordered items. When an order is placed, customer shipping and billing data/information is passed from the customer database to both the warehouse and order databases to ensure that all required customer details associated with the order are logged. When orders are placed, the shopper typically receives both web page and email confirmations.

When an online storefront is used with a back-end ERP or CRM system, all data flows to/from the ES's centralized database rather than to the separate databases illustrated in Figure 2-23. Customer, product, order, and inventory data is still necessary for online sales, but the need to maintain separate databases is eliminated when a centralized ES database is used.

2.5.3 Online Payment Architecture and Infrastructure

Payment, of course, is an important part of online sales transactions, and *payment gateways* are often involved, especially for credit and debit card payments. As Figure 2-24a illustrates, e-commerce servers securely communicate with payment gateways and identify the payment type (credit card, debit card, ACH, etc.) and payment amount. The payment gateway establishes secure connections with the customer's bank (or credit card issuer) and the merchant's bank. The payment type and amount are sent to the customer's bank so that they can be checked against the customer's account balance, and the bank transfers the payment amount to the payment gateway. The payment gateway relays the payment to the merchant bank, and the merchant bank responds with a payment receipt confirmation. The payment gateway relays the payment confirmation to the e-commerce server, which sends an order confirmation to the customer as a web-page and/or email confirmation.

PayPal and Venmo are examples of payment gateways used for consumer-to-consumer (C2C) and other e-commerce transactions. Payment gateways are common in all types of electronic payment transactions, including pay-at-the pump gasoline sales and grocery/retail point-of-sale (POS) transactions.

Some businesses include *payment management servers* in their e-commerce infrastructures. These

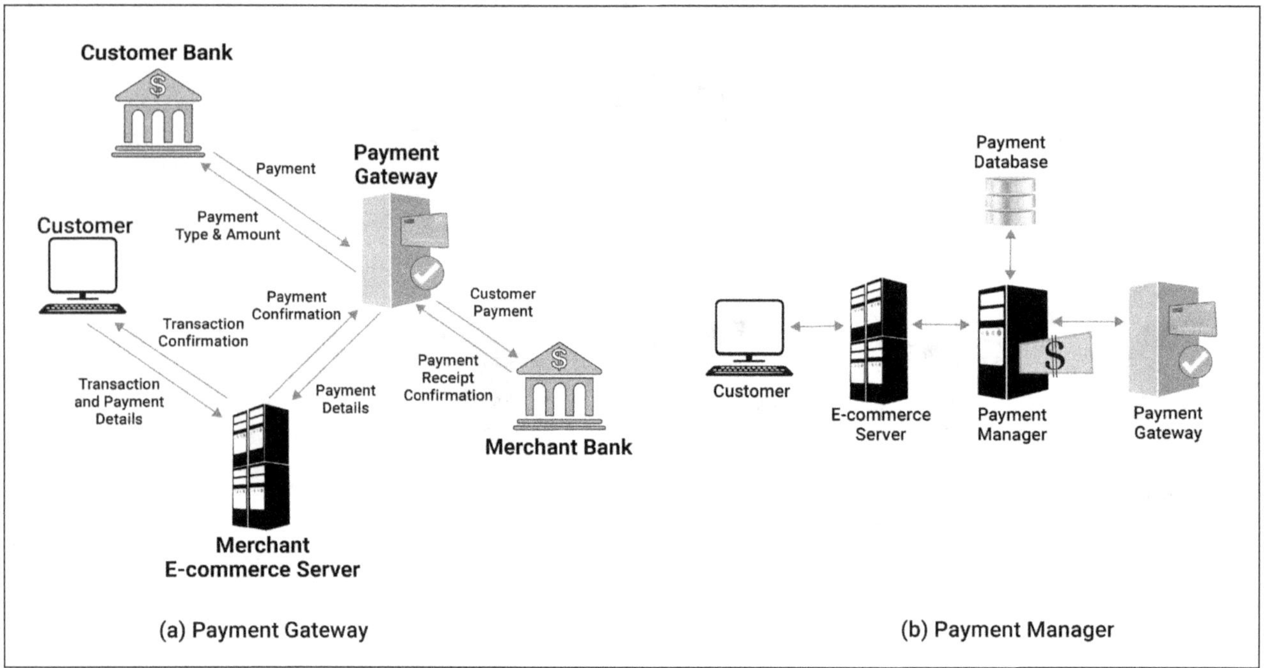

Figure 2-24: Conceptual depictions of a payment gateway and a payment manager in e-commerce infrastructure.

are found between the e-commerce server and payment gateway (see Figure 2-24b) to capture and store customer payment data (e.g., credit card or bank account details) to facilitate/automate future transactions.

2.6 SECURING ENTERPRISE NETWORK APPLICATIONS

Data created by e-commerce transactions and other enterprise network applications is a common attack target. It is important to secure data at rest (e.g., data stored in databases) and data in motion (data sent over network circuits). It is also important to secure the applications that capture, create, and process data.

In 2014, attackers using third-party contractor credentials installed malware in Target's POS system. The malicious code captured credit and debit card data as Target customers were checking out and relayed this information to the attackers. Basically, an application, not a database, was compromised to amass a trove of customer data to use in fraudulent ways.

Historically, enterprises have deployed elaborate network security defenses to protect insecure applications. A variety of these defenses are described in Chapter 12, including secure coding practices, patch management, application execution, monitoring, and other approaches that focus on application vulnerabilities.

Many software vulnerabilities are unintended flaws in applications or operating systems. These can result from programming errors or improper computer or security configurations. If left unaddressed, vulnerabilities (defects, bugs, log flaws, etc.) can be exploited by attackers.

2.6.1 Securing Distributed Applications

Today's enterprises usually have a mix of applications and platforms, from custom legacy apps to cutting-edge apps in cloud or hybrid environments. In today's enterprise networks, security requires protection for both old and new apps, regardless of their locations or environments.

Protecting the integrity and security of applications begins with developer awareness of common software vulnerabilities. Several organizations maintain lists of vulnerabilities, such as the Common Weakness Enumeration (CWE) and Open Web Application Security Project (OWASP) lists. Such lists help developers understand how/why software security safeguards are needed.

Secure coding practices are described in Chapter 12. Table 2-9 provides some examples. Table 2-10 identifies other mechanisms for securing enterprise network applications.

It is also important to harden server platforms and network infrastructure that support applications. Platform hardening includes installing software and security updates as soon as they are available and monitoring the services, protocols, and middleware that facilitate front-end/back-end server communications. Networking components (e.g., switches, routers, firewalls) also should be hardened and monitored to minimize unauthorized/unauthenticated data traffic.

As Figure 2-25 illustrates, protecting web applications includes consideration of the entirety of an application, including its back-end servers. E-commerce applications such as those illustrated in Figures 2-23 and 2-24 often include third-party code components (such as payment gateways) that have the potential to expose data to the outside world, so their security is an important part of end-to-end protection of the application.

Attackers know that if they can change how a program executes (which is what Target's attackers did), the change may go undetected. Attacks that are difficult to see are difficult to stop, and

Table 2-9: Examples of secure coding practices and recommendations.

Secure Coding Technique	Description
Input Validation	Applications properly validate input and only accept input from known and trusted sources. Input that cannot be validated or that comes from sources that cannot be authenticated or trusted should not be processed.
Authentication and Authorization	Application users and developers/coders wishing to modify an application should invariably be authenticated and authorized as having appropriate rights to use or modify the application before access to the application is allowed.
Encryption	Input and output of applications that maintain, process, transmit, or store sensitive data should be encrypted. Whenever possible, use secure communication protocols (e.g., HTTPS) and communication channels (e.g., VPNs) for data in motion (DIM). Also encrypt data at rest (DAR).
Code Management	Implement and maintain application change management processes, including version control processes, that document application modifications. Include comments in the program code to document all changes and (re)design decisions.
Vulnerability Management	Patch applications and/or application components for known security vulnerabilities as soon as the vulnerabilities are discovered. Test all patches/updates to ensure that they do not adversely affect application functionality.
Quality Assurance	Utilize quality assurance techniques (such as source code audits, application scanning and auditing, and penetration testing) to identify and eliminate vulnerabilities prior to placing application code changes in production.

Table 2-10: Examples of application security controls in enterprise networks.

Security Control	Description
Session Logging	Whenever possible, ensure that application use is logged. Maintain logs for all user accesses of an application, including time of access and access duration. Leverage log files to identify anomalous use of the application.
Application and Web Firewalls	*Application firewalls* use predefined policies and rules to monitor and block suspicious incoming requests or systems calls. *Web application firewalls (WAFs)* are application firewalls that protect web apps by filtering, monitoring, and blocking any malicious HTTP/HTTPS traffic sent to the application; they also prevent unauthorized data from exiting the app.
Runtime Monitoring	Monitoring applications while they are executing can alert security personnel to anomalous software behavior or anomalous use of the application. When anomalous behavior is detected, the application should be isolated or quarantined before other applications are affected. Service-level runtime monitoring should also be used.

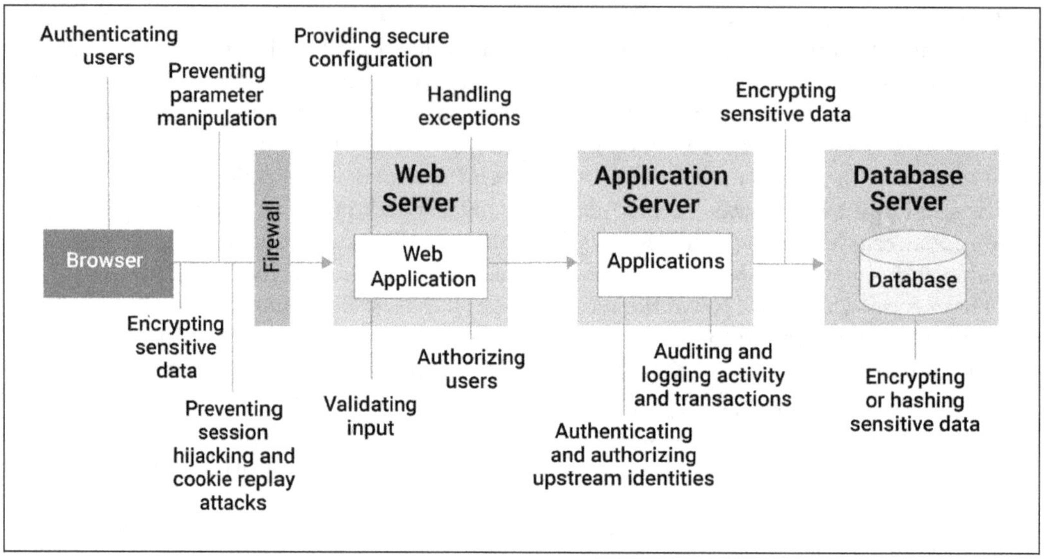

Figure 2-25: Examples of security mechanisms for web and distributed client-server applications.

until recently, monitoring programs as they run has been rare. Today, security experts recommend software monitoring and tools that increase the visibility of software code execution.

In a nutshell, application vulnerabilities and attack surfaces must be considered to fully protect an application, and with software fully ingrained in today's business operations, appropriate steps must be taken to ensure its integrity. When applications are secured, businesses are less likely to be disrupted by malicious actors.

2.6.2 Additional Application Security Considerations

Malware and denial-of-service (DoS) attacks are some of the most potent threats to enterprise network applications. As such, they warrant being briefly introduced here despite being addressed more fully in other chapters, including Chapters 11 and 12. Zero trust security and enterprise mobility management are reminders that the cloud and remote workers are extensions of today's enterprise networks.

Malware

Malware is short for "malicious software." Malware is intrusive software (program code) that is designed by hackers to infect user devices or software by installing malicious code that enables them to gain unauthorized access to a network and/or steal or cause extensive damage to data and systems. Some malware turns devices into bots used in DoS or other attacks. Examples of malware include adware, malvertising (malicious advertising), ransomware, rootkits, rogue software, scareware, spyware, trojans, viruses, wipers, and worms. Today, malware code and tools are available for sale on the dark web, along with known application and network vulnerabilities. And AI is being used to both create new malware and make existing malware more potent. Because malware can affect both application performance and availability, appropriate anti-malware security mechanisms should be in place.

Denial-of-Service Attacks

A denial-of-service attack is a cyberattack in which the perpetrator seeks to make a computer (server), application, or network resource unavailable to its intended users. When it succeeds, a DoS attack disrupts the services that servers normally provide. The disruption can be temporary or indefinite. DoS attacks typically involve flooding the targeted server with superfluous (and bogus) requests for services in sufficient volumes to overload the system and prevent some or all legitimate service requests from being fulfilled. This can make an application unavailable to legitimate users while the attack is under way. Firewalls, intrusion protection systems (IPSs), routers, and other technologies that can examine and filter incoming traffic can be configured to detect or deflect DoS attacks.

Zero Trust Security

Zero trust security is widely viewed as an appropriate response to growing numbers of remote users and their devices and increasing use of cloud-based assets located outside enterprise-owned network boundaries. Experts expect this to become the dominant network security model in the years ahead.

When followed, zero trust security principles require authentication and authorization of both devices and users before access to requested applications or computing resources is granted. The process used to authenticate/authorize devices is separate and independent from the process used to authenticate and authorize individual users. Neither devices nor users are trusted because of their geographic location (or presence on an internal network).

Zero trust security represents a shift to a more application-centric perspective of enterprise network security. Traditional cybersecurity defenses focused on hardware, software, and networking equipment owned and managed by the organization. Zero trust security, however, also includes users, assets, and resources outside traditional network boundaries.

Enterprise Mobility Management

The proliferation of mobile clients (smartphones, tablets, wearables, etc.) and their use in business applications has led to the establishment of *enterprise mobility management (EMM)* practices in many organizations. Basically, EMM is a set of services and technologies designed to secure corporate data, applications, and intellectual property that is implemented on employees' mobile devices. For example, if an employee's device is lost or stolen, EMM technologies may lock or wipe the device, or both. EMM technologies may also require a device user to use multifactor authentication to access applications and/or data.

EMM includes several important subsets, including MDM, MAM, and MIM. These are briefly introduced in Table 2-11 and are described more fully in Chapter 10.

Widespread business adoption of EMM, MDM, MAM, and MIM serves as a reminder that today's enterprise networks include mobile users and cloud applications. These practices provide insights into how security can be deployed on the client device side of distributed client-server applications.

Table 2-11: Summary overviews of EMM's MDM, MAM, and MIM components.

EMM Component	Brief Description
MDM (mobile device management)	MAM is a subset (and predecessor) of EMM that enables mobile devices to be managed remotely to ensure compliance with an organization's security policies.
MAM (mobile application management)	MAM is a subset of EMM that enables organizations to manage applications on employee mobile devices. Organizations can create separate containers for business and personal applications on employee devices and implement robust security mechanisms to protect the business applications. MAM also controls the deployment and updating of mobile apps and enables organizations to selectively remove apps and their associated data from a device.
MIM (mobile identity management)	The primary goal of this EMM subset is to ensure that only trusted devices and users can access the organization's applications or data. MIM has various forms, including user and device certificates, app code signatures, and authentication. It can play an important role in zero trust security initiatives. The primary goal of MIM is to ensure that only trusted devices and users can access enterprise applications or data.

SUMMARY

Enterprise networks exist to support applications that enable employees to perform their jobs. Today's enterprises support numerous types of applications, including COTS, custom, and open-source software as well as DBMSs and mobile apps. Specialized applications such as virtual desktops are also common.

Both horizontal and vertical market software are common parts of an organization's application architecture, and major ES software vendors have industry-specific versions of their products for specific markets/industries (verticals). Because of their crucial role in supporting business processes, operations, and best practices, ESs are usually considered mission-critical applications that command priority on enterprise network circuits.

ERP, CRM, SRM, and SCM systems are widely used ESs and support boundary-spanning and interorganizational applications. Some of these systems leverage EDI links to external business partners. The tiered architecture of ES software facilitates ES deployment as distributed client-server applications. It also facilitates cloud deployment of ES software tiers and fully hosted cloud versions of ESs.

In client-server computing, an application is split into tasks that are performed on separate computers over a network. Client software enables client devices to connect, interact, and send service requests to servers. Servers are typically faster and more powerful than the client devices they interact with and are the controlling entities in client-server communications. Today, servers are usually housed in data centers and are dedicated to specific functions. Server virtualization is also common. It enables a single physical server to be transformed into a "cloud" with numerous virtual servers; this contributes to the on-demand scalability of cloud-based applications.

There are multiple ways to distribute the processing work of client-server applications among clients and servers. For many applications, servers perform most or all processing, but clients do most of the processing for some. The distribution of processing is associated with different names, such as zero client, thin client, cooperative processing, thick client, and P2P.

Communication software and protocols enable clients and servers to exchange messages and data while distributed applications are being processed. Differences in client and server hardware configurations and OSs can require middleware for additional communication capabilities.

Service-oriented architecture (SOA) is a type of software design where application components provide services, self-contained business functions, to other software components over a network.

ES software's architecture makes it well suited for client-server networks and for deployment using various combinations of on-premises, private, hybrid, and public cloud services. SaaS, PaaS, and IaaS are categories of cloud services commonly used by businesses.

Business websites can be implemented in private, hybrid, or public clouds. Their components are usually found in enterprise network public zones that are separate from DMZ, private, and remote access zones. Many businesses have e-commerce sales channels that enable shoppers to interact with e-commerce servers using secure connections. Payment gateways are involved in most online transactions.

Malware and DoS attacks are some of the more important threats to enterprise network applications. The increasing importance of remote work and cloud applications and services is pressuring businesses to adopt software-centric and application-centric cybersecurity views. Secure coding practices and runtime visibility for applications are consistent with this perspective. Zero trust security and EMM also provide insights for securing important business applications.

KEY TERMS

Application
Client device
Client-server computing
Client software
Cloud computing
Customer relationship management (CRM)
Electronic data interchange (EDI)
Enterprise resource planning (ERP)
Hybrid cloud
Infrastructure as a service (IaaS)
Interorganizational system (IOS)
Middleware
Platform as a service (PaaS)
Private cloud
Public cloud
Server virtualization
Service oriented architecture (SOA)
Software as a service (SaaS)
Supplier relationship management (SRM)
Supply chain
Supply chain management (SCM)
Virtual private cloud (VPC)

REVIEW QUESTIONS

1. What is an application? Briefly describe each of the following types of applications: COTS, custom, horizontal market, vertical market, open-source, mobile app, virtual desktop, and DBMS.
2. How are enterprise systems (ESs) different from other business applications? Why are they considered mission-critical applications? Why may they be considered interorganizational systems (IOSs)?
3. What is ERP? Why do organizations adopt ERP systems?
4. What is CRM? What are common capabilities of CRM software?
5. What is SRM? What are common capabilities of SRM software?
6. What is SCM? Identify several common SCM software capabilities.
7. What are the distinguishing characteristics of EDI? What are examples of EDI documents exchanged by business partners?
8. What is client-server computing? How do clients differ from servers?
9. What is client software? Explain how mobile apps transform user devices into clients.
10. Identify examples of servers used to support client-server applications in enterprise networks.
11. What is server virtualization? How does it contribute to application scalability and performance?
12. Briefly describe each of the following software architecture tiers: presentation logic, application logic, data logic.
13. Explain how/why multi-tier (n-tier) software architectures are well suited to client-server applications.
14. Briefly describe how processing work is distributed among clients and servers in each of the following types of client-server computing: host-based processing, server-based processing, cooperative processing, client-based processing, peer-to-peer processing.
15. Identify examples of back-end and front-end servers in client-server networks.
16. Briefly explain the role(s) of TCP/IP protocols in client-server computing. Identify examples of application layer, transport layer, and network protocols.
17. What is middleware, and how does it support applications on a variety of client devices and servers?
18. What is SOA? What is a service? Identify examples of services.
19. What is cloud computing? How does the cloud abstract and hide the details of client-server computing infrastructure and applications?
20. What is network virtualization, and how does it contribute to the scalability of cloud services?
21. Why are cloud services attractive to businesses? Briefly describe each of the following: private clouds, public clouds, hybrid clouds, community clouds, and virtual private clouds (VPCs).
22. Briefly describe and provide examples of each of the following: SaaS, PaaS, and IaaS.
23. Briefly describe the role of each of the following zones in enterprise network architectures: public, DMZ, private, remote access.
24. Briefly explain the role(s) of e-commerce servers in online sales transactions.
25. How are payment gateways used in e-commerce gateways? What do they do, and how do they differ from payment managers?
26. What are the primary causes of application software vulnerabilities? What steps can be taken to increase the security of applications?
27. What is malware, and why is it a device and application security concern?
28. What are DoS attacks, and why are they server and application security concerns?
29. What are the distinguishing features of zero trust security?
30. What is EMM, and how does it contribute to application security? Briefly describe each of the following subsets of EMM: MDM, MAM, and MIM.

PROBLEMS AND EXERCISES

Exercise 2-1 Do some Internet research on virtual desktops and desktop-as-a-service (DaaS). Develop a professionally formatted 1000- to 1500-word document, or an 8- to 10-slide presentation, that summarizes the following:

- How virtual desktops differ from traditional desktops
- Why businesses are adopting virtual desktops
- How businesses are using virtual desktops
- How/why virtual desktops can lower a business's IT costs
- How/why virtual desktops contribute to enterprise network security

Your document/presentation should identify at least three recommended online sources (and their URLs) for learning more about virtual desktops and DaaS. It should also include a complete list of all sources/references used to develop your document or presentation, using APA or MLA format.

Exercise 2-2 Do some Internet research that focuses on the types of business applications that are most likely to be located in private clouds or VPCs. Your research should focus on determining the types of applications that businesses have been reluctant to move to public cloud environments and the reasons why they have been reluctant to do so. Summarize your findings in a professionally formatted two- to five-page document or five- to eight-slide presentation that includes a reference list (including URLs) in APA or MLA format of the sources used.

Exercise 2-3 Do some Internet research on the business use of community clouds. Find examples of business community clouds (business-focused use cases). Develop a professionally formatted 750- to 1250-word document or six- to eight-slide presentation that:

- Explains how community clouds differ from private and public clouds
- Identifies several different ways that businesses are using community clouds
- Summarizes the advantages and disadvantages of community clouds
- Summarizes security challenges associated with community clouds

Your document/presentation should identify at least two recommended online sources (and their URLs) for learning more about the business use of community clouds. It should also include a complete list in APA or MLA format of all sources/references used to develop your document (including URLs).

Exercise 2-4 Do some Internet research on application firewalls and web application firewalls (WAFs). Develop a professionally formatted 750- to 1250-word document or six- to eight-slide presentation that:

- Explains how application and web application firewalls work
- Identifies examples of rules used to block incoming requests or outgoing data
- Identifies and briefly describes the threats these firewalls protect against
- Identifies and briefly describes the security limitations of these firewalls

Your document/presentation should identify at least two recommended online sources (and their URLs) for learning more about application and web application firewalls. It should also include a complete list in APA or MLA format of all sources/references used to develop your document (including URLs).

Exercise 2-5 Do some Internet research on enterprise mobility management (EMM) and its various components: MDM, MAM, MIM, etc. Develop a 1000- to 1500-word document or eight- to ten-slide presentation that:

- Explains why businesses have embraced EMM
- Briefly describes why a business's EMM program may include MDM, MAM, MIM, and other components
- Explains why employees may resist EMM and MDM policies and requirements
- Explains how EMM programs and policies affect bring-your-own-device (BYOD) programs and policies
- Explains how EMM and its components contribute to the protection/security of enterprise applications

Your document/presentation should identify at least one recommended online source (and its URL) for learning more about EMM in today's businesses. It should also include a complete list in APA or MLA format of all sources/references used to develop your document (including URLs).

CHAPTER REFERENCES

Altvater, A. (2017). What Is N-Tier Architecture? How It Works, Examples, Tutorials, and More. Stackify. Retrieved from: https://stackify.com/n-tier-architecture/

Bigelow, S. J., & Gillis, A. S. (2021). What Is Server Virtualization? The Ultimate Guide. TechTarget. Retrieved from: https://searchservervirtualization.techtarget.com/definition/server-virtualization

Cloudflare. (n.d.). What Is OWASP? What Is the OWASP Top 10? Retrieved from: https://www.cloudflare.com/learning/security/threats/owasp-top-10/

Donohoe, A. (n.d.). What Is a Client Server Network? Techwalla. Retrieved from: https://www.techwalla.com/articles/what-is-a-client-server-network

HEAVY.AI. (2021). Client-Server. Retrieved from: https://www.omnisci.com/technical-glossary/client-server

IBM. (n.d.). The Future of EDI: An IBM Point of View. Retrieved from: https://www.ibm.com/watson/supply-chain/resources/future-of-edi/

i-SCOOP. (n.d.). Big Data as a Service (BDaaS): Benefits, Evolutions and Market Trends 2025. Retrieved from: https://www.i-scoop.eu/big-data-action-value-context/big-data-as-a-service-bdaas/

Johnson, J., & Shiff, L. (2021). What Is Microservice Architecture? Microservices Explained. BMC Software. Retrieved from: https://www.bmc.com/blogs/microservices-architecture/#

Kapko, M. (2017). What Is EMM? Enterprise Mobility Management Explained. Computerworld. Retrieved from: https://www.computerworld.com/article/3230510/what-is-enterprise-mobility-management-emm.html

Leichter, W. (2020). 5 Essential Steps for Enterprise Application Security. Dark Reading. Retrieved from: https://www.darkreading.com/application-security/5-essential-steps-for-enterprise-application-security/d/d-id/1338833

Luenendonk, M. (2019). What Is Middleware and How Does It Work? Cleverism. Retrieved from: https://www.cleverism.com/what-is-middleware-and-how-does-it-work/

Markus, M. L. (2007). Building Successful Interorganizational Systems. In Chen, C.S., Filipe, J., Seruca, I., & Cordeiro, J. (Eds.), *Enterprise Information Systems VII*. Springer, Dordrecht. https://doi.org/10.1007/978-1-4020-5347-4_4

Mell, P. M., & Grance, T. (2011). The NIST Definition of Cloud Computing. Special Publication (NIST SP) 800-145. National Institute of Standards and Technology. Retrieved from: https://www.nist.gov/publications/nist-definition-cloud-computing

MITRE. (n.d.). Common Weakness Enumeration. Retrieved from: https://cwe.mitre.org/

Mixon, E., & Harder, J. (2020). What Is Virtual Desktop Infrastructure? VDI Explained. TechTarget. Retrieved from: https://searchvirtualdesktop.techtarget.com/definition/virtual-desktop-infrastructure-VDI

MuleSoft. (n.d.). What Is an ESB? Retrieved from: https://www.mulesoft.com/resources/esb/what-esb

Software Development Community. (2019). What Is Service-Oriented Architecture? Medium. Retrieved from: https://medium.com/@SoftwareDevelopmentCommunity/what-is-service-oriented-architecture-fa894d11a7ec

MINICASE: Walmart GoLocal

In August 2021, Walmart announced its launch of Walmart GoLocal, an initiative designed to assist local merchants in fulfilling customer orders using Walmart's Spark delivery service. Walmart provided a cloud-based e-commerce application to small and medium-size companies in July 2021 and a month later rolled out the GoLocal app to enable local merchant customers to have their orders delivered by Spark.

When a customer uses the GoLocal app to place an order, the Spark delivery service is notified, and local Spark contract workers are dispatched to the merchant's location to pick up the ordered items and deliver them. Order-to-delivery duration can range from a few hours to a couple of days, depending on the size and contents of the order.

Walmart contends that it will deliver anything that customers order from local merchants using the GoLocal app. It also contends that the Spark service reflects the scalable commerce and last mile delivery capabilities that the company has developed over the past decade. Essentially, GoLocal represents commercialization of Walmart's delivery platform. It is a delivery-as-a-service cloud application that helps local businesses of all sizes get their products to customer doorsteps.

Walmart's GoLocal app serves several purposes. First, it is a lifeline for small businesses in local communities, especially rural areas, that struggle to deploy their own delivery operations. Second, it taps into the surge in community interest in supporting local businesses that emerged during the COVID-19 pandemic. Third, the app combats traditional criticisms of Walmart as not caring about local companies and driving them out of business. Fourth, GoLocal positions Spark to compete with Uber, DoorDash, and other delivery services in local markets.

Although Spark was originally envisioned as a local service for delivering Walmart products ordered online, it gained traction as an alternative to Walmart's curbside pickup option for local shoppers during the pandemic by enabling residential deliveries.

During the pandemic, noticing that a sizeable percentage of curbside pickup customers were using Uber to get to its stores, Walmart was inspired to build out its Spark delivery service. The GoLocal app enticed contract workers to become Spark drivers and earn additional income by delivering local merchant products to local customers. In many communities, GoLocal lured drivers away from Uber, DoorDash, and other local delivery services to work for Spark and has made Spark the preferred delivery service.

GoLocal provides a revenue stream to Walmart outside its core retail businesses and puts Walmart on the strategic path to monetizing cloud services, which is something that Amazon, its main competitor, has done effectively with Amazon Web Services and its other cloud offerings. Amazon, of course, has its Prime delivery service to keep its products out of Spark delivery vehicles and has developed its own local delivery program to entice merchants to use Amazon as their online sales channel. Walmart also has Walmart+ to compete with Amazon Prime.

Walmart hopes that the GoLocal name will inspire local shoppers to view the retail giant as more of a friend than a foe of local businesses. In addition to helping local merchants meet e-commerce, fulfillment, and delivery challenges, Walmart hopes that GoLocal will help Spark mature as a delivery service. Eventually, Walmart hopes to add driverless vehicles and drone deliveries to its Spark delivery network. Of course, arch-rival Amazon also has big plans for these technologies.

Minicase Questions

1. Explain how/why GoLocal can be considered a delivery-as-a-service cloud application.
2. Small businesses often rely on cloud services and social media to provide an online presence and offer information about themselves to the local market. Identify a small business in your local community that might benefit from joining Walmart's GoLocal delivery service and explain how/why adding the app to its website or Facebook page might be beneficial.
3. What is/are the best way(s) to categorize Walmart's GoLocal cloud service: SaaS, PaaS, IaaS, or something else? Explain your reasoning.
4. If you were a small business owner thinking about adding the GoLocal app to your website or Facebook page, what are some of the questions you would want to have answered before signing up?
5. If you were Walmart, what steps would you take to ensure that the GoLocal app was secure and to protect the security of merchants who used the app? If you were a small business owner, what security guarantees would you be looking for?

Minicase References

D'Innocenzio, A. (2021). Walmart to Offer Delivery Service to Others. *Savannah Morning News*. August 25, p. A10.

Edelson, S. (2021). Walmart's New GoLocal Delivery Service Solution Targets Outside Retailers Big and Small. *Forbes*, August 24. Retrieved from: https://www.forbes.com/sites/sharonedelson/2021/08/24/walmarts-new-golocal-delivery-as-a-service-solution-targets-sellers-and-retailers-big-and-small/

Walmart. (n.d.). Walmart GoLocal. Retrieved from: https://one.walmart.com/content/go-local/home-page.html

Chapter 3

Enterprise Network Data

LEARNING OBJECTIVES

After reading and studying this chapter, you should be able to:

- Describe the business value of enterprise data.
- Briefly describe how various types of enterprise data are digitized.
- Describe the differences between structured and unstructured data.
- Briefly describe the characteristics of Big Data and Big Data processing platforms.
- Identify and briefly describe the major types of logical data collections supported in enterprise networks.
- Identify and briefly describe the various data storage technologies used in enterprise networks.
- Identify and briefly describe the various aspects of data governance.
- Briefly describe why attackers target enterprise data.
- Identify and briefly describe several types of data breaches.
- Identify and briefly describe several enterprise data security controls.

3.0 INTRODUCTION

Enterprise data deserves attention for numerous reasons. Applications supported on enterprise networks capture and process data, and some applications, including ESs and IoT systems, generate large volumes of data. Data is also the target of most network attacks.

Any discussion of enterprise data must acknowledge the reality that vast amounts of data are being captured and stored by today's businesses, and most only analyze a small fraction of what they have. Data storage costs (per terabyte) continue to decline, especially in cloud data centers, making it inexpensive for businesses to amass ever-increasing data volumes. The maturation of Big Data processing platforms and AI also fuels business data capture.

While technological advancements are contributing factors, businesses capture and analyze data because it has business value. Examples of valuable business data are identified in Table 3-1.

Several types of data are identified in Table 3-1, but business value is their common denominator. Some of this data is unstructured (e.g., social media posts), while other data is structured (such as customer and transaction data). Structured data has been traditionally stored in relational databases, while unstructured data is better suited for NoSQL databases.

Relational and NoSQL databases and data warehouses are "logical" data repositories that reside on physical data storage media, such as those included in storage area networks (SANs) and data centers. Business data warehouses often include both relational and NoSQL databases, sometimes in sufficient volumes to be considered Big Data. Increasingly, businesses are storing part or all of their data in cloud data centers. Some cloud providers have data warehouse services.

Big Data processing and analysis often involves the simultaneous processing of both structured

Table 3-1: Examples of valuable business data.	
Type of Data	**Business Value**
Social data	Social media posts about businesses are tracked and analyzed to understand customer sentiments toward them and their products or services.
Customer data	This is used to understand shopping behaviors, both in-store and online, to improve targeted marketing, increase conversion rates, and lower customer acquisition costs.
IoT sensor data	IoT data is used to improve logistics and materials movement in supply chains, warehouses, and manufacturing facilities. It is also used to increase operational efficiencies, reduce costs, and improve capacity utilization.
Sales data	Sales transactions are analyzed to identify patterns, trends, and opportunities to better serve customers and improve sales processes.
Procurement data	Purchasing and procurement data is analyzed to reveal patterns, trends, and opportunities to improve procurement and purchasing processes and identify opportunities to reduce costs.
Website data	This is used to determine how visitors got there and their movements after they arrive, which can help businesses improve website design or layout and increase e-commerce revenues.

and unstructured data. Businesses analyze Big Data to reveal previously unnoticed patterns and actionable insights. Digitizing structured and unstructured data facilitates the ability to combine and simultaneously process both types of data.

Digitizing converts data from its original form to representative strings of bits (binary digits) needed for processing, storage, and transmission. Digitized data is encoded in symbols/signals when transmitted on network circuits. Knowing and understanding how different types of data are digitized is important.

Because it has value, the quality, integrity, and security of business data are important. Businesses typically have data governance structures and processes to oversee data consistency, reliability, availability, integrity, and security. Data security is important for both stored data (data at rest) and transmitted data (data in motion), and encryption is widely used to protect both.

3.1 DATA/INFORMATION ARCHITECTURE AND DIGITIZATION

The data/information domain of EA (Enterprise Architecture) should fulfill business needs. A business requires data/information to support processes and operations, fuel business intelligence (BI) activities, drive business performance, and make strategic decisions. Today, a wide variety of data is generated, captured, stored, and transmitted in enterprise networks, and it is important for EA analysts and architects to assess the operational and strategic relevance and value of data. Data that is critical to business operations and strategic initiatives should receive special consideration in enterprise networks for transmission, storage, and security.

3.1.1 Data and Information Architecture

EA sometimes separates data/information architecture into two subdomains: data architecture and information architecture.

- Data architecture consists of the standards, policies, rules, or models that govern how the organization collects, stores, and integrates data. It documents the types and sources of the organization's logical and physical data assets and the resources used to manage them.
- Information architecture describes how the organization's data is structured, collected, stored, and maintained, both technically and from a business perspective. It includes blueprints for semantically and physically integrating the organization's data using

data models and data flows. It also focuses on connections between business strategy and data. It provides guidance on how data should be structured, classified, associated, and deployed to enable the generation of strategically relevant information and insights into how the organization's application and technical architectures could/should be aligned with its business architecture.

Data quality and data governance processes are important data/information architecture considerations. ES master data management and the organization's use of data analytics, BI, and enterprise reporting tools are other important considerations.

3.1.2 Data Digitization

Digitization is the process of converting diverse forms of data and information, such as audio, images, documents, text, and video, into binary code (see Figure 3-1). The conversion process should produce binary code that represents the original source with as much accuracy and conformity as possible. When accuracy and conformity are maximized, converting binary code back to its original form after it is transmitted, processed, or stored produces a result that is indistinguishable from the original prior to conversion.

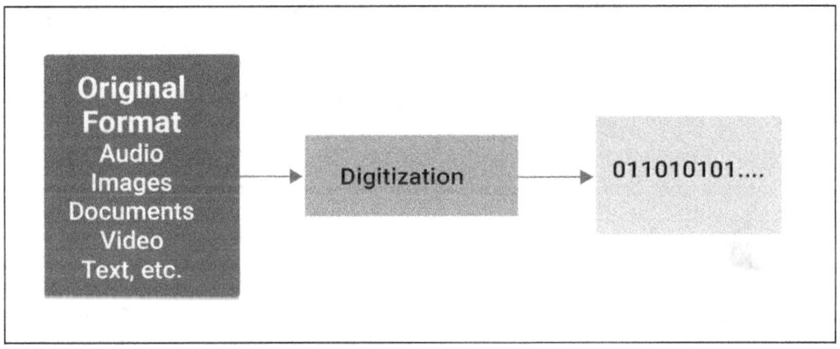

Figure 3-1: A high-level depiction of the process of digitizing data.

The conversion process (digitization) involves representing the original data by sequences of *binary digits (bits)*, zeros (0s) and ones (1s), that are organized into discrete units, usually multibit groups called *bytes*. The capacities of computer memory (RAM) and storage devices are measured in bytes (such as *megabytes [MB]*, *gigabytes [GB]*, or *terabytes [TB]*) to reflect the amounts of digitized data they can handle, and the bandwidth (capacity/speed) of network circuits is measured in bits per second (e.g., *megabits per second [Mbps]* or *gigabits per second [Gbps]*).

Enterprise data is converted into a digital format to facilitate processing, storage, and transmission over network circuits. Digitized data is considered computer-readable because it is in the form that computers use for processing tasks.

In addition to preparing data for processing, digitization facilitates the storage, transmission, and intermingling of data, regardless of its original form. Because digitized data can be easily accessed, copied, shared, and processed, it is the preferred format for business data. Figure 3-1 indicates a wide variety of data that is digitized, and bar and QR codes and IoT sensor data are as well.

Digitizing Audio

Audio data is based on sound. Sound sources emit analog waveforms such as those depicted in Figure 3-2.

As you may recall from biology, human ears convert sound waves into electrical pulses that are carried on nerves to the brain, where they are interpreted and "heard." An analogous conversion process occurs when sounds are digitized and carried by symbols/signals on network circuits to computing or storage devices. While it is possible to represent sound waves as other analog waveforms, such as those used in the past for AM or FM radio broadcasts, today it is more common to convert sound waves to binary code to facilitate transmission on network circuits and for storage.

Digitizing sound enables podcasts, music, telephone calls, voice mail, and other sound-based

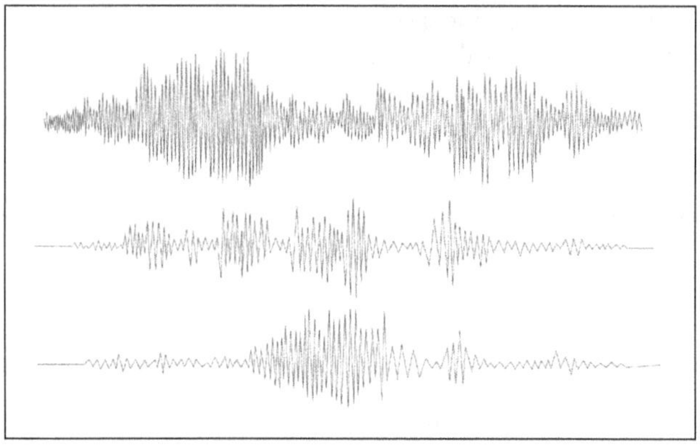

Figure 3-2: Examples of sound waveforms. Source: reklamlar/iStock. Stock illustration ID:1193081525

information to be transmitted and saved in a computer-readable form that can be copied and/or converted back to their original form on demand. The quality (accuracy and conformity to the original sound) of the digitized data is dependent on the digitization process that is used.

The digitization process for audio data is a type of quantization. **Quantization** is the process of approximating a continuous signal, such as an analog sound waveform, using a discrete set of symbols or integer values. It involves sampling the sound wave (such as those illustrated in Figures 3-2 and 3-3), rounding each sample to an integer value, and converting each integer value to binary code. Usually, it is the height (amplitude) of the audio wave that is sampled at regular intervals (see Figure 3-3), and *samples per second* is used to identify the number of wave samples that are collected each second.

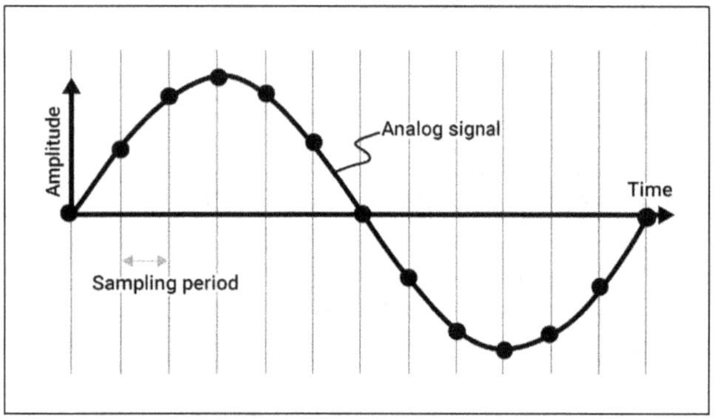

Figure 3-3: Waveform sampling.

Pulse Code Modulation

Pulse code modulation (PCM) is the most widely used quantization process for digitizing audio data. It is a three-step method to digitally represent analog wave samples and is the standard form of digital audio for computers, CDs, phone calls, and other purposes. In PCM, the first step is *sampling* (see Figure 3-3). This involves measuring the amplitude of the sound wave at regular intervals. *Quantizing* is the second step. Here, each amplitude sample is rounded to the nearest value in the integer range. In the third step, *encoding*, the integer value is converted to binary code (see Figure 3-4).

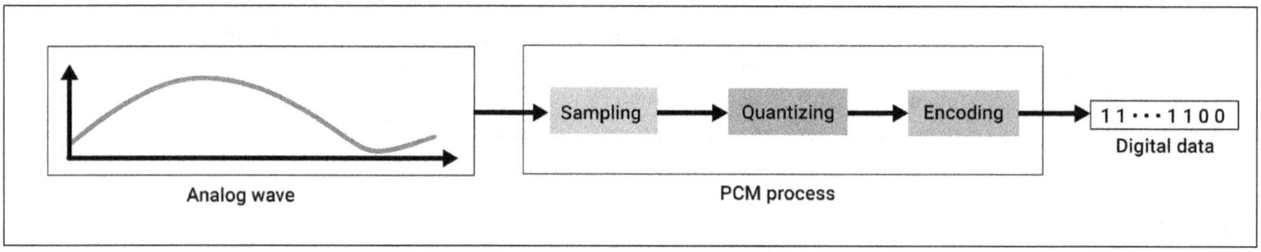

Figure 3-4: How PCM converts an analog sound wave to digital data.

In devices, analog to digital conversion, as illustrated in Figure 3-4, is usually done by an integrated circuit called a *PCM analog-to-digital converter (ADC)*. A *PCM digital-to-analog converter (DAC)* converts the digital data back to an analog wave; essentially, its job is to reproduce the original sound from the binary data it receives.

The number of bits in the binary code that represents each sample measure is called *bit depth*. In PCM, bit depth determines the total number of integer values that are available to quantize each sample and corresponds to the sample's *resolution*. Bit depth is also one of the determinants of

Table 3-2: Relationships among bit depth, integer ranges, and bit combination ranges.			
Bit Depth	**Total Number of Values**	**Example Integer Range**	**Bit Combination Range**
1	$2 = 2^1$	0–1	0–1
2	$4 = 2^2$	0–3	00–11
3	$8 = 2^3$	0–7	000–111
4	$16 = 2^4$	0–15	0000–1111
5	$32 = 2^5$	0–31	00000–11111
6	$64 = 2^6$	0–63	000000–111111
7	$128 = 2^7$	0–127	0000000–1111111
8	$256 = 2^8$	0–255	00000000–11111111
9	$512 = 2^9$	0–511	000000000–111111111
10	$1024 = 2^{10}$	0–1023	0000000000–1111111111

PCM *fidelity* (the degree to which the digitized data accurately represents the original sound wave). Greater bit depth means greater resolution or precision of each wave height sample; it also means that more bits are generated each time a sample is taken. This increase is illustrated in Table 3-2.

Common bit depths for PCM are 8, 16, 20, and 24 bits. In digital telephony, the standard bit depth is 8, and the integer value of each amplitude is represented as a combination of 8 bits. Compact Disc Digital Audio has a bit depth of 16, and DVD-Audio and Blu-ray Disc may have a bit depth of 24. An audio recording with a bit depth of 24 can represent more nuances of the audio than a recording with a bit depth of 16 because a 16-bit recording has a resolution/integer value range of 65,536 (2^{16}), while a 24-bit recording has a resolution/integer value range of 16,777,216 (2^{24}).

Sampling rate is the other determinant of PCM fidelity. The *Nyquist–Shannon sampling theorem* suggests that PCM ADCs should provide a sampling rate that is at least twice that of the highest frequency of the analog wave that is sampled. For example, in telephony, the average human produces sounds that range from 300 cycles per second (300 Hz) to 3400 cycles per second (3400 Hz). To be in accord with the Nyquist-Shannon theorem, telephony applications typically use a sampling rate of 8000 samples per second, which is more than twice the highest voice frequency.

Because a symphony orchestra can produce a wider range of sounds than the average human voice, a higher sampling rate is needed to be in accord with the Nyquist-Shannon theorem. And, since the highest sound frequencies produced by a symphony orchestra are about 22,050 Hz, the theorem indicates that a sampling rate of 44,100 samples per second is needed.

PCM's bit rate, the number of bits generated per second, is reflected by the following formula:

$$\textit{Bit rate} = \textit{Sampling rate} \times \textit{Bit depth}$$

In digital telephony, 8000 samples are taken each second, and each sample is converted into an 8-bit binary code. Hence, a total of 64,000 bits is produced each second. To record a symphony orchestra performance on a CD, the sampling rate is 44,100. When a bit depth of 16 is used, 705,600 bits per second are generated. Higher bit rates occur when recording Blu-ray Discs.

Since PCM's binary code provides an approximation rather than an exact replica of the original sound, it is important to understand how its fidelity (accuracy) can be improved. Greater conformity to the original sound can be achieved by (1) increasing the sampling rate (taking more samples per second), (2) increasing the bit depth (increasing the number of integer values available to measure each amplitude sample), or (3) increasing both the sampling rate and the bit depth. Doing either 1 or 2 in isolation is often enough to make the reproduced sound indistinguishable from the original.

Data Compression

Audio files can be saved in uncompressed or compressed formats. When audio files are small or short in duration, saving them in an uncompressed file format may be feasible. Uncompressed PCM file formats include PCM files (a raw audio format), WAV files on Windows, and audio interchange file format (AIFF) files on MacOS. However, when the duration of sound information is extensive, such as a lengthy podcast or musical performance, the digital audio files that are produced can be very large. To make them more compact, data compression is commonly used.

Data compression is a process used to reduce the number of bits needed to represent data. This has traditionally been used to reduce the size of files saved to storage media or to speed up file transfer rates on enterprise network circuits. Data compression involves re-encoding the file data into a form that uses fewer bits. It enables the original file to be transferred or stored in a more compact format and later re-created (decompressed) and used.

Compressed audio files can have lossless or lossy formats. *Lossless* compressed audio formats store audio data in less space (50% to 60% of the original) without losing any information and enable the original audio to be re-created from the compressed version without discernible differences. Lossless audio file formats include *Apple Lossless Audio Codec (ALAC)*, *Free Lossless Audio Codec (FLAC)*, *MPEG-4 Audio Lossless Coding (MPEG-4 ALS)*, and *Windows Media Audio Lossless (WMA Lossless)*.

Lossy audio file formats enable the greatest reduction in the size of original uncompressed files, to an average of 5% to 20% of the original, but can result in a noticeable reduction of audio quality. The lossy compression process removes some audio information and simplifies the data. Most techniques strive to remove the parts of the original sound that have the least effect on perceived quality and to minimize the amount of audible noise (usually experienced as a hiss) added by the compression process. *MP3* is probably the best known lossy audio compression file format, but the *Advanced Audio Codec (AAC)* format used on the iTunes Music Store is also well known. Both offer a range of degrees of compression.

Digitizing Images

Numerous types of images are transmitted on network circuits and saved to storage devices. This includes photographs, charts, drawings, web page content, document images, screen captures or snips, and medical images. Many smartphone users liberally use the cameras in their devices to take pictures (or capture videos) to embed in text messages, send as email attachments, or upload to social media platforms. Since many image transmittals involve enterprise network circuits, businesses are having to accommodate growing volumes of image traffic and storage.

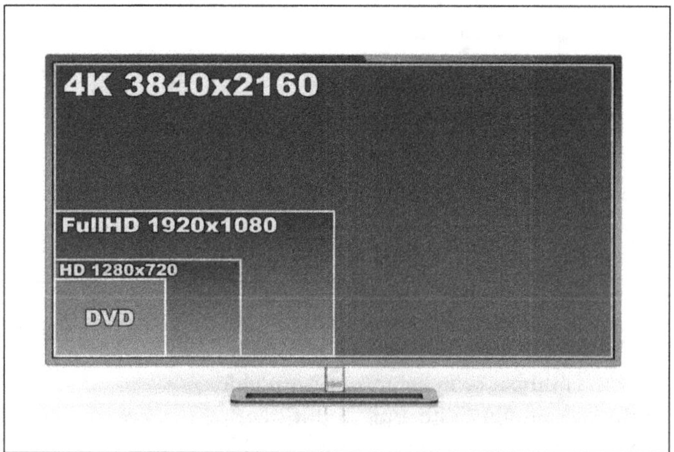

Figure 3-5: Some common pixel grids used by computer and television monitors. Source: scanrail/iStock.com. Stock photo ID:529369253

Two types of graphics are used to represent images: raster and vector. Most images displayed on computer and device screens are *raster graphics*. Pictures produced by digital cameras are raster graphics.

Raster graphics is an offshoot of television technology, with images constructed much like those on television screens. A raster graphic is made up of a collection of tiny, uniformly sized *pixels (pixel elements)*, which are arranged in a two-dimensional grid called a *bitmap*. Examples of bitmap array sizes are identified in Figures 3-5 and 3-6. As grids get bigger, more pixels are available to represent the

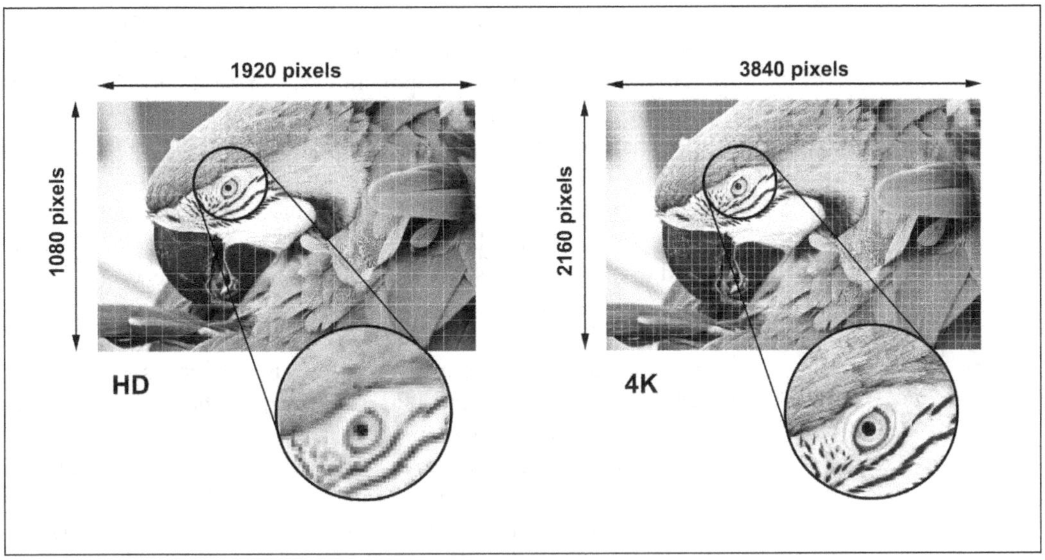

Figure 3-6: Number of pixels and screen resolution. Source: scyther5/iStock. Stock photo ID:475777175

image. For example, a 640 x 480 grid has 307,200 pixels, while a 3072 x 2048 grid (from a 6.3-Megapixel digital camera) has 6,291,456 pixels.

The number of pixels per image determines an image's *resolution*, the amount of detail that can be depicted in the image. Figure 3-6 provides an example of how resolution affects the crispness of an image on a display screen.

For transmittal and storage, bits are used to represent each pixel. If each pixel is represented by a single bit (0 or 1) and is limited to displaying two colors, such as black and white, a 640 x 480 image would include 307,200 bits, whereas a 3072 x 2048 image would have 6,291,456 bits. However, when multiple bits (e.g., 8, 16, 24, or 32) represent each pixel, the pixel can display a wider range of colors. For example, when 8 bits are used to indicate the color of a pixel, each pixel can display 256 (2^8) different colors or shades of a single color (such as grayscale). When 24 bits are used, each pixel can have more than 16 million different states (2^{24} = 16,777,216), such as colors or shades.

The number of bits used to represent the color of a pixel (or pixel component) is called *color depth*. Color depth is also known as bit depth and is usually provided in *bits per pixel (bpp)*. Table 3-3 demonstrates how color depth and bitmap size combine to determine the number of bits in an image; the general formula is:

Total bits per image = Bitmap dimensions x Color depth

Table 3-3: Some common bitmap dimensions and color depths for raster graphics.

Bitmap Dimensions (Resolution)	Number of Pixels per Image	Color Depth	Number of Bits per Image
640 x 480	307,200	1-bit	307,200
		8-bit	2,457,600
1280 x 720	921,600	1-bit	921,600
		8-bit	7,372,800
		16-bit	14,745,600
1920 x 1080	2,073,600	1-bit	2,073,600
		8-bit	16,588,800
		16-bit	33,177,600
		24-bit	49,766,400
3840 x 2160	8,294,400	1-bit	8,294,400
		8-bit	66,355,200
		16-bit	132,710,400
		24-bit	199,065,600

Today, each pixel in a raster graphic display usually has three components—one phosphor for each of the three primary colors: red, green, and blue (see Figure 3-7). The bright-

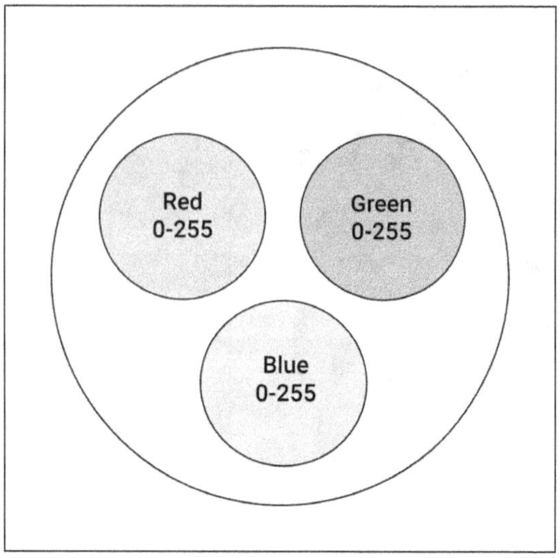

Figure 3-7: Each phosphor in a true color 24-bit pixel can display 256 shades of color.

ness of each component is adjustable, and additive mixing of red, green, and blue enables other colors to be displayed. In a 24-bit (*true color*) pixel, each component can represent 256 (2^8) different shades (brightness levels) of the color it represents. For each component, the separate 8-bit values range from 00000000 (0 or off) to 11111111 (255 or fully illuminated [very bright]).

The pixel is bright blue when the brightness level for the blue phosphor is 11111111 (255), while the brightness level for the red and green phosphors are 00000000 (0). The pixel is bright yellow when the brightness levels for both red and green are 11111111 (255), and the brightness level for blue is 0 (00000000). Displays with a 32-bit color depth combine an opaqueness component with the red, green, and blue components; that component has 256 (2^8) opaqueness levels.

As Table 3-3 illustrates, image sizes can be large, especially for high-resolution true color displays. Like audio files, image files may be compressed for storage or transmission over network circuits. Also, like audio files, images may be converted into either lossless or lossy file formats. Lossless and lossy image compression are briefly described in Table 3-4.

Raster graphics (bitmap) images typically can be scaled down (reduced in size) with little or no loss of quality. Enlarging, however, often causes a bitmap image to look "pixelated," or blocky. For this reason, vector graphics are more common for images that need to be enlarged or reduced without loss of quality.

Vector graphics images are described by straight and curved lines, geometric shapes, and other collections of line segment groupings. They are saved and stored using geometric formulas. Because the processes used to render and reproduce vector images are more complex than those used for raster graphics, raster images are more common than vector graphics.

Sometimes, a combination of raster and vector graphics is used to create image files. Examples using this combination include Encapsulated Postscript (EPS) and Portable Document Format (PDF) files.

Table 3-4: Characteristics and examples of lossless and lossy image compression.

Type	Description	Examples
Lossless	The goal of lossless image compression is to represent the uncompressed image with the smallest number of bits without sacrificing image quality. Lossless image compression ratios are typically less than 5:1; the compressed file is no smaller than one-fifth the size of the original.	*Graphics Interchange Format (GIF)* *Free Lossless Image Format (FLIF)* *JPEG-2000* *JPEG-LS* *Portable Network Graphics (PNG)* *Tag Image File Format (TIFF)*
Lossy	When lossy image compression is used, some data from the original image file is lost and cannot be recovered when the file is decompressed. In other words, the loss is irreversible. Once an image is compressed using lossy compression, there is no going back. However, lossy image compression can result in significantly smaller files than lossless compression. Compression ratios range between 10:1 and 20:1, with the compressed file one-tenth to one-twentieth the size of the original.	*Joint Photographic Experts Group (JPEG)* *Better Portable Graphics (BPG)* *High Efficiency Image Format (HEIF)* *Multiple-Image Network Graphics (MNG)*

Digitizing Video

Video traffic on the public Internet and in enterprise networks continues to expand at dramatic rates. Typically, at any given moment, more than half the Internet traffic is video traffic. This includes movie streams (such as Netflix), television live streams (such as Hulu), and sports live streams (such as ESPN+). The use of video for online advertising, e-learning, telemedicine, real-time video surveillance, and videoconferencing (such as Zoom meetings) also contributes significant video traffic.

Digitizing video involves capturing, storing, and using video in digital formats. Digital video cameras capture moving images and convert them to binary code. Digital video sometimes consists of sequences of digital photographs (images) captured at a rate of 30 pictures (frames) per second or higher. However, capture rates as low as 24 or as high as 60 *frames per second (fps)* may be used.

Cameras in smartphones and tablets are examples of digital video cameras. So are the webcams in laptop computers, standalone webcams, and most cameras in video surveillance systems. High-resolution digital video cameras are common for professional sports live streams and television broadcasts. These often have 60 fps capture rates to enable high-quality replay reviews. Also, rather than continuously sending entire frames, many digital cameras create digital code that identifies how a frame differs from the previous one so not as much data needs to be transmitted.

Because digital video consists of bits that represent sequences of images, bit generation rates, and uncompressed file sizes, are very large. Very high speed network circuits are needed for uncompressed video streams, and storage requirements for uncompressed video can be massive.

For example, a 4K true color (24-bit) digital video camera with a 60 fps capture rate generates more than 159 billion bits each second (see Table 3-5). The bit generation rate is calculated by the following formula:

Video bit rate = Image dimensions x Color depth x Images per second

Like images, lossy compression can be used to reduce the size of video files, and most videos transmitted over networks are compressed using lossy video compression. Basically, lossy video compression algorithms analyze the video stream and discard information that the human eye is unable to perceive.

Reasonable quality (from a human perspective) is possible when video compression ratios are between 20:1 (where the compressed file is about one-twentieth the size of the original) and 100:1 (where the file is about one-one-hundredth the size of the original). Lossy versions of *JPEG* and *Motion Picture Experts Group (MPEG)* formats exist for video compression. *H.263*, *H.264*, and *H.265* are video compression standards for videoconferencing applications.

Table 3-5: Examples of video capture and bit generation rates.

Format	Image Dimensions (Resolution)	Pixels per Image	Color Depth	Bits per Image	Images per Second	Bits per Second
HD	1280 x 720	921,600	8-bit	7,372,800	60	43,988,000
			16-bit	14,745,600		87,936,000
Full HD	1920 x 1080	2,073,600	8-bit	16,588,800	60	995,328,000
			16-bit	33,177,600		1,990,656,000
			24-bit	49,766,400		3,981,312,000
4K	3840 x 2160	8,294,400	8-bit	66,355,200	60	39,813,120,000
			16-bit	132,710,400		79,626,240,000
			24-bit	199,065,600		159,252,480,000

A narrated PowerPoint presentation that contains both images and audio can be converted to a digital video using PowerPoint's Export feature. Basically, the process converts files from one digital format to another.

The Export feature supports several format and quality options, from Standard (852 x 480) to 4K (3840 x 2160), and the resulting video is typically an *MPEG-4 Part 14 (MP4)* file that enables streaming over the Internet. While usually used to store video and audio, MP4 also can be used to store subtitles and still images.

Digitizing Text

Alphanumeric is a term used to describe data that consists of both letters and numbers. In the early days of computing, almost all network traffic was alphanumeric data, and techniques for converting alphanumeric data to binary code have been used for decades.

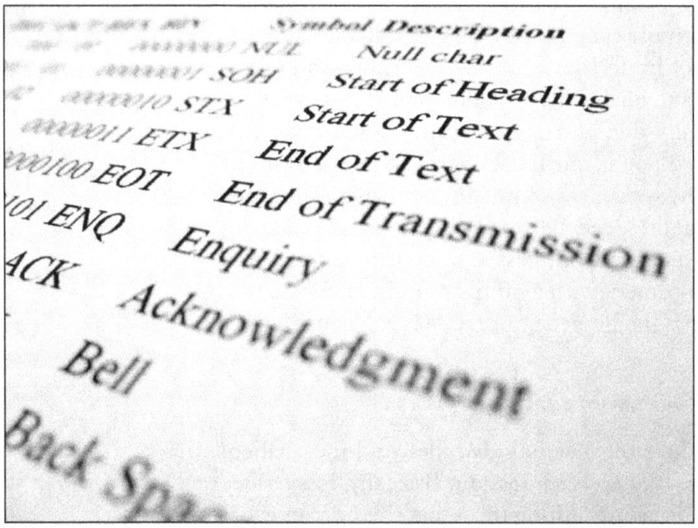

Figure 3-8: Examples of communication symbols in character sets. Source: kr7ysztof/iStock. Stock photo ID:91290152

In computers, alphanumeric data (such as lowercase a–z and uppercase A–Z letters and the digits 0–9); punctuation marks (e.g., !, ?, ;, :, “, ‘, ., and comma [,]); special characters (e.g., >, <, =, +, -, *, %, &, $, #, @, [, }, and /); and other keys on a QWERTY keyboard (e.g., Space, Enter, and Tab) are each assigned a specific binary value using a *character code* or *character set*. When converted to binary, each character or symbol is represented as a fixed-length string of bits, like those associated with the data communication symbol examples in Figure 3-8.

Over the years, multiple character sets have been developed for alphanumeric data, including those identified in Table 3-6. Both Unicode and UTF-8 can represent significantly more characters than ASCII or IRA, but both are backward compatible with both IRA and ASCII; this essentially makes them extensions of IRA and ASCII to accommodate characters and symbols used in the world's major languages. IRA and ASCII were devised for the English language. EBCDIC is an alphanumeric character set that IBM developed for the operating systems on its larger computers.

There are both 7- and 8-bit versions of ASCII, but today, the 8-bit version is most common. The 7-bit version is essentially the IRA. Text files (files saved with a .txt extension) use the IRA

Table 3-6: Some widely used character sets.

Character Set Name	Bits per Character	Total Number of Characters
International Reference Alphabet (IRA)	7	128 (2^7)
American Standard Code for Information Interchange (ASCII)	8	256 (2^8)
Unicode Transformation Format 8-bit (UTF-8)	8*	256 (2^8)*
Extended Binary Coded Decimal Interchange Code (EBCDIC)	8	256 (2^8)
Unicode	16	65,536 (2^{16})

*Supports variable length encoding, which allows a character to be represented by multiple bytes.

character set and have limited formatting capabilities. They do not support special formatting such as boldface, italics, or a wide variety of fonts. Examples of programs that can open and edit text tiles are Microsoft Notepad, TextEdit (on a Mac), and Notepad++.

Universal Character Set (UCS) enables a character or symbol to be represented by 1 byte (UTF-8), 2 bytes (UTF-16), or 4 bytes (UTF-32). Because it can represent so many different characters and symbols, UCS can support the different languages spoken around the world.

Revisions to Unicode enable it to support variable-length encoding of characters and symbols. Unicode 6.0, released in 2010, was the first character set to support emoji.

Online text-to-binary converters, such as the ASCII/UTF-8 and Unicode to binary converters available on the RapidTables website (https://www.rapidtables.com/convert/number/ascii-to-binary.html), provide a hands-on demonstration of alphanumeric data digitization.

Alphanumeric data can be compressed to reduce the size of stored or transmitted files. Lossless compression is commonly used to ensure that an exact duplicate of the original file can be reproduced from the compressed file.

Lempel-Ziv data compression schemes are used for both stored and transmitted alphanumeric data. Some are used to "zip" (compress) individual files or sets of files (folders) prior to uploading them to a website or sending them as email attachments. Files and folders also can be zipped to conserve storage space.

Some Lempel-Ziv data compression versions enable alphanumeric data streams to be compressed and decompressed by modems or other transmission devices without creating .zip files. Compression ratios between 3.5:1 and 4.5:1 are common when Lempel-Ziv compression is applied to ASCII data streams. These compression ratios are lower than those for other data (e.g., audio, image, or video) but are still significant reductions in size from the uncompressed data.

Digitizing Barcodes and QR Codes

Barcodes, such as the universal product code (UPC) in Figure 3-9 and quick response (QR) codes, are widely used in businesses. Barcodes are used to track warehouse inventory and parcel deliveries and to record sales in point-of-sale (POS) systems. They are also found on coupons scanned at checkout stations.

Figure 3-9: Universal product code barcode. Source: emptyclouds/iStock.com. Stock photo ID:173563308

The 12 decimal digits in a UPC code (see Figure 3-9) create a unique identifier for the product, and the pattern of black lines and white spaces in the barcode represent the 12-digit decimal number. Barcode scanners convert the pattern to binary code.

Each digit (0–9) is represented by a unique pattern of two bars and two spaces, with black bars representing 1s and white spaces (bars) representing 0s in the binary code. Thick black bars represent a string of 1s (several 1 bits in a sequence), and wider white spaces represent a string of 0s.

When the barcode is scanned, the bars and spaces that represent each of the 12 decimal digits are converted to a 7-bit binary code; a total of 84 bits is created for the 12 decimal values. There are two guide bars on either end of the barcode that frame the bars and spaces representing the 12 digits. Each guide bar converts to 101. There is also a central guide bar that separates the 12 digits into two six-digit segments; it converts to 01010. When the bits for the guide bars are added to the 84 bits that represent the 12 digits, a total of 95 bits of binary code are generated each time a UPC barcode is scanned.

Once scanned, product details from the product database display on POS checkout screens and are printed on receipts. Since each scan implies a product sale, it also updates the inventory level.

Figure 3-10: Examples of commonly used barcode types and formats. Source: Evgenii_Bobrov/iStock Stock illustration ID:840496010

A wide range of barcodes are used by today's businesses. These vary in format, the amount of information they convey, and the number of bits generated when scanned. Examples are included in Figure 3-10.

QR Codes, like those in Figure 3-11, are more complex than barcodes and may hold hundreds of times more data/information. This makes them suitable for a wide range of uses. QR codes on product packaging enable access to product information beyond what can be included on the packaging.

Figure 3-11: Examples of QR codes. Source: Happy_vector/iStock Stock illustration ID:1008469132

QR codes are used for contactless airline and event e-tickets and public transportation passes. Numerous restaurants use QR codes to enable customers to access menus using their mobile devices. QR codes are also used in mobile payment systems.

Readers/scanners convert QR codes to binary code for transmission or storage. Because most applications require exact reproductions of the original QR code data/information, their binary codes are typically transmitted/saved in uncompressed form or use lossless compression.

As Figure 3-11 illustrates, there is a wide variety of QR types and formats. QR codes also vary in size.

Digitizing IoT Sensor Data

IoT sensors generate a lot of data traffic on the public Internet and in enterprise networks. Estimates/projections for the number of IoT-connected devices vary, but those on the conservative side claim that there were about 10 billion active IoT devices by the end of 2021 and there will be at least 25 billion by 2030. IoT use in businesses is the focus of Chapter 9.

IoT devices and applications usually communicate and interact via the cloud; however, those used in business facilities often involve edge technologies that strive to minimize the amount of data passed to the cloud. Being able to communicate with IoT applications via the cloud enables users to access/use them from remote locations. For example, a worker may check and adjust the temperature settings of the smart thermostat in their home during their evening commute.

Most IoT devices include one or more *sensors* that monitor the status and changes to conditions of certain things where they are located. The primary role of a sensor is to measure some aspect of the physical world and to convert the measurement into computer-readable binary code.

Numerous types of sensors are used in IoT applications and systems, including temperature, motion, humidity, pressure (used to detect leaks), proximity, gas, and optical sensors. Sensor data is translated into computer-readable (and manipulable) binary code and is transmitted to IoT control services (usually in the cloud) that alert IoT device owners/users (or others) when conditions require their attention or intervention.

Most IoT sensors that monitor naturally occurring analog data (such as temperature or movement) are equipped with *microcontrollers* that include an analog-to-digital converter (ADC) that uses a sampling, quantizing, and encoding process akin to PCM (see section 3.1.2). Waveform samples are converted to a fixed-length string of bits (often 8-bit strings capable of representing 256 [2^8] different physical states). Some IoT microcontroller ADCs produce 9-, 10-, or 16-bit codes. Some IoT sensors produce analog output that is subsequently converted to binary code for transmission or storage.

AI and the IoT are converging to enable greater autonomy for IoT systems and applications, but sensor data is the primary trigger of AI-facilitated adjustments and reactions to changing conditions. The convergence of AI and the IoT is very important for applications such as driverless vehicles and autonomous robots in warehouses and manufacturing facilities, and greater autonomy will require substantial increases in the volumes of IoT data carried by the Internet, enterprise networks, and other communication networks.

3.2 STRUCTURED AND UNSTRUCTURED DATA

Enterprise data is often categorized as structured or unstructured, or somewhere in between: semi-structured. Some of the major differences between structured and unstructured data are summarized in Table 3-7.

Table 3-7: Some of the major differences between structured and unstructured data.

Structured Data	Unstructured Data
Data that can be stored in tables with rows and columns and can be mapped to predefined fields	Exists in a variety of formats and usually stored in its native format
Easy to access and searchable; often organized and stored in relational databases to facilitate searches and queries	Does not have a predefined model and may be difficult to search or query; often stored in NoSQL databases
Often quantitative data, such as numbers and things that can be counted, which enables the data to be classified or clustered and analyzed using probabilities and statistical methods	Often qualitative data that is challenging to analyze using conventional tools based on probabilities and statistics; alternative analytical approaches, such as data stacking, may enable insights into frequencies of similar data and anomalies
Often commingled and stored in data warehouses after being extracted from original sources and cleansed	Often stored in data lakes in its original format after undergoing a basic cleaning
Examples include alphanumeric data, data in spreadsheet files, ES data, and data in relational databases	Examples include audio, image, and video files; social media posts; text messages; email messages; and word processing documents

3.2.1 Structured Data

In businesses, structured data often refers to data that resides in a field within a file or database record. Structured data is often stored in tables that have meaningful rows and columns. Examples of structured data include spreadsheet files and tables in relational databases. Each of these formats have structured rows and columns that can be sorted.

Structured data has a *data model*—a model of how data can be stored, accessed, and processed. With a data model, each field (column) in the table is discrete and can be accessed individually or jointly along with data from other fields. A data model enables data to be aggregated from various locations in the spreadsheet or database.

Structured data is considered a traditional type of logical data representation because the earliest versions of database management systems (DBMSs) could store, access, and process data stored in tables by leveraging data models. Historically, the first types of data stored in databases were alphanumeric data made up of text and numbers (such as names, addresses, credit card numbers, locations, dates, account balances, quantities, prices, etc.).

3.2.2 Unstructured Data

Most new data that businesses are capturing and storing is unstructured data. Today, more than 75% of enterprise data is unstructured data, and that percentage is growing. It is a primary reason why most businesses analyze only a small fraction of the data that they have amassed.

Examples of unstructured data include social media posts, text messages, email messages, surveillance video, podcasts, and word processing documents. Unstructured data typically requires more bandwidth than structured data when transmitted over network circuits and is a primary driver of business adoption of cloud storage.

Unlike structured data, unstructured data often lacks a predefined data model or is not organized in a predefined manner; it is often stored in its original format. Unstructured data may have a native, internal structure, but its irregularities and ambiguities make it difficult or impossible to assess using traditional data manipulation and analysis tools designed for structured data.

3.2.3 Semi-Structured Data and Metadata

Semi-structured data is a third data category that falls somewhere between structured and unstructured data. Semi-structured data is often considered to be a type of structured data that does not fully conform to the formal structures or data models associated with relational databases or spreadsheets. However, it contains tags or other identifying markers to separate semantic elements and/or to enforce hierarchies of fields within records or hierarchies of records. It is sometimes said to have a self-describing structure.

A smartphone photo is a commonly cited example of semi-structured data because it typically has a time stamp and/or a location tag and other identifying tags that enable it to be found by a search. XML and CSV files are also identified as semi-structured data.

Metadata is another important type of data. *Metadata* is data about data. It provides information about a specific field in a database or a specific set of data. Examples of metadata in relational databases include table names, field names, the type of data (e.g., text, numeric, date) in a field, and field size (length). Metadata for a set of photos could identify when and where the photos were taken and the objects or people in them. Such metadata provides structured information about photos that would otherwise be unstructured data.

When structured, unstructured, semi-structured, and metadata is digitized, it can be transmitted, stored, processed, and commingled for analysis by Big Data processing platforms. The ability of businesses and other organizations to extract value from comingling unstructured and semi-structured data has been one of the main drivers of Big Data processing.

3.2.4 Big Data

Declining data storage costs and the ability to leverage the cloud to store vast quantities of data have fueled businesses' appetite for amassing ever-increasing volumes of data. However, most organizations still analyze only a small fraction of the data they have accumulated, despite the maturation of platforms and tools capable of processing large data sets.

Big Data is the term used to describe the large volumes of structured, unstructured, and semi-structured data that today's businesses are capturing and storing daily. The term refers to data sets that are too large or complex for traditional data management processes to handle and for traditional processing tools to process.

Big Data Attributes

Several characteristics are used to describe Big Data, including volume, velocity, variety, variability, and veracity (see Table 3-8).

Businesses with Big Data processing platforms and analytics are best positioned to capitalize on their large data sets. Such platforms enable deeper understanding of customer behaviors and purchasing habits and other patterns that can be leveraged to boost sales, develop new products, and add value. Big Data is also leveraged to better understand security vulnerabilities and fraudulent activities that threaten enterprise network assets.

Table 3-8: Some of the key attributes of Big Data.

Characteristic	Brief Description
Volume	Organizations collect, transmit, and store data from a variety of sources, including business transactions, IoT devices, industrial equipment, social media, and many more. In the past, storing the massive amounts of data could be a problem, but inexpensive cloud storage platforms, such as data lakes, have alleviated much of the problem. Today, the volume of data is doubling approximately every 18 months, but because the rate of data acquisition is increasing, doubling will happen more quickly in the future. Experts predict that by 2025, there will be more than 180 zettabytes (180,000,000,000,000,000,000,000 bytes or 180,000,000,000 terabytes) of data.
Velocity	The accelerating rate of business adoption of IoT systems and applications contributes to accelerating data generation and flow rates. Some types of data, such as data from RFID tags, sensors, and process controls, add the most value when they are handled in real time or near real time. Ideally, the rate at which Big Data is processed should also be accelerating.
Variety	Data comes in a variety of formats—structured, unstructured, and semi-structured. Over time, the variety of data being captured, stored, and analyzed by businesses has increased, and it is likely to continue to increase in the years ahead. Increasing variety fuels business adoption of data lakes.
Variability	This stems from unpredictable data flows from different sources, flows whose rates may change frequently and can range from a trickle to a flood. Although challenging, it is important for businesses to have the ability to quickly respond to changing data flow rates. A surge in social media data, for example, may mean that something important is trending that requires business attention and a possible response. Enterprise networks should have sufficient bandwidth to handle data surges alongside daily, seasonal, and event-triggered peaks in data traffic.
Veracity	This refers to the quality of data and its sources. If data sources are inaccurate or cannot be trusted to provide valid data, their ability to contribute business value is limited. When data with varying degrees of structure comes from many different sources, it may be difficult to cleanse, transform, match, link, commingle, compare, or associate. Big Data is most likely to be helpful to a business when the various types of data flowing into the organization can be connected, correlated, or hierarchically arranged, but data sources must be trustworthy.

Big Data Processing Platforms

Two common types of Big Data processing platforms are Hadoop clusters and SAP HANA.

A *computer cluster* generally refers to a collection of computers that work together as a single system. A Hadoop cluster is a specialized type of computer cluster that is frequently used to simultaneously store and process structured and unstructured data. Basically, a **Hadoop cluster** is a collection of networked computers, called nodes, that perform parallel computations on large data sets.

Hadoop clusters are typically implemented as servers and storage technologies in data centers. Although they perform complex processing tasks, they are relatively inexpensive to implement because they do not require specialized hardware.

Horizontal scaling makes Hadoop clusters suitable for Big Data processing. **Horizontal scaling** refers to adding computers to a cluster and distributing data processing activities across the different computers so they can perform the activities in parallel. For example, structured data processing activities can be performed on some of the computers in a Hadoop cluster, while unstructured data is processed by other computers in the cluster. Server virtualization, introduced in Chapter 2, is a form of horizontal scaling.

Horizontal scaling is contrasted with **vertical scaling**, which involves adding more power to existing computers or replacing them with more powerful computers. For example, vertical scaling could involve upgrading the CPUs in an existing server. However, it could also mean replacing an existing server with one equipped with more powerful CPUs or processing capacity. Replacing existing servers with SAP HANA servers combines horizontal and vertical scaling.

SAP HANA is an in-memory database engine that is used for real-time analysis of large data sets that reside entirely in memory. It is sometimes described as a high-capacity, column-oriented, in-memory relational DBMS that can hold up to a petabyte of data in memory.

Typically, SAP HANA® is physically implemented as a data center appliance or horizontally scalable cluster that primarily functions as a database server. However, because it has extract, transform, load (ETL) capabilities, it can be used to cleanse and update data warehouse data in addition to processing it. SAP HANA is also used as an application server to run SAP ERP and other ES applications. These applications perform well on SAP HANA because their entire databases can be run in memory.

Both memory capacity and the use of column-oriented data in in-memory databases enable SAP HANA to be used as a Big Data processing platform. In-memory databases are described in Appendix 3-2. Hadoop clusters and SAP HANA are described in further detail in Appendix 3-1.

There are several important considerations for Big Data processing platforms in today's businesses. First, business interest in AI-enabled applications, such as machine learning and natural language processing, is an important driver of Big Data acquisition and processing. Big Data fuels machine learning and continuous improvement of AI algorithms. Second, businesses seek Big Data processing platforms and AI applications that can analyze continuous streams of all types of data—structured, unstructured, and semi-structured. Third, to control costs, businesses prefer commodity storage and server hardware that scales horizontally and can be widely distributed, ideally among fault tolerant clusters with thousands of nodes.

Increasingly, Big Data processing platforms are important components in enterprise network architectures. These platforms and their underlying technologies will continue to evolve, but commingling and parallel processing of diverse types of digitized data is likely to continue to be used.

3.3 LOGICAL DATA COLLECTIONS

3.3.1 Databases

Traditionally, businesses have organized their data in one or more databases. However, as noted in section 3.2.4, a wide variety of data is being captured by today's businesses, and data capture and storage rates (and volumes) are increasing. Much of the new data is unstructured or semi-structured and is less suitable than structured data for being organized, saved, and managed by relational databases. And some types of digitized data (e.g., alphanumeric and barcode) are more easily organized as structured data in relational databases than others (e.g., audio, images, video, or sensor).

Databases are primarily logical arrangements of data that are stored on various physical storage media. Generally, any collection of data is considered a database, regardless of how or where it is stored. This makes a file cabinet containing employee payroll information a database as much as the data/information stored on a hard drive or in the cloud.

Some databases, including NoSQL, in-memory, and blockchains, are often coupled with specific physical storage configurations, such as Hadoop clusters, SAP HANA, or a distributed network of computers. Others, like data warehouses (DWs) and data lakes, have physical-sounding names but are fundamentally logical collections and arrangements of data.

Several of the more important types of databases that enterprise networks support are briefly described in this section. They are described more fully in Appendix 3-2.

Relational Databases

Relational databases have been used in businesses since the 1970s, and their popularity surged after Structured Query Language (SQL) was developed in the 1980s. They remain popular because they enable large amounts of structured data to be organized in tables that can be manipulated and queried by query languages and analyzed by business analytics and business intelligence (BI) tools. They are sometimes called SQL databases to distinguish them from NoSQL databases.

NoSQL Databases

Not Only SQL (NoSQL) databases are preferable to relational databases for unstructured and semi-structured data. They support a variety of nontabular data types and organizational schemes, including graph-based, document-oriented, column-oriented, and key–value pairs.

NoSQL databases enable the creation of files (often called documents) that lack precisely defined structures. They also enable:

- The addition of new attributes to file entities without having to change existing files
- Storage of files with unique structures
- The creation of multiple databases with different structures for entities

These characteristics make a NoSQL database more appropriate than a relational database for storing data like news articles, social media posts, text messages, email, images, videos, podcasts, and other types of unstructured data that do not neatly conform to relational database table structures.

In-Memory Databases

An **in-memory database (IMDB)** is capable of storing large data sets in a computer's main memory. This eliminates the need (and required time) to transfer database data in pieces from a storage device to main memory for processing. Memory limitations in traditional database and application servers have contributed to increased business use of computer clusters (Hadoop) and SAP HANA for Big Data processing.

IMDBs are well suited to applications that require rapid response times and real-time data management, such as securities trading, banking, e-commerce, geospatial processing, processing sensor data streams, and machine learning. They are also useful for real-time management of enterprise network routers and switches. IMDBs are sometimes called real-time databases (RTDBs) or main memory databases (MMDBs).

3.3.2 Data Warehouses (DWs) and Data Lakes

A **data warehouse (DW)** includes data that is integrated, time-variant (historical), and nonvolatile. DWs can be physically implemented in storage area networks (SANs) or data centers (discussed in section 3.4), but, like databases, they are logical data collections and arrangements.

Traditionally, DWs have included data extracted from structured data sources. Today, however, they are increasingly being used to also house unstructured and semi-structured data, especially by businesses interested in Big Data processing. DWs have traditionally been used for BI and analytics, and their contents are often "mined" to identify important patterns and trends across time.

Data lakes are among the newer, and larger, logical collections of data in enterprise networks. Data in a data lake comes from disparate sources and often includes a mix of structured, semi-structured, and unstructured data. Businesses create data lakes as repositories for data they do not currently need or plan to immediately analyze.

Like a natural lake, a data lake can be fed by multiple continuously flowing streams, in this case, real-time flows of structured, unstructured, and semi-structured data. Data lakes enable businesses to amass large pools of unrefined raw data for later processing and analysis, including data with unidentified or unknown business value. Data lakes may be fed by data from both relational and NoSQL databases. Alternatively, data lake data may flow to relational and NoSQL databases for processing. Data lakes are often attractive destinations for digitized audio, image, video, IoT sensor, and social media data.

Data lakes invariably rely on cloud storage. Major cloud providers, including AWS, Azure, and Google Cloud Platforms, offer managed data lake services. They are relatively inexpensive, are highly scalable, and can be integrated with other cloud services and applications, such as BIaaS (BI as a Service).

3.3.3 Centralized, Distributed, Replicated, Partitioned, and Blockchain Databases

Various types of databases are used in today's businesses. Some are used at specific locations, and others are used across most or all locations. Several deployments of databases are briefly described in this section, including centralized databases and various types of distributed databases.

Centralized versus Distributed Databases

Both centralized and distributed databases may be supported by enterprise networks. A **centralized database** is located and maintained at a single enterprise network location. Users access the database via network connections (see Figure 3-12a).

A **distributed database** is a collection of different databases at different enterprise network locations that is organized in a way that makes it appear as a single database to its users. Figure 3-12b provides a conceptual depiction of a distributed database.

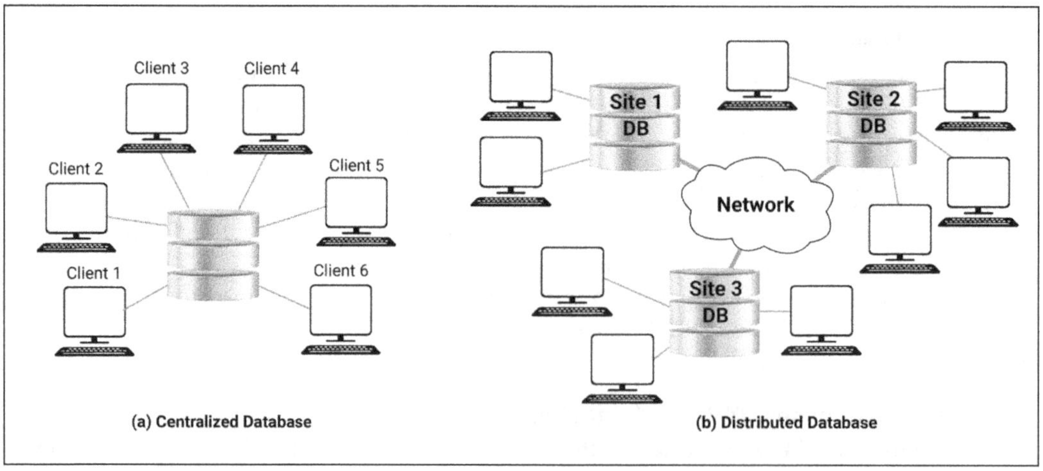

Figure 3-12: Conceptual depictions of a centralized database and a distributed database.

Replicated and Partitioned Databases

Most distributed databases in today's enterprise networks are replicated databases. In a **replicated database**, the database is copied to two or more network locations. In Figure 3-13, copies (replicas) of the principal database are located at sites A and B. The key advantages of this arrangement are availability, resilience, and business continuity. If a server, data storage equipment, or communication link failure occurs at one location, users can continue to access the database at another location.

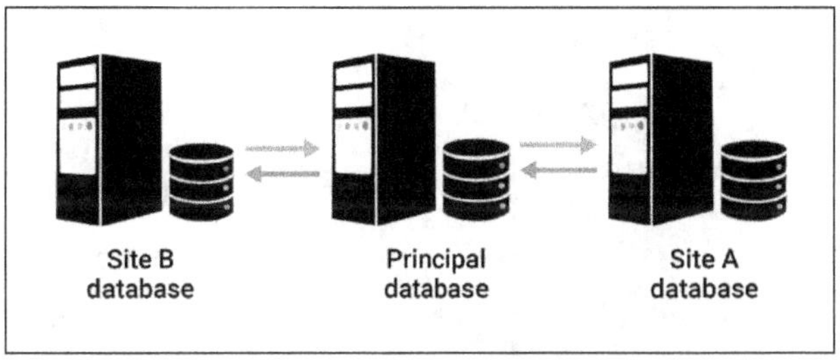

Figure 3-13: An example of database replication.

Some distributed databases are partitioned databases. In a **partitioned database**, the database exists as distinct and nonoverlapping segments that are dispersed across network locations. Typically, there is little data duplication because each partition is a nonoverlapping subset of the database. NoSQL databases that store several different types of unstructured or semi-structured data across different servers or locations are sometimes considered partitioned databases.

Blockchain Databases

A **blockchain** is a database that is shared among a network of computers (see Figure 3-14). While a blockchain can be viewed as a logical collection of data because it is distributed across the computers in the network, it is challenging to separate its logical structure from its physical deployment.

Basically, a blockchain is a digital ledger that is transparent and accessible to all computers in the network. It is a list of transactions that is constantly being updated. It is supported by a private or public P2P (peer-to-peer) network of computers that uses the same process (algorithm) to verify each transaction. Processing work is distributed across the network to ensure that there is no single point of failure.

A blockchain is controlled by a central node to ensure that only trustworthy computers can add new data to the database. Data/information is stored in blocks that are uniform in size. Each block includes hashed information (a hash code) from the previous block in the database to provide cryptographic security. Hashing, hash codes, and their use in securing data are described in Chapter 12.

Fuller descriptions of blockchain databases and the other databases discussed in this section are provided in Appendix 3-2.

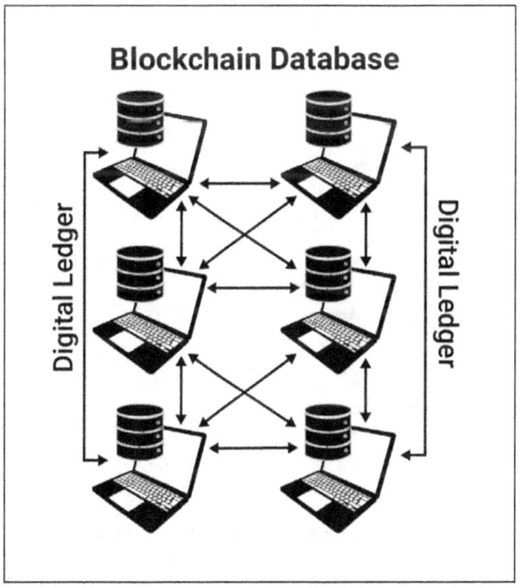

Figure 3-14: Conceptual depiction of a blockchain database.

3.4 ENTERPRISE DATA STORAGE

An organization's logical data collections (databases, DWs, and data lakes) are stored in digital form on storage devices. PC and laptop hard drives in employee computers may contain some enterprise data, but their limited capacities (typically measured in gigabytes and terabytes) constrain their use for many applications. Like many individuals, employees may supplement the storage limits of their personal devices with external hard drives and virtual storage options such as Google Drive or Microsoft's One Drive.

Enterprise network applications that most or all employees use typically support on-premises or cloud-based data centers or storage area networks (SANs) whose capacities may be measured in petabytes (quadrillions of bytes) or more. Smaller organizations, however, may use smaller network-attached storage (NAS) systems to support their shared applications.

Figure 3-15: A network-attached storage system. Source: 300dpi Stock photo ID:517709366

3.4.1 Network-Attached Storage (NAS) Systems

Small enterprises sometimes satisfy their storage needs via one or more on-premises **network-attached storage (NAS) systems**—specialized data storage servers with multiple disk drives that can support multiple users (see Figure 3-15). Increasingly, however, SANs and cloud data centers are more common than NAS systems in small business networks.

3.4.2 Storage Area Networks (SANs)

A **storage area network (SAN)** is a high-speed network of data storage devices that are accessed by servers. Client devices interact with SAN servers to access data stored in SAN storage devices. To client devices, the different storage devices in the SAN appear to be locally attached. Figure 3-16 provides a conceptual depiction of a SAN.

A variety of storage technologies, including disk arrays, optical disk jukeboxes, tape libraries, and SSD pools, may be included in a SAN to store a wide variety of data types (including audio, image, video, and alphanumeric data). Over time, optical jukeboxes and tape libraries have become less common, and today, most SANs consist of disk arrays (Figure 3-17) and SSD pools.

Solid state drives (SSDs), like the one in Figure 3-18, perform the same storage functions as disk drives but store data on interconnected flash-memory chips that retain data even when they are not powered. Because they use electrical circuitry and have no moving parts, SSDs provide faster data access than disk drives; data access can be up to 10 times faster, and saving data is up to 20 times faster. Despite their advantages, SSD deployment has been slowed by their costs. SSD cost per terabyte remains higher than that for hard disk drives (HDDs) but is expected to equalize with HDD cost in 2026 and be lower after that. So, SSD appears to be the wave of the future.

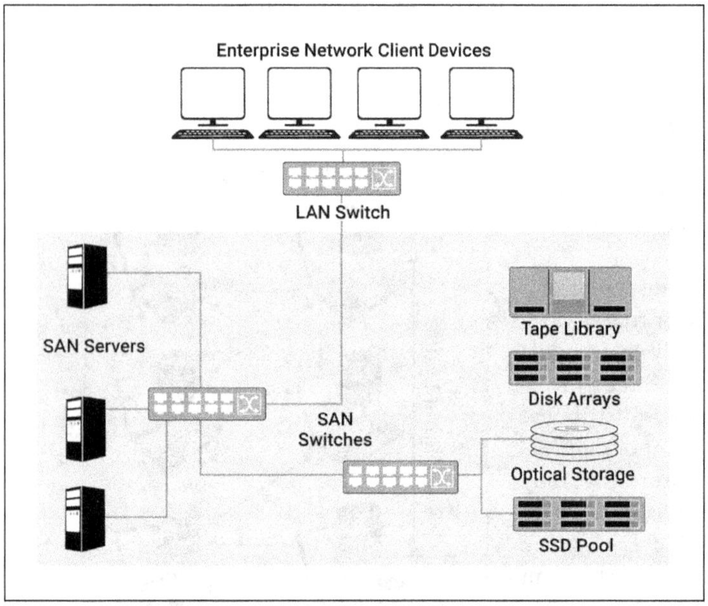

Figure 3-16: Conceptual diagram of a storage area network.

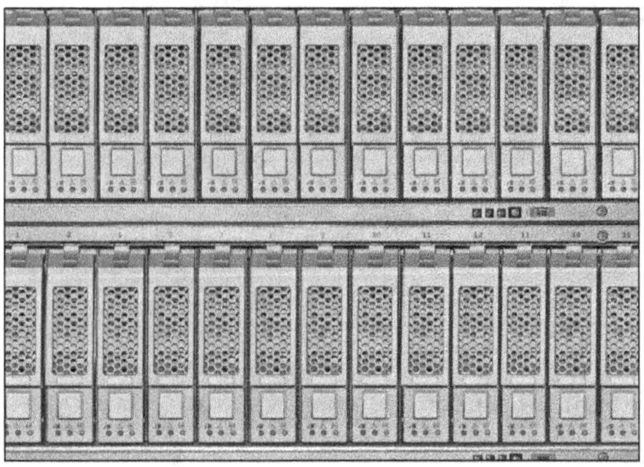

Figure 3-17: Disk drives in a storage area network. Source: tupikov/iStock. Stock photo ID:89228399

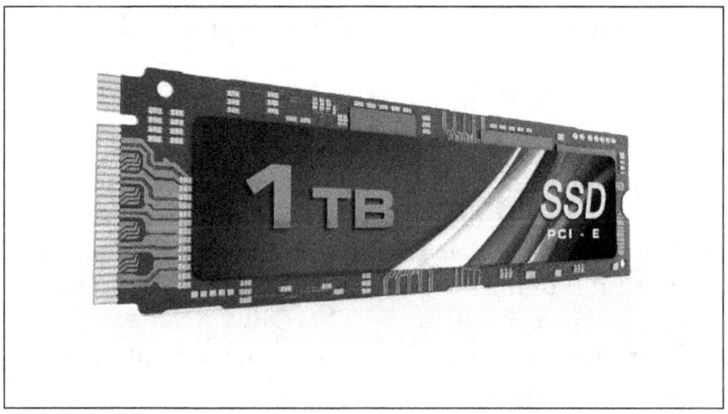

Figure 3-18: Example of a solid-state drive. Source: adventtr/iStock. Stock illustration ID:652966516

The network locations of storage devices in SANs are typically independent of client (user) locations. Employees dispersed across multiple locations may have access to a single SAN. SAN storage devices also can be distributed across multiple locations. Some businesses have redundant SANs at different network locations to eliminate the potential for a single point of failure and to ensure data availability when network disruptions occur. Having redundant SANs provides resilience and contributes to business continuity.

3.4.3 Data Centers

A **data center** is a large group of networked servers and storage hardware that provides storage, processing, and distribution of large amounts of data for one or more organizations. Data centers are the primary infrastructure component of the cloud, but on-premises data center deployments continue to be common in enterprise networks. Data centers typically have very high speed/bandwidth connections to the Internet and to backbone networks in the enterprises they support. High-speed connections facilitate data and data processing results transfers.

Figure 3-19: Aisles in a data center. Source: gorodenkoff/iStock. Stock photo ID:1148233863

A data center may occupy one room, one or more floors of a building, or an entire building. Server and storage equipment is typically mounted in rack cabinets, which are typically placed in rows that form corridors or aisles (see Figure 3-19).

Data centers vary in complexity and extent of component redundancies. Data center tiers have been developed to provide a standardized ranking system for the reliability of data center infrastructure. Traditionally, this classification has ranked facilities from 1 to 4, with 1 being the least and 4 the most reliable infrastructure. Recently, a fifth level has been added. These tiers are described more fully in Appendix 3-3.

Data centers typically include redundant power supplies and cooling systems. Redundant Internet/network connections, internal power grids, wiring, networking equipment (switches and routers), fire suppression, and security controls are also common.

Some organizations have a private on-premises data center for their data storage and processing needs. Others choose to be tenants in cloud providers' data centers.

3.4.4 Cloud Storage

As noted in Chapters 1 and 2, the cloud is an important part of most enterprise networks and can be viewed as an extension of on-premises infrastructure. Over 90% of today's businesses rely on the public cloud for applications and/or storage services, and nearly 70% use a hybrid combination of public and private clouds. As of 2020, more than 50% of all corporate data was stored in the cloud.

Cloud storage is a data storage model in which data is stored in logical pools whose physical storage spans multiple storage devices and servers that are sometimes distributed across multiple data centers.

Cloud storage infrastructure is owned and managed by providers who are responsible for keeping their tenants' data available, accessible, and secure. Although cloud storage infrastructure typically consists of distributed devices and data management resources, tenants are provided with a unified, single-entity experience.

Relative to on-premises data storage, cloud storage offers several business advantages, including:

- Lower costs from not having to purchase, install, and maintain storage and processing equipment. Staff reductions for on-premises infrastructure may also occur.
- On-demand scalability from being able to add or reduce storage infrastructure in response to changing needs.
- Higher reliability, especially for large, geographically dispersed, high-tier data centers that shield tenants from outages and downtime.
- Flexible pricing. Cloud providers offer different service tiers and service level agreements (SLAs). Support for mission-critical applications and data that require high availability, fast speeds, and security can be acquired at higher priced service tiers. Lower service and price tiers may be sufficient for less important data and applications.

Enterprise cloud storage refers to cloud storage purchased from a cloud service provider (CSP) to address the storage needs for all or most of an organization. Enterprise cloud storage is used to store application data, back up important data, facilitate content distribution or disaster recovery, and archive data. Organizations often adopt cloud storage to combat high or increasing on-premises storage costs, avoid costly upgrades to on-premises infrastructure, or address increasing data management complexity for unstructured, semi-structured, and Big Data.

Private, public, and hybrid clouds were introduced in section 2.4.3 of Chapter 2 as different ways of deploying applications and computing infrastructure. To recap, a *public cloud* is a multi-tenant cloud computing environment available via the public Internet. A *private cloud* provides computing infrastructure used by a single organization, and a *hybrid cloud* is a combination of a private and public cloud.

Relative to traditional on-premises IT infrastructure, all cloud options usually offer greater scalability and affordability. Adopting any one of these storage types does not prevent an organization from adopting the others, and an increasing number of businesses have all three. The storage implications of each of these options are identified in Table 3-9.

Table 3-9: Characteristics and storage implications of different deployments of cloud storage.

Cloud Storage Option	Characteristics and Storage Implications
Public cloud	*Public clouds* are the best known and most pervasive cloud computing model for data storage. In these clouds, the infrastructure components (storage devices, servers, networking components) are housed in data centers owned and managed by providers such as Microsoft Azure, Google Cloud Platform, and Amazon Web Services (AWS). Public clouds are multi-tenant, and business subscribers share their infrastructure with other organizations; however, each tenant's data is isolated from that of other tenants. Each tenant rents needed storage devices and servers, and their rental fee is based on the services they use.
Private cloud	A *private cloud* is created for and used by a single organization. It can be housed in a data center facility owned and managed by the organization or in a data center owned and managed by a third-party provider. In either case, the storage devices, servers, and IT resources that the organization uses are located on a private network that only serves that organization. Because it is not shared, a private cloud is the easiest cloud storage option to customize to meet the needs of the organization that it serves. Private clouds are attractive to heavily regulated organizations, such as those in financial services and healthcare. Targeted customization facilitates strong security, regulatory compliance, and high performance. Virtualization enables private clouds to scale in response to growing demands and facilitates flexible adaptation.
Hybrid cloud	*Hybrid clouds* combine public and private cloud infrastructure, often in a purposeful attempt to reap the advantages/benefits of both. These clouds enable the movement of data and applications between the private and public clouds in response to changing needs. A hybrid cloud deployment can enable sensitive financial reports to be run in a private cloud while less important applications and data are supported in a public cloud. By providing the flexibility to choose the most appropriate cloud environment for its various types of data and applications, a hybrid cloud can enable a business to satisfy its needs more effectively than it could with just a private or public cloud.

As noted in Chapter 2, some public cloud providers offer *virtual private cloud (VPC)* services. These provide a private cloud computing environment within a shared, rather than single-tenant, infrastructure. VPCs strive to provide the advantages and benefits of private clouds within the public cloud.

Cloud storage prices vary and usually depend on the volume and type of data stored and the data protection requirements. Additional costs may be incurred for data retrieval (for archived data) and high-frequency updates. Because different providers have different pricing models, most businesses shop for the services that best fit their needs.

Data lakes are cloud storage solutions that enable businesses to amass large volumes of data for future processing. DWs have traditionally been deployed on premises or in private clouds, but numerous CSPs offer DW services, often as VPC services. Some CSPs also offer DW data processing services, such as *BI as a service (BIaaS)* and *Big Data as a service (BDaaS)*.

Because a variety of logical databases and storage requirements are associated with data/information architectures in today's organizations, data governance processes are commonly used to provide oversight of business data.

3.5 DATA GOVERNANCE

Data is an important business asset that should be appropriately managed and protected to ensure that it serves the needs of the organization. Some businesses have Chief Data Officer (CDO) or comparable executive level positions to oversee the collection, storage, management, and security of enterprise data, and most have data governance processes and structures that typically include a governance team or steering committee.

Data governance is the process of managing the availability, usability, integrity, and security of enterprise data. It is widely viewed as a quality control discipline for assessing, improving, monitoring, managing, maintaining, protecting, and using data. It establishes internal standards and policies that control data formats and usage, and it strives to ensure that data is consistent, trustworthy, and not misused.

As Figure 3-20 illustrates, data governance may be multifaceted. Master data management is important in organizations that use enterprise systems (ESs), and metadata management is important for DWs and data lakes.

Metadata management includes the creation of policies, processes, and procedures for ensuring that data from different data sources can be integrated, shared across applications, linked to comparable data from other sources, maintained, and analyzed. It typically strives for consistent data element names, data elements formats, and data access permissions.

The increasing variety of data types and sources being captured and analyzed by businesses has elevated the importance of metadata management. Data in data lakes often has little or no metadata when it is captured, and data scientists add metadata to the data prior to analyzing it. Metadata policies and processes provide guidance to data scientists when adding metadata to data lake data to facilitate the data's potential to be integrated with data from other sources for Big Data processing and advanced analytics.

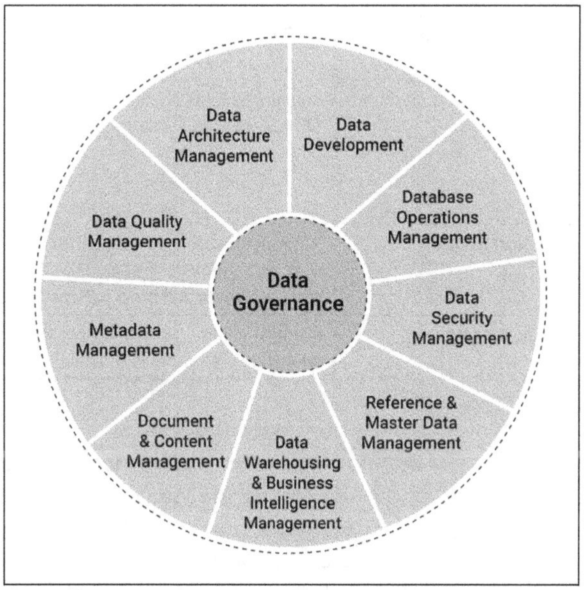

Figure 3-20: Common aspects of data governance in today's businesses.

Data development (ensuring that the business has the data it needs to meet its objectives) and data architecture management are important in organizations that embrace EA. Data quality management and data security management are important in all organizations.

Like data governance, data quality management is multifaceted. It includes quality assurance processes that discover inconsistencies (such as missing or inaccurate data) and data anomalies (such as outliers). It also includes data cleansing activities that contribute to effective DW and BI management and database operations management.

3.6 DATA SECURITY

Data is the lifeblood of today's data-driven businesses. As such, it must be protected and secured. As noted in Figure 3-20, data security management is an important aspect of data governance. Securing enterprise network data begins by acknowledging that data is the target of most enterprise network security breaches. Examples of commonly targeted data are identified in Table 3-10. These targets are compiled from multiple sources identified in the chapter references.

Table 3-10: Types of enterprise data that attackers frequently target.

Type of Business Data	Target Examples	Why is this a target?
Personal information	Customer and employee data: • Social Security numbers • Account numbers • Birthdates • Financial information • Phone numbers • Email addresses • Healthcare information	Can be sold on the dark web and/or used for: • Identity theft • Tax fraud • Extracting money from financial accounts and/or purchasing gift cards • Opening new accounts • Making fraudulent purchases • Making fraudulent insurance claims • Impersonating individuals and requesting money from their friends and contacts • Extortion • Data ransom
Data infrastructure	Data servers and storage	To store/hide data and applications for free on infrastructure that someone else is paying for
Product information	Confidential designs and prototypes of new products	Can be used by competitors to get a jump on the market and undercut the designer's or developer's sales
Corporate account data	• Employee login credentials • Executive email accounts	• Can be used to impersonate an employee and gain access to enterprise networks and databases; can be used for account takeovers; can be sold on the dark web • Can be used to impersonate executives and disrupt business operations
Network control	Network operating system (NOS) administrator or network management systems (NMS) administrator IDs and passwords and other network login credentials	Can be sold on the dark web and/or used for ransomware attacks that make servers, data, and accounts inaccessible until ransom is paid
Trade secrets	Business plans, business forecasts, market analysis, marketing plans, and intellectual property (IP)	Can be sold to competitors to give them an edge in the market; IP can be sold to agents in developing countries

3.6.1 Data Breaches

A **data breach** is an incident that involves unauthorized or illegal access, viewing, or retrieval of data by an individual, group, or software system. Basically, it is an intentional or unintentional release of confidential, private, or secured data to an untrusted entity without the knowledge of the data owner.

Intentional data breaches are purposeful enterprise network attacks whose goals are to steal data and possibly publish it to an illegal or unsecured location. These attacks typically target data in secure databases or repositories in enterprise networks, and attackers typically try to gain access to the network through Internet or other network connections. Some attackers install *card skimmers* at pay-at-the-pump gas pumps or ATMs and use them to illegally capture credit and debit card information to sell to other bad actors on the dark web.

Perpetrators of intentional data breaches often use social engineering to learn employee login credentials or to compromise employee devices with malware. Phishing and business email compromise (BEC) may be used to imbed code on employee devices that enables the attacker to access the enterprise network. Data loss is a common result of intentional data breaches, and the perpetrators may sell or use stolen information to impersonate authorized users to gain access to databases.

Unintentional data breaches occur when employees or other legitimate network users negligently put the network and its data assets at risk. They may, for example, access unsecured websites, unknowingly download malware-infected apps, use unsecured Wi-Fi networks to connect to the enterprise network, or lose their smartphone or laptop.

Data breaches often cause financial losses, diminished brand image, reduced customer/client trust, and other undesirable business outcomes. This motivates most businesses to be vigilant about securing their data and protecting it from intentional and unintentional breaches.

3.6.2 Data Protection

Data security is the process of protecting sensitive data and information from unauthorized access. This has always been important, but technological advances, including the IoT, continue to make it a front-burner issue for businesses. In some industries, including financial services and healthcare, government regulations require data security vigilance and safeguards.

Some of the more common data security controls used in enterprise networks are briefly described in Table 3-11. These and other data security controls are described more fully in Chapters 11 and 12.

Table 3-11: Examples of data security controls used in today's enterprise networks.

Data Security Control	Description
Authentication	Authentication is the process of verifying an enterprise network user or device to ensure that it is really them. This is considered a frontline defense against unauthorized access to the network or its data. *Multifactor authentication* (such as sending a one-time access code to a previously verified smartphone or email address when a user logs on) is common. *Single-sign-on* mechanisms that associate users or devices with network and data resources as they connect to the network are other common authentication controls. *Breached password detection* mechanisms that notify users if/when their credentials have been accessed are also associated with authentication controls.
Access control	Access control is a security technique that regulates who or what can view, access, or use resources in a computing environment. Access controls come in various forms, including discretionary and role based. *Discretionary access controls* associate users with one or more groups that have certain access and usage rights to network resources and data. *Role-based access control* assigns access and usage rights based on organizational roles and duties.
Encryption	Data encryption uses an algorithm to scramble data so it cannot be read by someone without the encryption key required to unscramble it. This is used to ensure that if someone gains unauthorized access to data, they will not be able to use it. Encryption is used to protect stored data (*data at rest*) and data passed over enterprise network circuits (*data in motion*). Encryption keys must be securely managed, and critical data should be backed up, and encrypted, at secure off-site locations.
Tokenization	Tokenization is like encryption, but instead of scrambling data with an algorithm, tokenization replaces sensitive data with random characters. The relationship between the randomized data and the original data (the token) is stored in a separate protected database table.
Data masking	Data masking does not transform data into an unreadable form but hides the data by obscuring letters and numbers with proxy characters, like a string of dots for a password on a login screen or a string of Xs to obscure all but the last four digits of a credit card number.

Table 3-11, Continued.

Data Security Control	Description
Backups	A **data backup** involves making a copy of the data and storing it on a separate system or medium in another location, or in the cloud. Backups enable lost or corrupted data to be recovered, and doing regular data backups can help ensure data availability and business continuity.
Data deletion	When data becomes obsolete, outdated, or unimportant, or is no longer needed, it should be permanently cleared from a database or storage device because of the potential to cause harm if it falls into the wrong hands. For example, old user passwords should be deleted because many users reuse their passwords across multiple sites. This means that they might be used to breach another organization's network or data. Data should be deleted rather than merely erased. While erasure overwrites data on a storage medium, it often hides the data in such a way that makes it relatively easy to retrieve.
Physical access controls	This includes access controls for the physical locations where data is located, such as data centers, on-premises server rooms, and server and storage cabinets. Security personnel, key card entry, and biometric authentication, such as retinal scans or hand/thumb/fingerprint recognition, are examples of data security physical access controls.

Best practices in data security include managing access to sensitive data, encrypting all important data, and robust authentication processes. They also include regular testing of data security defenses; educating users about phishing and other attack tactics that target enterprise networks and data; having incident response plans and procedures to minimize the effect of data breaches; and having data recovery plans that include regular backups at one or more secure sites at other geographic locations. Businesses in industries where data security is heavily regulated should also conduct periodical compliance audits.

SUMMARY

Data is the lifeblood of today's businesses. Because it has value, data is being captured, stored, and analyzed at increasing rates. For transmission over enterprise network circuits, processing, and storage, data is *digitized*—converted to fixed-length strings of bits, 0s and 1s. Digitization processes can vary for different types of data (e.g., audio, image, video, alphanumeric, barcode, and sensor), but all such processes produce binary code that represents the original data.

Data compression is widely used to reduce the number of bits required to represent data. Lossless compression enables exact replicas of the original data to be reproduced from compressed data, but when lossy compression is used, some of the original data is lost and cannot be recovered.

Business data is often categorized as structured, unstructured, or semi-structured data. Structured data conforms to tabular formats, such as the rows and columns in spreadsheets or relational database tables, and has well-defined data models. Unstructured data, such as images and social media posts, exists in a variety of forms and lacks a well-defined data model to facilitate searching or sorting. Semi-structured data is a form of structured data that lacks a well-defined data model. Increasing volumes and varieties of each of these types of data have produced very large data collections, Big Data, that are easiest to process using specialized platforms, such as Hadoop clusters and SAP HANA.

Relational databases, NoSQL databases, DWs, and data lakes are examples of logical data collections that businesses use. Relational databases have traditionally been used to organize structured business data, and NoSQL databases are common for unstructured and semi-structured data.

DWs and data lakes are common in today's enterprise networks. A DW is a central repository of integrated data from different sources that is primarily used to support BI. Data lakes store structured, unstructured, and semi-structured data in their native formats for future business use and analysis.

Centralized, distributed, replicated, and partitioned databases may be supported on enterprise networks. Blockchain databases are also increasingly common, as businesses develop applications for which a transparent digital ledger shared by a network of computers makes sense.

An organization's logical data collections are physically stored on storage technologies in SANs, data centers, and the cloud. Disk arrays continue to be the most common type of physical storage, but despite their higher cost, SSDs have gained traction because of superior I/O performance.

Data centers can be located on premises or in private, public, and hybrid clouds. Public clouds are the most common form of cloud storage infrastructure, but some organizations prefer to be sole tenants in private clouds. Data warehouses have traditionally been created in private clouds, whereas data lakes are typically created in public clouds.

Organizations establish data governance structures and processes to ensure that their data is appropriately managed and protected. Data governance includes oversight of data availability for BI and decision-making, data quality and integrity, metadata management, and data security.

Data is the primary target of most intentional enterprise network security breaches. However, data can also be compromised or corrupted by unintentional or negligent acts of enterprise network users. Data security controls include authentication, access controls, encryption, tokenization, data masking, backups, data deletion, and physical access controls.

KEY TERMS

Alphanumeric
Blockchain
Centralized database
Cloud storage
Data backup
Data breach
Data center
Data compression
Data encryption
Data governance
Data lake
Data security
Data warehouse
Digitization
Distributed database
Hadoop cluster
Horizontal scaling
In-memory database
Network-attached storage (NAS) systems
Partitioned database
Quantization
Replicated database
SAP HANA
Storage area network (SAN)
Vertical scaling

REVIEW QUESTIONS

1. Provide examples of data with business value and briefly describe the value of each example.
2. How does data architecture differ from information architecture?
3. What is digitization? Why do businesses prefer digitized data?
4. What is quantization? What is PCM, and how does it digitize audio?
5. Identify and briefly describe the factors that determine PCM bit rates. Explain how bit depth and sampling rate effect the resolution and fidelity of PCM sound wave samples.
6. What is data compression, and why is it used? How does lossless compression differ from lossy compression? Identify examples of lossless and lossy audio files.
7. What is a bitmap in raster graphics? How are bitmaps related to image resolution?
8. What is pixel color depth, and how is it related to the range of colors a pixel can display? Explain how bits per image are related to color depth and bitmap dimensions.
9. Describe the components of true color pixels and explain how they combine to display color images.
10. Identify examples of lossless and lossy image compression file formats. Briefly describe how vector graphics differ from raster graphics and identify image file formats that use both raster and vector graphics.
11. Identify and briefly describe each of the factors used to compute video bit rates. Explain how lossy video compression is accomplished and why it is used.
12. What is alphanumeric data, and how are character sets used to digitize it? Identify examples of widely used character sets.
13. How is Lempel-Ziv data compression used in enterprise networks?

14. How is a barcode converted to binary code? Why do QR codes have a wider range of uses than barcodes?
15. How do A/D converters in IoT sensor microcomputers digitize sensor data?
16. How is structured data different from unstructured data? Identify examples of structured data. Identify examples of unstructured data.
17. What is semi-structured data? What is metadata? Identify examples of semi-structured data. Identify examples of metadata.
18. What is Big Data? Briefly describe the meaning of each of the following attributes of Big Data: variety, volume, velocity, variability, and veracity.
19. What is a computer cluster? What is a Hadoop cluster? How/why can a Hadoop cluster serve as a Big Data processing platform?
20. How does horizontal scaling differ from vertical scaling? How are these different scaling approaches related to Big Data processing?
21. What is SAP HANA®? What makes it useful as a Big Data processing platform?
22. What are the distinguishing characteristics of each of the following databases: relational, NoSQL, in-memory, centralized, distributed, replicated, partitioned, and blockchain?
23. How are data warehouses (DWs) different from data lakes?
24. Briefly describe the major characteristics of each of the following: network-attached storage (NAS), storage area network (SAN), and data center.
25. What is cloud storage? What are the characteristics and advantages of cloud storage infrastructure?
26. Briefly describe the characteristics of public, private, and hybrid cloud storage.
27. What are blockchains, and how are businesses using them?
28. What is data governance, and what does it encompass?
29. Identify types of data that are frequent targets of attackers and briefly explain why each type is targeted.
30. What is data security? Identify and briefly describe common data security controls used in enterprise networks. Also identify and briefly describe data security best practices.

PROBLEMS AND EXERCISES

Exercise 3-1 Bit depth is sometimes defined as the total number of discrete items, symbols, characters, or states that can be represented by a fixed number of bits. This is typically stated as a power of 2 (e.g., 2^1, 2^2, 2^3, etc.). For example, 2^2 can represent four discrete items (or four different symbols, characters, or states), each of which is represented by two bits: 00, 01, 10, 11; whereas 2^3 can represent eight discrete items, symbols, characters, or states, each of which is represented by three bits: 000, 001, 010, 011, 100, 101, 110, 111.

Given this definition, determine the bit depth needed to represent:

- The digits 0–9 (10 different characters)
- 256 different analog wave amplitude levels
- 1024 different colors
- 4 billion different IPv4 addresses

Exercise 3-2 A PCM digital-to-analog converter (DAC) receives 8-bit codes over a communication circuit and uses the binary code to re-create the original sound wave. This is done in three steps. The first identifies the binary code representing each of the sender's waveform samples, the second converts the binary code to a decimal integer value, and the third uses the integer value to reproduce the sound. The first two steps are illustrated in this problem/exercise.

Step 1. Complete the following table by converting the binary value of each sample's wave height to its decimal value. Guidance on how to convert binary values to decimal values is available at https://www.wikihow.com/Convert-from-Binary-to-Decimal. A number of binary-to-decimal converters are available, including the one at https://www.rapidtables.com/convert/number/.

Step 2. Draw a sketch of the analog wave represented by the ten decimal wave heights. ***Note:*** Put the sample number on the X-axis and the decimal integer value of the wave height on the Y-axis.

Sample Number	8-bit Binary Value	Decimal Integer Value of Wave Height
1	11100000	
2	11101111	
3	11111111	
4	11100100	

5	11001001	
6	11000000	
7	10101000	
8	01111001	
9	10001111	
10	10100111	

Submit your completed table and an electronic copy of your sketch.

Exercise 3-3 When examining mammograms, radiologists often deal with four to six images at a time. For a reasonable digital representation of a mammogram, a pixel array of 3000 x 4000 is needed, and 12-bit grayscale is used for each pixel.

- How many bits are needed to represent a single mammogram image?
- How many bits are needed to represent four mammogram images?

Exercise 3-4 Explain why lossy compression algorithms are not recommended for reducing the file sizes of medical images.

Exercise 3-5 A high-definition digital video camera produces an uncompressed video stream of 60 frames per second. Each frame has a resolution of 1,280 x 720 pixels (921,600 pixels). If an 8-bit binary number is used to represent each pixel's color:

- How many bits are needed to represent the pixels in one frame?
- How many bits are needed to represent one second of video (60 frames)?

Exercise 3-6 A Full HD digital video camera produces an uncompressed video stream of 60 frames per second. Each frame has a resolution of 1980 x 1020 pixels (2,073,600 pixels), and a 24-bit binary number is used to represent the color of each pixel.

- How many bits are needed to represent the pixels in each frame?
- How many bits are needed to represent one second of video (60 frames)?

Exercise 3-7 The *Encyclopedia Britannica* includes approximately 50 million words. Its average word length is 6.5 characters (which includes the letters in the words, spacing, and punctuation).

- Approximately how many total characters are in the encyclopedia?
- If 8-bit code, such as ASCII or UTF-8, is used to represent each character, how many bits are needed to represent the entire contents of the encyclopedia?
- If you had a perfect connection, how long (in seconds) would it take you to download the encyclopedia over a 25 Mbps (25,000,000 bps) connection?
- If you had a perfect connection, how long (in seconds) would it take you to download the encyclopedia over a 1 Gbps (1,000,000,000 bps) connection?

Exercise 3-8 Go to Online Labels.com (https://www.onlinelabels.com/tools/barcode-generator) and use the UPC-A option to re-create the bar code shown in Figure 3-9. Take a screenshot or snip of the barcode you create to verify your work on this website. Then go to Barcode Lookup.com (https://www.barcodelookup.com) and enter the barcode number to identify the product that has this barcode. Take a screenshot or snip of the product to verify your work on this website.

Exercise 3-9 When calculating its total data traffic and storage requirements, a corporation determined that the business office at one of its enterprise network locations generates an average of 75 GB of data traffic per employee per month. There are 50 employees at this location. Use the converters at KylesConverter.com (http://www.kylesconverter.com/) to assist in converting gigabytes to bits, gigabytes to terabytes, and terabytes to bits.

- How many bits of data traffic are generated by one employee each month?
- How many bits of data traffic are generated by all 50 employees each month?
- Assuming that each month is 30 days, how much data (in bits) does the business office at this location generate in an average day?
- On average, how much data (in bits) does the business office at this location generate each second?
- If all data traffic generated by the location were logged and stored, how many terabytes of storage would be needed to store the data traffic generated by the business office at this location in one year? If the data were stored in uncompressed form, how many bits would be stored in a year?

CHAPTER REFERENCES

Convertb1nary. (n.d.). Convert Text to Binary Code! Retrieved from: https://www.convertbinary.com/text-to-binary/

F-Secure. (n.d.). Why Do Hackers Want Your Personal Information? Retrieved from: https://www.f-secure.com/us-en/home/articles/why-do-hackers-want-your-personal-information

Goldman, M. (2007). Lectures on Digital Color. Everett Public Schools. Retrieved from: https://www.everettsd.org/cms/lib/WA01920133/Centricity/Domain/992/Java/DigiColor.pdf

Jareth. (2020). How Do Hackers Make Money from: Your Stolen Data? Emsisoft. Retrieved from: https://blog.emsisoft.com/en/35541/how-do-hackers-make-money-from-your-stolen-data/

Olavsrud, T. (2023, March 24). What Is Data Governance? Best Practices for Managing Data Assets. *CIO.* Retrieved from: https://www.cio.com/article/202183/what-is-data-governance-a-best-practices-framework-for-managing-data-assets.html

Petzold, C. (2000). Bit by Bit by Bit. In *Code: The Hidden Language of Computer Hardware and Software*. Microsoft Press Store by Pearson. Retrieved from: https://www.microsoftpressstore.com/articles/article.aspx?p=2263500

Price, D. (2015). How Much Data Is Produced Every Day [Infographic]? CloudTweaks. Retrieved from: https://cloudtweaks.com/2015/03/how-much-data-is-produced-every-day/

UptimeInstitute. (n.d.). Tier Certification. Retrieved from: https://uptimeinstitute.com/tiers

Velimirovic, A. (2021). Data Center Tiers Explained. Retrieved from: https://phoenixnap.com/blog/data-center-tiers-classification

V-Soft Consulting. (n.d.). What Do Hackers Want from Your Business? Retrieved from: https://blog.vsoftconsulting.com/blog/what-do-hackers-want-from-your-business

MINICASE: Big Data and Avis Budget Group (ABG)

Competition is fierce in the rental car industry. For more than a decade, the Avis Budget Group (ABG) has focused its efforts on being a leading vehicle renting services company through data-driven decision-making and strategizing. It has leveraged Big Data to identify new opportunities and increase revenue.

In 2009, consultants from CSC Consulting Group convinced ABG that it was sitting on a treasure trove of data that could be mined to identify new opportunities and insights. By that time, ABG had amassed data on hundreds of millions of rental transactions for more than 40 million customers. With Big Data becoming a standard part of the IT lexicon at that time, ABG began to realize that there might be something of value in its massive database. It turned to CSC, an IT services provider known for helping businesses launch Big Data initiatives, for assistance.

CSC realized that ABG's transaction data could be analyzed to reveal opportunities to enhance customer experience and revenue through real-time actions, such as special offers and services, at rental locations. CSC also noticed that ABG was capturing increasing volumes of unstructured data from customers through its social media channels, emails, website, and call centers. However, none of the unstructured data was being directly connected to rental vehicle transactions. ABG's structured transaction data and unstructured data were in separate data pools.

With CSC's help, ABG embarked on a new customer relationship management (CRM) and loyalty program. The program initially involved a customer valuation approach and a model to identify ABG's most valuable customers. This model enabled ABG to better understand the characteristics of these customers.

The model was applied to ABG's customer database, which included data from more than 40 million customers. Mimicking widely used CRM methods, customers were ranked into value segments, and the most attention was initially devoted to customers in the top value segments. They received special offers designed to maintain their loyalty. ABG also focused on those who had the potential to become high-value customers in the future.

Many of the patterns that emerged from the initial number crunching were unsurprising, but others were intriguing and got ABG's marketers thinking about how customers' perceptions could be influenced by differentiating their experiences while renting a vehicle. Since renters usually consider rental vehicles to be commodities, providing differentiating experiences at all phases of the rental process (from making a rental decision to interactions while picking up and returning vehicles) was viewed as an opportunity for winning repeat business and making ABG the preferred rental option for customers.

Rental process speed and efficiency were more important to business customers than to vacationers and other leisure customers, who were more concerned with service friendliness and having a stress-free experience during vehicle pickup and return. The early number crunching showed ABG that there were opportunities to provide offers that met customers' needs and to create relationships that they wanted. However, doing so required ABG to make both business and technological changes, some of which were costly and took several years to implement.

By studying its data, ABG gained a 360-degree view of its customers. This included their demographics, rental history, service issues, feedback, and much more.

ABG's Big Data initiative has increased the company's customer loyalty and revenues. It has also improved ABG's profitability and has convinced the company that differentiated customer service and experience are keys to increased customer loyalty.

ABG labels its CRM customer segmentation approach a "customer lifetime value" strategy. It takes a long-term view of the company's relationship with customers that extends beyond a vehicle rental transaction. Rental transactions are, of course, very important, and its transaction database is critically important to ABG's data-driven operations, but customer visits to the company's website and website analytics that provide insights into the types of vehicles, vehicle features, and amenities that customers consider before making a rental reservation are also important.

Initially, almost all the data collected by ABG came from internal sources, but now it is exploring further expansion of its data reservoir to include a wide range of external, open-source data. To accommodate a wider array of data, much of which is unstructured or has unknown business value, ABG's Big Data processing capabilities will have to scale.

When ABG began its Big Data journey, it lacked the analytics infrastructure and organized processes it needed to leverage its data. This inhibited its ability to use data to improve customer experience, drive long-term relationships and value, and improve marketing ROI. In response, ABG created a marketing science unit that included customer data integration specialists focused on CRM analytics and reporting.

Now ABG can develop three- to five-year projections for a wide range of business operations. It can also predict the likelihood of a specific customer renting a vehicle during the next year and the profit they are likely to generate. This has enabled ABG to modify the company's customer contact strategy.

ABG's frontline and customer-facing employees now have a web-based dashboard that enables them to personalize their interactions with customers. Data is being used to influence every decision that ABG makes and to customize decisions made about customers. Big Data empowers frontline employees to identify the best ways to market and relate to individual customers.

ABG's customer-centric Big Data infrastructure continues to evolve, and it contributed to the company's decision to acquire car-sharing company Zipcar. It increased ABG's confidence that it could quickly learn how to best engage and win over this new type of customer.

By leaning into data, ABG has expanded the range of digital services it offers to customers. ABG's smartphone app has extensive capabilities. The company has used insights from its data to modify in-vehicle infotainment and to add virtual local guides.

Big Data platforms contribute to ABG's operations through digital alerts (e.g., for predictive vehicle maintenance), regional demand predictions, fleet placement recommendations, and competitive pricing. ABG monitors real-time data about its 600,000+ fleet of vehicles, including telematics data from GPS systems, data from IoT-enabled sensors, and data from vehicle safety systems (e.g., braking and lane departure). The company aspires to have a fully connected fleet and to know what is happening in each vehicle in real time, including its speed, mileage, tire pressure, and GPS coordinates.

To realize its vision of a fully connected future, ABG has created an advanced enterprise data hub for fleet management decisions. The platform enables monitors to unlock, lock, and immobilize vehicles. It also provides a platform for enhancing services and identifying ways to reduce costs, increase profitability, and determine optimal times to sell vehicles to used vehicle businesses.

ABG has engaged with cloud services (especially AWS) to continue its trajectory as a data-driven business. Scalability is important because ABG wants to accommodate thousands of fields of sensor data (per vehicle) in real time, and to accommodate new onboard IoT devices. ABG is determined to have a data lake that is both clean and usable. It wants to continue to build on its Big Data success, and a cloud-based architecture is critical for doing so.

Real-time data from vehicles, and from a variety of Oracle and IBM databases, streams into ABG's data lake. Some is being leveraged in today's Big Data processing, and the rest is being captured and retained for potential use and analysis in the future. An enterprise data catalog has been created to provide data scientists with information about data location, lineage, and business context, and to provide self-service access and visualizations.

The data lake should help ABG further build out its analytics efforts. The company has grown comfortable having terabytes of information moving rapidly from its vehicle fleet to the cloud. It is also comfortable reacting in real time and pushing more data out to customers via the mobile app. ABG aspires to enable all employees to have a better understanding of how its data can be used to better manage the vehicle fleet, while also providing customers with high-quality rental and reservation experiences.

Minicase Questions

1. Discuss how ABG's transition to being a data-driven business reflects each of the different "Vs" of Big Data identified in section 3.2.4.
2. Discuss how and why ABG's combined use of data warehouses and a data lake contributes to the company's ability to be a data-driven organization.
3. Identify two examples of data used by ABG that you consider to be innovative or forward thinking. Explain why you are impressed by them and how they improve ABG's operations and competitiveness.
4. If you were a data analyst at ABG empowered to identify an innovative use of data to improve customer experience or day-to-day operations, what would you look at (i.e., describe your innovation and its effect on customers or operations)?

Minicase References

Berg, B. (2014). A Case Study in Data-Driven Marketing—Avis Budget Group. BB Direct. Retrieved from: https://www.bbdirect.com/about/blog/A-Case-Study-in-Data-Driven-Marketing--AvisBudget-Group_AE625.html

Dan, A. (2014). How Avis Budget Group Uses Data to Drive Its Marketing. *Forbes*. Retrieved from: https://www.forbes.com/sites/avidan/2014/03/26/how-avis-budget-group-uses-data-to-drive-its-marketing/?sh=299fb2587a7e

IdeaConnection. (2019). Big Data Boost for Vehicle Rental Company. Retrieved from: https://www.ideaconnection.com/open-innovation-success/Big-Data-Boost-for-Vehicle-Rental-Company-00728.html

Chapter 4

Network Communication Models

LEARNING OBJECTIVES

After reading and studying this chapter, you should be able to:

- Identify and briefly describe the composition of EA's technical architecture.
- Explain the business value of enterprise network frameworks.
- Identify the layers of the OSI and TCP/IP models.
- Briefly describe the major communication functions performed at each layer of the OSI model.
- Identify and briefly describe the major communication functions and protocols at each layer of the TCP/IP model.
- Identify and briefly describe important networking and security technologies for each layer of the TCP/IP model.

4.0 INTRODUCTION

Enterprise Architecture (EA) helps keep us focused on the business rationale for enterprise networks. Chapter 2 describes how enterprise networks support applications, and Chapter 3 describes how various types of data are digitized for transmission on network circuits, storage, and processing. Both chapters provide insights into why cloud applications and cloud storage have become important parts of business networks.

This chapter introduces EA's technical architecture, specifically its networking and communication components. It also introduces the frameworks/models that guide the deployment of networking and communication technologies.

Chapter 4 provides an overview of the Open Systems Interconnection (OSI) and the TCP/IP (Transmission Control Protocol/Internet Protocol) models, and it introduces important communication functions, protocols, technologies, and security issues for the different layers of the TCP/IP model.

This chapter lays the groundwork for Chapters 5, 6, and 7. Chapter 5 provides a closer look at the Transport and Network layers of the TCP/IP model, and Chapters 6 and 7 focus on how Data Link layer and Physical layer communication functions are carried out in wired and wireless networks. This chapter also serves as a backdrop for Chapter 8's discussion of wide area networks.

4.1 THE VALUE OF LAYERED COMMUNICATION MODELS

Chapter 1 noted that EA's technical architecture serves as the foundation for the other EA architectural components (see Figure 4-1). It provides the technical platforms required to run the applications and create information from data required for operational and strategic decision-making. It includes the processing technologies (e.g., servers), storage technologies, and

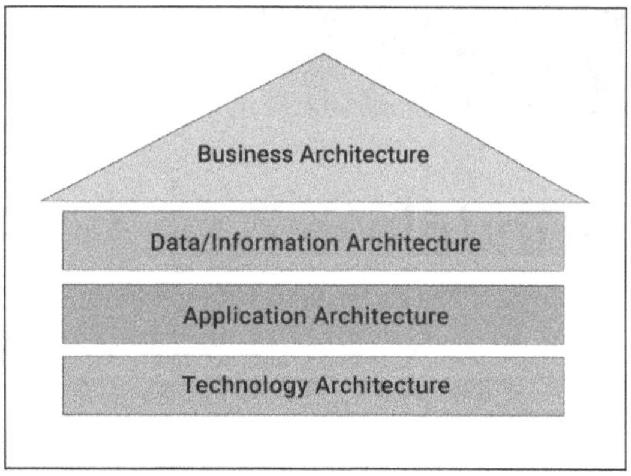

Figure 4-1: The foundational nature of EA's technical architecture.

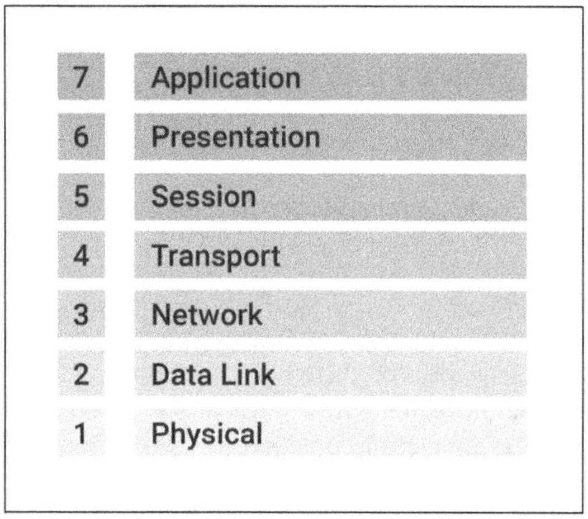

Figure 4-2: The OSI model's seven layers.

networking and communication technologies needed to support distributed applications.

More specifically, EA's technical architecture encompasses the collection of computers, networks, storage technologies, operating systems (OSs), platforms, and database management systems (DBMSs) that support the application architecture and run the programs, applications, services, and other solutions that the organization uses to transform data into information.

The technical architecture also includes the communication protocols and middleware that enable business applications to interoperate, as well as the networking equipment (such as routers, switches, and modems) that supports wide area network (WAN) connections among the organization's geographically dispersed locations. Client devices (desktop systems, laptops, tablets, smartphones, etc.) and servers that provide services to client devices (application servers, database servers, email servers, web servers, etc.) are also a part of EA's technology architecture. Client and server devices are key components of local area networks (LANs) and backbone networks (BNs) at the organization's different locations.

Two major frameworks (models) promote understanding of relationships among the networking and communication technologies included in an organization's technical architecture: the Open System Interconnection (OSI) model and the TC/IP (or Internet) model. These models help us understand how and why today's enterprise networks are organized the way they are and how their different parts interoperate to support applications. Both are layered communication models.

The OSI model divides data communication into seven layers (see Figure 4-2), sometimes called "abstraction" layers because they strive to ensure interoperability within the communication system regardless of the specific technologies that it contains. In addition to facilitating understanding of networks, this model serves as a useful reference for software developers by enabling them to create software applications in an abstracted manner and without having to know the details of the networks on which the applications are deployed.

The OSI model provides a big-picture view of how networks operate, from the physical hardware that serves as network infrastructure to the applications that the network supports. It has two major components: the basic reference model and protocols.

The *reference model* describes the seven layers in the model. *Protocols* allow each layer of a network-attached device to communicate with the corresponding layer of another device. For example, protocols enable a user in Atlanta to compose an email in Outlook and send it to a colleague in Sydney, Australia, who uses Gmail, because both email applications (Outlook and Gmail) use the same protocols to transfer email messages over the Internet.

In the OSI reference model, each layer works with the layers immediately above and below it. For example, Layer 4 (Transport) works with Layer 5 (Session) and Layer 3 (Network). The communications work done at each layer is affected by and affects the work done at the layers immediately above and below. So, in our example, the communication functions performed at Layer 4 are affected by the work done at Layer 5 and affect the work done at Layer 3.

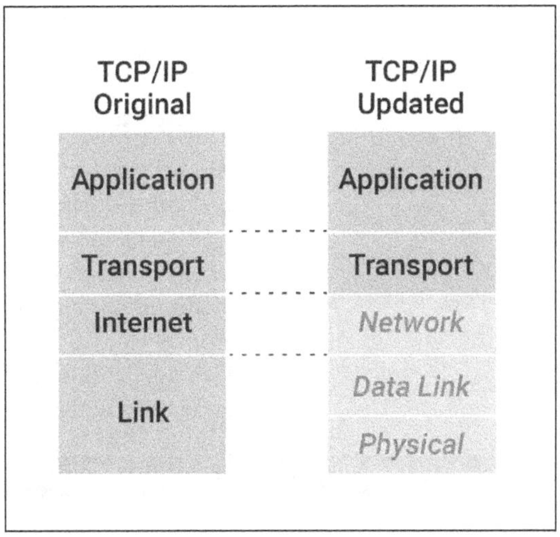

Figure 4-3: Original and updated versions of the TCP/IP model.

Compartmentalizing communication functions by layers is valuable when something goes wrong and troubleshooting communication problems is required. Having distinct layers and division of work enables network professionals to pinpoint specific layers to begin their troubleshooting activities. Issues with a user's web browser are likely to be labeled as a "Layer 7 problem," and when a PC loses its Internet connection, troubleshooting is likely to begin at Layer 1 by checking network cable connections before moving to Layer 3 to determine if the network's router is working correctly. The TCP/IP model provides comparable troubleshooting assistance.

The TCP/IP (Transmission Control Protocol/Internet Protocol) model was initially a four-layer model, but today it is more commonly viewed as a five-layer model (see Figure 4-3). It is named for the most common protocols used at its Transport and Network layers. Because TCP and IP are central communication protocols used on the Internet, the TCP/IP model is also called the Internet model.

This model correctly assumes that the Internet is an important component in today's enterprise networks, and it is widely used to explain how the Internet works. The updated TCP/IP model is important to the flow of discussion in Chapters 5, 6, 7, and 8.

Although it has fewer layers than the OSI model, the TCP/IP model also provides a high-level look at how networks support applications. Like the OSI model, communication functions and protocols are identified for each TCP/IP layer, and the functions performed at a layer are affected by and affect the functions performed at the layers immediately above and below it. There is considerable overlap between Layers 1, 2, and 3 of the two models, but differences at the upper layers.

Independence among applications, user devices, and networks is a metaphor that the OSI and TCP/IP models facilitate. This is beneficial to network users, software developers, and businesses.

Users have 24/7/365 access to applications regardless of their locations and devices, which provides flexibility. For example, if a user wants to switch from Microsoft Office to Google Workspace applications, they are not required to use a different network to do so; they just switch applications. Similarly, a user can switch from a wireless to a wired network connection or from a PC to a tablet without affecting their ability to access or use an application.

The level of abstraction that the models provide to developers is also beneficial. The models facilitate layered software architectures (like those described in Chapter 2) while also enabling developers to modify applications (at the Application layer) without having to worry about how they will be supported by the other (lower) layers.

Independence among applications, devices, and networks enables businesses to change ISPs or cloud providers without disrupting their employees' abilities to access and use needed software. The models also are beneficial to businesses because they provide more granular network security and facilitate the deployment of layered defenses. Incoming data, for example, can be examined for malware and other threats to devices, applications, and data at lower layers in the models before being passed to upper layers and applications. This contributes to stronger protections against potential disruptions to business continuity.

As you can see, layered models are valuable for numerous reasons. They facilitate understanding of how networks support applications. They contribute to independence among users, applications, and network infrastructures. They enable developers to focus on applications without having to also consider the networks that will support them. They facilitate troubleshooting of network connectivity issues, and they facilitate the layering of security defenses. Looking more closely at layered models results in further appreciation of their benefits.

4.2 OSI MODEL

The Open Systems Interconnection (OSI) model is a product of the Open Systems Interconnection initiative at the International Organization for Standardization (ISO). In 1984, the ISO formally adopted the OSI model as an international standard. Table 4-1 summarizes the major communication functions performed at the OSI's seven layers.

The OSI model is a conceptual model that describes networking/telecommunication functions independently from the underlying technology infrastructure. The model's upper layers deal primarily with application issues, and most are only implemented in software. The lower layers handle data transport activities that are implemented in software and hardware.

Table 4-1: A summary of the major data communication functions at each layer of the OSI model.

Layer	Name	Description
7	Application	This top-of-stack layer is sometimes called the end user layer. It provides access to network resources and includes the networking processes that interact directly with users to provide support for email, network data sharing, file transfers, directory services, and other distributed information services. This layer allows users to access software applications. Application programming interfaces (APIs), web browsers, and streaming services are found at this layer.
6	Presentation	The Presentation layer includes processes that make data more presentable and understandable by an application. Data is translated and formatted at this layer so that applications, networks, and devices can understand what they're receiving. Characters are encoded and decoded, data is compressed and decompressed, and data is encrypted and decrypted at this layer.
5	Session	The Session layer controls the opening and closing of communication sessions between devices, including those between a client and a server or between two servers. The Session layer is also responsible for establishing pathways (such as VPN tunnels) between communicating devices and for authenticating and authorizing communication between specific apps and servers. This layer serves as a communication moderator that controls the dialogue between devices during sessions, enforces response times, and terminates sessions.
4	Transport	The Transport layer coordinates the transfer of data between devices during communication sessions. Because it focuses on providing reliable data/message delivery, it is considered the heart of the OSI model. This layer provides/specifies mechanisms for error control and flow control, such as data transfer rates, data duplication checks, and the resending of information that fails to be delivered or contains errors. It uses service-point addressing (port addresses) to ensure that data is delivered to the recipient's appropriate service/process. Basically, this layer functions as a digital post office that coordinates data transfers between communicating devices.
3	Network	This layer determines the most efficient route for data to take from source to destination when senders and receivers are in different networks. It implements logical addressing to distinguish between the source and destination networks and network endpoints. Outgoing data that is too large to fit in a single packet is fragmented (divided into packets), and incoming data that has been fragmented is extracted and reassembled into information that is consumable at higher levels, including the application layer. Error and flow controls specified by the Transport layer are implemented at this layer. Network congestion controls are also implemented at this layer.
2	Data Link	This layer provides an avenue for node-to-node data transfers of frames (containers for single network layers packets) between two physically connected devices in a local network. It has two sublayers: media access control (MAC) and logical link control (LLC). The MAC sublayer determines how devices in the network gain access to a medium and permission to transmit data; it uses MAC (physical) addresses to identify senders and receivers in the network. Data is transmitted sequentially, and senders expect acknowledgments of data receipt from recipients. The LLC layer controls frame synchronization, flow control, and error checking for data transmission between devices in the network. It also identifies and encapsulates network layer protocols for frames whose recipients are in other networks.
1	Physical	This layer is responsible for transmitting and receiving data symbols (signals that represent bits). Senders convert bits in Data Link layer frames into electrical, radio, or optical signals at this layer, and recipients convert the signals they receive into bits. The type of signaling used to represent bits determines transmission rate (bit rate, such as bits per second) and bitstream synchronization.

The OSI model works because *logical connections* are established between the corresponding layers of devices during communication sessions. These connections are illustrated as dashed arrows in Figure 4-4.

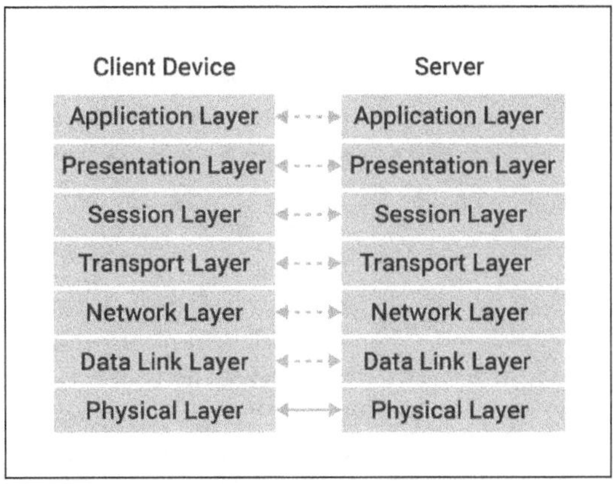

Figure 4-4: Logical connections between corresponding layers in the OSI model.

Logical connections ensure that receivers understand and correctly act on the data/messages they receive from senders. In Figure 4-4, for example, the logical connection established at the Application layer ensures that the user request is delivered to the correct server or service. If the client requests a web page, its request is delivered to a web server. If the client uses ASCII/UTF-8 to encode characters in a server request, the logical connection at the Presentation layer ensures that the server uses ASCII/UTF-8 to decode the characters in the request.

The Physical layer requires the use of physical circuits between devices to enable bitstreams to be transmitted and received. However, even here, logical connections may be used to ensure that receivers properly interpret transmitted symbols. Some WAN services, including T-1 and OC-3 services (described in Chapter 8), establish logical connections at the Physical layer.

Header fields added by senders at each layer tell receivers how data should be handled. As Figure 4-5 illustrates, a sender communicates what it wants the receiver to do at the Application layer by adding an application header (AH) to the data/message that is being sent. When a layer adds a header to the data/message it receives from the layer above it, the process is called **data encapsulation**.

After an AH is added, the data is handed down to the Presentation layer, where a presentation header (PH) is added to inform the Presentation layer at the receiver what it needs to do with the data. As the data descends layer by layer to the Physical layer, other headers are added to the data to ensure that appropriate data handling occurs at each corresponding layer by the receiver. The Data Link layer adds both a header and a trailer. Receivers use the trailer for error checking.

Receivers receive the sender's bitstream at the Physical layer and pass the data/message to the Data Link layer, where it is converted to frames and checked for errors. The sender's data link header and trailer are removed before the data is passed to the Network layer. **De-encapsulation** is the process that a receiving device uses to sequentially remove protocol headers layer-by-layer as their contents are interpreted and acted upon. When the AH is removed, the sender's data is passed to the appropriate application or service.

To sum up, the OSI model specifies how senders and receivers communicate over a network to support applications. Senders add header fields to messages and data to communicate how receivers should handle them. The information embedded in the headers serves as logical connections between corresponding layers in senders and receivers. Comparable activities occur in the TCP/IP model.

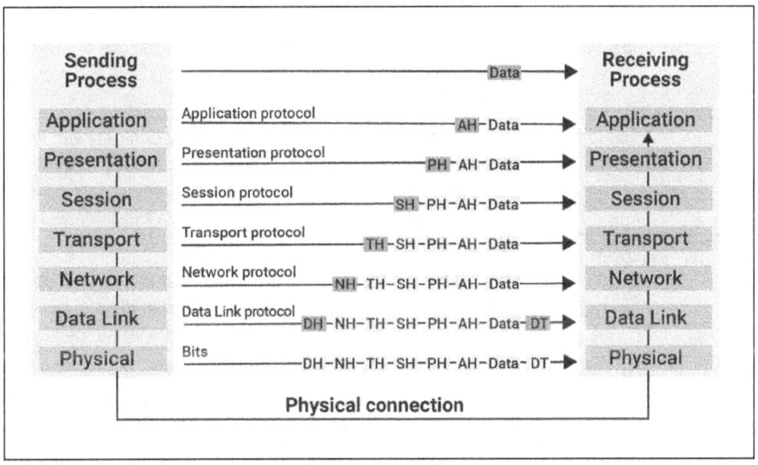

Figure 4-5: Logical connections between corresponding layers are enabled by data/message headers.

4.3 TCP/IP MODEL

Enterprise applications often involve the movement of data from a network at one location to a network at a different location. The five-layer TCP/IP model provides a framework for understanding how data is transmitted/received between different locations and describes the protocols to do so.

This model recognizes that reliable message delivery and communication are needed for some applications and that fast, although unreliable, communication is preferable for others. The model also recognizes that a mixture of logical addressing (e.g., IP addresses) and physical addressing (e.g., MAC addresses) is needed for communication between devices in different networks. It also recognizes the necessity of physical connections and communication paths between locations.

TCP/IP communication is often called *host-to-host* communications. A **host** is a hardware device that provides access to a network via a user interface, specialized software, a network address, and a protocol stack. In TCP/IP terminology, a host is simply a computer connected to a TCP/IP network.

Examples of hosts include personal computers, servers, network printers, and thin clients, such as mobile devices (e.g., smartphones and tablets). On a TCP/IP network, each host has a *host number* that uniquely identifies it within the network. An IP address can be decomposed to identify a host's subnet and host number.

The TCP/IP model provides a standard format for sending and receiving data that is specified in the five-layer model. Like layers in the OSI model, each TCP/IP layer provides basic functions needed to transfer data, and logical connections between corresponding layers in communicating devices are used. Sending hosts add headers to data/messages that enable corresponding layers in destination hosts to interpret the tasks/functions that should be performed on the data.

Like OSI model layers, each layer in the TCP/IP model only communicates and interacts with adjacent layers, those immediately above and below. Table 4-2 summarizes the major communication tasks/functions at each TCP/IP layer.

Data encapsulation and de-encapsulation processes occur as headers are added by senders and removed by receivers. The unit of information sent by the protocol at a particular TCP/IP (or OSI)

Table 4-2: Major communication functions performed at each layer of the TCP/IP model.

Layer	Name	Description
5	Application	Applications that require network communications are found at this layer. This layer uses application protocols, such as HTTPS, SMTP, and FTP, to support web, email, file transfer, and other services. This layer relies on the Transport layer to manage connections between hosts.
4	Transport	The Transport layer establishes the connection between applications running on different hosts and provides a channel for an application's communication needs. It uses TCP for applications that require reliable connections and User Datagram Protocol (UDP) for applications that require fast connections. It tracks processes running in applications via port numbers and uses the Network layer to move data between hosts.
3	Network	This layer creates the packets that move across the network. It also defines the addressing and routing structures used in the network. IP is the primary protocol at this layer; it defines IP addresses. IP addresses are added to TCP segments and UDP datagrams during packet creation to identify the packet's source and destination. IP destination addresses are used to route packets across networks to their final destinations.
2	Data Link	The Data Link layer is responsible for creating the frames that move between devices in local networks. Frames are created by encapsulating Network layer packets and adding MAC addresses that identify the source and destination devices in the local network.
1	Physical	The Physical layer encodes and decodes the symbols used to represent the bits in a frame. Encoding involves representing and transmitting the bits as electromagnetic, radio, or optical signals over communication media. Decoding involves interpreting received signals and converting them back to the bits that they represent.

layer is called a **protocol data unit (PDU)**. A PDU consists of the data passed to the layer from the layer above it and the header fields that are added to the data at that layer. During the data encapsulation process, the PDU created at one layer is encapsulated in the PDU created at the layer beneath it.

Figure 4-6 illustrates the PDUs at different TCP/IP layers and their distinctive names. When TCP is used at the Transport layer, the PDU created at that layer is called a segment and consists of data passed to the Transport layer from the Application layer and TCP header fields.

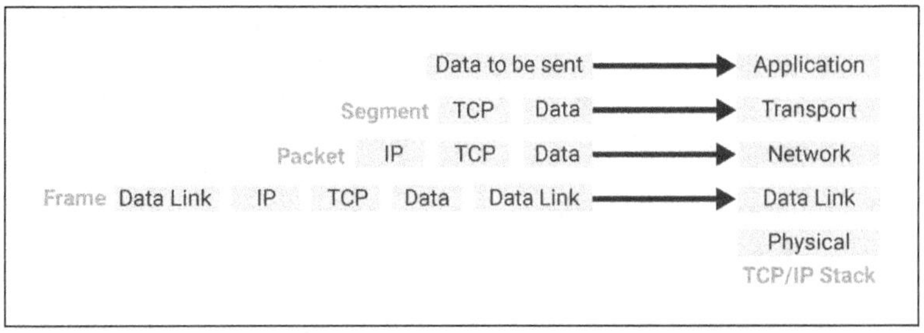

Figure 4-6: Headers added at TCP/IP layers produce PDUs with distinctive names.

When a segment is passed to the Network layer and an IP header is added, it becomes a *packet*, and when a packet is passed to the Data Link layer and a Data Link header and trailer are added, it becomes a *frame*. Like the trailer added at the Data Link layer of the OSI model, the trailer added by this layer in the TCP/IP model is used for error checking.

The TCP/IP model uses three different types of addressing. *Port numbers* are included in Transport layer headers to identify applications in communicating hosts; these numbers serve as application addresses. Logical *IP addresses* are included in Network layer header fields when packets are created, and physical *MAC addresses* are included in Data Link layer headers when frames are created. They are illustrated in Figure 4-7's partial decomposition of an Ethernet frame. Each of these addressing types has an important role in host-to-host communications.

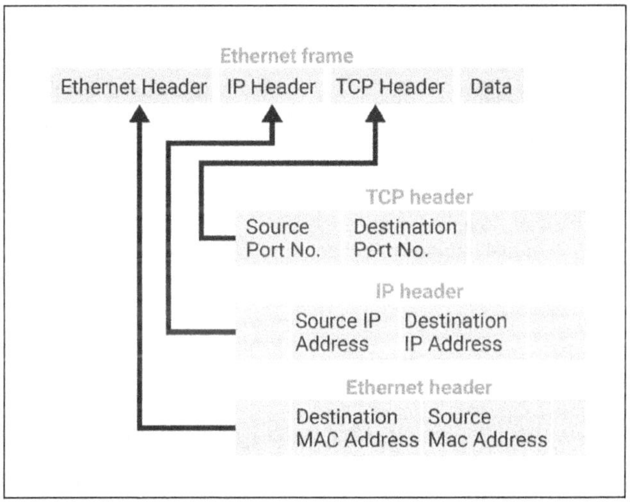

Figure 4-7: Port numbers and IP and MAC addresses are included in header fields added during TCP/IP data encapsulation.

Figure 4-8 illustrates data encapsulation and de-encapsulation in TCP/IP hosts and provides a summary overview of the PDUs at the Transport, Network, and Data Link layers.

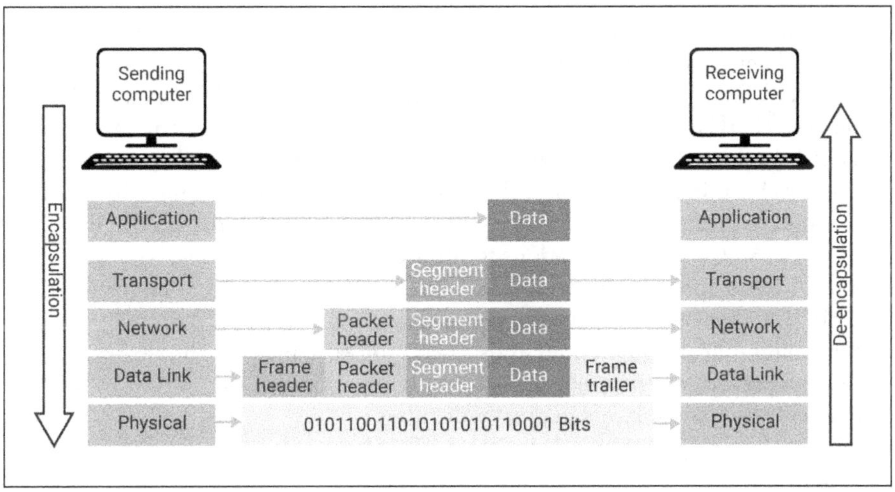

Figure 4-8: Data encapsulation and de-encapsulation in TCP/IP hosts.

4.3.1 Similarities and Differences Between the OSI and TCP/IP Models

There is considerable overlap between the OSI and TCP/IP models, especially at their lower levels. You can observe this in the descriptions of the Network, Data Link, and Physical layers in Tables 4-1 and 4-2. As Figure 4-9 illustrates, TCP/IP's Transport layer includes functions performed by the Transport layer in the OSI model and some of the functions and tasks performed by the OSI model's Session layer. In addition, the TCP/IP Application layer incorporates the functions performed by OSI's Application and Presentation layers and some functions performed by the Session layer.

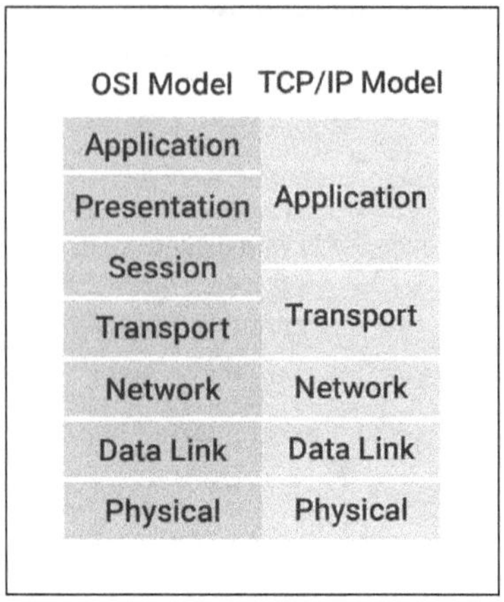

Figure 4-9: How the layers of the TCP/IP model map to OSI model layers.

The OSI model is more generic and encompassing than the TCP/IP model, but the TCP/IP model arguably better reflects the realities of today's Internet-connected enterprise networks. Both facilitate understanding of how applications are supported on networks. They also provide guidance for developing communication standards and protocols that networking equipment vendors use to create standards-compliant technologies.

Standards have inspired competition among network hardware manufacturers, including price competition. Competition is especially keen among makers and vendors of Layer 3 (Network), Layer 2 (Data Link), and Layer 1 (Physical) networking equipment. The availability of Layer 3 routers and Layer 2 switches from numerous vendors has kept their costs reasonable. Routers, switches, and Layer 1 cabling are commodity items, and this enables businesses to negotiate attractive prices that contribute to lower overall networking costs.

A closer look at the similarities and differences of the OSI and TCP/IP models is provided in Appendix 4-1.

4.4 TCP/IP LAYERS: Functions, Protocols, and Technologies

The TCP/IP model consists of a suite of communication protocols and a set of rules and procedures for connecting devices over the public Internet and other TCP/IP networks (including private intranets and extranets). The model's main purpose is to connect two remote machines (hosts) and enable them to exchange data/information. The hosts may be in different networks and have different computing architectures.

TCP and IP are the two main protocols in the TCP/IP model, but a wide range of other protocols are included in the model's protocol suite. Some of them are introduced in this chapter, but others will be discussed at relevant junctures in subsequent chapters. The model's collection of protocols serves as an abstraction layer between applications and the routing and switching fabrics of the Internet and local networks that support them.

The Defense Advanced Research Projects Agency (DARPA), the research branch of the U.S. Department of Defense (DoD), created the TCP/IP model in the 1970s for use in ARPANET, a WAN that preceded the Internet. TCP/IP was originally designed for use with the Unix OS, but TCP/IP support has been included in all of the OSs developed since that time. The TCP/IP model and its protocols are maintained by the *Internet Engineering Task Force (IETF)*. The IETF uses *requests for comment (RFCs)* for modifications to the TCP/IP model and its protocols.

As noted in section 4.1, the updated version of the TCP/IP model divides communication functionality and protocols into five layers: Application, Transport, Network, Data Link, and Physical. Each layer's primary communication functions, most used protocols, major technologies, security concerns, and security defenses are introduced and briefly described in the following sections. Chapters 5, 6, and 7 will address the layers in greater detail.

4.4.1 Application Layer

Communication Functions

The Application layer provides standardized data exchange for client-server and other distributed applications. It defines the services that applications need, but not the applications themselves. Application layer protocols provide services to application software running on hosts. For example, when a host launches a web browser, TCP/IP's HTTPS (or HTTP) protocol enables a web browser running on a user device to pull a web page from a web server. Basically, the Application layer provides an interface between a host's application software and the network.

Unlike the OSI model, the TCP/IP model does not consider the specifics of formatting and presenting data and does not have layers (or sublayers) between the Application and Transport layers that handle data formatting and presentation. The TCP/IP model delegates these functions to APIs and libraries. Accordingly, TCP/IP's Application layer is considered a combination of the OSI model's Session, Presentation, and Application layers (see Figure 4-9).

The TCP/IP model's Application layer includes protocols that most applications use to provide services or exchange data over the logical network connections established by Transport layer protocols. Some Application layer protocols provide network support services, such as routing, domain name services, host configuration, and network management.

Examples of widely used Application layer protocols include Hypertext Transfer Protocol Secure (HTTPS), Simple Mail Transfer Protocol (SMTP), Domain Name Services (DNS), Dynamic Host Configuration Protocol (DHCP), and Simple Network Management Protocol (SNMP). These and other Application layer protocols are identified in Figure 4-10.

Protocols

Protocols associated with specific client-server applications or common services are identified by *well-known port numbers* assigned by the Internet Assigned Numbers Authority (IANA). For example, HTTPS uses TCP port 443 because it is supported by TCP at the Transport layer. SNMP typically uses UDP ports 161 and 162 for Transport layer services. Clients connecting to a server service fill the Source Port field in Transport layer headers (see Figure 4-7) with ephemeral port numbers that are randomly assigned for a particular communication exchange.

Although they have some awareness of Transport layer connections (such as destination port numbers), Application layer protocols generally treat Transport layer protocols and protocols at lower layers as black boxes that provide necessary network connections. Likewise, Transport and lower-layer protocols treat Application layer protocol specifics as a black box. While there are some exceptions to this general rule, the Application layer typically has limited awareness of what happens at other layers.

The TCP/IP model distinguishes between user protocols and support protocols at the Application layer. Examples of each type are identified in Figure 4-9. User protocols support network user applications, such as web browsing, file transfers, and email. Support protocols provide behind-the-scenes services to applications, systems, network processes, and other TCP/IP protocols. Table 4-3 provides brief descriptions of the protocols included in Figure 4-9.

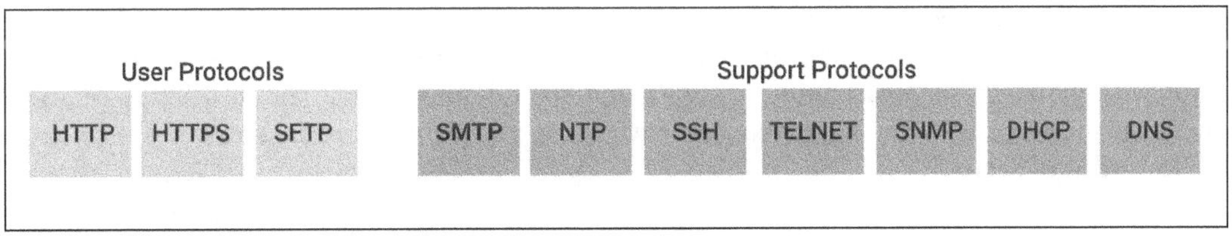

Figure 4-10: Examples of widely used TCP/IP Application layer protocols.

Table 4-3: Key characteristics of some widely used Application layer protocols.	
Protocol	**Key Characteristics**
HTTP (Hypertext Transfer Protocol)	HTTP defines a set of rules for transferring text, graphics, images, sound, video, and other multimedia included on web pages. It provides a way to publish and retrieve Hypertext Markup Language (HTML) pages. HTTP is a request/response protocol between clients and servers and uses TCP port 80 as the destination port in TCP headers. Today, websites that only support HTTP are flagged by browsers as insecure.
HTTPS (HTTP Secure)	HTTPS combines normal HTTP interaction over an encrypted Transport Layer Security (TLS) or Secure Sockets Layer (SSL) connection between client and server. Today, TLS is most common. Most browsers use HTTPS by default and include warnings when users try to access insecure websites that only support HTTP. TCP port 443 is the default destination port for HTTPS in TCP headers.
SFTP (Secure [or SSH] File Transfer Protocol)	SFTP enables file access, file transfer, and file management over a TCP/IP network. SFTP uses TCP port 22 for server connections, authentication, and data transfers.
SMTP (Simple Mail Transfer Protocol)	SMTP is used to move (send and receive) email on and across networks. It is typically used with Post Office Protocol 3 (POP3) or Internet Message Access Protocol (IMAP) to save messages in a server mailbox and download them periodically from the server to user email apps, such as Gmail and Outlook. SMTP mail servers traditionally used TCP port 25. SMTPS is a secure version of SMTP that uses TCP port 465.
NTP (Network Time Protocol)	NTP is used to synchronize the clocks of communicating computer systems on data networks. NTP uses time stamps to document the order of network events and occurrences. It uses UDP port 123 for Transport layer services.
SSH (Secure Shell)	SSH is used for creating a secure connection between a client and server when the client initiates the connection. TCP port 22 is used for SSH. Most applications have replaced SSH with TLS.
TELNET	TELNET is a command-line client-server program used to virtually access a remote computer and provide a two-way, text-based communication channel. The protocol may be used to remotely manage an account or device. For example, a user may use TELNET to communicate with the computer that hosts their website to manage website files. TELNET uses TCP port 23. Because TELNET communication sessions are unencrypted and therefore insecure, clients such as PuTTY that combine TELNET and SSH are most common.
SNMP (Simple Network Management Protocol)	SNMP is used by network administrators to manage and monitor network-connected devices (such as routers, switches, servers, firewalls, and wireless access points) in TCP/IP networks. It provides a mechanism for network devices to relay relevant information to network management consoles and databases. It typically uses UDP ports 161 and 162 for Transport layer services.
DHCP (Dynamic Host Configuration Protocol)	DHCP is used to automate the process of configuring devices on IP networks. It is used by a client to communicate with a DHCP server, which dynamically assigns an IP address and other network configuration parameters to network devices so they can use TCP/IP services and protocols to communicate with devices in other TCP/IP networks. The protocol uses UDP port 63 for Transport layer services.
DNS (Domain Name System)	The DNS is a hierarchically organized system of computers and databases that makes the resolution of domain names to IP addresses possible. The protocol helps Internet users and devices access websites using human-readable hostnames instead of numeric IP addresses. By default, the protocol uses UDP port 53 to serve DNS queries. TCP port 53 is the fallback when the protocol is unable to use UDP to communicate.

Technologies and Security

Like technologies at all TCP/IP model layers, Application layer technologies are deployed to enhance network performance, efficiency, and security. There is a limited range of hardware-only technologies for the Application layer but an extensive array of services deployed as software or as combinations of hardware and software.

Application layer hardware technologies include servers, application layer switches, content switches, load balancers, application firewalls, and some hardware encryption devices. Many of these capabilities can be implemented as software and may or may not be supported on a dedicated hardware device.

Servers

As noted in Chapter 2, a server is technically a software process that supports an application or provides a service. This may be most easily observed in virtual servers. However, servers are commonly deployed as hardware devices in enterprise networks and cloud data centers, although virtualization software is typically used to transform the physical machines into virtual server clouds.

Examples of servers associated with Application layer user protocols include web servers and e-commerce servers. Examples of servers for Application layer support protocols include DHCP servers, DNS servers, and email servers.

Load Balancers

Load balancing is the systematic distribution of network or application traffic across servers in a server cluster, server farm, or data center to efficiently handle client service or resource requests.

A *load balancer* is a hardware and software or software-only solution located between client devices and servers that handles client requests; it receives client requests and distributes them to the servers available to fulfill them (see Figure 4-11). Basically, a load balancer acts as a traffic cop that routes client requests in a manner that maximizes response speed and capacity utilization and ensures that no one server is overworked.

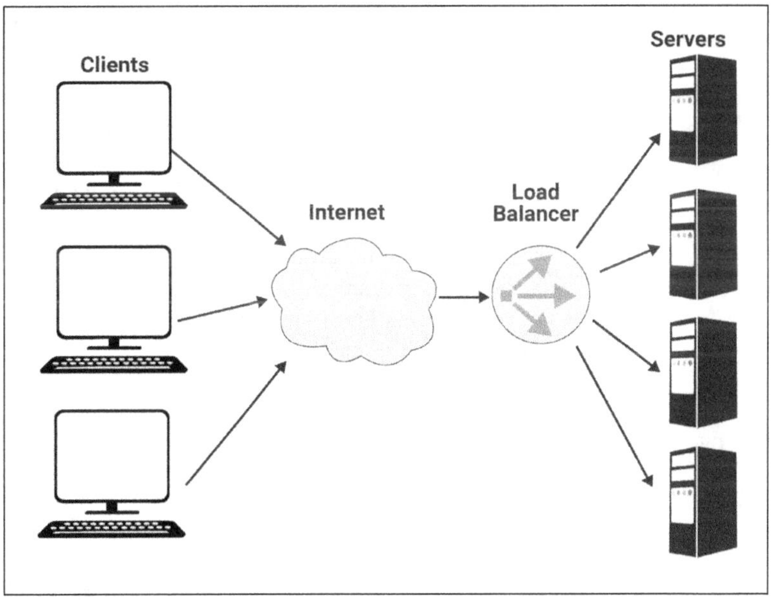

Figure 4-11: An example of Application layer load balancing.

Switches, Firewalls, and Encryption

An **Application layer switch** is a type of multilayer switch that uses Application layer information such as a URL, session ID (used in HTTPS), or cookie to make switching decisions. These are called *Layer 7 switches* by the OSI model and are sometimes called *web switches*. Like load balancers, they are typically deployed at server locations to expedite delivery of client requests to servers. Different types of Application layer switching services are identified in Table 4-4.

Table 4-4: Types of switching services used by Application layer switches.

Switching Service	Brief Description
Cookie Switching	In cookie switching, the switch forwards a client's request to a server, or another destination based on information in the cookie header.
URL Switching	This involves forwarding a client's request to a server, or another destination, using information in the URL text string in the packet's Application layer header.
Session ID Switching	This connects a client to the same server based on the information in a session ID, such as those used in HTTPS SSL communication sessions between clients and servers.
Content Switching	A **content switch** inspects the contents of incoming packets and bases its switching decisions on the results of its deep packet inspections. It may base its switching decisions on Transport layer port numbers and/or the processing loads of available servers in their switching decisions. Content switches are often used for load balancing among groups of application servers.

An **Application layer firewall** implements rules to block or allow data/messages to and/or from an application. These firewalls do more in-depth inspection of packet contents than firewalls used at lower layers in the TCP/IP model. They strive to prevent the executable malicious code from reaching or infecting the applications that they protect. Most application firewalls can be remotely managed and are regularly updated to ensure that they can identify and respond to newly discovered threats or vulnerabilities.

Application layer firewalls can be active or passive:

- Active application layer firewalls actively inspect and compare the contents of all incoming requests against known threats, such as cross-scripting, cookie or parameter tampering, and SQL injections. Only "clean" requests are passed to the application.
- Passive application layer firewalls inspect incoming requests for known threats but do not deny requests that fail inspection from being passed to the application; instead, they send alerts/alarms to warn network administrators of potential problems. Basically, these firewalls function as intrusion detection systems (IDSs) for applications.

Web application firewalls (WAFs) filter, monitor, and block HTTP and HTTPS traffic to and from web servers and web applications. Like a load balancer, a WAF sits between client devices and web servers. A content switch may be configured to function as a WAF. Because WAFs provide protection at Layer 7 of the OSI model, they are sometimes called *Layer 7 firewalls*.

Encryption is usually deployed as software but can also be implemented in hardware or as a combination of hardware and software. **Hardware encryption** involves the use of a processor that is dedicated to encryption and authentication, and it enables encryption and decryption processes to be performed more rapidly than is possible using software. It also makes encryption processes more difficult to hack.

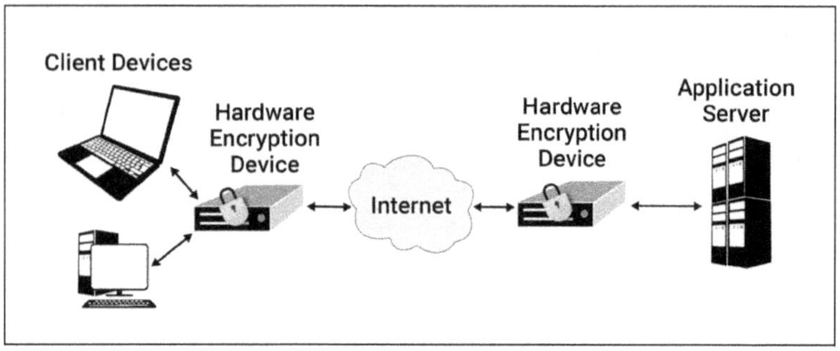

Figure 4-12: A conceptual diagram of Application layer hardware encryption.

Hardware encryption can be deployed at any level in the TCP/IP protocol stack but is most common at the Physical, Network, and Application layers. Figure 4-12 illustrates how hardware encryption might be used at the Application layer. Pairs of hardware encryption devices are used to encrypt and decrypt messages and data transferred between clients and servers. The U.S. military makes heavy use of hardware encryption to protect data transfers on its networks.

Transport Layer Security (TLS) is a cryptographic protocol that provides host-to-host communications security. It is widely used by client-server applications (including email, instant messaging, and voice over IP) to prevent eavesdropping or tampering. It is also used to secure Application layer protocols. For example, HTTPS uses TLS by default.

Although it has "Transport Layer" in its name, TLS is located between the Application and Transport layers in the TCP/IP model. It is maintained by the Internet Engineering Task Force (IETF) standard and builds on earlier SSL (Secure Sockets Layer) specifications. The latest version of TLS, TLS 1.3, was defined in 2018. TLS is usually implemented on top of TCP to encrypt Application layer protocols, but it is also used with other Transport layer protocols. Because it runs on top of TCP, it essentially bridges the Application and Transport layers.

Protecting the security of an application, especially mission-critical applications such as ESs, is a business priority. Hence it is not surprising that security technologies are found at the Application layer. Application security issues and defenses are described more extensively in Chapter 12. Security controls at lower layers of the TCP/IP model also contribute to protecting applications.

4.4.2 Transport Layer

Communication Functions

As noted in Table 4-2, the Transport layer establishes, and monitors communication channels that applications use to exchange data. It uses port numbers to define how data should be delivered to applications on destination hosts. This layer also provides flow and error control mechanisms for connection-oriented applications that require reliable communication channels and less reliable but potentially faster delivery channels for connectionless applications.

A network **port** is a process-specific or application-specific software construct that serves as a communication endpoint for Transport layer protocols. The IANA has standardized port numbers for specific applications and services; they are called *well-known ports*. Port numbers identify applications and services at a specific network address or host.

The Transport layer provides two types of data delivery services: connection-oriented and connectionless. A **connection-oriented service** involves the creation and termination of host-to-host communication sessions and data exchanges. Connection-oriented services typically enable receiving hosts to deliver data to the Application layer in its correct order. A **connectionless service** does not require a host-to-host communication session for data transfer.

Connection-oriented Transport layer protocols, such as TCP, are usually considered reliable data delivery services because they include mechanisms for receivers to acknowledge successful data delivery as well as mechanisms to notify senders to retransmit missing or corrupt data. Connectionless protocols, such as UDP, do not require delivery acknowledgments, error checking, or error recovery.

Protocols

The two most common Transport layer protocols are the Transmission Control Protocol (TCP) and the User Datagram Protocol (UDP). Stream Control Transmission Protocol (SCTP) is another well-known Transport layer protocol.

TCP is a connection-oriented protocol that establishes a connection between a sender and a receiver before data is sent. It is reliable; data sent using TCP is guaranteed to be delivered to the receiver. If data is lost or corrupted in transit, TCP ensures that it is resent.

To provide a reliable data delivery service, TCP strives to ensure the following:

- Delivered data can be reassembled into the order in which it was transmitted.
- Duplicated data can be identified and discarded.
- Missing or corrupted data is resent by the sending host.
- Data delivery is not impeded by network traffic.

The mechanisms that TCP uses to provide reliable data delivery are described in Chapter 5.

UDP is a connectionless protocol that does not require acknowledgment of transmitted datagrams. **Datagram** is the term used to refer to the basic transfer unit (protocol data unit [PDU]) that connectionless communication services use. UDP is widely used for applications, Application layer protocols, and network services where data delivery speed is more important than reliable data delivery.

Like TCP segments, UDP datagram headers include source and destination port numbers to identify the application or service to which transmitted data should be delivered. However, because it is a connectionless protocol, UDP headers are more compact than TCP headers. The formats of both TCP and UDP headers are identified in Chapter 5.

UDP is suitable for applications where error checking and recovery are unnecessary or are performed by the application. Time-sensitive Application layer protocols such as DNS and DHCP use UDP, and applications that UDP supports often keep sending datagrams until they get a response.

Like TCP, *Stream Control Transmission Protocol (SCTP)* is a connection-oriented Transfer layer protocol, but it uses UDP for data transfer. SCTP ensures in-order data transmission; data is transferred in the same order as it is received from the Application layer over the communication channel.

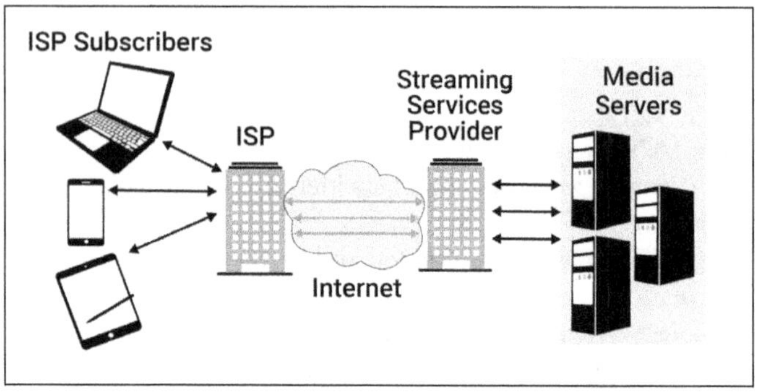

Figure 4-13: A conceptual depiction of SCTP multistreaming.

Unlike TCP, which only allows a single connection between endpoints, SCTP supports multiple connections between two endpoints. Establishing connections between endpoints is more complex than in TCP, but the use of UDP facilitates fast data transfers after the connections are established.

In Figure 4-13, the ISP and Streaming Services Provider are the two endpoints, and after SCTP connections are established, data is transferred in order as a UDP datagram stream over each communication channel. Each stream is a logical unidirectional connection.

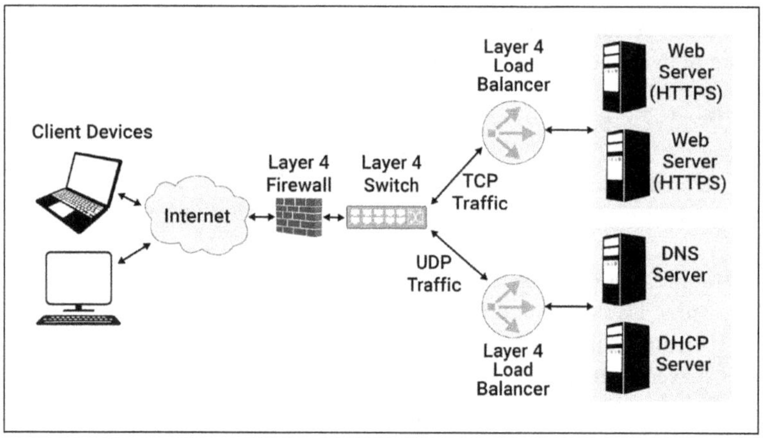

Figure 4-14: A conceptual depiction of Layer 4 switches, firewalls, and load balancers.

Figure 4-14 depicts how SCTP might be used to support multiple simultaneous data/message streams between a streaming services provider (such as ESPN+, Hulu, or Netflix) with numerous media servers and an ISP with numerous residential subscribers (such as Bulloch Solutions in Statesboro, Georgia).

Technologies and Security

There are several important Layer 4 technologies. These include Layer 4 switches/gateways, load balancers, and firewalls (see Figure 4-14). Like Application layer technologies, these technologies may be deployed solely in software but are more commonly a combination of hardware and software.

A **Layer 4 switch** is a multilayer switch that uses the port numbers in Transport layer headers for switching decisions and directing incoming traffic to specific applications, services, or hosts (servers). It extracts and analyzes information from Transport layer protocol headers to efficiently route network traffic. In Figure 4-14, the Transport layer protocol, TCP or UDP, is the basis of switching decisions.

A **Layer 4 load balancer** uses port numbers in Transport layer headers to distribute incoming client requests across available servers. Like other load balancers, it strives to optimally distribute incoming requests to facilitate quick responses from servers. Layer 4 load balancers often use simple load balancing algorithms that consider basic information about available servers, such as counts of current server connections and response times.

Layer 4 firewalls are most often used in conjunction with connection-oriented protocols, such as TCP and SCTP. **Layer 4 firewalls** filter traffic based on source and destination IP addresses, ports, and protocols; they also actively track network connections (communication sessions) and allow/deny traffic to pass based on the state of those sessions. These firewalls keep track of each active connection and constantly check its validity using a process called *stateful packet inspection* or *dynamic packet filtering*.

When stateful inspection is used, the firewall examines the contents of a packet and compares them to the contents of packets that have previously passed through the firewall during the communication session. If there are differences, the firewall may terminate the communication session and force the client and server to reauthenticate and establish a new communication session.

4.4.3 Network Layer

The Network layer enables connections between independent networks and enables packets to be transported across network boundaries from one network to another. This layer is called the Internet layer in the four-layer TCP/IP model that preceded the updated five-layer model. Internetworking and logical addressing are some key communication functions that this layer performs.

Communication Functions

Internetworking involves transferring data from one network to another. The network-to-network transfer process is called *routing* and is supported by host identification and host addressing. These capabilities enable data to be transferred from a host in one network to a host in another network via logical communication channels called *virtual circuits*.

Host addressing is the process that allocates logical Network layer addresses to hosts. Logical host addresses are needed to identify hosts and the networks and subnets in which they are located. Host addressing processes are described more fully in Chapter 5.

IP addresses are the logical host addresses used in TCP/IP networks. A host needs an IP address to use the TCP/IP network to create, send, and receive Network layer PDUs (called *packets*). Source (sender) and destination (receiver) IP addresses are included in Network layer headers.

The Network layer provides a connectionless (and unreliable) transmission service between hosts. Each packet is treated as a datagram that can be independently routed from sending to destination host. Routing is performed by a *router*—a networking technology deployed as software or a hardware/software combination—that transfers packets between networks.

Network layer protocols carry data for all Transport layer protocols. Transport layer protocols are identified by protocol numbers in Network layer headers. Because the Network layer only provides connectionless and potentially unreliable data transfer, connection-oriented applications rely on connection-oriented Transport layer protocols, such as TCP, to provide reliable data delivery.

When sender and receiver hosts are in different networks, packets are forwarded from a router in the sender's network to an appropriate next-hop router for further relaying to the destination network. A router in the destination network delivers the packet to the destination host. Because packets may be forwarded across multiple networks before reaching their destinations, the Network layer is considered the layer that establishes the Internet.

Protocols

Figure 4-15 identifies several protocols at TCP/IP's Network layer. Some of these (such as ICMP and IGMP) are located at the border of the Network and Transport layer and are sometimes described as running on top of IP. Other protocols (such as ARP and RARP) are described as being located at the border of the Network and Data Link layer because they identify current associations between logical IP addresses and physical (MAC) addresses in hosts.

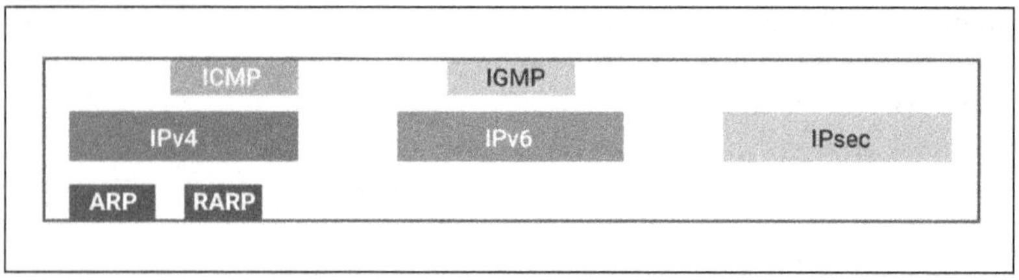

Figure 4-15: Examples of Network layer protocols.

Internet Protocol (IP) is the principal Network layer protocol. It defines two logical host addressing systems: IPv4 and IPv6. *Internet Protocol version 4 (IPv4)* uses 32-bit IP addresses and can uniquely identify slightly more than four billion hosts. *Internet Protocol version 6 (IPv6)*, standardized in 1998, uses 128-bit addresses and has more *quality of service (QoS)* capabilities than IPv4. Differences between IPv4 and IPv6 are described more fully in Chapter 5.

IP addresses include network, subnet, and host components to enable hosts to be uniquely identified within a subnet and network. These components facilitate packet transfers across networks and delivery to destination hosts. Routers use the network components of destination IP addresses when making next-hop decisions. The router in the destination network uses the subnet and host components of the IP address to identify the host that should receive the packet.

IP is an encapsulating protocol. When TCP segments and UDP datagrams are passed from the Transport layer, an IP header is added to each segment or datagram to create a packet. The IP header includes both sender and destination IP address fields, as well as several other fields. IP packet formats are identified and briefly described in Chapter 5.

IPsec (Internet Protocol Security) is a secure Network layer protocol suite that authenticates and encrypts packets in an IP network to provide secure host-to-host communication. Numerous virtual private networks (VPNs) use IPsec to secure packets sent over the Internet. IPsec is also used to secure data in transit on private internal networks.

The IPsec protocol suite includes protocols for mutually authenticating endpoints at the start of a communication session. It also includes protocols for negotiating encryption keys used during communication sessions. After mutual authentication has taken place and session keys have been determined, IPsec adds an IPsec header to IP packets. IP packet payloads are encrypted, and the packet's original IP header may also be encrypted. IPsec is described more fully in Chapter 5.

Internet Control Message Protocol (ICMP) is used to communicate information about network connectivity issues to the source of unsuccessful data transfer. Routers and other networking technologies use ICMP to communicate transmission issues to senders. For example, if a TCP segment is not delivered, ICMP may provide details to the sender that may be useful in determining why the transmission was unsuccessful. It is also used to send messages such as "Destination unreachable" or "Source Quench" (which is used for flow control by informing the sender that the receiver cannot handle packets at the rate they are currently being sent). ICMP sends control messages in packets with an 8-byte ICMP header.

Ping is a utility that uses ICMP messages to report network connectivity information and the speed of data relay between a sending and destination host. *Tracert* is another utility that uses ICMP messages; it is used to identify the routing of a packet from sender to destination.

Unfortunately, ICMP can be exploited by network attackers. Ping scans or sweeps can help attackers discover potential targets. In addition, if attackers succeed in compromising network equipment, they can use ICMP to send behind-the-scenes control messages to network devices. Misconfigured network equipment can open the door to ICMP-based attacks, including ICMP floods, a type of distributed denial-of-service (DDoS) attack.

The **Internet Group Management Protocol (IGMP)** is a Network layer protocol that allows several devices to share an IP address and receive the same data from a sender. It is used for multicasting on IPv4 networks and enables devices to join a multicasting group.

Multicasting occurs when a specific group of devices in a network receive the same messages or packets. It should not be confused with *broadcasting*, in which all devices in a network receive the same messages/packets. Devices in an IP network use IGMP to join or leave a multicast group. IGMP adds a header to an IP packet for IGMP messages.

Like ICMP, IGMP works on top of IP; this accounts for its placement in Figure 4-16. In IPv4, IGMP uses addresses that are set aside for multicasting. They are outside the range of IPv4 addresses assigned to individual hosts. In IPv6, *Multicast Listener Discovery (MLD)* is the protocol for multicasting.

Address Resolution Protocol (ARP) is used to identify the Data Link layer address (MAC address) associated with an IPv4 address. An IP packet is delivered to a host via Data Link layer frames that include the host's MAC address. Basically, ARP maps an IPv4 address to the MAC address of a device in a destination network. In IPv6, *Neighbor Discovery Protocol (NDP)* is used instead of ARP.

ARP is a request-response protocol whose messages are encapsulated in Data Link layer frames. This makes it more of a Data Link layer protocol than a Network layer protocol and accounts for its placement at the border of the Network and Data Link layers in Figure 4-15. It is used within the boundaries of a single network and is never routed across network boundaries.

ARP can be exploited by network attackers using ARP spoofing (ARP poisoning) to intercept data frames, modify network traffic, and potentially stop traffic from reaching its destination. In ARP spoofing, the attacker sends a falsified ARP request to a destination network's router that enables the attacker's MAC address to be listed as a legitimate device on the network. This opens the door to other types of attacks, such as man-in-the-middle, denial-of-service, or session hijacking.

Reverse Address Resolution Protocol (RARP) translates a Data Link layer (MAC) address to a Network layer (IP) address. It is used to discover/identify the IPv4 address currently associated with a MAC address. RARP is obsolete and has been replaced by BOOTP, DHCP, and *InARP (Inverse Address Resolution Protocol)*. InARP is a protocol extension to ARP.

Routing protocols define the rules that routers use for transferring packets from source to destination networks and control the updating of the routing tables that routers use to select the best route or path to a destination network. Although routing protocols determine how IP packets are routed across networks, they are located at other layers in the TCP/IP model. Routing protocols are introduced in Appendix 4-2 and are addressed more fully in Chapter 5.

Technologies and Security

Routers are the predominant Network layer technology. However, there are other important technologies at this layer, including Layer 3 switches, IPsec gateways, NAT gateways, and packet filtering firewalls. While these technologies can be deployed as software-only solutions, they are commonly implemented as hardware and software devices.

Routers

A **router** is a computer or networking device that transfers (forwards) packets between computer networks. They direct traffic on the Internet. A packet is forwarded from a router in a sending host's network to routers in other networks on the Internet until it reaches the router in the destination network that delivers the packet to the destination host. Routers are also used on private TCP/IP networks to forward data between hosts in different subnets.

A router has two or more interfaces (circuit connections) that provide pathways to/from different networks. A router may have different types of physical interfaces for different types of physical layer connections, such as Ethernet cables, fiber optic cables, or wireless transmission.

When a router receives a packet on one of its interfaces, it reads the destination address in the

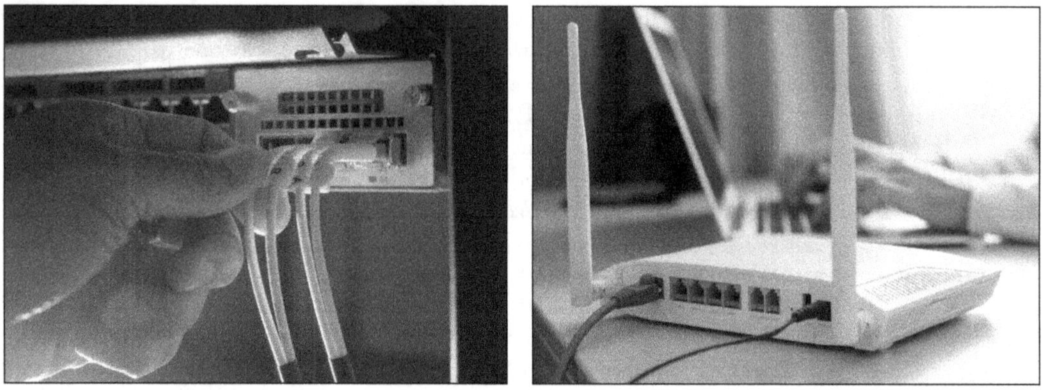

Figure 4-16: Examples of enterprise network and Wi-Fi routers. Source: iStock/ Stock photo ID:1270583054, Source: iStock/ AnuchaCheechang/ Stock photo ID:1085926502

IP header and consults its routing table to identify the interface to use to send the packet to the next router (the *next hop*) along its path to the destination. Routers exchange information about routes to destination networks using routing protocols.

Routers vary in complexity and configuration. *Wi-Fi routers* in home and small office networks are used to forward IP packets to/from these networks and ISP networks. Routers that transfer packets between an organization's LANs or subnets are called *interior* routers, and the router that connects an organization to an ISP or another WAN is called a *border (or edge)* or *exterior* router. A router that is part of the Internet's fiber optic backbone is called a *core* router. Some router examples are shown in Figure 4-16.

A router's performance is measured by its filtering and forwarding rates. *Filtering rate* measures how many packet headers it can read per second to identify the packets' destinations and determine their next hops. *Forwarding rate* measures the number of packets it can transmit per second on outgoing circuits. As you might suspect, core routers have some of the highest filtering and forwarding rates.

The software that runs a router has two major parts called *planes*, which are identified in Table 4-5.

Table 4-5: Router table control and forwarding planes.

Router Plane	Brief Description
Control	The *control plane* maintains a routing table that lists the route that should be used to forward a packet to a destination network and the interface on which it should be transmitted. Control-plane software logic builds the *forwarding information base (FIB)*—routing table—that the forwarding plane uses.
Forwarding	The *forwarding plane* forwards packets between incoming and outgoing circuit interfaces. It reads the destination address in the packet header, matches the destination to entries in the FIB, updates the header, and transmits the packet on the appropriate interface to the next-hop router.

Distinct control and forwarding planes facilitate the creation of software-defined networks. Software-defined networking (SDN) was introduced in Chapter 1 and is described more fully in Chapter 10. In SDN, the control plane is managed separately and externally to the physical router, which enables the router to devote its full processing capability to forwarding packets.

Switches, Gateways, and Firewalls

A **Layer 3 switch** is a multilayer switch that combines the functionality of a switch and a router and is used to support *virtual LANs (VLANs)*. It has Layer 3 routing capabilities that enable it to transfer packets between VLANs or subnets and to other networks. Like a router, it can read IP packet headers and make forwarding decisions based on the packets' destination IP addresses. However, it can also read VLAN tags (IDs) in Data Link layer frames and use them for Layer 2 or Layer 3 forwarding. Because they support Layer 2 switching, Layer 3 switches more closely resemble switches than routers, especially in their number of interfaces.

Layer 3 switches were originally designed for use in large networks and corporate intranets, and this is where they continue to be most common. They typically only support routing for IP networks and do not include interfaces for non-IP WANs, which constrains their use in some enterprise networks. Layer 3 switches may be more costly than Layer 2 switches and are often more challenging to configure and manage.

An *IPsec gateway* is a router that supports IPsec protocols. An IPsec gateway may be called an *IPsec VPN router*, an *IPsec VPN gateway*, or another name. Regardless of what it is called, an IPsec gateway is the technology that uses IPsec protocols to encrypt IP packet payloads or both the payload and the original IP packet header. The IPsec gateway at the receiving network decrypts the packets and passes them to the local network for delivery. A conceptual depiction of IPsec gateways is provided in Figure 4-17.

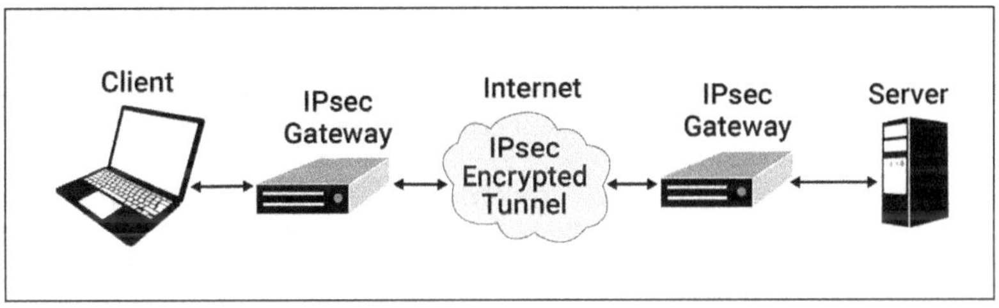

Figure 4-17: Conceptual depiction of IPsec gateways.

Tunneling over the Internet or another IP network involves protecting transmitted data by repackaging (encapsulation) and encrypting it during transit over nonsecure networks, such as the public Internet. Encapsulating a packet in an IPsec packet insulates it from other Internet traffic, and encryption makes its data unreadable by surveillance agents or malicious actors. Tunneling is often described as analogous to transporting cash between two banks in an armored car over public roadways—the armored vehicle provides a secured container (tunnel) for the cash being transported.

Network Address Translation (NAT) involves modifying a sender's IP address (source address) in the IP header of transmitted packets. In simple terms, NAT substitutes the private IP address of a device in a private TCP/IP network with an IP address that is routable on the public Internet. NAT is commonly supported by Wi-Fi routers in home and small business networks.

Most home Wi-Fi networks allocate private IPv4 addresses, like those in Figure 4-18, to user devices. Private IP addresses cannot be routed on the public Internet because they do not uniquely identify the network. A NAT-enabled Wi-Fi router, however, has a routable public IP address assigned by an ISP. Devices with private IP addresses are able to share the router's public IP address to transfer packets to/from other networks.

Routers with NAT capabilities are called *NAT gateways*. They are sometimes called *NAT servers* or *NAT firewalls*. Basically, a NAT gateway "hides" or "masquerades" the private IP addresses of devices in its local network and makes the packets they send to the public Internet anonymous.

The router tracks active connections and the destination IP addresses and ports to which packets are sent. When a reply is returned to the router, it uses its connection tracking log to identify the device that should receive it.

With NAT, a user in the private network can browse public Internet websites, but a user in another network cannot browse a website in the private network. Hence, NAT contributes to anonymous browsing by hosts in the private network while shielding them from attackers.

Packet filtering is a firewall technique used to control network access by monitoring outgoing and incoming packets and allowing them to pass or discarding them based on rules applied to IP

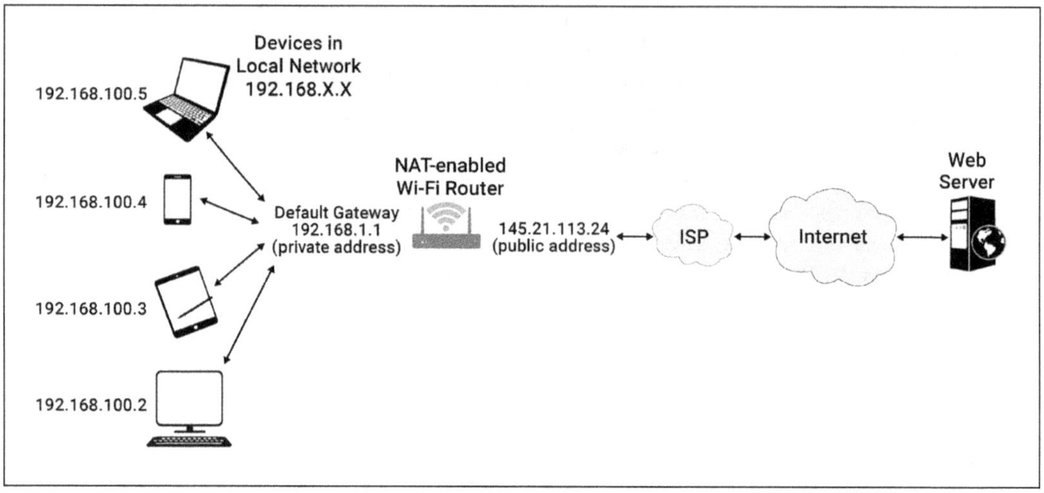

Figure 4-18: Conceptual depiction of a NAT gateway.

addresses, Transport and Application layer protocols, and port identifiers. Packets are allowed in (or out) when they comply with predefined rules; otherwise, they are dropped (not sent or delivered). This is conceptually depicted in Figure 4-19.

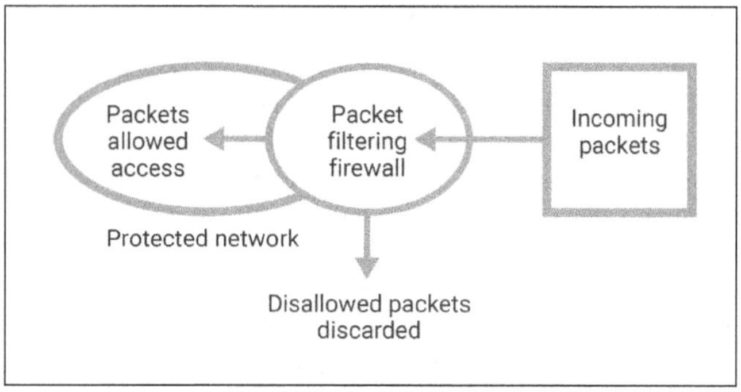

Figure 4-19: Conceptual depiction of incoming packet filtering in a firewall.

When decisions are based on IP addresses, a *packet filtering firewall* checks source and destination addresses in IP packet headers. When both are included on the firewall's approved *access control list (ACL)*, or *whitelist*, the packet is allowed to pass through the firewall if it also complies with firewall rules for protocols and ports.

Firewall rules can be defined to only allow access to familiar or well-known IP addresses and deny access to unknown or unrecognized IP addresses. Most routers have integrated filtering capabilities and can be used as packet filtering firewalls. They may also be configured to serve as IPsec gateways or NAT servers.

4.4.4 Data Link Layer

TCP/IP's Network layer is designed to be hardware independent to enable it to be implemented on top of any Data Link layer architecture and Physical layer technology. This is also largely the case for the Transport layer, but TCP must be "aware" of the maximum size of Data Link layer frames when determining how to fragment (segment) data received from the Application layer. While there is not complete independence between upper and lower TCP/IP layers, there is enough to enable making changes at the Data Link and Physical layers that have minimal effects on upper layers.

Communication Functions

The "link" in "data link" refers to all hosts that are directly accessible to a particular host without having to involve a router. These are other devices (hosts) in the local network or subnet.

The primary function of the Data Link layer is to move data between hosts in the local network. Physical addresses uniquely identify devices in the local network. These addresses are included in Data Link layer header fields and are used by switches or Data Link layer protocols to deliver frames to their destinations.

Physical addresses are hardcoded in the network adapters that enable devices to connect and use the local network. When an adapter is manufactured, it is equipped with a hardwired address that uniquely identifies it. The address is called a physical address because it is part of the adapter's circuitry. A device equipped with both an Ethernet and Wi-Fi adapter has two physical addresses, one for each adapter.

In addition to supplying devices with physical addresses, adapters perform other important functions, including *framing*, that is, adding Data Link layer headers and trailers to IP packets passed from the Network layer to create Data Link layer PDUs (*frames*). Adapters are also involved in *access control* (implementing procedures that control how and when devices transmit their data) and *error detection* (determining whether data is changed in passage between hosts). Adapters include transceiver circuitry used to transmit and receive frames. All of these functions are controlled by device drivers, firmware, and specialized chipsets in the adapters, and, collectively, they add reliability to data transmissions over the local network's physical circuits.

As Figure 4-20 illustrates, the Data Link layer has two sublayers: LLC and MAC. These work in concert to perform this layer's communication functions. The *LLC (logical link control)* sublayer manages error detection, flow control, and frame synchronization. The *MAC (media access control)* sublayer manages encapsulation and access/use of the medium used to transmit data.

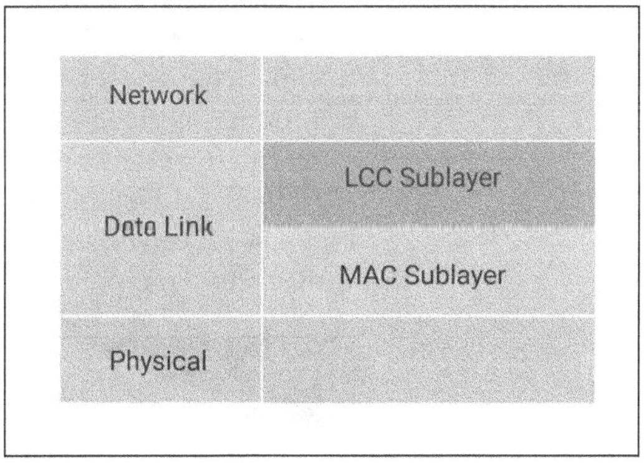

Figure 4-20: Data Link layer sublayers: LLC and MAC.

The LLC establishes and controls logical connections between the devices on the local network. It hides local network details from the Network layer to enable different technologies (e.g., both wired and wireless devices) to work seamlessly with the Network layer. In sending hosts, the LLC accepts IP packets from the Network layer and passes them to the MAC sublayer for framing. In receivers, the LLC identifies and removes frames with errors. The LLC sublayer is defined in IEEE standard 802.2.

The MAC sublayer is responsible for encapsulating packets passed from the Network layer in Data Link layer frames. The format of the frames that are built is dependent on the device's active adapter. For example, when a device is connected to an Ethernet network, Ethernet frames are created; when it is connected to a Wi-Fi network, Wi-Fi frames are created. Ethernet and Wi-Fi frame formats are described in Chapters 6 and 7.

The MAC sublayer adds both a header and a trailer to the IP packets. The frame header includes source and destination MAC address fields and control fields. The addresses specify the frame's creator and destination. Control fields convey frame handling information to the destination device. Senders include an error check code in the frame trailer that the destination device uses to check for errors. Frames with errors are discarded.

Access control determines when a device can transmit data and exert control over the communication link. Data Link layer protocols are the main determinants of access control processes. In wired Ethernet LANs, *Carrier Sense Multiple Access with Collision Detection (CSMA/CD)* is the official Data Link layer protocol. In Wi-Fi LANs, *Carrier Sense Multiple Access with Collision Avoidance (CSMA/CA)* is the official protocol.

Protocols and Standards

As noted, CSMA/CD and CSMA/CA are the "official" Data Link layer protocols identified in IEEE standards. These are the most common Data Link layer protocols. Other Data Link layer protocols, including Point-to-Point Protocol (PPP), are briefly described in Appendix 4-3.

Both CSMA/CD and CSMA/CA are formally recognized in standards formulated and maintained by the Institute of Electrical and Electronics Engineers (IEEE). IEEE standard 802.3 is the general standard for Ethernet, and IEEE standard 802.11 is the general standard for Wi-Fi. The current standard for Ethernet is IEEE standard 802.3-2018, and the current standard for Wi-Fi is IEEE standard 802.11ax (or Wi-Fi 6). These standards are discussed more fully in Chapters 6 and 7.

Technologies and Security

Network Adapters

Network adapters and Layer 2 switches are the most important Data Link layer technologies. A **network adapter** is a computer hardware component that provides an interface between the computer and a network. It enables a computer or another network device to connect to a local network and to transmit and receive data. A device requires an adapter to communicate with other devices in the local network, including the router that serves as a gateway for communicating with devices in other networks. Adapters are needed to connect to both wired (e.g., Ethernet) and wireless (e.g., Wi-Fi) LANs, and devices that can connect to both Ethernet and Wi-Fi have two adapters, one for each network.

Mobile devices, including smart phones, tablets, and laptops, typically have built-in Wi-Fi; laptops may also have built-in Ethernet adapters. As Figure 4-21 illustrates, connecting a laptop to an Ethernet network (or to an Ethernet port in a Wi-Fi router) can be as simple as plugging an Ethernet cable into the computer's Ethernet (RJ45) port. Plug-in Wi-Fi adapters, like that in Figure 4-21, can be added to laptops without built-in adapters. Plug-in Ethernet adapters are also available for laptops, tablets, and smartphones.

Figure 4-21: Examples of built-in adapters (left) and plug-in adapters (right). Source (left): Visual Field/istock/Stock photo ID:172161962. Source (right): FORGEM/istock/Stock photo ID:939548926

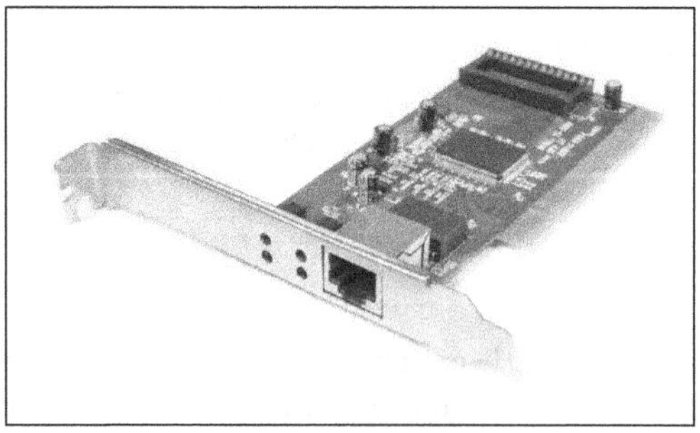

Figure 4-22: Example of an Ethernet network adapter card for a desktop computer. Source: indigolotos/istock/Stock photo ID:46657882

Like laptops, most desktop computers have adapters that are integrated (built into) their motherboards, providing an Ethernet port to connect to the local network. *Network adapter cards* (which are also called *network interface cards [NICs]* or *network interface controllers* [*NICs*]) like that illustrated in Figure 4-22 can be installed in motherboard expansion slots to provide network connectivity to desktop computers without built-in adapters.

A network adapter's circuitry implements specific Data Link and Physical layer standards (such as Ethernet or Wi-Fi) and protocols (such as CSMA/CD or CSMA/CA). This also provides a base that enables the device to support the TCP/IP protocol stack.

Layer 2 Switches

A **Layer 2 switch** operates at Layer 2, the Data Link layer, and uses physical (MAC) addresses to forward frames within the local network. It is primarily responsible for transferring Data Link layer frames over Physical layer connections; however, it may also be configured to detect errors in the frames it receives. It serves as the central connection point for devices in a local network.

In Ethernet LANs, each device connects to a switch via an Ethernet cable. The cable attaches to an interface (port) in the switch, such as the one shown in Figure 4-23.

Each switch has a limited number of interfaces. Small switches with 4 to 16 ports may be sufficient for smaller businesses. Larger switches with 24, 32, 36, 48, or 52 ports are common in larger networks. Small switches may be tabletop units, but most are rack mountable.

Figure 4-23: An example of an Ethernet switch with numerous ports. Source: vnosokin/ istock/ Stock photo ID:89332176

A Layer 2 switch must know the MAC address of the adapter in each device that connects to it. It "learns" the MAC addresses by copying the ones in the frames received from connected devices and uses them to create and maintain a *forwarding table*. The forwarding table associates each MAC address with the port (interface) used for its connection (see Figure 4-24).

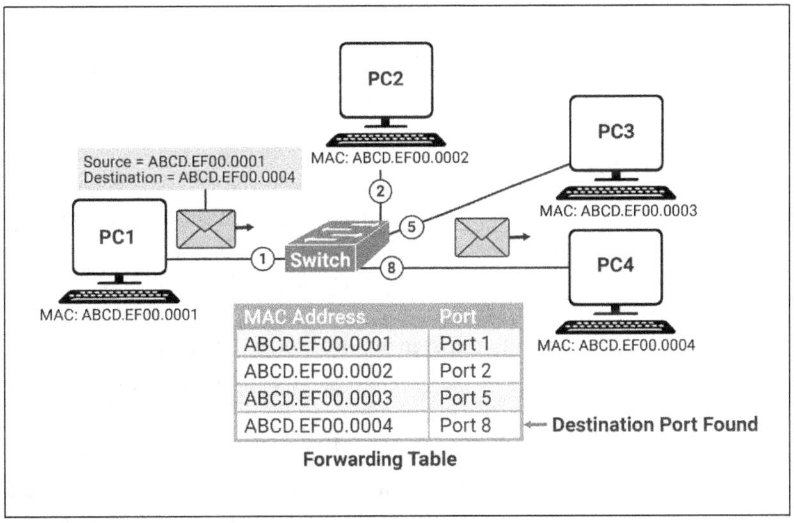

MAC Address	Port
ABCD.EF00.0001	Port 1
ABCD.EF00.0002	Port 2
ABCD.EF00.0003	Port 5
ABCD.EF00.0004	Port 8

Figure 4-24: Layer 2 (Data Link layer) switch operations.

When a frame is received, the switch identifies the MAC address of the destination in the frame header and transmits the frame on the interface listed for the MAC address in the forwarding table. Unlike switches at other layers (e.g., Layer 3 or Layer 4 switches) or multilayer switches, a Layer 2 switch bases its frame forwarding decisions on MAC addresses. It also lacks mechanisms for filtering or prioritizing frames on the basis of IP addresses, Transport layer ports, or sending/receiving applications.

Layer 2 switches also support broadcast traffic. By default, any broadcast frames that a switch receives are forwarded out to all ports except the one on which they were received. This defines the switch's default *broadcast domain*. A Layer 2 broadcast frame is a frame with the following destination MAC address: FFFF.FFFF.FFFF (or ff:ff:ff:ff:ff:ff or ff-ff-ff-ff-ff-ff).

Additional Layer 2 switch capabilities, switching modes, and support for broadcasting are briefly described in Appendix 4-4.

Virtual Switches and VLANs

Today, most Layer 2 switches are Power over Ethernet (PoE) switches capable of both transferring data and providing power to attached devices. Many also support virtual LANs (VLANs). A *virtual LAN* is a logical and administratively defined grouping of switch ports in the same broadcast domain. Multiple VLANs can be established in a broadcast domain.

VLANs are supported by *virtual switches* defined on a physical switch, and each virtual switch creates a new broadcast domain (a VLAN). Because traffic from one VLAN cannot pass directly to another VLAN via a Layer 2 switch, a Layer 3 switch or router is used to forward packets between VLANs. Devices in a VLAN can communicate with other devices in the same VLAN via its virtual switch at Layer 2.

Additional VLAN fundamentals are discussed in Appendix 4-5.

Network Bridges

A **network bridge** is a network device that connects two LANs or LAN segments and controls the transfer of data between them. When one or both networks are wireless, the bridge is called a *wireless bridge*. Today, bridges are not widely used, but they remain useful in some circumstances, including those that require a change from one type of communication medium to another.

Like a switch, a bridge bases forwarding decisions on MAC addresses. The bridge knows the MAC addresses of devices in both LAN segments or LANs and forwards a frame from one network to the other when the destination MAC address is not in the same network/segment as the source MAC address. Basically, a bridge uses a "forward if not local" forwarding decision.

Unlike switches, bridges are software rather than hardware based. Switches typically rely on application-specific integrated circuits (ASICs) to achieve faster forwarding speeds than is possible with the software used to implementing bridging. Also, switches have several forwarding modes, but bridges only perform store-and-forward forwarding without error checking. In addition, bridges do not support VLANs.

4.4.5 Physical Layer

The Data Link layer relies on the Physical layer to transfer data from one device to another over the local network's physical communication medium. Physical media are the "pipes" that carry the symbols (signals) that represent bits in Data Link layer frames. These pipes should not alter the symbols and bits that they carry, and destination devices are typically able to exactly reproduce the frames they receive.

Data transfer requires several elements:

- Physical media (e.g., cables) and associated connectors and interfaces
- The representation of bits on the media (symbols/signals)
- Transmitter and receiver circuitry on adapters and network devices

Control information (transmission framing) is added by some WAN transmission services to create Physical layer frames. This encapsulates Data Link layer frames in Physical layer frames.

Communication Functions

A Data Link layer frame is represented as a stream of bits (a *bitstream*) on physical transmission media. These bits are encoded as symbols/signals transported over a network's communication medium.

Signaling is arguably the most important communication function that the Physical layer performs. This involves creating the electrical, optical, or radio wave symbols/signals that represent bits in Data Link layer frames. Symbols/signals are sent sequentially on the network's communication medium, one at a time. Destination devices receive transmitted symbols/signals on the Physical layer link, identify the bits they represent, and pass the bits up to the Data Link layer as complete frames. This is conceptually depicted in Figure 4-25.

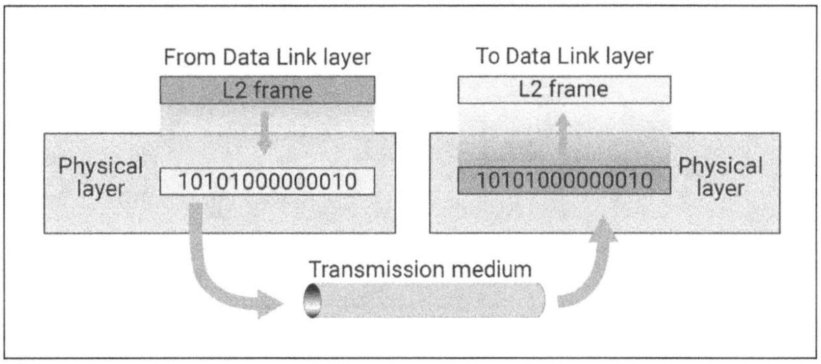

Figure 4-25: A conceptual depiction of Physical layer signaling and transmission framing.

Three basic types of physical media are used in local networks to transmit the representation of a frame's bits: copper cable, fiber optic cable, and wireless. Bit representation (the type of signal used to represent bits) is dependent on the medium that is used. On copper cables, the signals are electrical pulses. On fiber optic cables, the signals are light patterns. For wireless media, the signals are radio waveforms (waveforms in the radio wave portion of the frequency spectrum).

Transmission rate regulation and bit synchronization are other important communication functions at the Physical layer and are briefly described in Table 4-6.

Table 4-6: Some important Physical layer transmission functions.

Transmission Function	Summary Description
Transmission rate regulation	*Transmission rate* refers to the number of bits per second (bps) sent over the physical medium; it is also called the *bit rate*. This also defines the duration of a *symbol* (signal) on the medium. In data communications, a *symbol* is a waveform or transmission medium state that persists for a fixed time duration. Each symbol represents one or more bits. For example, if each symbol represents a single bit and the bit rate is 100 Mbps (100,000,000 bps), the duration of each symbol on the transmission medium is 0.00000001 seconds (one one-hundred millionth of a second). However, if the bit rate is 100 Mbps and each symbol represents four bits, each symbol's duration on the medium is 0.00000025 seconds.
Bit synchronization	A sender and receiver must be synchronized at the symbol level to ensure that the number of bits expected per second is the same as the transmission rate. The Physical layer synchronizes the transmission and reception of bits by providing a clock that controls both sender and receiver and thereby provides bit-level synchronization.

Data transfer between devices at the Physical layer has directionality. Directionality specifies the direction of the flow(s) of symbols/signals between devices. When one device is always the sender and the second device is always the receiver, the transmission mode is called *simplex transmission*. When both devices can be a sender or receiver, but cannot simultaneously send and receive, the transmission mode is called *half-duplex transmission*. When both devices simultaneously send and receive, the transmission mode is called *full-duplex transmission*. These modes are illustrated in Figure 4-26.

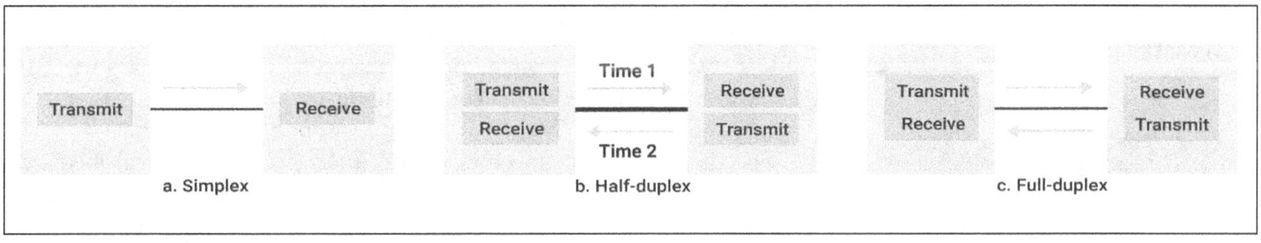

Figure 4-26: Conceptual depictions of simplex, half-duplex, and full-duplex transmission.

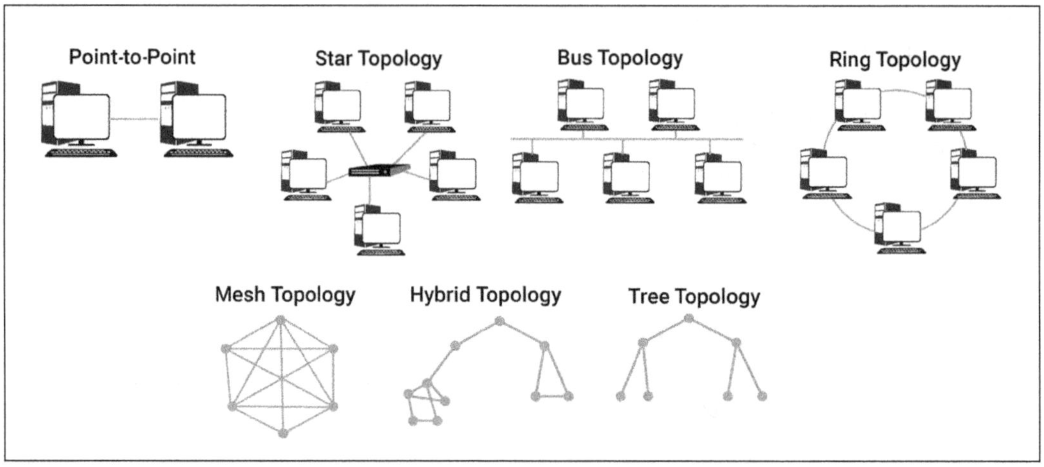

Figure 4-27: Examples of physical topologies in local networks.

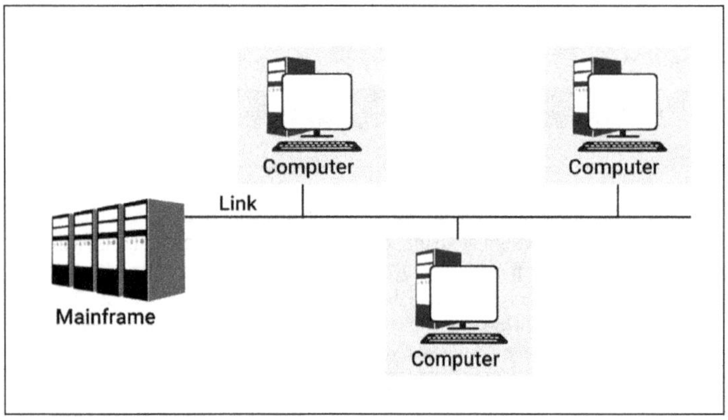

Figure 4-28: Example of a multipoint configuration.

Additional Physical layer considerations include physical topology and link configuration. **Physical topology** considers the interconnection structure of a local network. It includes the placement of devices and how the devices physically and logically transfer data. Examples of physical topologies in networks are illustrated in Figure 4-27. The star topology is most common in LANs.

Link configuration considers the number of devices that connect to a communication link. In a *point-to-point* configuration (like that in Figure 4-27), the link is a direct connection between two devices. In a *multipoint* configuration (like that illustrated in Figure 4-28), two or more devices share a single communication link to a specific destination device.

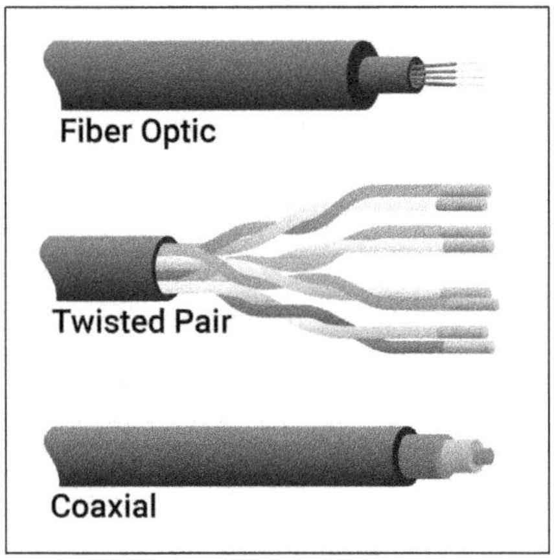

Figure 4-29: Examples of cables used in local networks. Source: hobrath/istock/Stock illustration ID:1059658092

Physical Layer Technologies

Cables are used for Physical layer connections in both wired and wireless networks. The three most common types are twisted-pair, coaxial, and fiber optic cables (see Figure 4-29). Twisted-pair and coaxial cables are copper-based cabling. Ethernet cables are twisted-pair cables. Fiber optic cable is used in LANs, backbone networks, and WANs. In LANs, fiber optic cables are primarily used to connect servers and routers to switches.

Connectors, located at the ends of cables, enable cables to be plugged into network adapter, switch, and router ports. Ethernet cables use RJ45 connectors (Figure 4-30a) to connect to device interfaces. LC, SC, and ST connectors (Figure 4-30b) are used on fiber optic patch cables.

Specifications for connectors, device interfaces, and physical media are addressed in Physical layer standards defined and maintained by electrical and communications engineering organizations, including the ISO,

NIST, and IEEE. Other organizations that have defined Physical layer standards include the International Telecommunication Union (ITU) and the Electronic Industries Alliance/ Telecommunications Industry Association (EIA/TIA). The nature of these standards and their applications are briefly discussed in Appendix 4-6.

Hubs, repeaters, amplifiers, media converters, modems, and analog-to-digital converters are other Physical layer technologies.

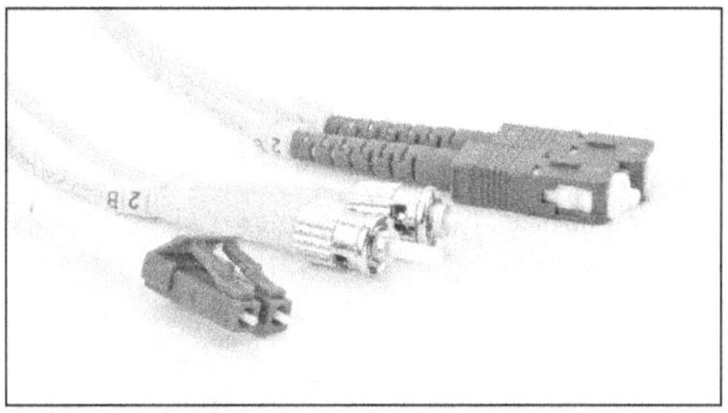

Figure 4-30: Example of an RJ45 Ethernet cable connector (left) and examples of LC, SC, and ST connectors (right) for fiber optic cables. Source (left): deepblue4you/istock/Stock photo ID:157532921. Source (right): Yanawut/istock/Stock photo ID:980935198

Physically, a hub resembles a switch (see Figure 4-31). Like a switch, a hub has a fixed number of RJ45 interfaces for Ethernet cable connections to devices. Prior to the widespread switch adoption, hubs were common in Ethernet LANs. Today, they are significantly less common and are primarily used to enable several devices to share a single cable connection to a switch.

Figure 4-31: A four-port hub. Source: Alysta/istock/ Stock photo ID:139984728

Hubs and switches are not interchangeable, and Figure 4-32 illustrates why. With a switch, when computer 1 sends a frame to computer 4, the switch reads the destination MAC address in the frame header, consults its forwarding table, and transmits the frame out the appropriate exit port. A hub would simply broadcast computer 1's frame on each of its ports (including the port on which the frame was received) and rely on connected devices to sort out the intended destination. Because it

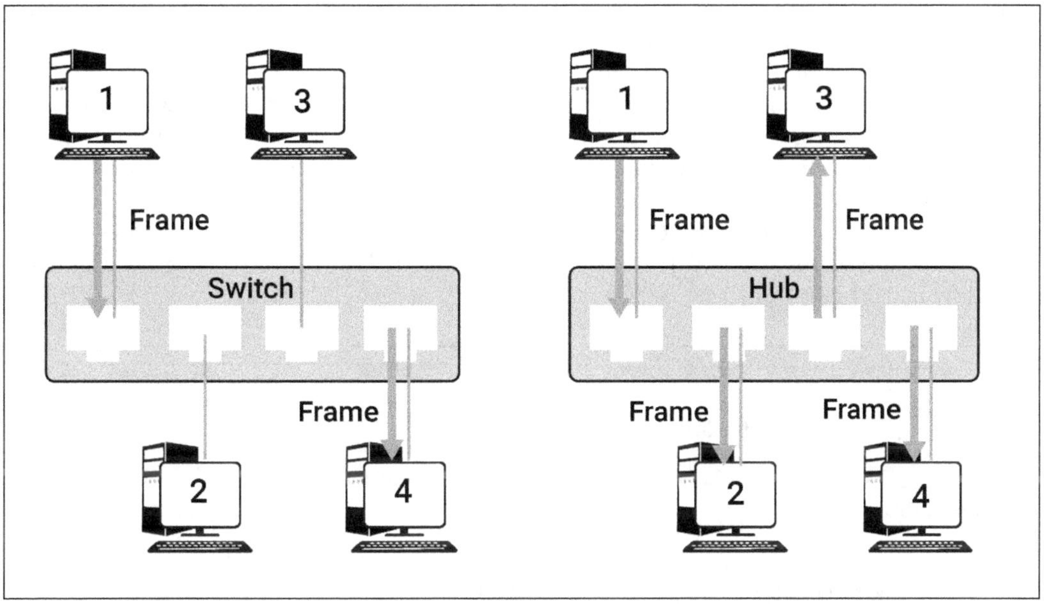

Figure 4-32: A conceptual depiction of the differences between hub and switch operations.

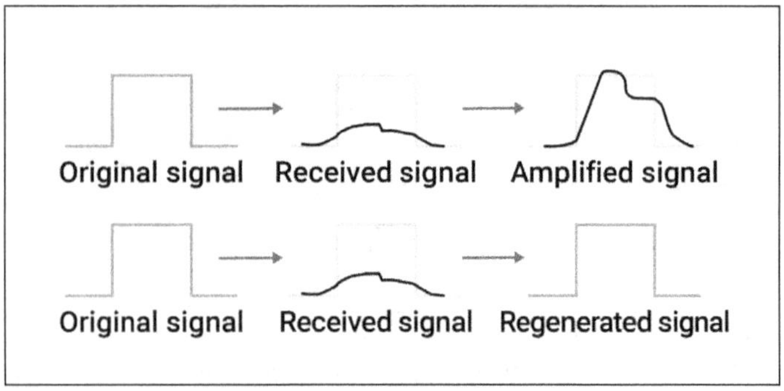

Figure 4-33: Signal attenuation, amplification, and regeneration.

doesn't read or use MAC addresses in frame headers, a hub is appropriately identified as a Physical layer technology.

Repeaters and amplifiers are used to strengthen signals on communication media. They are needed because the further signals travel on a communication medium, the weaker they become. Signal weakening is called signal *attenuation*, and it happens on all transmission media.

Differences between amplifiers' and repeaters' original and attenuated signals are illustrated in Figure 4-33. Amplifiers strengthen attenuated signals, even those that do not closely resemble the original signal. A repeater, however, strives to regenerate the original signal and restore it to its original form.

Figure 4-34: An example of a media converter.

Source: Artush/istock/Stock photo ID:187371047

Amplifiers and repeaters are used to extend the distance that signals can travel over communication media. To improve communication efficiency and reliability, regeneration and amplification capabilities are incorporated in many Physical layer and Data Link layer devices, including adapters, switches, hubs, media converters, modems, and codecs.

A **media converter** is a device used to connect transmission media that would otherwise be incompatible. In enterprise networks, media converters are primarily used to integrate copper and fiber cabling; however, some are used to convert from wired to wireless media.

Figure 4-34 provides an example of a media converter with an RJ45 port for an Ethernet cable and a SC port for a fiber optic cable. This device could receive a light pulse on the fiber optic cable and convert it to a corresponding electrical signal on the Ethernet cable.

Although less common today than in the past, a variety of modems remain in use, including dial-up modems, DSL modems, and cable modems. A *modem* (modulator/demodulator) converts (modulates) digital signals from a computing device's serial communication interface to analog signals transmitted on network circuits, and vice versa. Modems are always used in pairs (see Figure 4-35).

Analog-to-digital converters (ADCs) were introduced in Chapter 3. ADCs are widely used in IoT sensors to monitor analog data from their surroundings. They convert analog data/signals to digital signals (Figure 4-36).

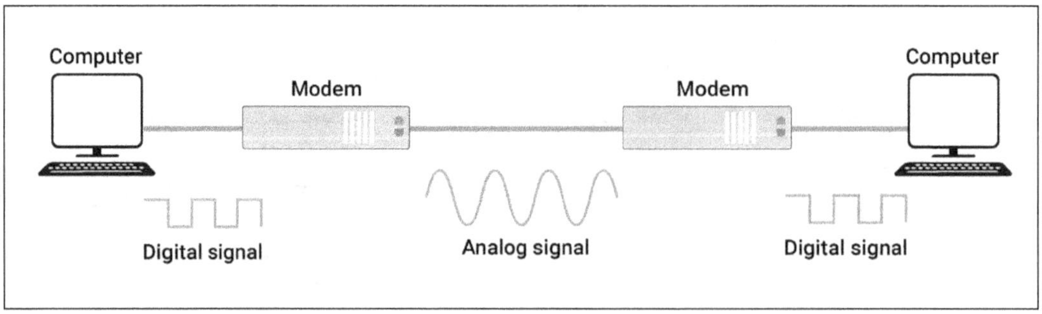

Figure 4-35: Signal modulation and demodulation.

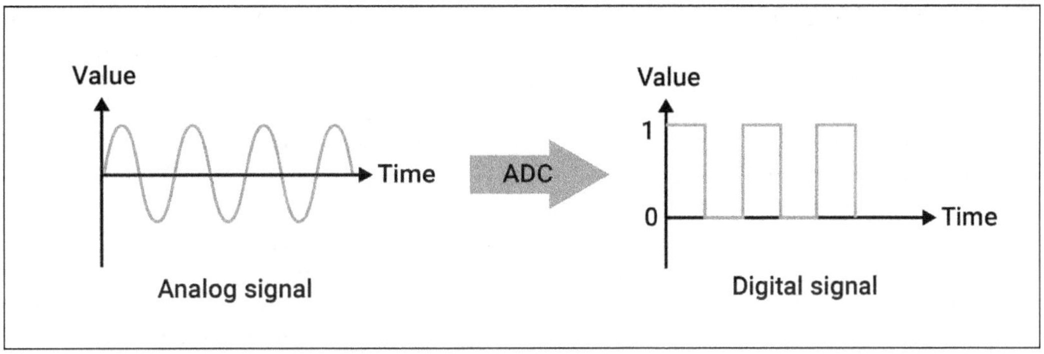

Figure 4-36: Signal conversion by an analog-to-digital converter.

Some *codecs* (coders/decoders) have ADC capabilities, but many simply convert analog data inputs into representative strings of bits that can be represented by what symbol/signal is used on the communication medium.

Like modems, codecs are used in pairs. The sending codec encodes the analog signal in a stream of bits that is used by the receiving codec to reproduce the original analog signal. The bitstream may be represented by digital signals on electronic circuits (such as Ethernet cables), light pulses on fiber optic cables, or radio (or other) waveforms on wireless media.

Physical Layer Security

An important first step to protecting Physical layer technologies is to limit access to a network's physical infrastructure, including network cabling and equipment, to authorized personnel. Anyone who gains access to the physical cabling and network equipment can compromise a network's integrity and security. Physical security also involves protecting network assets from theft, vandalism, natural and manmade disasters, and accidental damage.

When intruders succeed in gaining access to physical assets, they are positioned to "wiretap" traffic on transmission media and use the information they glean for other types of attacks. Hackers that succeed in attaching a packet sniffer (a program that can intercept and log network traffic) to a network may be able to bypass most of the other security safeguards deployed by network administrators, especially if data traffic is not encrypted.

MAC address filtering is security control that spans the Physical and Data Link layers. This involves identifying and maintaining a list of authorized MAC addresses. Such lists are used to control network access. Switches and wireless access points can be configured to ignore or discard frames from devices with MAC addresses that are not on the authorized list.

Protecting a network's physical assets is discussed more fully in Chapter 11.

SUMMARY

Enterprise network components map most directly to the EA technology architecture. Two layered communication models, the OSI and TCP/IP models, facilitate understanding of how networks work. These models influence networking standards and contribute to price competition among hardware manufacturers. Both models have distinct and largely independent layers that facilitate troubleshooting activities when communication problems occur and contribute to the development of applications with multi-tier software architectures.

The OSI model has seven layers and continues to serve as a useful reference for software developers that enables them to focus on applications without having to know the details of the networks that support them. The five-layer TCP/IP model is more protocol oriented but closely aligns with the Internet's dominant role in today's networks.

Application, Transport, Network, Data Link, and Physical layers are included in both the OSI and TCP/IP models. Network users interact with distributed applications at the Application layer, and messages/data exchanged by clients and servers are encapsulated (packaged) as PDUs at the Transport, Network, and Data Link layers by adding headers at each layer. The headers added by senders contain addressing and control information that informs how corresponding layers at receivers should handle the received message/data. Bits that represent Data Link layer frames are encoded as symbols/signals on the network's physical communication medium.

The TCP/IP model is considered a protocol stack because each layer above the Physical layer has layer-specific communication protocols. These protocols play important parts in the communication functions performed at each layer. HTTPS, SMTP, and DNS are examples of Application layer protocols; TCP and UDP are Transport layer protocols; IP and IPsec are Network layer protocols; and CSMA/CD and CSMA/CA are examples of Data Link layer protocols.

Networking technologies are frequently mapped to TCP/IP layers. For example, web and e-commerce servers, application firewalls, and load balancers are considered Application layer technologies, whereas routers, Layer 3 switches, and packet filtering firewalls are considered Network layer technologies. Layer 2 switches (e.g., Ethernet switches), Wi-Fi access points, and network adapters are important Data Link layer technologies, and cables, connectors, hubs, repeaters, and modems are examples of Physical layer technologies.

Security mechanisms can be deployed at all TCP/IP layers. For example, web application firewalls (WAFs) are used at the Application layer, and encryption can be deployed by applications at the Application layer, or via secure protocols at the Transport, Network, or Data Link layer. MAC address filtering can be used at the Data Link layer to prevent unauthorized devices from accessing the network and its assets. Physical access controls are commonly used to protect a network's servers, storage technologies, networking equipment, and cabling.

The communication functions, protocols, and networking/security technologies introduced in this chapter are described more fully in Chapters 5, 6, and 7. Chapter 5 provides a closer look at TCP/IP's Application, Transport, and Network layers. And Chapters 6 and 7 consider the Data Link and Physical layers for wired and wireless LANs.

KEY TERMS

Address Resolution Protocol (ARP)
Application layer switch
Application layer firewall
Connectionless service
Connection-oriented service
Content switch
Data encapsulation
Datagram
De-encapsulation
Hardware encryption
Host
Internet Protocol Security (IPsec)
Internet Control Message Protocol (ICMP)
Internet Group Management Protocol (IGMP)
Layer 2 switch
Layer 3 switch
Layer 4 firewall
Layer 4 load balancer
Layer 4 switch
Load balancing
Media converter
Multicasting
Network adapter
Network Address Translation (NAT)
Network bridge
Packet filtering
Physical topology
Port
Protocol data unit (PDU)
Reverse Address Resolution Protocol (RARP)
Router
Transport Layer Security (TLS)

REVIEW QUESTIONS

1. What aspects of enterprise networks are encompassed by EA's technical architecture?
2. Why are layer communication models valuable?
3. Identify the major communication functions performed at each layer of the OSI model.
4. What are *logical connections*, and why are they important?
5. What is a *host*? How are hosts identified in TCP/IP networks?
6. Briefly describe *data encapsulation* and *de-encapsulation* processes in TCP/IP hosts.
7. Identify several commonalities and differences between the OSI and TCP/IP models.
8. Identify examples of Application layer protocols for the TCP/IP model.
9. Briefly describe the characteristics of each of the following: load balancers, Application layer switches, and Application layer firewalls.
10. What is hardware encryption?
11. What is TLS, and how does it contribute to application security?
12. What communication functions are performed at the Transport layer?
13. What is a network port? What are well-known ports?
14. How do connection-oriented services differ from connectionless services?
15. How does TCP contribute to reliable data delivery? How does UDP differ from TCP?
16. What is a datagram? Identify examples of applications that use UDP.
17. What is SCTP, and how does it differ from TCP and UDP?
18. Briefly describe Layer 4 switches, Layer 4 load balancers, and Layer 4 firewalls.
19. What is *stateful packet inspection (dynamic packet filtering)*?
20. What communication functions does the Network layer perform?
21. Identify differences among IPv4, IPv6, and IPsec.
22. How does ICMP differ from IGMP? How does multicasting differ from broadcasting?
23. What communication functions do ARP, RARP, and routing protocols perform?
24. Briefly describe the characteristics of each of the following: routers, Layer 3 switches, IPsec gateways, NAT gateways, and packet filtering firewalls.
25. What communication functions are performed at the Data Link layer? What happens at the LLC and MAC sublayers?
26. What are access controls? Why are CSMA/CD and CSMA/CA important Data Link layer protocols?
27. Why are network adapters important Data Link layer technologies?
28. How do Layer 2 switches make switching decisions?
29. What are virtual switches? What are VLANs? What are network bridges?
30. What communication functions does the Physical layer perform?
31. Briefly describe each of the following: symbol, transmission rate, bit synchronization, transmission directionality, physical topology, and link configuration.
32. Briefly describe each of the following: cables, connectors, hubs, repeaters, amplifiers, media converters, modems, analog-to-digital converters, and codecs.
33. Briefly describe Physical layer security.

PROBLEMS AND EXERCISES

Exercise 4-1 Explain how (and why) an organization's technology architecture is influenced by its business architecture, data/information architecture, and application architecture.

Exercise 4-2 Wireshark is a widely used packet sniffing tool that is used to capture and analyze data traffic in TCP/IP networks. It can be downloaded from the Wireshark.org website (https://www.wireshark.org/download.html) for installation on personal computers and laptops with Ethernet or Wi-Fi adapters. If you lack access to Wireshark in a campus lab, download and install the current version on your personal computer or laptop. Learn Wireshark basics, navigation, and uses from online or printed tutorials such as the following:

- Sunny Dimalu the Cyborg. (2020). Wireshark Tutorial for Beginners (2022): From Absolute Basics | Packet Capture | Kali Linux [Video]. https://www.youtube.com/watch?v=DCqbOhWSFus
- Vinsloev Academy. (2020). Learn Wireshark in 10 minutes—Wireshark Tutorial for Beginners [Video]. https://www.youtube.com/watch?v=lb1Dw0elw0Q
- Viatto. (2019). How I Use Wireshark [Video]. https://www.youtube.com/watch?v=7CYpjf19GkA
- Orgera, S. (2020). How to Use Wireshark: A Complete Tutorial. Lifewire. https://www.lifewire.com/wireshark-tutorial-4143298
- Neasbitt, C. (n.d.). Wireshark Tutorial [Slideshow]. University of Georgia. https://cobweb.cs.uga.edu/~perdisci/CSCIx250-F15/Slides/wireshark_lecture.pdf

Launch Wireshark and capture packets going through your network adapter for 20 to 30 seconds. Click Protocol ( ) to sort your captured packets

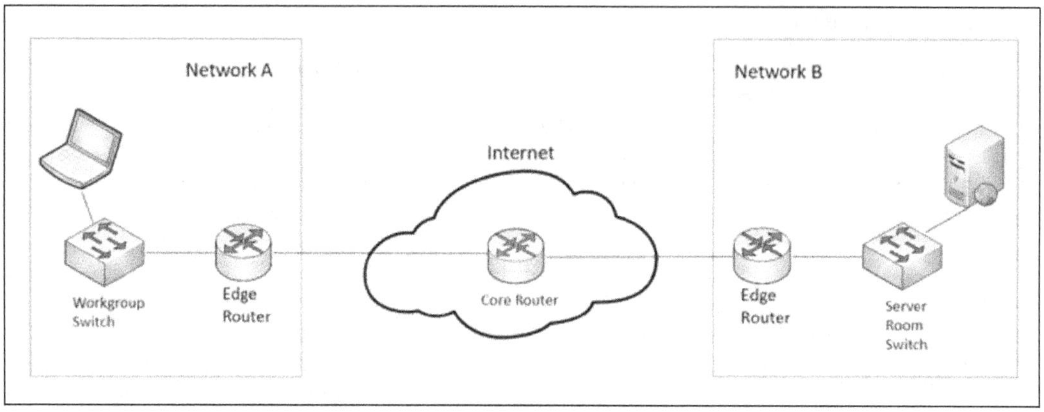

Figure 4-37: Internet connections between two networks.

TCP/IP Model Layer	Security Controls	Brief Descriptions	Recommendations & Reasons
Application			
Transport			
Network			
Data Link			
Physical			

alphabetically by protocol. (*Note:* Clicking Time will restore the packets to their original order.) List all the protocols included in your set of captured packets, associate each with its TCP/IP model layer, and identify protocols that were not mentioned in this chapter.

Exercise 4-3 Network diagrams are useful for visualizing network topologies and other networking concepts. Visio is a widely used tool for creating network diagrams. If you have access to Visio through your university, consult one or more online tutorials to learn how to use Visio to create network diagrams:

- Video: Create a Network Diagram (https://support.microsoft.com/en-us/office/video-create-a-network-diagram-a2360cd9-5c9d-4839-b4f6-17b485e02262)
- Use Visio or another network diagramming tool to re-create Figure 4-37.

Exercise 4-4 Create a table in a Word document that looks like the table above. In the Security Controls column, list at least three security mechanisms identified in this chapter for each layer. In the Brief Descriptions column, provide a two- to three-sentence description for each security control in your list. In the Recommendations & Reasons column, identify which security control at each layer you think is the most important to deploy and provide a two- to three-sentence reason for each of your recommended choices.

Exercise 4-5 Zero-trust security initiatives require authentication for every user and every device every time to grant access to the network or a network resource. Do some online research on zero-trust security that enables you to clearly describe how it works and how users and devices are authenticated. Map what you learn about zero-trust security to the layers of the TCP/IP model. Summarize the results of your research in a 500- to 750-word report or a four- to six-slide presentation. Specify a minimum of two online sources in a references section using APA or MLA format.

CHAPTER REFERENCES

Dominguez, J. A. (2002). An Overview of Defense in Depth at Each Layer of the TCP/IP Model. SANS Institute. Retrieved from: https://www.giac.org/paper/gsec/2233/overview-defense-in-depth-layer-tcp-ip-model/103817

Drury, A. (n.d.). Introduction to Content Switching—Application and Virtual Server Load Balancing via Deep Packet Inspection. Firewall.cx. Retrieved from: https://www.firewall.cx/networking-topics/general-networking/961-cisco-switches-content-switching.html

Highteck.net. (n.d.). OSI Physical Layer. Retrieved from: http://www.highteck.net/EN/Physical/OSI_Physical_Layer.html

Howtonetwork.com. (n.d.). Network Fundamentals—Layer 2 Technologies. Reality Press. Retrieved from: https://www.howtonetwork.org/design/ccda/chapter-1-network-fundamentals/network-fundamentals-layer-2-technologies/

Network Educator. (n.d.). Define Network Topology? Retrieved from: https://www.networkeducator.com/network-topology

OmniSecu.com. (n.d.). Five Layered TCP/IP Model. Retrieved from: https://www.omnisecu.com/tcpip/five-layered-tcpip-model.php

Sheldon. (2021). TCP/IP vs OSI: What's the Difference Between the Two Models? FS. Retrieved from: https://community.fs.com/blog/tcpip-vs-osi-whats-the-difference-between-the-two-models.html

SlideToDoc. (n.d.). Datalink Layer. Retrieved from: https://slidetodoc.com/datalink-layer-data-link-layer-provides-a-welldefined/

Solomon, M. G., & Chapple, M. (2005). Securing TCP/IP. In *Information Security Illuminated* (pp. 135–164). Jones and Bartlett. Retrieved from: https://samples.jblearning.com/076372677X/chapple06.pdf

Williams, L. (2023). TCP/IP vs OSI Model—Difference Between Them. Guru99. Retrieved from: https://www.guru99.com/difference-tcp-ip-vs-osi-model.html

Zimmerman, J., & Spurgeon, C. E. (2013). Ethernet Switches. O'Reilly. Retrieved from: https://www.oreilly.com/library/view/ethernet-switches/9781449367299/ch01.html

MINICASE: Professional Vision Clinic (PVC)

Professional Vision Clinic (PVC) is an optometry practice in a small city in the southeast United States. Over the last decade, the practice has grown from a single optometrist with six office personnel at a single location to a business that employs four optometrists (all with OD credentials), seven optometry assistants, and 23 office personnel in three locations in the city. The practice's patient/client base has also demonstrated significant growth, despite competition from more than a dozen other optometry practices as well as numerous opticians.

Technology has contributed to PVC's growth. The practice has been a trendsetter in the city in the deployment of optometry technology and has usually been the first to adopt and invest in digital optometry equipment (such as digital retina cameras) and optometry software solutions (such as optical point-of-sale, optometry practice management [for managing patient records], ophthalmology electronic health records, and vision billing [for filing insurance claims] software). The practice takes pride in being able to share digital images and electronic patient records across locations to enable its patients/clients to make appointments and receive the services that they need at whatever location is most convenient for them.

To minimize expenses, PVC has chosen to locate the servers and storage equipment that the practice needs in-house at its largest office location. The largest office has two LANs, one to serve desktop systems used by front-office personnel and in exam and patient consultation rooms and a second that connects digital optometry equipment to their servers. Each of the other two office locations have two LANs as well with a similar setup.

A high-level illustration of the major networking equipment at PVC's three locations is provided in Figure 4-38. The switches and router at each location are in a single rack. The main office includes a second rack that holds PVC's servers and storage devices.

During the last decade, PVC migrated from symmetric DSL (a type of DSL for business subscribers) offered by a local ISP to higher speed cable modem service from a different ISP. Three years ago, PVC transitioned from cable modems to 1 Gbps connections, and the connections are provided via fiber. Each location has a fiber to Ethernet media converter to support its wired LANs. Although Wi-Fi is provided at each location for the convenience of its patients, PVC does not use Wi-Fi to support its internal operations.

To avoid the expense associated with having an IT specialist on staff, PVC outsources its network support needs to a local IT services firm that specializes in providing support for the clients of the ISP that PVC uses. PVC has been satisfied with the firm's responsiveness whenever it has experienced internal or external connectivity issues; the firm quickly dispatches one or more service technicians and usually has someone on site and working to resolve the networking problem within 30 minutes.

Soon after installing and beginning to use digital retina scanning and other digital optometry equipment, PVC realized that storage would be an ongoing challenge. The company quickly exhausted its available storage capacity, and despite adding more storage devices and capacity, it did not take long for PVC to realize that storing all images and readings onsite would overwhelm its available space for networking hardware.

PVC currently uses hosted data storage from its ISP to address its burgeoning data storage requirements. Images captured during office hours at the different locations are aggregated on the storage equipment at the main office and are uploaded to the ISP's data center once a day, typically in the early evening. Over time, as the volume of data stored by the ISP has increased, so have PVC's storage costs. As a result, PVC is considering moving to a fully cloud-based storage solution using AWS or another enterprise storage solution provider with lower per-gigabit storage fees than their ISP.

Because PVC must sometimes share patient records and images with eye surgeons and other eye care specialists, the practice's patient records must comply with HIPAA requirements. Sometimes, such records and images are also needed for insurance claim filings. HIPAA requires encrypted data transmission among service providers and recommends, but does not require,

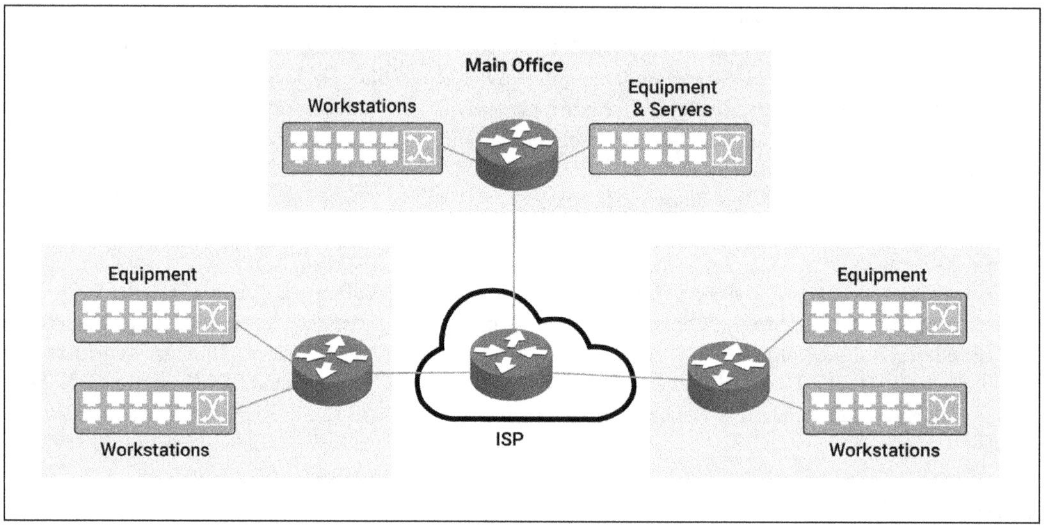

Figure 4-38: Connections among LANs across PVC's office locations.

encryption for stored data. Upon returning from a state optometry association conference, one of the practice's optometrists voiced the need to bolster the practice's security defenses at all defense in depth layers. She also recommended replacing routers with Layer 3 or Layer 4 switches to enable the creation of VLANs and to improve the overall performance of PVC's enterprise network.

PVC remains committed to being among the first adopters of advancements in digital optometry equipment and both front- and back-office optometry software solutions. It continues to be the most popular choice for optometry services in its community and thinks that its attitudes toward being an early adopter of technology are a driver of its success.

Minicase Questions

1. The company that provides the optometry software solutions that PVC is currently running in-house has announced a fully hosted cloud-based platform that includes all the solutions that the practice currently uses. Since this would be identical to what it currently has in place, PVC has begun the due diligence to compare the pros and cons of moving from its in-house system to the cloud-based system. Identify and briefly describe the major factors that PVC should consider before migrating to a fully hosted cloud platform.
2. TCP/IP clients are installed on all network-attached devices at PVC. As a result, the practice uses numerous protocols in the TCP/IP protocol stack.
    - Which Application layer protocols is PVC probably using?
    - Should PVC use TLS when sending retina scan images to/from servers at the main office? Why or why not?
    - Which TCP/IP Transport layer protocol is PVC most likely to use for communications between its main office and other locations? Why?
    - Which IP version is PVC most likely to use in its enterprise network? Why?
    - Are the routers at PVC's locations likely to support IPsec? Why or why not?
    - Which Data Link layer protocol(s) is/are used to support PVC's wired and Wi-Fi networks?
3. Identify and briefly describe the pros and cons of replacing PVC's routers with Layer 3 switches to support VLANs. Would replacing the routers be advisable if the Layer 2 switches at PVC locations had to be replaced with VLAN-compliant Layer 2 switches?
4. Identify at least one security mechanism that you think PVC should have at each layer of the TCP/IP model to protect its enterprise network. For each layer, briefly explain why you think PVC should have the security mechanism(s) that you have identified.

Chapter 5

Enterprise Networks and the Internet

LEARNING OBJECTIVES

After reading and studying this chapter, you should be able to:

- Briefly describe Internet architecture, autonomous systems (ASs), and Internet service providers (ISPs).
- Briefly describe Internet domains, domain names, and the Domain Name Service (DNS).
- Briefly describe the Dynamic Host Configuration Protocol (DHCP).
- Identify and briefly describe Application layer browser, file transfer, and email protocols.
- Identify and briefly describe communication functions that the Transport layer performs.
- Describe how TCP creates, maintains, and terminates communication sessions.
- Describe how UDP differs from TCP.
- Identify and briefly describe communication functions that the Network layer performs.
- Identify and briefly describe the characteristics and components of IP addresses.
- Briefly describe the differences between IPv4, IPv6, and private IP addresses.
- Briefly describe IPsec's Transport and Tunnel modes.
- Briefly describe dynamic routing and differences between distance vector, link-state, and path vector routing protocols.
- Identify and briefly describe several Transport and Network layer technologies.
- Briefly describe intranets and extranets.

5.0 INTRODUCTION: The Internet and Today's Businesses

The Internet is an important part of enterprise networks. Businesses leverage the Internet's publicly available infrastructure, protocols, and applications to support their processes and applications. Businesses also rely on the Internet to integrate cloud services with their intranets. The Internet facilitates the creation of sophisticated interorganizational systems, including SCM (supply chain management) and extranets, to support collaborative relationships with business partners that may be global in scope.

All types and sizes of businesses use the Internet as an e-commerce platform to sell products and deliver services. For tech companies, including Amazon, Google, and Instagram, the Internet is central to core business models. Internet marketing is commonly used to advertise products and services, and for some companies, the only form of marketing is digital marketing.

Businesses use Internet technologies and protocols to create private intranets for internal applications, collaborative communication platforms, and virtual desktops. They also support some enterprise system (ES) deployments.

It is mind-boggling to consider how today's businesses would operate without the Internet. Most business strategies focus on making more, not less, use of the Internet to support and improve companies' processes, operations, and competitiveness. Unplugging is rarely an option. The Internet has transformed many companies into e-businesses that interweave people, processes, and things.

The Internet is an ever-growing and evolving network of networks, and its many facets are challenging to fully grasp. However, considering its architecture and the communication functions that its primary protocols perform provides some of the scaffolding that is needed.

This chapter begins with a summary overview of Internet architecture, ISPs, and Internet domains, before taking a closer look at several Application, Transport, and Network layer protocols introduced in Chapter 4.

The formats and contents of Application, Transport, and Network layer headers are identified to provide insights into logical connections between corresponding TCP/IP layers in communicating hosts. This chapter also focuses on routing protocols, Transport and Network layer technologies and security, intranets, and extranets.

5.1 INTERNET ARCHITECTURE AND INTERNET SERVICE PROVIDERS

The Internet enables hosts in different networks to communicate and exchange data. Basically, any device with an IP address is a host, so "host" is a broad term that encompasses laptops, smartphones, tablets, desktop computers, servers, printers, wearables, IoT devices, and other devices. Most hosts access the Internet via a local network, such as a Wi-Fi or Ethernet LAN, but some gain access via WANs, such as mobile network operator (MNO) cellular networks (see Figure 5-1). Routers enable packets to be exchanged among LANs, WANs, and the Internet.

Interconnections among the networks that make up the Internet enable communication paths to be established between hosts in different networks. A sending host creates a *packet* (a Network layer PDU) by adding a header to each PDU passed down from the Transport layer. The header includes an IP address that identifies the destination host. Routers use the destination address to

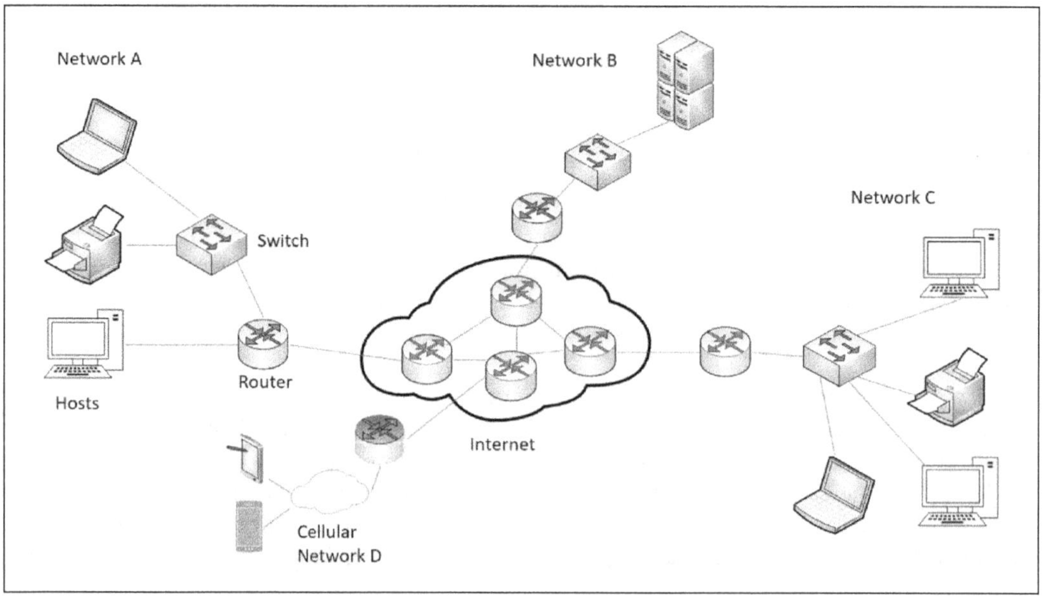

Figure 5-1: Some of the basic hardware components of the Internet.

make routing/forwarding decisions when transferring the packet to its destination. This process is facilitated by the Internet's architecture, which includes autonomous systems, ISPs, and domains.

Basically, the Internet is a global collection of separate, but interconnected, networks. Each network is part of a single administrative domain called an autonomous system (AS), and each host is associated with an AS. Architecturally, the Internet is a collection of ASs (see Figure 5-2).

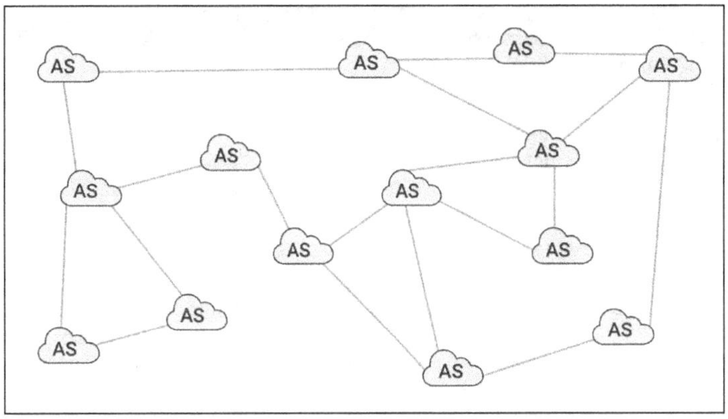

Figure 5-2: The Internet as a collection of autonomous systems.

5.1.1 Autonomous Systems

An **autonomous system (AS)** is a large network or group of networks that has a unified routing policy. Each AS is identified by a unique number assigned by the Internet Assigned Numbers Authority (IANA). An *AS routing policy* identifies the AS's *IP address space* (the list of IP addresses that it controls) and the list of the other ASs to which it directly connects. An AS appears to other ASs as having a single interior routing plan and identifies the destinations that can be reached through it. An AS uses Border Gateway Protocol (BGP) to announce its routing policy to the Internet.

IP addresses and BGP are considered the glues that bind the Internet's ASs together. IP provides a standard addressing scheme (IP addressing) and BGP provides the global routing framework.

An AS allocates IP addresses in its address space to the hosts in its network(s). Hence, a host is a member of an AS. When a host communicates with a host in a different AS, each packet that the sender creates traverses the Internet by hopping from AS to AS until it reaches the AS with the destination IP address. There, internal routers deliver the packet to the destination host.

A post office in a town provides a useful analogy for an AS. A piece of mail goes from post office to post office until it reaches the post office in the destination town. There, the post office delivers the mail to the correct address. Just as a town's post office is responsible for handling mail to/from the various addresses in the town, an AS is responsible for delivering packets to/from hosts with IP addresses in its IP address space.

Typically, each AS is operated by a single large organization, such as an Internet service provider (ISP), a large technology company, a university, or a government agency. Most ASs connect to several other ASs, but some do not. When an AS only connects to one other AS and shares the same routing policy, it may be considered a subnetwork of the AS to which it connects.

The range of IP addresses assigned to an AS or ISP is governed by the Internet Corporation for Assigned Names and Numbers (ICANN). The actual allocation of IP addresses to hosts within an AS or ISP's network is controlled by the AS or ISP. Additional information about ASs is provided in Appendix 5-1.

5.1.2 Internet Service Providers (ISPs)

An **Internet service provider (ISP)** is an organization (usually a company) that provides Internet connections and services to individuals and organizations. It provides Internet access for business and residential networks and some transit services for other ISPs. Each ISP is an AS, with its own business policies, internal network topologies, services, and customers/subscribers.

An ISP is the vehicle that enables businesses and individuals to access everything on the Internet. In addition to Internet access, ISPs may provide software (such as browsers), email services,

Table 5-1: Characteristics of Tier 1, 2, and 3 ISPs.	
ISP Category	**Brief Description**
Tier 3	Tier 3 ISP networks are primarily engaged in delivering Internet access to end customers. These are usually "last mile" providers that connect consumers to the Internet and service the connection to their home or office. They provide an "on-ramp" to the Internet for their business and residential customers via cable, fiber, DSL, or wireless access networks. Their coverage is limited to specific countries or subregions, such as a metropolitan area or a local community. Tier 3 ISPs may utilize and pay higher tier ISPs for access to the Internet.
Tier 2	Tier 2 ISPs provide connections between Tier 1 and Tier 3 ISPs. They typically have regional or countrywide reach, and they primarily provide transit services for smaller (Tier 3) ISPs. Transit basically means allowing data traffic to cross the ISP's network. In some markets, such as larger metropolitan areas in the United States, Tier 2 ISPs compete with Tier 3 ISPs in the provision of Internet connection services for end users. Tier 2 ISPs peer with other Tier 2 networks but also purchase IP transit from Tier 1 ISPs for full access to the Internet. Examples of Tier 2 ISPs include Comcast, Sprint Communications, Virgin Media, and Vodafone. Some Tier 2 ISPs provide Internet network infrastructure (e.g., fiber optic cabling) in regions that they serve.
Tier 1	Tier 1 ISPs are the networks that serve as the Internet's backbone; hence, they are sometimes called backbone Internet providers. Tier 1 ISPs provide other ISPs with access to the Internet backbone. They own and manage their operating infrastructure, including the intermediate devices (e.g., routers and switches) that make up the Internet backbone. Examples of Tier 1 ISPs include AT&T, Verizon, Sprint, NTT, Singtel, PCCW, Telstra, Deutsche Telekom, and British Telecom.

and streaming services (such as TV Everywhere). Many ISPs host business websites and provide platforms and tools used to build and maintain them.

ISPs have various organizational forms. Some are commercial, some are nonprofit, and some are community based and municipally owned. Some commercial ISPs are privately owned, and others are publicly traded.

ISPs also vary by the size of their footprint. Many are local and serve one or more communities in a small area. Others have much larger footprints, including those that serve locations in multiple states (in the United States) or are national, international, or global in scope. Some countries, like the United States, have thousands of ISPs, while others have fewer than five, and some only have one.

Because there are so many ISPs in the United States, it's useful to categorize them. While there are no official or strict category definitions, three tiers are commonly identified (see Table 5-1).

Some Tier 1 ISPs are also NSPs that provide access to the Internet backbone. A **network service provider (NSP)** is a business that builds and maintains the Internet's primary infrastructure, including fiber optic lines between Internet exchanges (IXs) and undersea cables uses to route Internet traffic worldwide. The circuits that NSPs provide typically have very high transmission speeds and bandwidths to enable seamless data flows among the Internet and ISP networks.

In the United States, most NSPs are commercial entities, such as AT&T and Verizon. In some countries, NSPs are owned and operated by the government, but some international NSPs are privately owned. In the United States, NSPs and ISPs are usually separate companies, but in some countries, they are not. For example, India's Tata Communications and the EU's Tele2 are both NSPs and ISPs.

Connections Among ISPs

ISPs connect to each other through network access points (NAPs), Internet exchange points (IXPs), and other public or commercial facilities on the Internet backbone. Because the Internet consists of a relatively complex set of interconnections among separate networks, rules are needed to manage the technical and business aspects of the connections. These rules focus on peering and transit.

ISPs that connect to other ISPs at the same tier and allow data traffic to pass for free over each other's circuits are called *peers*. Allowing data packets to/from peers to cross your network for free is called *peering*. Since the transit cost incurred by an ISP is usually roughly equal to that of another ISP at the same tier, exchanging payments with peers doesn't serve a useful business purpose.

There are two types of peering: private and public. In *private peering*, there is a direct connection between two ISPs over a Physical layer link, such as a fiber optic cable, and there is a bilateral agreement about data traffic exchanges that is exclusive to that pair of ISPs. A high percentage of the Internet's traffic is exchanged between Tier 1 ISPs via private peering agreements.

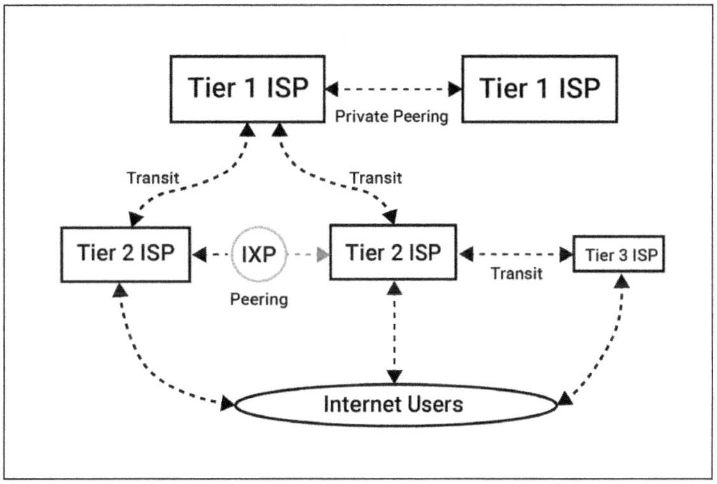

Figure 5-3: Depiction of ISP connections through peering and transit.

Public peering is the most common type of ISP peering. Historically, the first public peering exchange locations were *network access points (NAPs)*. Today, public peering occurs at both NAPs and approximately 250 nonprofit and commercial Internet exchange (IX) facilities worldwide. NAPs and IXs facilitate data traffic exchange among ISPs by consolidating connections for dozens or hundreds of ISPs (across all tiers) in a single physical location.

Like a NAP, an **Internet exchange point (IXP)** is a physical location through which Internet infrastructure companies such as NSPs can connect to ISPs, and ISPs can connect to other ISPs at the same tier or different tiers. Basically, an IXP is a collection of switches that forwards traffic between ISP networks. The way ISPs maintain an IXP's physical infrastructure and services using a cost-sharing arrangement is analogous to the arrangement that international shipping companies use for the Panama Canal and ports at which they load and/or unload cargo. An IXP shortens an ISP's communication paths to other ISPs and improves Internet access for its customers.

Transit is a simpler form of interconnection where Tier 1 ISPs and some large Tier 2 ISPs enable other ISPs to procure dedicated access to their networks via private leased circuit connections. Transit costs include both a fixed monthly cost for the leased circuit and a variable cost for data carried on the connection. For example, Tier 1 ISPs may have transit connections with Tier 2 and Tier 3 ISPs and receive monthly payments from them. A Tier 2 ISP may receive revenue monthly from transit connections with Tier 3 ISPs. Figure 5-3 illustrates transit and peering relationships.

Business Connections to ISPs

Businesses connect to ISPs in various ways. Like consumers, businesses often have several broadband service options for connecting to ISPs, including digital subscriber line (DSL), cable modem, fiber to the home (FTTH), and Gigabit Ethernet connections. Often, ISPs offer special services to businesses that are not available to other customers, such as T1 lines, OC-3 fiber optic circuits, and 10- or 40-Gigabit Ethernet services.

A business may have a single connection to an ISP or have single or dual connections to two or more ISPs (see Figure 5-4). These options are described in Table 5-2.

ISPs often have dual- or multihomed connections with other ISPs and IXPs. Cloud data centers typically have dual-homed, single multihomed, or dual multihomed connections to ISPs to ensure continuous access for their customers.

Adding links and routers increases the monthly ISP expenses but also increases the reliability

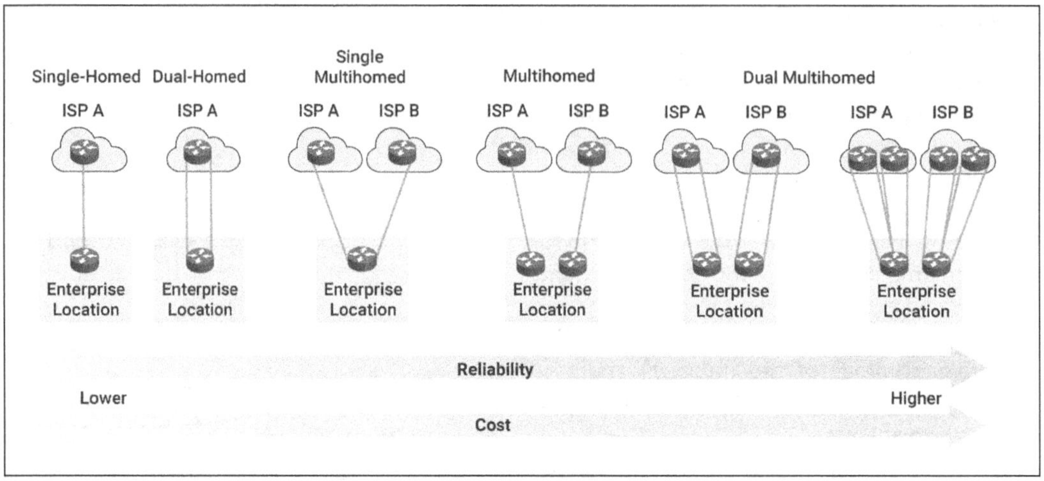

Figure 5-4: ISP connection options for businesses.

Table 5-2: Examples of business connections to ISPs.	
Connection Type	**Brief Description**
Single-homed	A business has a *single-homed* connection when it has a single link to a single ISP.
Dual-homed	A business has a *dual-homed* connection when it has two links to the same ISP.
Multihomed	*Multihoming* occurs when a business connects to two or more ISP networks.
Single multihomed	This occurs when a business's router supports single-homed connections to two different ISPs.
Dual multihomed	When a business has two edge routers at its locations and each router has a dual-homed connection to a different ISP, it has a *dual multihomed* connection.

of Internet access. Dual multihomed connections are among the most expensive options, but here, even when an ISP's entire network fails, the business can still access the Internet through the second ISP.

To manage costs, some businesses with dual- or multihomed connections use different types of circuits or connection services for their ISP connections. One of them, typically the one with the highest transmission capacity/speed (and cost) is the primary connection, and the lower capacity/speed (and less expensive) connection is a secondary or backup connection. In some cases, the secondary/backup connection is only used when the primary link is overloaded or fails.

5.1.3 Internet Domains and Domain Names

In networking, a **domain** is a logical organization of connected physical network resources and users that typically includes servers, desktops, printers, and other devices and provides a mechanism for authorizing and authenticating users for network access. Administrators can control which resources individual users can access and each user's level of access.

An **Internet domain** is also an administrative structure, in this case, one that is used for organizing, delivering, and accessing services on the Internet. *Domain* and *domain name* are often used interchangeably for Internet domains because the administrative structure governs how Internet domains are named.

Internet domains are set up in accordance with the Domain Name System (DNS). They are identified by unique IP addresses that make it possible for an Internet-connected device to

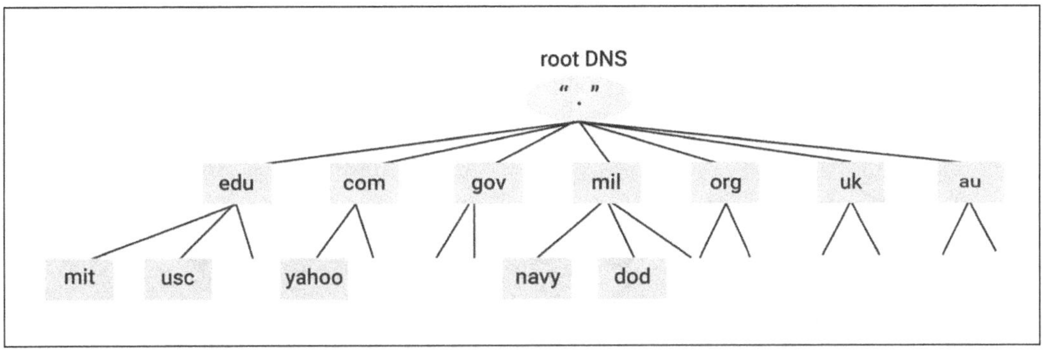

Figure 5-5: Examples of Internet domain top and second levels.

directly communicate with a specific domain. To further simplify such communications, the DNS uses a hierarchical naming structure that enables Internet users to access a domain's content by its domain name rather than its IP address. For example, DNS makes it possible for browser users who use Amazon.com to connect to Amazon's website without knowing Amazon's IP address.

By 2019, there were more than 330 million registered domain names. They identify networks, websites (e.g., Amazon.com), email services (such as Gmail.com), and other IP resources.

Internet domains are organized in a tree structure, and a given domain may include multiple subdomains. Top-level domain designations are administered by the IANA, and top-level domain names include purpose or geographic identifiers. For example, in Figure 5-5, *uk* is an example of a geographic commonality, and *com* is an example of a purpose commonality.

The second level of a domain name identifies an instance or network within the domain whose domain name is associated with a unique IP address. For example, in Figure 5-5, for mit.edu, *mit* identifies the second-level instance, and *edu* identifies the top-level domain.

Host naming schemes extend the Internet domain tree structure to subdomains and/or hosts within second-level domains. For example, for the host name *case.esa.georgiasouthern.edu*:

- edu is the top-level domain.
- georgiasouthern.edu is the second-level domain name for Georgia Southern University.
- esa.georgiasouthern.edu is a second-level subdomain that identifies the university's Department of Enterprise Systems & Analytics.
- case.esa.georgiasouthern.edu is the host name of a particular device in the esa.georgia southern.edu subdomain.

To be findable in the DNS, domain names must be registered. ICANN is the ultimate authority on domain names, and its designated registry operators are responsible for maintaining the database of second-level domain names. Domain name registrations are not permanent and must be renewed, usually on an annual basis. The registration process is described in Appendix 5-2.

Domain Name System

The **Domain Name System (DNS)** is a decentralized and hierarchical naming system for Internet-connected networks, services, hosts, and other Internet or IP network resources that provides translation services between domain names and IP addresses.

Its hierarchical system of globally distributed DNS servers acts as a giant directory for resolving domain names to IP addresses and IP addresses to domain names, regardless of where the domains are located. The DNS is comparable to an online directory that maps a person's name to a phone number or email address. Most importantly, it translates readable and easy to remember domain names into the numerical IP addresses needed for host-to-host communications.

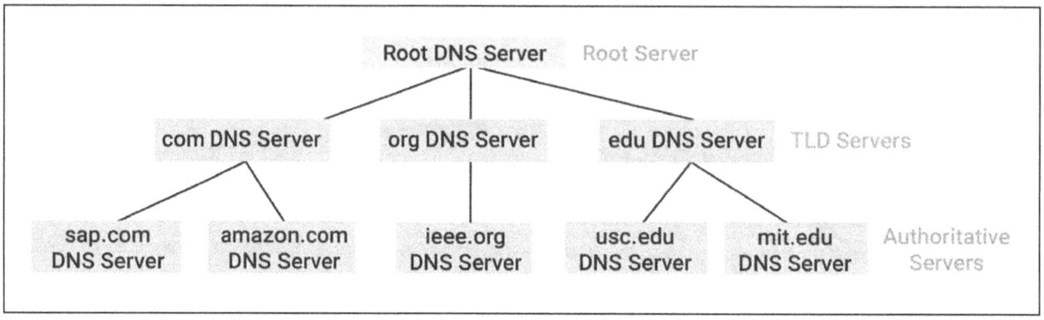

Figure 5-6: Examples of authoritative, top-level domain, and root servers in the DNS name server hierarchy.

The DNS implementation includes name servers and the DNS protocol. A **DNS name server** is a server that stores DNS records for a domain and responds with answers to queries against its database. Like the domain name hierarchy, DNS servers are hierarchically structured (see Figure 5-6) with root servers, top-level domain (TLD) servers, and authoritative servers.

Each name server is responsible for a subtree of the domain name hierarchy, called a *zone*, and includes and maintains DNS database records for its portion of the hierarchy. The hierarchical structure illustrated in Figure 5-6 can be extended to virtually any depth by delegating a portion of an authoritative server to a subordinate name server. For example, the mit.edu DNS server could delegate responsibility for portions of its domain name space to subordinate name servers associated with the university's major academic and research divisions.

As noted in Chapter 4, the DNS protocol is a TCP/IP Application layer that typically (but not always) uses UDP at the Transport layer. The protocol governs communication exchanges between hosts and DNS servers and often gets credit for domain name to IP address translations.

A host in a TCP/IP network is configured with a DNS client and the IP address of one or more local DNS servers to enable it to utilize the DNS. A local server is sometimes called a DNS *resolver* because it includes software for extracting information from other name servers in response to client requests. A typical client request is for the IP address for a specific domain or subdomain name.

Multiple steps can be involved in responding to a client request. Figure 5-7 illustrates an eight-step process (described in Table 5-3) where the involvement of a DNS root server is required; however, fewer than eight steps may be needed. UDP facilitates the rapidity of the process, regardless of how many steps are needed.

To keep up with Internet growth and changes, the DNS database is updated continuously. This requires DNS name servers to send updates to other servers when new second-level domains or subdomains are added to the domain name hierarchy and when other name changes occur.

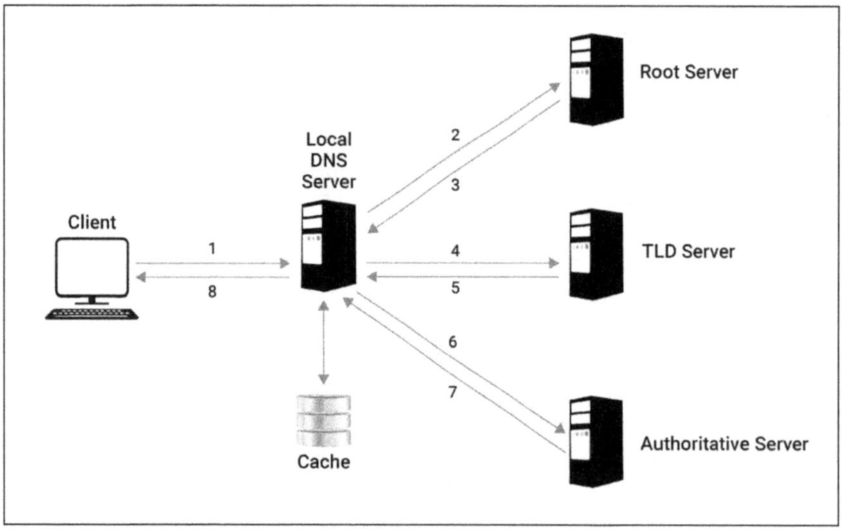

Figure 5-7: Typical steps the DNS uses to respond to client requests.

Table 5-3: Description of steps in Figure 5-7 and how they would be used to identify a specific IP address.

Step #	General Description	Role in Finding IP Address for CNN
1	The client sends a request to the local DNS server for the IP address for a domain name. The local DNS server's resolver software checks to see if the domain name and its IP address are in its cache or database. If it has the IP address, it returns it to the client; if it does not, it queries other name servers until the IP address is identified.	The client sends a request to its local DNS server for the IP address for CNN.com.
2	If the domain name is not in the local DNS server's cache or database, the server sends a query to a root server.	If the local name server does not have CNN.com in its cache, it sends a query to a root server responsible for the .com domain.
3	The root server returns the name and IP address of a top-level domain (TLD) server responsible for the destination host's domain.	If the root server does not have CNN in its database, it refers the local DNS server to a TLD server for the .com domain.
4	The local name server sends a query to the TLD server identified by the root server.	The local DNS server sends a query to the .com TLD server.
5	If the TLD server knows the domain name, it returns the IP address to the local DNS server. If not, it returns the name and IP address of an authoritative server to the local name server.	If the .com TLD server does not have CNN.com in its database, it refers to the local name server for an authoritative server for the CNN.com domain.
6	The local DNS server sends a query for the IP address to the authoritative server.	The local name server sends a query to the authoritative server for CNN.com.
7	The authoritative server returns the IP address for the domain name to the local name server.	The authoritative server returns the IP address for CNN.com to the local DNS server.
8	The local DNS server adds the domain name and IP address to its cache and sends the requested IP address to the client.	The local DNS server adds CNN.com to its cache and returns the IP address to the client.

5.1.4 Dynamic Host Configuration Protocol (DHCP)

For stability and efficient functioning, permanent IP addresses are often assigned to important network components such as servers and routers. IP addresses are usually not permanently assigned to Internet user devices. Most of these devices are allocated a temporary IP address that may change over time; it is dynamic.

The Dynamic Host Configuration Protocol (DHCP) is a TCP/IP Application layer protocol that is used to allocate IP addresses to hosts. It was developed to alleviate issues associated with the limited number of assignable IPv4 addresses (a little more than 4 billion) and an ever-growing number of Internet-connected devices.

Private IPv4 addresses continue to be widely used in residential Wi-Fi networks, and DHCP is widely used in these networks to allocate private IP addresses to connected devices. In many Wi-Fi networks, device connections are temporary, and device users often jump between online and offline applications. Hence, it makes sense to use DHCP.

TCP/IP host configurations include the IP address of the DHCP server for the local network; in a residential Wi-Fi network, the Wi-Fi router is typically the local DHCP server. The DHCP protocol is used when a device logs on or joins the network and needs an IP address. A DHCP server manages a pool of IP addresses, and when a device logs off or is idle, its IP address can be returned to the pool and potentially be assigned to another device. This arrangement enables a network to accommodate many devices with a limited pool of assignable IP addresses.

DHCP is a client request/server response protocol in which a client that needs an IP address can send a request when booting up, returning from sleep mode, or joining a network. In addition to an IP address, a DHCP server may provide clients with other important network parameters, such as the IP addresses of the local DNS server and router. The client-server communication exchange is illustrated in Figure 5-8; it is supported by UDP at the Transport layer.

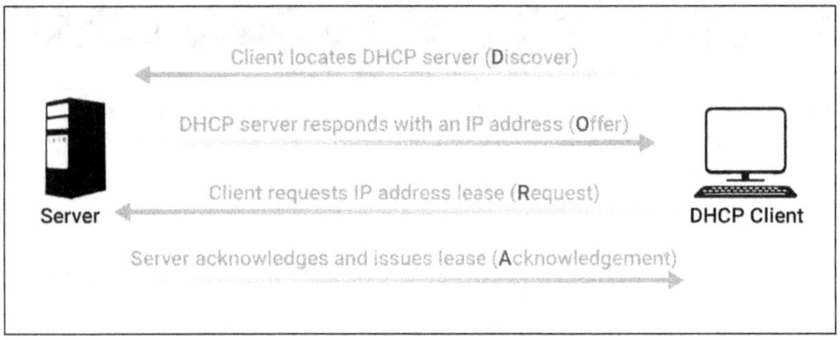

Figure 5-8: DHCP client-server message exchange.

The process begins when the client broadcasts a DHCPDISCOVER message to request an IP address. A DHCP server responds with a DHCPOFFER message that includes an IP address and other important configuration parameters. The client responds to the Offer message with a DHCPREQUEST indicating its acceptance of the offered IP address. The server then sends a DHCPACK message that acknowledges the client's acceptance of the IP address.

Clients "lease" their assigned IP addresses for specific amounts of time. If the client device is still active when the lease expires, it sends a Request message to extend its lease on the IP address.

DHCP is an important behind-the-scenes support protocol in TCP/IP networks that facilitates network operations. Technically, it is an Application layer protocol, but its greatest effect is at the Network layer, where sending hosts construct IP packets.

5.2 APPLICATION LAYER PROTOCOLS

As noted in Chapters 2, 3, and 4, distributed client/server applications are common in enterprise networks. Some are tailored to the unique needs of specific organizations, but others are general purpose and are supported by Application layer protocols, such as those introduced in Chapter 4. This section provides a closer look at web browser, file transfer, and email protocols.

5.2.1 Web Browser Protocols

HTTP

Hypertext Transfer Protocol (HTTP) is a transaction-oriented client-server protocol that was created to support distributed applications that include hypertext. *Hypertext* is text that contains links to other text. Hypertext documents are interconnected by hyperlinks. A *hyperlink* enables a user to jump to another hypertext document via a screen touch, mouse click, or other link selection action.

The HTTP protocol governs the transfer of information required to make hypertext jumps. It can also be used for various types of data transfers, including text, hypertext, image, audio, video, and other Internet-accessible data/information.

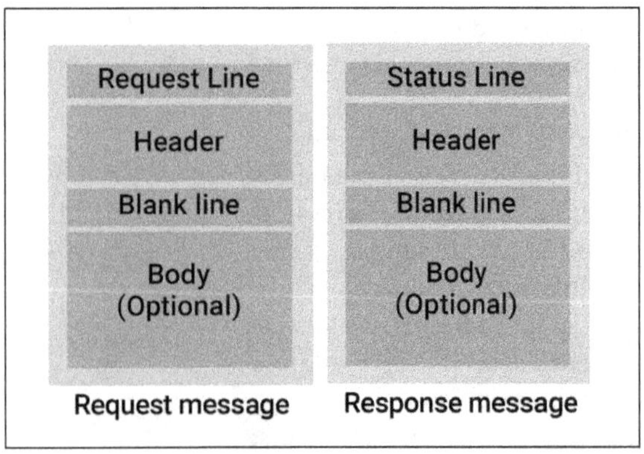

Figure 5-9: An overview of the formats of HTTP request and response messages.

HTTP supports transactions between web browsers and web servers. Although it uses TCP to provide reliable connections between clients and servers, HTTP is a *stateless protocol.* This means that the server is not required to track or retain session or status/state information about the client requests it handles. Each client request is executed independently, without knowledge of prior requests from the same client.

Two types of messages are used in HTTP transactions: request messages and response messages. The general formats of both messages are illustrated in Figure 5-9. When the client requests a web page, "GET" is included in the Request Line and the URL of the web page is included in the Header field. The requested web page is included in the Body of the web server's response message. Appendix 5-3 considers transactions between web browsers and web servers in more detail.

HTTPS

Hypertext transfer protocol secure (HTTPS) is a secure version of HTTP that uses encryption for data transfer security. Today's web browsers typically flag non-HTTPS websites as insecure to dissuade users from connecting to them.

Technically, HTTPS is not a separate protocol from HTTP, and the formats of request and response messages are the same. The basic difference is HTTPS's use of TLS/SSL encryption. TLS/SSL certificates are used to verify website authenticity, and encryption secures message exchanges.

The TLS protocol was introduced in Chapter 4. It uses asymmetric encryption and public key infrastructure (PKI) to secure data transfers. Asymmetric encryption and PKI are described in Chapter 11.

A TLS/SSL handshake is used to establish a secure connection between the client and web server. During this process, the client receives the website's TLS/SSL certificate, which contains the site's public key. The client uses the public key to encrypt request messages and to decrypt web server response messages.

5.2.2 File Transfer Protocols

Because the HTTP protocol can be used to transfer text, hypertext, audio, images, video, and other Internet-accessible information, HTTPS is used to transfer a wide range of files in today's networks. However, other file transfer protocols exist and are sometimes used for file transfer.

File Transfer Protocol

File Transfer Protocol (FTP) is a TCP/IP Application layer protocol that was created to support file transfers. It is a client-server protocol that uses two separate connections between a client and a server: one for data transfer, and the second for the exchange of control messages before, during, and after file transfers.

Like HTTP, FTP uses unencrypted (plaintext) messages. This makes it vulnerable to sniffing or interception, especially over insecure connections such as public Wi-Fi connections. Some applications require users to provide a username and password to authenticate, but anonymous connections to servers are also allowable.

Because of security vulnerabilities, FTP is rarely used today. As of 2021, it was no longer supported in many web browsers, including Firefox and Chrome. It has been replaced with HTTPS and more secure versions of FTP, including FTPS, FTP over SSH, and SFTP, that employ encryption to protect message exchanges and file transfers. Because two of these, FTP over SSH and SFTP, use SSH, it is briefly summarized below.

SSH

Network administrators use Secure Shell (SSH) to remotely manage applications and systems. It enables them to log in to remote computers, execute commands, and move files from one computer to another. SSH has replaced insecure terminal emulation and login applications such as Telnet and is used instead of FTP for file transfers.

SSH employs the client-server communication model and includes a suite of security-oriented utilities that require strong passwords, public key authentication, and encrypted message exchanges. SSH is widely used because of its encryption and versatile set of utilities.

SSH is used in enterprise network and cloud data centers and is supported by data center servers and networking technologies. SSH is used for secure remote access to computing resources, remote execution of commands, delivery of software updates/patches, and other network management tasks, including the management of routers, servers, SSH clients, virtualization platforms, and backup processes.

FTP versions that use SSH are described in Table 5-4. FTPS, which uses TLS, is also described.

Table 5-4: Secure versions of FTP.

Secure FTP Protocol	Key Characteristics
FTP over SSH	FTP over SSH adds security to FTP by establishing an SSH tunnel between a client and an FTP server prior to data transfer. Once established, FTP handles the data transfer, and the SSH tunnel ensures the security of the data in transit. Because it is challenging to set up and use two FTP ports, FTP over SSH is less widely used than SFTP or FTPS.
SSH FTP or Secure FTP (SFTP)	SFTP is an SSH extension that secures data transfer between an SFTP server and an SFTP client over any reliable data stream. SFTP assumes a secure communication channel, such as an SSH tunnel, after the SFTP server has authenticated the client. Because it only requires a single port (22) to establish a connection between a client and server, SFTP is easier to implement than FTP, FTPS, or FTP over SSH. Because SFTP is one of the most widely used protocols for remotely accessing and transferring files over the Internet, it is described in more detail in Appendix 5-4.
FTP Secure (FTPS)	FTPS is an extension to FTP that adds security via TLS. It supports both TLS and SSL (Secure Sockets Layer) cryptographic protocols, server-side TLS/SSL certificates and PKI, and client-side authorization certificates. FTPS also supports numerous widely used encryption ciphers. Like HTTPS, FTPS servers provide a public key certificate when establishing connections to clients. If the server's certificate is not signed by a trusted CA, the FTPS client generates a warning that prompts the user to accept or reject the connection.

5.2.3 Email Protocols

Common email protocols in use include SMTP, IMAP, and POP. SMTP is a protocol that is more oriented toward transferring outgoing messages to email servers, whereas IMAP and POP are oriented toward retrieving incoming messages from email servers.

SMTP

SMTP (Simple Mail Transfer Protocol) is a TCP/IP Application layer protocol that mail servers use to send, receive, or relay email between email senders and recipients. When an Internet user creates an email message, SMTP is used to send it to the user's email server. The server determines the destination, establishes a connection to the email server in the destination network, and uses SMTP to relay the message to the destination server (see Figure 5-10).

Since its introduction in the early 1980s, SMTP has been updated, modified, and extended numerous times. The current version provides extensions for authentication, encryption, and international email exchange.

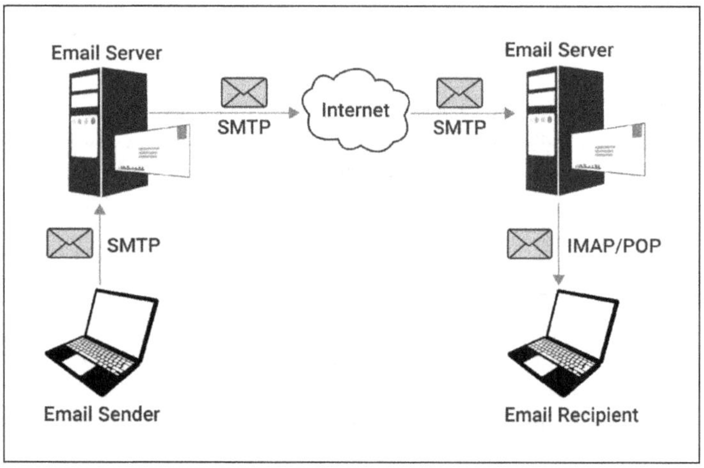

Figure 5-10: Role of SMTP in Internet email.

SMTP is a connection-oriented Application layer protocol that TCP typically supports. An SMTP communication session consists of commands originated by an SMTP client or server and responses from an SMTP server.

An *email client* (a *mail user agent [MUA]*) needs to know the IP address of the email server to establish a communication session with it. This address is included in the client's configuration and is often listed/specified as a DNS server.

The software on an SMTP server that receives outgoing email messages from clients is called a *mail submission agent (MSA)*. For security, email clients use TCP port 587 to transfer outgoing encrypted messages to the server; however, many servers also accept unencrypted (plaintext) email messages from clients on port 25.

The MSA delivers the email message to its *mail transfer agent (MTA)*, the software used to relay email to the destination SMTP server. Often, the MSA and MTA agents run on the same server, but different machines can be used.

To handle incoming email messages from other servers, SMTP servers also have *mail delivery agent (MDA)* software that saves messages in the mailbox format that the server uses. Once messages are delivered to the destination email server, they are stored for batch retrieval by authenticated email clients (MUAs) using Internet Message Access Protocol (IMAP) or the Post Office Protocol (POP)—see Figure 5-11.

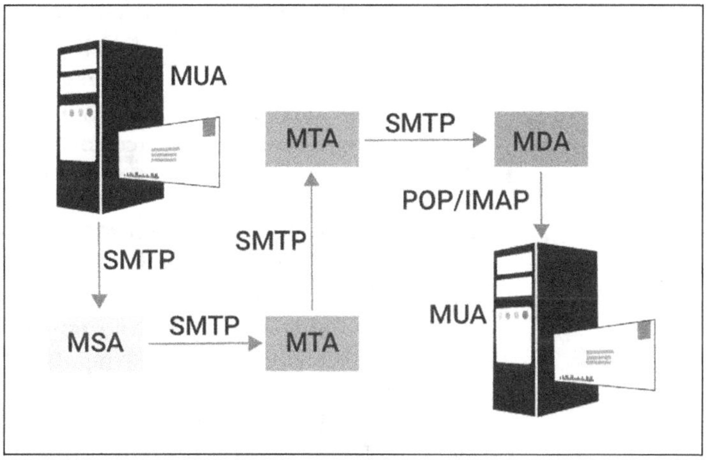

Figure 5-11: Host-to-host email transfers using SMTP.

SMTP is essentially a delivery protocol. In normal use, email is "pushed" to a destination mail server as it arrives. The routing of email messages is based on the destination server, not on the individual email users to which messages are addressed. Other protocols, such as IMAP and POP, enable email users to retrieve messages from servers and to manage their email boxes.

In today's enterprise networks, SMTP servers typically require client authentication before access is granted. This enables email users to log in and access their email from multiple devices and locations. *SMTP AUTH* is an SMTP extension that provides client authentication at login.

IMAP and POP

IMAP is a TCP/IP Application layer protocol that allows an email client to access email on an email server. Incoming email messages to an email server are stored in client email boxes. Each client retrieves/downloads messages using an email retrieval protocol, which today would most commonly be IMAP or POP.

Email clients using IMAP generally leave messages on the server until they are deleted. With IMAP, messages remain on the server after retrieval and must be explicitly deleted by email users. IMAP has largely replaced POP for email retrieval and management.

POP also supports download and delete operations for email messages. In its original form, POP clients would connect to the email server, retrieve all messages, store them on the client computer, and delete them from the server. The current version, POP3, gives clients the option of leaving email messages on the server after download.

5.3 TRANSPORT LAYER FUNCTIONS AND PROTOCOLS

The Transport layer links applications to the networks on which they are used, serves as a communication intermediary between applications and networks, and frees applications from having to know networking or communication protocol details. It provides applications with an abstraction of network connections and enables application developers to focus on their applications without having to worry about how networks support them.

The Application layer protocols described in sections 5.1 and 5.2 rely on Transport layer protocols for message/data transfers. As noted in Chapter 4, the Transport layer supports both connection-oriented and connectionless communication exchanges between clients. TCP is used with connection-oriented applications that require reliable data exchanges. UDP is used for connectionless applications where speed is preferred over reliability.

Both TCP and UDP use port numbers to identify applications and services. When a sending host creates a Transport-layer PDU, it adds a TCP or UDP header to the data passed down from the Application layer. The header includes Source Port and Destination Port fields (see Figure 5-12). The Destination Port identifies the application that should receive the data. For some applications, the numbers in the Source Port field may be random, arbitrary, and meaningless. Destination ports, however, are usually well-known port numbers in IANA's registry.

5.3.1 Transmission Control Protocol

TCP provides host-to-host connectivity and reliable data exchanges. Today, most Internet users have multiple applications simultaneously running on their devices. Once opened, an email application may continuously retrieve incoming messages from the email server. Similarly, web browsers often remain open to facilitate rapid access to favorite websites or search engines.

Connections to streaming applications (such as those for music or sporting events) may be persistent to enable users to monitor their streams as they do other online or offline computing tasks. When an Internet user uses numerous applications at the same time, it is the responsibility of the Transport layer to ensure appropriate data and message deliveries.

TCP and UDP headers include more than source and destination port fields (see Figure 5-12). To provide reliable data transfers, TCP headers have more fields than UDP headers. These additional fields contribute to TCP segmentation and session management activities, which are essential to TCP's provision of reliable data transfers.

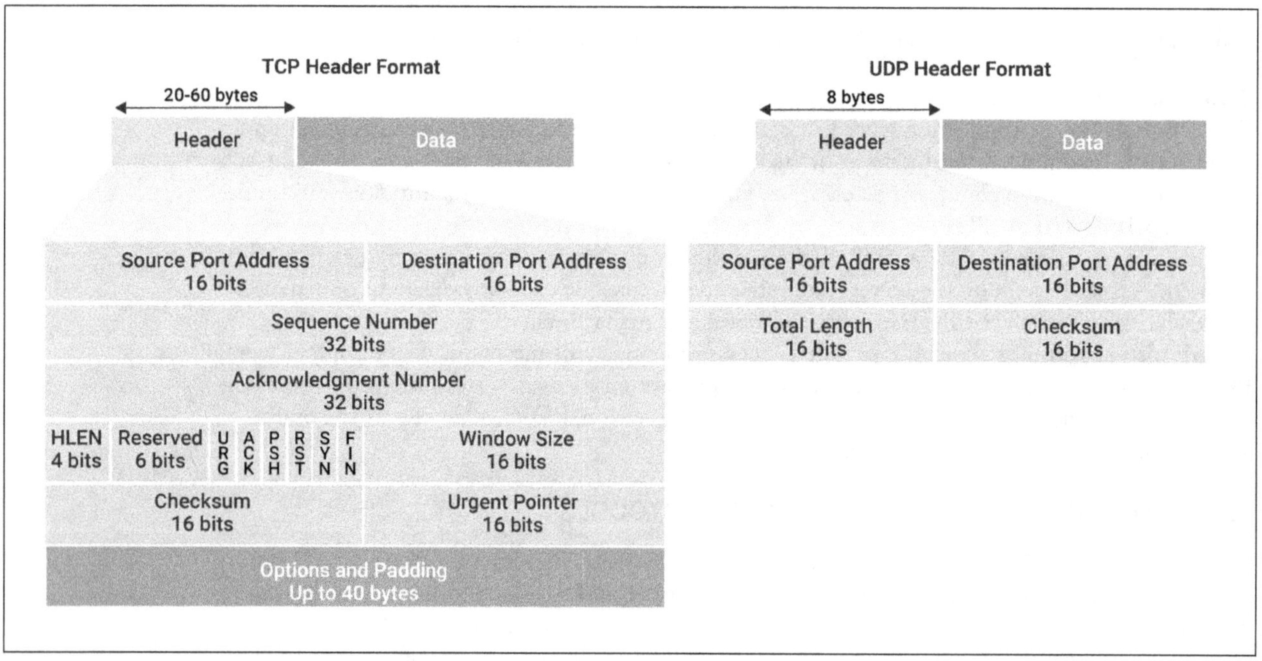

Figure 5-12: The formats of TCP and UDP headers.

Segmentation

Some application messages and data blocks are small enough to be transmitted in a single Data Link layer frame, but others are too large and must be broken into smaller pieces to fit into multiple frames. Application data is broken into smaller pieces at the Transport layer of senders' hosts and can be recombined by the Transport layer of receivers.

The process used to break application data into pieces is called **segmentation.** The segmentation process ensures that an application's outgoing messages or data is divided into pieces that will fit into the local network's Data Link layer frames.

When determining segment size, TCP considers the sizes of the header fields that will be added at the Transport, Network, and Data Link layers. However, it is unaware of frame sizes in the destination host's local network; a host's segment size determination also involves negotiations with the destination host when TCP connections are established.

A TCP header, like that illustrated in Figure 5-12, is added to each application data segment (see Figure 5-13). The Sequence Number field in the TCP header enables senders to number the segments they create and is used to ensure segment delivery to receivers.

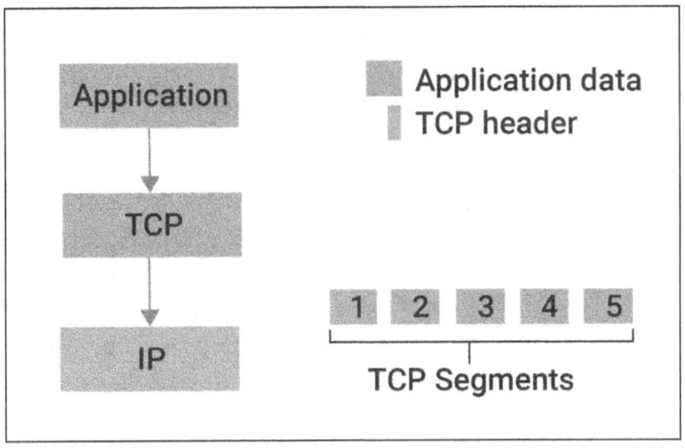

Figure 5-13: TCP segmentation and application data encapsulation.

When incoming segments are received, TCP is responsible for delivering them to the appropriate application. Some applications require segments to be recombined into their original message or data block before being delivered. Others require the delivery of segments as they arrive.

Web browsers usually want segments to be delivered as they arrive. This explains why the initial display of a requested web page may have a fuzzy appearance that comes into focus as additional segments are delivered to the browser. In contrast, email clients usually only retrieve and display fully intact messages after all segments have been received and recombined.

Session Management

In TCP/IP networks, a *session* is considered a conversation between two hosts, such as a client and a server. TCP establishes, maintains, and terminates sessions. It conducts the "handshaking" involved with establishing and terminating the logical host-to-host connections, and from the time a session is established to when it is terminated, TCP manages/maintains the session to ensure that all data that a sender transmits is delivered to the receiver.

Once a session is established, the sender transmits its segments in sequential order until all have been delivered to the other host. After all data has been transferred, the session termination process is initiated. Between sessions, servers usually enter a "listening" mode, during which they wait for a client connection request.

Session Establishment

In TCP/IP networks, a *handshaking* process is used to establish a session. Three segments/frames are exchanged in a *three-way handshake* (see Figure 5-14) that is described in Table 5-5. SYN and ACK fields in TCP headers (Figure 5-12) are important in session establishment.

Sequence number determination, maximum segment size, and window size (the amount of data the receiver is willing to store in its buffer) are other parameters shared between hosts during the three-way handshake.

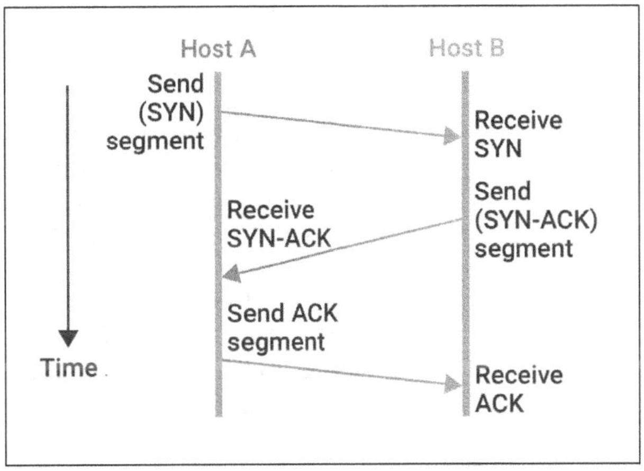

Figure 5-14: TCP's three-way handshake for establishing host-to-host sessions.

Table 5-5: Explanation of session establishment in the three-way handshake.	
Step	**Description**
1	The handshaking process begins when the session-initiating host sends a SYN (synchronize) segment to the destination (remote) host. This TCP segment is a connection request. This segment also identifies the sequence number to be used when the upcoming data transfer begins.
2	The remote host replies to the sender with a SYN-ACK segment. This acknowledges the sender's request to connect (ACK) and verifies the sequence number that will be used to start the data transfer (SYN).
3	The session initiator sends an ACK segment to the remote host, verifying the receipt of the SYN-ACK segment from the other host and signifying that the session has been established.

Managing/Maintaining Established Connections

Application layer protocols and services that use TCP can be stateful or stateless. Stateless host-to-host transactions include distinct connect, data transfer, and disconnect processes. HTTPS is an example of a stateless protocol. SSH, however, is a stateful protocol whose host-to-host connections have indeterminate durations that are maintained by keep-alive messages.

A **stateful connection** is one in which information about the connection between two systems is retained for future use or reference. In TCP, a stateful connection is kept open until terminated, even though the two hosts may not continuously exchange messages or data. After a stateful connection is established, TCP uses *keep-alive* timers in connected hosts to maintain the connection. When a host's timer reaches zero, it sends a keep-alive probe to the other host. When a reply to its probe is received, the host knows that the connection is still active.

Keep-alive messages are one of the TCP features that enable Internet users to have multiple concurrent connections to different hosts. Multiple application processes can remain open and running while users interact with other online or offline applications.

During an active session, these are the primary TCP responsibilities:

- Provide reliable in-order transport of data without data loss
- Control the flow of segments between sender and receiver
- Adjust to network congestion or degradation of network performance

Sequence numbers in TCP headers provide receiving hosts with a means of knowing whether they have received the entirety of a sender's message or data block. They enable destination hosts to identify and react to missing segments. They also enable receivers to rearrange segments received out of order into the sequence in which they were transmitted. In short, segment sequence numbers contribute to reliable data delivery.

Acknowledgments and Retransmission

Sequence and Acknowledgment Number fields in TCP headers are among the features that make TCP a connection-oriented protocol. When data is sent through a TCP connection, these fields help remote hosts keep track of the connection and ensure that segments are not lost.

TCP utilizes acknowledgments, timeouts, and retransmissions to ensure error-free, sequenced data delivery. Retransmission is not difficult to understand. Basically, when one host sends data to another, it retains a copy of the data in its buffer until the recipient acknowledges its receipt. If an acknowledgment is not received within a reasonable time (a timeout period), the sender automatically retransmits the data using its retained copy.

Retransmission may also be triggered when:

- The receiver determines that expected data has not arrived and notifies the sender. Sequence numbers help receivers identify missing segments.
- The receiver determines that the data has arrived, but in a damaged condition, and notifies the sender. The Checksum field in TCP headers is used to detect damage.

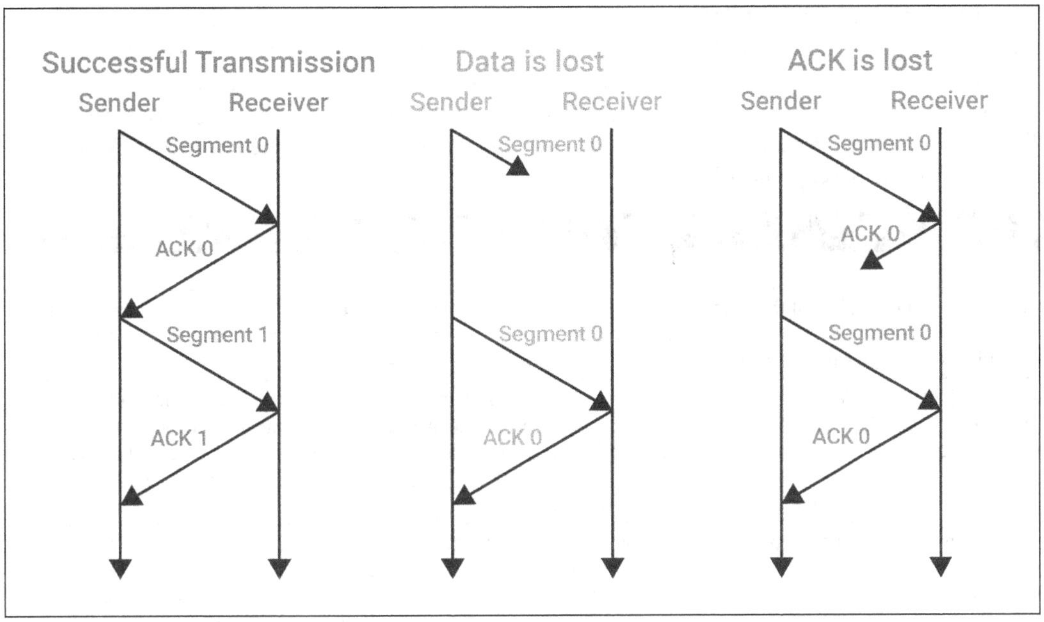

Figure 5-15: Examples of TCP acknowledgments and retransmission.

- The sender determines, often through an out-of-band means (such as an ICMP message), that the transmission was unsuccessful. ICMP was introduced in Chapter 4.

Figure 5-15 illustrates retransmission and positive acknowledgment. If transmission is successful, the sender receives an acknowledgment before its timeout period expires. If it is not, the sender retransmits the data.

Figure 5-15 also illustrates that retransmission can be triggered by lost data (missing segments) or lost acknowledgments. Network congestion, traffic load balancing, or unpredictable network behavior may cause IP packets to be delayed, lost, duplicated, delivered out of order, or corrupted. When Data Link layer error checking detects corrupted data, damaged frames are usually discarded rather than passed to the Network layer, and discarded frames become missing segments at the Transport layer.

Several types of acknowledgments are used in networking protocols. They are identified and briefly described in Table 5-6. Cumulative acknowledgment is most common for TCP, but selective acknowledgment is used for some TCP connections.

Table 5-6: Types of acknowledgements used in networking protocols.

Type of Acknowledgment	Description
Positive Acknowledgment (ACK)	With *positive acknowledgment* (ACK), the receiver notifies the sender which frames, segments, or messages were received correctly. This implicitly informs the sender which packets were not correctly received and need to be retransmitted.
Negative Acknowledgment (NACK)	With *negative acknowledgment* (NACK), the receiver explicitly notifies the sender which frames, segments, or messages were damaged or received incorrectly and need to be retransmitted.
Selective Acknowledgment (SACK)	In *selective acknowledgment* (SACK), the receiver explicitly lists which frames, segments, or messages in a data stream are acknowledged (either negatively or positively). Positive selective acknowledgment is an option in TCP.
Cumulative Acknowledgment	In *cumulative acknowledgment*, the receiver acknowledges that it correctly received a frame, segment, or message in a data stream, which implicitly informs the sender that the previous packets were also correctly received. TCP uses cumulative acknowledgment with its TCP sliding window protocol.

ARQ Protocols and Sliding Windows

Automatic Repeat reQuest (ARQ) protocols use acknowledgments and retransmission to provide reliability to unreliable networks, such as IP networks. These protocols can be used at either the Data Link or Transport layer, but today, they are most common at the Transport layer. At the Transport layer, the retransmission is triggered by unacknowledged segments. Table 5-7 describes several types of ARQ protocols.

Table 5-7: ARQ protocols.

ARQ Protocol	Description
Stop-and-Wait	Stop-and-wait is the simplest ARQ protocol. When it is used, the sender transmits one frame (segment) at a time and waits until it receives an acknowledgment before sending the next frame (segment) in the sequence. No additional frames are sent until reception of the previous one is confirmed via an acknowledgment message.
Go-Back-N	Go-Back-N is more complex. When used, the sender transmits frames (segments) in sequence and sets a retransmission timer for each frame. The sender continues sending frames until its timer expires for one of the transmitted frames. Then, the sender retransmits the unacknowledged frame and all those that follow it in sequence. This continues until all the sender's frames are acknowledged. This protocol can result in numerous frames being transmitted and acknowledged multiple times, so receivers must be able to identify and discard duplicate frames.
Selective Repeat	Selective Repeat ARQ minimizes the transmission and receipt of duplicate frames. When used, the sender transmits a specified number of frames (called *window size*) in sequence, setting a timer for each frame, until its window is emptied. It then begins transmitting frames in the next window. If the timer expires for a frame, the sender transmits the remaining frames in its current window, retransmits the unacknowledged frame, then picks up where it left off in the frame and window sequence. This version of ARQ is considered a sliding window protocol. It is more efficient than Go-Back-N ARQ in that it only requires the retransmission of unacknowledged frames.

In a simple ARQ protocol, such as stop-and-wait, the sender stops after every frame (segment) and waits for an ACK. If no ACK or a NACK is received, the frame is retransmitted. Although this ensures that frames are received in the correct order, it is inefficient and constrains throughput. The time it takes for an ACK to be received is significant compared to the time needed to send a packet and contributes to lower overall throughput than is theoretically possible.

Sliding window protocols improve throughput and efficiency by allowing a specific number of segments (frames), a *window*, to be sent without having to wait for an ACK. Each transmitted segment (frame) has a sequence number, and each ACK includes the sequence number of the segment being acknowledged. Senders track which segments have been acknowledged and send more segments as ACKs are received. In this way, the window slides along the stream of segments (frames) being transferred to the receiver.

TCP uses variants of Go-Back-N or Selective Repeat ARQ in which cumulative acknowledgments are used instead of acknowledging individual segments. With *cumulative acknowledgment*, the receiver sends a single acknowledgment in response to a finite number of segments received to signify that it correctly received all previous segments. Additional information on TCP's use of ARQ protocols and sliding windows is provided in Appendix 5-5.

Session Termination

After transferring all its data, the session-originating host terminates the session. The session termination process is called a *four-way handshake* and is illustrated in Figure 5-16.

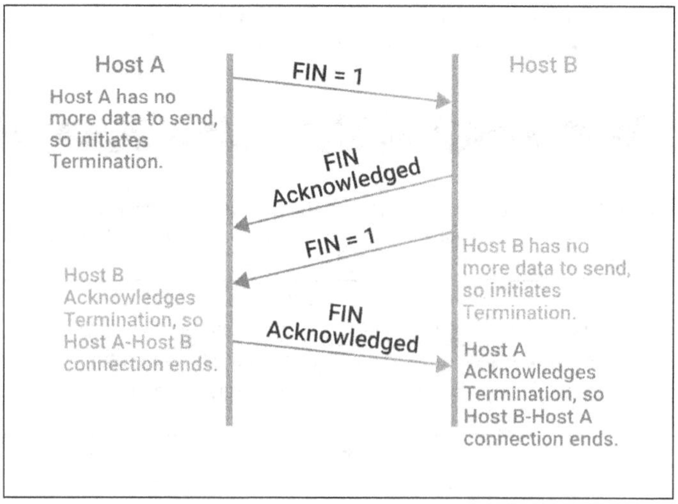

Figure 5-16: TCP session termination: The four-way handshake.

The session termination process begins when the session-originating host sends a TCP segment with the FIN flag set to 1 in the header to indicate its desire to end the session. The host then enters a FIN-WAIT state, during which it continues to receive data segments and acknowledgments from the other host, including an acknowledgment for its FIN segment. When the other host completes its data transfer, it sends a FIN segment to the first host. The first host then sends an acknowledgment for the FIN segment to signify the end of the session.

To sum up, TCP performs several important functions in TCP/IP networks. It connects applications to networks; segments application data into pieces; establishes, manages, and terminates host-to-host sessions; and provides reliable data transfer over unreliable IP networks. Essentially, it enables connection-oriented communications on connectionless networks.

Information in the fields of TCP headers is used to implement the protocol's capabilities. The Destination Port, Sequence Number, Acknowledgment Number, ACK, SYN, and FIN fields are especially important. Appendix 5-6 includes a summary of the purposes/roles of the contents of each of the fields in TCP headers (Figure 5-12).

5.3.2 User Datagram Protocol

Some applications do not require connection-oriented communication. Such applications perform acceptably when connectionless communication is used and typically use UDP instead of TCP. Relative to TCP, User Datagram Protocol (UDP) is a simpler protocol that increases transfer speeds by not requiring a formal two-way connection before data transmission begins. UDP PDUs (*datagrams*) are sent directly to receivers without establishing communication sessions, which enables UDP connections to be low-latency.

UDP is suitable for applications where error checking and correction are unnecessary or performed by the application. UDP is used for time-critical data transmissions, protocols, and applications where dropped packets are preferable to having to wait for packets whose delivery is delayed by retransmissions. It is used for DNS lookups, online gaming, and video streaming.

UDP is well suited for stateless applications that do not require the sender or receiver to retain information. For such applications, senders typically do not expect acknowledgment of packet receipt and are tolerant of data loss. UDP headers lack Sequence Number and Acknowledgment Number fields to indicate the transmission order of datagrams or to confirm their receipt. These features result in UDP being considered a "best-effort" data communication mode.

Numerous Application layer protocols use UDP, including, DNS, DHCP, Simple Network Management Protocol (SNMP), Network Time Protocol (NTP), Routing Information Protocol (RIP), and Open Shortest Path First (OSPF). It is also used for streaming media applications (such as movies), real-time videoconferencing, multiplayer online games, and voice over IP (VoIP), where transmission speed takes precedence over datagram loss.

Table 5-8: UDP header fields and their roles.

UDP Header Field	Brief Description
Source Port	The Source Port identifies the port number of the sender. When set to 0, the sender indicates that it does not expect a response from the destination host.
Destination Port	This identifies the port address of the application/service in the receiving device to which the datagram data should be delivered. Well-known port numbers from 0 to 65,535 are used in this header field.
Length	Length identifies the combined length (in bytes) of the UDP header and the datagram's encapsulated data. This field's limit is based on the IP protocol used for data transmission.
Checksum	Checksum enables the receiver to cross-check the integrity of both the header and the payload. Its use is optional in IPv4 but mandatory in IPv6. When it is not used, each of the field's 16 bits are set to 0.

As Figure 5-12 illustrates, UDP headers include fewer fields than TCP headers. The four fields in UDP headers are briefly described in Table 5-8. UDP headers include a Checksum field for ensuring datagram data integrity, but this is not always used. They also include a Destination Port number field to identify the application or service that should receive datagram data. Basically, UDP just adds port addressing to IP to facilitate connectionless communication over unreliable IP networks.

Because both TCP and UDP run on the same network, some businesses experience performance issues with TCP-supported applications when the use of UDP-supported real-time applications increases. Increased UDP usage contributes to increased TCP segment loss and can cause TCP to compensate by decreasing window size and slowing its data transfer rates. This can be problematic for POS, accounting, ES, and database systems that are crucial for smooth business operations.

5.3.3 Technologies and Security

Important Transport layer technologies were introduced in Chapter 4. These include Layer 4 switches, load balancers, and firewalls. **Layer 4 switches** are multilayer switches that base switching decisions on the information in the Destination Port fields of TCP and UDP headers that identifies the application or service that should receive the segment's or datagram's data.

A **Layer 4 load balancer** uses information in TCP and UDP header fields to manage data traffic. Like other load balancers, it strives to optimally distribute incoming requests across available servers to provide optimal application availability and responsiveness. Simple load balancing algorithms that consider the request queue lengths at servers and average response times are commonly used to distribute incoming requests.

In addition to filtering packets on destination ports and protocols, Layer 4 firewalls actively track TCP connections (sessions) and allow/deny traffic based on the state of those sessions. They keep track of each active connection and constantly check its validity using a process called stateful packet inspection. They are also known as session firewalls or session filtering firewalls.

5.4 NETWORK LAYER FUNCTIONS AND PROTOCOLS

As noted in Chapter 4, the two main functions of the Network layer are logical addressing and routing. IP addresses, whether IPv4 or IPv6, are logical addresses that, at a given moment in time, are associated with specific Internet-attached devices.

IP addresses are needed for host-to-host communications in TCP/IP networks, and address allocation services, such as DHCP (see section 5.1.4), and address lookup services, such as DNS (see section 5.1.3) play crucial roles in Internet operations. Also, routers base packet forwarding decisions on IP addresses in the Destination Address fields in IP headers.

IP is often considered the keystone of the TCP/IP protocol stack. Both TCP and UDP run on top of IP. TCP strives to provide reliable data delivery over IP networks, while UDP does not. Both Transport layer protocols pass their PDUs (TCP segments and UDP datagrams) to the Network layer, where IP appends a header to form an IP packet (or IP datagram).

Like other TCP/IP protocol headers, the contents of IP header fields enable Network layer communication functions to be performed. Figure 5-17a illustrates IPv4 header fields and Figure 5-17b depicts the fields in IPv6 headers. Appendix 5-7 provides descriptions of each of the fields in IPv4 and IPv6 headers.

The Source Address and Destination Address fields in an IP header respectively identify sending and destination hosts. These fields, of course, are directly related to the Network layer's addressing functions. Many of the other fields are related to packet routing and the possibility of packets being fragmented during routing. Some header fields (such as Time to Live and Hop Limit) are included to address transmission or network failures.

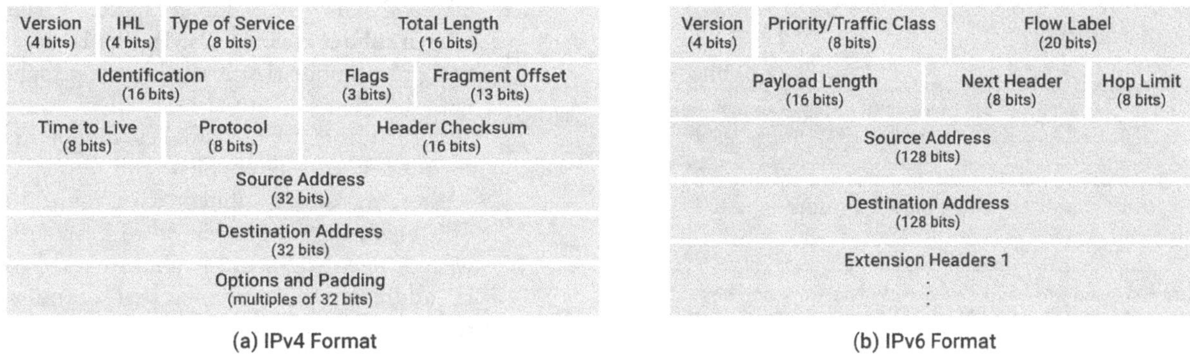

Figure 5-17: IPv4 and IPv6 header formats.

Unlike a TCP header, an IP header does not include fields (such as SYN, ACK, and FIN) that can be used to establish, maintain, or terminate host-to-host connections. The absence of such fields indicates that IP is a connectionless protocol that does not guarantee packet delivery. Source and destination addresses are the primary indicators of logical host-to-host connections at the Network layer.

5.4.1 Addressing

Network layer addresses are logical, software-based addresses that are changeable but provide a means for differentiating networks and hosts within networks. IP addresses are assigned in a hierarchical manner. A host always resides in a specific network, and if that network has subnets, it also resides in a specific subnet. A host's IP address identifies its network and subnet, and this information enables packet transfer from a host in one network or subnet to a host in another.

IP Addresses

An **Internet Protocol (IP) address** is a set of numbers given to a computer or device to enable it to communicate with other computers or devices over a TCP/IP network such as the Internet. An IP address is needed to send or receive data/messages from other hosts, and it makes communication over the Internet possible.

Two types of IP addresses are common in today's enterprise networks, IPv4 and IPv6. Although a transition from IPv4 to IPv6 has been under way for nearly three decades, a complete transition to IPv6 will take awhile, so it is important to understand both IPv4 and IPv6 addressing.

Before 1993, classful addressing was used for IPv4 addresses, but this has been replaced by classless IP addressing. If you are curious about how classful addressing worked, you are encouraged to consult Appendix 5-8.

Classless IPv4 Addressing

Classless addressing was introduced in 1993 as *Classless Inter-Domain Routing (CIDR)*. Prior to 1993, organizations received IP address space allocations based on their size and classification. All organizations in each class received the same number of IP addresses to allocate to hosts in their networks, and numerous organizations were allocated more addresses than they needed or could use. In addition to fixed-size networks, classful addressing also had fixed sizes for subnets within the networks. As more organizations and networks connected to the Internet, it became clear that classful IP addressing was inefficient, was wasteful, and needed to be replaced by classless IP addressing.

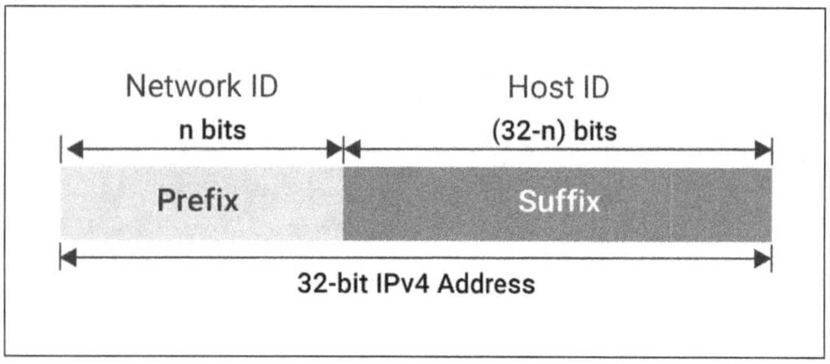

Figure 5-18: An IPv4 address includes network and host identifiers.

Classless addressing enables organizations to efficiently use IP address space. **Variable-length subnet mask (VLSM)** is an IP network design technique that is used to create subnets with different subnet masks. It allows network administrators to use smaller subnet masks for subnets with fewer hosts and to use larger subnet masks for subnets with more hosts. This enables an organization to have subnets with different sizes and to allocate its block of IP addresses in a manner that best fits its requirements.

An organization can request a block of IP addresses with 1, 2, 4, 8, 16, 32, 64, 128, or 256 addresses, or more as long as the requested block is a power of 2. This enables the organization to have sufficient addresses to satisfy its needs without having an excess number of unused or wasted addresses.

In IPv4, an IP address is 32 bits in length. "Dotted quad" notation, such as 167.200.129.55, is used for IPv4 addresses. Here, each decimal number in the address converts to an 8-bit binary number; with four numbers in the address, it converts to a 32-bit address, in this case 10100111 .11001000.10000001.00110111 (but the separating periods are dropped).

Classless IPv4 addressing divides the 32-bit address into two parts: prefix and suffix. The prefix identifies the network that contains the host, and the suffix defines the host within the network. This is illustrated in Figure 5-18.

Addresses in the same network (block) have the same prefix; however, each host in the network (block) has a different suffix. Since the length of a prefix (n) can vary (from 0 to 32), the size of the suffix is 32 minus the length of the prefix (32 – n).

In classless IPv4 addressing, the length of the prefix is included with each address to facilitate the determination of subnet and host portions of an address. The length of the prefix (n) is added to the last byte/octet of the IPv4 address and is separated by a slash. Doing this is called *slash notation* or *Classless Inter-Domain Routing (CIDR) notation.*

The IPv4 address 167.200.169.28/26 is an example of a CIDR notation. The "26" after the slash indicates that the first 26 bits of the IP address identify the host's network, and if the network ID is 26 bits in length, the length of the suffix (the host ID) is 6 bits (32 bits – 26 bits = 6 bits), the last 6 bits of the 32-bit IPv4 address.

Knowing prefix and suffix lengths enables the number of hosts in the same address block (network) to be calculated. If the suffix is 6 bits in length, the number of hosts in the same block (network) is 64 ($2^6 = 64$). This information can also be used to identify the IP addresses of the first and last hosts in the same block.

Subnetting, Variable Length Subnet Mask (VLSM), and Supernetting

Some of the addressing concepts developed for classful addressing, including subnetting and supernetting, continue to be used for classless IPv4 addressing and for IPv6 addresses. A **subnet** (or *subnetwork*) is a logical subdivision of an IP network. **Subnetting** is the process of dividing a single large network into multiple small networks known as subnets.

As previously noted, in VLSM, network administrators can divide an available IP address space into subnets of different sizes and efficiently allocate the organization's block of IP addresses to meet the needs of the organization or network. VLSM is the de facto standard for how today's IP networks are designed and administered.

Table 5-9: Using VLSM to divide an IPv4/24 address space into different size subnets.				
Business Unit	**Computers**	**VLSM Subnet Mask**	**Total Addresses**	**Assignable Host Addresses**
Sales and Marketing	120	/25	128	126 (128-2)
Product Development	50	/26	64	62 (64-2)
Purchasing	25	/27	32	30 (32-2)
Accounting	10	/28	16	14 (16-2)

Suppose, for example, that a network administrator in a business organization has the IPv4 address space of 167.200.169.28/24 to allocate among the four different departments identified in Table 5-9: Sales and Marketing (120 computers), Product Development (50 computers), Purchasing (25 computers), and Accounting (10 computers).

An IPv4 address range with a /24 CIDR notation could have a total of 256 host addresses ($2^8 = 256$). However, in IPv4, subnet masks take one or more bits from the host address portion of an IP address, which constrains the total number of addresses that can be assigned to hosts with the same VLSM subnet mask. The network address and broadcast address for each block represented by a VLSM mask reduce the total number of addresses that can be assigned to hosts in the block by two, as shown in the last column of Table 5-9.

In our example, the network administrator can use VLSM to divide the total available address space (256 addresses) into four subnets to align with the organization's business units: one with a /25 mask, one with a /26 mask, one with a /27 mask, and one with a /28 mask. As Table 5-9 illustrates, the subnetwork with the /25 mask would have 126 assignable addresses, the subnet with the /26 mask would have 62 assignable addresses, the subnet with the /27 mask would have 30 assignable host addresses, and the subnet with the /28 mask would have 14 assignable host addresses.

Supernetting is the opposite of subnetting. In **supernetting**, multiple smaller networks (or subnets) are combined into a bigger network that is called a *supernet* or *supernetwork*.

Supernetting is mainly used for *route summarization*, where routes to multiple networks (or subnets) with similar network prefixes are combined into a single routing table entry that encompasses all of the networks. For example, all subnets in Table 5-9 can be represented by 167.200.169.28/24 in a routing table because this was the address space used to create the variable-length subnets. This reduces the size of routing tables as well as the sizes of routing table updates exchanged by routing protocols.

In summary, classless addressing and VLSM improve IP address space allocation and contribute to more efficient routing and increased use of classless routing protocols that improve Internet performance. VLSM is supported by Border Gateway Protocol (BGP), Open Shortest Path First (OSPF), and Routing Information Protocol (RIP) versions 2 and 3. Routing tables and protocols are discussed in section 5.4.2.

Private IP Addresses

The Internet Assigned Numbers Authority (IANA) reserved several IPv4 address ranges for use in private networks. These are illustrated in Table 5-10. Any private network that needs or chooses to use IP addresses internally can use the addresses in these ranges without permission or coordination with the IANA or an Internet registrar.

Table 5-10: IPv4 addresses reserved for use in private networks.	
Private IP Address Space	
From	**To**
10.0.0.0	10.255.255.255
172.16.0.0	172.16.255.255
192.168.0.0	192.168.255.255

A private IP address is only unique within the network in which it is used because the same address can be simultaneously used in two or more networks. This makes a private IP address unrouteable on the public Internet. All IPv4 addresses outside the private ranges are considered public IP addresses and are routable. ISPs automatically block attempts to use private addresses on the Internet to avoid potential IP address conflicts.

Private IP addresses are used in most home networks and some small business networks. The two most common networks in homes are 192.168.0.0 and 192.168.1.0.

As noted in Chapter 4, Network Address Translation (NAT) is supported in most residential Wi-Fi routers. This enables an ISP to allocate a single public IP address to the Wi-Fi router (typically a dynamic IP address allocated by an ISP's DHCP server), and NAT enables devices connected to the Wi-Fi router to share the router's public IP address for their Internet communications. Most residential Wi-Fi routers also provide DHCP services (allocating private IP addresses to connected devices) and function as the local network's router and DNS server.

Because the IPv6 address space is huge, there is less need for private IPv6 addresses. However, private IPv6 address spaces are addressed in RFC 4913 to enable organizations that want private IPv6 addresses to have them. If you are interested in learning more about private IPv6 addresses, you are encouraged to consult Appendix 5-9.

IPv6 Addresses

IPv6 was developed by the Internet Engineering Task Force (IETF) to address long-anticipated problems of IPv4 address space exhaustion. Rapid Internet growth in the early 1990s demonstrated that more addresses would be needed than what was available in the IPv4 address space. Today, accelerating growth of the IoT continues to fuel the need for more IP addresses.

Today, the number of IoT devices that require IP addresses surpasses the total number of IPv4 addresses by a factor of five or more. Smartphones, smartwatches, smart TVs, and smart appliances connect to the Internet, and the number of Internet-connected devices increases every day. Continued growth is speeding up the transition to IPv6.

Currently, it is common for enterprise networks to support both IPv4 and IPv6 addressing. IPv6 addressing is supported on less than half of the global Internet. Hence, supporting both IPv4 and IPv6 enables an enterprise to access the entirety of the public Internet.

IPv6 uses 128-bit addresses. Theoretically, this allows 2^{128}, or approximately 3.4×10^{38} (340,282, 366,920,938,463,463,374,607,431,768,211,456) or *340 undecillion* IPv6 addresses.

Instead of IPv4's decimal notation (e.g., 192.168.1.100), IPv6 uses *hexadecimal notation*, such as that illustrated in Figure 5-19. Each 128-bit address has the format x:x:x:x:x:x:x:x, where x, called a segment, is a hexadecimal value between 0 and FFFF, and segments are separated by colons, not periods. Each of the eight hexadecimal values converts to 16 bits.

The first 64 bits identify the Network and Subnet ID portions of the IPv6 address. Together, they make up the *IPv6 prefix* used to delimit the block of host addresses in the network. All hosts/clients in an IPv6 network share the IPv6 prefix. The prefix is typically allocated to the network by an ISP and is usually a static network identifier that does not change.

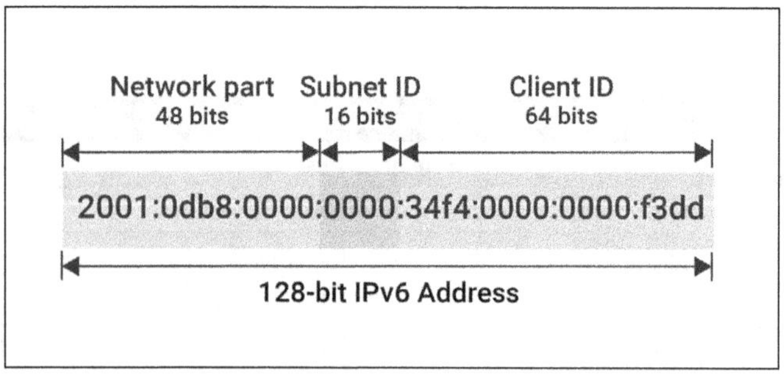

Figure 5-19: IPv6 address characteristics.

The last 64 bits represent the host (client) within the network. The 64-bit Client ID portion of the address is also called the *interface identifier* because it is usually derived from the adapter's 48-bit MAC address. Typically, converting a MAC address to a 64-bit IPv6 address is accomplished by adding 16 bits to the MAC address using IEEE's EUI-64 MAC address modification process; EUI stands for *Extended Unique Identifier*. Alternatively, the interface identifier may be obtained from a DHCPv6 server in the network, established randomly, or manually assigned by a network administrator.

IPv6 allows a single device to be connected to multiple networks at the same time. The protocol's autoconfiguration feature enables multiple addresses to be simultaneously assigned to the same device. This feature enables the device to generate an IPv6 address when it is turned on or joins a network and searches for an IPv6 router. When a router is found, a complete IPv6 address can be generated that includes both a Network ID and a Client ID.

IPv6 has several advantages over IPv4, including eliminating the need to support NAT in home and other local networks. IPv6 enables unique public addresses for all devices in the local network to be autoconfigured from device MAC addresses. This contributes to easier network administration while also eliminating the need for DHCP.

As Figure 5-17 illustrates, the IPv6 header format is simpler than that for IPv4. This contributes to more efficient packet routing. IPv6 utilizes quality of service (QoS) routing and "flow labeling" to efficiently prioritize and handle network traffic. IPv6 also supports multicast addressing, which enables multimedia streams and other bandwidth-intensive data to be sent to numerous destinations at the same time. Each field in an IPv6 header is described in Appendix 5-7.

When implemented correctly, IPv6 is more secure than IPv4. IPsec is built into IPv6 and includes authentication, confidentiality, and data integrity features. IPsec is also used to improve IPv4 security, but its use is optional, not required.

Although IPv6 use is prevalent among cloud service providers and ISP consumer access networks, the transition from IPv4 to IPv6 is still under way. For now, it is important to understand both IPv4 and IPv6 addressing and protocols. In many networks, IPv6 is neither faster nor more secure than IPv4, and although IPv6 routing is becoming more common, it is not dominant in many business networks. IPv6 is not accommodated by all VPN solutions, and this constrains its use in some intranets and extranets.

IPsec

Chapter 4 introduced IPsec (Internet Protocol Security) as an important Network layer protocol in the TCP/IP model. IPsec is incorporated into IPv6, which means that communication between two IPv6 endpoints is either authenticated, encrypted, or both.

IPsec operates in two different modes: Transport and Tunnel. As Figure 5-20 illustrates, an IPsec header is added to the original IP packet in either mode. In the Transport mode, the IPsec header is added between the original packet's IP and TCP headers. In the Tunnel mode, the IPsec header is added before the original packet's IP header, but after a new IP header. This means that the original packet is encapsulated in a new IP packet.

In addition, in the *Transport mode* (a.k.a. the IPsec *Host-to-Host mode*), only the original packet's payload (its TCP header and data) is encrypted and/or authenticated. In the *Tunnel mode* (a.k.a. the *Gateway-to-Gateway* or *Gateway-to-Host mode*), the entirety of the original IPv6 or IPv4

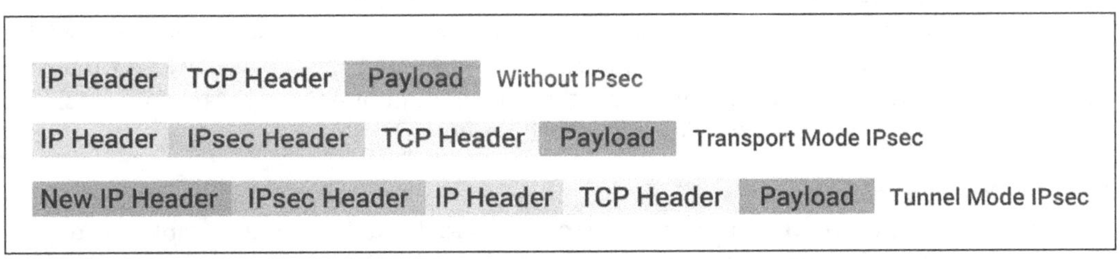

Figure 5-20: IPsec Transport and Tunnel modes.

packet is encrypted, including its IP header. Additional details about IPsec and these two modes are provided in Appendix 5-10.

5.4.2 Routing

Routing is the other major communication function performed at the Network layer. Routing enables internetworking, the forwarding of packets from one network to a different network. Routers use destination IP addresses in IP headers to determine how packets should be forwarded.

On the Internet and other TCP/IP networks, **routing** is the process of selecting a path for data transfers between networks or across multiple networks. Often, multiple intermediate nodes (routers) are involved in host-to-host data transfers, with each intermediate node making a routing decision and forwarding the packet to another intermediate node until it reaches its destination.

Packet forwarding is the process of transmitting a packet from one node (router) to another after a routing decision is made. Transmission occurs at the Physical layer and requires router hardware to create the symbols/signals that represent the packet's bits on the communication medium. However, routing is a software-based process that can occur independently of router hardware. The ability to separate routing and packet forwarding processes is the basis of software-defined networking (SDN).

The routing process relies on routing tables that maintain a record of routes to various destination networks. Routing tables can be created and maintained by network administrators, but this rarely happens and is only done for a network's internal routers. More commonly, routing tables are established and maintained dynamically via routing protocols.

A **routing table** is a summary of all networks known by a router. Table 5-11 is an example. As this table illustrates, a routing table includes a list of destination networks, the IP address of the next hop (the next router [node] on the path to the destination network), and the interface (circuit) via which packets to the destination network should be transmitted.

Table 5-11: Routing table example.

Destination		
Network	**Next Hop**	**Interface**
10.0.0.0	10.0.0.1	2
11.0.0.0	11.0.0.1	1
12.0.0.0	11.0.0.2	1
13.0.0.0	13.0.0.4	3
14.0.0.0	13.0.0.2	3
15.0.0.0	13.0.0.2	3
16.0.0.0	10.0.0.2	2

In Table 5-11, the router has three interfaces (circuit connections): 1, 2, and 3. Two networks (11.0.0.0 and 12.0.0.0) are reachable via interface 1, and two others (10.0.0.0 and 16.0.0.0) are reachable via interface 2. Three networks (13.0.0.0, 14.0.0.0, and 15.0.0.0) are reachable via interface 3. If the router receives a packet whose destination IP address is in the 10.0.0.0 network, the packet will be forwarded to that network's router whose IP address is 10.0.0.1 via interface 2.

Routing and routing tables are built on the assumption that the allocation of IP addresses within an IP address space (a network or subnet) is structured, and that devices with similar addresses are located close to one another. Structuring IP address space allocation, classless addressing, and supernetting enables a single routing table entry to represent the route to a large group of devices. This contributes to network efficiency and facilitates the work of routing protocols.

A **routing protocol** specifies how routers communicate with each other and share routing table updates. Such communication and sharing keep routers informed about paths and best routes to destination networks. Supernetting minimizes the amount of information that needs to be shared when router table updates are *advertised* (shared with other routers).

Dynamic Routing Protocols

Dynamic routing involves the automatic construction and updating of routing tables via routing protocols. It enables the Internet to act (nearly) autonomously, and it helps data traffic avoid network blockages and failures. Routing protocols were briefly introduced in Chapter 4, and BGP was identified in Section 5.1.1 as the required protocol for forwarding packets between and among the Internet's autonomous systems (ASs).

As illustrated in Figure 5-21, there are two major categories of dynamic routing protocols: Interior Gateway Protocols (IGPs) and Exterior Gateway Protocols (EGPs). Distance vector and link-state protocols are the two categories of IGPs used for routing among networks in an AS. They are described in Table 5-12. Path vector routing protocols are EGPs (such as BGP) used for routing across ASs.

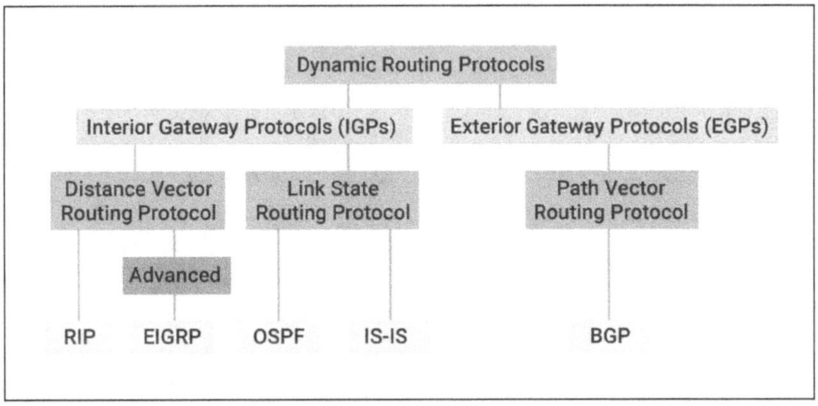

Figure 5-21: Dynamic routing protocol categories.

Table 5-12: Characteristics and examples of distance vector and link state IGPs.

IGP Type	Description	Example
Distance Vector Protocols	Distance vector protocols use "distance" to determine the best route to a given destination. "Distance" is usually measured in hops, but it can be based on delay (how long it takes a packet to reach a destination), packet loss, or another distance metric. When hops are used, each intermediate node involved in transferring a packet is a hop, and the route with the fewest hops to the destination is considered the best route. "Vector" shows the direction to the network; this usually specifies the interface on which the packet should be transmitted. Routers have a limited number of interfaces, and an interface may be used to transfer packets to multiple destinations (Table 5-11). Routers that support distance vector protocols send their entire routing table at regular intervals to the neighboring routers to which they directly connect. RIP is one of the oldest and best known distance vector protocols.	Routing Information Protocol (RIP)
Link-State Protocols	These are sometimes called shortest-path-first protocols: OSPF is one of the best known and most widely used link-state routing protocols. Link-state routing protocols strive to provide a complete picture of the network topology within the AS. They know more about how networks and routers are physically deployed within an AS than a distance vector protocol. In link-state routing, every router constructs a map (graph) of the connections among routers, and the network uses its map to calculate the shortest/best route to every other router in the network. Therefore, link-state protocols only make sense for interior routing. With new networks and routers being added to the public Internet daily, it is impossible for a link-state router to construct a map of the entire Internet. Link-state protocols use characteristics of the links that connect routers in the network to build and maintain a routing table. They consider each link's transmission speed, cost (e.g., number of hops), and current congestion (packet cues at hops) to determine the best (shortest/fastest) route to the other routers in the network. The Dijkstra algorithm is typically used for best route calculations that determine the "shortest" route timewise to each of the other routers. When a link-state protocol router detects a change, it notifies its neighboring routers. Neighbor routers are updated only when link states change and affect best route calculations. Unlike distance vector protocols, link-state protocols only advertise routing table updates when needed rather than at regular intervals.	Open Shortest Path First (OSPF)
Hybrid Routing Protocols	EIGRP is considered an advanced distance vector and hybrid routing protocol that combines elements of distance vector and link-state routing. Cisco initially developed it as a proprietary routing protocol for use in ASs whose infrastructure is dominated by Cisco routers (which is a considerable number of ASs), but it was converted to an open standard in 2013 and was formally recognized by the IETF in 2016. By combining factors used by distance vector and link-state algorithms for best route calculations, EIGRP can result in better routing performance than is possible by using either type of algorithm alone. It also uses encrypted messages for router table updates.	Enhanced Interior Gateway Routing Protocol (EIGRP)

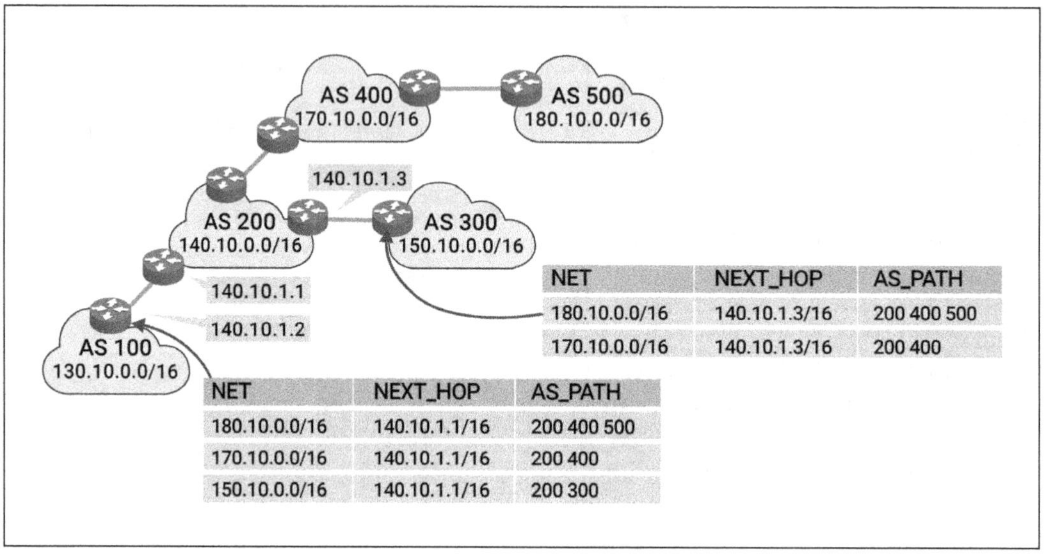

Figure 5-22: Path vector routing table example.

Interior Gateway Protocols (IGPs) are used to transfer packets within an AS. As noted previously, each AS can choose its own internal topology and interior routing protocol. One AS may choose a distance vector protocol, such as RIP, and an adjacent AS may choose a link-state protocol, such as OSPF. IGPs advertise routes to different networks within the AS's network and use algorithms to determine the best routes to destination networks.

Exterior Gateway Protocols (EGPs) are used to forward packets over the Internet to networks with different AS numbers. They enable devices in one AS to communicate with devices in another.

Path Vector Protocols, such as BGP, are used for updating the routing tables of the AS border routers that transfer packets between and across ASs. In this type of routing, a router knows the IP address of the next router along the path to a destination AS but does not know the entire path.

AS *border routers* advertise the reachability of other networks. Because an AS border router typically has a limited number of neighbors (as few as one), it has a limited number of entries in its routing table. Hence, numerous destination networks are reachable via an adjacent (neighbor) AS's border router. This is illustrated in Figure 5-22. The next hops for the border routers in AS 100 and AS 300 are border routers for AS 200; this means that for these two networks, all other ASs on the Internet are reachable via AS 200.

Because a path to a destination network may change (due to a link failure or router crash), an alternative path to reach the network may be available via another nearby AS. When paths change, routing table changes are communicated to neighbor routers so that they can update their routing tables with the new reachability information. The addition of new destinations (such as adding new networks to the public Internet) also triggers updates to path vector routing tables because each new network must be reachable via at least one existing AS.

Basically, path vector routing focuses on best paths rather than on best routes. *Best route algorithms* (such as those used in distance vector and link state protocols) factor in route costs (such as number of hops) and/or link states (such as current transmission speeds and delays) to identify the fastest routes to destinations. *Best path determinations* are primarily concerned with being able to reach another AS rather than how rapidly it can be reached.

A path vector protocol is needed for the public Internet because it is impossible for distance vector or link-state routing protocols to monitor all the routes and link states for a collection of networks as extensive as the Internet. Only path vector protocols that focus on network reachability make sense.

BGP is the path vector protocol EGP uses to exchange routing information on the public Internet. It is called Border Gateway Protocol because an AS border router must communicate and share routing table updates with at least one other border router in another AS.

The Internet requires each AS to have at least one border router that runs BGP and connects to at least one other BGP router in another AS. When a pair of BGP routers in adjacent AS's agree to exchange network reachability (routing) information, the routers become BGP peers.

Because a limited amount of information is required to advertise network reachability updates, and because these updates are only shared with peers, path vector routing conserves network bandwidth. In addition, because BGP supports CIDR (Classless Inter-Domain Routing), paths to destination networks in BGP routing tables can be highly summarized to include fewer entries that identify paths to other ASs. This is reflected in the 180.10.0.0/16 entries in the tables in Figure 5-22; in each table, this entry summarizes a path to three other ASs and avoids the need for having separate router table entries for each of the different ASs that can be reached via that entry. Summarization is also used in VLSM. For example, 167.200.169.28/24 summarizes a path to each of the four subnets listed in Table 5-9 and enables a single router table entry to identify how each subnet can be reached.

BGP version 4 (BGP4) is the current standard for routing among the Internet's ASs. BGP4 is the first BGP version to support CIDR. Unlike most routing protocols, which use UDP to transfer routing table updates, BGP4 establishes TCP sessions between peers for routing table updates.

5.4.3 Technologies and Security

Several Network layer technologies were introduced in Chapter 4, including routers, Layer 3 switches, IPsec gateways, NAT gateways, and packet filtering firewalls. This section provides some important additional observations about some of these and related technologies.

Technically, routing is a software-based function, but it is typically carried out by software installed on a physical device called a **router**. A router is connected to two or more circuits (has two or more interfaces), and each circuit connects to a different network. When a router receives a packet via one of its interfaces, it reads the destination IP address in the IP header, identifies the packet's best route/path to its destination in the routing table, and transmits the packet on the appropriate outgoing interface. A routing protocol keeps the routing table up to date. A router's performance is measured by filtering and forwarding rates. *Filtering rate* measures how many routing decisions can be made per second. *Forwarding rate* measures the number of packets per second the router can transmit on its interfaces.

A **Layer 3 switch** is a multilayer switch that combines the functionality of a switch and a router. It is used as a switch to forward packets among devices and VLANs in the local network but also includes routing software that enables it to forward packets to another TCP/IP network. In today's enterprise networks, Layer 3 switches are primarily used for routing traffic within and among VLANs and large subnets.

An **IPsec gateway** is essentially a router that supports the IPsec protocol. Depending on the mode, an IPsec gateway encrypts the original packet's data/message or encrypts the entire original packet. An IPsec gateway is considered a type of VPN gateway. A **VPN gateway** connects devices in two or more networks using VPN infrastructure. Although a VPN gateway can be a router, server, or firewall, in most cases it is a physical router.

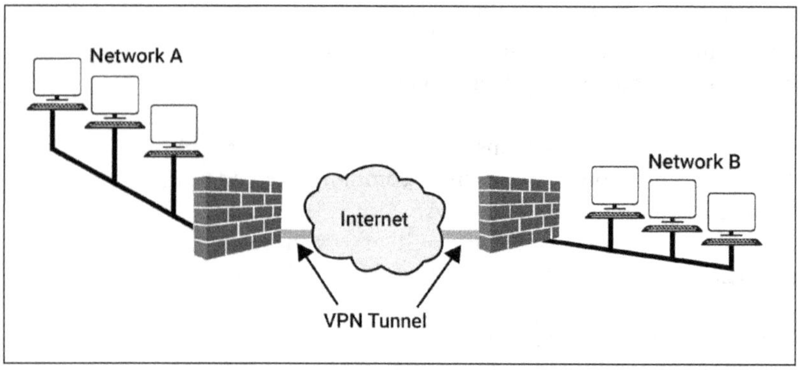

Figure 5-23: Conceptual depiction of VPN gateway deployment.

VPN gateways establish VPN tunnels through the public Internet (see Figure 5-23). A **virtual private network (VPN)** is an encryption-based communication method that connects a remote office or worker to an organization's private network over the Internet or another shared public network. Encryption protects data passed between VPN endpoints, and only authorized technologies/devices at either end of the connection can decrypt the data. VPNs can be implemented at TCP/IP's Application, Network, or Data Link layer, but IPsec is usually deployed at the Network layer.

Packet filtering is a firewall technique used to control network access by monitoring outgoing and incoming packets and allowing them to pass or halting them based on source and destination IP addresses, Transport and Application layer protocols, and port identifiers. Routers can be configured to perform packet filtering. Packets are allowed in or out when they comply with predefined rules; otherwise, they are dropped (not sent or delivered).

Transport and Network layer technologies and protocols make important contributions to enterprise network security and privacy. Intranets and extranets are also used by many businesses to provide secure private data transfers.

5.5 INTRANETS AND EXTRANETS

Intranets and extranets are private networks that use TCP/IP protocols and technologies. Intranets are created to serve the internal needs of organizations and their employees and are sometimes called "corporate" or "private" webs. Extranets allow authorized users from business partners to have restricted access to a subset of intranet resources.

Basically, an **intranet** is a private computer network for facilitating communication, collaboration, and information and computing resource sharing. As Figure 5-24a illustrates, TCP/IP infrastructure is important in intranets and extranets. This figure also illustrates that an organization's intranet or extranet is separated from the public Internet by a firewall.

Employees typically use browser interfaces to interact with intranet or extranet servers. An intranet server is usually configured as a portal that provides secure access to a wide variety of information, apps, computing resources, collaboration tools (such as videoconferencing), email, and computing services.

Intranet access and maintenance is usually centrally administered. Employees are assigned login credentials (user IDs and passwords) to access the network, and these credentials are required to access the intranet whether or not employees are working on site or remotely.

As shown in Figure 5-24a, an organization's public web server is different from the private server that supports the intranet portal. The public web server is located outside the firewall to enable access by Internet users.

Like intranets, extranets are private networks. They are sometimes described as intranet extensions that enable authorized external users to access the organization's intranet. However, such descriptions are somewhat misleading because authorized outsiders are typically permitted to access only small parts of an intranet in a highly restricted manner.

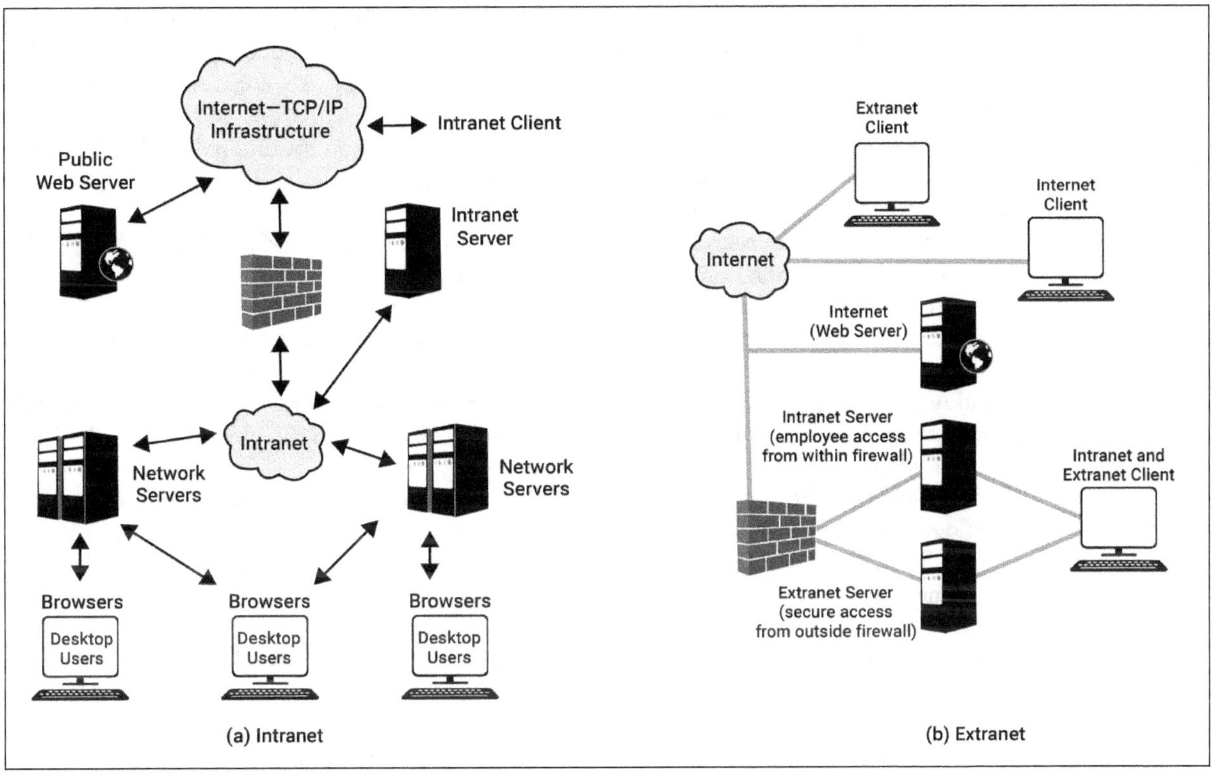

Figure 5-24: Conceptual depictions of an intranet and an extranet.

In simple terms, an **extranet** is a private network that provides secure communications between trusted business partners. Extranets serve a key role when communication is required between/among business partners. Figure 5-24b provides a conceptual depiction of an extranet.

Trusted business partners may include customers (who are permitted to view/track order status), suppliers (who are permitted to monitor inventory levels of the materials they supply), computer hardware/software vendors with contractual obligations to provide technical support/maintenance, consultants, and other trusted companies that do business with the organization. Extranets often support supply chains by facilitating communication, coordination, and collaboration among supply chain partners.

Like intranets, extranets rely on TCP/IP protocols and infrastructure. Typically, authorized outsiders connect to an extranet server via the firewall that separates the organization's intranet from the public Internet. The extranet server is usually configured as a portal that provides access to a limited range of intranet resources. Many organizations require remote workers and extranet users to use VPNs to connect to their intranets and extranets.

SUMMARY

Businesses leverage the Internet's publicly available infrastructure, protocols, and applications to support their processes and applications and to integrate cloud services with their network infrastructures. They subscribe to various Internet access services from one or more ISPs to access and utilize the Internet's TCP/IP protocols and technologies in intranets and extranets.

Several structured architectural elements enable networks to interconnect and transfer data over the Internet, including ASs, ISPs, domains, and structured naming and addressing schemes. The ICANN and IANA oversee several of these elements, including AS number assignments, the DNS, and IP address space allocations.

An AS is a large network or group of networks with a common routing policy. An AS is permitted to choose its internal routing protocol but is required to use BGP to exchange data with other ASs. An ISP is typically an AS.

ISPs are arranged in tiers and interconnect via peering, transit services, IXPs, and NSPs. ISPs offer an array of connection options and services for businesses. To ensure continuous access, businesses often have multihomed connections with more than one ISP.

Domain names are structural elements of the hierarchical DNS that translates domain names into numerical IP addresses. IPv4 and IPv6 addresses are logical addresses allocated to hosts and networking technologies. IPv4 addresses are often dynamically assigned to user devices by DHCP servers, but IPv6 addresses are usually mathematically derived from the physical (MAC) address of a host's adapter.

Browser, file transfer, and email applications are supported by Application layer protocols and technologies. HTTPS supports browser applications, and most client-server file transfers involve HTTPS, SSH, or secure versions of FTP, such as FTPS and SFTP. Email clients use SMTP to transfer messages to email servers; server-to-server email transfers also use SMTP. Email clients use IMAP or POP to retrieve messages from inboxes on email servers.

Internet applications and services rely on Transport layer and Network layer protocols. Destination port numbers in Transport layer headers identify applications/services. TCP and UDP are the most used Transport layer protocols.

TCP is used to support connection-oriented applications on connectionless IP networks. It establishes host-to-host communication sessions prior to data transfer and includes multiple mechanisms, such as segmentation, acknowledgments, and retransmission, to provide reliable data transfers over unreliable IP networks.

UDP is used for connectionless applications, such as DNS, where speed is more important than reliability. UDP headers have simple formats that can be quickly read and processed, and UDP PDUs are called datagrams.

Both TCP and UDP run on top of IP and pass their segments/datagrams to the Network layer, where IP appends a header to each of them to create IP packets. Logical addressing and routing are the Network layer's most important communication functions.

Addressing involves the assignment of logical IP addresses to Internet hosts. Today, a host typically has an IPv4 and an IPv6 address. IPv4 addresses are commonly expressed in a dotted decimal form (e.g., 192.168.1.14) that converts to 32-bit addresses, while IPv6 addresses, like MAC addresses, include hexadecimal values that convert to 128-bit addresses. IP addresses include network, subnet, and host ID components to signify the networks and subnets in which hosts are located. Classless addressing and CIDR notation are used for both IPv4 and IPv6.

IPsec can be used with IPv4 but is required for IPv6. IPsec has two modes: Transport and Tunnel. The Transport mode encrypts an IP packet's data payload. The Tunnel mode encrypts the entire IP packet and encapsulates it in a new packet with a new IP header.

Routing selects a path/route for IP packets between or across multiple networks. Multiple intermediate nodes (routing) may be involved in packet routing and forwarding. Dynamic routing enables the Internet to function autonomously.

IGPs and EGPs are the two major categories of routing protocols. IGPs are used for internal routing in an AS, and EGPs are used for routing between or across ASs. Distance vector and link-state protocols are IGPs. Distance vector algorithms consider hop counts or other "distance" measures to identify best routes. Link-state algorithms consider link conditions (e.g., transmission speeds, delays) to identify best routes.

EGPs use path vector routing protocols to determine the best path to a network in a destination AS; these protocols focus on network reachability (best path) instead of best/fastest route. The Internet requires an AS to use BGP to transfer packets to an adjacent AS.

Layer 4 switches, load balancers, and firewalls are important Transport layer technologies. Routers, Layer 3 switches, packet filtering firewalls, IPsec gateways, and VPN gateways are important Network layer technologies. Internet technologies and protocols are used to create intranets and extranets. Intranets are private networks designed for use by employees. Extranets enable authorized outsiders to have highly restricted access to a subset of intranet resources; they are primarily designed and used for B2B (business-to-business) purposes.

KEY TERMS

Autonomous system (AS)
Domain
Domain name server
Domain name system
Dynamic routing
Exterior gateway protocols (EGPs)
Extranet
Internet domain
Interior gateway protocols (IGPs)
Internet exchange point (IXP)
Internet Protocol (IP) address
Internet service provider (ISP)
Intranet
IPsec gateway
Layer 3 switch
Layer 4 load balancer
Layer 4 switch
Network service provider (NSP)
Packet filtering
Router
Routing
Routing protocol
Routing table
Segmentation
Stateful connection
Subnet
Subnetting
Supernetting
Variable-length subnet mask (VLSM)
Virtual private network (VPN)
VPN gateway

REVIEW QUESTIONS

1. What is an AS? How/why are ASs fundamental components of Internet architecture?
2. What are ISPs? How/why are ISPs important parts of Internet architecture?
3. Briefly describe each of the following: Tier 3 ISP, Tier 2 ISP, Tier 1 ISP, NSP, and IXP.
4. Briefly explain each of the following: peers, peering, transit, private peering, and public peering.
5. Identify and briefly describe the various ways that businesses connect to ISPs.
6. What is an Internet domain? How are domains and subdomains organized on the Internet, and how do they map to the DNS?
7. Briefly describe the communication functions that DNS performs.
8. Briefly describe the communication functions that DHCP performs.
9. How does HTTPS differ from HTTP? Why is HTTPS both a browser and a file transfer protocol?
10. Identify and briefly describe examples of secure file transfer protocols.
11. Briefly describe the communication roles of each of the following: SMTP, IMAP, and POP.
12. Identify and briefly describe the major communication functions performed at the Transport layer. How do Transport layer header fields support these functions?
13. Briefly describe how TCP establishes and terminates host-to-host communication sessions.
14. How do segmentation, sequence numbering, acknowledgments, retransmission, and ARQ protocols contribute to reliable data transfers?
15. Why do UDP headers include fewer fields than TCP headers? Identify examples of applications supported by UDP.
16. What communication functions are performed at the Network layer?
17. Why are Network layer addresses (IP addresses) logical addresses? How are networks, subnets, and hosts identified in IP addresses?
18. Briefly describe each of the following: classless addressing, VLSM, subnet, supernet, and private IP address.
19. How do IPv4 addresses differ from IPv6 addresses? How are the two types of addresses assigned to hosts?
20. Relative to IPv4, what are the advantages of IPv6? How is IPsec related to IPv6?

21. Briefly explain the differences between IPsec's Transport and Tunnel modes.
22. How is routing different from packet forwarding?
23. What is dynamic routing, and why is it used on the Internet?
24. What are routing protocols? How do EGPs differ from IGPs?
25. How are distance vector protocols different from link-state routing protocols? Identify at least one example of each type.
26. What are path vector protocols, and how do they differ from IGPs?
27. Briefly explain the role and importance of BGP4 in today's Internet.
28. Identify and briefly describe several hardware/software technologies deployed at the Transport and Network layers.
29. Briefly describe the characteristics and business roles of both intranets and extranets.

PROBLEMS AND EXERCISES

Exercise 5-1 At a Windows computer command line, type: ipconfig /all. ***Note:*** On a Windows computer, the command prompt is included in the Windows System folder. The results will resemble figure 5-25.

Note: On a Windows 11 computer, you can find comparable information by navigating to the Network and internet settings screen, selecting Advanced network settings, and selecting Hardware and connection properties. The results obtained will resemble figure 5-26.

Create a Word document and insert a screenshot or snip of the configuration of your computer's active network adapter. Beneath your screenshot or snip, provide your answers for the following by using the section of your results for your active adapter (Ethernet or Wi-Fi) to:

- Identify the adapter's MAC address(es).
- Identify your device's logical Network layer address.
- Identify the value that would be included in the Source Address field of IPv4 packets created by your computer.
- Identify the value that would be included in the Source Address field of the Data Link layer frames created by your computer.
- Identify the device in the list that your computer would contact when its lease expires.
- Identify the device in the list that your computer would contact to identify the IP address of the network that includes a host with which you want to communicate.
- Identify the device in the list that your computer would contact to send packets to computers in other networks.

Exercise 5-2 Ping is a tool that can be used to identify the reachability of computers in your network or other networks attached to the Internet. It can also be used to identify the amount of time it takes to get a response from the other host. Ping sends a small packet to the other computer. Like *ipconfig*, ping is used at the command prompt. Due to security concerns, not all networks support ping, since it can be used to identify IP addresses associated with URLs and determine whether another host is active and reachable. Such networks will not respond to ping requests.

- At the command prompt, type *ping* followed by the IP address for your network's Default Gateway—the router that serves your local network. ***Note:*** To identify the IP address for your Default Gateway, refer to Exercise 1. Your results should resemble figure 5-27. Document the completion of this step by adding a screenshot or snip of your results for pinging your network's router to a Word document.
- At the command prompt, type *ping* followed by *amazon.com*. Note that the round-trip time is more than that obtained when you pinged your local router because amazon.com is in a different network. Also note that your ping results identify amazon.com's IP address. To verify your completion of this step, add a screenshot or snip of your ping results to your Word document.
- At the command prompt, type *ping* followed by *unsw.edu.au* (the domain name for the University of New South Wales in Sydney, Australia). Include a screenshot or snip in your Word document to verify the completion of this part of this exercise. Students in the United States should note that the round-trip time is higher than those for their previous pings because the university's network is on a different continent.

Exercise 5-3 You can use nslookup at the command prompt to issue a DNS request to identify the IP address of a network that includes a particular domain name. For example, typing *nslookup* followed by the domain name for Home Depot (homedepot.com) produces the results shown in figure 5-28.

Use nslookup at the command prompt to identify the IP address for Slack.com and another website of your choice. Note that your DNS request may return more than one IP address. To verify completion of this exercise, include screenshots or snips of your nslookup results in a Word document.

```
Wireless LAN adapter Local Area Connection* 1:

   Media State . . . . . . . . . . . : Media disconnected
   Connection-specific DNS Suffix  . :
   Description . . . . . . . . . . . : Microsoft Wi-Fi Direct Virtual Adapter
   Physical Address. . . . . . . . . : F0-57-A6-08-2A-C9
   DHCP Enabled. . . . . . . . . . . : Yes
   Autoconfiguration Enabled . . . . : Yes

Wireless LAN adapter Local Area Connection* 2:

   Media State . . . . . . . . . . . : Media disconnected
   Connection-specific DNS Suffix  . :
   Description . . . . . . . . . . . : Microsoft Wi-Fi Direct Virtual Adapter #2
   Physical Address. . . . . . . . . : F2-57-A6-08-2A-C8
   DHCP Enabled. . . . . . . . . . . : Yes
   Autoconfiguration Enabled . . . . : Yes

Wireless LAN adapter Wi-Fi:

   Connection-specific DNS Suffix  . : vyvebroadband.net
   Description . . . . . . . . . . . : Intel(R) Wi-Fi 6E AX211 160MHz
   Physical Address. . . . . . . . . : F0-57-A6-08-2A-C8
   DHCP Enabled. . . . . . . . . . . : Yes
   Autoconfiguration Enabled . . . . : Yes
   Link-local IPv6 Address . . . . . : fe80::ad3e:3c1e:5ba8:88ee%11(Preferred)
   IPv4 Address. . . . . . . . . . . : 192.168.0.197(Preferred)
   Subnet Mask . . . . . . . . . . . : 255.255.255.0
   Lease Obtained. . . . . . . . . . : Tuesday, January 16, 2024 10:28:29 AM
   Lease Expires . . . . . . . . . . : Tuesday, January 16, 2024 11:28:43 AM
   Default Gateway . . . . . . . . . : 192.168.0.1
   DHCP Server . . . . . . . . . . . : 192.168.0.1
   DHCPv6 IAID . . . . . . . . . . . : 149968806
   DHCPv6 Client DUID. . . . . . . . : 00-01-00-01-2C-EE-A5-F0-F0-57-A6-08-2A-C8
   DNS Servers . . . . . . . . . . . : 192.168.0.1
   NetBIOS over Tcpip. . . . . . . . : Enabled

Ethernet adapter Bluetooth Network Connection 2:

   Media State . . . . . . . . . . . : Media disconnected
   Connection-specific DNS Suffix  . :
   Description . . . . . . . . . . . : Bluetooth Device (Personal Area Network) #2
   Physical Address. . . . . . . . . : F0-57-A6-08-2A-CC
   DHCP Enabled. . . . . . . . . . . : Yes
   Autoconfiguration Enabled . . . . : Yes
```

Figure 5-25

Name:	Wi-Fi
Description:	Intel(R) Wi-Fi 6E AX211 160MHz
Physical address (MAC):	f0:57:a6:08:2a:c8
Status:	Operational
Maximum transmission unit:	1500
Link speed (Receive/Transmit):	351/324 (Mbps)
DHCP enabled:	Yes
DHCP servers:	192.168.0.1
DHCP lease obtained:	Tuesday, January 16, 2024 10:58:53 AM
DHCP lease expires:	Tuesday, January 16, 2024 11:58:53 AM
IPv4 address:	192.168.0.197/24
IPv6 address:	fe80::ad3e:3c1e:5ba8:88ee%11/64
IPv4 default gateway:	192.168.0.1
IPv6 default gateway:	
DNS servers:	192.168.0.1 (Unencrypted)
DNS domain name:	vyvebroadband.net

Figure 5-26

```
Pinging 192.168.0.1 with 32 bytes of data:
Reply from 192.168.0.1: bytes=32 time=4ms TTL=64
Reply from 192.168.0.1: bytes=32 time=6ms TTL=64
Reply from 192.168.0.1: bytes=32 time=3ms TTL=64
Reply from 192.168.0.1: bytes=32 time=4ms TTL=64

Ping statistics for 192.168.0.1:
    Packets: Sent = 4, Received = 4, Lost = 0 (0% loss),
Approximate round trip times in milli-seconds:
    Minimum = 3ms, Maximum = 6ms, Average = 4ms
```

Figure 5-27

```
Non-authoritative answer:
Name:    homedepot.com
Address:  35.201.95.83
```

Figure 5-28

Exercise 5-4 You can use *ipconfig/displaydns* at the command prompt to show the contents of your computer's DNS cache. The DNS cache is basically a list of the Internet domains and their associated IPv4 or IPV6 addresses that your computer consults prior to sending a request to the DNS for an IP address. When you visit a new website, your DNS cache is typically updated. The results returned when this command is used resemble figure 5-29 but may be quite lengthy, depending on your recent online activity.

Type *ipconfig/displaydns* at the command prompt to view the contents of your computer's DNS cache. Include one or more screenshots or snips of your results in a Word document to verify completion of this exercise.

```
Record Name . . . . . : ns3-06.azure-dns.org
Record Type . . . . . : 28
Time To Live  . . . . : 51
Data Length . . . . . : 16
Section . . . . . . . : Additional
AAAA Record . . . . . : 2a01:111:4000:700::6


ocsp.digicert.com
----------------------------------------
Record Name . . . . . : ocsp.digicert.com
Record Type . . . . . : 5
Time To Live  . . . . : 718
Data Length . . . . . : 8
Section . . . . . . . : Answer
CNAME Record  . . . . : ocsp.edge.digicert.com
```

Figure 5-29

Exercise 5-5 You can use the *tracert* command at the command prompt to identify the number of routers (hops) involved with transferring a tracert packet to another network attached to the Internet. Because tracert information can be used maliciously by attackers, numerous networks do not respond to tracert packets for security reasons. Figure 5-30 displays the results from typing tracert unsw.edu.au, (the domain name for the University of New South Wales in Sydney, Australia) at the command prompt.

These results show that 24 routers were involved in transferring the tracert request from a host in the United States to the UNSW network.

- At the command prompt, type *tracert facebook.com*. To verify completion of this activity, include a screenshot/snip of your tracert results in a Word document.

```
Tracing route to unsw.edu.au [202.58.60.194]
over a maximum of 30 hops:

  1     2 ms     2 ms     2 ms  arrisatom.vyvebroadband.net [192.168.0.1]
  2     *        *        *     Request timed out.
  3    11 ms    11 ms    11 ms  10.1.2.9
  4    20 ms    21 ms    19 ms  host-24-112-127-40.vyvebroadband.net [24.112.127.40]
  5    20 ms    19 ms    20 ms  172.29.0.10
  6     *        *        *     Request timed out.
  7    19 ms    22 ms    19 ms  be2790.ccr42.atl01.atlas.cogentco.com [154.54.27.165]
  8    40 ms    41 ms    41 ms  be2690.ccr42.iah01.atlas.cogentco.com [154.54.28.130]
  9    61 ms    60 ms    62 ms  be3851.ccr22.elp02.atlas.cogentco.com [154.54.2.6]
 10    70 ms   113 ms    71 ms  be3872.ccr32.phx01.atlas.cogentco.com [154.54.26.53]
 11    75 ms    76 ms    78 ms  be2932.ccr42.lax01.atlas.cogentco.com [154.54.45.162]
 12    80 ms    76 ms    76 ms  be3360.ccr41.lax04.atlas.cogentco.com [154.54.25.150]
 13    76 ms    76 ms    76 ms  38.142.35.186
 14   256 ms   254 ms   256 ms  45.112.244.198
 15   256 ms   255 ms   256 ms  xe-0-2-0.cr1.sy4.nsw.au.coloau.net.au [103.52.116.52]
 16   259 ms   284 ms   254 ms  45.112.247.3
 17     *        *        *     Request timed out.
 18   259 ms   259 ms   256 ms  172.31.128.26
 19   254 ms   255 ms   255 ms  45.112.244.161
 20   258 ms   257 ms   264 ms  103.52.119.68
 21   262 ms   258 ms   254 ms  103.52.119.69
 22   265 ms   258 ms   261 ms  172.16.44.5
 23   257 ms   254 ms   254 ms  172.16.16.36
 24   258 ms   254 ms   253 ms  202.58.60.194

Trace complete.
```

Figure 5-30

- Use tracert to identify the number of hops to another Internet domain of your choosing, and include a screenshot/snip of your results in your Word document. ***Note:*** You may have to try this for several domains to get results—mit.edu is a domain that typically returns tracert results.

Exercise 5-6 You can use Wireshark to view your computer's interactions with the DNS to identify the IP address for a website. Completing this exercise will demonstrate that your computer will issue a DNS request for the IP address of a website that is not in its DNS cache. Wireshark and its use were introduced in the exercises for Chapter 4. Some preliminary activities are necessary before using Wireshark:

- Use *ipconfig /All* at the command prompt to identify the IP addresses for your computer and your network's DNS server.
  a. What is your computer's IP address?
  b. What is the IP address of your network's DNS server?
- Type *ipconfig /flushdns* at the command prompt to empty your computer's DNS cache.

Next, open Wireshark and type *ip.addr==your IP address* (e.g., ip.addr==192.168.0.111) in the filter in the upper left hand corner of the screen, as shown in figure 5-31. This will

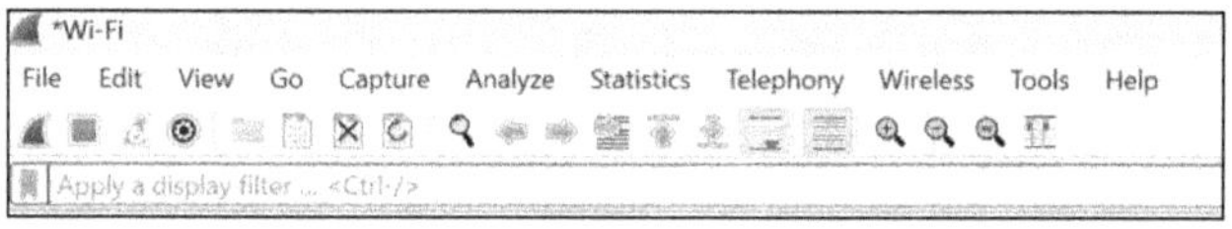

Figure 5-31

limit your capture to the packets coming from or going to your device. Then double-click your active adapter (Ethernet or Wi-Fi) and begin to capture packets.

Use your web browser to visit www.icann.org, and stop your packet capture after the web page has loaded. Locate the DNS query and response messages for www.icann.org in your packet list.

- What Transport layer protocol was used for the DNS query?
- What Transport layer protocol was used for the DNS response?
- What source and destination ports are specified in the DNS query?
- What source and destination ports are specified in the DNS response?
- What IP address for icann.org is specified in the DNS response message?
- What destination IP address is specified in the DNS query?
- What destination IP address is specified in the DNS response?

Locate the HTTP GET message for www.icann.org in your packet list.

- What is the source IP address?
- What is the destination IP address?

CHAPTER REFERENCES

Antoniou, S. (2022). Dynamic Routing Protocols: Distance Vector and Link State. Pluralsight. https://www.pluralsight.com/blog/it-ops/dynamic-routing-protocol

Biagioni, E. (2016). Computer Networks Notes 3: Transport Layer. University of Hawaii. https://www2.hawaii.edu/~esb/2016spring.ics651/notes3.html

Chan, W. (n.d.). IPv6: Internet Protocol Version 6. University of Hawaii. http://www2.hawaii.edu/~esb/prof/proj/ipv6/wilsonch/IPv6.html

Geeks for Geeks. (n.d.). Services and Segment Structure in TCP. https://www.geeksforgeeks.org/services-and-segment-structure-in-tcp/

Haden, Rhys. (n.d.). TCP. Data Network Resource. http://www.rhyshaden.com/tcp.htm

Hiley, C. (2023). IPv4 vs IPv6: What Are They and What's the Difference? Cybernews. https://cybernews.com/what-is-vpn/ipv4-vs-ipv6/ Neha, T. (2019). Classful IP Address ing in IPv4. Binary Terms. https://binaryterms.com/classful-addressing-in-ipv4.html

Ingargiola, G. (n.d.). CIS307: Structure and Naming in the Internet. Temple University. https://cis.temple.edu/~giorgio/old/cis307s00/readings/autonomsys.html

Loshin, P., & Cobb, M. (n.d.). Secure Shell. TechTarget. https://searchsecurity.techtarget.com/definition/Secure-Shell

The TCP/IP Guide. (n.d.). IPsec Modes: Transport and Tunnel. http://www.tcpipguide.com/free/t_IPSecModesTransportandTunnel-2.htm#Figure_119

Thousand Eyes. (n.d.). ISP 3 Tier Model. Cisco Systems. https://www.thousandeyes.com/learning/techtorials/isp-tiers

Triangles. (2021). Understanding the Internet. *Internal Pointers*. https://www.internalpointers.com/post/understanding-internet

XYZ Network. (2018). ISP, POP, NSP, NAP, MAE, IXP. http://xyznetwork.blogspot.com/2018/08/isp-pop-nsp-nap-mae-ixp.html

MINICASE: Web3

Web3 (Web 3.0) is often described as the next generation of the Internet and is contrasted with the preceding generations: Web 1.0 and Web 2.0. The Web 1.0 era began in the early 1990s, soon after businesses and the public were given access to the Internet. In those days, Internet users could visit static websites and look at their content; there was little or no user interaction with the websites other than viewing the information they contained. Business websites primarily functioned as online billboards, before the first e-commerce servers emerged in the mid-1990s and enabled businesses to begin using the Internet as a new online sales channel.

Most Web 1.0 participants were consumers of content rather than creators. Content creators were typically developers who built read-only websites.

The Web 1.0 era lasted from 1991 to about 2004, but beginning around 1999, there was a significant uptick in interactivity and website "stickiness" aimed at lengthening how long users remained on websites and increasing the likelihood of them making purchases. And online purchasing volumes grew year after year.

Most of today's Internet users have only experienced the web in its current form, Web 2.0 or Web2. Web 2.0 is an interactive and social web, and individual users contribute to content creation. User-generated content (UGC) is an important part of Web 2.0—purchasers did not have the ability to post personal testimonials about their experiences with products, services, restaurants, hotels, and so forth., before Web 2.0.

The year 2007 is often considered an inflection point in the evolution of IT because many of today's popular social media platforms first appeared in or around 2007. The iPhone also made its debut then.

You can see common patterns in the evolution of popular applications such as Facebook, Twitter, LinkedIn, and YouTube. A developer or company launches a popular app with a slick user experience to help it become very popular very fast. At first, the developer/company focuses on growth and locking in new users rather than monetization, but eventually attention turns toward making a profit. Outside investors, especially venture capitalists, often push the company toward incorporating advertising in the app, selling the personal data of app users, or both. Accumulating user data enables Web 2.0 companies (including Facebook, Google, Instagram, and Twitter, for example) to personalize the ads that app users see and increase revenue. In the meantime, company founders may be enriched through IPOs or selling the company to another company.

Centralizing and exploiting user data for profit is how the web and Big Tech work today. This is central to how Web 2.0 is engineered to function. In Web2, users have little, if any, control over their personal data and how it is captured, stored, used, and sold. Companies track and store user data without user consent, and the data is "owned" and controlled by the companies that own the platforms. The massive creation and accumulation of data by Web 2.0 companies and applications has fueled the explosion of public cloud services and massive centralized data centers.

The treasure trove of user data that has been amassed also attracts malicious actors who want to steal and profit from the data. Like it or not, Web 2.0 applications and platforms have created a side industry to keep up with data breaches and inform users when their data has been compromised. These companies have essentially found a way to capitalize on Web. 2.0 vulnerabilities.

The ability of users to interact with centralized websites and be cocreators of their content, which makes Web 2.0 popular, also contributes to its shortcomings. Web3 seeks to address these shortcomings by rethinking how developers architect applications and how users interact with them.

In many ways, Web3 looks like Web 2.0. In Web3, traditional web servers support websites and continue to have Web2 functionalities. However, the website's Web3 applications connect to a blockchain network, such as Ethereum, Fantom, or Solana, or a decentralized peer-to-peer network. Because Web3 apps use a blockchain or peer-to-peer network, they are decentralized and transparent. This makes them fundamentally different from Web 2.0 applications, and the differences transform Web3 app creators and users into co-owners of the applications.

Web3 developers avoid building and deploying applications that run on a single server and/or store data in a single database hosted or managed by a single cloud service provider. Being based on blockchain or decentralized peer-to-peer networks (or a combination of the two) makes Web3 apps *dapps* (decentralized apps).

A true Web3 app has no single controller (server). By using a blockchain or peer-to-peer network, instead of a central server controlled by a profit-minded owner, Web3 apps add considerable reliability, transparency, and security to user data. The redundancy that exists in such networks helps ensure that Web3 apps are not disrupted by node or link failures. And, because a blockchain is a distributed ledger system, user transactions are recorded to all computers in the network instead of a single server. This makes the database transparent and very difficult or impossible to hack. Hence, Web3 app users have greater insight into how their data and privacy are being protected.

Web3 apps need access to a lot of servers, and even though many servers are included in the public cloud, Web3 app developers are reluctant to use them because of centralization concerns. To date, Web3 apps are usually deployed on thousands of rented "bare metal" servers across a variety of providers. However, many of them lack ideal Web3 server configurations and don't have the fast disk read speeds and sufficient storage space that blockchain apps need. Servers with traditional solid-state drives and less than 4TB of storage are insufficient for production-grade, high-traffic Web 3.0 workloads.

Decentralization, instead of reliance on central servers, is one of the hallmarks of Web3. Ideally, this means that Web3 app users will be able to directly communicate with one another without their messages flowing through central servers. It also means that Web3 users can send and receive money without the involvement of a central payment server and that cryptocurrencies, NFTs, and other digital assets can be used for payments.

SpiritSwap is an example of a Web3 app. It is a decentralized finance website running on a blockchain, but its web application is hosted on a traditional web server from a well-known public cloud services provider (AWS). SpiritSwap requires a browser extension wallet, such as a Coinbase Wallet, to connect and authenticate with the web application. The wallet functions as a single-sign-on tool and contains the user's digital assets. It also includes a hexadecimal address that uniquely identifies the wallet and user. Once connected, a SpiritSwap user can swap and trade digital assets, not unlike a trader on the NY Stock Exchange, with every swap/trade being added to the blockchain. The wallet also enables SpiritSwap users to directly transfer pay-per-use payments to the app's creators without the involvement of a central payment server.

Helium is another interesting example and provides insight into how Web3 can transform Internet infrastructure. Basically, Helium is a decentralized hotspot network for IoT devices that rewards hotspot owners with cryptocurrency tokens. A Helium hotspot costs about $500 and can share its bandwidth with nearby devices—such as smart appliances, pet collars, and parking meters—that need to periodically send small amounts of data to maintain their Internet connections. However, unlike traditional Wi-Fi hotspots, Helium hotspots have a much greater footprint, up to 200 times greater. Helium hotspots reward their owners with cryptocurrency tokens, which can be sold or bought on cryptocurrency markets. The more a hotspot is used by nearby devices, the more tokens it generates/mines for its owner.

More than half a million Helium hot spots were in use by early 2022, with more being added every day. Although they can be used by anyone, early adopters have primarily been companies such as Lime (to keep track of its scooters) and Victor (to keep track of Internet-connected mousetraps).

So, as SpiritSwap and Helium illustrate, Web 3.0 promises to be a decentralized version of today's Internet. Its decentralization promises to wrest control of apps from "Internet behemoths" (Big Tech firms) and give it to app developers and users. In the near term, Web 3.0 apps will be added to Web 2.0 websites, but with the rollout of Web3 apps over time, Internet users will increasingly control their data, identity, and destiny through the creation of applications with native payment mechanisms that are verifiable, self-governing, distributed, secure, and robust.

Minicase Questions

1. As you have learned from reading this chapter, the architecture of today's Internet includes numerous components that are highly structured, including autonomous systems, ISP tiers, IP addresses, Internet domains and the DNS, and the TCP/IP protocol stack. Will Web 3.0 make these architectural structures obsolete, or will it extend them in new ways? Explain your reasoning and identify any online sources you use to develop an answer to this question.
2. Continued reliance on central servers, databases, and cloud services by Web 2.0 apps contributes to the need for robust cybersecurity mechanisms to protect applications and user data. Briefly summarize why Web3 apps offer greater security than web2 apps and discuss whether new Transport and Network layer protocols and security technologies will be needed for a full transition to Web 3.0. Explain your reasoning and identify any online sources you use to develop your answer.
3. Native payment systems are a part of most Web3 apps, and many allow for payments in cryptocurrency. Some apps reward developers with one or more spendable tokens for contributing several lines of code to app updates and pay-per-use payments by app users that go directly to the app owners instead of through traditional intermediary or banking systems. Are native payment systems that bypass the banking system a plus or a minus for Web3 apps? Explain your thinking and identify any online sources you use to develop your answer.
4. Do some online research and identify a popular Web3 app that you think does a good job of illustrating the potential of Web3 to benefit businesses. Briefly describe the app, what it does, and how businesses are using it. *Hint:* One of the references for this minicase introduces some popular Web3 apps; it can provide a starting point for additional online research that can assist in developing an answer for this item.
5. Given what you have learned about Web 3.0, do you think it has the potential to deliver on its promise to deliver a decentralized Internet that will give users more control over their personal data and finances? Why or why not? Explain your reasoning and identify any online sources you use to develop your answer.

Minicase References

Dabit, N. (2021). What Is Web3? The Decentralized Internet of the Future Explained. Free Code Camp. Retrieved from: https://www.freecodecamp.org/news/what-is-web3/

Dogra, S. (2021). Web3 Explained: What Is It, Why Jack Dorsey, Elon Musk, and Everyone Else Is Talking About It. *India Today*. Retrieved from: https://www.indiatoday.in/technology/features/story/web3-explained-what-is-it-why-jack-dorsey-elon-musk-and-everyone-else-is-talking-about-it-1891480-2021-12-23

Neuroth, J. (2021). How Infrastructure Providers Can Enable Web 3. *The New Stack*. Retrieved from: https://thenewstack.io/how-infrastructure-providers-can-enable-web3/

Rastogi, S. (2021). Top Web 3 Apps You Should Know. Developer Updates. Retrieved from: https://www.developerupdates.com/blog/top-web-3-apps-you-should-know

Roose, K. (2022, February 6). Maybe There's a Use for Crypto After All. *New York Times*. Retrieved from: https://www.nytimes.com/2022/02/06/technology/helium-cryptocurrency-uses.html

Chapter 6

Wired Networks in Business Facilities

LEARNING OBJECTIVES

After reading and studying this chapter, you should be able to:

- Briefly explain why wired networks are common in business facilities.
- Identify and briefly describe Data Link layer functions and protocols in wired networks.
- Identify and briefly describe Physical layer functions and protocols in wired networks.
- Identify and briefly describe important Data Link layer and Physical layer technologies in wired networks.
- Identify and briefly describe each of the major components of the Ethernet architecture.
- Identify and briefly describe important fields in Ethernet frame headers.
- Briefly describe media access control in Ethernet LANs.
- Briefly describe error detection and control in Ethernet LANs.
- Briefly describe backbone network (BN) switches and cabling.
- Briefly describe how core layer BNs differ from distribution layer BNs.
- Identify and briefly describe security threats and controls for wired LANs and BNs.

6.0 INTRODUCTION: Wired Networks in Today's Businesses

Numerous changes are afoot in business facility networks. Wireless LANs are on the upswing, along with increasing use of mobile devices. However, there are wires in wireless infrastructure, and Wi-Fi continues to be a wireless extension of wired LANs in many facilities.

Ethernet is arguably the only important wired LAN architecture, and it continues to evolve to accommodate higher transmission rates required for time-sensitive and bandwidth-intensive applications. Despite the increasing prevalence of Wi-Fi and other wireless networks, it is misleading to claim that the importance of Ethernet has been eclipsed.

Business adoption and use of cloud services has caused many organizations to rethink the need for extensive and expensive on-premises data centers. Today, they are an option, not a requirement, especially since it is typically easier and less costly to scale networking and application processing infrastructure via cloud services. And resulting cost savings free up money for enhancing Ethernet and wireless infrastructures in business facilities.

Businesses often lease copper and fiber optic circuits from ISPs for single- and multihomed connections and Internet access. Examples of services supported on leased circuits are described in Chapter 8. Compared to cabling used in business facilities, ISP connections and those used to create private WANs have slower transmission speeds that often turn them into enterprise network bottlenecks. Also, such connections require payment of monthly fees, and businesses may pay a premium to upgrade to higher speed connections. Cabling that supports wired infrastructure in business facilities is typically owned and maintained by the business. It typically supports high transmission speeds and has no recurring costs other than the electricity that powers it.

In short, it is important to understand wired network infrastructure in today's businesses, especially the wired LANs that directly support employees and the backbone networks (BNs) that distribute network traffic between and across LANs. Network cables are sometimes called *guided media*. Copper and fiber optic cabling are the most common types of guided media and provide high-speed circuits for supporting distributed applications and transferring massive volumes of internal data traffic.

Cabling is one of several important parts of wired infrastructure. This chapter also focuses on network adapters and Ethernet switches that support both Data Link and Physical layer communication functions. The Ethernet architecture and protocols are discussed, as well as types of symbols/signals used to represent data bits on Ethernet cables. BN infrastructure and wired network security are also considered. The chapter begins with a closer look at communication functions performed at the Data Link and Physical layers.

6.1 DATA LINK LAYER FUNCTIONS AND PROTOCOLS

Prior to the Internet, email, file sharing, client-server applications, and printer sharing were supported internally on local business networks. Today, only printer sharing continues to be commonly supported internally, while email, file sharing, and multi-tier client-server applications usually involve the Internet or cloud services.

Like the OSI model, the five-layer TCP/IP model includes separate Data Link and Physical layers that have distinct communication functions and protocols. TCP/IP's Network layer is designed to be hardware independent and compatible with any Data Link layer architecture (e.g., Ethernet or Wi-Fi) and Physical layer technology. Hence, it is important to consider TCP/IP Data Link and Physical layer protocols and technologies for both wired and wireless local networks.

The "Link" in "Data Link" refers to all other hosts that are directly accessible to a host without having to involve a router. Essentially, these are devices in the same subnet or LAN and reflect the Data Link layer's primary communication function: transferring data between devices in the local network.

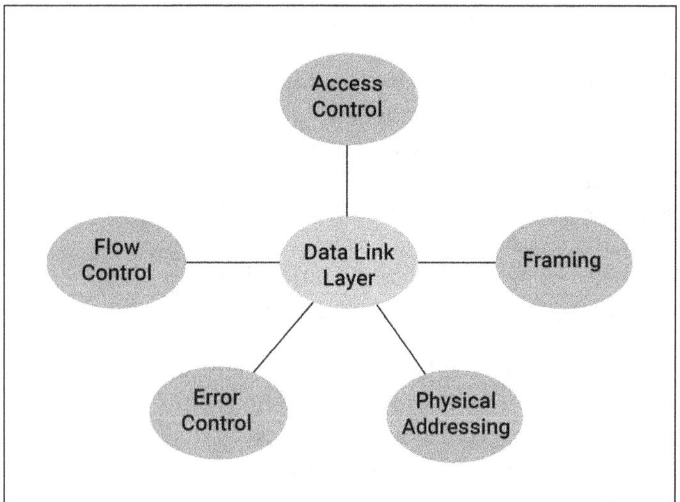

Figure 6-1: Important Data Link layer communication processes and functions.

The efficiency and reliability of data transfers in the local network stem from several Data Link layer processes identified in Figure 6-1. As noted in Chapter 3, physical (MAC) addresses are used to forward frames between devices in local networks. These addresses are hardwired in network adapters when they are manufactured and enable adapters (devices) to be uniquely identified in networks. Network adapters also implement other Data Link layer processes identified in Figure 6-1, including framing, access control, flow control, and error control. Collectively, these processes add efficiency and reliability to data transfers in local networks. They are briefly described in Table 6-1.

Network adapters also create and receive the symbols/signals used to represent bits on LAN circuits. Because doing so involves Physical layer processes, network adapters provide a hardware/

Table 6-1: Data Link layer processes implemented by network adapters.

Data Link Layer Process	Summary Description
Framing	Framing is the process of encapsulating Network layer IP packets in Data Link layer PDUs (frames). This involves adding Data Link layer headers and trailers to IP packets.
Access Control	This process includes procedures used to control how and when devices in the local network transmit data.
Flow Control	Speed matching is commonly used in wired networks to ensure that receivers sample the communication medium at the same rate that senders are transmitting and are not overwhelmed by the data they are sent.
Error Control	These procedures are used to enable receivers to identify whether transmitted data has been changed in transit over the communication medium.

software bridge between the Data Link and Physical layers. An adapter's Physical layer functions are controlled by device drivers, firmware, and specialized chipsets.

As noted in Chapter 3, the Data Link layer has two sublayers that work in concert to perform the layer's communication functions: LLC and MAC. The *logical link control (LLC)* sublayer manages framing, error detection, and flow control. The *media access control (MAC)* sublayer manages access control.

IEEE standard 802.2 defines the communication roles of the LLC sublayer. This layer establishes and controls logical connections between hosts in the local network and assists the Transport layer with the provision of connection-oriented and connectionless services in the local network. It hides local network details from the Network layer to enable the Network layer to work seamlessly with different Data Link layer protocols and Physical layer technologies. In sending hosts, the LLC accepts IP packets from the Network layer, adds an LLC header (see Figure 6-2), and passes the partially created frames to the MAC sublayer, where a MAC header and trailer are added to complete each frame. The LLC serves as a managing buffer between TCP/IP's upper "executive" layers (e.g., the Transport and Network layers) and lower "shipping department" layers (MAC sublayer and Physical layer). Both LLC and MAC header fields are more fully described in Appendix 6-1.

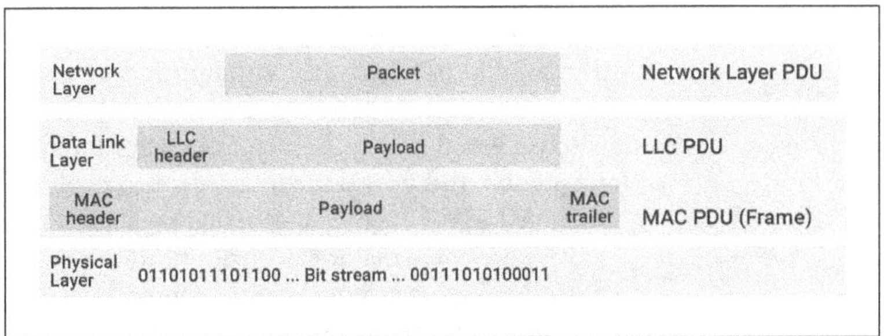

Figure 6-2: LLC and MAC sublayer PDUs.

6.1.1 Framing and Physical Addressing

The MAC sublayer serves as an interface between the LLC sublayer and the Physical layer. It encapsulates the LLC PDU by adding a MAC header and MAC trailer. The format of the MAC header is dependent on the device's active network interface (adapter). For example, if the device is connected to an Ethernet network, an Ethernet frame is created; if connected to a Wi-Fi network, a Wi-Fi frame is created. The format of Ethernet frames is described later in this chapter; Wi-Fi frame formats are described in Chapter 7.

MAC headers contain source and destination address fields (MAC addresses) and control fields. The source address field includes the sender's MAC address, and the destination address field contains the MAC address of another device in the local network. Receivers use control fields to process the frame. They use the trailer field to detect data transmission errors. Each frame has a maximum size that cannot be exceeded because communicating devices must allocate memory space (buffers) to the data being transferred. Ensuring that frames are neither too small (*runts*) or too large (*giants*) is an aspect of Data Link layer *flow control.*

MAC addresses are permanently etched (burned) into network adapters. Today, laptop and desktop computers are typically equipped with both Ethernet and Wi-Fi adapters, and each adapter has a unique 48-bit MAC address. As noted previously, MAC addresses are commonly expressed in hexadecimal form (such as 00:1b:63:9d:45:e6 or 00-1B-63-9D-45-E6), and each hexadecimal value in the address converts to 8 bits. At any given moment, only one adapter is used to connect to a local network and to build MAC sublayer frames, so only one MAC address is used at any given moment by devices with more than one adapter.

6.1.2 Access Control

The MAC sublayer provides access to the physical communication medium. Access control is used to determine when a device can transmit its data and exert control over the communication link.

Media access control is the method used to allocate access to the communication medium and prevent devices from transmitting at the same time, which would cause data collisions. Technically, there are two parts to media access control: data link control and multiple access control using media access protocols. **Data link control** is responsible for reliable transmission over the communication link and involves framing, flow control, and error control. When devices have a dedicated link between them, data link control is typically sufficient for reliable data transmission. In the absence of a dedicated link, multiple access control is required to prevent multiple devices from simultaneously trying to seize control of the communication channel and transmit.

Multiple access control protocols are used at the MAC sublayer to enable connected devices to access and use a shared communication channel. Today, they are especially important in Wi-Fi and other wireless networks but are relatively unimportant (but still sometimes used) in fully switched wired networks, such as most of today's Ethernet LANs. In wired LANs, the continued recognition and use of media access protocols is a carryover from early networks, such as those illustrated in Figure 6-3, that relied on shared buses and hubs.

There are three major categories of multiple access control protocols: random-access protocols, controlled-access protocols, and channelization protocols. They are summarized in Table 6-2.

As noted in the introduction, Ethernet is the most common type of wired LAN in enterprise networks. Other types of wired LANs exist, such as token passing LANs, but they are very rare. Early Ethernet LANs were shared bus or shared media hub LANs (such as those illustrated in Figure 6-3), but almost all of them have been replaced by fully switched Ethernet LANs, in which media sharing is no longer an important issue. Despite these advancements, CSMA/CD, a random-access protocol, remains the "official" Ethernet protocol, even though it is only deployed for backward compatibility with older implementations and/or half-duplex links.

Carrier Sense Multiple Access with Collision Detection (CSMA/CD) is based on *Carrier Sense Multiple Access (CSMA)*, which strives to avoid data collisions by requiring a device to "sense" the state

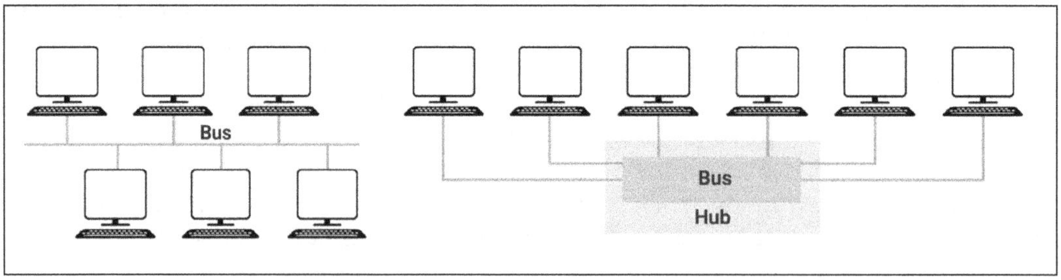

Figure 6-3: Shared media bus and hub networks.

Table 6-2: Types of multiple access protocols used in today's networks.	
Category	**Brief Description**
Random-access protocols	**Random-access protocols** (also known as contention protocols) treat all network-attached devices as equals (none have priority). Devices transmit, or delay transmitting, data depending on the communication media's state (busy or idle). There is no fixed sequence (order) for when a device can transmit, and there are no fixed time slots for devices to use the medium.
Controlled-access protocols	**Controlled-access protocols** allow only one device to use the medium at any given time to avoid data collisions. Some require a device to make a reservation to transmit; some use a polling mechanism; and others pass tokens to devices to signify when they can transmit. These protocols often involve a central controller that functions like a music conductor who orchestrates when a particular musician can play.
Channelization protocols	**Channelization protocols** enable the available bandwidth of the communication link to be simultaneously shared by multiple devices using time slots, frequency bands, or codes. Historically, these protocols have been popular in cellular networks as a means of enabling multiple users to use the network at the same time.

of the medium (busy or idle) before transmitting data. If the medium is idle, the device can transmit; if the medium is busy, the device must wait until it becomes idle.

CSMA/CD goes beyond CSMA by recognizing that collisions may happen when devices are far apart. For example, if two devices (*A* and *B*) are far apart, *A* may sense that the channel is idle and begin transmitting, even though *B* has already started transmitting because of propagation *delay*—the time it takes *B*'s transmission to reach *A*. The CD (collision detection) part of CSMA/CD requires devices to stop transmitting when a data collision is detected and typically involves requiring the devices to return to the step of sensing the medium before transmitting.

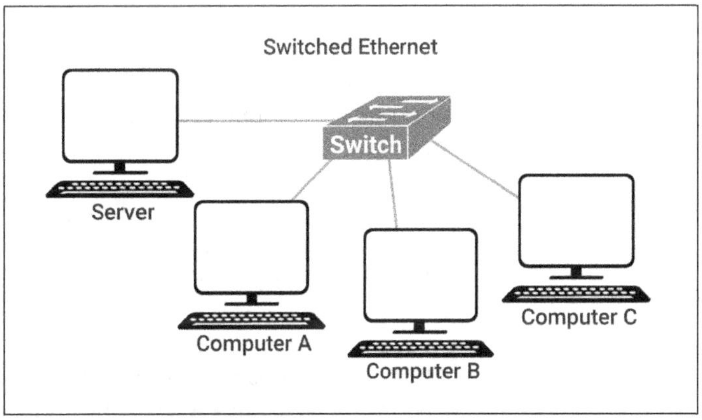

Figure 6-4: A switched Ethernet network.

In a switched Ethernet network, such as that illustrated in Figure 6-4, each device connects to an Ethernet switch by a dedicated Ethernet cable. Basically, switches create a dedicated link between two devices in the local network. Since the communication medium is not shared, a multiple access control protocol, such as CSMA/CD, is not needed. Here, CSMA/CD is turned off as a MAC sublayer protocol. CSMA/CD is still useful, however, if the dedicated link only supports half-duplex transmission.

6.1.3 Error Detection

Prior to the Internet, both error detection and correction functions were usually performed at the Data Link layer in local networks. Error detection processes identified frames containing data transmission errors, and error correction processes leveraged the ARQ protocols described in Chapter 5.

Today, error detection continues to be performed at the Data Link layer, but error correction is handled by the Transport layer. In most LANs, when a recipient detects an error in a frame, the frame is discarded (removed from the network) and is not passed to the Network layer. Missing frames become missing segments at the Transport layer, and missing acknowledgments trigger sender retransmissions. While it remains possible to configure local networks to handle error detection and correction at the Data Link layer, in today's networks, it makes more sense to utilize the Transport layer for error correction and flow control.

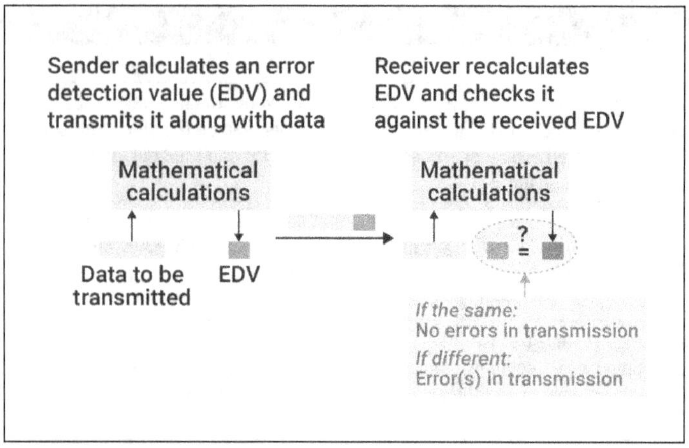

Figure 6-5: A conceptual depiction of the error detection process in local networks.

In local networks, frame recipients can detect errors because frame senders include an error check code in each frame's MAC trailer field. Figure 6-5 summarizes the process that is used.

Basically, the sender performs a mathematical calculation on the frame's data and puts the results of its calculation in the trailer field before passing the frame to the Physical layer. The mathematical calculation serves as an *error detection value* (*error check value*). The receiver performs the same mathematical calculation on the frame's data and compares its results to the error detection value (EDV) added by the sender. If the receiver's EDV matches the sender's, the receiver concludes that the frame is error-free. If the EDVs are different, the frame is flagged as having errors.

Error Checking Techniques

The process illustrated in Figure 6-5 applies to many types of error checking schemes used in today's networks, including parity checking, checksums, and cyclic redundancy checks. All error checking/detection methodologies involve sending extra bits that receivers use to determine whether bits have changed while in transit. You may recall from Chapter 5, checksum fields are included in TCP, UDP, and IPv4 headers to enable error detection, but they are not always used.

Parity checking is one of the older and simpler error checking techniques. When this technique is used, one additional bit (a parity bit) is added to each byte or data unit (see Table 6-3). The value of the parity bit is based on the number of 1s bits in the data unit and is set to make the total number of 1s in the data unit (including the parity bit) either an even or odd number.

Parity checking is used in asynchronous serial data communication applications, where parity bits are typically generated and checked at hardware interfaces. It is also used internally in computers on PCI and SCSI buses and microprocessor caches, where data can be easily/quickly retransmitted when an error is detected.

Parity checking is effective when an odd number of bits are changed in original data in transit between sender and receiver, but if an even number of bits are changed, an error will not be detected. With an error detection rate of about 50%, parity checking is not very effective.

Checksums and CRCs are other types of EDV calculations. A *checksum* is calculated by summing the decimal values of bytes in a data block, dividing the sum by 255, and using the remainder as the EDV. Approximately 95% of errors can be detected by checksums.

In Ethernet LANs, senders calculate and include a cyclic redundancy check (CRC) in each frame's MAC trailer field, which is often identified as the *Frame Check Sequence* field (see Figure 6-6).

Table 6-3: Parity checking examples.

Original Data	Even Parity Bit	Even Parity Transmission	Odd Parity Bit	Odd Parity Transmission
10101010	0	101010100	1	101010101
01101110	1	011011101	0	011011100
10010011	0	100100110	1	100100111
01011101	1	010111011	0	010111010

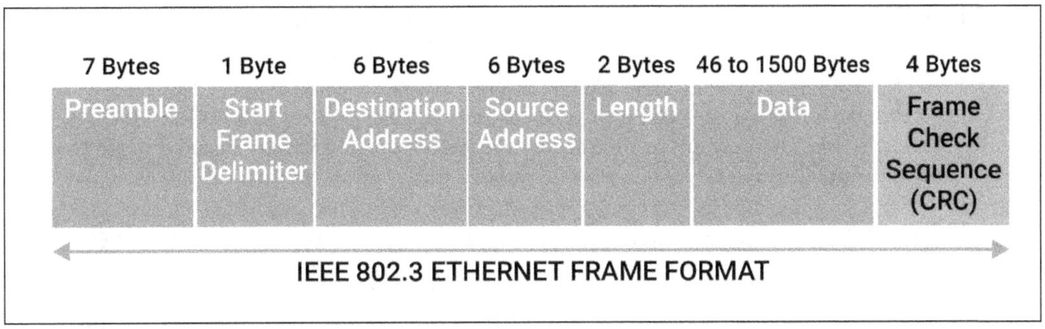

Figure 6-6: In Ethernet frames, the error detection (check) value is included in the FCS field.

CRC involves binary division of the frame's data bits. In CRC, the data bits are treated as one long binary number, and polynomials are used to determine divisors that produce division remainders that are 8, 16, 24, or 32 bits in length. Ethernet uses CRC-32, and 32-bit remainders serve as EDVs.

Figure 6-7 provides a conceptual depiction of the CRC calculation process. Here, the division produces a 3-bit remainder that is added to the frame. When the receiver's remainder (EDV) is the same as the sender's, the frame's data is considered error-free.

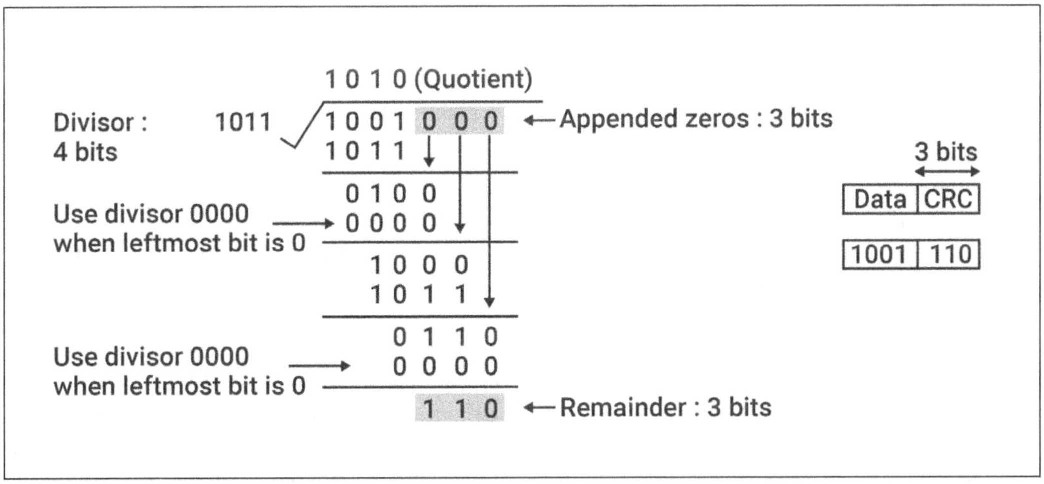

Figure 6-7: An example of binary mathematics used to calculate a CRC.

CRC is one of the most popular error checking schemes, and CRC-32 is very robust; it detects approximately 99.99999998% of data transmission errors. As a result, if an Ethernet frame's data is corrupted during transmission, it will almost always be detected.

Error Recovery and Correction

Today, TCP/IP hosts in most LANs are configured to detect errors at the Data Link layer and to handle error recovery at the Transport layer. When the host detects an error in a received frame, it discards the frame (removes it from the network). When TCP is used, a missing frame becomes a missing segment, and an ARQ protocol (usually selective ARQ) triggers its retransmission.

Forward error correction (FEC) is used in some networks and on some types of circuits. FEC uses EDVs that enable receivers to both detect and correct errors without retransmission of the data. The EDVs contain sufficient information about the original data to enable the receiver to recover it from frames that contain errors. For some FEC techniques, the number of error checking bits sent with the data is roughly the same as the number of data bits.

FEC is often used in satellite communications, where signals may travel hundreds or thousands of miles. It is also used in noisy environments, where high-powered machinery and power sources make data communication errors impossible to avoid.

6.2 PHYSICAL LAYER COMMUNICATION FUNCTIONS IN WIRED NETWORKS

The Physical layer of TCP/IP performs the communication functions required to transfer data from one host to another over a physical communication medium. Physical media are the "pipes" that carry the bits that represent frames. Ideally, bits are not altered as they travel through the pipes and receivers are able to determine and exactly reproduce the data they are sent.

In wired networks, the representation and transfer of frames requires:

- physical media (e.g., cables) and associated connectors/interfaces
- symbols (signals) that represent bits on the communication medium
- transmitter and receiver circuitry in network devices

As Chapter 8 explains, some cable-based ISP transmission services add control information to frames passed down from the Data Link layer. This is called *transmission framing*. Transmission framing is not common in wired LANs.

On physical media, a MAC sublayer frame is represented as a bitstream—an ordered sequence of bits. Bits are encoded as symbols (signals) transmitted on the physical medium, and the signals/symbols that are used are a function of the medium (e.g., copper or fiber optic cable).

6.2.1 Signaling

Signaling involves the creation of electrical or optical signals that represent bits on physical media. Signaling is typically recognized as the most important Physical layer communication function.

The Physical layer must generate the electrical, optical, or wireless signals that represent the 1s and 0s on the media. The method used to represent bits is called the *signaling method*, and Physical layer standards define what type of signal represents a 0 and what type of signal represents a 1.

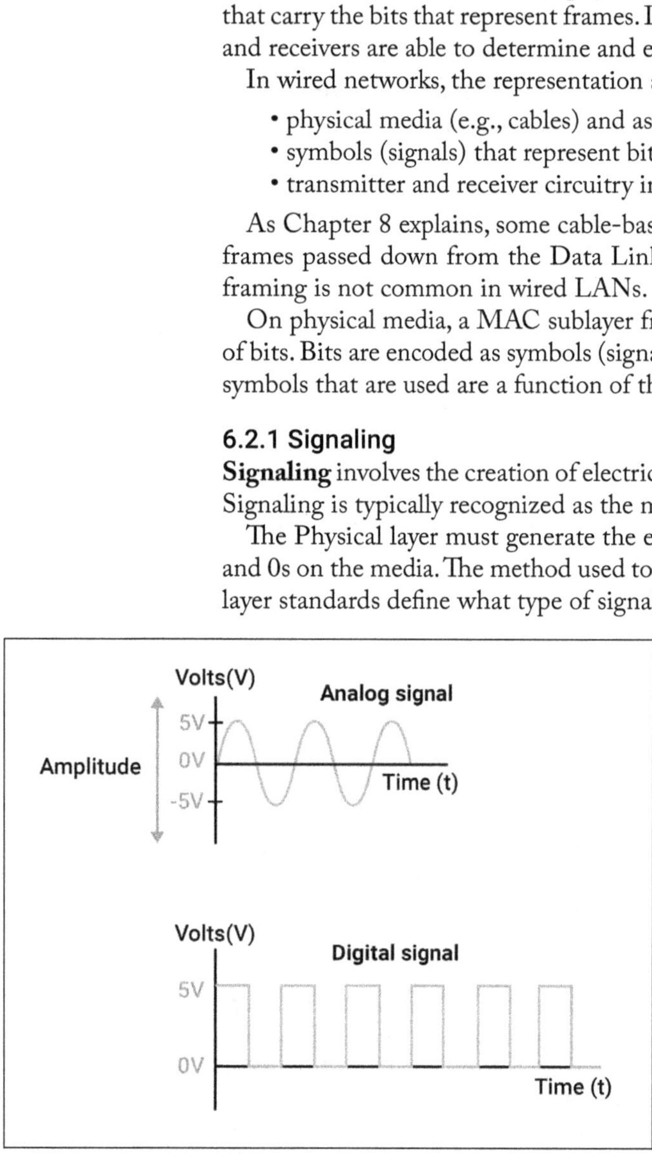

Figure 6-8: Examples of analog and digital signals on copper cables.

In wired LANs, signals are transmitted sequentially on the cables that connect senders and receivers. Recipients must interpret the signals they receive, translate them to the bits they represent, reassemble the sender's frame, and pass the frame to the Data Link layer.

Different levels of electrical signals or optical pulses can be used to differentiate 1s and 0s. When copper cables are used, the signals are electrical pulses. When fiber optic cabling is used, the signals are light pulses or patterns. In wireless LANs, the signals are radio waveforms; these are described in Chapter 7.

On copper cables, signaling involves changing the voltage level of an electrical current. Data can be represented on electronic circuits as analog signals with continuously varying voltage levels or by digital signals with discrete voltage levels (see Figure 6-8).

Almost all wired LANs are Ethernet LANs, which transmit digital signals. Digital signals are also used on T-1 circuits that some businesses use to connect to ISPs. In digital subscriber line (DSL) connections to ISPs, analog signals are used to represent bits.

On fiber optic cables, LED or laser sources transmit light pulses that represent bits. As Figure 6-9 illustrates, senders often convert outgoing electronic signals to digital light pulses, and receivers convert incoming light pulses to electronic signals. Media conversion circuitry makes this possible.

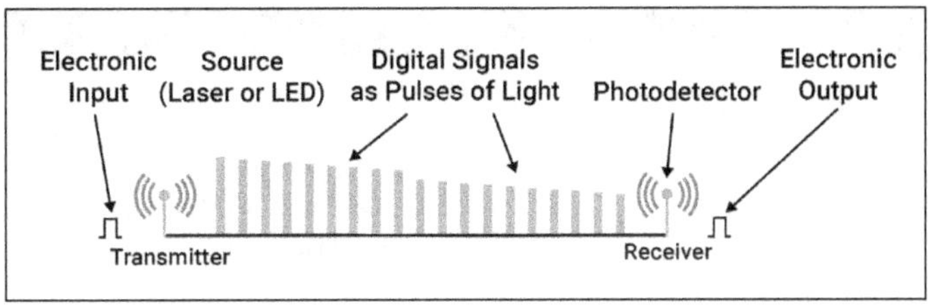

Figure 6-9: Signaling and signal attenuation on fiber optic cable.

Figure 6-9 also illustrates an important Physical layer transmission reality: transmitted signals weaken as they travel on the medium; the further they travel, the weaker they get. This is called signal attenuation. In networking, signal attenuation means signal weakening or loss; it is a natural consequence of signals traveling long distances over communication media. Signal attenuation happens in both wired and wireless networks, and it happens to both analog and digital signals.

Line Encoding

A signaling method includes a set of symbols that defines how 1s and 0s are represented on the communication media. In networking, a **symbol** is a transmission medium state or waveform that persists for a specific time duration.

Line encoding refers to signaling methods that represent bits as digital signals on communication media. On copper cables, line encoding involves the use of a voltage or current pattern to represent 1s and 0s on the media. Common types of line encoding include unipolar, bipolar, and Manchester line encoding. These types are illustrated in Figure 6-10 and described in Table 6-4.

For a signaling method to work, senders and receivers must agree on the symbols used to represent bits. Hence, a sender and receiver must be on the same page about the line encoding being used.

Senders and receivers must also agree on the number of symbols transmitted per second. **Symbol rate** is the number of symbol changes per unit of time. It specifies the number of transmission state (or waveform) changes per time unit (usually per second). Symbol rate is sometimes called *baud rate*, but this is an older data communication term that is considered outdated; it has been replaced by symbol rate in the data communications lexicon.

On copper or fiber optic cables, symbol rate is sometimes called *pulse rate* and may be expressed in pulses per second. For digital line encoding techniques used on copper cables, each symbol (pulse) represents a single bit (see Figure 6-10), and the symbol rate specifies the number of bits that are transmitted or received per second.

When analog signaling is used on copper cables, symbol rate identifies the number of waveform changes on the circuit per second and is sometimes

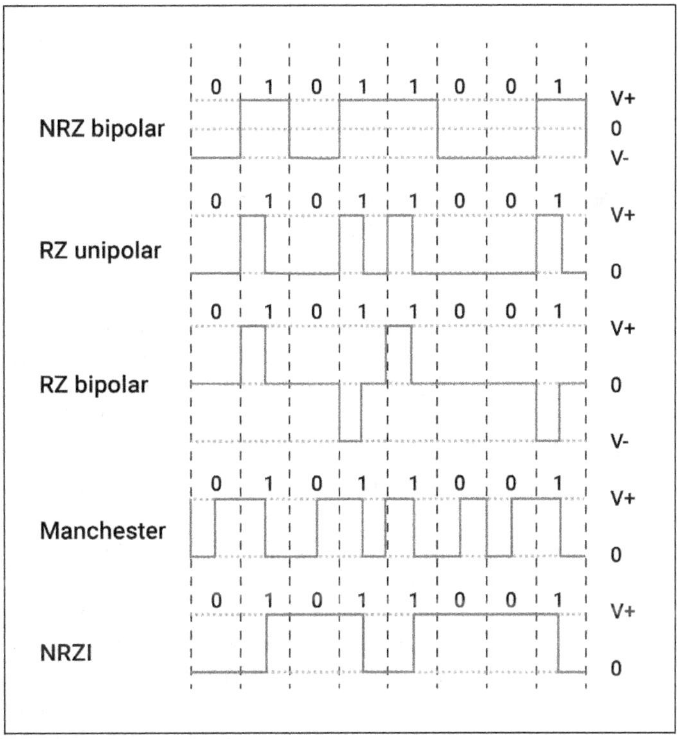

Figure 6-10: Line encoding examples.

Table 6-4: Line encoding examples.	
Line Encoding Method	**Description**
Unipolar encoding	*Unipolar encoding* has two voltage states, with one of the states being 0 volts and the other being either a negative (−v) or positive (+v) voltage level. Because it has a 0 volts state, unipolar encoding is also called *return to zero (RTZ)* or *RZ unipolar* encoding (see Figure 6-10). Unipolar line encoding works well where the signal path is short (such as inside a computer) but is less suitable when signals must travel longer distances.
Bipolar encoding	*Bipolar encoding* has two voltage states; it has a +v (positive voltage) state and a -v (negative voltage) state and does not have a 0 volts state. In Figure 6-10, *non-return-to-zero (NRZ) bipolar* is an example. Some bipolar encoding schemes, such as *RZ bipolar* in Figure 6-10, have three voltage levels; a 0 bit is represented by a zero (0) volt level and a 1 bit is represented by alternating polarity pulses. Alternating the polarity for 1 bits helps senders and receivers stay synchronized when long strings of 1s are transmitted. Bipolar line encoding is also called *alternate mark inversion (AMI)*; AMI is used on T1 circuits.
Non-Return-to-Zero Inverted (NRZI)	*NRZI* is a type of NRZ encoding in which each 1 bit changes the state of the previous bit (toggles) and each binary 0 keeps the same state as the previous bit, or vice versa. NRZI is used in 100 Mbps (and faster) Ethernet LANs. NRZI unipolar is illustrated in Figure 6-10.
Manchester encoding	In *Manchester encoding,* there is a transition at the middle of each bit period (bit interval). The mid-bit period transitions help senders and receivers stay synchronized. A low to high transition represents a 1, and a high to low transition represents a 0 (see Figure 6-10). Manchester encoding is (was) used in 10 Mbps Ethernet LANs.

called *modulation rate*. Each symbol usually represents multiple bits, and the total number of bits transmitted per second is calculated by multiplying the symbol rate by the number of bits each symbol represents. For example, if the symbol rate is 4000 symbols per second and each symbol represents eight bits, a total of 32,000 bits (4000 x 8) are transmitted each second. Because analog signaling is less common in wired LANs than in wireless LANs, analog signal modulation is described in Chapter 7.

Bit Synchronization and Bit Rate Control

In addition to agreement regarding symbols and symbol rate, a sender and receiver must be synchronized to ensure correct receipt of transmitted signals. Bit and frame synchronization techniques help receivers correctly decode transmitted signals. Bit-level synchronization is usually achieved by providing a clock that controls the sender's transmission pace and the receiver's monitoring of the communication link. The receiver "samples" the transmission state of the communication medium at the same rate that the sender transmits symbols.

Transmission rate measures the total number of bits that can traverse the communication medium each second and is often called *bit rate*. This can be expressed as bits per second (bps) but is more commonly kilobits per second (Kbps), megabits per second (Mbps), or gigabits per second (Gbps).

When digital line encoding is used, bit rate is a function of the duration of a symbol on the transmission medium. Each symbol persists for a fixed time duration. For example, if NRZ bipolar encoding is used, each symbol represents a single bit, and the symbol rate is 100 million symbols per second, the bit rate is 100 Mbps (100,000,000 bps), and the duration of each symbol on the transmission medium is 0.00000001 seconds (one one-hundred millionth of a second).

Bit interval is the amount of time required to transmit a single bit. When each symbol represents a single bit, bit interval and symbol duration are the same. If 100 million symbols are transmitted per second, the duration of each symbol on the medium is 0.00000001 seconds, and the bit interval is also 0.0000001 seconds (one one-hundred millionth of a second).

When analog signaling is used on copper cables, the relationships among bit rates, bit intervals, and symbol duration are less clear-cut. For example, if the circuit's bit rate is 100 Mbps and each symbol represents four bits, each symbol's duration on the medium is 0.00000025 seconds. While it might be tempting to infer that a bit interval is one-fourth of the symbol duration (since each symbol represents four bits), this glosses over the fact that each symbol is a specific waveform that only persists for a fixed time on the medium (symbol duration) and represents a specific combination of four bits.

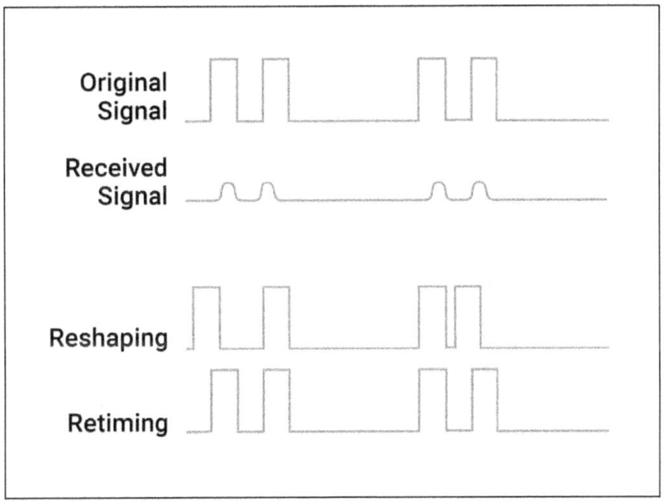

Figure 6-11: Signal reshaping and retiming are important aspects of signal regeneration.

6.2.2 Signal Regeneration and Errors

As noted in the previous sections, signals weaken as they travel on communication media. Long distances between senders and receivers can also affect their ability to remain synchronized. When signal attenuation or synchronization differences are significant, receivers may have difficulty correctly interpreting incoming signals. To compensate, signal regeneration is common in wired networks. **Signal regeneration** is a type of signal processing that involves recovering/restoring the signal's original characteristics, including its symbol shape and timing. This is illustrated in Figure 6-11.

In wired networks, a device that performs signal regeneration is called a *repeater*. A repeater includes circuitry required to recover a signal's original characteristics and timing from a weakened incoming signal. After re-creating the signal, a repeater transmits the signal on an outgoing circuit. This is conceptually illustrated in Figure 6-12.

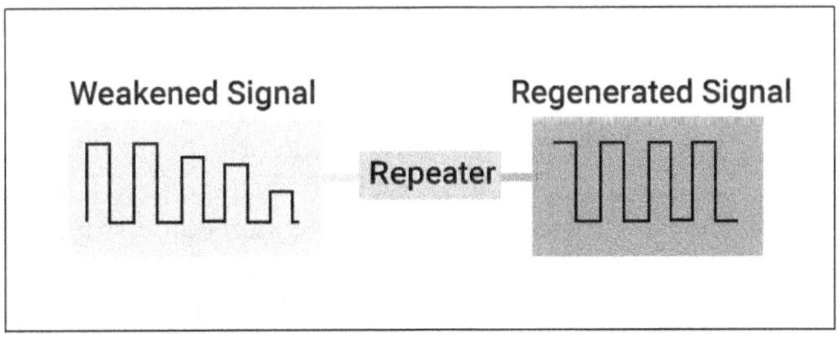

Figure 6-12: Repeaters regenerate signals weakened by signal attenuation.

A repeater is usually a two-port Physical layer device that receives an incoming signal on one interface and transmits the reconstructed signal on its other interface. Signal regeneration capabilities, however, are commonly included in other network devices that have more than two ports, including switches and routers. They are also common on adapters to ensure that received signals are restored to their original form.

Cabling standards specify maximum distances that signals should travel without regeneration, and, typically, the higher the bit rate the shorter the distance. For example, standards for 100 Mbps Ethernet LANs specify a maximum cable length of 100 meters, but those for 40 Gbps Ethernet LANs specify a maximum cable length of 30 meters. Repeaters are sometimes called *line drivers* because they can be used to extend distances between senders and receivers beyond the maximums specified in standards.

Signal Erosion, Noise, and Transmission Errors

In addition to weakening, signals erode as they traverse communication media (see Figure 6-13). Significant erosion can affect receivers' ability to accurately interpret incoming symbols, so using repeaters to reconstruct eroded signals can positively affect network efficiency. Noise can erode or distort a transmitted signal, and noise removal is considered a part of signal regeneration.

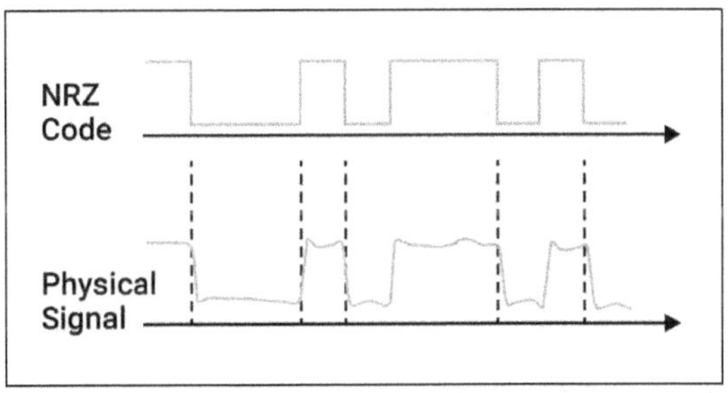

Figure 6-13: Signal erosion is common as signals traverse copper cables in wired networks.

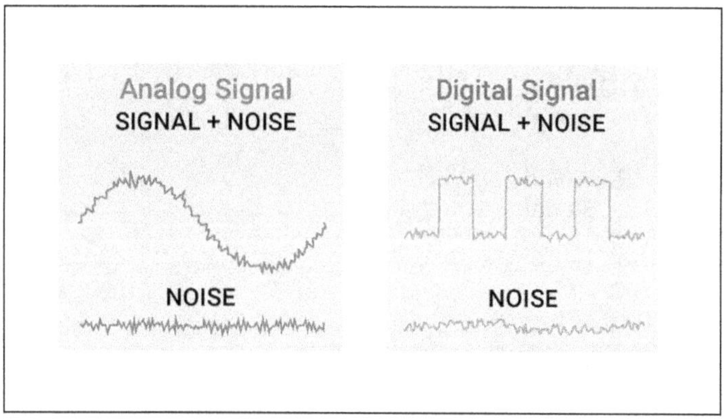

Figure 6-14: Noise on copper cables can alter the shape of both analog and digital signals.

As Figure 6-14 illustrates, noise manifests as analog waveforms (signals) that affect the shape of both digital and analog signals. When a transmitted symbol and noise are simultaneously present on a cable, the two signals combine and may cause the transmitted symbol to become significantly eroded or distorted (see Figure 6-15).

The reason why analog signals are affected by noise is easily explained. Since both the transmitted symbol and noise have analog waveforms, they combine to form a new waveform with characteristics of both. The explanation for why a digital signal is misshaped by analog noise waveforms is a little more involved but boils down to this: despite the use of discrete voltage levels to represent symbols (1s and 0s), digital signals consist of combinations of analog waveforms. If you are curious about how digital signals are made from analog signals, you are encouraged to read Appendix 6-2.

Noise and Errors

In networking, **noise** is an unwanted disturbance of a transmitted signal. Noise is frequently the result of unwanted and/or disturbing energy from natural or man-made sources and is often random rather than persistent. It can come from sources that carry electricity, such as motors, lights, and power cables, and can be created by lightning, bad connections, and radio waves.

Noise is typically distinguished from *interference* (signals from other transmission sources on the communication medium that disrupt a transmitted signal) and from *distortion* (unwanted changes in the shape of a transmitted signal caused by communication equipment or changes in the communication path). Noise, interference, and distortion can affect the quality of a transmitted signal and cause data transmission errors and are reasons why error detection and correction processes are needed. Figure 6-15 provides an example of how noise can cause transmission errors.

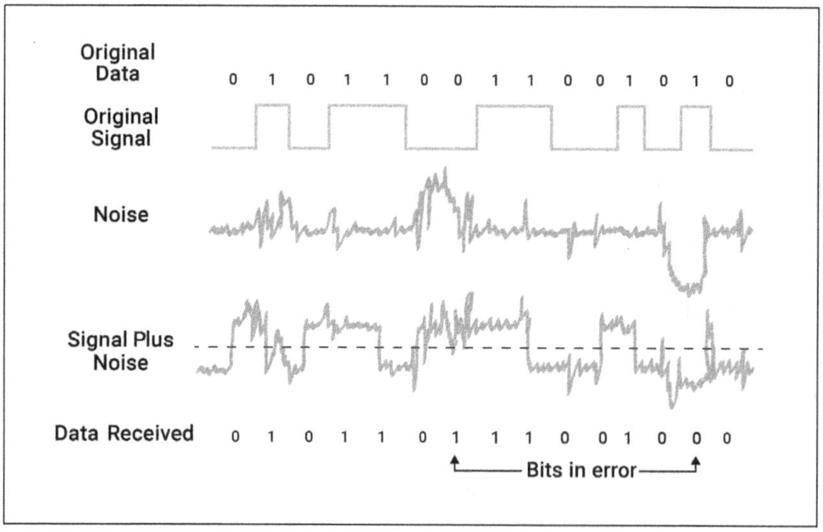

Figure 6-15: Noise that significantly distorts a signal can cause receivers to misinterpret the transmitted symbols.

Two major types of network errors are commonly identified: *corrupted data* (data that has been changed in transit across circuits) and *lost data* (data that is not delivered/received). The frequency of errors is often a function of the type of circuits that are used and the presence (and strength) of noise and other error sources. In wired networks, errors are more common on copper circuits than on fiber optic circuits because light signals are less susceptible to interference from other electronic devices, which can cause data transmission errors.

Typically, network errors occur in bursts. For a **burst error**, more than one bit in a data unit is changed (flipped) by the error-causing condition; these errors typically manifest in numerous bits being corrupted in clumps. A **single-bit error** happens when only one bit in a data unit (such as a byte, character, or data block) is changed from 1 to 0 or from 0 to 1. Today, burst errors are more common than single-bit errors, and each error may corrupt 100 or more bits.

Error Sources

Table 6-5 identifies some of the most common types and sources of network errors, their effects, and how their effects can be mitigated or prevented. Detrimental affects from some error sources

Table 6-5: Data communication error sources, causes, and remedies.

Error Source	Characteristics	Causes	Prevention Measures
Attenuation	Weak or undetectable signal on circuit.	Erosion of transmitted symbols and weakening of signal strength as it traverses the communication link.	Repeaters and other signal regenerators. Decrease distance between senders and receivers. Increase signal strength. Abide by EIA/TIA structured cabling standards and IEEE cable run specifications.
White (Gaussian) noise	Inescapable background noise on electrical and electronic circuits, such as hiss or static. This is rarely strong enough to cause data transmission errors.	Movement or agitation of electrons.	Increase signal strength or signal-to-noise ratio.
Impulse noise	Signal spikes that manifest as clicks or crackling noise. This is the most common cause of data transmission burst errors.	Voltage changes in adjacent lines, lightning strikes, fluorescent lights, poor circuit connections.	Shield or move the wire.
Crosstalk	This occurs when a circuit picks up a signal in an adjacent circuit; experienced on landline phone lines when other conversations are heard in background. Like white noise, signal strength in adjacent circuits is typically too low to be bothersome or cause data transmission errors.	Communication distance, proximity of adjacent wires, increased signal strength in adjacent wires, high-frequency signals, wet or damp conditions. In multiplexing, this can result from guard bands that are too small.	Shield wires; increase size of multiplexer guard bands.
Echoes	An echo is a signal reflection that occurs when a transmitted signal returns (reflects back) to the transmitter rather than terminating at the receiver. Transmission errors may occur when signal strength is sufficient to be detected; signal strength is typically too low to cause errors.	Poor circuit connections.	Fix or replace connections; fix, tune, or replace transmitting and receiving equipment, especially if it and communication links have been poorly maintained.
Intermodulation noise	Occurs when signals in adjacent circuits combine to form a new signal that affects or interferes with the signal in the circuit; it is like harmonics in music.	Variations in equipment adjustments or circuit connectors, such as RJ45 connectors on Ethernet cables.	Make communication equipment adjustments, replace connectors, move/separate circuits.
Jitter	Minute variations in the amplitude, frequency, or phase of analog signals. Some jitter is natural (generating a pure carrier signal is impossible), but some is periodic or random. On telephone calls, jitter can cause sound volume to fluctuate.	Rapid amplitude and/or phase changes can cause the transmitted signal to be impaired and/or incorrectly interpreted by the receiver.	Tuning or replacement of transmitting and/or receiving equipment.
Line outages	Loss of carrier signal and data transmission capability.	Faulty communication equipment, short circuits, storm damage to circuits or facilities.	Replacement of faulty equipment and sources of short circuits. Moving elevated circuits underground.

(such as white noise, crosstalk, and echoes) are rare, and impulse noise is the most common source of burst errors.

Line outages can be catastrophic causes of errors and incomplete transmission. Communication links sometimes experience temporary failures, but line outages caused by storms, or natural or man-made catastrophes, can cause lengthy network disruptions, especially when they affect a network's sources of electricity—signals cannot be propagated without electricity. Data centers typically have redundant power supplies (e.g., generators and battery backup) to compensate for power loss, and many also have dual- or multi-homed ISP connections to compensate for link failures.

Error Prevention and Reduction

Noise is sometimes controlled by improving the communication medium's *signal-to-noise ratio (SNR)*. This involves increasing the strength of the signal and/or reducing or suppressing the medium's noise level. This is one of a variety of techniques used to prevent or reduce errors.

Shielding (covering wires with an insulating coating) is an effective way to reduce or prevent errors caused by impulse noise, intermodulation noise, and crosstalk. Most types of copper cables used in local networks are available with different amounts of shielding. For example, both shielded twisted-pair (STP) and unshielded twisted-pair (UTP) Ethernet cables are available from most cable vendors. Generally, STP is more expensive than UTP and can be more difficult to install; however, it is often the best option in noise-prone environments.

Moving cables away from noise sources (such as power cables, heavy equipment, or lights) can reduce impulse noise, intermodulation noise, and crosstalk. Conduit and cable trays are often used to isolate network cables from noise sources. Proper maintenance or replacement of networking equipment can reduce detrimental effects from several error sources, including echoes, jitter, intermodulation noise, and white noise.

6.2.3 Cabling Standards

Specifications for connectors, device interfaces, and physical media are addressed in Physical layer standards. Because Physical layer technologies are designed and developed by engineers, Physical layer standards are defined and maintained by electrical and communications engineering organizations, including the following:

- The Institute of Electrical and Electronics Engineers (IEEE)
- The International Organization for Standardization (ISO)
- The National Institute for Standards and Technology (NIST)
- The American National Standards Institute (ANSI)
- The International Telecommunication Union (ITU)
- The Electronics Industries Alliance/Telecommunications Industry Association (EIA/TIA)

National telecommunications authorities such as the U.S. Federal Communications Commission (FCC) formally adopt standards defined by these organizations.

Physical layer standards address several aspects of the technologies used at this layer, including the mechanical and functional properties of connection interfaces, physical and electrical properties of communication media, and how bits are represented as symbols on communication media. These standards are implemented in network adapters, cable connectors, switch interfaces, and network cabling.

ANSI/TIA-568 standards are among the most important standards for wired LANs, and they address the following:

- Subsystems of a structured cabling system (see Figure 6-16 and Table 6-6)
- Definitions of cabling elements (e.g., horizontal cable, telecommunication outlets, etc.)

- Minimum requirements for telecommunications cabling
- Connector pin assignments for twisted-pair cabling
- Media types and performance specifications for the newest generations of horizontal and backbone cabling
- Recommended cabling topology and distances
- Installation methods and networking practices
- Connecting hardware performance specifications
- The life span of a telecommunications cabling systems technology (which should exceed 10 years)

Structured cabling refers to building or campus telecommunications infrastructure that consists of multiple standardized elements. ANSI/TIA-568 structured cabling standards address the six telecommunication subsystems illustrated in Figure 6-16 and briefly described in Table 6-6.

These standards are used to deploy Ethernet LANs and BNs in business facilities whose infrastructure includes cross-connects, patch panels, cable terminations, and the conduit/cable trays used to organize horizontal cabling that connects work areas to telecommunications closets. Conduit is also used for backbone (vertical) cabling that connects telecommunications closets to equipment rooms and building entrances.

Other important Physical layer standards are identified and briefly described in Appendix 6-3.

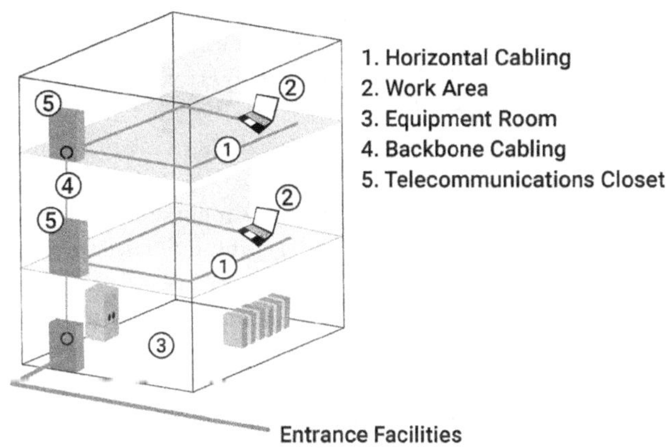

Figure 6-16: Structured cabling subsystems.

Table 6-6: Structured cabling subsystems.

ANSI/TIA-568 Subsystem	Summary Overview
Work area	This includes user equipment (computers, printers, copiers, telephones, etc.) and the cables (e.g., Ethernet cables, fiber optic patch cables, etc.) that connect the user equipment to communication jacks/outlets. Work areas connect to telecommunications rooms via horizontal cabling.
Horizontal cabling	Horizontal cabling extends from work area communication jacks/outlets to a telecommunications room on the same floor. The cabling often runs through conduit or cable trays beneath raised floors or above ceilings.
Telecommunications room	A telecommunications room houses cable terminations (such as switches and patch panels) for horizontal and backbone cables. It also includes patch cables and/or jumpers that connect cable terminations.
Backbone cabling	Backbone cabling interconnects telecommunications rooms, equipment rooms, and building entrances. This includes backbone cables (usually optical fiber cables), mechanical terminations (e.g., connectors for fiber optic cables that enable them to connect to cable terminations), and patch cables used for connecting different backbone components.
Equipment room	The equipment room houses equipment (such as servers, storage devices, and telephone equipment) that supports users in the building. It also provides cable terminations, cross-connections, and connections between backbone cabling and the building entrance facilities.
Entrance facilities	A building entrance is the point at which external cabling and/or wireless services connect to a building's equipment room and internal cabling. Entrance facility components include internal and external demarcation points, connection points, protection devices, cables, and other equipment that connects the building to network access providers (such as ISPs) or private cabling/wireless providers.

6.3 DATA LINK AND PHYSICAL LAYER TECHNOLOGIES

There are a number of important technologies at the Data Link and Physical layers of wired networks. Repeaters, cables, connectors, and media converters are some of the most important Physical layer technologies, and adapters and Layer 2 switches are important Data Link layer technologies.

6.3.1 Adapters

As noted in Chapter 4, adapters are needed to connect to local networks. Today, adapters are commonly included components on device motherboards, but some plug into motherboard expansion slots or USB ports. Adapters serve as the interface/bridge between the Network and Physical layers and perform both Data Link (e.g., physical addressing, frame building, and error detection) and Physical layer (e.g., symbol transmission) functions.

Network adapters perform frame building (data encapsulation) and error checking/detection at the Data Link layer. They also implement data link and media access controls. The adapter's MAC address (its 48-bit serial number and unique identifier) is stored in read-only memory (ROM) on the adapter.

Network adapters include *transceivers* that create, transmit, and receive the symbols/signals that represent bits on communication media. They also include serial/parallel conversion circuitry that, when receiving, converts serial transmission from the communication medium to parallel transmission used internally among motherboard components, and, when transmitting, reverses the process.

Most network adapters are configured to autodetect and automatically adjust symbols/signals, bit rates, and duplex settings on connecting circuits to switches. Ethernet adapters automatically toggle to using data link controls on full duplex circuits or to CSMA/CD media access control on half-duplex circuits.

Adapter circuitry includes a controller that works like a mini CPU or microprocessor that determines how it performs. The controller implements the Data Link standard (e.g., Ethernet or Wi-Fi) and thereby helps support the TCP/IP protocol stack in the local network. A closer look at adapter components and operations is included in Appendix 6-4.

Most Ethernet controllers are designated as 10/100/1000 (or 100/1000/10000) controllers. They can support bit rates of 10, 100, or 1,000 Mbps (or 100/1,000/10,000 Mbps) and the line encoding schemes associated with the different speeds. Some include a TCP offload engine that enables processing of the entire TCP/IP stack to be offloaded to the adapter's controller, including TCP retransmission (ARQ) protocols.

Adapters in wired networks also include the physical interface to the communication medium. In Ethernet LANs, this is an RJ45 interface for twisted-pair cable or an SC, ST, or LC interface for fiber optic cable.

6.3.2 Cabling and Connectors

The two most common types of cables in wired LANs are twisted-pair and fiber optic cables, but some LANs also include coaxial cables, and some include hybrid cabling that usually combines coaxial and fiber optic cables. Twisted-pair and coaxial cables are examples of copper cabling. The various types of cables are introduced and briefly described in section 4.4.5 in Chapter 4.

Twisted-pair cables are the primary type of cable used to connect user equipment to telecommunication jacks/outlets in work areas in buildings. They are also the most common type of horizontal cabling between work areas and telecommunications rooms. Unshielded twisted-pair (UTP) is most common, but in noisy environments, shielded twisted-pair (STP) may be used to provide additional protection from error sources. As Figure 4-30 in section 4.4.5 illustrates, twisted-pair cables include four wired pairs (eight total wires).

When electric current is passed through pairs of wires that are twisted together, an electromagnetic field is created around them that helps protect transmitted data from external error sources, including interference from adjacent pairs of wires. In some locations, this electromagnetic field may not provide enough protection from error sources, and more costly STP may be needed. As Figure 6-17 illustrates, in STP cabling, a metal sheath encases each pair of wires.

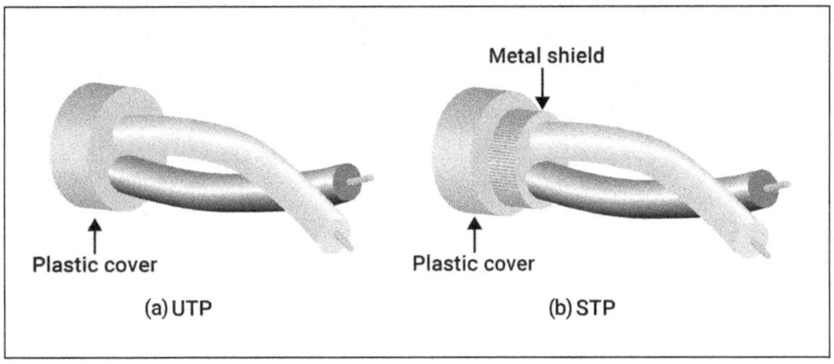

Figure 6-17: The difference between UTP and STP.

ANSI/TIA-568 standards address UTP and STP cables. They specify categories (such as Cat5, Cat6, and Cat8) for cables associated with Ethernet standards (see Table 6-7) and identify the specifications and capabilities of different types of Ethernet cables.

Table 6-7: Examples of twisted-pair cables used in Ethernet LANs.

	Cat5e	Cat6	Cat6a	Cat8
Frequency	100 MHz	250 MHz	500 MHz	2000 MHz
Maximum Transmission Speed	1 Gbps	1 Gbps	10 Gbps	40 Gbps
IEEE Ethernet Standard	1GBASE-T	1GBASE-T	10GBASE-T	40GBASE-T
Number of Wires	8	8	8	8
Connector Type	RJ45	RJ45	RJ45	RJ45

As Figure 6-18 illustrates, twisted-pair Ethernet cables include eight wires (four pairs) in a single cable that ends with an RJ45 connector on each end. The color scheme for wire pairs can vary by the ANSI/TIA-568 standard (category), but four colors are used (e.g., green, blue, orange, brown), and in each pair, one of the wires is solid and the other has white bands. Pin assignments for the individual wires vary by termination standard, of which there are two: T568A and T568B (see Figure 6-18). T568B is typically used for new network installations, but T568A may be used to ensure backward compatibility with older office equipment or to comply with government contract requirements.

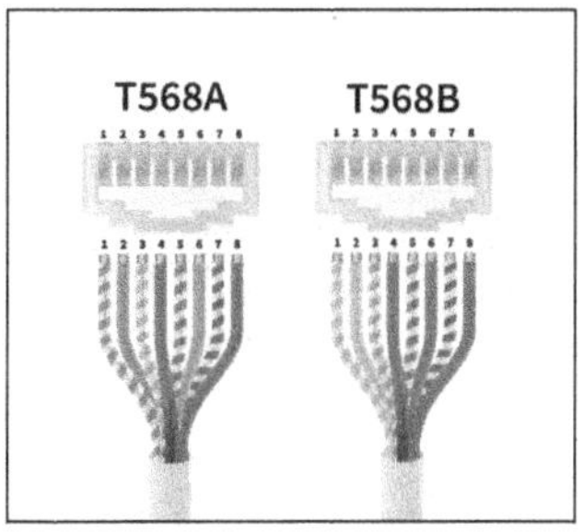

Figure 6-18: Example of ANSI/TIA-568 pin assignment schemes for twisted-pair cables in an RJ45 connector. Source: Evgenii_Bobrov/iStock/Stock illustration ID:1139342284

Photos of RJ45 connectors and ST, SC, and LC connectors used on fiber optic patch cables are included in section 4.4.5 in Chapter 4. ST, SC, and LC connectors are common for fiber optic patch cables used to interconnect switches, servers, and routers. *SC (subscriber connector)* is widely used because it is inexpensive to produce and simple to use. *LC* (alternatively known as the *Lucent connector*, *little connector*, or *local connector*) is frequently preferred in high-performance networks, such as those in data centers. *ST (straight tip)* connectors may also be used. Optical fiber connectors are commonly spring-loaded to ensure connection stability.

Because optical fiber polishing and tuning procedures are needed, connectors are usually added to optical fiber by patch cable manufacturers; however, sometimes installers perform assembly and polishing operations. Optical fibers and connectors are commonly used for backbone cabling in buildings, equipment rooms, and building entrances (see Figure 6-16 and Table 6-6).

SC, LC, and ST connectors are used on both single-mode and multimode fiber optic cable. Optical fiber is the glass (or plastic) portion of a fiber optic cable; it is the light-carrying core of the cable and is surrounded by cladding to keep the light from escaping as it travels through the core.

Table 6-8: Comparison of single-mode and multimode fiber optic cables.

Type	Core Diameter	Diameter with Cladding	Light Source	Standards/Grades
Single-mode	9 micrometers (μm)	125 μm	Light Amplification by Stimulated Emission of Radiation (LASER)	OS1 (1,310 nanometer wavelength) OS2 (1,550 nanometer wavelength)
Multimode	50 μm or more	125 μm	Vertical-Cavity Surface-Emitting Laser (VCSEL). Prior to VCSEL, LED was used.	OM1–OM5 (See Table 6-9)

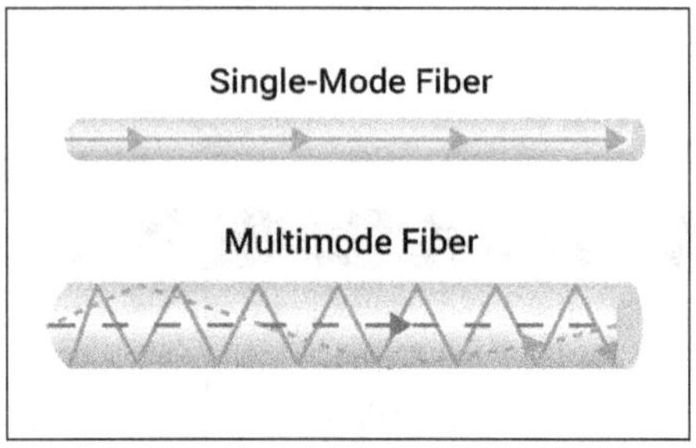

Figure 6-19: Depiction of light beam paths in single-mode and multimode fiber.

Single-mode fiber has a smaller core than multimode (see Table 6-8); its diameter is one-tenth the diameter of a human hair, and its smaller core limits light dispersion and enables signals to be sent over longer distances than multimode. As light travels through the core in multimode fiber, it bounces off the cladding (see Figure 6-19). When multiple light beams are transmitted at the same time, each beam will have a different path, and the different beams will reach the end of the fiber at different times.

As Table 6-9 indicates, five different grades of multimode fiber are commonly identified: OM1, OM2, OM3, OM4, and OM5. The OM stands for "optical multimode." Each grade has a specified bandwidth range and distance limitation. OM4 and OM5 provide the greatest transmission speeds over the longest distances, and OM1 provides the lowest speed and shortest distance.

Table 6-9: Multimode fiber optic table grades.

Multimode Designation	Maximum Lengths			
	1 Gbps	10 Gbps	40/100 Gbps	400 Gbps
OM1	300m	30m	NA	NA
OM2	600m	150m	NA	NA
OM3	1000m	300m	100m	100m
OM4	1100m	550m	150m	150m
OM5	1100m	550m	150m	150m

In sum, optical cables have different core diameters, use different light sources, and are available in different grades.

Fiber optic cables are also widely used to interconnect buildings on a business or university campus. For example, in Figure 6-16, the cable that connects the building to the outside world may be a fiber optic cable that includes multiple optical fibers. Such cables may contain 144 single-mode or multimode optical fibers, but all are either single-mode or multimode fibers and not a mixture of the two.

6.3.3 Media Converters

Media converters were introduced in section 4.4.5 in Chapter 4. They enable different types of cabling (e.g., twisted-pair and fiber optic cable) to be used in the same wired network.

A common type of media converter converts the electrical signals utilized on UTP Ethernet cables to light waves in fiber optic cabling. The deployment illustrated in Figure 6-20 would enable the two switches to be hundreds of meters apart (beyond the maximum specified in ANSI/TIA-568 standards); similar arrangements would enable a server, router, or user device to connect to a switch over a considerable distance. Basically, this enables media converters to serve as network extenders.

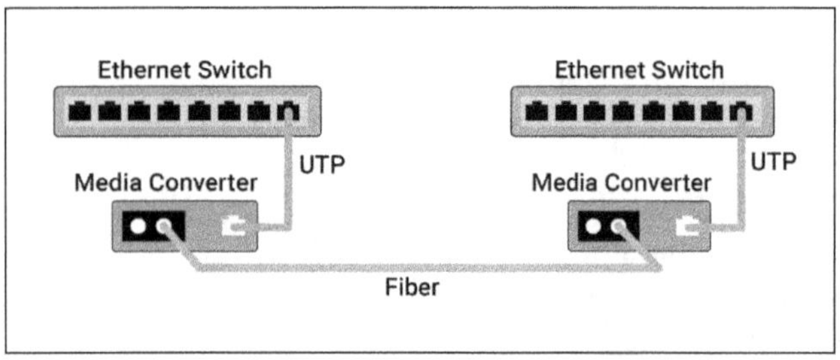

Figure 6-20: Example of UTP to fiber media conversion.

A data center may include a rack-mounted media conversion chassis that includes multiple UTP and fiber ports and transceivers (see Figure 6-21). Additional types of media converters include UTP to coaxial cable converters, UTP to wireless converters, and single-mode to multimode cable converters. Often, organizations that claim to have a fiber optic backbone liberally deploy media converters that enable the distribution of traffic to/from LANs over fiber optic cabling.

Figure 6-21: Switch or media converter with both RJ45 and fiber optic ports. Source: iStock/wisawa222/Stock photo ID:637345096

6.3.4 Switches

Layer 2 (Data Link layer) switches were introduced in section 4.4.4 in Chapter 4. In addition to making frame forwarding decisions, Layer 2 switches function as signal regenerators that reconstruct symbols that have eroded during transfer over incoming circuits. They can also be configured to detect and remove errored or fragmented frames from the local network. Some switches may also be media converters.

Each device connects to a switch via a copper or fiber optic Ethernet cable; UTP is most common. The cables attach to switch interfaces (*ports*). In Figure 6-22, RJ45 ports are illustrated, but some switches have SC, ST, and LC ports for multimode or single-mode fiber optic cables.

Figure 6-22: An example of a 24-port Ethernet switch. Source: vnosokin/istock/ Stock photo ID:89332176

Each switch has a limited number of connection ports. Small switches with five, eight, or 16 ports may be sufficient for wired networks in small businesses or homes, but switches with 24, 32, 36, 48, or 52 ports are more common in larger networks. Switches can be standalone (tabletop) or rack-mountable, but most are rack-mountable.

Unless configured as part of a multilayer switch that also considers VLAN tags, destination IP addresses, or port addresses in Transport layer PDUs, a Layer 2 switch only uses MAC addresses in the Destination Fields of frame headers to make forwarding decisions.

Layer 2 switches are usually configured to maximize forwarding speed, but most support several forwarding modes including those described in Table 6-10. Most switches are configured for cut-through forwarding but can also be configured to operate in a fragment-free or store-and-forward mode.

Table 6-10: Switching modes in Layer 2 switches.

Switching Mode	Brief Description
Cut-through	In the *cut-through forwarding* mode, the switch only reads the Destination Address in the frame header before beginning to transmit the frame on the interface for the device with the specified MAC address. In this switching mode, frames with data transmission errors are forwarded to recipients, which forces receivers to detect and remove errored frames from the network. Since errored frames are rare in today's LANs, it makes sense to configure switches to operate in the cut-through mode, the fastest forwarding mode.
Fragment-free	In this mode, the switch receives and examines the first 64 bytes of the Ethernet frame before making the forwarding decision. Sixty-four bytes is the smallest allowable Ethernet frame size; any frame less than this minimal size is a fragment, and in this switching mode, fragments are not forwarded. Frame fragments can result from malfunctioning adapters or data transmission errors. Today, this mode is rarely used.
Store-and-forward	In this switching mode, the switch waits for the entire frame to be received and placed in a buffer, where it is checked for errors before forwarding. Frames with errors are not forwarded. This is the slowest forwarding mode but is sometimes the best to use in noisy environments.

As noted in section 4.4.4 of Chapter 4, Layer 2 switches also support broadcast traffic. When default settings are used, any broadcast frames that a switch receives are forwarded out of all ports except the one on which they were received. This defines the switch's default *broadcast domain.*

A broadcast frame has the following Destination Address: FFFF.FFFF.FFFF (or ff:ff:ff:ff:ff:ff or ff-ff-ff-ff-ff-ff). When a device transmits a broadcast frame, the switch knows to transmit it on each interface except that on which it was received. Broadcast frames originate at devices attached to a switch; they do not originate at the switch.

Now that you have a better understanding of Data Link and Physical layer communication functions, protocols, signaling, and technologies in wired networks, you are positioned to appreciate how they are implemented in Ethernet LANs and backbone networks.

6.4 ETHERNET LANs

Ethernet is the dominant wired LAN architecture in today's organizations and arguably the only wired LAN and backbone network architecture that warrants attention.

A **LAN architecture** consists of the design principles and rules that define the structure of a LAN. This includes hardware (adapters, cabling, connectors, switches, media converters, etc.), software (such as that used at LLC and MAC sublayers), topology (the physical and logical way that network devices are interconnected), communication protocols (such as data link and media access controls), and the sequence of operations.

6.4.1 Ethernet Architecture

The primary hardware components of an Ethernet LAN are:

- Ethernet adapters in client devices, servers, printers, storage equipment, etc.
- Ethernet cables (UTP, STP, fiber optic)
- Ethernet switches

Because Ethernet LANs continue to evolve, there are multiple IEEE standards for Ethernet LANs.

Ethernet Standards

IEEE 802.3 provides an umbrella for the various Ethernet standards that define Physical and Data Link layer specifications for Ethernet networks with different transmission speeds. Some of the best known standards and their associated names and transmission speeds are identified in Table 6-11. Table 6-12 identifies various physical specifications for Ethernet and their associated media, media standards, and reach (distance).

Table 6-11: Examples of well-known Ethernet standards.

Ethernet Standard	Known Name	Speed
IEEE 802.3	Ethernet	10 Mbps
IEEE 802.3u	Fast Ethernet	100 Mbps
IEEE 802.3z or 802.3ab	Gigabit Ethernet	1000 Mbps
IEEE 802.3ae	10 Gigabit Ethernet	10 Gbps
IEEE 802.3ba	100 Gigabit Ethernet	100 Gbps

As may be observed in Table 6-12, the first number in the name of the physical standard (e.g., 1000BASE-T) represents the speed of the LAN in Mbps. "BASE" refers to *baseband transmission*, which means that the transmitted signals do not share the cable/circuit with other signals and occupy the entire physical channel. The final part of the physical implementation name refers to the cabling used to carry signals. So, for example, 1000BASE-T means twisted-pair cabling is used, the speed of the network can reach 1,000 Mbps, and baseband signaling is used.

Table 6-12: Examples of Ethernet physical implementation specifications.			
Physical Implementation	**Medium**	**Medium Standard**	**Reach (Distance)**
10BASE-T	UTP or STP	CAT-3	100 m
100BASE-T	UTP or STP	CAT-5	100 m
1000BASE-T	UTP or STP	CAT-5e	100 m
2.5GBASE-T	UTP or STP	CAT-5e	100 m
5GBASE-T	UTP or STP	CAT-6	100 m
10GBASE-T	UTP or STP	CAT-6A	100 m
25GBASE-T	STP	CAT-8	30 m
40GBASE-T	STP	CAT-8	30 m
1000BASE-SX	Multimode fiber	OM1, OM2	220 m to 550 m
1000BASE-LX	Multimode fiber	OM2	550 m
1000BASE-LX	Single-mode fiber	OS1, OS2	5 km
1000BASE-LX10	Single-mode fiber	OS1	10 km
1000BASE-EX	Single-mode fiber	OS1	40 km
1000BASE-ZX	Single-mode fiber	OS2	70 km
1000BASE-BX10	Single-mode fiber	OS1, OS2	10 km

Line Encoding

Different types of line encoding are used to represent bits on Ethernet cables. Manchester encoding (see Figure 6-10) is used on 10 Mbps (10BASE-T) Ethernet LANs, but few of these LANs still exist. 100Base-T (Fast Ethernet) Ethernet LANs use 4B/5B encoding with NRZI encoding. (NRZI is illustrated in Figure 6-10.)

4B/5B (a.k.a. 4B 5B or 4b/5b or 4b 5b encoding) is a type of block coding that processes groups (blocks) of bits rather than simply creating a symbol/signal for each individual bit. In 4B/5B, a fifth bit is added to each group of four bits. There are 2^4 (16) different four-bit groups (see Table 6-13), and a fifth bit is added to each group to create its corresponding 4B/5B code. Then NRZI encoding is used to represent 4B/5B codes on the Ethernet cable (see Figure 6-23). Receivers convert the 4B/5B code back to the original four bits.

4B/5B encoding helps senders and receivers to stay synchronized by avoiding long strings of 0s that can cause synchronization drift. NRZI's inversion of successive 1s also helps synchronization. Similar types of block coding are used in higher speed Ethernet LANs. For example, 8B/10B is used in Gigabit Ethernet LANs.

Table 6-13: 4B/5B codes for four-bit strings.			
Binary	**4B/5B Code**	**Binary**	**4B/5B Code**
0000	11110	1000	11010
0001	01001	1001	10011
0010	10100	1010	10110
0011	10101	1011	10111
0100	01010	1100	11010
0101	01011	1101	11011
0110	01110	1110	11100
0111	01111	1111	11101

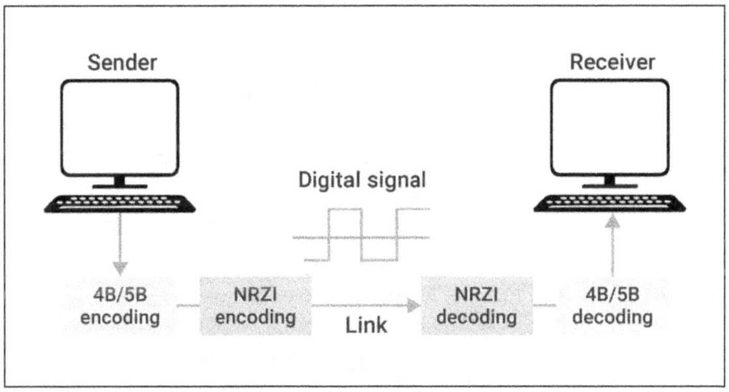

Figure 6-23: Fast Ethernet (100Base-T Ethernet) combines 4B/5B encoding with NRZI line coding.

Physical and Logical Topology

Physical topology considers the interconnection structure of a local network. As noted in section 4.4.5 of Chapter 4, this includes the placement of the network's physical devices, the method used to connect the devices using cables, and the type of cabling that is used. Depictions of the physical topologies that have been used in Ethernet LANs are shown in Figure 6-24.

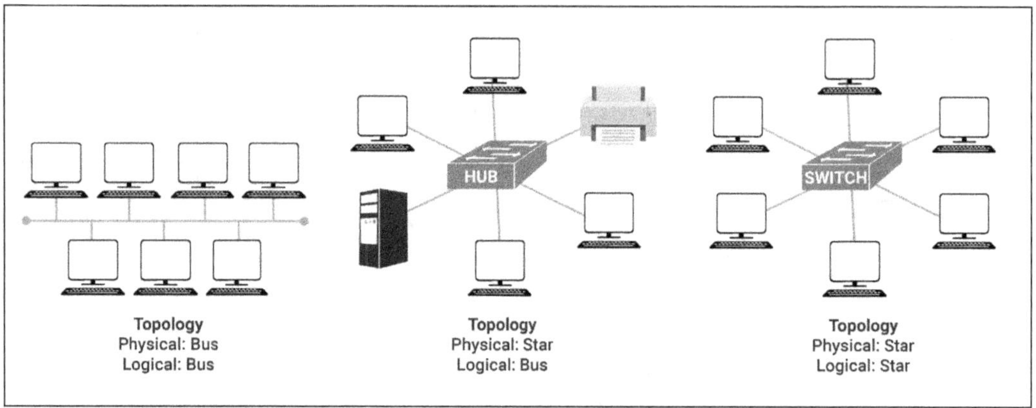

Figure 6-24: Historical progression of physical and logical topologies in Ethernet LANs.

Logical topology emphasizes how data is transferred between devices rather than the layouts of the physical paths that data follows. It addresses line discipline (when a device can transmit), the ordered delivery of frames to receivers, error control, and flow control. Logical topologies are more closely associated with Data Link layer protocols than physical topologies.

The earliest Ethernet LANs had both physical and logical bus topologies. The physical bus was usually a coaxial cable. Network-attached devices had Ethernet adapters with coaxial cable interfaces, and a coaxial cable from each device's adapter connected to the physical bus via a T-connector. The physical bus was a shared circuit, and every device in the network received every transmitted frame. CSMA/CD, a random-access protocol, was used to provide line discipline in this and hub-based shared media Ethernet LANs.

CSMA/CD

CSMA/CD (Carrier Sense Multiple Access with Collision Detection) is based on CSMA, the random-access, contention-based protocol introduced in section 6.1.2. CSMA works on the principle that only one device can use the shared medium to transmit data at a single point in time; otherwise, a data collision will occur that will result in frame corruption or loss.

CSMA requires the device to check the medium for in-progress data transmissions before beginning to transmit. If it "senses" an in-progress transmission, the device will wait for the transmission to end before beginning to transmit its data. However, if other devices are also waiting and begin transmitting, data collisions occur and corrupt the transmitted frames. Hence, collision detection (CD) is needed to detect and recover from data collisions.

In CSMA/CD, when data collisions are detected, all transmitting devices cease transmitting, and each device waits a specific time, called *backoff time*, before retransmitting. A *backoff algorithm*, supported by software embedded in Ethernet adapters, is used to calculate the backoff time.

CSMA/CD continued to be important in the hub-based physical star topologies that replaced physical bus topologies in the next generation of Ethernet LANs. In physical appearance, a hub looks like a switch, with RJ45 ports that connect client devices via Ethernet cables. However, that is where the resemblance between a hub and switch ends.

In a shared media hub, devices connect to an internal shared bus, which is often called "a bus in a box." As with physical bus LANs, all connected devices receive every transmitted frame. Hence, CSMA/CD continued to be an appropriate line discipline in hub-based Ethernet LANs.

Today's switched Ethernet LANs have both a physical star and a logical star topology. The Ethernet cable that connects a device to a switch is not shared with any other and is the only medium available for CSMA/CD to monitor. Usually, the Ethernet cable supports full-duplex transmission, with one of the four pairs of wires used to transmit and a second pair used to receive. This enables a device to simultaneously transmit and receive without being disrupted by collisions.

This configuration eliminates the need for a device monitor to "sense" the communication medium before transmitting and reduces the potential for data collisions. A contention-based protocol, such as CSMA/CD, is unnecessary. Framing and sender-receiver synchronization are sufficient data link controls in today's switched Ethernet LANs.

As mentioned in section 6.1.2, CSMA/CD continues as the "official" Ethernet protocol but is disabled and not used in switched Ethernet networks. Today it is only used with half-duplex circuits or in legacy hub-based Ethernet LANs.

6.4.2 Ethernet Frame Formats

The format of traditional Ethernet frames is illustrated in Figure 6-25, and the contents of each field are briefly described in Table 6-14. The MAC address of a frame's recipient (the Destination address) is conveniently located near the beginning of the frame, and when CSMA/CD is used, this location enables recipients to quickly determine whether a frame can be ignored (if it is addressed to a different device) or received and processed. The device only needs to read the first two fields of the frame before making the "receive or ignore" decision. The intended recipient(s) must process the entire frame, but the others can ignore it.

To accommodate virtual LANs (VLANs) in Ethernet LANs, the traditional 802.3 frame format is modified in compliance with IEEE's 802.1Q standard, the networking standard for VLANs in Ethernet LANs.

802.1Q defines a VLAN tagging system for Ethernet frames. It also defines the procedures that switches and other networking equipment use for handling frames with VLAN tags. 802.1Q adds a

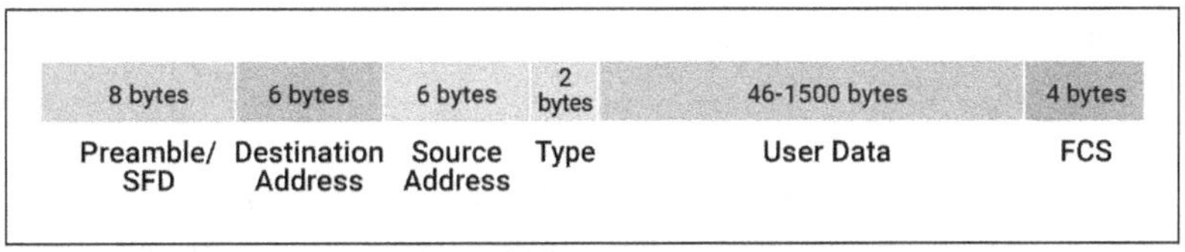

Figure 6-25: Format of traditional 802.3 (Ethernet) frames.

Table 6-14: Brief descriptions of the fields in a traditional Ethernet 802.3 frame.	
Field Name	**Field Description**
Preamble	This facilitates synchronization of sender and receiver network adapter clocks.
Start Frame Delimiter (SFD)	This identifies where the receiver's Ethernet software should begin reading the frame.
Destination Address	The MAC address of the frame recipient.
Source Address	The MAC address of the sending device.
Type	This identifies the kind of packet (PDU) in the data field and is also called the Ether Type field.
User Data	This carries the Network layer PDU plus networking overhead.
Frame Check Sequence (FCS)	The sending device's Ethernet adapter calculates an EDV and places its results in this field. The frame recipient performs the same calculation on the bit stream and compares its EDV to that in this field. If the bitstream has been changed during transmission, the match will fail and the frame will be discarded.

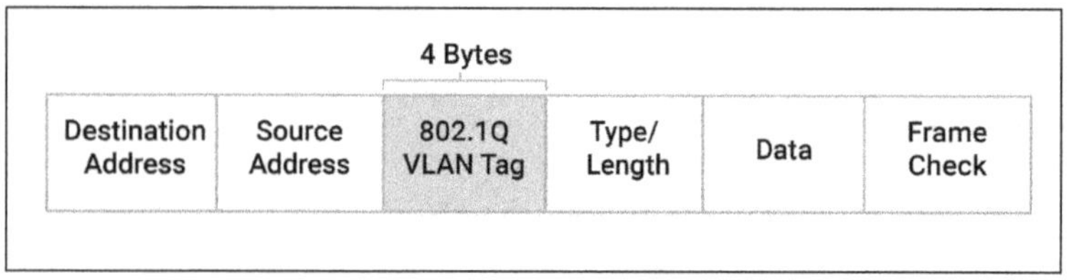

Figure 6-26: VLAN tags in 802.1Q frames.

32-bit field between the Source Address and Type fields (see Figure 6-26) and extends the maximum frame size by four bytes.

The VLAN tag field has four segments. Three of the segments are used by switches and other networking equipment to support VLANs, and the other, a VLAN ID, identifies the VLAN to which the frame belongs. VLAN tags are described in further detail in Appendix 6-5.

VLANs and other modifications to traditional Ethernet frame formats illustrate Ethernet's evolution and suggest that future modifications are likely.

6.4.3 Power over Ethernet (PoE)

Power over Ethernet (PoE) refers to standards and technologies that enable both electric power and data signals to be carried to LAN devices on twisted-pair Ethernet cables. With PoE, network devices do not need a separate power supply or power cord. PoE is widely used to power wireless access points (WAPs) in Wi-Fi LANs, IP security/surveillance cameras, and an increasing array of other devices, including computer motherboards.

Table 6-15: PoE standards and specifications.

	PoE	PoE+	PoE++	PoE++
IEEE Standard	802.3af	802.3at	802.3bt	802.3bt
Switch Port Power				
Maximum Port Power	15.4W	30W	60W	100W
Port Voltage Range	44V-57V	50V-57V	50V-57V	52V-57V
Powered Device Power				
Maximum Power to Device	12.95W	25.5W	51W	71W
Voltage Range to Device	37V-57V	42.5V-57V	42.5V-57V	41.1V-57V
Cables				
Supported Cables	Cat3/Cat5/Cat6	Cat5/Cat6	Cat5/Cat6	Cat5/Cat6
Twisted Pairs Used	2 pairs	2 pairs	2 or 4 pairs	4 pairs

Some types of PoE use two pairs of wires in Cat5 or Cat6 Ethernet cables to power devices (e.g., devices in 100BASE-T LANs), but others enable power to be carried on all four pairs (see Table 6-15). Today, PoE is also used in 1000BASE-T and 10GBASE-T Ethernet LANs.

As shown in Table 6-15, PoE standards address several different power and voltage levels. It also illustrates that there are 60W and 100W versions of PoE++. Generally, higher power and voltage levels enable a wider range of devices to be powered. Some computer manufacturers have products with motherboards that can be powered by PoE++ switches and midspan technologies.

Today, Ethernet switches that do not support PoE are rare. However, PoE midspans can be added to non-PoE switches to provide power to devices (see Figure 6-27). PoE midspans resemble switches and have RJ45 ports for device connections. They enable non-PoE switches to continue to be used for data connections while providing power to connected devices. Many PoE midspans share the same rack as the non-PoE switches they support, but some are located close to the devices they power. PoE extenders can also be used to enable powered devices to be located further from switches or midspans than structured cabling standards allow.

PoE has several important network design implications. First, PoE enables device locations to be decoupled from a facility's existing power grid; devices do not have to be located near electrical receptacles, and this increases the flexibility of their deployments. Second, increases in maximum port power and power to devices enable a growing range of devices to be powered by Ethernet cables; this increases PoE versatility. Third, PoE also provides a greener deployment option for wired networks, with lower total power consumption and a smaller carbon footprint than most non-PoE alternatives.

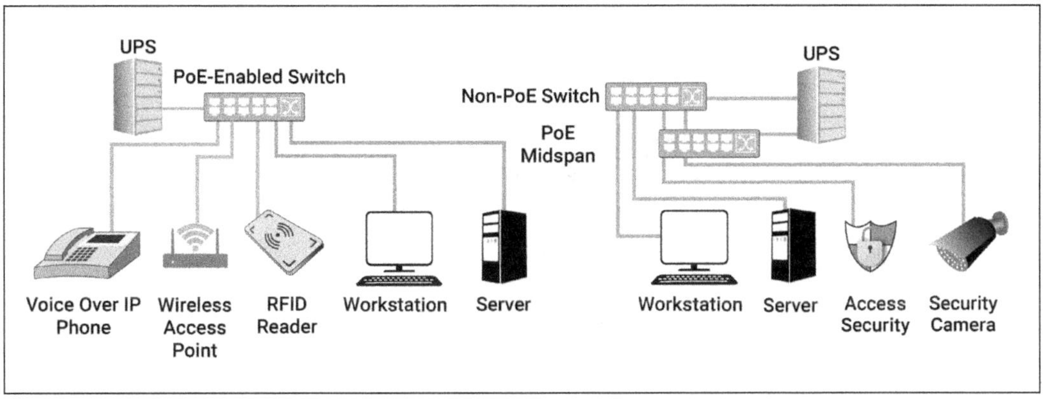

Figure 6-27: PoE switch and midspans configurations.

PoE is another example of Ethernet's adaptation to advancing technologies. As PoE continues to evolve, some pundits foresee a future where most or all data center devices are powered by PoE. This can benefit everyone and explains why PoE has gained traction in many enterprise networks.

6.5 BACKBONE NETWORKS

Enterprise networks routinely include wired backbone networks that interconnect LANs within buildings and across buildings in a single campus. Distributing data traffic to/from Ethernet and Wi-Fi LANs is a primary function of backbone networks. This makes backbone networks important elements in enterprise network architectures.

In networking, a **backbone** is network infrastructure that interconnects different networks and provides a pathway for them to exchange data. A backbone network can connect different networks in the same building, networks in different buildings in a campus environment, or networks at geographically distributed locations.

Ideally, a backbone's pathway capacity (and transmission speed) is greater than those in the networks it interconnects. This is common within buildings or on campuses but is less common in business WANs. Structured cabling standards (discussed in section 6.2.3) identify locations within buildings where LANs interconnect. A telecommunication room can serve a single LAN or provide an interconnection point for two or more LANs. An equipment room interconnects a building's telecommunication rooms and its infrastructure serves as a building backbone that distributes data traffic to/from the building's LANs.

Figure 6-28a is a logical depiction of a backbone in a building. This might be a four-story building with two LANs on each floor or a single-story building with eight LANs. A switch that interconnects all LAN switches in a building is sometimes called a building distribution switch. It may be in the building's equipment room, and a single connected router may serve all LANs in the building.

An organization with multiple buildings at the same location may create a *campus area network (CAN)* by interconnecting the buildings' distribution switches (see Figure 6-28b). As noted in Chapter 8, when a business uses carrier services to create a backbone that interconnects its different locations in a single metropolitan area, the network may be called a *metropolitan area network (MAN)*. A backbone that interconnects business locations spread across a considerable area is typically called a wide area network (WAN). Terminology aside, it is important to observe the importance of the scope and scale to which the term "backbone" is applied.

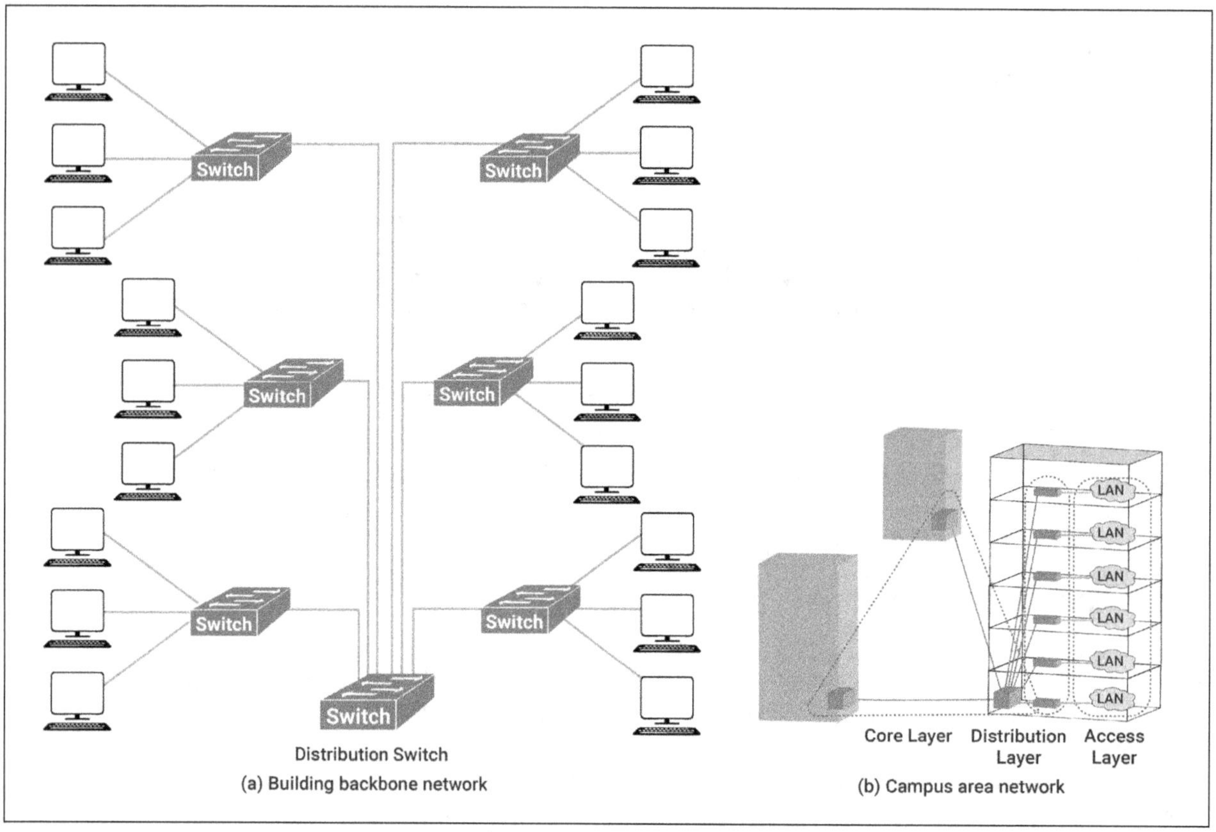

Figure 6-28: Logical diagrams of a building backbone network and a campus area network.

Best practices for backbone networks include having at least two, but not more than three, layers of switches. This conforms to the three-layer hierarchical model that was first championed by Cisco (see Figure 6-29). In this model, user devices connect to access layer switches, and the distribution layer forwards data to/from access layer switches, while the core layer forwards data to/from distribution layer technologies. In today's business networks, it is common to use fiber optic cable to interconnect such switches.

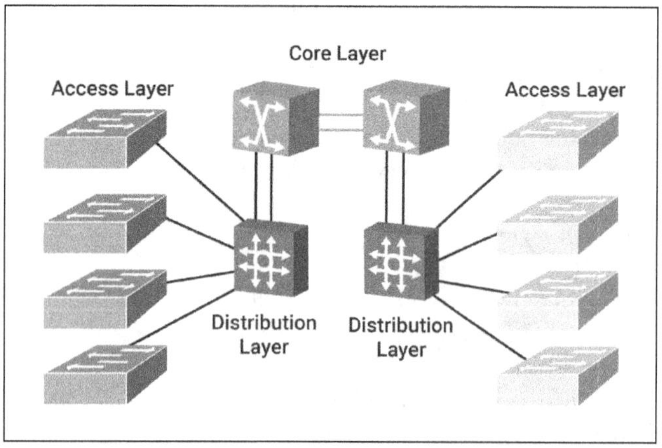

Figure 6-29: Logical depiction of the three-layer hierarchical model.

Generally, distribution switches have higher filtering and forwarding rates than access layer switches, and core layer switches have even higher filtering and forwarding rates. A business with a switched Ethernet backbone may use 10/100/1000 switches at the access layer, 10 GbE (10 Gigabit Ethernet) switches at the distribution layer, and 40 GbE (40 Gigabit Ethernet) switches at the core layer.

The three-layer hierarchical model has several important implications. First, it often relegates Layer 3 (Network layer) switching/routing to the core layer to achieve higher levels of route summarization and to improve router performance by facilitating advanced

Figure 6-30: Backbone equipment rack example. Source: thexfile-photo/istock/Stock photo ID:917266980

Figure 6-31a: Server blades in a data center server chassis. Source: kjekol/iStock/ Stock photo ID:160581566

Figure 6-31b: Ethernet blade switches for a chassis switch. Source: AlexLMX/iStock/ Stock photo ID:1222653751

quality of service (QoS) routing and reducing unnecessary packet processing. Second, having a distinct distribution layer helps ensure consistent application of an organization's security policies across its LANs. Third, the model facilitates the deployment of VLANs, including those that span buildings or locations.

Physically, distribution and access layer switches may be housed in one or more equipment racks, like that in Figure 6-30. Most switches are rack-mountable, and it makes sense to organize them in equipment racks or cabinets. Backbone and core layer switches often have fewer ports than the access layer switches. Fewer ports are needed because they interconnect other switches.

Some organizations prefer chassis switches to racks for interconnecting networks. A chassis switch is like chassis used for servers (Figure 6-31a) but accepts networking components, such as the Ethernet switch modules in Figure 6-31b. The slide-in switch modules, called blades, plug into the chassis switch backplane, which provides interconnection and power circuitry. Blades for routers or WAN interfaces may also be included in a chassis switch.

6.5.1 Routed Backbones

There are two major backbone network architectures: routed and switched. A **routed backbone** uses Network layer (IP) addresses and routers to forward packets. It is sometimes called a *subnetted backbone* because the network's IP space is divided into subnets.

Figure 6-32 includes a logical depiction of a routed backbone. Here, each backbone switch has an associated router that serves the interconnected LANs and subnets, and its routing table summarizes their IP address space. These routers connect to a core router whose routing table identifies routes among the network's subnets and summarizes the entire network's address space. The core router also has an interface to the edge router that provides Internet access.

A core layer router might double as a border router and support both BGP and the organization's internal routing protocol. However, as Figure 6-32 illustrates, an organization may choose to have a clean separation of interior and exterior routing by using separate routers for core layer routing and Internet access.

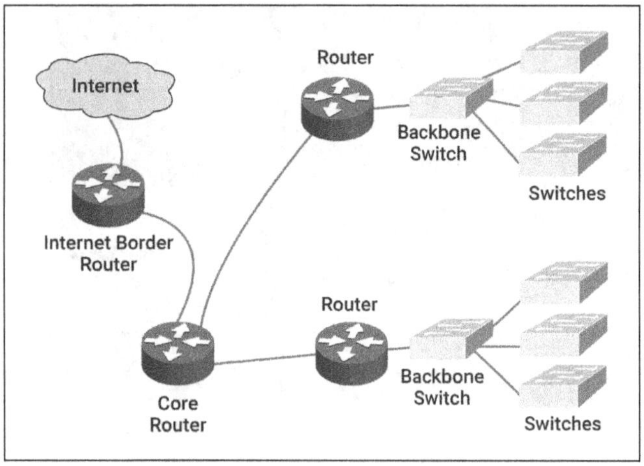

Figure 6-32: An example of a routed backbone network.

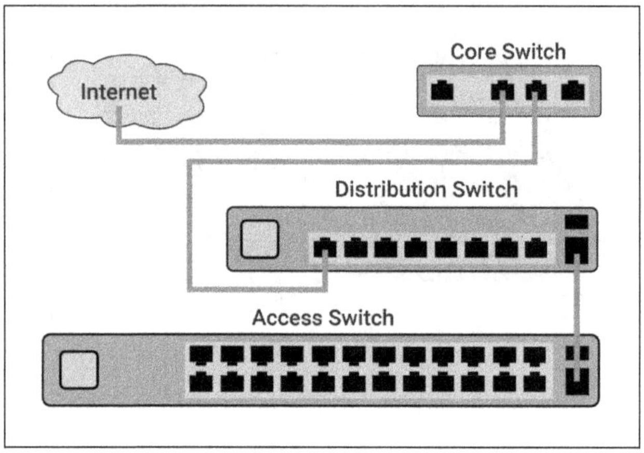

Figure 6-33: Examples of switched backbone network connections.

Routed backbone architectures are useful in networks that have multiple subnetworks or include network segments at different locations. Distributed routing protocols are used to identify the best paths to other networks, both internally and externally.

Because switching involves less processing than routing, a routed backbone may be slower than a switched backbone. However, judicious decisions about subnetting, router filtering and forwarding rates, and routing protocols can narrow performance differences.

6.5.2 Switched Backbones

A **switched backbone** network typically conforms to the three layer-hierarchical model (Figure 6-33). This facilitates the use of Layer 2 switching throughout much of the network, which typically translates into speedy data transfers across the backbone.

Switched backbones are common at the distribution layer, and structured cabling standards assume switched backbones in buildings. Increasingly, switched backbones also have a core layer.

As Figure 6-33 illustrates, core layer switches provide a pathway to the Internet via Layer 3 switching capabilities or an interface to a border router. Layer 3 switches provide switched connections between devices in the same subnet or VLAN but also have IP routing intelligence that enables them to serve as routers.

A Layer 3 switch can support routing protocols, inspect incoming packets, and make routing decisions based on destination addresses in IP headers. Originally, Layer 3 switches were conceived to improve routing performance on large networks and intranets by implementing router logic in integrated circuitry rather than software. This can lower latency. Layer 3 switches can support routing among VLANs and can simplify VLAN configuration by not requiring a separate router for each VLAN.

An organization may create different VLANs to support its different functions/departments (e.g., marketing, finance, and operations), members of its executive team, and process/project teams whose members are distributed across functional areas or locations. VLANs may also be created to support different types of data traffic, such as voice traffic (IP telephony), video traffic, image traffic, etc., with each type of traffic being assigned different QoS settings within VLAN tags.

Traditionally, subnetting has been more closely associated with routed backbones and VLANs have been more closely aligned with switched-backbone networks. Today, however, it is most common for a VLAN to be associated with a particular subnet rather than distributed across subnets. Hybrid backbone architectures frequently have routed core layers and switched distribution layers, and some organizations use VLANs in some network segments but not others.

6.6 WIRED NETWORK RESILIENCE AND SECURITY

LAN security, both wired and wireless, primarily focuses on Data Link layer and Physical layer security issues and controls. However, because Network layer PDUs are handed to the Data Link and Physical layers for framing and transmission, security mechanisms utilized at upper layers of the TCP/IP model are also part of the story.

Network resilience and business continuity are Data Link and Physical layer security considerations. A network is *resilient* when its infrastructure is resistant to disruption, can continue to operate in a degraded mode when damaged, can quickly recover from network or link failures, and/or can scale in response to rapid or unpredicted changes in demand. Basically, **network resilience** is the degree to which a network can quickly recover from network disruptions and maintain services when disruptions occur.

Circuit redundancy can be used at all layers of the three-layer hierarchical model to improve resilience. When a switch has separate connections to two or more switches at the layer above it, it can move traffic from the connection it normally uses to another if there is a failure. Redundant circuits from devices to access layer switches can also be provided, but this is rarely done, especially today when many devices have both Ethernet and Wi-Fi adapters to enable both wired and wireless connections.

Figure 6-34 illustrates redundant connections among access and distribution layer switches. It also illustrates multihomed Internet connections.

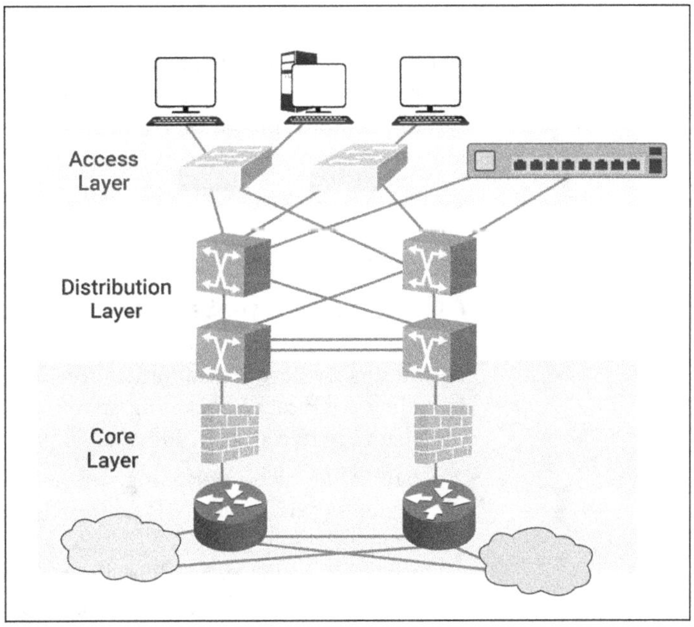

Figure 6-34: Circuit redundancy contributes to network resilience.

Redundant power supplies, backup battery storage systems, UPS systems, backup generators, and redundant links to internal and external electrical grids also contribute to network resilience. So does ready availability of spare plug-and-play (PnP) switches, routers, servers, storage devices, repeaters, media converters, patch cables, etc., to replace failed counterparts.

Vigilant monitoring can often quickly identify (and sometimes prevent) link, switch, and other network infrastructure failures and trigger remedy processes. When coupled with readily available replacement or backup components, many Physical layer issues can be avoided.

Environmental issues that can affect network operations and internal electric grids include fire, smoke, water damage, abnormal temperatures, humidity, dust, and poor ventilation, and reasonable steps should be taken to protect network infrastructure from them. "Noisy" environments and other causes of transmission errors and data loss may be impossible to avoid, but using STP and isolating cables from noise sources (such as lighting and heavy machinery) can improve network efficiency and performance.

6.6.1 Physical Layer Security

Protecting wired networks begins with controlling access to telecommunication rooms, equipment rooms, data centers, and other spaces that contain critical network infrastructure. Only authorized personnel should be permitted in these spaces. Today, physical access controls often include multifactor authentication, such as door locks that require both passcodes and biometric identification

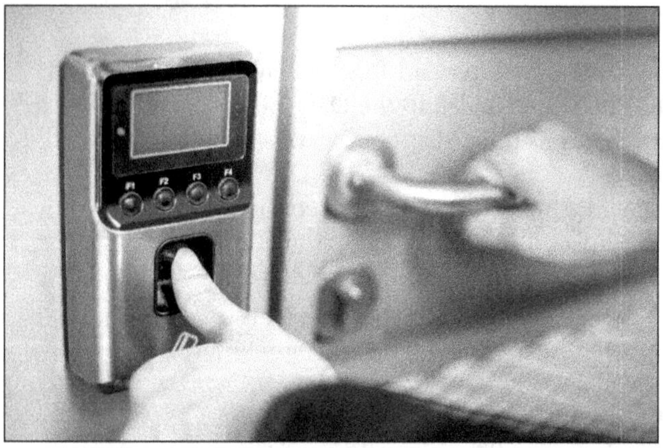

Figure 6-35a: Biometric access control example.
Source: Zephyr18/iStock/Stock photo ID:1187676181

Figure 6-35b: Network cable conduit (on ceiling) and cable trays.
Source: PixHouse/iStock/Stock photo ID:187276343

(see Figure 6-35a). A wide range of biometric identifiers may be used, including finger/thumbprint and hand scans, retina scans, and facial geometry or face recognition systems. Some entry systems combine biometric identification with badge readers, and some employee badges include location tracking/human movement capabilities.

Network cable conduit and cable trays, such as those illustrated in Figure 6-35b, can keep network cabling out of harm's way and increase its security. Other facility security controls are identified in Chapter 11.

6.6.2 Data Link Layer Security

Some attackers attempt to compromise Data Link layer software and protocols. Vigilant network monitoring by network administrators is needed to identify and thwart Data Link layer attacks, including ARP cache poisoning/spoofing, MAC address flooding, MAC address flooding/spoofing, spanning tree attacks, and VLAN hopping.

- In ARP cache poisoning, the attacker attempts to associate their device's MAC address with a valid IP address by sending bogus ARP messages to the network's router.
- In MAC address flooding, the attacker floods a switch with fake MAC addresses to force it to modify its forwarding table to include the attacker's MAC address.
- In MAC address spoofing, the attacker hunts for valid MAC addresses to pose as a valid device on the network's router.
- The Spanning Tree Protocol (STP) is designed to close switching loops in a network but can be exploited by attackers to destabilize forwarding tables.
- VLANs have several vulnerabilities, and VLAN hopping is a common type of attack; when it succeeds, the attacker can gain access to other VLANs in the network.

These attacks are described more fully in Appendix 6-6. They are often precursors to other and potentially more damaging types of attacks. Switch port security features and settings can prevent several of them.

Zero trust initiatives and principles (introduced in Chapter 2) can bolster network defenses at the Data Link and Physical layers. When used, authentication and authorization of both devices and individual users is required before access to a network resource is granted. Neither devices nor users are trusted because of location (such as being connected to a wired internal network) or ability to provide valid login credentials (which may be illegally obtained by attackers). By requiring both user and devices to undergo separate authentication and authorization processes, malicious actors are less likely to succeed in carrying out Data Link layer attacks.

Data Link and Physical layer vulnerabilities underscore the value of layered security defenses. Focusing security initiatives on upper layers of the TCP/IP protocol stack and ignoring the lower layers (or vice versa) leaves vulnerabilities for savvy attackers to exploit. Maintaining a holistic perspective on enterprise network security is the best way to confront cybersecurity realities.

SUMMARY

Wired networks continue to be an important part of enterprise networks despite the increasing prevalence of wireless technologies. Copper and fiber optic cabling used in LANs, BNs, and CANs offers very high transmission speeds that wireless networks have yet to reach.

Much must happen at the Data Link and Physical layers to enable local networks to have Internet access. The Data Link layer is responsible for transferring messages among devices in the local network, including to/from the network's router. Framing, physical addressing, access control, and error detection are important responsibilities at this layer.

Two Data Link layer sublayers facilitate these operations: the LLC and MAC. The LLC serves as a bridge between the Network layer and the MAC sublayer. The MAC sublayer plays important parts in framing and error detection. It interfaces with the Physical layer and controls when devices transmit, as well as the symbols/signals that adapters use to represent a frame's bits on communication media. Symbols/signals used on copper cables vary by voltage level, polarity, and symbol rate. Light pulses represent bits on fiber optic cables.

Transmission errors are more common on copper circuits than on fiber optic circuits, largely because of a greater range of error sources. Attenuation occurs on both types of cables. Signal regenerators are widely used in wired networks to compensate for signal attenuation and erosion and to enable transmitted signals to exceed distance maximums specified by structured cabling standards.

Adapters, switches, cabling, and connectors are other important Data Link and Physical layer technologies. Adapters include the circuitry and software required to send/receive frames, transmit signals, and detect errors; MAC addresses are hardcoded into adapters. Ethernet cable, with RJ45 connectors at each end, connects a device's adapter to an Ethernet switch. Switches base forwarding decisions on destination MAC addresses in received frames.

Ethernet is the most common wired LAN architecture. Ethernet standards, frame formats, media access controls, and transmission rates have evolved over the years to accommodate technology advances. Increasing use of PoE in enterprise networks also reflects Ethernet's evolution.

BNs are widely used to distribute data traffic to/from LANs. BNs may be found within buildings and interconnecting buildings on multibuilding campuses. BNs are often deployed to comply with the three-layer hierarchical model. Routed, switched, and hybrid backbones are common.

Redundant links and equipment contribute to network resilience, and physical security controls are used to protect network infrastructure at business facilities. This includes restricting access to telecommunication rooms, equipment rooms, data centers, and other spaces with critical network infrastructure to authorized personnel. Protecting network infrastructure against damage from floods, fires, and environmental hazards is also important.

Vigilant network monitoring is an important Physical layer and Data Link layer security control. Data Link layer threats include ARP poisoning, MAC address spoofing, and VLAN attacks. Appropriate switch and port configurations can thwart potential attackers. Zero trust security controls can also enhance security at these layers.

KEY TERMS

Backbone
Burst error
Channelization protocols
Controlled-access protocols
Data link control
LAN architecture
Line encoding
Media access control
Multiple access control protocols
Network resilience
Noise
Power over Ethernet (PoE)
Random-access protocols
Routed backbone
Signaling
Signal regeneration
Single-bit error
Switched backbone
Symbol
Symbol rate

REVIEW QUESTIONS

1. Identify and briefly describe the communication functions performed at the Data Link layer.
2. Briefly describe the communication roles of the LLC and MAC sublayers.
3. How does media access control differ from data link control? What are media access protocols?
4. Briefly describe the differences between random-access, controlled access, and channelization protocols.
5. What is CSMA/CD? How does it differ from CSMA?
6. What is an EDV, and how is it used to detect transmission errors?
7. Briefly describe each of the following EDVs: checksums, cyclic redundancy checks, parity checks.
8. What does signaling involve? What is a signaling method? What is signal attenuation?
9. What is a symbol? What is line encoding? Identify and briefly describe several line encoding techniques used on copper wires.
10. What are the differences between symbol rate, bit rate, and bit interval?
11. What is signal regeneration? How do signal regenerators reconstruct signals? Why are signal regenerators called line drivers?
12. What is noise? Why are both analog and digital signals affected by noise? What is interference? What is distortion?
13. What is corrupted data? What are burst errors?
14. Identify and briefly describe several major sources/causes of network errors.
15. Identify and briefly describe several common approaches for preventing errors.
16. What happens to errored frames in local networks? How is error recovery and correction typically handled?
17. What is structured cabling? What subsystems do ANSI/TIA-568 structured cabling standards address?
18. What data communication functions do network adapters perform? Identify and briefly describe several important adapter components.
19. What are the characteristics of twisted-pair cables? How does UTP differ from STP?
20. What connectors are used on Ethernet cables? What connectors are used on fiber optic cables? How does single-mode fiber optic cable differ from multimode fiber optic cable?
21. What are media converters? How are they used in local networks?
22. Briefly describe the characteristics of Layer 2 switches and how they operate. Briefly explain how switching mode affects switch performance and how switches handle broadcast traffic.
23. What is specified in a LAN architecture?
24. Identify several well-known Ethernet standards (e.g., Fast Ethernet). Also briefly decode/explain the meaning of 100Base-T and 1000Base-SX.
25. Fast Ethernet (100Base-T Ethernet) combines 4B/5B encoding with NRZI line coding. Explain what this means.
26. Briefly describe the format of 802.3 frames. How are Ethernet frame formats modified to accommodate VLANs?
27. What is PoE? Identify examples of devices powered by PoE. Identify several PoE network design implications.
28. What is a backbone? Briefly describe the differences between building and campus BNs.
29. Identify several BN best practices. Briefly describe the differences between routed and switched backbones.
30. What is network resilience? Briefly explain how circuit and switch redundancy, PnP devices, and backups contribute to network resilience.
31. Briefly summarize the major elements of Physical layer security.
32. Identify examples of Data Link layer attacks and approaches used to prevent them.

PROBLEMS AND EXERCISES

Exercise 6-1 Using the following description, create a network diagram using Visio or another network diagramming tool (such as EdrawMax, SmartDraw, Lucidchart, or Creately). If you have never used Visio, consider viewing one or more online videos about using Visio to create a network diagram.

Create a diagram that includes the following elements. If using Visio, use Network and Peripherals shapes and the shapes search box to search for other needed shapes. The diagram should include the following:

- Five switches
- One access point
- One laptop
- Two tablets
- One smartphone
- One router
- Two servers
- One storage device
- One network printer
- Eight desktop PCs
- One scanner
- Four VoIP phones
- One Internet cloud

Specific Guidance:

- One of the switches should be labeled Backbone Switch, and each of the other four switches should have a single circuit that connects it directly to the Backbone Switch. The router should have a circuit that connects it to the Backbone; it should also have a link to the Internet cloud.
- The Wi-Fi access point (labeled Access Point) should have a circuit that connects it to one of the other four switches; this switch should be labeled PoE Switch. The smart phone, tablets, and laptop should be grouped near the labeled Access Point to depict this network segment as a Wi-Fi LAN.
- A labeled Email Server, Database Server, Network Printer, and Storage Device should be the only devices connected to a second switch that connects to the Backbone Switch. Each of these devices should have its own circuit to connect to this switch, which should be labeled Server Switch.
- Four PCs should connect to a third switch, labeled Employee LAN Switch, that connects to the Backbone Switch. Each PC should have its own circuit that connects it to the Employee LAN Switch. (Four total circuits should be shown.)
- Four PCs and four VoIP phones should connect to the fourth switch, labeled Administrative LAN Switch, which connects to the Backbone Server. Each PC should have a circuit that connects it to the switch. Each VoIP phone should also have a circuit that connects it to the switch.
- The labeled Scanner should directly connect to one of the desktop PCs. It should not directly connect to a switch.

Deliverable: The deliverable for this exercise is a network diagram that conforms to the specified requirements.

Exercise 6-2 AgSouth is renovating a warehouse in downtown Statesboro, GA, to expand the campus of its southeastern headquarters. A telecommunications closet will be included in the new space, which will house an equipment rack for the building's backbone network. The equipment rack will include four 24-port 10/100/1000 Ethernet switches, a building distribution switch, and a router. The building distribution switch will connect to a core layer switch located in another building on the campus via an underground fiber optic cable.

- Use Visio or another network diagramming tool to develop a logical diagram for the backbone network. (Your diagram may resemble Figure 6-28a but with fewer switches.)
  a. Include a title on your diagram: e.g., "Building Backbone Network for AgSouth."
  b. Label each access-layer switch "24-port 10/100/100BASE-T Ethernet Switch."
  c. Label the building distribution switch "Gigabit Ethernet Backbone Switch."
- Use cdw.com or another data communications equipment vendor to identify a switch to use as the building distribution switch. On your diagram or in a separate Word file, identify the make, model, and price of the switch you are recommending as the backbone switch.
  a. The backbone switch must be a *managed* switch.
  b. The backbone switch *must be* rack-mountable. It should not be a chassis switch or a chassis blade.
  c. The backbone switch should have a limited number of ports, ideally no less than 12 ports and no more than 16.
  d. The backbone switch you recommend should have at least two 10 Gbps uplinks; at least one of them should be a 1000Base-X SFP interface for a fiber connection.
  e. The backbone switch you recommend should support Layer 3 routing and VLANs.
  f. You should provide a clickable link to the switch vendor's web page that identifies the switch's specifications.
- Use cdw.com or another data communications equipment vendor to identify a 24-port 10/100/1000BASE-T switch to use as a LAN switch. On your diagram or in a separate Word file,

identify the make, model, and price of the 24-port Ethernet switch.

a. The access layer switch must be a 10/100/1000 *managed* switch.
b. The access layer switch must be *rack-mountable*; it should not be a chassis switch or a chassis blade.
c. The access layer switch must have 24 ports and at least one 1G uplink, ideally with a 1000Base-X SFP interface to support a fiber connection.
d. The access layer switch should support VLANs.
e. You should provide a clickable link to the switch vendor's web page that identifies the switch's specifications.

Deliverables: The deliverables for this exercise include a diagram of the building backbone network and clickable links to your recommended backbone switch and LAN switch.

CHAPTER REFERENCES

aastha98. (n.d.). Multiple Access Protocols in Computer Network. Geeks for Geeks. Retrieved from: https://www.geeksforgeeks.org/multiple-access-protocols-in-computer-network/

Bhardwaj, R. (n.d.). Network Vulnerabilities and the OSI Model. AAR Technosolutions. Retrieved from: https://ipwithease.com/network-vulnerabilities-and-the-osi-model/

The Fiber Optic Association. (n.d.). Fiber Optic Jargon Illustrated. Retrieved from: https://www.thefoa.org/tech/ref/Management/jargon-illustrated.html

Katiyar, S. (n.d.). Difference Between Unipolar, Polar, and Bipolar Line Encoding Schemes. Geeks for Geeks. Retrieved from: https://www.geeksforgeeks.org/difference-between-unipolar-polar-and-bipolar-line-coding-schemes/

What-When-How. (n.d.). Error Control (Data Communications and Networking). The-Crankshaft Publishing. Retrieved from: http://what-when-how.com/data-communications-and-networking/error-control-data-communications-and-networking/

MINICASE: New Construction at Southeastern State University—LAN & BN Design & Cost Estimates

Southeastern State University (SSU), a public university, has received funding from the state legislature to add a wing to its College of Business (COB) building. The building wing will include three classrooms, three computer labs, and offices for a COB department that will move to the new wing. The new office space will include 11 faculty offices, an office for the department's graduate and lab assistants, and a server room (a telecommunications room with server rack space and a router to interface with the university's campus backbone network). A preliminary floor plan for the first floor of the new wing is illustrated in Figure 6-36.

The SSU campus has a core-layer fiber optic backbone network that interconnects its buildings.

Important Information about Classrooms, Labs, Office Area, and Server Room

Classrooms

Each classroom and lab depicted in Figure 6-36 will be equipped with the following:

- An instructor's console/workstation
- A ceiling mounted projection and classroom lighting control system
- A high-speed network printer
- Riser (raised) floors
- Sufficient computer and electrical interfaces needed to handle the maximum number of occupants planned for each classroom
- PCs with 100/1000/10000 Ethernet cards

Each classroom will be equipped to support Wi-Fi access to the Wi-Fi network that will support the new building wing. Only the instructor's workstation/console in each classroom will use Cat 6 cabling to connect to a switch in the server room.

A power source and charging station will be located at each student seat in the classroom to ensure power for student laptops, tablets, and mobile devices.

Each classroom will accommodate a maximum of 32 students at tables like those found via the following link: https://smartdesks.com/seminar-tables-with-tubular-column-leg-base-202.html

Note: The instructor's console/workstation, the projection/lighting system for each classroom, and the PCs for Labs A, B, and C will be funded from other sources and are not included in the cost estimates for this project.

Labs

With the exception of Lab A, each PC and instructor workstation will connect to its switch (located in the server room) via Cat 6 UTP cable.

Lab A will be equipped with high-end, large-monitor workstations. Each workstation and the instructor's workstation/console in Lab A will connect to a 1000Base-F switch in the server room using multimode fiber optic cable.

Labs B and C will be general-purpose labs. The computers in these labs will connect to switches in the server room using Cat 6 UTP.

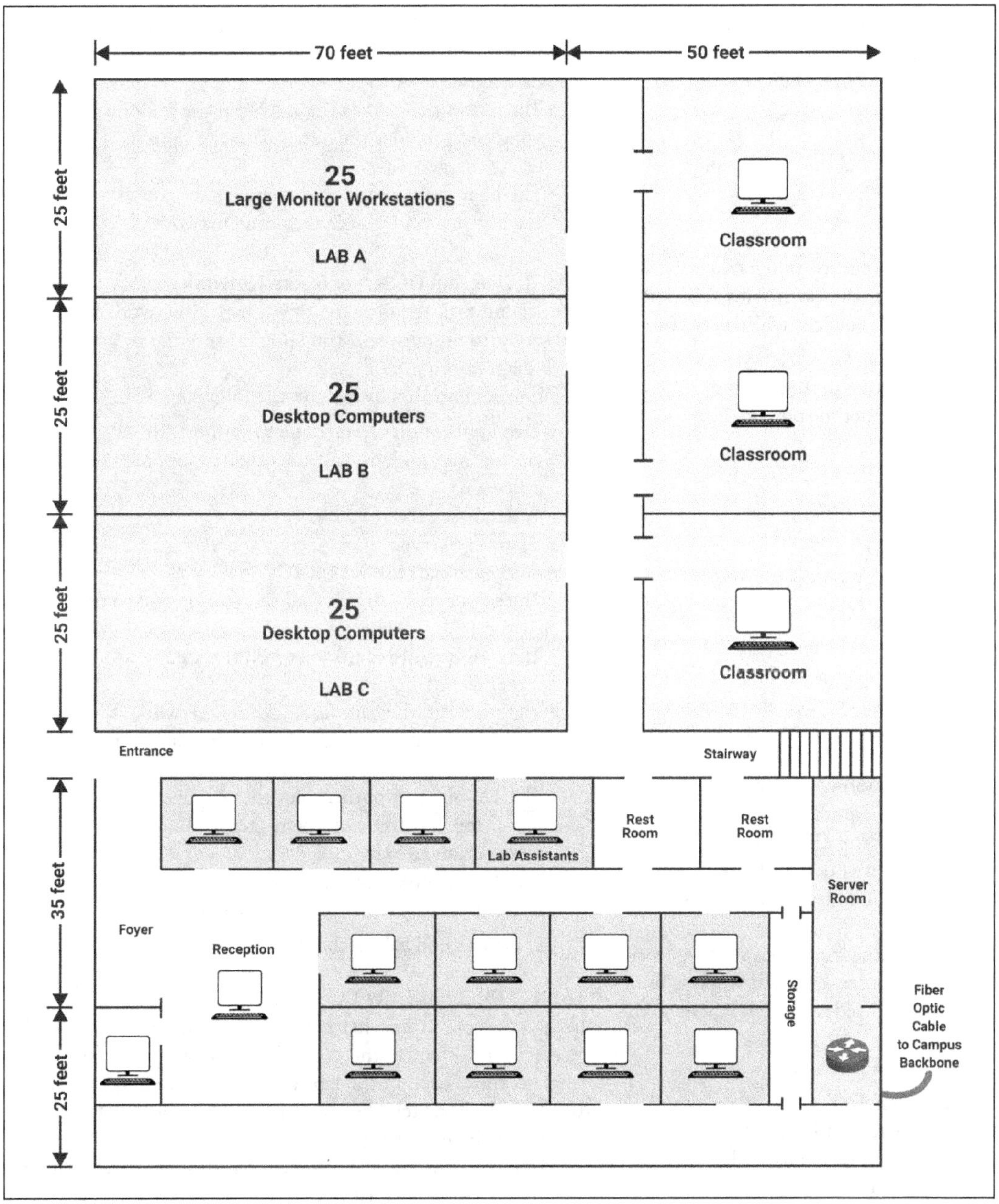

Figure 6-36: Layout of first floor of the new wing of the COB building.

Office Area

The office area on the first floor of the new wing of the COB building will include an office for a department chair, administrative assistant, and 10 faculty members; it will also include an office for student assistants. These offices are illustrated in the lower third of Figure 6-36.

General Information About the Office Area

- All PCs in the office area are equipped with 100/1000/10000 Ethernet cards.
- Each faculty office will have four electrical receptacles and two RJ-45 wall jacks.
- The Lab Assistants room will include six computers and a network printer.

- The reception area will include a PC and an office copier with an Ethernet adapter.
- The office area will be supported by a dedicated Ethernet switch in the server room (which is adjacent to the office area).
- Each PC, the network printer, and the office copier will connect to the switch via Cat 6 UTP.

Server Room

The server room will include racks (already purchased) that will house the access switches that serve the classrooms, labs, office area, and wireless overlay network. The racks will also house the following:

- Two application (file) servers: one to support the classrooms and labs, and the other to support the office area
- A database server
- A storage server
- Storage devices
- An uninterruptible power supply system
- The building backbone distribution switch

Each access-layer (LAN) switch connects to the backbone distribution switch using 1 Gigabit Ethernet (1 GbE) fiber optic patch cable.

Fiber 1 GbE patch cable will connect the backbone distribution switch to the router that interfaces with the campus network.

Task 1: Diagram of Building Backbone Network

Your first task is to create a logical diagram of the building backbone network for the new wing of the COB building at SSU. You should use Visio or another network diagramming tool to create it. Your diagram should include descriptive labels for all network components.

This diagram should illustrate access switches that will serve the labs, classrooms, server room, office area, and wireless overlay network and the cabling that is used to connect them to the building distribution switch.

This diagram should include the following:

- Seven labeled access-layer switches
- Two 16-port 1000Base-F switches for Lab A
- A 24-port 10/100/1000 Base-T switch for Lab B
- A 24-port 10/100/1000 Base-T switch for Lab C
- An 8-port 10/100/1000 Base T switch for the instructors' consoles in the classrooms and labs
- A 24-port 10/100/1000 Base-T switch for the office area
- An 8- or 12-port 1000Base-F server room switch
- A 16-port 1000Base-F switch to serve as the building distribution switch
- Labeled 1 GbE fiber optic cables that connect the access-layer switches and server room switch to the building distribution switch
- A labeled 1 GbE fiber optic cable that connects the router (to the campus backbone) to the building distribution switch
- The router that serves the LANs in the building wing and provides the gateway to the campus backbone network.
- The fiber optic circuit that connects the router to the campus's core-layer backbone network.

Task 2: Diagram Of Server Room Network

The second task requires creating a logical network diagram of the server room network. You should use Visio or another network diagramming tool.

This diagram should include the following:

- Two application servers: one to support the classrooms and labs, and the other to support the office area
- A database server
- A storage server
- A storage area network (SAN)
- The server room switch (All servers connect to this switch.)
- The building distribution switch (located in the server room)
- The router to the campus backbone network
- The 1 GbE fiber optic cables used to connect the servers and SAN to the server room switch
- The 1 GbE fiber optic cables that connect the server room switch and the router to the building distribution switch
- The 1 GbE fiber optic cable that connects the router to the campus backbone network

All devices and cables should be labeled.

TASK 3: PRELIMINARY COST ESTIMATES

Using cdw.com or another major data communications vendor, research and identify the costs for a 24-port Ethernet switch (such as those used in the labs and office area) and the 16-port 1000BASE-F switch that will serve as the building backbone switch for the new wing.

Each switch must be managed, rack-mountable, and support VLANs. The 24-port Ethernet switch should include at least one 1 GbE uplink to enable it to connect to the building backbone switch by fiber optic cable.

DELIVERABLES

To recap, for this minicase you should create a logical diagram of the building backbone network, a logical diagram of the server room network, and cost estimates for an Ethernet switch and the switch to be used as the building backbone switch.

Chapter 7

Wireless Networks in Business Facilities

LEARNING OBJECTIVES

After reading and studying this chapter, you should be able to:

- Identify wireless networks found in business facilities.
- Describe Data Link and Physical layer functions and protocols in wireless networks.
- Describe the characteristics of analog waveforms and the modulation processes used to encode data on them.
- Identify and briefly describe the major aspects of Wi-Fi architecture.
- Briefly describe media access controls in Wi-Fi networks.
- Identify and briefly describe error sources and error controls in wireless networks.
- Briefly describe CSMA/CA's distributed coordination function (DCF) and point coordination function (PCF).
- Identify and briefly describe important fields in Wi-Fi headers.
- Briefly describe the contributions of QAM, MIMO, and OFDM to the evolution of Wi-Fi networks.
- Identify and briefly describe Wi-Fi security threats and security controls for business and residential WLANs.
- Briefly describe the evolution of Wi-Fi security standards and protocols.
- Briefly explain how/why private 5G networks are used in business facilities.

7.0 INTRODUCTION: Wireless Networks in Today's Businesses

Wi-Fi is common in homes and business facilities. Customers, clients, and visitors expect Wi-Fi connections at restaurants, hotels, grocery and retail stores, airports, doctors' offices, hospitals, hair salons, and other business locations and are adept at joining available networks. They often connect to nonsecure guest networks, but secure connections are sometimes available.

Many businesses also have secure Wi-Fi networks to support their operations and employees. ESs and other mission-critical applications are commonly supported on mobile devices and wireless infrastructure in business facilities, which is often robust to handle the large volumes of data they generate and to ensure adequate application performance. Advanced analytics, AI, and the IoT are also increasingly supported on wireless infrastructure in business facilities.

Businesses use various types of wireless networks (see Table 7-1). Bluetooth and Zigbee are used in wireless personal area networks (WPANs) to support communications between devices that are close to one another, and some businesses use wireless MAN (WMAN) or wireless WAN (WWAN) services to support their operations. IoT sensors and applications are increasingly common in today's business facilities; most rely on Wi-Fi for Internet access, but some are supported by cellular network and non-Wi-Fi hotspots (e.g., Helium).

Table 7-1: Common types of wireless networks.

	Wireless LAN (WLAN)	Wireless MAN (WMAN)	Wireless WAN (WWAN)	Wireless PAN (WPAN)
Type	Local area network	Metropolitan area network	Wide area network	Personal area network
Use	Provide Internet access within a building or limited outdoor area	Provide communications between different locations in a metropolitan area	Provide communications between geographically dispersed locations	Transmit signals between devices in limited areas
Example(s)	Wi-Fi (IEEE 802.11)	WiMAX (IEEE 802.16) or Clearwire	4G, LTE, 5G cellular networks; ViaSat satellite network	Bluetooth or Zigbee

A business with multiple locations in a metropolitan area may use a wireless Internet service provider (WISP), such as Clearwire, to create a WMAN. Outside the United States, WiMAX (IEEE 802.16) is widely used to support WMANs in urban areas.

Wireless WAN technologies and services are described in Chapter 8, and WPAN technologies and protocols are included in Chapter 9's discussion of the IoT. This chapter primarily focuses on Wi-Fi infrastructure and protocols but also introduces private cellular networks and radio access networks (RANs), which are gaining traction in business facilities.

The deployment of 5G cellular service has the potential to change user preferences and default configurations for mobile devices, and the deployment of RANs in business facilities may fuel a migration away from Wi-Fi. However, Wi-Fi technologies, protocols, and security continue to evolve, and this standard's prevalence in homes and businesses is likely to endure.

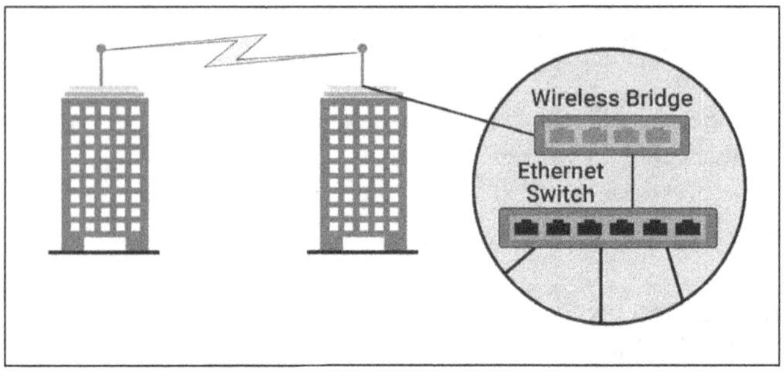

Figure 7-1: A wireless bridge can be used to connect networks in two buildings.

Other types of wireless infrastructure are used in enterprise networks, including wireless bridges between buildings (see Figure 7-1). Basically, these are media converters that transform symbols transmitted on cables to corresponding wireless symbols, and vice versa.

Wireless infrastructure often adds complexity to network management. Relative to Ethernet, Wi-Fi is more challenging to configure and maintain, especially when reliable connection speeds, performance levels, and security and the ability to accommodate a wide range of mobile devices are all desired. Wi-Fi security standards and protocols continue to evolve, and security-focused best practices guide Wi-Fi administration in most businesses, but security challenges persist.

This chapter begins by considering how communication functions at the Data Link and Physical layers are handled differently in wireless networks than in wired networks. Understanding these differences is important in understanding Wi-Fi network architecture, protocols, and security, as well as RANs.

7.1 DATA LINK AND PHYSICAL LAYER FUNCTIONS IN WIRELESS NETWORKS

As noted in Chapters 4 and 6, physical addressing, framing, media access control, and error handling are important Data Link layer communication functions, and representing bits as symbols/signals is a critical Physical layer function. These functions are performed in both wired and wireless networks, but there are important differences in how they are addressed.

7.1.1 Wired and Wireless Network Differences at Layers 1 and 2

As Figure 7-2 illustrates, the general communication functions identified in IEEE 802 standards are carried out in IEEE 802.11 (Wi-Fi) networks, but some additional considerations are involved. Communication functions performed at the LLC and MAC sublayers and the Physical layer in wired networks are discussed in sections 6.1 and 6.2 of Chapter 6, and there is no need to recap them here.

In 802.11 Wi-Fi networks, the Data Link layer continues to be responsible for flow framing, physical addressing, error detection, and flow control, but is also responsible for implementing wireless access protocols and reliable data delivery. Contention-based, random-access protocols, such as CSMA, can be used, but the ability of devices to "hear" data traffic on the shared communication media is less certain, and access protocols need to shift away from collision detection to collision avoidance. This makes media access control in wireless networks more complex than in wired networks.

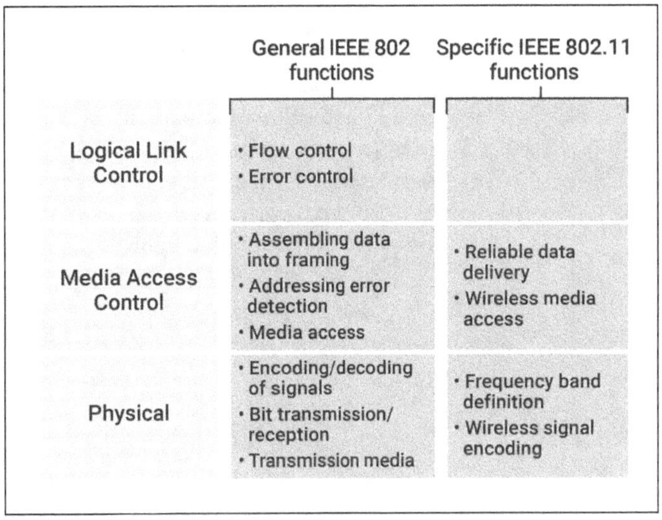

Figure 7-2: Additional Data Link and Physical layer communication functions in Wi-Fi (802.11) networks.

Data delivery is also less certain in wireless networks and is affected by transmission range, signal interference, collisions, attenuation, and other factors. To compensate, Wi-Fi frames include sequence numbers to enable receivers to identify missing frames, request retransmission of corrupted frames, and reorder frames into their original transmission sequence.

At the Physical layer, Wi-Fi involves more than representing bits as symbols and signals. Wi-Fi requires frequency band (e.g., 2.4 GHz or 5 GHz) and channel definition, and senders and receivers must be on the same page about the type of signal encoding (waveform modulation) that is used. Evolving Wi-Fi standards often mean communicating devices may not support the latest or fastest type of signaling.

In short, things are different at the Data Link and Physical layers in wireless networks. Although adding flexibility and convenience for mobile device users, wireless networks can be more challenging for network personnel to understand and manage.

7.1.2 Wireless Signals: Some Basic Physics

Chapter 6 described how bits are represented by symbols/signals on copper and fiber optic cables. On Ethernet cables, voltage levels and polarity are used to create the symbols/signals that represent bits, and electricity is required to propagate the signals.

Radio Wave Propagation

Electricity is also required in wireless networks. Electricity that flows through transmitter antennae causes electrons to vibrate and produce radio waves (see Figure 7-3). Radio waves travel through the air and cause receiving antennae to vibrate and produce electric current.

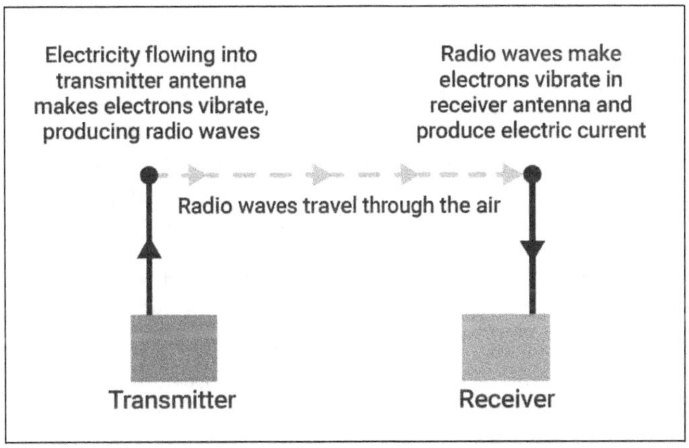

Figure 7-3: A high-level overview of radio signal creation and reception.

To tie this back to Chapter 6, if bits are encoded on an Ethernet cable by a line encoding scheme such as NRZ-I, and the cable's electric current is used to create radio waves, receivers can reproduce and interpret the original line encoding from received radio waves. While this is an overly simplistic depiction of all that is happening, it provides a picture of what is going on.

Wi-Fi and the Frequency Spectrum

The term *radio waves* is interpreted more narrowly and precisely by physicists than by everyday Wi-Fi and cellular network users. For physicists, the term refers to a specific range of the electromagnetic spectrum. In Figure 7-4, radio waves are found on the left side of the spectrum and are separated from the visible light range of the spectrum (the "visible spectrum") by the microwave and infrared portions of the spectrum. Ultraviolet light, X-rays, and Gamma rays have higher frequencies than visible light.

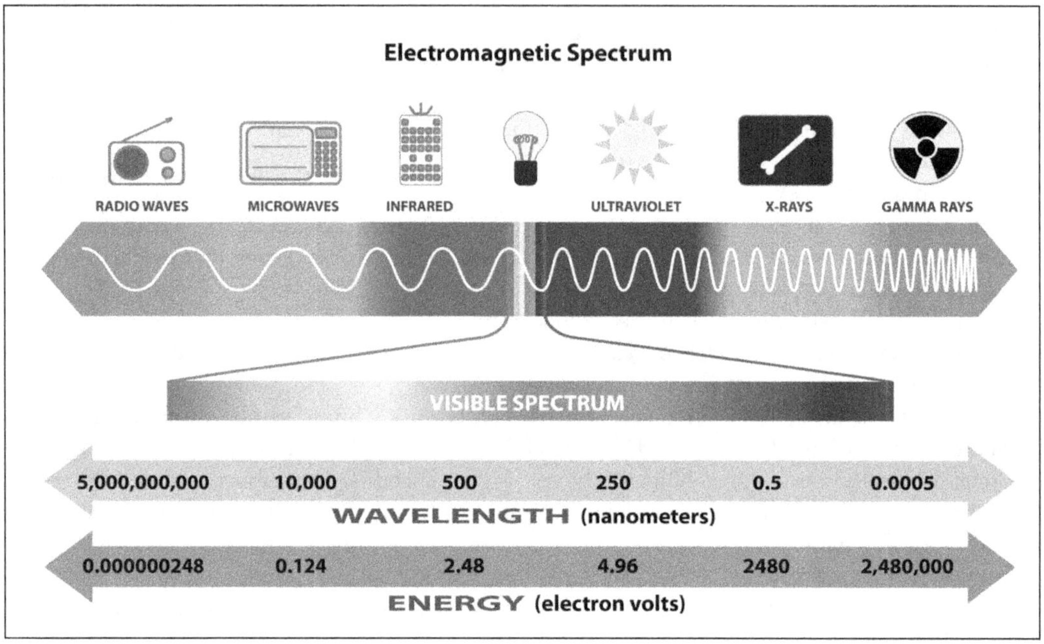

Figure 7-4: The electromagnetic spectrum. Source: Coolvectormaker/iStock/ Stock illustration ID:1311362176

As you move from left to right in Figure 7-4, wavelengths get shorter, and energy gets higher. The bands from radio waves through visible light are classified as *non-ionizing radiation*. This means that they lack sufficient energy to break chemical bonds or remove electrons from atoms. Frequencies above the visible light band are *ionizing radiation* that can break chemical bonds, remove electrons from atoms, and cause other mischief, such as nuclear reactions. In the overall scheme of things, Wi-Fi radio waves are low energy and harmless.

Licensed and Unlicensed Spectrum

Government regulation of electromagnetic frequencies used for communication constrains how wireless spectrum and technologies can be used. If there is too much activity in a specific frequency band, transmitted signals can interfere with one another, sometimes to the point of making transmissions indiscernible. Like other countries, the United States has a government agency, the Federal Communications Commission (FCC), that is tasked with allocating radio wave spectrum.

Most of the radio spectrum is *licensed* by the FCC to certain users. Companies pay a licensing fee for the exclusive right to use an assigned frequency in a specific geographical area. In exchange for the licensing fee, companies are assured that other organizations cannot legally interfere with their transmissions.

Unlicensed parts of the spectrum can be used for communications without FCC permission. The amount of unlicensed and publicly available spectrum is small and limited, and there's greater potential for transmission interference as parts of the spectrum get crowded. However, unlicensed spectrum, including that used for Wi-Fi, is free, and since it is publicly owned, there are few rules that must be followed. It also opens the door to innovation and the development of new applications that facilitate device connectivity or provide devices with more capabilities.

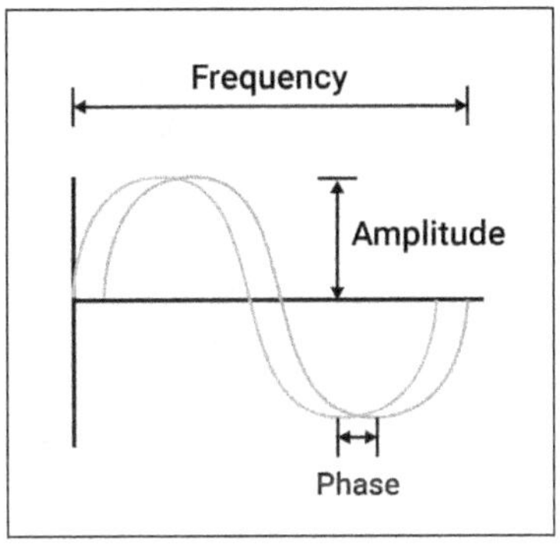

Figure 7-5: Radio waves and other analog waves differ in amplitude, frequency, and phase.

Encoding Bits on Radio Waves

Radio waves are analog waveforms and have three fundamental characteristics: amplitude, frequency, and phase (see Figure 7-5).

- Amplitude relates to the height of the wave relative to a zero point (like an x-axis in a two-dimensional graph); it is often equated with signal strength, with higher amplitudes being stronger signals.
- Frequency relates to the rate at which the signal repeats (again relative to an x-axis); this is sometimes called the wave's period and is measured in cycles per seconds (Hertz). Wi-Fi signals are measured in Gigahertz (billions of cycles per second).
- Phase is how much a signal is shifted along the x-axis with respect to another signal (such as the previous signal) or an ideal or reference signal.

Understanding amplitude, frequency, and phase is a prerequisite for understanding how data is encoded on radio waves and other analog waveforms.

Figure 7-6 illustrates analog waves with different amplitudes. If a sender can transmit both a low-amplitude and a high-amplitude signal, and if a receiver can receive both the low- and high-amplitude signals, one amplitude can represent a 1 bit, and the other can represent a 0.

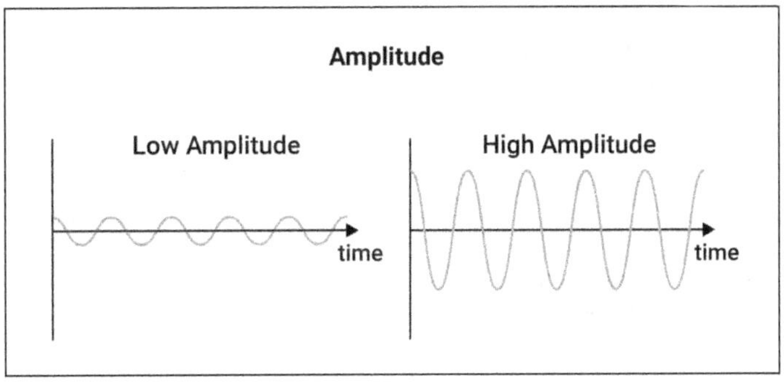

Figure 7-6: Analog waves with different amplitudes. Source: petrroudny/iStock/ Stock illustration ID:1355274014

Figure 7-7 illustrates analog waves with different frequencies. If a transmitter can transmit both a low-frequency and a high-frequency signal, and a receiver can receive both the low- and high-frequency signals, one frequency can represent a 1 bit, and the other can represent a 0.

Similarly, when a sender can transmit signals with two different phases, such as those illustrated in Figure 7-5, and receivers can receive signals with two different phases, one signal phase can represent a 1 and the other can represent a 0. Basically, when a sender and a receiver agree on which signal represents a 1 and which signal represents a 0, data can be transferred.

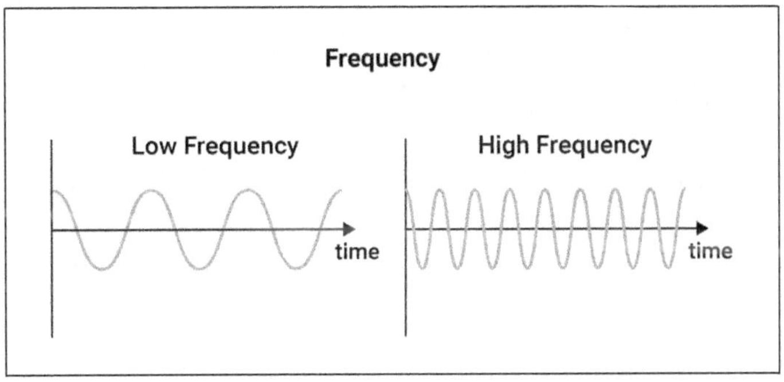

Figure 7-7: Analog waves with different frequencies. Source: petrroudny/iStock/ Stock illustration ID:1291557151

Carrier Waves

Before we take a closer look at encoding bits on radio waves, it is important to introduce carrier signals. In telecommunications, a **carrier signal** (a.k.a. *carrier wave* or *carrier*) is an analog waveform that is modulated (changed) for the purpose of carrying data or conveying information. Like any other analog wave, a carrier wave has an amplitude, frequency, and phase that can be changed to represent bits.

Chapter 6 introduced CSMA (carrier sense multiple access), a media access control protocol. It requires devices to determine whether the communication medium is busy or idle before beginning to transmit. So, how does a device know when the medium is idle or busy? When analog signals are used, the medium is idle when the only signal on it is the carrier signal. When a device "senses" anything other than the carrier signal on the medium, the medium is busy, and the device refrains from transmitting until only the carrier signal is present.

You can think of a carrier signal as a base signal that exists on the communication medium when no data is being transferred. However, it is also a signal that can be changed (modulated) to represent bits.

Modulation

Modulation is the process of varying one or more properties of a carrier signal with a separate signal, called a *modulation signal*, that contains data to be transmitted. In analog modulation, an analog modulation signal is impressed upon the carrier signal by altering the carrier signal's amplitude, frequency, phase, or a combination thereof.

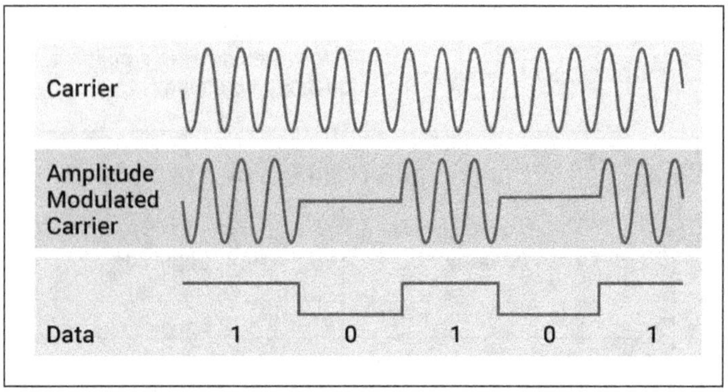

Figure 7-8: Amplitude modulation example.

Amplitude modulation (AM) modifies the amplitude of the carrier. Figure 7-8 illustrates a type of amplitude modulation called *amplitude-shift keying (ASK)*. In ASK, a symbol, representing one or more bits, is transferred by transmitting a fixed-amplitude analog wave at a fixed frequency for a specific time duration. In Figure 7-8, a 1 is represented by the presence of the carrier for a predefined number of carrier wave cycles (three in this example), and the absence of the carrier for the same number of cycles represents a 0.

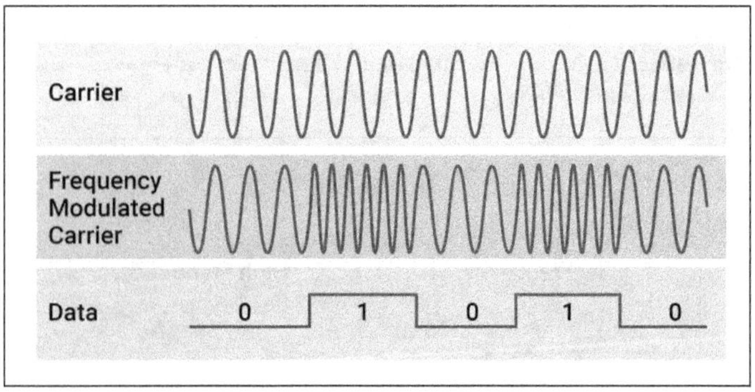

Figure 7-9: Frequency modulation example.

In *frequency modulation (FM)*, the modulating signal modifies the frequency of the carrier wave. In Figure 7-9, the original carrier frequency for a specific number of cycles (three in this example) represents a 0, while a higher frequency for the same number of cycles represents a 1. The type of FM illustrated in Figure 7-9 is called *frequency-shift keying (FSK)*.

Phase modulation (PM) modifies the phase of the carrier signal to represent a 1 or 0. The phase of the signal is measured relative to the phase of the preceding bit. The type of phase modulation illustrated in Figure 7-10 is called *phase-shift keying*

(PSK). Here, the bits being represented are timed to coincide with a specific number of carrier cycles (three cycles in this example). In Figure 7-10, when the phase is constant at the beginning of every third cycle, a 0 is represented, and when the phase changes at the beginning of the third cycle, a 1 is represented. PSK is used in Wi-Fi and Bluetooth networks. It is also used in radio frequency identification (RFID) applications.

Chapter 6 mentioned that sometimes analog signaling is used on copper cables instead of line encoding. When it is used, the signal's amplitude is measured by voltage and polarity (e.g., from +5v to -5v), and when PM is used, the waveform may differ in both phase *and* polarity.

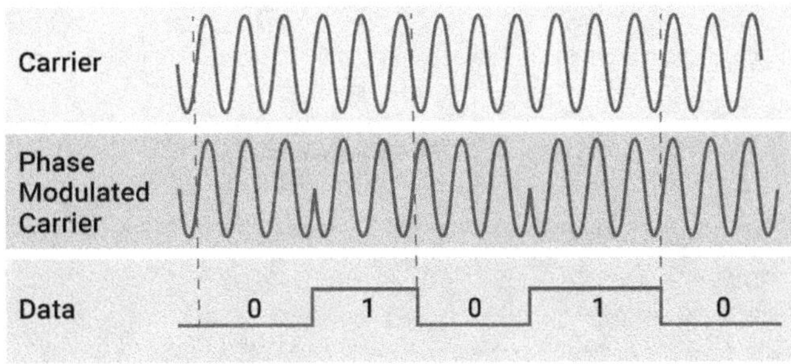

Figure 7-10: An example of phase modulation.

Modems

A **modulator** is a device that performs modulation. A **demodulator** is a device that performs demodulation. *Demodulation* is the inverse of modulation; it separates the modulation signal from the carrier signal. A **modem** (short for *modulator–demodulator*) can perform both modulation and demodulation. It sits between two networks (e.g., between a home Wi-Fi network and an ISP's network) and serves as the local shipping and receiving station for data transfers between the networks.

Wi-Fi routers are sometimes called wireless modems because they are equipped to modulate and demodulate radio waves. Wi-Fi adapters and access points also have antenna and transceiver circuitry that modulates and demodulates radio waves.

Modems are also used on wired connections. For example, *DSL modems* are used on landline telephone wires, and *cable modems* are used on coaxial cables (such as those from CATV providers). Fiber optic modems also exist; a *fiber optic modem (FOM)* transmits/receives light pulses instead of electronic waveforms.

Multiple Level Modulation

Most modems have *multiple-level (M-level) modulation* capabilities and routinely transmit analog symbols/signals that represent multiple bits. With M-level modulation, symbols/signals with more than two amplitudes, frequencies, or phases are transmitted. For example, when a modem transmits four different amplitudes, each different symbol can represent a two-bit combination (00, 01, 10, 11). This is illustrated in Figure 7-11.

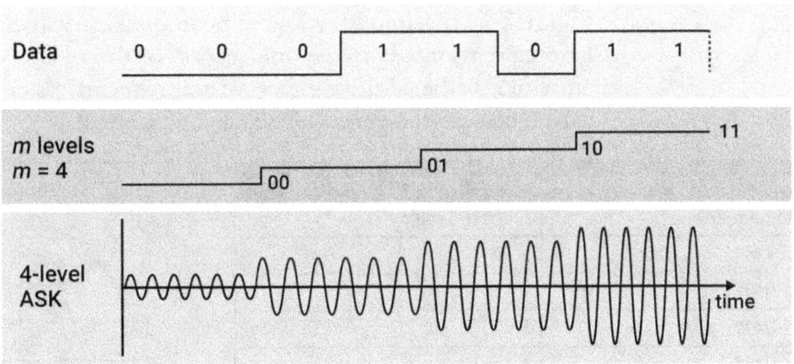

Figure 7-11: Multiple-level amplitude shift keying.

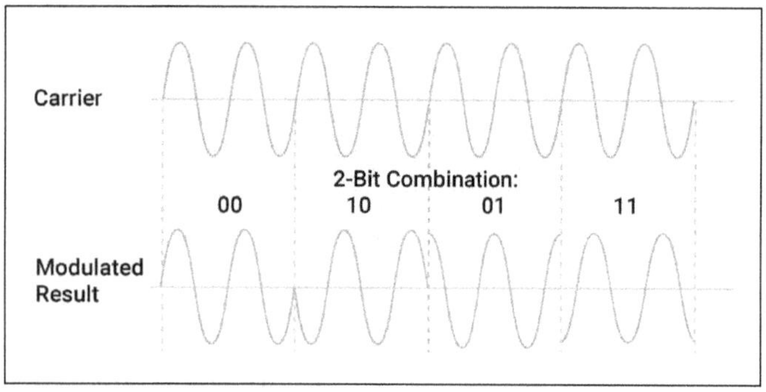

Figure 7-12: Quadrature phase-shift keying (QPSK) uses four phase shifts to represent two-bit combinations.

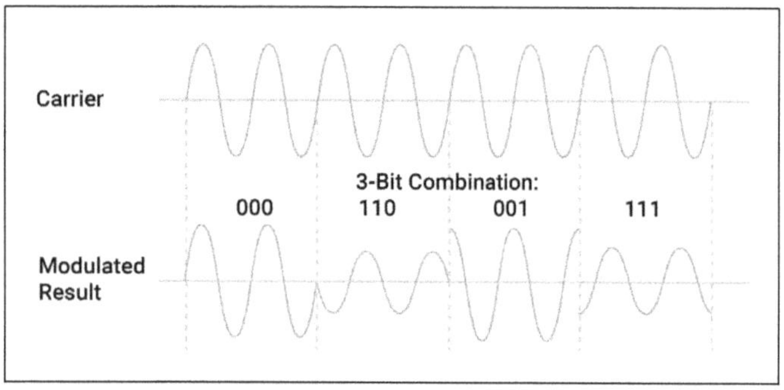

Figure 7-13: Multilevel PSK combined with ASK. Only four of eight three-bit combinations are depicted.

Quadrature phase-shift keying (QPSK) is a form of PSK in which each transmitted symbol/signal represents two bits. It uses four phase shifts (0, 90, 180, or 270 degrees) and is illustrated in Figure 7-12.

Quadrature Amplitude Modulation

Quadrature amplitude modulation (QAM) is a family of modulation methods that combine AM and PM to represent bits. The use of both ASK and PSK is a distinguishing character of QAM. QAM is used in Wi-Fi and other wireless networks; it is also used in fiber optic communications.

Two carrier waves with the same frequency that are out of phase with one another by 90° are used; this condition is known as *quadrature* or *orthogonality*. M-level ASK is used to encode multiple-bit combinations on each carrier wave, and the transmitted signal combines (adds) the two modulated carrier waves. The orthogonality of the two carriers enables receivers to coherently separate and demodulate them.

Figure 7-13 illustrates how phase and amplitude shifts can be combined to represent three-bit combinations. It illustrates a modulation technique called 8 QAM that combines two amplitude levels and four phase shifts to represent three-bit combinations.

The QAM family has many members (see Table 7-2), distinguished by the number of bits represented by each transmitted symbol/signal. The current generation of Wi-Fi (Wi-Fi 6) supports 1024 QAM, which is one of the reasons why its bit rates are higher than the previous generation.

The combination of phase and amplitude shifts for QAM modulation schemes is illustrated by *QAM constellation maps*. Figure 7-14 illustrates constellation maps for 16 QAM and 64 QAM. Figure 7-15 illustrates the four-bit combination associated with each point in a 16 QAM constellation; points closer to the intersection of the x- and y-axes are indicative of symbols with lower amplitudes. The additive effects of the two carriers create angles that differ from the orthogonal carrier phases (the perpendicular x- and y-axes).

Table 7-2: Transmission capabilities of different types of QAM.

Modulation	Bits per Symbol
8 QAM	3
16 QAM	4
32 QAM	5
64 QAM	6
128 QAM	7
256 QAM	8
512 QAM	9
1024 QAM	10
2048 QAM	11
4096 QAM	12

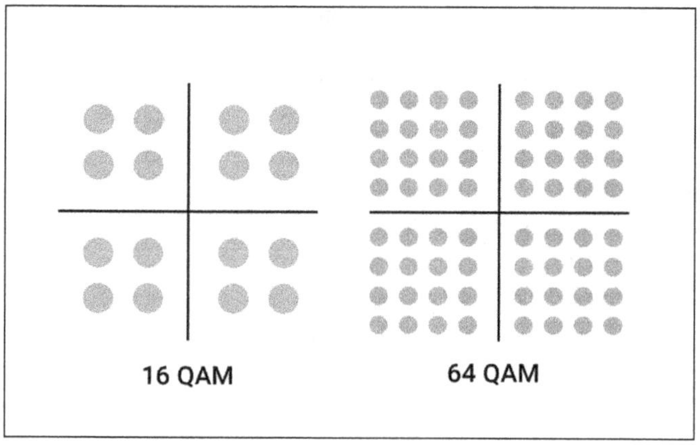

Figure 7-14: Examples of QAM constellation maps.

As you can mentally visualize, the constellation maps for the higher modulation levels used in Wi-Fi networks (such as 256 QAM and 1024 QAM) would be very dense. The ability to support very dense constellation maps demonstrates the sophisticated modulation and demodulation capabilities of Wi-Fi adapters and access points.

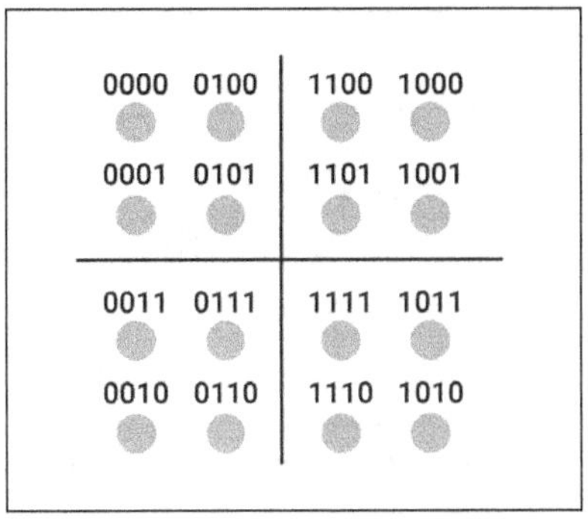

Figure 7-15: In 16 QAM, each point in the constellation represents four bits.

7.1.3 Media Access Control

A wireless communication channel is a shared medium, and media access control (MAC) is required to coordinate the transmissions of devices sharing the channel. The goals of wireless MAC protocols include maximizing throughput, minimizing latency and delays, and avoiding data collisions. Several factors constrain the achievement of these goals.

When radio waves are propagated (transmitted), they typically radiate out in all directions and may quickly attenuate. Sender-receiver communication is possible when they are not too far apart. The receiver must be in the sender's *communication range*, and the transmitted signals must be strong enough to be accurately detected and decoded (see Figure 7-16).

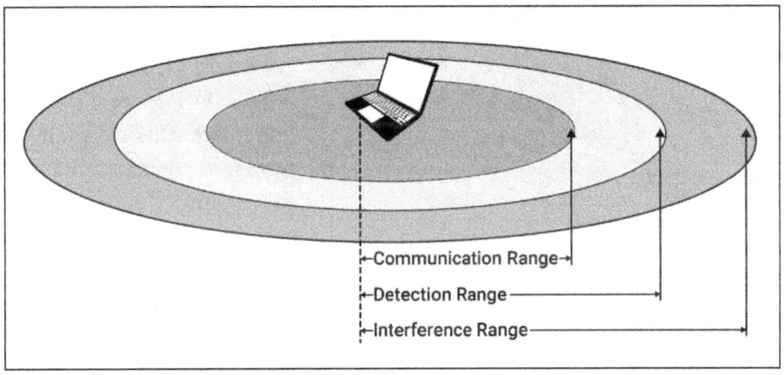

Figure 7-16: Wireless signal communication (transmission), detection, and interference ranges.

Receivers located outside a sender's transmission range that can detect a sender's weakened signals are in the transmitter's *detection range*. Reliable communication between a receiver in the detection range and the sender is impossible because the transmitted signal can be too attenuated to be accurately detected and decoded, and an excessive number of errors may be detected. So, radio waves in the detection range are detectable but may be unintelligible.

Transmitted signals beyond the detection range are in an *interference range*. A transmitter's signals are severely attenuated in this range, and receiving devices typically cannot detect a sender's transmission. However, there may be enough residual strength in the signals to contribute background noise to other signals that are transmitted/received by devices in the interference range. Examples of communication ranges for different types of wireless networks are provided in Table 7-3.

Table 7-3: Transmission ranges for different wireless technologies.

Wireless Technology	Communication Range
Wi-Fi	Up to 100 meters
Bluetooth	Up to 10 meters
Zigbee	10–100 meters
RFID	1 meter
4G/LTE/5G Cellular	1 to 10 Km

Communication ranges for cellular service base stations are called "cells," and their transmission radii (ranges) are usually significantly greater than those for Wi-Fi networks. However, cell phone users know that signal strength is also important for data services and avoiding dropped calls. Four bars are better than one, and when your device is beyond the transmission range of the closest tower, "no service" is displayed. Many data services bog down with one- or two-bar service levels.

Most Wi-Fi users know that the further a device is from a Wi-Fi router or access point, the slower its connection speed. Both distance and attenuation are factors. Attenuation accelerates when Wi-Fi signals pass through walls, especially thick reinforced concrete walls or timber walls.

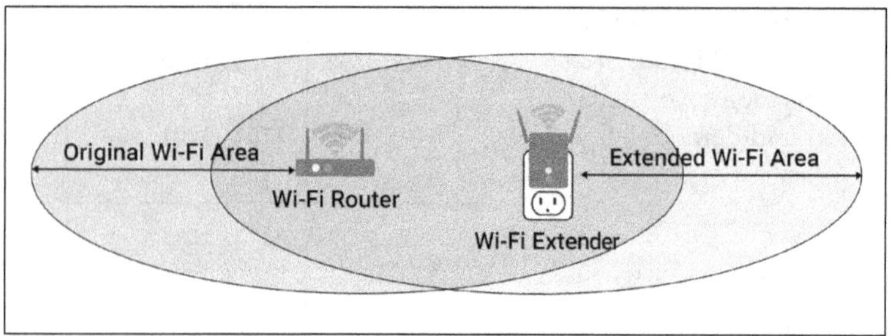

Figure 7-17: Wi-Fi extenders may be used to expand the Wi-Fi coverage area.

Wi-Fi signals can also be affected by Bluetooth signals, baby monitors, microwave ovens, televisions, and other Wi-Fi networks that are nearby. Wi-Fi extenders (repeaters) are used in some homes and businesses (see Figure 7-17); they rebroadcast Wi-Fi signals and enable devices that are outside the normal coverage area to use the network.

Transmission ranges also contribute to "hidden node" issues in wireless networks. Figure 7-18 helps to visualize what a hidden node is. In Figure 7-18, each of the three devices (Nodes A, B, and C) is within the transmission range of the network's access point, but each node is also outside the transmission range of the other two nodes. These nodes are "hidden" from each other despite being able to communicate with the access point.

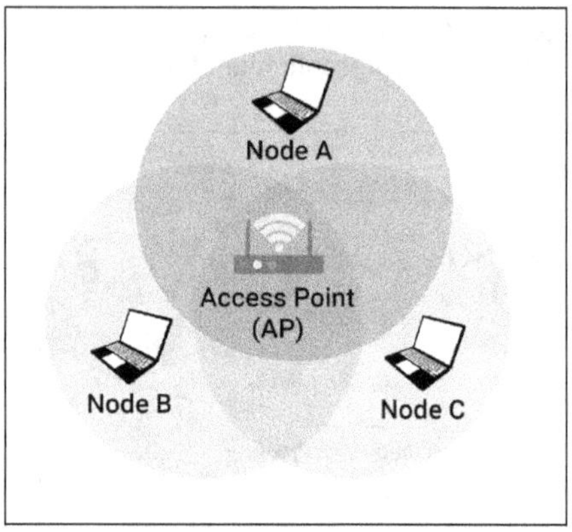

Figure 7-18: Examples of hidden nodes in a Wi-Fi network.

In a Wi-Fi network, there is a *hidden node problem* when two or more nodes are outside each other's transmission range but are inside the access point's transmission range. If the devices have data to transmit and begin to transmit their data when they "sense" that the medium is not busy, their simultaneous transmissions will cause data collisions.

Section 7.2.3 describes how Wi-Fi media access controls are structured to accommodate hidden nodes. Table 7-4 provides a summary overview of MAC techniques used in wireless networks.

Table 7-4: Wireless media access control techniques and where they are used.

Wireless MAC Techniques	Brief Description	Where Used
Random-Access (contention)	CSMA and similar random-access techniques enable a device to transmit its data when the shared channel is not being used by another device.	These techniques are best suited to networks, such as Wi-Fi, that primarily carry data. Wi-Fi's DCF uses them.
Coordination (channelization)	These techniques use multiple access protocols such as code division multiple access (CDMA) to enable multiple devices to simultaneously transmit over the same communication channel.	These techniques are most suitable for wireless voice networks, such as cell phone networks.
Polling	These techniques use a central node that coordinates access to the shared communication channel by polling network devices and/or allocating time slots in which they can transmit data.	This is used for Bluetooth and Zigbee applications. It is also used in Wi-Fi's PCF.

7.1.4 Error Sources and Controls

As you may have guessed, factors that add complexity to media access control in wireless networks are also potential sources of data transmission errors. Wireless signals can be affected by *internal interference* (such as collisions of hidden node transmissions), external interference (such as strong signals from nearby Wi-Fi networks or high-power interference sources), and attenuation.

Error Sources

Table 7-5 identifies and briefly describes sources of errors in wireless networks.

Signals that interfere with Wi-Fi or other wireless transmissions can make it difficult or impossible for receivers to correctly interpret a sender's transmission. Since both are analog waveforms, when a significantly strong interfering signal combines with a Wi-Fi signal, the additive results could alter the transmitted signal's amplitude or phase and cause the receiver to conclude that frames contain errors.

Table 7-5: Examples of error sources in wireless networks.

Error Source	Description
Attenuation	When electromagnetic energy of any type encounters matter, some of it is lost in the form of heat; this happens in both wired and wireless networks and can cause data transmission errors. Often, Wi-Fi signals can penetrate several walls while maintaining acceptable error rates; however, this is not always the case, and when it is not, attenuation can be a significant source of errors.
Other transmitters	When a very powerful transmitter using one frequency band is near a receiver using another frequency band, the transmitter may overwhelm a receiver's filters and inject substantial noise. This is sometimes called *front-end overload*. Because wireless computer networks are often deployed near Bluetooth devices, microwave ovens, satellite television dishes, cell phones, and other wireless signal transmitters, front-end overload may be a source of data transmission errors.
Narrowband interference	Narrowband interference occurs when the frequency band used by another transmitter overlaps in part (or totally) with that used by a wireless computer network. Signals in the overlapping bands may combine or interfere and cause data transmission errors.
Spread-spectrum interference	This can occur when two or more nearby transmitters switch between narrowband frequencies (channels) or simultaneously spread their signals across an entire common frequency band. Competing spread spectrum transmission sources can produce error-causing interference.
Multipath interference	When electromagnetic radiation, such as Wi-Fi radio waves, reflects off of or diffracts around objects, it takes multiple paths from the transmitter to the receiver. Since these paths typically have different lengths and the signals taking different paths may have different signal strengths, destructive interference that causes errors may occur at the receiver. This is sometimes called *self-interference*.
Natural background noise	For example, using infrared signals for wireless bridges may result in poor performance if the bridges are located near sources of direct sunlight. Atmospheric noise, lightning, solar storms, and galactic noise are other potential sources of wireless signal interference and transmission errors.
Path loss (dispersion)	The intensity of electromagnetic energy reaching a receiver is decreased by distance even in free space. In an auditorium or arena, transmitted signals both attenuate and become more dispersed the further they travel. The combination of dispersion and attenuation can cause data transmission errors.
Motion	If two communicating objects/devices are moving with respect to each other, the frequency of the electromagnetic energy changes according to the Doppler effect. This has the potential to cause data transmission errors in wireless networks that support roaming or handoffs among coordination nodes.
Data-dependent effects	Some modulation schemes can lose clock synchronization in the face of certain long bit patterns (i.e., long strings of 0s or 1s).

Error Controls

Appropriate error controls help to mitigate the challenges to successful data transfers. This can involve forward error correction, cyclic redundancy checks (CRCs), and ARQ.

Forward error correction (FEC) was introduced in Chapter 6 as an error control mechanism used in noisy environments and for satellite communications, where transmitters and receivers may be thousands of miles apart. Basically, FEC schemes require senders to send both EDVs and sufficient information about the original data to enable receivers to reconstruct the original data when transmission errors are detected.

Convolutional coding is a form of FEC used in Wi-Fi networks that support orthogonal frequency division multiplexing (OFDM). OFDM was first used in fourth generation (802.11n) Wi-Fi networks and continues to be used in more recent Wi-Fi generations.

Convolution coding enables receivers to reconstruct data that has been mildly corrupted by interference. Senders perform logical mathematic operations on a frame's data, and the resultant convolutional code is added to the frame after it is constructed but before it is transmitted. If the receiver detects an error, the convolutional code helps receivers identify bits that have been changed in transit. Mildly corrupted frames can be reconstructed by receivers, but convolution coding is insufficient for more severely corrupted frames. Such frames will be identified at the Data Link layer by the cyclic redundancy checks included in the Wi-Fi frame's FCS field.

When the CRC value calculated by a receiver does not match the CRC result in the FCS field, the receiver does not send a required Acknowledgment (ACK) to the sender. This causes the sender to retransmit the frame. In Wi-Fi networks, error detection and ARQ retransmissions occur at the Data Link layer. This contributes to reliable frame delivery in Wi-Fi networks and represents a difference between Wi-Fi and Ethernet. In an Ethernet network, error detection occurs at the Data Link layer, but ARQ retransmissions are handled by the Transport layer.

Hybrid ARQ (HARQ) is used in some wireless networks. It uses a combination of FEC and ARQ. FEC corrects many errors when this combination is used, but when it cannot correct all errors, retransmission is requested. HARQ is used in Bluetooth networks and 5G cellular networks, and it may be used in future Wi-Fi generations. It is described more fully in Appendix 7-1.

Understanding wireless transmission issues and how they are addressed is valuable preparation for taking a closer look at Wi-Fi networks.

7.2 802.11 WI-FI NETWORKS

Wi-Fi technology is ubiquitous. Today, there are more Wi-Fi devices in use than people on the planet, and more than half of the Internet's traffic traverses Wi-Fi networks. Wi-Fi's roots are traced to 1985, when the FCC opened several unlicensed bands of wireless spectrum, but the work on developing a Wi-Fi standard began in 1997. The IEEE 802.11 Wi-Fi standard has also continued to evolve since then, with each new generation bringing higher speed connections and improved capabilities. A closer look at Wi-Fi's history is provided in Appendix 7-2.

7.2.1 Wi-Fi Architecture

The 802.11 standard calls every computer, both fixed and portable, and every mobile device with a Wi-Fi adapter a *station*. It also describes the architecture of Wi-Fi networks as incorporating several components, including access points (APs), basic service sets (BSSs), ad-hoc independent basic service sets (IBSSs), and extended service sets (ESSs) that use distribution systems (DSs) to interconnect APs. DSs can be wired or wireless; a wireless distribution system (WDS) enables wireless interconnection of APs. The 802.11 standard also addresses connections between Wi-Fi networks and wired networks.

Basic Service Sets (BSSs)

A *basic service set (BSS)* is a wireless network topology that allows stations to communicate through a shared medium called an access point (AP). A BSS is sometimes called a "Wi-Fi cell," and an AP is sometimes called a "base station." A BSS also manages how its wireless stations take turns using the shared medium and is a basic building block for more complex WLANs.

As Figure 7-19 illustrates, a BSS contains a single AP and the connected stations within its communication range. A simple BSS includes one AP but may contain multiple stations. A BSS's communication range is known as its *basic service area (BSA)*.

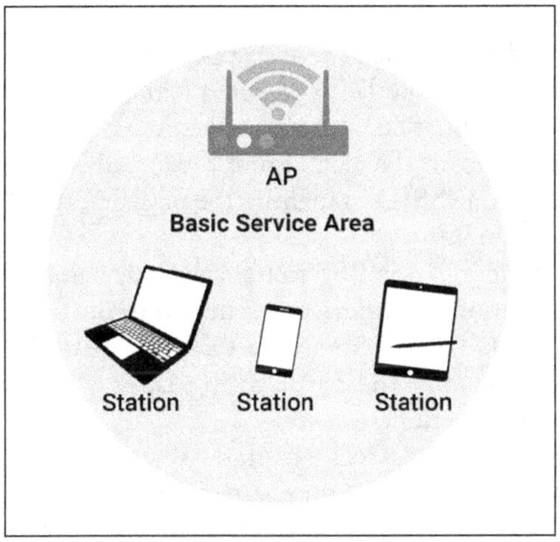

Figure 7-19: An 802.11 basic service set (BSS).

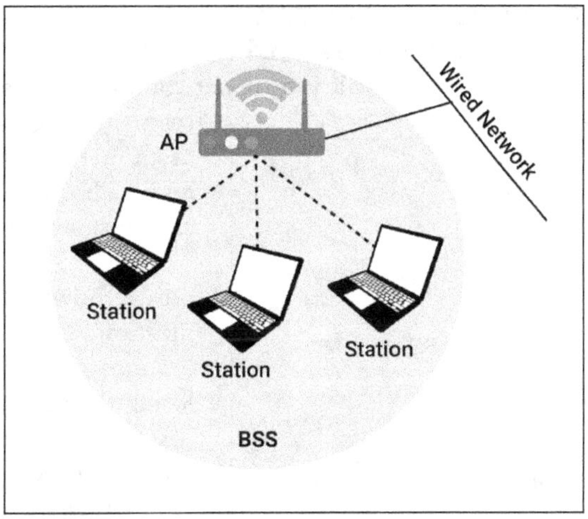

Figure 7-20: A BSS's AP connects the BSS to a wired network.

The AP in a BSS usually connects to a wired network (see Figure 7-20) to allow its wireless stations to communicate with devices connected to the wired network. This configuration makes the AP an internal and external communication coordinator for BSS stations.

Each BSS is uniquely identified by a *basic service set identifier (BSSID)*. Technically, the BSSID is the MAC address of the AP that serves the BSS, but, as Wi-Fi users know, a Wi-Fi network typically has a logical name to identify it in the list of available networks. The network's logical name is called its **service set identifier (SSID)**; this is broadcast by an AP to facilitate the process of finding and joining the network. When wireless device users consult their list of available networks, they see the SSIDs broadcast by nearby APs. Device users select an SSID to join the network and may configure their settings to automatically connect to a specific network.

Independent Basic Service Sets (IBSSs)

In a BSS, stations/devices communicate through the AP; they do not communicate directly with another station. To transfer frames to another station in the BSS, a device sends its frames to the AP, which forwards them to the destination station.

An **independent basic service set (IBSS)** is an 802.11 service set that allows wireless devices (stations) to directly communicate with each other without going through an AP (see Figure 7-21). Unlike a BSS, an IBSS does not contain an AP. An IBSS is also called an *ad hoc network* and is sometimes described as a type of peer-to-peer network with a point-to-point topology.

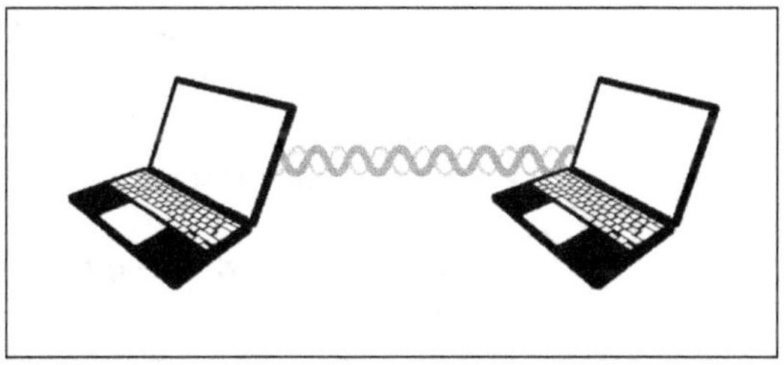

Figure 7-21: Depiction of station-to-station communication in an 802.11 IBSS.

An IBSS is considered the simplest type of Wi-Fi network identified in the 802.11 standard. While rarely used, it enables stations to connect and transfer frames where other Wi-Fi infrastructure (APs) is unavailable. IBSS may be used by small businesses that do not require Internet access. It can also be used to create a Wi-Fi network in remote areas and locations without Wi-Fi infrastructure. Because devices must be within each other's transmission range to communicate, the scope of an IBSS is limited. An IBSS can be implemented easily and quickly with no associated communication costs.

Extended Service Sets (ESSs)

An **extended service set (ESS)** is a WLAN that includes multiple APs and appears to users as a single, seamless, facility-wide network. It consists of two or more BSSs within a logical network segment (such as an IP subnet or VLAN) and is often described as an interconnected set of BSSs (see Figure 7-22). All APs in an ESS broadcast the same SSID to identify the network; this is sometimes called an *ESSID*.

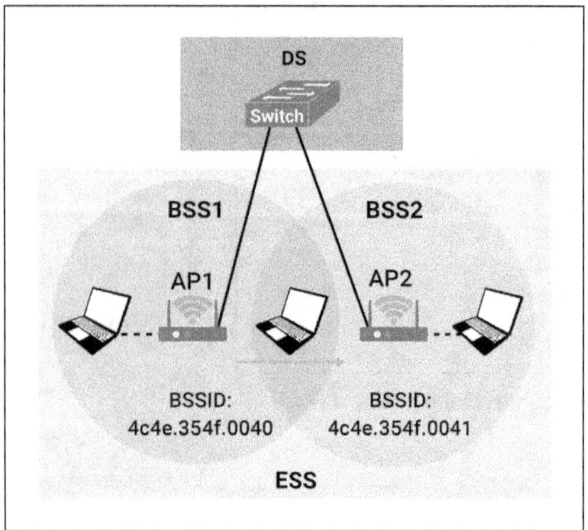

Figure 7-22: A simple example of an extended service set (ESS) and its key characteristics.

An ESS enables devices in one BSS to transparently communicate with devices in another, or devices connected to the organization's wired network(s). An ESS also enables mobile device users to move (roam) among the participating BSSs without losing their network connection.

Central authentication of devices facilitates roaming capabilities. Devices authenticate when they join the network, and their authentication can follow them as they move among BSSs. Handoffs between APs are usually transparent to device users and are handled at Wi-Fi's LLC sublayer.

As Figure 7-22 illustrates, the BSSs in an ESS interconnect via a distribution system (DS). The APs in the different BSSs may connect to a switch via Ethernet cable, but wireless distribution system technologies exist. When APs connect to a switch, the switch has a role that is equivalent to a distribution-layer switch that interconnects LANs. In today's enterprise networks, APs often connect to PoE switches to enable the APs to receive power via Ethernet cables.

Specialized switches called Wi-Fi controllers are common in ESSs. A **Wi-Fi controller** monitors and manages the APs in a WLAN and enables stations to be authenticated, connect to the network, and roam among BSSs. They can assist Wi-Fi network managers in identifying nonauthorized (rogue) APs and contribute to WLAN performance by requiring that APs in adjacent BSSs use nonoverlapping channels. This reduces signal interference. Many APs can operate in managed or unmanaged modes, but when connected to Wi-Fi controllers, most or all APs are managed.

APs are also classified as "fit" or "thin" or "fat." A *thin AP* lacks a complete operating system. It offloads responsibilities for routing, DNS, and DHCP services to Wi-Fi controllers and only retains AP capabilities. In contrast, a *fat AP* has an operating system and can function as a DHCP server, DNS server, VPN gateway, and firewall. Most Wi-Fi routers in residential networks are fat APs, while most managed APs in business facilities are thin APs.

Distribution and Integration Services

Distribution and integration services enable APs to be integrated in an ESS and extend wired network services to the wireless network (see Figure 7-22). Managing mobile station associations with APs is an important part of these services; this includes association, reassociation, and disassociation services, which are summarized in Table 7-6.

Station services, including authentication services, are other important DS services. These are described in Appendix 7-3.

Table 7-6: Summaries of distribution, integration, association, disassociation, and reassociation services.	
Service	**Brief Summary**
Distribution	A station uses this service every time it sends MAC frames to a device located in another BSS or wired network. This provides the DS with sufficient information to determine the correct destination BSS for frames being transferred between stations in different BSSs. The 802.11 standard does not specify how the DS delivers the data to a destination BSS but identifies distribution as the service that enables this.
Integration	The integration service enables the delivery of MAC frames through a portal between a DS and a non-802.11 LAN. It performs all required address space or media translations that the destination network requires. The details associated with integration services are dependent on how a DS is implemented in an organization.
Association	A station uses the association service to establish a connection with an AP. A station cannot use the DS to transfer data until an association with an AP is established. Association is the first step to enabling a station to move among BSSs in an ESS. Association maps a station to the DS via an AP. A station can associate with only one AP, but an AP can associate with multiple stations.
Disassociation	A station or AP uses the disassociation service to terminate an existing association. Basically, this is a notification service that its recipient (a station or AP) cannot refuse. Stations should disassociate when exiting the network. An AP may disassociate all its stations when it undergoes maintenance or reconfiguration.
Reassociation	The reassociation service enables a station to change the state of its current association. It also provides the functionality required to support a station's movement from one BSS to another; it enables a station to change its association from one AP to another. The reassociation service keeps the DS informed of the current mapping between an AP and a station as the station moves from one BSS to another within an ESS. A station always initiates the reassociation service; an AP does not.

Mesh Basic Service Sets (MBSSs)

In 2012, the 802.11 standard was extended to include mesh basic service sets (MBSSs). This Wi-Fi topology can be used in situations where wired networks are not possible and APs cannot be interconnected to create an ESS. An MBSS enables wireless distribution of network traffic.

Wi-Fi meshes are increasingly popular in residential networks. Two types of MBSSs are common. One uses wireless extenders to expand the network's communication range (see Figure 7-23a). They are placed near the edge of the mesh router's communication range, and devices connect to a nearby extender with the strongest signal. Extenders serve as wireless repeaters that rebroadcast Wi-Fi frames, and the mesh router serves as the network's wireless distribution system (WDS). The wireless connection between an extender and the mesh router is called a *Wi-Fi backhaul*. The result is a wireless "umbrella" that enables devices to roam within the WLAN's extended communication range.

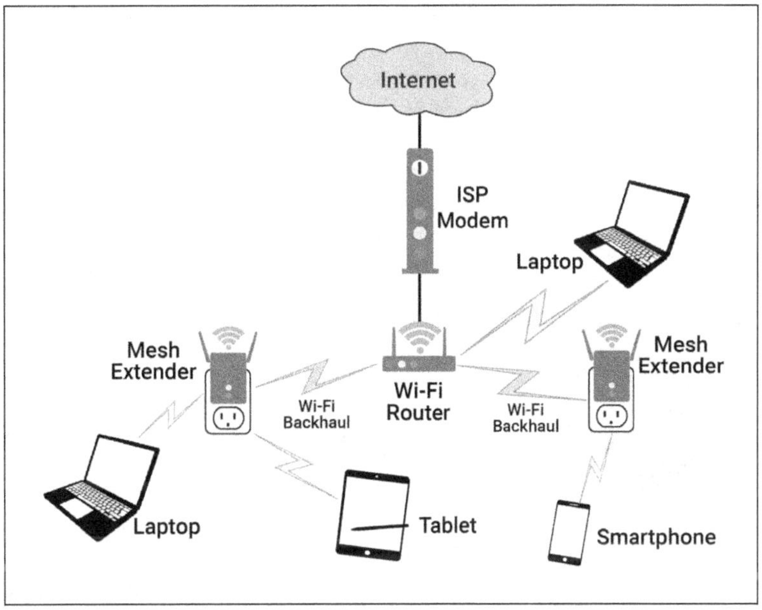

Figure 7-23a: An example of an 802.11 MBSS with extenders.

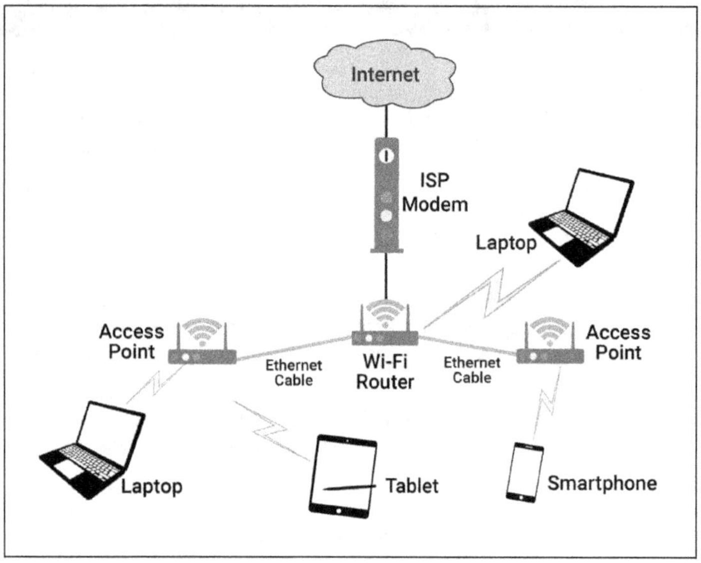

Figure 7-23b: A Wi-Fi mesh with wired APs.

An alternative MBSS topology is illustrated in Figure 7-23b. APs connect to the Wi-Fi router by Ethernet cables. This is considered a better option for MBSSs in business offices because Ethernet cables provide more reliable connection speeds and APs can accommodate more connected devices than mesh extenders. In this deployment, the Wi-Fi router functions as a WDS and as a fat AP or Wi-Fi controller that handles DHCP, DNS, routing, and VPN gateway services for thin APs.

7.2.2 Wi-Fi Physical and Logical Topology

Like hub-based Ethernet, a Wi-Fi BSS has a physical star topology (see Figure 7-20), and because the AP provides a shared medium for stations to communicate, it has a logical bus topology. IBSSs, however, have a logical point-to-point topology (see Figure 7-21).

Because stations in a BSS share a common communication medium, appropriate Data Link layer protocols are needed to minimize the potential for data collisions.

7.2.3 Wi-Fi Media Access Control

The 802.11 standard identifies carrier sense multiple access with collision avoidance (CSMA/CA) as the official Data Link layer protocol in Wi-Fi networks, but this may not be the only media access control that adapters in devices and APs support. CSMA/CA requires a device to associate with an AP prior to using it to transfer data. In an ESS, association maps the device to a BSS AP and enables it to use the network's distribution services.

Access Point Association

To connect to the wireless network, a station sends an association request to an AP. The AP checks the device's compatibility with the network and may also check its authentication credentials. In everyday terms, this means that when a device attempts to join an available Wi-Fi network, it is the AP that permits or denies the association request. An AP can reject association requests from devices that cannot be authenticated.

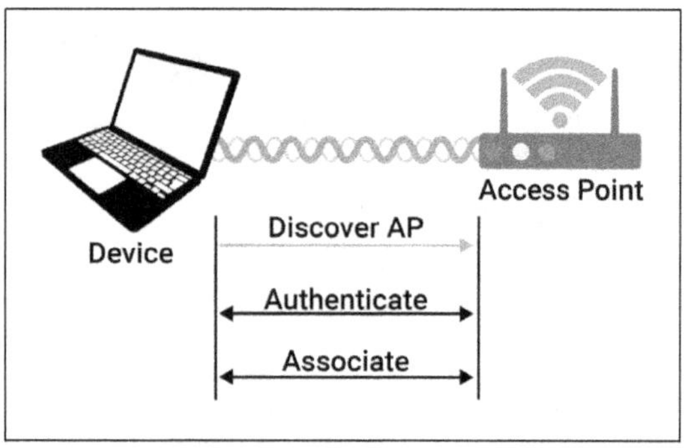

Figure 7-24: AP discovery and station authentication precede association.

Joining a Wi-Fi network is a three-step process: AP discovery, authentication, and association. This is illustrated in Figure 7-24.

Scanning is an important 802.11 part of AP discovery. A Wi-Fi adapter performs *scanning* to search for and identify an available AP to associate with. Two types of scanning are supported: active and passive. They are described in Table 7-7 and illustrated in Figure 7-25. Mobile devices in new locations often use passive scanning to identify nearby Wi-Fi networks.

APs that operate in both Wi-Fi frequency ranges (2.4 GHz and 5 GHz) may broadcast two SSIDs—one for the 2.4 GHz range and one for the 5 GHz range—and the second may have a -5G tag

Table 7-7: Active and passive scanning in Wi-Fi networks.

Type of Scanning	Description
Active	In *active scanning*, the device transmits a *probe frame* on all active channels. APs within the device's transmission range respond with *probe response frames* that include the information needed to create an association request. Generally, responses are received from multiple APs in an ESS. The adapter associates with the AP with the highest connection speed and strongest signal, which is often the closest.
Passive	With *passive scanning*, a device's adapter monitors the Wi-Fi frequency band(s) for a *beacon frame* broadcast by an AP. A beacon frame includes the information needed to send an association request to the AP.

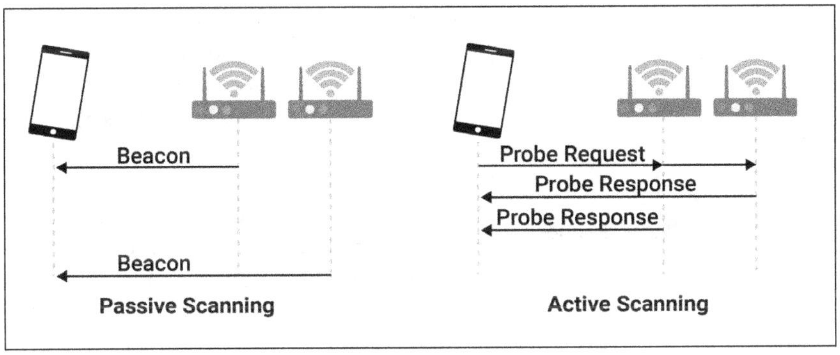

Figure 7-25: AP discovery may involve both passive and active scanning.

to indicate the 5 GHz range. These ranges are described more fully in section 7.3.1. After available APs are discovered and devices are authenticated, the association process can be completed.

Distributed Coordination Function (DCF) and Point Coordination Function (PCF)

Because a station associated with an AP may be a "hidden node" for one or more other stations in the BSS, CSMA/CA employs two media access controls: the distributed coordination function (DCF) and the point coordination function (PCF). DCF is the "normal" form of Wi-Fi access control. It is contention-based and is used for most data traffic within a BSS. PCF works in concert with DCF and is a controlled-access approach that provides hidden nodes an opportunity to transmit.

DCF is used in both IBSSs and BSSs. Like CSMA, DCF requires devices to monitor ("sense") the communication medium before starting to transmit and to refrain from transmitting when the shared medium is being used by another device.

Media access in PCF is centralized and controlled by the AP. The AP sends poll frames to devices in the BSS that support PCF (not all devices support PCF), and when a device receives the poll, it transmits a frame. If a polled device does not have data to transmit, it sends a null frame to the AP. Devices that only support DCF cannot access the medium while the AP operates in PCF mode.

To provide access to DCF-only devices when both PCF and DCF are used, the AP alternates between operating in PCF and DCF modes. Each PCF interval is followed by a DCF interval; together, they make a *superframe* (see Figure 7-26). A superframe is sometimes called a *beacon interval* because the AP broadcasts a beacon approximately every 100 ms to identify the start of a *contention-free period (CFP)*, during which the AP operates in PCF mode. The CFP is followed by a *contention period (CP)*, during which the AP operates in DCF mode. The continuous repetition of PCF CFPs and DCF CPs enables both hidden and nonhidden stations to use the shared medium.

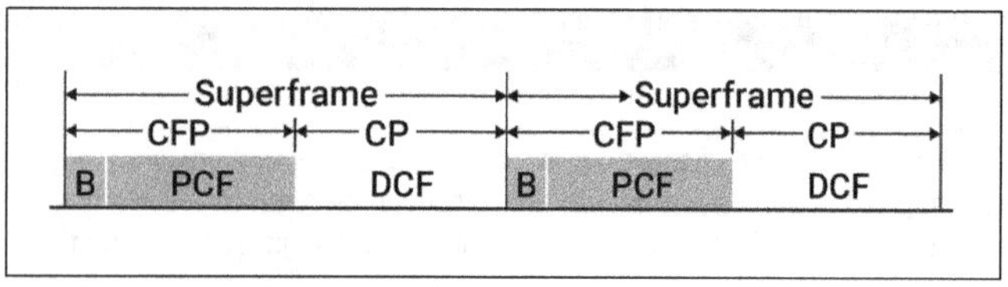

Figure 7-26: Superframes are used in Wi-Fi networks that support both the DCF and the PCF.

DCF is the Wi-Fi MAC protocol identified in the IEEE 802.11 standard and is officially called CSMA/CA. The process depicted in Figure 7-27 illustrates how DCF uses RTS and CTS frames to avoid data collisions. DCF requires a station with data to transmit to first check the medium to determine if it is idle or being used. If the medium is being used, the station pauses for a short time (*backoff time*) before again checking the status of the medium. If the medium is free, it transmits a *request to send (RTS)* frame, and if the destination is available to receive data (e.g., is not receiving data from another device), it will respond with a *clear to send (CTS)* frame. Upon receipt of the CTS, the device with data to transmit begins to transmit its data.

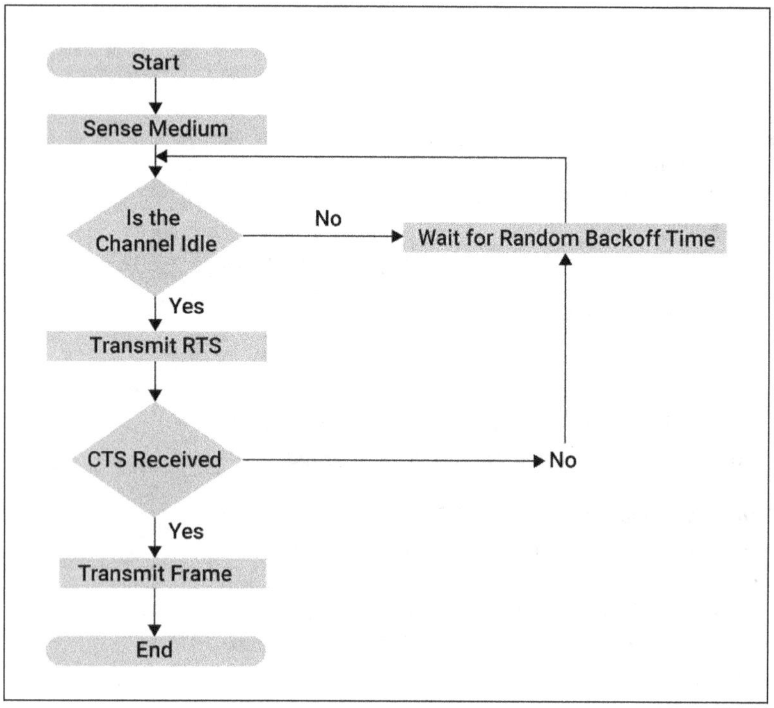

Figure 7-27: DCF/CSMA/CA overview.

The required exchange of RTS and CTS frames prior to transmission is a collision avoidance mechanism and is another example of how Wi-Fi differs from Ethernet. Ethernet's CSMA/CD protocol allows a device to begin transmitting as soon as it determines that the medium is idle and includes mechanisms for recovering from collisions. Wi-Fi's CSMA/CA requires RTS–CTS exchange to prevent collisions.

PCF is best suited for high-traffic networks, where the possibility of data collisions from hidden nodes is significant. In low-traffic networks, collisions are less likely, and requiring stations to wait before receiving a poll (or until the CFP ends) can reduce rather than improve latency. Here, PCF may be unnecessary, even when there are hidden nodes, and is typically not supported. This is why DCF is most common and is equated with CSMA/CA. Both DCF and PCF are described in more detail in Appendix 7-4.

7.2.4 Wi-Fi Frame Format

Figure 7-28 illustrates the format of an 802.11 Data Link layer frame. When compared to the format of 802.3 (Ethernet) frames (described in Chapter 6), one of the biggest differences is the number of address fields.

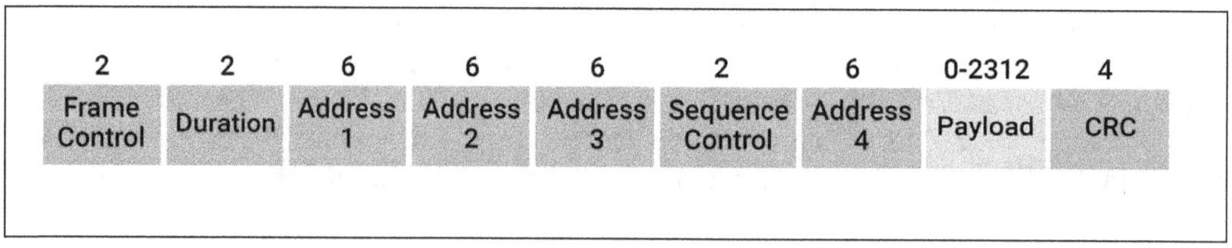

Figure 7-28: The format of Wi-Fi data frames.

Ethernet frames include two Address fields: the destination and source addresses. On the other hand, 802.11 data frames have four addresses. Three of these Address fields are used in BSSs and ESSs, but one is only used in ad hoc networks (IBSSs). Each of the addresses is six bytes (48 bits) in length—the standard length of IEEE 802 MAC addresses.

The Frame Control field identifies the frame's type (e.g., management, control, data) and subtype (e.g., beacon, association request). The Duration field is used to reserve the medium for a specific amount of time to ensure that other devices do not transmit during that time; it is also used to specify the duration of a transmission in response to an RTS frame.

The Sequence Control field is used for frame sequence numbers, which contribute to reliable frame delivery and assist in Wi-Fi's Data Link layer ARQ retransmissions. The Payload field includes the LLC PDU, and the CRC field is equivalent to an Ethernet frame's FCS field. It includes a CRC-32 EDV used for error detection. The Wi-Fi frame format is discussed in greater detail in Appendix 7-5.

In business facilities, Wi-Fi networks offer users convenient Internet access, but much happens behind the scenes to enable such convenience, and revisions to the 802.11 standard have brought new capabilities to APs, Wi-Fi adapters, and their respective antennas. These revisions have contributed to improving Wi-Fi networks.

7.3 EVOLVING WI-FI STANDARDS

Revisions (amendments) to the original 802.11 standard have produced successive Wi-Fi generations. Because the first three generations are considered obsolete, Table 7-8 only considers generations four through seven. Wi-Fi generation 6e represents a revision to the 802.11ax amendment in response to the opening of an unlicensed portion of the 6 GHz frequency spectrum. Taking a closer look at Table 7-8 contents reveals how successive Wi-Fi generations have delivered faster transmission speeds and expanded capabilities.

Before unpacking Table 7-8, it is important to note that each successive Wi-Fi generation is backward compatible with previous generations. This enables older devices to connect to and use technologies that support newer generation Wi-Fi networks, even though they lack the technical capabilities to take full advantage of the features that the newer generation supports.

On a practical level, this means that replacing a residential Wi-Fi router with one that supports Wi-Fi 6 or 7 will not enable laptops, tablets, or smartphones equipped with Wi-Fi 4 or Wi-Fi

Table 7-8: Comparison of Wi-Fi generations four through seven.

	Wi-Fi Generation				
	Wi-Fi 4	**Wi-Fi 5**	**Wi-Fi 6**	**Wi-Fi 6e**	**Wi-Fi 7**
Launch Year	2007	2011	2019	2021	2023
IEEE 802.11 Amendment	802.11n	802.11ac	802.11ax		802.11be
Data Rate Maximum	1.2 Gbps	3.5 Gbps	9.6 Gbps		46 Gbps
Bands (GHZ)	2.4 and 5	5	2.4 and 5	6	2.4, 5, and 6
Channel Size(s)—MHz	20, 40	20, 40, 80, 160	20, 40, 80, 160		Up to 320
Modulation	OFDM	OFDM	OFDMA		OFDMA
QAM	64 QAM	256 QAM	1024 QAM		4096 QAM
MIMO	4 x 4 MIMO	4 x 4 MIMO DL MU-MIMO	8 x 8 UL/DL MU-MIMO		16 x 16 MU-MIMO
Security	WPA2	WPA2	WPA3		WPA3
Sources: IEEE, Intel Corporation, Wi-Fi Alliance					

5 adapters to connect and transfer data at Wi-Fi 6 speeds. This also means that it is important to pay attention to the Wi-Fi adapter generation when replacing a laptop, tablet, or smartphone with a newer one. Sometimes, continuing to use older devices with newer Wi-Fi routers will slow connection speeds for all devices, including newer ones.

Table 7-8 identifies several reasons why newer Wi-Fi generations support higher data rates. This includes support for denser QAM constellations and advances in the ability to use multiple-input and multiple-output (MIMO) on Wi-Fi's shared radio spectrum. Shifts from OFDM to OFDMA and the ability to support larger channels are other reasons for increasing data rates across generations.

Support for higher QAM schemes partially accounts for increased maximum data rates across Wi-Fi generations. As noted in section 7.1.2, increases in the density of QAM constellation maps translates to the ability to represent more bits per symbol (see Figure 7-14). Hence, even if the symbol rate (symbols per second) remains constant, when each symbol represents a larger number of bits, the data rate (in bps) increases.

Multiple-input and multiple-output (MIMO) is a method for multiplying the capacity of shared radio spectrum by using multiple transmission and receiving antennas to exploit multipath propagation. When Wi-Fi radio waves reflect off or diffract around objects, they take different paths to receiver antennas. MIMO takes advantage of this phenomenon and has been supported in Wi-Fi networks since Wi-Fi 4.

Initially, MIMO referred to the use of multiple antennas at the transmitter and the receiver, such as those depicted in Figure 7-29. MIMO is often contrasted with *single-input and single-output (SISO)*, in which both the transmitting and receiving devices have single antennas. Before Wi-Fi 4, a single antenna was the norm for wireless adapters and APs. Since Wi-Fi 4, Wi-Fi adapters and APs have been equipped with four or more antennas.

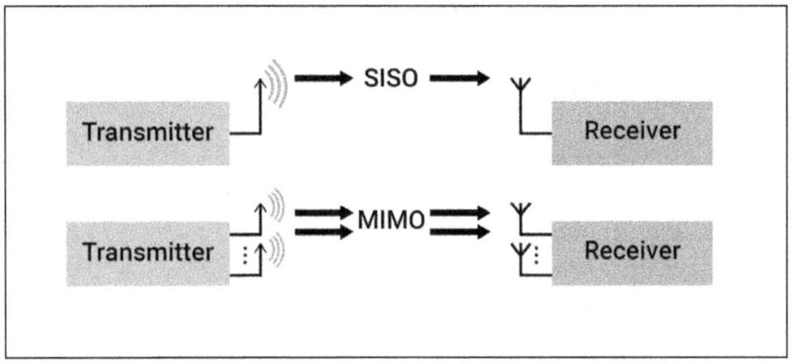

Figure 7-29: SISO (single-input and single output) vs. MIMO (multiple-input and multiple-output)

4 x 4 MIMO (see Table 7-8) means that wireless transmitters and receivers are each equipped with four antennas. *16 x 16 MIMO* (supported in Wi-Fi 7) refers to 16 antennas in transmitters and receivers. *Multi-user MIMO (MU-MIMO)* enables an AP or a Wi-Fi router to deploy its multiple antennas to support simultaneous connections with two or more devices. *Downlink MU-MIMO (DL MU-MIMO)* enables an AP to use its different antennas for simultaneous transmissions to a device; *uplink MU-MIMO (UL MU-MIMO)* enables a device to use its different antennas for simultaneous transmissions to an AP.

Today, MIMO is usually described as a technique that leverages OFDM to enable simultaneous transmission and receipt of multiple signals over the same radio band. OFDM is the focus of section 7.3.2, and understanding it is facilitated by understanding Wi-Fi frequency bands and channels.

7.3.1 Wi-Fi Frequency Bands and Channels

Since Wi-Fi 4, 802.11 networks have operated in the 2.4 GHz and 5 GHz frequency bands. Table 7-8 shows that Wi-Fi 6e and Wi-Fi 7 also use the 6 GHz frequency band allocated for unlicensed use in 2020 by the FCC. These bands are subdivided into channels where actual transmissions occur.

Wi-Fi Frequency Bands

Many residential Wi-Fi routers are *dual-band* APs that can support devices in both the 2.4 GHz and 5 GHz ranges. Some broadcast slightly different SSIDs (see Figure 7-30) to differentiate the two bands, but some do not. Typically, a device only connects to the AP (router) in one of the two bands. This means that some devices in a Wi-Fi network may communicate with the AP in the 2.4 GHz band while others are using the 5 GHz band to communicate with the AP. Devices typically try to automatically connect to their preferred frequency band, which is usually the 5 GHz band.

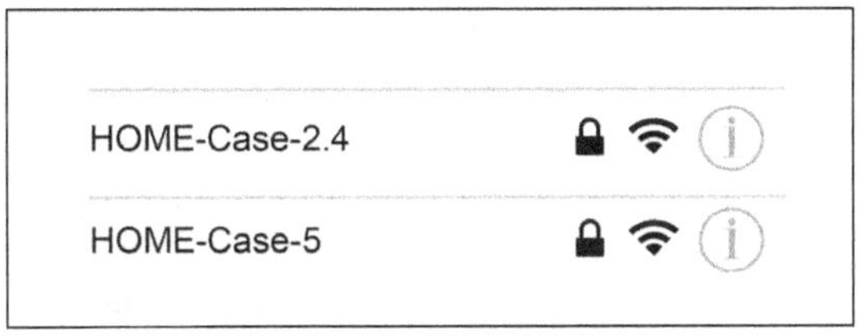

Figure 7-30: 2.4 GHz and 5 GHz connection options in an available networks list.

As Figure 7-31 illustrates, 5 GHz signals have a shorter wavelength than 2.4 GHz signals. It also illustrates the well-known formula $f=1/\lambda$ by showing that more waves are sent by higher frequencies (smaller λs) per second than lower frequencies. If each complete wave represents one bit, more bits per second can be transmitted by using higher frequency signals. In Wi-Fi, this means that a modulated 5 GHz carrier can transfer more data per second than a modulated 2.4 GHz carrier.

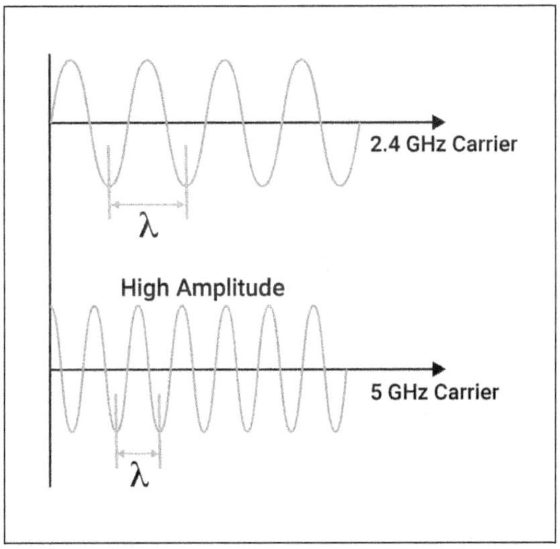

Figure 7-31: Wavelength differences between 2.4 GHz and 5 GHz Wi-Fi signals enable more symbols per second for 5 GHz connections.

Relative to 2.4 GHz, 5 GHz Wi-Fi offers faster uploads and downloads because more symbols can be transmitted per second. However, 5 GHz signals lose more power (attenuate) than 2.4 GHz signals when they travel to/from devices, especially when they pass through walls. (Higher frequency signals generally suffer greater power loss than lower frequency signals when they pass through solid or semi-solid objects.) In a dual-band Wi-Fi network, the 2.4 GHz network typically has a greater transmission range than the 5 GHz network, but the differences are more pronounced when one or more walls separate devices from the AP (router).

On a practical level, this means that 5 GHz is better than 2.4 GHz Wi-Fi for bandwidth-hungry applications like high-definition video streaming or online gaming, but the receiving device or gaming console should be close to the Wi-Fi router or AP and not in another room.

Wi-Fi Channels and Channel Bonding

The 2.4 GHz and 5 GHz Wi-Fi frequency bands are subdivided into smaller bands called channels. A **Wi-Fi channel** is the radio band through which data is transferred.

The 2.4 GHz band is divided into 14 channels (see Figure 7-32), but channel 14 is rarely used, and in North America, only channels 1 to 11 are. Each 2.4 GHz channel is 20 MHz wide, and includes an additional 2 MHz *guard band* that increases each channel to 22 MHz.

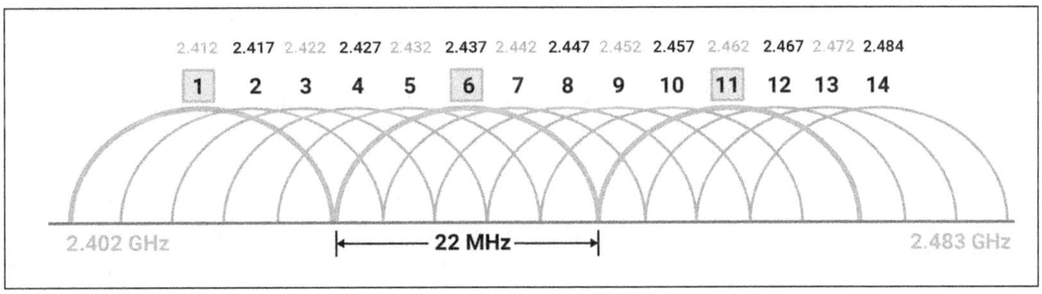

Figure 7-32: Wi-Fi channels in the 2.4 GHz range.

Examples of 20 MHz channels in the 5 GHz Wi-Fi band are illustrated in Figure 7-35. In the United States, 20 MHz channels in three ranges may be used. (The channels in each range increase by increments of 4.) The first range has channels that range from 32 to 68, but channels 32 and 68 from this range are rarely used, and channels 36, 40, 44, and 48 are the most widely used channels in residential Wi-Fi networks. The second range has channels that range from 96 to 144, but channel 96 is rarely used, and the channels have operating restrictions to avoid interference with weather radar and military applications. The third range has channels that range from 149 to 173, but channels 169 and 173 are rarely used. Some of these (149, 153, 157, and 161) are used in mesh networks in buildings.

Figure 7-32 also illustrates that adjacent channels overlap. For example, channels 2, 3, and 4 each begin within channel 1's 20 MHz frequency band and thereby overlap with some of channel 1's frequency band. Only channels 1, 6, and 11 do not overlap with one another, and they are the only nonoverlapping Wi-Fi channels used in North America. Residential Wi-Fi routers usually automatically select the best performing channel based on what is being used in other nearby Wi-Fi networks; however, this may be one of the overlapping channels.

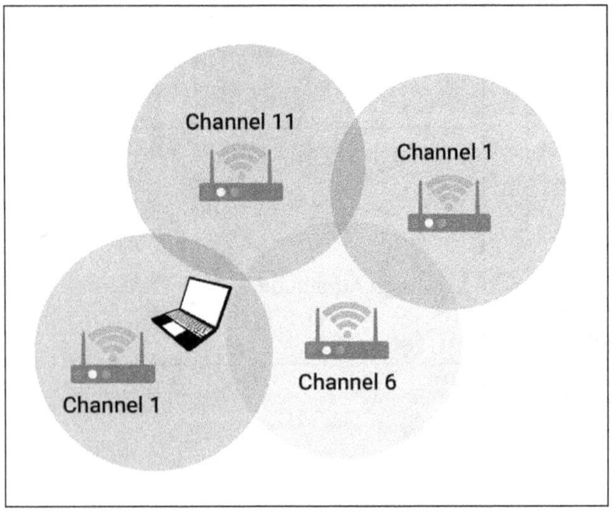

Figure 7-33: An example of nonoverlapping 2.4 GHz channel allocation in a business facility.

In business facilities, the channels that adjacent APs use are usually centrally controlled by network administrators, and allocation patterns are followed to minimize the potential for signal interference. An example of an allocation pattern is provided in Figure 7-33.

Channel bonding enables adjacent channels in a frequency band to be combined to increase throughput between wireless devices. Wi-Fi 4 introduced channel bonding and enabled 40 MHz width channels to be created. Wi-Fi 5 extended channel bonding to allow 80 MHz or 160 MHz channels. Figure 7-34 shows how two nonoverlapping 40 MHz channels can be created by combining channels in the 2.4 GHz range, and Figure 7-35 shows how channel bonding can be used to create 40 MHz, 80 MHz, and 160 MHz nonoverlapping channels in the 5 GHz range.

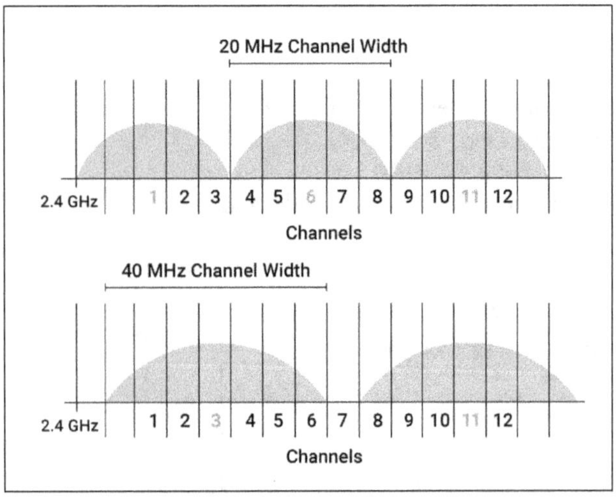

Figure 7-34: Channel bonding in the 2.4 GHz range.

According to Shannon's formula [C=B*log2(1+S/N)], higher bandwidth translates into higher channel capacity. So, using channel bonding to create higher bandwidth Wi-Fi channels equates to being able to transfer a higher volume of data (throughput) each second through each channel. A potential downside to channel bonding is the reduction of nonoverlapping channels in the frequency band.

Some Wi-Fi devices, especially older ones, only support 20 MHz channels. This means that channel bonding can be impractical in networks with older devices.

In the United States, the only 20 MHz channels in the 5 GHz frequency band that are permitted in mesh networks in buildings are 36, 40, 44, 48, 149, 153, 157, 161,

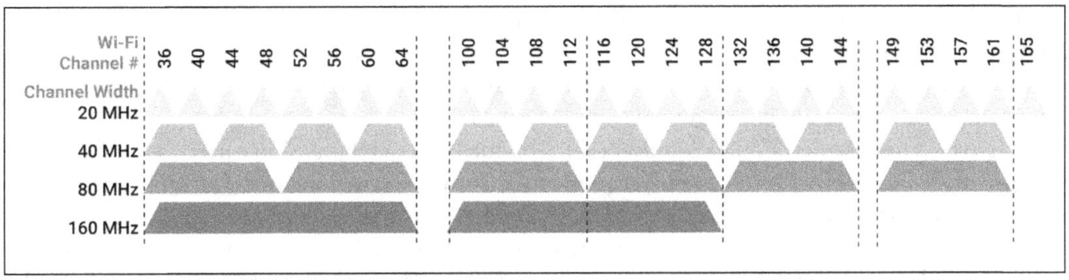

Figure 7-35: Examples of nonoverlapping 5 GHz Wi-Fi channels and channel bonding used in the United States.

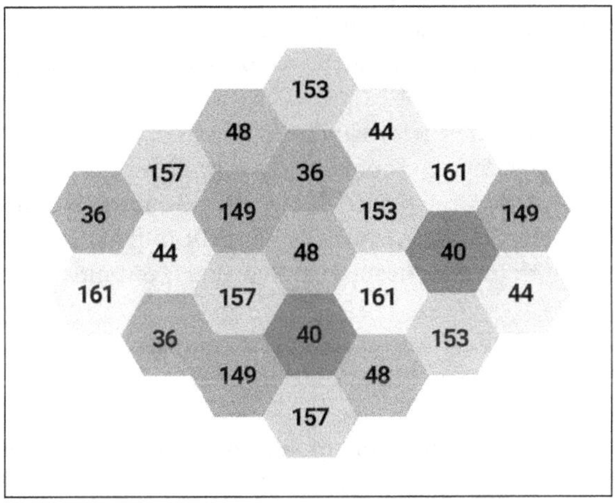

Figure 7-36: An example of a deployment of nonoverlapping 5 GHz channels in a single-story business facility, such as a warehouse.

and 165. Figure 7-36 illustrates how these channels might be deployed in a business facility. These restrictions make some of the 40 MHz, 80 MHz, and 160 MHz channels impractical in the United States.

7.3.2 Orthogonal Frequency-Division Multiplexing (OFDM)

Orthogonal frequency-division multiplexing (OFDM) is a data transmission method that subdivides a channel into smaller channels called *subcarriers* or tones. This is conceptually illustrated in Figure 7-37. OFDM has been supported in Wi-Fi networks since Wi-Fi 2, and its use has evolved in successive Wi-Fi generations to support smaller subcarriers. While primarily used for wireless communication, OFDM can also be used for fiber optic and wired communications.

When an undivided 20 MHz Wi-Fi channel is used, each bit in a Wi-Fi frame is transmitted sequentially (serially), one after the other. In OFDM, subcarriers can be used to simultaneously transmit bits (in parallel) and transfer the frame more rapidly.

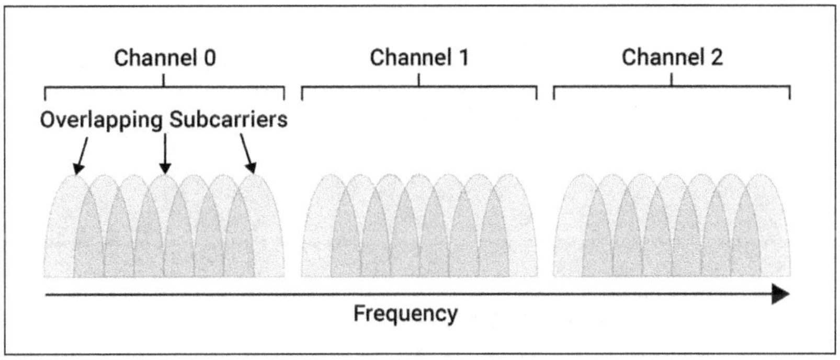

Figure 7-37: OFDM subdivides a channel into subchannels that are used simultaneously to carry data.

OFDM enables efficient use of a channel's total bandwidth by using closely spaced subcarriers. Sixty-four subcarriers are created, and the frequency range of each one is 312.5 KHz. They may be overlapping but are still orthogonal, or separate, and they are allocated and modulated in a way that cancels out subchannel interference.

OFDMA, supported in Wi-Fi 6 and Wi-Fi 7, divides a channel into 256 carriers with frequency ranges of 78.125 KHz. **Orthogonal frequency-division multiple access (OFDMA)** enables a channel's subcarriers to be assigned to different devices. This reduces the need for devices sharing the same channel to have to wait or take turns transmitting data. It also is helpful when a device needs a low, but consistent, stream of data and when many devices are connected to the same AP or Wi-Fi router. OFDMA also provides a way to support a growing number of IoT devices.

Resource Units (RUs) are key components of OFDMA spectrum allocation. With OFDMA, a channel can be divided into multiple RUs with different subcarrier widths. A client device/station can only be assigned to one RU, so an RU is basically a set of subcarriers allocated to a connected device.

Valid OFDMA RU allocations for a 20 MHz channel width include 26, 52, 106, and 242 subcarriers. As Figure 7-38 illustrates, when only one device is connected to the Wi-Fi network, all 242 subcarriers, the entire channel, can be allocated to the device. Here, all 242 subcarriers are allocated to a single RU for one device. When there are two users, the channel can be split into two RUs with 106 subcarriers. Four RUs with 52 subcarriers can support four users, and nine RUs with 26 subcarriers can support nine users.

Although there are fixed combinations, RU allocation across the channel can mix and match to meet the communication needs of connected stations/devices. In addition, an AP can communicate with each RU at a different data rate and power level.

As Table 7-8 indicates, OFDMA is part of the combination of advancements that have contributed to the evolution of Wi-Fi networks. Support for denser QAM constellations and MU-MIMO are other reasons for improvements in Wi-Fi network performance. Wi-Fi security has also improved. OFDM and OFDMA are discussed in greater detail in Appendix 7-6.

It is important to remember that both wireless devices and APs (or Wi-Fi routers) must support a specific Wi-Fi generation to take full advantage of that generation's capabilities and potential data rates. If some devices are a generation or two (or more) behind the others, the network's performance usually matches that of its oldest components.

Practically, this means that the Wi-Fi networks in business facilities frequently do not align with the prevailing Wi-Fi standard. However, the new standards for the different Wi-Fi generations provide a roadmap for improving WLAN performance.

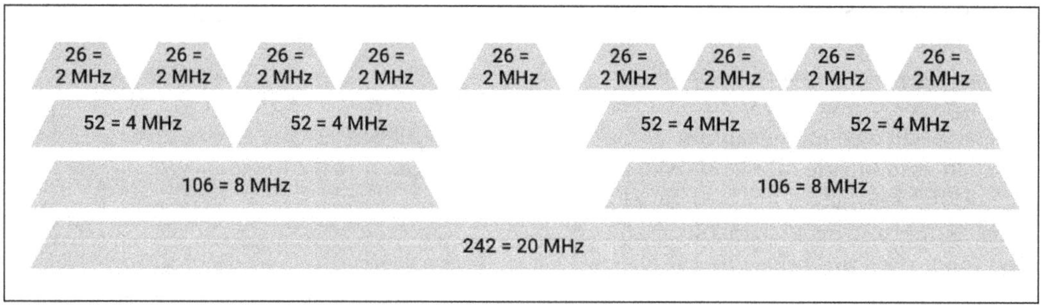

Figure 7-38: Valid RU allocations for a 20 MHz channel in OFDMA.

7.4 WI-FI SECURITY

Because of their nature, Wi-Fi networks have numerous vulnerabilities. For example, Wi-Fi transmission signals can be intercepted by any wireless device within range of the transmitter. This does not mean that Wi-Fi networks should be feared or considered highly susceptible to attacks; however, flawed deployments should be avoided, and secure Wi-Fi protocols, such as WPA3 (see Table 7-8), should be used to ensure that attackers don't get much, if anything, from intercepted signals. Implementing industry-standard security mechanisms and best practices enables Wi-Fi to be a valuable part of enterprise network infrastructure.

7.4.1 Wi-Fi Threats and Attacks

Table 7-9 identifies and briefly describes some of the more common types of Wi-Fi infrastructure network attacks. Additional Wi-Fi network vulnerabilities are identified and described in Appendix 7-7. Examples of Wi-Fi security best practices are summarized in Table 7-10. Two important observations are needed. First, attackers often try to compromise Wi-Fi user devices via stolen credentials or malware to gain access to an enterprise network, and bogus APs or hotspots are often involved. Second, Wi-Fi users may be unaware that they are being victimized when an attack is occurring.

Table 7-9: Examples of Wi-Fi infrastructure network security threats and attacks.

Security Threat	Brief Description
Channel interference attack	This is a type of denial-of-service (DoS) attack where users are unable to use the network when the attack is underway. The attacker places an AP in the Wi-Fi network's coverage area that emits an illegally strong signal on the same channels as those used in the legitimate network. This causes interference that disrupts the transmissions of both the network's legitimate APs and user devices and causes users to lose connectivity to the network.
Evil twin attack	In an evil twin attack, the attacker gathers information about a network AP and impersonates it. The attacker uses a stronger broadcast signal than the one generated by the legitimate AP, which causes user devices to connect to the bogus AP instead of the real one. This positions the attacker to use packet sniffers and specialized tools to capture and read data transferred by users, including credit card numbers, login credentials, and other personal information.
Karma attacks	A Karma attack is a type of evil twin attack in which an attacker's device listens to probe requests and mimics the SSID being requested to trick unsuspecting devices into believing that they have found a trusted Wi-Fi connection. The connection creates a man-in-the middle (MITM) situation (see below) where the attacker sits between the victim's device and the Internet, intercepting traffic.
Man-in-the-middle (MITM) attack	An MITM attack is similar to an evil twin attack, but here, an MITM AP masquerades as an AP to which users connect and that is connected to the enterprise network that provides Internet access and access to corporate network services. As with an evil twin, all data transferred to/from the enterprise network via the AP can be intercepted by the attacker and may position the attacker to capture sensitive data transferred to/from enterprise services, such as financial applications and transaction databases.
Malware and ransomware	Attackers routinely target enterprise network users via phishing, spear phishing, business email scams, etc. They use these methods to enable them to install malware or ransomware so they can steal login credentials and gain access to corporate networks, or so they can use the devices in DoS and other types of attacks. Antimalware software, user training, zero trust mechanisms, and other preventative measures can be used to combat these attacks.
Mobile device theft	Not all attackers rely on gaining access to your data via wireless means. By physically stealing your device, attackers could have unrestricted access to all of its data, as well as any connected cloud accounts.
Rogue hotspots	These are used to fool devices into connecting to a false AP and facilitate evil twin, Karma, and MITM attacks.
Unauthorized access to infrastructure network	In corporate environments, a private Wi-Fi network is usually connected to the wired corporate network to provide employee access to internal services and the Internet. Hence, a compromised Wi-Fi network may mean a compromised corporate network. VLANs, network segmentation, and other network segregation measures may help.
Source: Compiled from multiple sources in Chapter References list.	

Table 7-10: Examples of Wi-Fi infrastructure network best practices.

WLAN Security Best Practice	Brief Summary
Maintain a list of authorized APs	Being able to separate rogue from authorized APs starts with a complete list of the network's authorized APs and their MAC addresses (BSSIDs).
Detect authorized APs	Network vulnerability scanning and other security tools should be configured to detect authorized APs and alert network administrators when an unauthorized AP is detected.
Use a wireless intrusion detection system (WIDS)	A WIDS is a specialized intrusion detection system that can be configured to detect unauthorized APs. In addition to network scanning, a WIDS can be configured to monitor traffic anomalies that may signal channel interference or protocol-level attacks.
Disable Wi-Fi access on devices that don't need it	If there is not a business reason for a device to have Wi-Fi access, make sure it stays off the WLAN. This reduces the network's attack surface and can be viewed as being like disabling ports and services on devices and switches when doing so increases network security. For example, servers and desktops typically connect to the organization's wired network and do not need a wireless connection.
Limit wireless access on client devices	For devices without an essential business purpose, configure their wireless access to only allow access to authorized networks. This is only practical for wireless devices that never leave the business facility; it is impractical for employees who need their laptops, tablets, or smartphones for business travel or remote work.
Disable ad hoc network capabilities on wireless clients	Disabling ad hoc (IBSS) capabilities on enterprise WLAN devices can prevent them from being used for peer-to-peer transfers of data to unauthorized wireless devices.
Disable wireless peripheral access to enterprise devices unless there is a legitimate business reason why it is needed	Unless there is a business purpose for allowing wireless peripheral access to an authorized enterprise device (e.g., Bluetooth or NFC connections), turn this off as a connection option to reduce the associated security risks.
Leverage Advanced Encryption Standard (AES) algorithms and keys	AES is supported in the enterprise editions of WPA2 and WPA3. WPA3-Enterprise supports 196-bit encryption in ESSs. By using the strongest available AES encryption for wireless data, any data intercepted in transit is worthless to attackers.
Use wireless authentication protocols, such as EAP/TLS, that require mutual multifactor authentication	Extensible Authentication Protocol–Transport Layer Security (EAP/TLS) is a protocol that requires mutual, multifactor authentication. This helps to ensure that wireless clients and APs authenticate one another before an association request is approved.
Create a separate WLAN for personal or untrusted devices	Enterprise access from this network should be treated as untrusted and monitored, filtered, and audited accordingly. There are typically few, if any, reasons why a guest network should communicate with a corporate network. Ideally, there should be no pathway from a guest network to the corporate network.
Use an intelligent wireless controller	A Wi-Fi controller orchestrates the provisioning, functionality, and management of an ESS's APs. APs throughout the network register with the controller, which allows the entire network to be centrally configured and managed. A Wi-Fi controller also helps mitigate against rogue and MITM APs and sources of channel interference. Some controllers have the intelligence and capabilities to detect AP-associated threats and send alerts to network administrators. Some also have automatic mitigation features that are triggered when a suspicious event is recorded; other controllers have features that help pinpoint the physical location of suspicious or interfering devices, enabling their quick discovery and deactivation.
Employ an authentication, authorization, and accounting (AAA) system to record user activity	When using WPA2 or WPA3 in the enterprise mode, APs redirect user login credentials to a centralized AAA server (such as a RADIUS server), to authenticate (only enable access to permitted users), authorize (provide connectivity only to allowed services), and log (record activity while connected) user activities. Such systems enable network administrators to regulate network restrictions on a per-user basis and record any prohibited activity that may occur.
Use an authentication portal	A Wi-Fi network can require additional levels of security beyond those associated with initial authentication and encryption mechanisms. For example, once connected, users can be directed to a mandatory login web page configured to deny access to any network services that are not associated with their login credentials.
Sources: Compiled from multiple sources on the chapter reference list.	

7.4.2 Wi-Fi Security Controls

Table 7-9 is not an exhaustive list of Wi-Fi infrastructure network threats and attacks (others are identified in Appendix 7-7), it is a representative list. There are also numerous ways to secure Wi-Fi networks in business facilities. They cluster into two main categories:

- Reducing the network's attack surface—For example, utilizing encryption best practices to protect wireless data
- Using tools, approaches, and common sense, comparable to those in wired networks—For example, using specialized vulnerability scanning and wireless intrusion detection systems

Examples of security best practices for Wi-Fi infrastructure networks are summarized in Table 7-10.

Today, supporting remote workers means extending enterprise networks to the remote networks they use to perform their job duties. This includes home networks as well as those in public spaces. Several of the security controls identified in Table 7-10 can be deployed in home networks, such as restricting access to authorized users using WPA3. Other security controls to protect home networks and workers who need to use Wi-Fi networks in public spaces are identified in Appendix 7-7.

7.4.3 Wi-Fi Security Protocols

Wi-Fi security standards and protocols have evolved since early generation 802.11 networks, but only WPA2 and WPA3 have been supported in Wi-Fi 4 and later generations. Today, to be certified by the Wi-Fi Alliance, devices must support WPA2 or WPA3. Some of their important features are summarized in Table 7-11.

Table 7-11: Some of the key differences between WPA2 and WPA3.

	WPA2	WPA3
Release Year	2004	2018
Encryption Method(s)	CCM Mode Protocol (CCMP) and Advanced Encryption Standard (AES)	Advanced Encryption Standard (AES)
Session Key Size	128-bit	128-bit (WPA3-Personal) 192-bit (WPA3-Enterprise)
Cipher Type	Block	Block
Data Integrity	CBC-MAC	Secure Hash Algorithm
Key Management	Four-way handshaking mechanism	Simultaneous Authentication Among Equals handshake
Authentication	Preshared key (PSK) and 802.1x with EAP variant	Simultaneous Authentication Among Equals and 802.1x with EAP variant

WEP and WPA

Wired Equivalent Privacy (WEP) was introduced in 1999 to provide early Wi-Fi networks with security comparable to that in wired LANs. However, WEP was plagued by numerous security flaws, and despite efforts to improve it, the Wi-Fi Alliance officially retired WEP in 2004 after Wi-Fi Protected Access (WPA) was introduced. WPA introduced a 128-bit key for encryption, the four-way handshaking mechanism used for key management, and the use of a preshared key for authentication.

WPA2

Like its predecessor, WPA2 ensures that data sent/received over the WLAN is encrypted, and that only people who know the network password can access and use the network. WPA2 introduced the Advanced Encryption Standard (AES) to encrypt data transfers over the network. AES is one of the strongest single-key (symmetric) encryption approaches used in today's networks.

WPA-PSK (preshared key) uses a single password shared between authorized users. While generally considered safe, it is only as safe as the trustworthiness of those who know the PSK. If the PSK is acquired by bad actors through nefarious means, the network can be compromised.

The *four-way handshaking mechanism* for key management that WPA introduced continues to be supported in WPA2. This involves the exchange of four messages between an AP and a wireless device. It enables an AP and a client device to prove that they know the PSK without explicitly identifying it. They send encrypted messages to each other, use each other's public keys to decrypt them, and thereby authenticate each other.

The enterprise edition of WPA2 (WPA2-Enterprise) is more secure than WPA2-PSK because it uses *Extensible Authentication Protocol (EAP)* to identify the best encryption to use for data transfers. EAP is a challenge and response-based protocol that requires a wireless device to authenticate itself to the AP prior to being allowed to connect. EAP enables personalized, encrypted tunnels to be created between the AP and different devices in the Wi-Fi network.

For data integrity, WPA2 introduced *cipher block chaining message authentication code (CBC-MAC)*. CBC-MAC is a technique for constructing a message authentication code from a block cipher. A block cipher algorithm (such as AES) creates a chain of blocks where the encryption of each block depends on the proper encryption of the previous block. This interdependence among blocks in the chain ensures that only the key for the block cipher can correctly decrypt the encrypted chain of blocks, and, when it does, it authenticates the message.

WPA3

WPA3 (Wi-Fi Protected Access 3) was released in 2018. It continues to use several Wi-Fi security mechanisms included in WPA2 while also introducing new ones, including Secure Hash Algorithms for data integrity and the Simultaneous Authentication of Equals for key management and authentication.

Secure Hash Algorithms (SHAs) are a family of hash functions for securing data. They are used to transform data to a fixed-size string that looks nothing like the original, and they use one-way functions that make them impossible to transform the hashed data back into the original data.

As discussed in greater detail in Chapter 12, encrypting login credentials (passwords) is a common use of SHAs. This enables a server to only keep track of the hash value for a specific user, rather than the actual password. Should an attacker succeed in hacking the server's password database, they will only find hash values, not passwords, and if the attacker tries to substitute a hash value for a password, the hash function will convert it to a different hash value and deny access.

SHAs are also used to create hash values for the contents of data files to detect data tampering by attackers. If an attacker accesses the file and attempts to make and save changes, the modified file's hash value will be different from the original's and will make the tampering noticeable.

Simultaneous Authentication of Equals (SAE) is a password-based authentication and key agreement method. Both a password and MAC address are used to authenticate a device that wants to join the network. To bypass this, an intruder would have to know the network password, and their device would have to have a recognized (valid) MAC address.

An SAE exchange occurs when a client device wants to connect to the AP. During the exchange, both the client and the AP create their own encryption key. The session key used to encrypt data passed between the device and AP is subsequently derived from the keys they create. In short, SAE provides a secure way to create a session key.

WPA3 also provides *forward secrecy* against eavesdroppers. Should an intruder succeed in joining the network, WPA3's *forward secrecy protocol* makes it impossible for them to snoop on data passed between the AP and a different device.

The ongoing evolution of Wi-Fi and Wi-Fi security means that Wi-Fi is likely to continue to be used in business facilities in the foreseeable future. Bluetooth and Zigbee will also continue to have niche roles in business networks. However, private 5G networks are gaining traction, especially in warehouses and manufacturing facilities.

7.5 PRIVATE 5G NETWORKS IN BUSINESS FACILITIES

For Wi-Fi, 5G refers to the 5 GHz frequency band. For cellular services, 5G means fifth generation, and it represents advances over 4G (fourth generation) capabilities. Some of the differences between 4G and 5G are summarized in Table 7-12, and a glimpse of 6G is provided.

Table 7-12: Some differences between 4G and 5G cellular services.

	4G	5G	6G
Year	2010	2020	2030
Average (practical) End-to-End Latency	100 ms	10 ms	1 ms
Theoretical download speeds	1 Gbps	10 Gbps	1 Tbps
Average (practical) download speeds	100 Mbps	300 Mbps	1 Gbps
Theoretical upload speeds	1.5 Gbps	10 Gbps	10 Gbps
Average (practical) upload speeds	50 Mbps	100 Mbps	1 Gbps

5G shares frequency space with LTE, and mobile network operators (MNOs) use frequency-division duplexing and time-division duplexing to enable 5G and LTE technologies to share overlapping frequencies. *5G New Radio (5G NR)* has opened the door to using 5G technologies in business facilities. 5G NR is a physical connection method for radio-based communication that enables wireless interconnections of APs in a 5G network. Relative to 4G, 5G NR offers higher speeds and includes improvements in OFDM that contribute to increased cell density (devices per cell) and more efficient use of frequency spectrum. More importantly, 5G NR services have the speeds, capacities, and latencies needed to support technologies such as robotics, self-driving vehicles, and ubiquitous IoT applications.

As Table 7-13 indicates, 5G occupies three separate frequency bands, and businesses have the option of using some or all of them to meet their needs. High-band 5G (also called *millimeter-wave band 5G*) is gaining traction in business facilities to support high-speed, low-latency services and

Table 7-13: 5G frequency bands and their coverage areas.

5G Band	Description
Low-band 5G	Low-band 5G operates in the 600–850 MHz frequency band. It offers lower connection speeds (50–250 Mbps) than the other 5G bands, but it provides a much bigger coverage area—up to hundreds of square miles. Applications that require long-distance transmissions or connections to rural areas without sophisticated 5G infrastructure can benefit from low-band 5G access.
Midband 5G	Midband 5G uses the 2.5–4.2 GHz frequency band and supports speeds from 100 Mbps to 900 Mbps per connected device. Its balance of speed and distance makes it a good fit for towns, small cities, and suburban areas, and its availability for private spectrum use is attractive to some businesses.
High-band 5G	High-band 5G operates in the frequency band of 25–39 GHz; this is part of the millimeter-wave spectrum, and the fastest 5G speeds (up to 3 Gbps) are found in this band. Its transmission range is limited (to about 1,500 feet from the transmitter), but it is an attractive, high-speed option for applications in restricted areas, such as a factory floor or warehouse. It is also practical for public communication services in high-density urban areas.

applications. 5G NR has two frequency ranges: Frequency Range 1 (FR1) and Frequency Range 2 (FR2). FR1 includes frequency bands within 410 MHz to 7,125 MZ; this encompasses frequency bands in the low-band and midband 5G in Table 7-13. FR2 includes frequency bands within 24,250 MHz to 71,000 MHz, which corresponds to frequencies in high-band 5G in Table 7-13.

Some U.S. businesses have created private 5G LANs that enable them to control their data in ways that commercial (MNO) 5G infrastructure typically does not. In a *public 5G network*, the spectrum is owned by (licensed to) an MNO, and 5G network service and management are the responsibility of the MNO.

A **private 5G network** is a 5G network dedicated to use by a single business or organization. Frequently, a private 5G network serves a single location, such as a manufacturing facility, hospital, college campus, or military base, with mission-critical applications or infrastructure.

A private 5G network (or nonpublic 5G network) is comparable to a public 5G network in many ways, including hardware and software, data encoding schemes, and frequency spectrum, but is only available to a business's employees and authorized business partners. To differentiate from Wi-Fi networks (WLANs), private 5G networks are usually called *radio access networks (RANs)*.

There are two broad categories of private 5G networks: dependent and independent. Some of the important differences between them are summarized in Table 7-14.

Table 7-14: Some of the differences between dependent and independent private 5G networks.

Private 5G Network Type	Brief Description
Dependent	A *dependent private 5G network* is built and maintained by an MNO. An MNO can either dedicate part of its licensed spectrum to the business or use *network slicing* (which enables the MNO to create multiple virtual networks in a single physical 5G network) to provide a virtual private 5G network for the business. Because the MNO installs, maintains, and manages user access to dependent private 5G networks, a business may not have full control of its data (which may not be stored at a business location).
Independent	To create an *independent private 5G network*, the organization is responsible for choosing, procuring, or leasing the spectrum it wants to use (low-band, midband, high-band; licensed, unlicensed, or both). It is also responsible for installing and managing network infrastructure and network access. Typically, the organization's data remains on site in an independent 5G network, and the organization has more control over its applications (such as robotics and autonomous vehicles). With this option, a business has more control over how it connects to public 5G networks and how external users are allowed to access the private network.

5G is often described as an enabler and game changer for industrial and commercial Internet of Things (IoT) applications because of its potential to be used to support factory floor robotic automation, real-time predictive maintenance applications, autonomous vehicles (AVs) in warehouses, and faster and more secure network connectivity. Additional business benefits of private 5G networks are summarized in Appendix 7-8.

So, there is growing evidence that private 5G networks will coexist with or replace Wi-Fi networks in business facilities. Currently, private RANs make more sense for new business facilities, but continued advances in 5G technologies and evidence of sustainable ROI for private 5G network investments could accelerate their rollout in existing facilities.

Today, Wi-Fi is a "known" technology whose components are readily available from network equipment vendors, and those components will continue to evolve to provide higher connection speeds and security. However, with accumulating evidence that private 5G networks may become preferred networks for some applications, private 5G networks are also discussed in Chapter 8.

SUMMARY

ESs and other mission-critical applications are commonly supported by wireless infrastructure in business facilities. Wi-Fi is pervasive, but Bluetooth and Zigbee support specialized applications, and private 5G networks are becoming more common. Wireless networks are touted for their convenience, but network managers face numerous challenges to make them efficient and secure in addition to convenient and easy to use.

Wi-Fi networks and wired LANs have several differences at the Data Link and Physical layers. The characteristics of radio waves, how they are propagated (transmitted), and what happens to them in transit from transmitters to receivers make wireless connections less reliable than wired connections, and Data Link layer protocols must compensate for this reality.

Wi-Fi signals are analog radio waves in the unlicensed 2.4 GHz and 5 GHz bands of the frequency spectrum. Data is encoded on carrier waves by manipulating (modulating) their fundamental characteristics: frequency, amplitude, and phase. QAM combines amplitude and phase modulation to represent multiple bits for each signal (symbol) change. As Wi-Fi has evolved, so has the density of the QAM constellation maps and the ability to represent more bits per symbol.

Wi-Fi 2.4 GHz signals have a longer transmission range than 5 GHz signals and are better at penetrating walls and maintaining connections over larger distances. However, 5 GHz Wi-Fi signals can transfer more data per second, which makes 5 GHz better for applications that require high transfer rates. Both 2.4 GHz and 5 GHz Wi-Fi networks have multiple channels but typically use nonoverlapping channels to avoid signal interference. Channel bonding can be used in both frequency ranges to increase bandwidth and data transfer, but this reduces the number of nonoverlapping channels.

OFDM and OFDMA enable efficient allocation of channel (and subchannel) spectrum to Wi-Fi devices and have contributed to the evolution of Wi-Fi networks. MIMO has been another important contributor to Wi-Fi advancements by enabling more devices to simultaneously connect to an AP.

Data collisions are harder to detect in wireless networks, and Wi-Fi media access controls are designed to avoid collisions. DCF is the default media access control used in Wi-Fi networks. It is a contention-based protocol that requires devices to verify that the medium is idle before transmitting and requires an RTS/CTS exchange to avoid collisions. The PCF is a second form of media access control that is also supported in some Wi-Fi networks. It is a controlled-access protocol that involves device polling coordinated by the AP. To enable DCF and PCF operation together, Wi-Fi divides time into superframes that include both controlled-access and contention-based intervals.

In a business facility, a Wi-Fi network is often an ESS that includes multiple BSSs. APs in the BSSs connect to a switch or Wi-Fi controller that distributes data traffic to/from the BSSs and to/from the business's wired network(s). Unlike Wi-Fi routers in residential networks, which combine AP, routing, and switching capabilities, APs in enterprise WLANs typically only have AP capabilities.

Like Wi-Fi itself, Wi-Fi security protocols have evolved. This evolution has been accompanied by stronger encryption and more secure and robust association and authentication processes. These processes help to protect Wi-Fi infrastructure networks from Wi-Fi's numerous security threats. WLAN security best practices also help to harden business Wi-Fi networks and thwart potential attackers.

The ongoing evolution of Wi-Fi makes it likely that it will continue to be entrenched in enterprise networks in the foreseeable future. Private 5G networks, however, demonstrate the potential to become preferred networks for some business applications.

KEY TERMS

Carrier signal
Channel bonding
Demodulator
Extended service set (ESS)
Independent basic service set (IBSS)
Modem
Modulator
Modulation
Multiple-input and multiple-output (MIMO)
Orthogonal frequency-division multiplexing (OFDM)
Orthogonal frequency-division multiplexing multiple access (OFDMA)
Quadrature amplitude modulation (QAM)
Quadrature phase-shift keying (QPSK)
Private 5G network
Service set identifier (SSID)
Wi-Fi channel
Wi-Fi controller

REVIEW QUESTIONS

1. Identify and briefly describe several types of wireless networks used by businesses.
2. Briefly describe how Data Link and Physical layer communication functions are different in wireless and wired LANs.
3. Briefly describe how wireless devices propagate (transmit) and receive radio waves.
4. Identify Wi-Fi's frequency spectrum, and briefly explain the advantages and disadvantages of unlicensed Wi-Fi spectrum.
5. Briefly describe each of the fundamental characteristics of radio waves: amplitude, frequency, and phase. Briefly describe carrier waves and briefly explain how data is encoded on carrier waves using amplitude, frequency, or phase modulation.
6. What is multiple layer modulation, and why is QPSK an example?
7. What are the distinguishing characteristics of QAM? What is a QAM constellation map? How is QAM constellation map density related to data rates?
8. Identify factors that complicate media access control in wireless networks. Also identify processes used to ensure reliable data delivery in wireless LANs.
9. What are the differences between communication (transmission) range, detection range, and interference range? Explain "hidden nodes" in the context of these ranges.
10. Identify several causes of transmission errors in wireless networks. Also, identify and briefly describe Physical and Data Link layer error controls used in Wi-Fi networks.
11. Briefly describe each of the following: BSS, BSA, BSSID, and SSID.
12. What are the distinguishing characteristics of an IBSS?
13. What is an ESS? What functions does a Wi-Fi controller perform in an ESS?
14. How does a fit/thin AP differ from a fat AP?
15. What is an MBSS? Briefly describe two alternatives for MBSS deployment.
16. What are Wi-Fi distribution system services? Identify and briefly describe the role(s) of DS services supported in Wi-Fi networks.
17. Briefly explain how active and passive scanning are involved in AP discovery and association.
18. Briefly describe DCF medium access control. Also, briefly describe the PCF.
19. How do Wi-Fi superframes support PCF and DCF?
20. Identify and briefly describe several distinguishing characteristics of 802.11 frame formats.
21. Briefly describe how each of the following has contributed to the evolution of 802.11 networks: QAM, MIMO, and MU-MIMO.
22. Briefly explain why a 5 GHz Wi-Fi signal supports a higher data transfer rate than a 2.4 GHz signal.
23. What is a Wi-Fi channel? What are nonoverlapping channels, and why are they used in ESS WLANs? What is channel bonding, and why is it used?
24. How do OFDM and OFDMA contribute to Wi-Fi network efficiency and performance?
25. Identify and briefly describe several Wi-Fi security threats and attacks.
26. Identify and briefly describe several Wi-Fi security best practices in business facilities.
27. Identify and briefly describe security enhancements that WPA2 and WPA3 introduced.
28. Briefly describe the differences between the following types of 5G networks: public 5G networks, private 5G networks, independent private 5G networks, and dependent private 5G networks.

PROBLEMS AND EXERCISES

Exercise 7-1 Testing Wi-Fi Connection Speeds. Several free Wi-Fi connection speed tests are available on the public Internet that enable you to determine the robustness of your Wi-Fi connection from different locations of your residence. Most of these tests work by receiving a fixed-sized download and sending a fix-sized upload to a single Internet server and using the duration of the download and upload as a measure of connection speeds. It is important to note that the broadband connection between your Wi-Fi router and ISP is typically the main bottleneck that limits the total possible connection speed for your network. This means that most Wi-Fi speed tests produce results showing connection speeds that are likely to be significantly lower than the maximum speeds that ISPs advertise.

This exercise illustrates the use of the Wi-Fi Speed Test at Optimum.com, so it starts by using your device (smartphone, tablet, laptop) and using your browser to navigate to the Optimum.com web page (https://www.optimum.com/internet/wifi/speed-test). Optimum has partnered with Ookla for Wi-Fi testing. Ookla uses secure third-party test servers for measuring data transfer rates and latencies. You can access Ookla's testing platform at https://www.speedtest.net/.

When testing your Wi-Fi speed, it is important to remember that many factors can affect your test results, including device distance from the Wi-Fi router; the total number of devices connected to the Wi-Fi router; the type of device you use to do the tests; and the Wi-Fi router's age and ability to support the later Wi-Fi generations' capabilities.

To directly test the speed of the link from the Wi-Fi router to your ISP, you can use an Ethernet cable to connect your laptop to one of the router's RJ45 ports. Running this test first enables you to determine the maximum connection speed that is possible for your network.

To test your Wi-Fi performance, you should use a portable device (e.g., a laptop, tablet, or smartphone) that is connected to your Wi-Fi network. To illustrate concepts from this chapter, you should run your Wi-Fi speed test multiple times from different locations in and around your residence. You should also repeat your sequence of tests using both the 2.4 GHz and 5 GHz connection options, if they appear as distinct options in your list of available Wi-Fi networks.

To get a clear picture of your device's Wi-Fi connection and performance, you should disconnect all other devices on your WLAN while doing the Wi-Fi speed test. If this is not possible (e.g., you may not want to turn off Wi-Fi connected IoT sensors), do your best to ensure that they are currently inactive or are using no data.

Testing Instructions

1. Create ideal test conditions by disconnecting other wireless devices from your WLAN. Connect your device to the network, ideally using the 5 GHz connection option if it is available. Get as close as you can to your Wi-Fi router (ideally within five feet), launch your device's browser, navigate to the Wi-Fi test page (https://www.optimum.com/internet/wifi/speed-test), and click the GO button to perform the test. Record your test results. (An example of a table for recording test results is provided below.)
2. Move as far away as you can from the Wi-Fi router while still in the same room. Repeat the Wi-Fi speed test and record your results.
3. Move to a room that is adjacent to the room with the Wi-Fi router, repeat the speed test, and record the results.
4. Move to a room that is farthest from the room with the Wi-Fi router, repeat the speed test and record the results.
5. Move to a location that is outside your residence but in an area where you can still connect to the network. Repeat the speed test and record your results.
6. Identify and describe the patterns that you observe in your test results.
   - Does the distance between the device and the Wi-Fi router make a difference?
   - Do walls make a difference in test results?

Device	Wi-Fi Band	Location	Ping (ms)	Jitter (ms)	Upload (Mbps)	Download (Mbps)
(e.g., laptop)	*(e.g., 5 GHz)*	Next to router				
		Same room				
		Adjacent room				
		Distant room				
		Outside residence				

Device	Wi-Fi Band	Location	Ping (ms)	Jitter (ms)	Upload (Mbps)	Download (Mbps)
(e.g., laptop)	*(e.g., 2.4 GHz)*	Next to router				
		Same room				
		Adjacent room				
		Distant room				
		Outside residence				

Additional Tests (Optional)

Disconnect your device from the 5 GHz band, connect to the 2.4 GHz band, and repeat the sequence of Wi-Fi speed tests specified in the instructions above. Record your results.

7. Identify and describe the patterns that you observe in your test results.
   - Does the Wi-Fi band (2.4 GHz versus 5 GHz) make a difference?
   - Does the distance between the device and the Wi-Fi router make a difference?
   - Do walls make a difference in test results?

Disconnect and power off the device used for the first round of results. Connect to the network using a different device, repeat the Wi-Fi speed tests, and record your results.

8. Identify and describe the patterns that you observe in your test results.
   - Does the type of device used for the tests make a difference?
   - Does the Wi-Fi band (2.4 GHz versus 5 GHz) make a difference?
   - Does the distance between the device and the Wi-Fi router make a difference?
   - Do walls make a difference in test results?

Exercise 7-2 Configuring Wi-Fi Router Security Settings
Overview: For this exercise, you will use an online Wi-Fi simulator that will enable you to modify the settings of a simulated Wi-Fi router. As you complete this exercise, you will (a) be saving screenshots/snips for the Wi-Fi router setting changes and (b) be providing explanations/descriptions of how the setting changes will affect how the Wi-Fi router works and its security. This exercise illustrates multiple concepts discussed in Chapter 7, especially those associated with Wi-Fi security.

Instructions

Open a Web browser and go to: https://ui.linksys.com/WRT54GS2/1.0.00/Basic.htm (or an alternative router simulation specified by your instructor).

Part A

1. Click the Wireless navigation link. Then click the Manual configuration option.
2. Change the Wireless Network Name (SSID) to Yourname's Network (where Yourname is your first and last name).
3. *Briefly describe what will happen* to your device's list of available networks when the network's SSID is changed to Yourname's Network.
4. Change the Wireless SSID Broadcast status from Enable to Disable.
5. *Briefly describe what will happen* to your device's list of available networks when the SSID Broadcast Status is changed to Disable.
6. Change the Channel number from its default setting (6) to one of the other nonoverlapping channel numbers for the 2.4 GHz Wi-Fi band.
7. Take a screenshot (or snip) displaying the new nonoverlapping channel number and other setting changes made in steps 2–6 to verify/document your setting changes.

Part B

Click Wireless Security (next to Basic Wireless Settings on the menu bar).

1. Change the Security Mode from Disabled to that for the *most secure* wireless security mode that is available.
2. Capture a screenshot/snip of the setting change made in Part B, step 1 (showing the most secure wireless security mode).
3. *Briefly describe* how the security setting change will affect what new users will have to do when they log onto the Wi-Fi network for the first time and the security of the frames that are transferred between their device and the Wi-Fi router.
4. Click the Wireless MAC Filter on the Wireless menu bar.
5. Click the Enable radio button, click the Permit only radio button, and take a screenshot/snip of the changes specified in this step.
6. Click the Edit MAC Filter List button. For MAC 01: add the Physical Address for your Wi-Fi adapter (or use: 08:C7:29:12:6B:10).
7. For MAC 02: and MAC 03: add the physical addresses (MAC addresses) of two other wireless devices (or use: 00:0D:83:B1:C0:8E and 34:31:8F:75:24:B1).
8. Capture a screenshot/snip of the Wireless MAC Filter list screen after making the changes specified in Part B, steps 6 and 7.
9. *Briefly explain* the impact of making the changes specified in Part B, steps 6 and 7.

Part C

Click Access Restrictions on the menu bar to open the Internet Access Policy screen.

1. Change the Status to Enable.
2. For Enter Policy Name: enter Yourname's Workweek Policy (where yourname = your first and last name)
3. Click the Edit List of PCs button and add the MAC addresses used in Part B, steps 6 and 7; set the IP Range from 192.168.1.1 to 192.168.1.100 in the Enter the IP Range of the PCs section near the bottom of the List of PCs window, then click the Save Settings button.
4. Return to the Policy screen, and for Days uncheck Everyday then uncheck Sun. and Sat.: leave M, T, W, Th, and F checked.
5. For Times, change the settings to from 06:00 AM to 06:00 PM.
6. In the Blocked Services section of the policy screen, click the first NONE button and select ping from the list. Click the second NONE button and select ftp.
7. In the Website Blocking by URL Address section of the policy screen, add www.facebook.com, www.twitter.com, www.instagram.com, and www.tiktok.com.
8. *Briefly describe* the consequences of making the changes specified in Part C, steps 1–7.
9. Take a screenshot/snip that displays the settings specified in Part C, steps 1–2 and 4–7.

Part D

Click Administration on the menu bar.

1. Change the router default password.
2. For Access Server, make sure that both options are checked and enable Wireless Access.
3. Change Remote Management to Enable; check the Use https checkbox.
4. Take a screenshot/snip displaying the changes specified in Part D, steps 1–3.
5. *Briefly explain* the consequences of making the settings changes specified in Part D, steps 1–3.

CHAPTER REFERENCES

Ankit87. (2023). IEEE 802.11 Mac Frame. Geeks for Geeks. Retrieved from: https://www.geeksforgeeks.org/ieee-802-11-mac-frame/

Bhatia, A. (2021). How Is a Private 5G Network Different from a Public 5G Network? *Insights*. Retrieved from: https://www.samsung.com/global/business/networks/insights/blog/0503-how-is-a-private-5g-network-different-from-a-public-5g-network/

Commotion Wireless. (n.d.). Learn Wireless Basics. Retrieved from: https://commotionwireless.net/docs/cck/networking/learn-wireless-basics/

Cybersecurity & Infrastructure Security Agency (CISA). (2021). Securing Wireless Networks. Retrieved from: https://www.cisa.gov/news-events/news/securing-wireless-networks

Devopedia. (n.d.). Hybrid ARQ. Retrieved from: https://devopedia.org/hybrid-arq

Eckhardt, D., & Steenkiste, P. (1996). Measurement and Analysis of the Error Characteristics of an In-Building Wireless Network. *SIGCOMM '96: Conference Proceedings on Applications, Technologies, Architectures, and Protocols for Computer Communications*, pp. 243–254. https://doi.org/10.1145/248156.248178

Edmondson, J. (2021). What Are the Different Types of Wireless Devices? Business Tech Weekly. Retrieved from: https://www.businesstechweekly.com/operational-efficiency/wireless-networks/wireless-device-types/

Farnell | element14. (2017). Wi-Fi Architecture, Implementation, and Applications. Newark. Retrieved from: https://www.newark.com/wi-fi-architecture-implementation-and-applications

Gamechanger007. (2014). Wi-Fi Basic and MAC frame. Secure Tech Point. Retrieved from: https://securetechpoint.wordpress.com/2014/11/16/wi-fi-basic-and-mac-frame/

Geier, J. (2001). Overview of the IEEE 802.11 Standard: IEEE 802.11 Services. Pearson Education InformIT. Retrieved from: https://www.informit.com/articles/article.aspx?p=24411&seqNum=7

Hammad, M. (2020). Introduction of Basic Service Set (BSS). Geeks for Geeks. Retrieved from: https://www.geeksforgeeks.org/introduction-of-basic-service-set-bss/

Hammad, M. (2020). Introduction of Independent Basic Service Set (IBSS). Geeks for Geeks. Retrieved from: https://www.geeksforgeeks.org/introduction-of-independent-basic-service-set-ibss/

Hong, T. (2020). End-to-End 5G Private Network Planning for Precise Industry Empowerment. ZTE Technologies. Retrieved from: https://www.zte.com.cn/global/about/magazine/zte-technologies/2020/6-en/Special-Topic/6.html

Huawei. (2021). Why Is the 5G Router Faster than 2.4G router? Retrieved from: https://forum.huawei.com/enterprise/en/why-is-the-5g-router-faster-than-2-4g-router/thread/772515-861?page=1

Jasuja, N. (n.d.). WPA2 vs. WPA3. Diffen. Retrieved from: https://www.diffen.com/difference/WPA2_vs_WPA3

Landman, N., Williams, C., & Ross, E. (2023). Secure Hash Algorithms. Brilliant. Retrieved from: https://brilliant.org/wiki/secure-hashing-algorithms/

Marketing Team. (2017). Spectrum Wi-Fi—How unlicensed spectrum boosts the development of Wi-Fi. *Tanaza Classic Blog*. Retrieved from: https://www.classichotspot.com/blog/unlicensed-spectrum-wifi/

MathWorks. (n.d.). What Is WLAN? Retrieved from: https://www.mathworks.com/help/wlan/gs/what-is-wlan.html

Meraki. (2023). Wi-Fi 6 (802.11ax) Technical Guide. Retrieved from: https://documentation.meraki.com/MR/Wi-Fi_Basics_and_Best_Practices/Wi-Fi_6_(802.11ax)_Technical_Guide

Myers, A.D., & Basagni, S. (2002). Wireless Media Access Control. University of Texas at Dallas. Retrieved from: https://ece.northeastern.edu/fac-ece/basagni/Classes/F016V81.503/WMAC.pdf

Noworatzky, D. (2019). Common Wi-Fi Security Threats and How to Mitigate Them. *TeleDynamics Think Tank*. Retrieved from: http://info.teledynamics.com/blog/common-wi-fi-security-threats-and-how-to-mitigate-them

Ranganathan, R., Kambalapally, V., & Kannan, K. (2020). Modelling Link Failure in the Presence of Extended Hidden Terminals over Multi-Hop Wireless Ad Hoc Networks. *SN Applied Sciences*, 2, Article 383. Retrieved from: https://link.springer.com/article/10.1007/s42452-020-2159-8

Remmert, H. (2022). What Can 5G Do For Business: Enterprise, Industry, and Transportation. Digi. Retrieved from: https://www.digi.com/blog/post/5g-for-business-enterprise-industry-transportation

RF Wireless World. (n.d.). WLAN DCF vs. PCF—Difference Between DCF and PCF Medium Access Types. Retrieved from: https://www.rfwireless-world.com/Terminology/WLAN-DCF-vs-PCF.html

RF Wireless World. (n.d.). WLAN MAC Protocol | WLAN MAC Frame Format | 802.11 Wi-Fi MAC. Retrieved from: https://www.rfwireless-world.com/Articles/WLAN-MAC-layer-protocol.html

Rimala, G. E., & Newth, J. D. (2021). 10 Things in Your Home That Interfere with and Block Wi-Fi Signals. Eye Networks. Retrieved from: https://eyenetworks.no/en/10-things-that-disturb-and-block-wi-fi-signals/

Sarraillé, J. (2015). Notes On Chapter Sixteen—Wireless Networking Technologies. California State University, Stanislaus. Retrieved from: https://www.cs.csustan.edu/~john/Classes/Previous_Semesters/CS3000_Communication_Networks/2015_02_Spring/Notes/chap16.html

Shaw, K. (2022). 802.11x: Wi-Fi Standards and Speeds Explained. *Network* World. Retrieved from: https://www.networkworld.com/article/3238664/80211x-wi-fi-standards-and-speeds-explained.html

Smith, C. (2015). 5GHz Channel Planning Guide/Best Practices. Extreme Networks. Retrieved from: https://community.extremenetworks.com/t5/extremewireless-identifi/5ghz-channel-planning-guide-best-practices/m-p/55925

Vocal Technologies. (n.d.). 802.11 Distributed Coordination Function (DCF). Retrieved from: https://www.vocal.com/networking/802-11-distributed-coordination-function-dcf/

Woligroski, D. (2011). LAN 102: Network Hardware and Assembly—Wireless Network Logical Topologies. Tom's Hardware. Retrieved from: https://www.tomshardware.com/reviews/local-area-network-gigabit-ethernet,3035-7.html

Wright, G., & Burke, J. (2021). Orthogonal Frequency-Division Multiplexing (OFDM). TechTarget. Retrieved from: https://www.techtarget.com/searchnetworking/definition/orthogonal-frequency-division-multiplexing#:~:text=Fiber%20optic%20transmission%20may%20use,the%20same%20base%20station%20simultaneously.

Zomaya, D. (2019). When to Use 20mhz vs. 40mhz vs. 80mhz. CBT Nuggets. Retrieved from: https://www.cbtnuggets.com/blog/certifications/cisco/when-to-use-20mhz-vs-40mhz-vs-80mhz

MINICASE: SSU COB Building Addition—Wi-Fi Network Design and Infrastructure Costs

Scenario: Southeastern State University (SSU), a public university, has received funding from the state legislature to add a multistory wing to its College of Business (COB) building. The first floor of the new wing will include three classrooms, three computer labs, and offices for a COB department that will move to the new wing. The new office space will include 11 faculty offices and an office for the department's graduate and lab assistants. The first floor will also include a server room (a telecommunications room with server rack space and a router to interface with the university's campus backbone network). A preliminary floor plan for the first floor of the new wing is provided in Figure 6-36 in the Chapter 6 minicase.

A Wi-Fi network will support all parts of the new wing. Current plans call for this to be an IEEE 802.11ax (Wi-Fi 6) wireless overlay network that will include at least 21 managed access points (powered by Power over Ethernet [PoE]) that will connect to a Wi-Fi controller. The Wi-Fi controller will connect to the building distribution switch with fiber optic cable—it will have a 1000BaseF port.

Task 1

Logical Diagram of Wi-Fi Network.

This task requires the creation of a logical network diagram of the wireless network in the new wing. Ideally, a network diagramming tool, such as MS Visio, should be used.

This diagram should include:

- 21 managed access points with PoE interfaces
- Three for each classroom

- Two for each lab
- Six to support the office area and Server Room
- A 24-port Wi-Fi controller with PoE ports
- 21 Cat5e STP Ethernet cables that connect the APs to the Wi-Fi controller
- The building distribution switch
- The Fiber 1 GbE cable that connects the Wi-Fi controller to the building distribution switch
- The router and fiber optic cable that link the building to the campus backbone network

Task 2

For Task 2, you will provide a cost estimate for the wireless infrastructure that will support the new wing of the COB building at SSU. When researching APs and the Wi-Fi controller, look for 802.11ax compliance. Look for Wi-Fi AP controllers comparable to a Planet Wireless AP Controller with 24-Port 802.3at PoE.

Cost estimates for the wireless LAN can be summarized in the following table.

Component	Quantity Needed	Cost per Unit	Total Cost
Managed Access Point with PoE	21		
24-Port Wi-Fi Controller with PoE	1		
1000BaseF fiber port upgrade for Wi-Fi controller (if it lacks a fiber port)			
Cat 5e STP Cable	21		

Total Costs for Wi-Fi Infrastructure: ____________________

Minicase Deliverables: The deliverable for Task 1 is a network diagram. The deliverables for Task 2 are Wi-Fi infrastructure cost estimates from cdw.com or another networking equipment vendor.

Chapter 8

Connecting Enterprise Network Locations: Wide Area Networks

LEARNING OBJECTIVES

After reading and studying this chapter, you should be able to:

- Briefly describe the importance of business wide area networks (WANs).
- Identify and briefly describe business WAN topologies and architectures.
- Briefly describe the characteristics, advantages, and disadvantages of dedicated circuit WANs.
- Identify the major types of dedicated circuits used in business WANs.
- Identify and briefly describe the characteristics, advantages, and disadvantages of packet-switched WANs.
- Identify and briefly describe the major types of packet-switching services used in business WANs.
- Identify and briefly describe the major types of wireless communication links used in business WANs.
- Briefly describe the characteristics and roles of radio access networks (RANs) in business WANs.
- Briefly describe the characteristics of SD-WANs and why they are adopted by businesses.
- Identify and briefly describe WAN security threats and issues.
- Identify and briefly describe WAN security controls.

8.0 INTRODUCTION: Business WANs

Chapters 6 and 7 focused on wired and wireless networks and how they are evolving to support higher connection speeds and data transfer capacities. Their evolutionary trends provide important context for considering how businesses interconnect facilities at different locations.

Businesses have more control and discretion over the networks in their facilities than over interconnections among geographically dispersed locations. They typically own the network infrastructure in their facilities and have some understanding of the ROI for their investments in that infrastructure. However, few companies own the circuits or services used to interconnect facilities at different locations; instead, they lease circuits from other companies (carriers) or subscribe to services that carriers offer. Hence, businesses have less control over the circuits and services that bind together networks at distributed facilities in their enterprise networks.

Lack of ownership makes it important for businesses to do due diligence on their interconnection options. They may have fewer alternatives in some locations than others and typically have little if any leverage over link capacities and how much they cost. Their due diligence includes getting a good grasp of the volumes of data being transferred to/from individual locations and selecting the

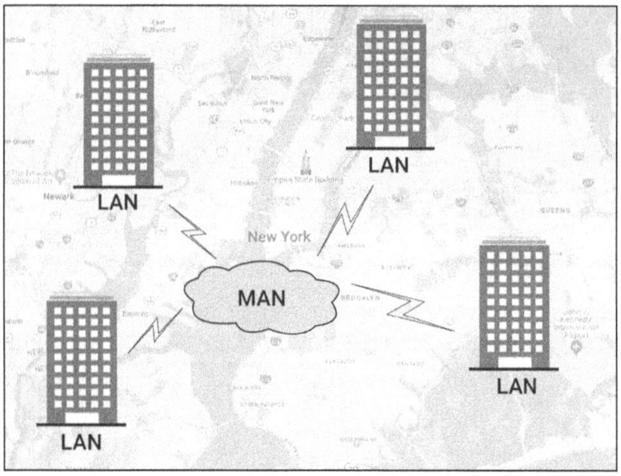

Figure 8-1: Conceptual depiction of a metropolitan area network (MAN).

connection options that best suit their needs. Often, the most affordable options have lower transmission speeds and capacities than the networks within their facilities. This means that wide area network (WAN) links or services have the potential to be bottlenecks that constrain the overall performance of an enterprise network.

There is no hard and fast description of what geographic expanse a business network must have to be considered a WAN. However, there is general agreement that WANs are more extensive than a cluster of buildings in a single location, such as a college or corporate campus or military base. As illustrated in section 6.5 of Chapter 6, such building clusters are often called *campus area networks (CANs)*. Businesses or other organizations with multiple interconnected buildings or campuses in a single urban/suburban area (see Figure 8-1) are sometimes said to have a *metropolitan area network (MAN)*. In the case of a sprawling metropolitan area such as Atlanta, Chicago, or Los Angeles, it is reasonable to ask whether such networks are better considered WANs. Today, *MAN* most commonly refers more to a business network that subscribes to a specific type of carrier service than to its expanse.

Another consideration is whether publicly available communication services are separate or a part of business WANs. Public Internet and cellular service provider (MNO) infrastructure is often leveraged by employees at different locations to use voice and data services to communicate, but such services may not be seen as parts of a business WAN, unless their communications are walled off from the public Internet or cellular services used by the public. As Chapter 7 introduced, private 5G networks have gained traction in business facilities and enterprise networks, and when they are truly private, they are likely to be considered a part of a business WAN. Extranets, private clouds, and VPNs may also be viewed as parts of business WANs because firewalls, access controls, and other technologies segregate them from the public Internet.

The public versus private distinction is important because business WANs have traditionally been viewed as private networks. This perspective persists, and it remains possible for businesses in the United States and other countries to create private WANs with limited or no connections to the public Internet or communication services. However, today, it is widely accepted that attempting to connect locations across a country or around the world with physical cables is no longer feasible. A variety of technologies have evolved that enable the public Internet to be used to complement or replace traditional enterprise WANs, and increasing adoption and use of cloud services has blurred traditional boundaries between business WANs and the Internet. As a result, this book takes the position that the Internet and cloud services should be viewed as important parts/extensions of enterprise networks.

In this book, a **wide area network (WAN)** is a geographically distributed network that interconnects local area networks (LANs) at multiple locations. By extension, a *business WAN* is a WAN that interconnects networks at geographically distributed business facilities (see Figure 8-2).

Without a WAN, LANs at a business's different locations would be a set of isolated networks. A WAN adds value to a business by enabling communications and resource sharing among the networks at its geographically separated sites and by facilitating coordinated business operations across locations.

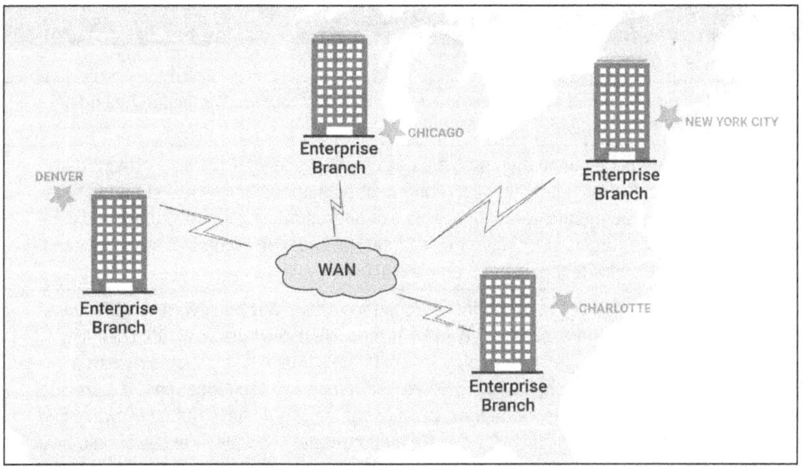

Figure 8-2: Conceptual depiction of a business WAN.

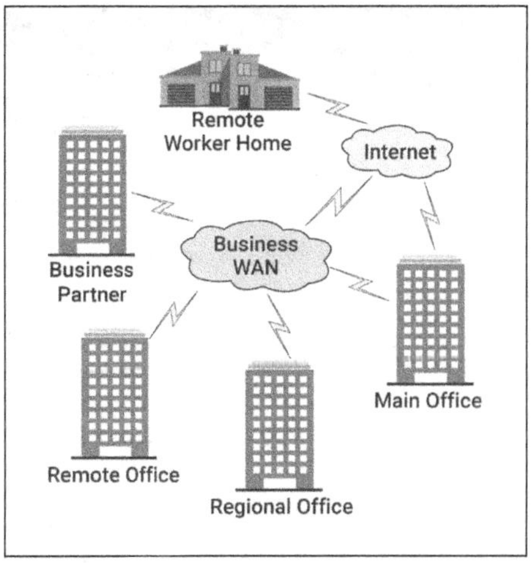

Figure 8-3: An expanded view of a business WAN.

Today, it is common to include employees working from home or remotely as parts of business WANs. Wi-Fi LANs in the homes of remote workers are often considered extensions of enterprise networks (see Figure 8-3). Expanded views of business WANs may also include business partners, such as suppliers, customers, distributors, e-commerce enablers, consultants, and network infrastructure providers.

As Figures 8-2 and 8-3 illustrate, like the Internet, a WAN is typically depicted as a cloud. This often provides a level of abstraction for the actual constellation of links, services, and network infrastructure used to interconnect different locations and users. A WAN cloud may include leased circuits, packet-switched services, VPNs, private RANs, or some combination thereof.

In addition to interconnecting geographically dispersed locations and users, business WANs have other identifiable benefits and advantages. Table 8-1 summarizes some of them.

Table 8-1: Examples of business WAN advantages.

Advantage	Description
Access to data	A WAN enables an organization's data to be accessible across locations even when it is stored in centralized data centers. Data can be stored in facilities that specialize in data storage, processing, backup, security, and shared access. This contributes to data synchronization across locations while minimizing the need for sophisticated data storage technologies at all locations.
Software/data updates	A business WAN enables software updates to be pushed to devices at different locations to help ensure that all devices and locations are protected by the latest security patches and have the most recent versions of the applications used to run the business. Database updates can similarly be automatically shared across locations within seconds.
Improved communication, collaboration, and productivity	When appropriately sized and configured, a business WAN can improve communication, collaboration, and employee productivity via real-time videoconferencing and other collaboration platforms. Such tools support virtual teams and remote workers and facilitate the inclusion of an organization's geographically dispersed subject matter experts in important communication exchanges. Travel expenses can be reduced, and better distribution of work across locations can be achieved.
Support for global business	When a business has locations or strategic partners in different countries, their activities can be better coordinated and controlled via a business WAN. Basically, a business WAN that is international in scope is a global business enabler.
High-bandwidth links	The connections that ISPs and carriers market to businesses typically have higher bandwidths than marketed to consumers. As business needs change, higher capacity circuits and services are available to accommodate growth.

Table 8-2: Example of WAN disadvantages.	
Disadvantage	**Description**
High setup costs	Setting up a business WAN for the first time and adding new sites can be costly. Costs include purchasing or leasing and installing equipment and cabling needed for WAN links.
Troubleshooting issues	Given their geographic scope, resolving WAN connection problems can be challenging. Providers often require subscribers to check and test their connection equipment and configuration settings before investigating other potential causes of link failures or other connection problems. This can be frustrating for subscribers and can delay timely problem resolution. Power outages, storm damage, and natural and man-made catastrophes can take provider circuits and equipment offline and affect part or all of the WAN.
Security issues	By not owning the circuits and technologies used to interconnect locations, there may be security problems and issues that businesses cannot directly address. Circuit owners often have challenges in closing security gaps because of the combinations of technologies they deploy to create links. Businesses should research track records and commitment to security when choosing providers to interconnect their locations. If a provider leverages public Internet circuits for interconnecting locations, its subscribers should have robust firewalls and antivirus protection in place beyond those used by the provider. Generally, robust security defenses should be in place at each location's connection to the WAN.

Business WANs also have downsides, some of which are identified in Table 8-2.

The potential for WAN link outages or failure means that businesses should consider having redundant WAN links. This is especially important for links that are crucial to business continuity or are most prone to disruption. Chapter 5 describes the business rationale for dual- and multi-homed connections to ISPs, but similar reasoning should be applied to WAN links.

Protecting the integrity of a business WAN involves more than redundant connections among locations. Robust security controls are also needed because WANs provide attackers with potentially exploitable attack surfaces. However, numerous technologies have emerged to provide businesses with secure Internet-enabled communications and transactions and secure Internet-WAN integration.

As noted in Chapter 5, intranets and extranets often leverage Internet technologies that enable employees and business partners to access an organization's private network and/or cloud resources. Today, cloud services may be viewed as virtual WAN facilities whose importance to day-to-day business operations and performance can surpass that of an organization's physical facilities. This makes the public Internet a logical extension of most business WANs.

As you make your way through this chapter, you will see that businesses have multiple options for creating WANs, including dedicated circuits, packet switching services, Carrier Ethernet services, and VPNs. You will also discover that businesses may use a combination of wired and wireless circuits to interconnect their different locations. Private *radio access networks (RANs)* may also be part of business WANs; they were introduced in Chapter 7. Businesses are also increasingly turning to *software-defined networking (SDN)* solutions to optimize their WAN connections. Software-defined WAN (SD-WAN) solutions have the potential to optimize network performance while controlling associated expenses.

8.1 WIDE AREA NETWORK TOPOLOGIES AND ARCHITECTURES

Basically, a **WAN architecture** is a WAN configuration that meets an organization's communication and data transfer requirements. It is the set of WAN circuits, services, and technologies that is best suited for an organization's environment and optimizes the performance of the organization's applications and business processes. Well-constructed WAN architecture adds value by facilitating employee productivity and business operations.

Today, WAN architectures often result from **WAN aggregation**, the process of consolidating the networks at different locations (campuses, branches, data centers, etc.) to create an enterprise WAN. WAN aggregation stitches the networks at different locations together to enable seamless communication among them. Physical and logical topologies are outcomes of WAN aggregation.

Like LAN topologies, a **WAN topology** describes the layout or arrangement of the network's components and connections and how communication occurs. Also, like LAN topologies, two perspectives are considered: physical and logical. Physical topology describes the physical deployment of network infrastructure that enables data to move from one location to another in the WAN, and logical topology describes how data is transferred over the infrastructure.

Although a WAN's physical topology can appear to be complex, most WANs are based on one or more simple topologies. A small company with few locations might implement a *flat topology* that consists of point-to-point connections between the business's locations. In Figure 8-4, leased circuits (wired or wireless) could be used to physically transport data between locations. Businesses sometimes have point-to-point circuits for connections with business partners such as suppliers or customers, and, historically, the first EDI systems (introduced in section 2.2.5 in Chapter 2) were deployed over point-to-point connections.

Figures 8-5a and 8-5b illustrate alternative flat topologies for a business WAN. In Figure 8-5a, each location is connected to two other locations via point-to-point circuits. The result is a loop or ring topology.

Full-duplex or half-duplex circuits can be used in WANs with ring topologies, but today, full-duplex circuits are most common. These enable data to flow in both directions over each point-to-point link. In WANs with ring topologies, data is typically routed to nonadjacent locations over the set of circuits with the shortest distances or latencies. If one of the links fails, the network remains intact because data can be rerouted to avoid the failed link, and if the router at a particular location fails, data can still be transferred among the other locations.

A *hub and spoke topology* can also be built using point-to-point circuits. Here, one location serves as a central hub to which each of the other locations connects (see Figure 8-5b). The result resembles a star or the hub and spokes of a wheel. In Figure 8-5b, the router at Location A serves as the hub, and those at the other locations are spoke routers. When a single circuit connects a spoke router to the hub router, it may be called a *single-homed hub-and-spoke topology*.

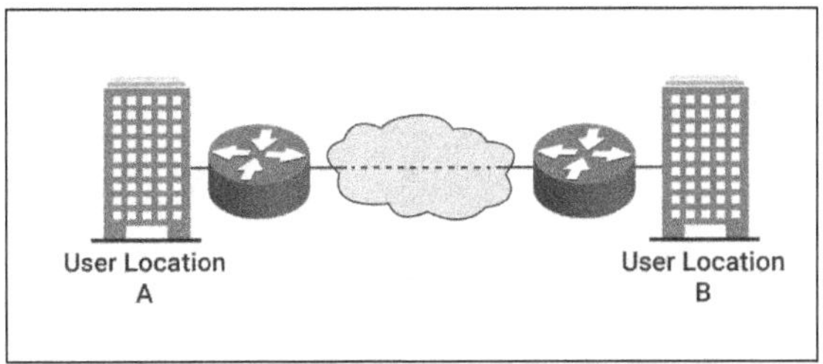

Figure 8-4: A depiction of a point-to-point WAN connection.

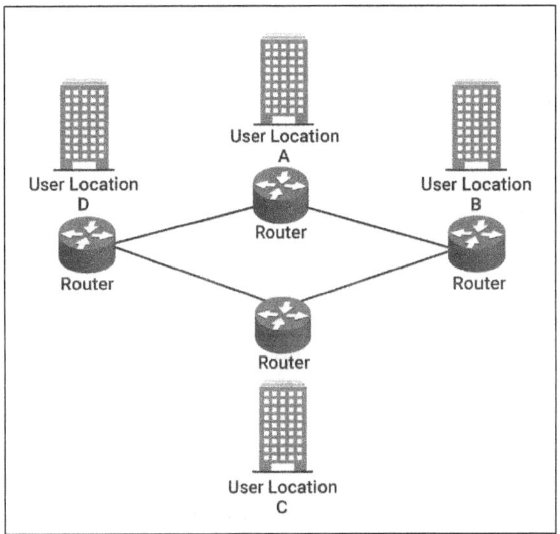

Figure 8-5a: An example of a ring (loop) WAN topology.

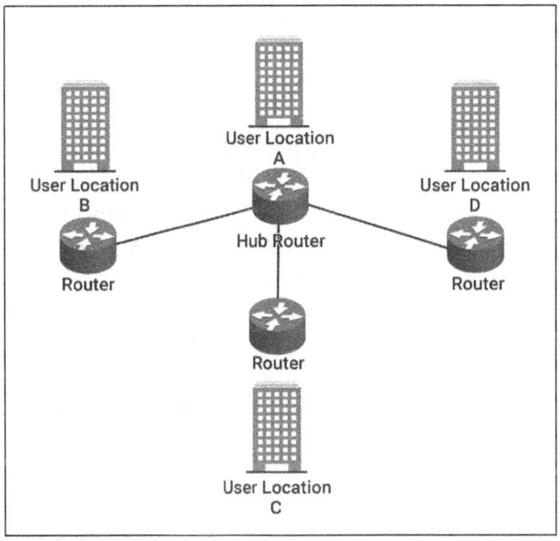

Figure 8-5b: An example of a hub-and-spoke (star) WAN topology.

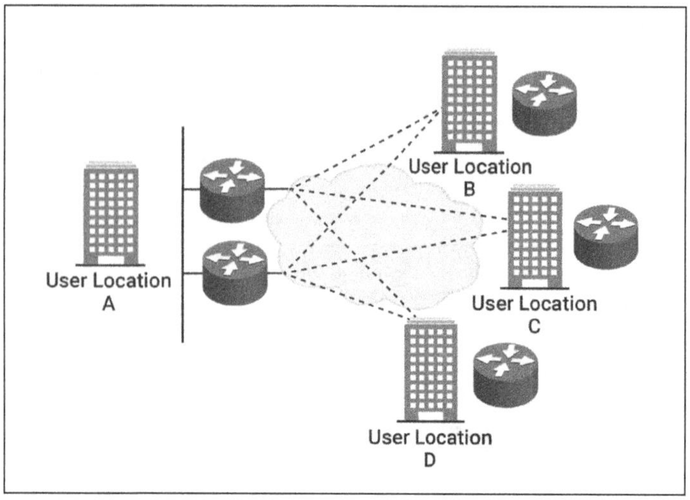

Figure 8-6: An example of a dual-homed hub-and-spoke WAN topology.

If poorly designed, the hub-and-spoke topology introduces the potential for the hub router to be a single point of failure that can disrupt the entire WAN. To compensate, businesses typically have one or more standby routers configured to automatically take over if the hub router fails. A link failure in a WAN with a star (hub-and-spoke) topology means that a location will be unable to communicate with other locations until the link is restored. Having an available backup, secondary, or standby link can compensate for a link failure, but they add costs to the network.

Some businesses deploy dual-homed hub-and-spoke topologies to address potential disruption from hub router or link failure. Dual-homed connections were introduced in Chapter 5's discussion of business connections to ISPs. As Figure 8-6 illustrates, in a *dual-homed hub-and-spoke topology*, each spoke router redundantly connects to two hub routers. Generally, one of the hub routers serves as the primary connection for spoke routers, and the second is a backup or standby hub router that is used if the primary router fails or becomes overloaded. Dual-homed topologies are more challenging to implement and maintain than single-homed topologies. They require more complex router configurations and connections to spokes. However, their redundancy helps ensure hub availability and enables load balancing for high traffic volumes.

Compared to a ring topology, a hub-and-spoke topology enables a WAN to be built with fewer point-to-point circuits. In Figure 8-5a, four point-to-point circuits are needed to create the ring topology. In Figure 8-5b, only three point-to-point circuits are needed to create the hub-and-spoke topology. Latencies in a hub-and-spoke topology may be lower and more predictable than those in a ring topology because data never needs to traverse more than two links to reach a destination.

While a mixture of circuit types (copper, fiber optic, wireless) can be used to create a ring or star topology, doing so introduces complexities that may require additional processing by routers (especially hub routers) and increased latencies.

A *full mesh topology*, such as that illustrated in Figure 8-7a, enables any location to directly communicate with any other location over a point-to-point connection. When you compare Figures 8-5a and 8-7a, you can see that a business with four locations could add two point-to-point connections to transform a ring topology into a full mesh WAN. Because data transfers between locations occur over a single link, full mesh topologies have average transmission latencies that are lower than those for ring and hub-and-spoke topologies. Should a single link in a full mesh fail, each location continues to be able to transfer data to all other locations via direct or indirect paths. The additional links make a full mesh more expensive than a hub-and-spoke or ring, and the additional expense may be challenging to justify in budget-conscious businesses.

A WAN can also be deployed as a partial mesh topology. Partial topologies can have a variety of very different configurations, but most ensure that there is a point-to-point connection between each pair of locations that consistently transfer data to one another in significant volumes. For a business with four locations, a partial mesh WAN topology might resemble Figure 8-7b. In this example, each location except C is connected to two other locations; location C only connects to

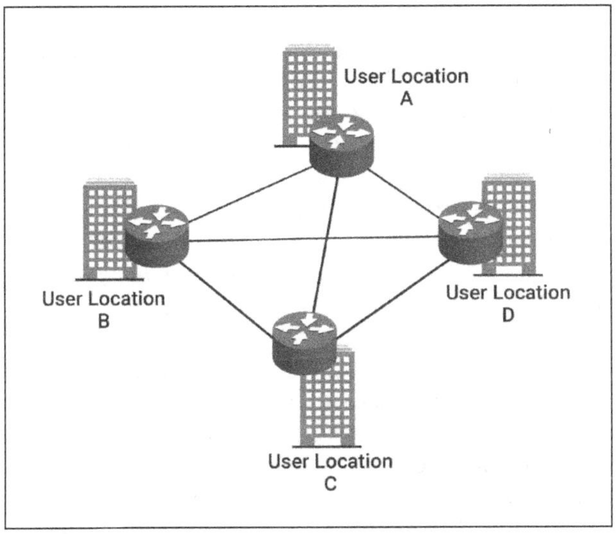

Figure 8-7a: An example of a full mesh WAN topology.

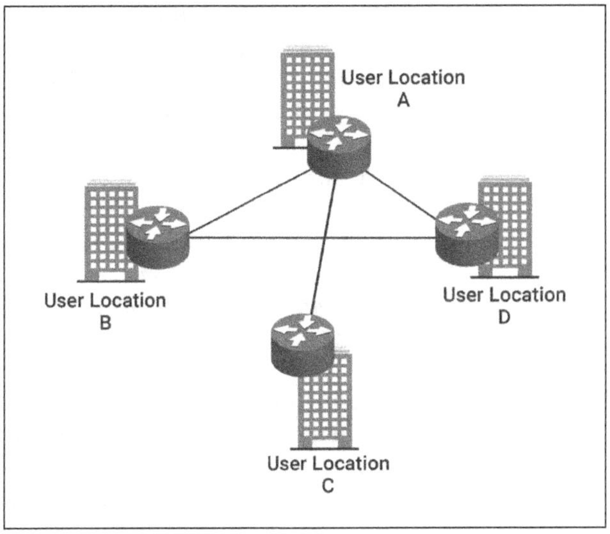

Figure 8-7b: An example of a WAN with a partial mesh topology.

location A. The connections among locations A, B, and D enable this part of the WAN to remain intact in the event of the failure of a single link.

Partial mesh topologies enable the number of hops and transmission latencies to be minimized for locations that are the sources/destinations of most data transfers. Relative to full mesh topologies, setup and ongoing communication expenses can be reduced in partial mesh topologies by not fully interconnecting lower data traffic locations.

As you can see, business WANs have various topology options. As will become clearer in subsequent sections of this chapter, a variety of physical and logical circuits are used to interconnect different locations in a business WAN.

8.2 WAN TECHNOLOGIES, STANDARDS, AND PROTOCOLS

As noted previously, a major difference between a LAN or CAN and a WAN is that an organization must obtain the circuits or services it needs to interconnect its different locations from one or more WAN service providers. The most prevalent providers are **common carriers**, organizations (typically businesses) that provide fee-based wired and wireless circuits and communication services to businesses and consumers. Examples of carriers include telephone, cable services, cellular services (MNOs), and satellite services companies. ISPs are sometimes considered common carriers and sometimes not; there are various legal and legislative issues still being sorted out. The situation is muddied by companies who provide both carrier and ISP services. Overall, though, WAN service providers provide the links that interconnect business locations, transport data, and may also provide Internet access.

Specialized terminology has traditionally been used to describe WAN connections to carrier networks. This includes terms such as *central office* (the local facility where customer connections to carrier networks terminate), *customer premises equipment* (the devices and wiring used at a location to connect to a carrier link), *local loop* (the circuit from customer premises equipment to the central office), and *demarcation point* (the point in a building that separates customer equipment from carrier equipment). These and other WAN terms are described in more detail in Appendix 8-1.

8.2.1 WAN Standards and Regulations

Operationally, most WAN communication functions occur at the Physical and Data Link layers of the TCP/IP and OSI models. WAN standards typically describe data transfer methods at the Physical layer and Data Link layer and include requirements such as data encapsulation/framing, flow control, and the physical addresses of WAN devices. Physical layer framing is used on some circuits.

Several organizations define WAN standards and oversee their revision processes. They include the *Electronics Industries Alliance (EIA)*, the *Institute of Electrical and Electronics Engineers (IEEE)*, the *International Organization for Standardization (ISO)*, and the *Telecommunications Industry Association (TIA)*. As noted in Chapters 6 and 7, these organizations also define and manage standards for LANs and backbone networks.

Most countries have a government agency that regulates voice and data communications. Some countries require businesses to use government-approved carriers and WAN service providers, and sometimes the carriers/providers are government owned and operated. The *Federal Communications Commission (FCC)* oversees voice and data communications in the United States. State *public utilities commissions (PUCs)* provide additional oversight within their borders. FCC and PUC regulations typically specify that WAN service providers must use public rights-of-way (such as those beside roads and train tracks) for their circuits and must be granted permission to place them in other locations.

As noted in Chapter 7, the FCC also licenses and allocates frequency bands used for voice and data communications. Often, specific bands are set aside for the exclusive use of WAN service providers, but providers must be formally granted licenses to use assigned frequencies. WAN service providers may also have to get PUC permission to operate in a state and to place, erect, or use cell towers or other wireless transmission towers in specific locations.

Like those for LANs and BNs, Physical layer standards for WANs address electrical, mechanical, operational, and functional connections. They address device interfaces, the symbols/signals used to encode data, and sender/receiver synchronization.

8.2.2 WAN Protocols

Since WANs primarily operate at the Data Link and Physical layers, protocols at these layers are most important. Like other Data Link layer protocols, those used in WANs specify the formats of the frames that are passed to the Physical layer for transmission. In IP-based WANs, LLC and MAC headers are added at the Data Link layer, and traditionally the frame format for the *High-Level Data Link Control (HDLC)* protocol or one of its variants has been used.

HDLC is a relatively simple protocol used for point-to-point connections that does not require a lot of configuration work to connect two locations. When used in point-to-point connections, the sending router encapsulates data from devices in the network in outgoing HDLC frames, and the receiving router de-encapsulates incoming HDLC frames so the data can be passed to devices in its local network.

Figure 8-8 illustrates the format of an HDLC frame. Each frame includes a beginning and ending delimiter (the Flag field) that facilitates synchronization between senders and receivers. The beginning delimiter is followed by an Address field, which can be used to specify the address of the destination network. The Address field is needed in multilink WANs (e.g., those with ring, hub-and-spoke, and mesh topologies) but does not need to be populated when the WAN

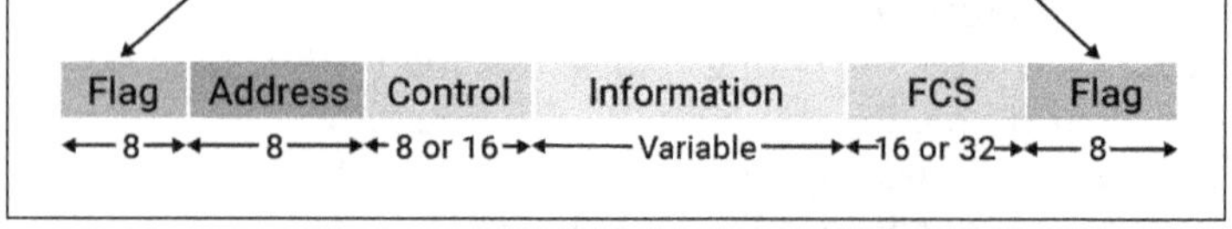

Figure 8-8: A depiction of the format of an HDLC frame.

consists of two locations connected by a single point-to-point connection. In that case, all transmitted frames traverse the link to the same destination.

The Control field specifies the frame's type: information, supervisory, or unnumbered. User data is carried in *information frames*; to ensure reliable delivery, these frames also include fields for sequence numbers and acknowledgments. *Supervisory frames* are primarily used for error and flow control. *Unnumbered frames* are used for setting up the link for data transfers and disconnections. Like Ethernet frames, HDLC frames include an FCS field that is used for error detection. HDLC uses CRC-16 or CRC-32 for error checking.

Point-to-Point Protocol (PPP) is another protocol used on various types of wired and wireless point-to-point circuits. It is based on HDLC and is very similar. ISPs have used PPP for dial-up access to the Internet because IP packets cannot be transmitted over a dial-up link without being encapsulated in Data Link layer frames with beginning and ending flags/delimiters. Dial-up Internet access uses public switched telephone network (PSTN) facilities to establish a connection to an ISP by dialing a telephone number on a conventional telephone line (a landline).

PPP is also common in digital subscriber line (DSL) connections. Many DSL service providers use PPP over Ethernet (PPPoE) to authenticate and manage subscriber connections; it encapsulates PPP frames in Ethernet frames and is used to establish a PPP connection over DSL. PPP is also used in cellular telephone and data services and in fiber optic point-to-point links in WANs.

The format of a PPP frame is illustrated in Figure 8-9, and it is easy to see its similarity to an HDLC frame. Basically, PPP adds a Protocol field between the Control and Information (Data) fields of an HDLC frame. The Protocol field specifies whether the Data field carries user data (an IP packet), link control data, or network control data.

Figure 8-9 illustrates how an IP packet (or another Network layer PDU) can be encapsulated in a PPP frame. Link Control Protocol (LCP) frames are used to establish, configure, and test the link; their role is like that of HDLC's unnumbered frames. Network Control Protocol (NCP) frames enable link endpoints to negotiate configuration parameters and services for different types of Network layer protocols, such as IP.

PPP's versatility and numerous dial-up networking features have made it the most popular dial-up networking protocol. It enables monitoring of the quality of dial-up connections, and if errors are excessive, connections are terminated. PPP also includes authentication mechanisms. *Password Authentication Protocol (PAP)* is a password-based authentication protocol that uses a two-way handshake. *Challenge Handshake Authentication Protocol (CHAP)* uses a three-way handshake and is a stronger authentication mechanism than PAP. HDLC does not support authentication.

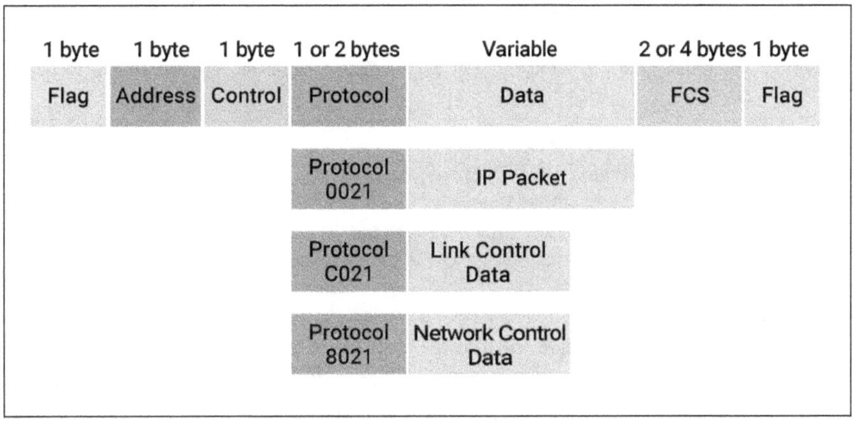

Figure 8-9: The PPP frame formats.

8.2.3 Physical Layer Framing

Physical layer framing is used on some point-to-point WAN circuits, including T1 and Synchronous Optical Network (SONET) circuits. This is primarily used for sender/receiver synchronization and timing over the physical circuit.

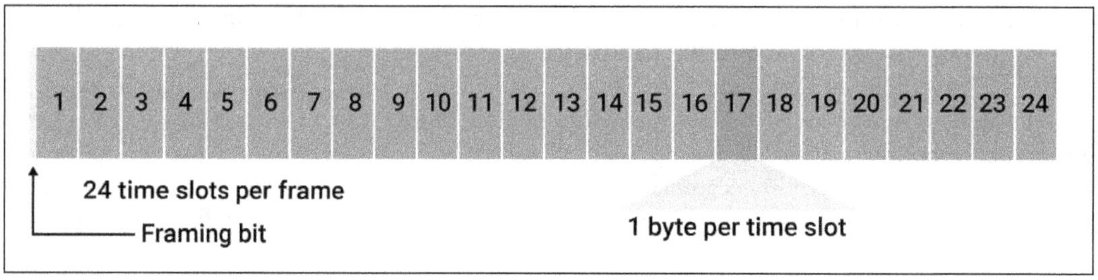

Figure 8-10: Physical layer framing on T1 circuits.

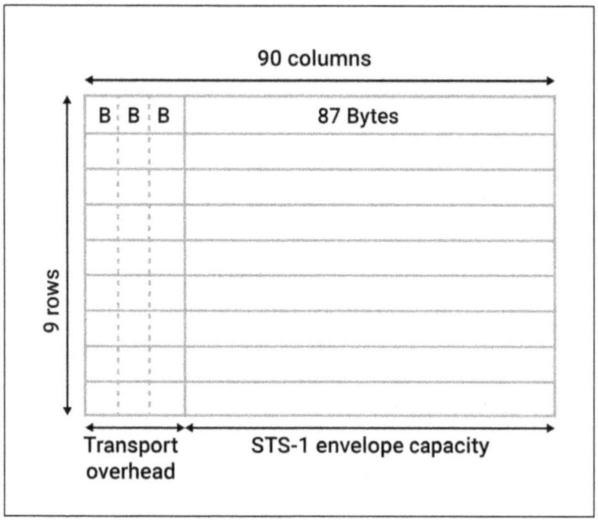

Figure 8-11: The format of a SONET frame.

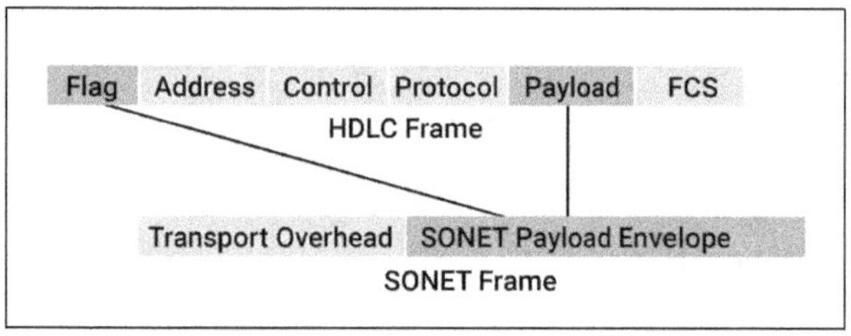

Figure 8-12: A conceptual depiction of the use of HDLC or PPP over SONET network links.

T1 frames are 193 bits in length (see Figure 8-10). Each frame begins with a frame bit and is followed by 24 time slots, each of which carries one byte of data. Since each frame is the same size and takes the same amount of time to transmit (125 microseconds), receivers receive a frame bit every 125 microseconds when data transfers are occurring.

Physical layer framing on SONET fiber optic circuits is more complex but also contributes to sender-receiver synchronization during data transfers. Figure 8-11 illustrates the structure of a SONET frame. Each frame is 810 bytes in length and has nine rows with 90 bytes in each row. The first three bytes in each row are transport overhead bytes, and each frame is transmitted row by row. The transport overhead bytes help maintain sender-receiver synchronization while frames are transmitted. With 810 bytes per frame and a new frame transmitted every 125 microseconds, 51.84 MB of data can be transferred each second over a SONET OC-1 circuit (see Table 8-4 in section 8.3.2).

Figure 8-12 illustrates how HDLC or PPP frames can be encapsulated by SONET Physical layer framing.

8.2.4 Business WAN Trends

Before focusing on the types of circuits and services used to create business WANs, it is important to consider three factors that are affecting business WAN evolution.

The first of these is Carrier Ethernet services as a competitor to traditional WAN services. In many communities, fiber optic networks have been installed by local and regional companies that are separate from carrier and WAN service provider networks and are offering high-speed Carrier Ethernet services at prices that are significantly lower than those of traditional providers. The attractiveness of Ethernet services to businesses consumers—and their popularity—has forced traditional carriers to add Ethernet services to their product lists.

Increasing business use of cloud services is the second factor. Today, cloud services are key components and logical extensions of business WANs. Growing business consumption of public cloud services has forced carriers and WAN service providers to incorporate technologies that facilitate fast, reliable, and secure access to cloud services for their business subscribers.

The third factor is increasing business adoption and use of radio access networks (RANs), especially private 5G networks like those introduced in Chapter 7. As they gain popularity, traditional WAN service providers are forging innovative partnerships with MNOs to meet the needs and desires of business customers.

Collectively, these factors are providing businesses with more leverage with WAN service providers. Like their business subscribers, WAN service providers are having to adapt to technological advances and changing circumstances. Enabling connections among geographically distributed business locations is no longer sufficient. And carriers are moving away from traditional circuits and services and embracing services that businesses want or need.

Today, businesses often leverage both traditional and new services in their enterprise WANs, so a basic understanding of both traditional and emerging WAN services is important. We begin by focusing on dedicated circuit WANs and circuits/services that they may include.

8.3 DEDICATED CIRCUIT WANs

A **dedicated circuit** is a data communication pathway between two network locations. The circuit may exist as a physical cable or a wireless link that serves as a point-to-point connection between two locations.

Traditionally, dedicated circuits have been used to create private business WANs. Businesses lease circuits owned by common carriers for point-to-point links between two locations. Lease cost (monthly cost) is based on a circuit's type, distance, and data carrying capacity.

A dedicated circuit can also exist logically in packet-switched networks, the public Internet, Ethernet services networks, and RANs. Logical dedicated circuits are usually called *virtual circuits* and predefine paths with guaranteed bandwidths through the network. For example, a VPN is sometimes considered a logical point-to-point connection.

The WAN topologies described in section 8.1 have traditionally been built using dedicated circuits. When physical cables are used, the carrier installs the equipment needed for a local loop connection at each location and configures the central office switch to enable the two endpoints to privately transfer data through the carrier's network.

Dedicated circuits are also called *private lines* because they are exclusively available to the subscriber 24/7. Although owned and managed by carriers, the point-to-point circuits in dedicated circuit WANs are private; they are not shared with other carrier subscribers.

Historically, many of the first dedicated circuits were voice-grade analog lines that required modems at each end. Today, most are digital lines, such as copper cable-based T-carrier services (e.g., T1 or T3 lines) or fiber optic cables used for SONET services.

From a business perspective, a dedicated circuit is justified when it is important to always have an uninterrupted connection between the two locations. When data is constantly exchanged between the locations and immediate data transfers are needed, a dedicated circuit is a reasonable connection option.

Given the monthly cost structure of dedicated circuits, typical and peak data transfer volumes should be considered when selecting among the different options. Ideally, the selected circuit is affordable and has the capacity needed but minimal excess capacity that will never be used. Some businesses supplement their dedicated circuits with inexpensive dial-up lines for redundancy and to help handle peak traffic volumes.

Because a business pays a monthly fee for each leased circuit, its total monthly costs for a dedicated circuit WAN include, among others, the sum of the fees paid for the circuits that are leased. The two most common types of dedicated circuit services in business WANs are T-carrier services and Synchronous Optical Network (SONET) services, which are implemented on physical cables. Wireless point-to-point connections may also be included in business WANs.

8.3.1 T-Carrier Services

T-carrier services is the name used in the United States for different levels of digital services provided over copper cables. The collection of available levels of digital services is called the *digital services hierarchy*. As Table 8-3 illustrates, digital services in the United States do not always match up with those in other countries.

Table 8-3: Digital services hierarchy levels in the United States, Europe, and Japan

Digital Service Level	United States	Europe	Japan
DS0	64 Kbps	64 Kbps	64 Kbps
DS1	1.544 Mbps - T1	2.048 Mbps - E1	1.544 Mbps - J1
DS3	44.736 Mbps - T3	34.368 Mbps - E3	32.064 Mbps - J3
DS4	274.176 Mbps - T4	139.264 Mbps - E4	97.728 Mbps - J4

In the United States, a T1 circuit (or DS1 circuit) provides a data rate of 1.544 Mbps. Most carriers also offer fractional T1 (FT1) services, which are sets of 64 Kbps (DS0) circuits. Popular FT1 services include 128 Kbps (2 bundled DS0 circuits), 384 Kbps (6 DS0 circuits), 512 Kbps (8 DS0 circuits), and 768 Kbps (12 DS0 circuits). FT1 services enable businesses to have digital connections between locations whose data transfer volumes average less than 1.544 Mbps, and to reduce the monthly expense associated with connecting the locations.

In the United States, T1 service cost depends on location and is driven by the number of T1 service providers and central offices. Since major cities have the most providers available, T1 pricing is the most competitive in and around them. Rural areas have the fewest providers and the highest T1 costs.

T1 costs in rural areas (locations more than 50 miles from a midsize city) vary but average approximately $350 to $450 a month. T1 costs in small cities are slightly lower, averaging about $300 to $400 a month. In midsize cities, the average monthly price is approximately $250 to $300, and in and around major cities, the average is usually in the $200 to $250 a month range.

One-time setup costs for a T1 circuit also vary per location but tend to range from $250 to $1,000 per location, partly driven by the likelihood of the business moving from a T1 circuit to a T3 (DS3 circuit) or a fractional T3 service (which are bundled T1 lines).

CSU/DSUs are other important T-carrier technologies. A **Channel Service Unit/Data Service Unit (CSU/DSU)** is a device (or software capability) that combines the communication functions of a Channel Service Unit (CSU) and a Data Service Unit (DSU). A *CSU* terminates the leased line at the customer's location. A *DSU* is responsible for the actual transmission and reception of signals on the leased line. It also provides buffering and flow control.

At the other end of the leased circuit, at the central office (CO), the carrier has a similar CSU that interfaces with the technologies used to access the carrier's network. This is illustrated in Figure 8-13. Additional details about CSU/DSUs and other T-carrier technologies are provided in Appendix 8-2.

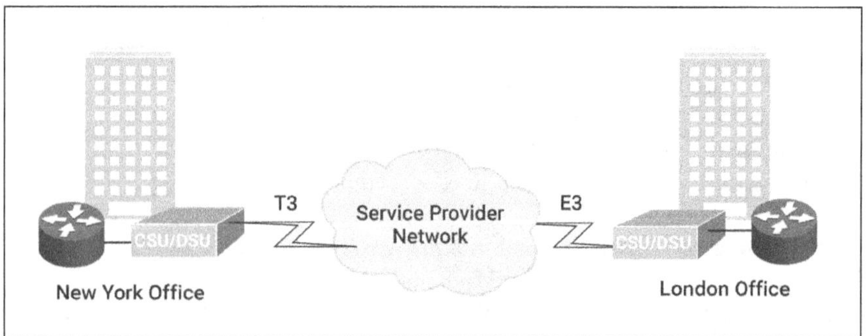

Figure 8-13: An example of how leased lines might connect locations in different countries.

8.3.2 SONET Services

Synchronous Optical Network (SONET) is a standardized digital communication protocol used on fiber optic cables. SONET was developed in the 1980s by the American National Standards Institute (ANSI), and its ability to convert electrical signals to optical signals for transmission over relatively long distances contributes to its continued use.

Like T-carrier services, there are different SONET optical carrier (OC) service levels characterized by different service rates (see Table 8-4). OC-3 services are most common in business WANs, and OC-12 services are second in popularity.

Table 8-4: SONET service levels.

Optical Carrier Level	Data Rate	Synchronous Transport Signal
OC-1	51.84 Mbps	STS 1
OC-3	155.52 Mbps	STS 3
OC-9	466.56 Mbps	STS 9
OC-12	622.08 Mbps	STS 12
OC-18	933.12 Mbps	STS 18
OC-24	1.24416 Gbps	STS 24
OC-36	1.86624 Gbps	STS 36
OC-48	2.48832 Gbps	STS 48
OC-96	4.97664 Gbps	STS 96
OC-192	9.95328 Gbps	STS 192
OC-256	13.27104 Gbps	STS 256
OC-384	19.90656 Gbps	STS 384
OC-768	39.81312 Gbps	STS 768
OC-1536	79.62624 Gbps	STS 1536
OC-3072	159.25248 Gbps	STS 3072

An OC-3 circuit has a data transfer capacity equal to 100 T1 lines. Average costs for an OC-3 line range from $3000 to more than $10,000+ per month, depending on the location. Businesses in major cities are most likely to have average prices near the lower end of this range, and businesses in rural areas may have monthly fees between $20,000 and $40,000 per month. The growing popularity of Ethernet services is putting pressure on providers to lower their prices for OC-3 connections, and in some cities, average prices have fallen to approximately $1500 per month.

With SONET, multiple digital data streams are simultaneously transferred over the fiber optic cable. LEDs and laser beams are used as light sources, and a 1 bit is indicated by the presence of light, while a 0 bit is indicated by the absence of light. A clock is used to coordinate the timing of signal transmission between network elements over SONET circuits. SONET uses a single clock, called the *Primary Reference Clock (PRC)*, to synchronize all the elements in the network. Like T-carrier services frames, a SONET frame takes 125 microseconds to transmit.

At SONET service subscriber locations, *terminal multiplexers* are the interfaces between the customer premises equipment and the OC circuit. They convert electrical to optical signals and vice versa. They get their name from being at the endpoints (termination points) of the OC circuit, and because they also perform multiplexing and demultiplexing. These and other SONET technologies are described in Appendix 8-3.

8.3.3 Wireless Point-to-Point Connections

Some business WANs include wireless point-to-point circuits. These may be private, but some are leased carrier circuits. Terrestrial microwave and satellite microwave links continue to be used in some WANs, but some businesses are using cellular services to create wireless WANs (WWANs).

As noted in Chapter 7, like radio waves, microwaves refer to a band of frequencies in the frequency spectrum. They fall between radio and infrared waves in the frequency spectrum (see Figure 8-14) in the 300 MHz to 300 GHz frequency range.

Usually, the terrestrial and satellite microwave links in carrier networks use microwaves in licensed frequency bands. These bands are allocated by the FCC and state PUCs in ways to ensure that carriers operating near one another will not interfere with each other's signals.

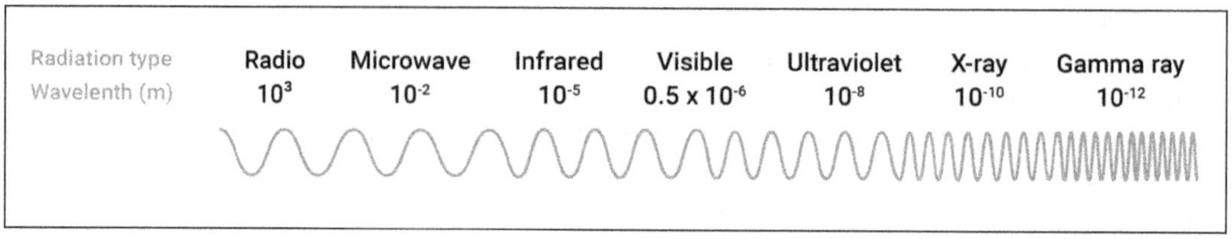

Figure 8-14: Where microwaves are found in the frequency spectrum.

Terrestrial Microwave

Terrestrial microwave links use line-of-sight paths between two points, and a focused signal beam is transmitted from one antenna to the other. In ideal situations, the endpoints can be up to 40 miles apart, but average spacing is 20 to 30 miles. When higher frequency microwave signals are used, the distance may be less than 10 miles.

In traditional microwave bands used for communications, data rates from 300 Mbps to 1 Gbps can be reached. Higher frequency bands, which cellular companies plan to use for wireless backhaul links, have the potential to support speeds that are 10 to 25 times higher.

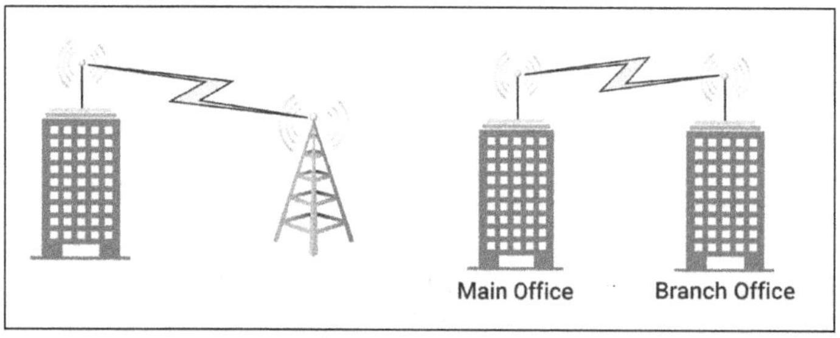

Figure 8-15: Microwave transmitter/receiver mounted on a communications tower.

Figure 8-15 illustrates how a business might connect a building at one of its locations to a carrier's freestanding transmission tower. It also illustrates how a private microwave link could be used to connect buildings at two geographically separated locations.

Terrestrial microwave links can be used to support communication in areas and terrains where the installation of cable would be very costly or difficult. They are widely used in mountainous areas and sometimes used to connect adjacent islands. In rural areas, landowners are usually more willing to allow wireless transmissions to cross their properties than to grant permission to install cables.

Because of their wavelengths, microwave signals are susceptible to weather conditions. For example, signals may be significantly corrupted or lost during heavy downpours. Also, concrete walls in buildings can block, and glass used for windows and exterior siding can corrupt, microwave signals. Exterior power lines can be sources of microwave signal interference.

Satellite Microwave Communications

Communications satellites overcome the line-of-sight limitations of terrestrial microwave links and enable wireless connections among widely separated geographic locations. This setup is illustrated in Figure 8-16.

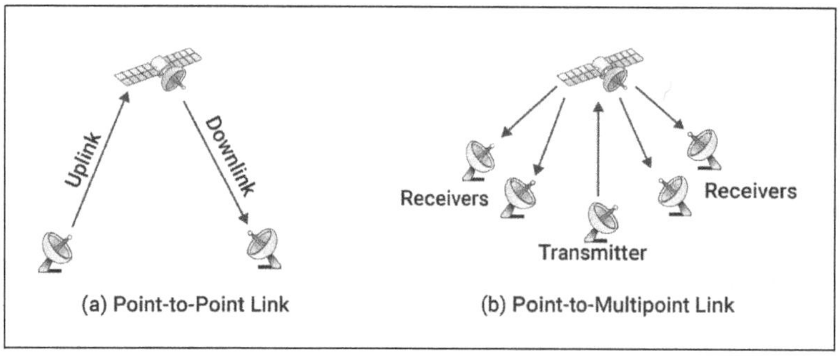

Figure 8-16: Examples of point-to-point and multipoint satellite links.

A **communications satellite** is a satellite that creates a communication channel between a transmitter and a receiver at different locations on Earth. It is typically equipped with a receiving antenna and a transmitting antenna. Frequency bands are allocated to communications satellites in pairs, with sufficient separation to avoid interference. An *uplink* frequency is used to transmit signals to the satellite, and a *downlink* frequency is used to transmit from the satellite to a receiving antenna on earth. If the same frequency were used for both uplinks and downlinks, the strong downlink signal being transmitted would interfere with the weaker uplink signal being received. The device at the satellite that converts the uplink signal to the downlink signal is a *transponder.*

In 2021, there were more than 2200 communications satellites in Earth orbit, not counting those used by the military. Most communications satellites are in *geostationary orbit* 22,300 miles (35,900 km) above the equator. Here, the satellite orbits the Earth at the same rate that the Earth rotates on its axis, and to ground stations, the satellite appears stationary at the same point in the sky. This enables ground station antennas to be permanently aimed at the same point in the sky, and there is no need to track the satellite's orbit. Additional discussion of communications satellites is provided in Appendix 8-4.

Fixed Wireless Access

Building-to-tower, building-to-building, and site-to-site microwave links, like those illustrated in Figure 8-15, are sometimes called *fixed wireless connections* because their infrastructure has permanence (is immobile) and is continually used for point-to-point communications between two network elements. They should not be confused with *fixed wireless access (FWA)*, which is an Internet access connection service available from some ISPs to provide businesses and homes with wireless last mile connectivity via 4G LTE or 5G services. FWA uses radio waves to create a line-of-sight connection between the provider's FWA transmitter/receiver antenna located on a tower or pole and an external antenna located on a subscriber's home or business, typically on a roof.

FWA can be a cost-effective alternative to wired Internet access services, especially in locations whose geographies or population densities make it difficult, impossible, or cost-prohibitive to install cabling. Because FWA can support high data rates and low latencies, it competes with satellite Internet services in many locations.

As 5G radio access networks continue to roll out, FWA services are expected to become more common, with local towers/poles providing last mile connectivity to provider networks. When combined with 5G cellular services, FWA provides a vehicle for creating fully wireless private 5G networks, including WWANs.

Leased lines from carriers can be used to create business WANs. T-carrier and SONET circuits provide dedicated point-to-point locations in some WANs. Wireless point-to-point circuits and FWA may also be included in business WANs. Hence, it continues to be possible for a business to create a private WAN using dedicated circuits. However, many businesses incorporate packet-switched services in their WANs, and some businesses rely solely on such services.

8.4 PACKET-SWITCHED NETWORKS (PSNs)

In a **packet-switched network (PSN)**, data is carried in packets that are routed over a shared network. Unlike dedicated circuit networks, PSNs do not require physical links between business locations. Instead, they enable locations to share circuits in the provider's network. Technically, the Internet is a PSN.

PSNs are attractive options for business WANs because of their costs. Because the circuits in the PSN are shared by subscribers, the monthly cost for interconnecting business locations is typically lower than the costs for dedicated circuit WANs. However, latencies (delays) and jitter (variability of delays) are typically higher in packet-switched networks than in dedicated circuit networks, especially when PSN traffic volumes are high. Generally, though, PSNs provide satisfactory data transport speeds for subscriber data transfers.

Traditionally, PSN subscribers were charged a fixed monthly fee to connect to the PSN and were charged a variable fee based on the volume of packets they transmitted over the network. Today, most carriers have fixed pricing for their PSNs.

Table 8-5: Some of the major differences between connectionless and connection-oriented PSNs.	
PSN Type	**Description**
Connectionless	A connectionless PSN requires the inclusion of a destination address in each packet. Switches/routers in connectionless PSNs use the destination address of a received packet to determine the outgoing interface/link on which the packet should be transmitted. The Internet is an example of a connectionless PSN.
Connection-oriented	A connection-oriented PSN requires the inclusion of route identifiers in packets. When a switch/router receives a packet, it consults a forwarding table that associates the packet's route identifier with an outgoing interface/link and then retransmits the packet on the correct link. MPLS (multiprotocol label switching) networks are examples of connection-oriented PSNs

Routers and switches in a PSN use addressing or route information in packets to determine the paths/links that packets traverse between locations. PSNs that base forwarding decisions on addresses are considered *connectionless systems*, and PSNs where forwarding is based on route identifiers are considered *connection-oriented systems*. The differences between the two are summarized in Table 8-5.

Virtual point-to-point connections can be created in a PSN for subscribers that require private connections. A **permanent virtual circuit (PVC)** is a connection from one location to a second location through the carrier's PSN. Figure 8-17 is an example. A PVC is usually implemented via route identifier in PSN forwarding tables.

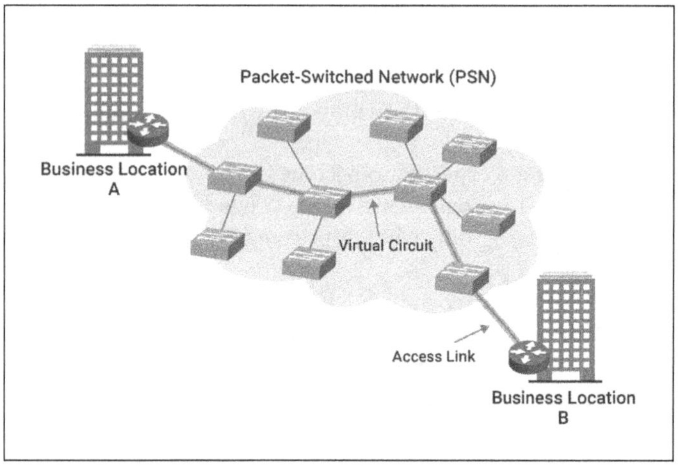

Figure 8-17: An example of a virtual circuit in a packet-switched network.

PVCs enable a business to establish the equivalent of a dedicated circuit WAN using a PSN's shared circuits. Packets from one location to another always follow the same path through the network, just as they would if the different locations were connected by leased point-to-point wired or wireless circuits. PVCs in PSNs can be deployed to create different WAN topologies (e.g., ring, hub-and-spoke, mesh).

The basic architecture of a PSN includes access links, packet assemblers/disassemblers, and the carrier's cloud of switches/routers. These parts are illustrated in Figure 8-18.

Access links are circuits that connect subscriber locations to the PSN. Businesses often lease these links from the carrier who owns and operates the

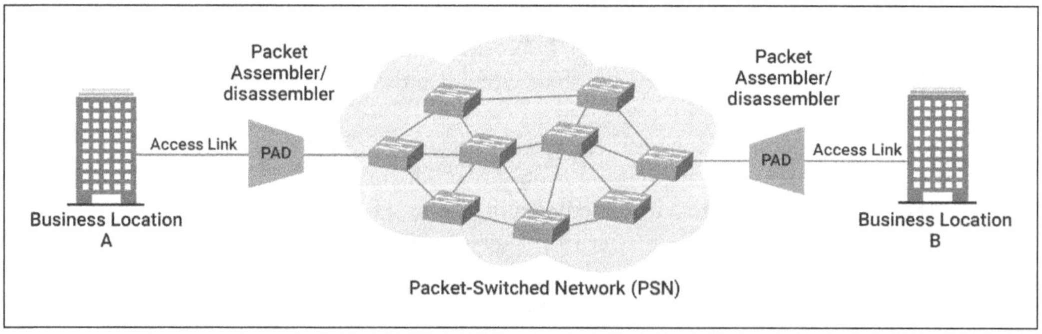

Figure 8-18: Key elements in PSN architectures.

PSN. T1 and fractional T1 lines have been popular access links for packet-switched services, but SONET and other types of circuits may be used as access links as well. Access links at subscriber locations can vary in type or speed; links for locations that generate/receive lower data volumes can use lower speed access links.

Packet assembler/dissembler (PAD) devices encapsulate frames from the network at a subscriber location to create the Data Link and Network layer packets used in the PSN. This typically involves placing a subscriber's Ethernet or Wi-Fi frames in the payload fields of the frames/packets.

To facilitate subscriber connections, carrier PSNs often have a point of presence (POP) at the central offices (COs) of local carriers. A CO may have several PSN POPs. Hence, a PSN subscriber can use a T1, FT1, or other type of access link to connect to a PSN's POP at a CO.

Frame Relay, MPLS, and Ethernet services are examples of packet-switched WAN services. Frame Relay was a popular PSN service for several decades, but it is no longer being installed or serviced by carriers in the United States. However, it is still used in some parts of the world, including some developing countries. Because frame relay is no longer an option for businesses in the United States, only MPLS, Ethernet, and VPN services are discussed.

8.4.1 Multiprotocol Label Switching (MPLS)

Multiprotocol label switching (MPLS) was developed in the 1990s, and businesses have used it to interconnect geographically dispersed locations (headquarters, branch offices, data centers, etc.) for more than two decades. MPLS networks can be used to transfer a wide range of data types (video, images, audio, text), and MPLS is "multiprotocol" because it is not picky about the Network layer PDUs carried in its packets.

MPLS networks are connection-oriented PSNs. MPLS packets include route identifiers, called *labels*, that determine how they are routed in the network. When a packet enters the MPLS network, it is assigned to a specific *forwarding equivalence class (FEC)*[1]; this is sometimes called a forwarding *class of service (CoS)*. A short bit sequence (label) is added to the packet to indicate its service class, and the label determines how the packet is routed through the network to its destination. When it reaches its destination, its label is removed (see Figure 8-19).

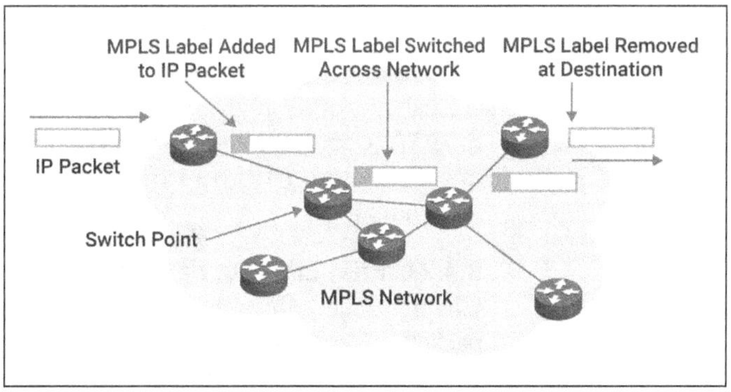

Figure 8-19: A conceptual depiction of an MPLS network.

An FEC assignment identifies the type of data carried in the packet and how it should be forwarded. All packets in the same FEC have the same label and are handled in the same way by the network. For example, packets carrying video or audio data might be assigned to a "real-time" FEC, packets carrying ERP or CRM data may be assigned to a "mission-critical" FEC, and packets carrying any other type of data (e.g., email) might be assigned to a "best effort" FEC. Basically, data associated with an organization's applications are assigned to FECs, and the assignments determine the labels that are added to packets and how they are forwarded.

Packets for real-time apps (those carrying video or audio data) could be assigned to fast (low-latency) routes to ensure adequate performance levels for the applications. Packets carrying mission-critical application data are typically assigned to the fastest, lowest latency routes to destinations, and packets for best effort applications can be assigned to slower, higher latency routes.

1 In other chapters of this book, FEC is used to signify *forward error correction*; when discussing MPLS, in this section, it refers to *forwarding equivalence class*.

FEC labels are associated with predetermined paths through the network to destinations called *label-switched paths (LSPs)*. MPLS router/switch forwarding tables associate FEC labels and outgoing interfaces/links. Hence, when a packet label is read, the router/switch can begin transmitting it on the appropriate link.

An MPLS strength is the ability to separate traffic based on the performance requirements of the applications supported on the network. Businesses like MPLS because it enables mission-critical applications to be supported on the network's fastest LSPs. Similar data traffic separation can be challenging to implement on connectionless PSNs, including the Internet. MPLS labels also enable switches/routers to make rapid forwarding decisions.

Traditional selling points for MPLS by carriers include scalability, superior bandwidth utilization, reduced likelihood of network congestion, application performance, and better user experience with applications. The biggest downside to MPLS is its expense. MPLS services are more expensive than Ethernet or VPN services with comparable connection speeds. In addition, MPLS does not provide encryption. If a subscriber's packets are not encrypted before they enter the carrier's network, the potential exists for them to be intercepted as they traverse the network.

MPLS was designed for organizations with multiple locations and one or more centrally managed data centers. MPLS was a good fit for business WANs before they started being extended by private, public, and hybrid clouds and by scalability requirements that were difficult for MPLS to address.

From 2019 to 2020, business use of MPLS declined by almost 25%. During that same time frame, the use of SD-WANs in enterprise networks increased from less than 20% to more than 40%. Like MPLS, SD-WANs are application-centric and facilitate the performance of mission-critical and other high-priority applications. For comparable data rates, the average cost for an SD-WAN connection is about one-quarter the average cost of an MPLS connection, so further migration from MPLS to SD-WANs is likely. Additional discussion of MPLS is provided in Appendix 8-5.

8.4.2 Carrier Ethernet Services

Chapter 7 describes the prevalence of Ethernet in business LANs and backbone networks. IP packets are encapsulated in Ethernet frames that are passed between devices in local networks. In dedicated circuit networks, Ethernet frames passed between WAN locations are typically encapsulated in HDLC or PPP frames as they make their way across links, and in MPLS networks, labels are added to and removed from Ethernet frames as they enter and leave the network. Encapsulating or modifying Ethernet frames can slow data transfers between locations.

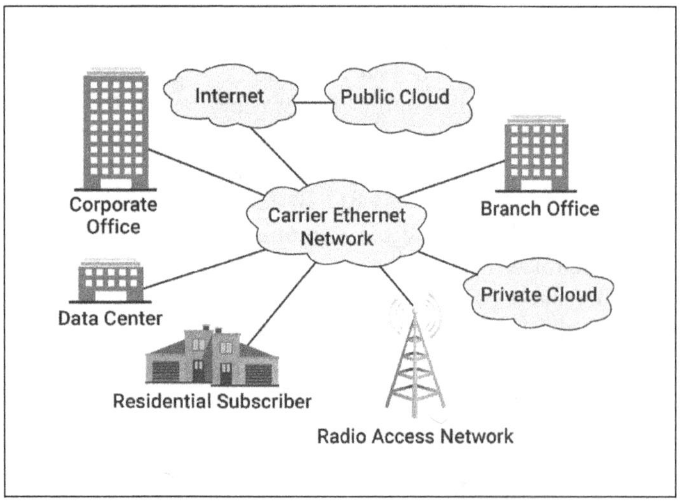

Figure 8-20: Business and consumer Ethernet service.

In many communities, local carriers have installed fiber optic cables, and federally backed rural broadband initiatives have brought fiber optic cabling to sparsely populated areas. Local fiber optic networks are separate from traditional carrier networks and are leveraging Ethernet services to provide businesses and consumers with low-cost, high-speed Internet connections.

For example, in the coastal regions of southeast Georgia and South Carolina, Hargray Communications has installed hundreds of miles of fiber optic cable that is being used to deliver Ethernet services to businesses and consumers. Businesses are using this resource to interconnect their different locations to create WANs. Their networks may also include public and private cloud services, third-party data centers, and private radio access networks (see Figure 8-20).

Competition from local carriers has caused traditional carriers to add Ethernet services. It has also led to the Carrier Ethernet standard, which provides guidance to carriers and other providers for the provision of Ethernet services to subscribers.

Carrier Ethernet enables an Ethernet LAN or backbone network at a business location to connect to an Ethernet service provider's network via a standard RJ45 interface. Essentially, it extends the subscriber's Ethernet LAN or backbone network to the service provider's network, enabling a business to create a WAN interconnecting its different locations that behaves like it is a single Ethernet network.

Network administrators at a business can manage their Ethernet WAN using VLAN (virtual LAN) tools that enable devices to be logically grouped regardless of their physical locations. Basically, an Ethernet WAN can be considered a geographically distributed VLAN (or set of VLANs).

Ethernet services are inexpensive. Businesses often choose Gigabit Ethernet (1 Gbps) or 10 GBE connections, and 1 Gbps connections usually cost less than $100 per month (per location). Consumers can connect their residential Wi-Fi networks to Ethernet services for comparable prices.

Some carriers are leveraging their existing MPLS networks to provide Ethernet services. This makes sense because, like LAN data traffic, Carrier Ethernet traffic is IP based, and because MPLS is used to enhance QoS (quality of service) in IP networks, it can be leveraged to ensure Ethernet service quality for business subscribers. Also, as business subscribers migrate away from traditional MPLS services, carriers can continue to justify their MPLS investments.

The device (or software) that serves as an interface between the LAN or backbone network at a subscriber location and the Carrier Ethernet network is called a *user network interface (UNI)* point. Carrier Ethernet establishes virtual circuits, called *Ethernet Virtual Circuits (EVCs)*, between subscriber locations.

A point-to-point EVC, like that illustrated in Figure 8-21a, is referred to as an *E-Line*. There are two types of point-to-point E-Lines: EPL and EVPL. An *Ethernet Private Line (EPL)* is a dedicated (private) connection between two points. An *Ethernet Virtual Private Line (EVPL)* is a shared E-line link between two locations.

Multipoint connections among three or more subscriber locations, such as those illustrated in Figure 8-21b, are called *E-LANs*. An E-LAN includes multiple EVCs and is essentially an Ethernet Services MAN or WAN that can be managed like a VLAN.

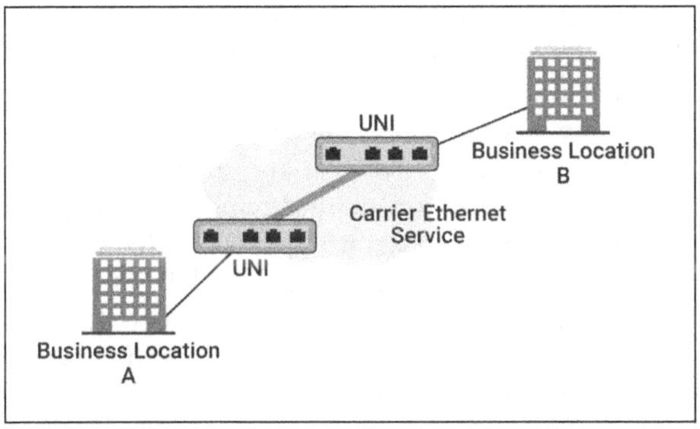

Figure 8-21a: A conceptual depiction of a point-to-point EVC (an E-Line).

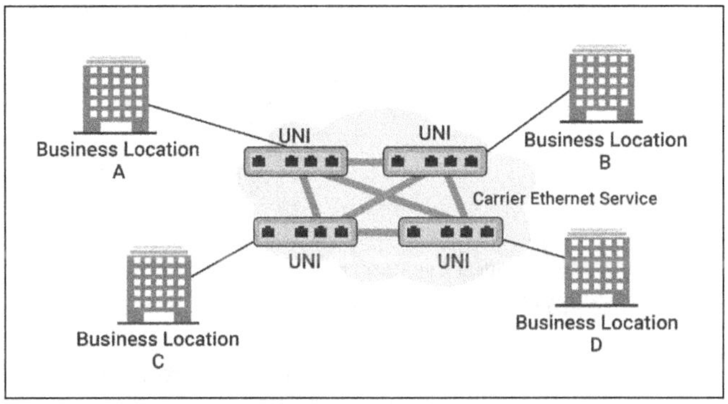

Figure 8-21b: A conceptual depiction of an E-LAN, a WAN established using Carrier Ethernet services.

8.4.3 Virtual Private Network (VPN) Services

VPNs were briefly introduced in Chapter 5 as services used by businesses to create secure virtual point-to-point connections over the Internet or another TCP/IP network. These services enable data to be transferred between business locations less expensively than is possible over leased circuits or most carrier PSNs. A conceptual depiction of a VPN connection between two business locations is provided in Figure 8-22.

To leverage VPN services, each location must have a connection to an ISP. A wide range of ISP connections may be used, including leased T- or OC-carrier circuits, leased wireless circuits, or less expensive options, such as a cable modem, DSL, FTTH (fiber to the home), or Ethernet services. As Figure 8-22 illustrates, each business location also needs a VPN router.

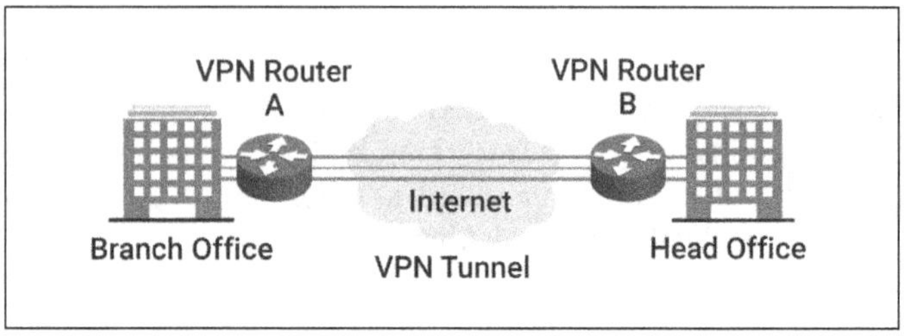

Figure 8-22: A conceptual depiction of using a VPN to connect the LANs at two business locations.

Three types of VPNs are common in enterprise networks: intranet VPNs, extranet VPNs, and remote access VPNs. Intranets and extranets are described in section 5.5 of Chapter 5. An *intranet VPN*, like that illustrated in Figure 8-22, creates VPN tunnels between business locations. A *VPN router* (which may be called a *VPN gateway* or *VPN server*) is located at each location.

An extranet VPN enables a trusted business partner (such as a supplier, customer, or consultant) to have a secure connection to a business location. As noted in Chapter 5, an extranet is sometimes considered a secure and limited extension of an organization's private network to a trusted partner. Typically, trusted partners have limited access to specified subsets of the private network's resources.

An extranet VPN can allow supply chain partners to share data/information required to control and coordinate the operations associated with their materials transfers. It might be used to securely exchange EDI documents or to support a vendor managed inventory (VMI) system, one of the types of SCM software mentioned in section 2.2.4 of Chapter 2. EDI is briefly described in section 2.2.5 in Chapter 2.

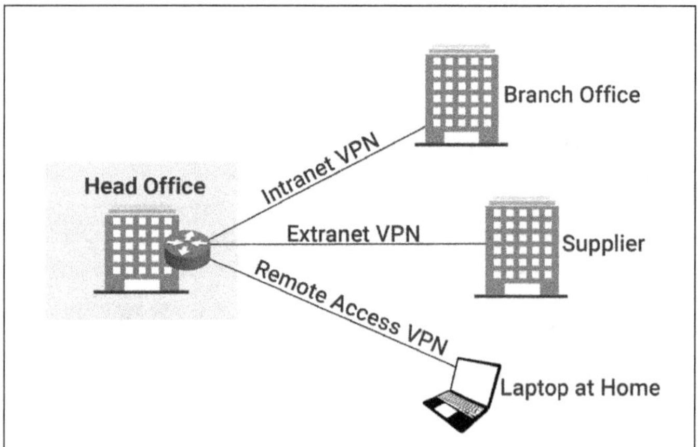

Figure 8-23: Conceptual depiction of the distinctions between intranet, extranet, and remote access VPNs.

The distinction between extranet and intranet VPNs is illustrated in Figure 8-23. Basically, an intranet VPN provides secure connections between a business's different locations, while an extranet VPN supports secure communications between an organization and a business partner, such as a supplier.

A *remote access VPN* provides a secure connection between a business location and the network in an employee's home or another remote location (see Figure 8-23). Remote workers use VPN software (or software clients) to establish a VPN tunnel to their employer's VPN gateway or router. They are typically required to provide login credentials to establish a VPN tunnel from their location to the employer's network.

Multipoint VPNs are used in some businesses to interconnect geographically distributed locations. These are often called *dynamic multiple VPNs (DMVPNs)* and are considered specialized forms of intranet VPNs. They are typically proprietary in nature and require VPN routers and software from the same vendor.

A DMVPN is usually a hub-and-spoke architecture, such as that illustrated in Figure 8-24. Typically, a VPN connects each spoke location to the hub to enable central management of the multipoint network. These connections are depicted as solid lines in Figure 8-24.

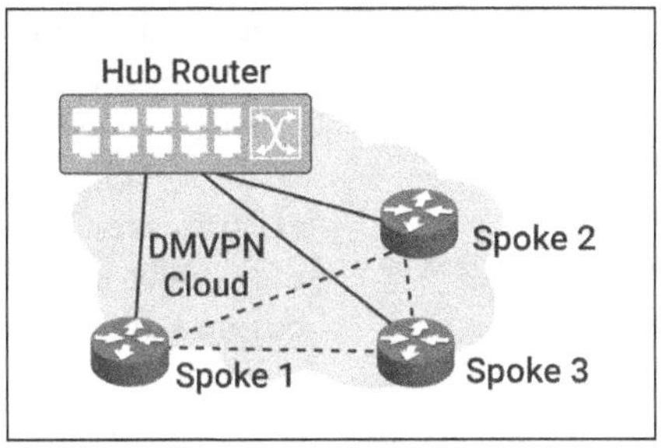

Figure 8-24: A conceptual depiction of a multipoint VPN network.

DMVPNs enable a temporary VPN connection to be established between a pair of spokes. This enables direct and secure communications between the two locations without having to go through the hub. Basically, a DMVPN is a centralized architecture that can provide VPN connections between branch locations on demand.

As noted in Chapter 5, a VPN tunnel is basically an encrypted packet or frame that is transferred over the virtual circuit between the networks at the two locations. A packet is encrypted (in part or whole) at the sending endpoint and decrypted at the receiving endpoint. When IPsec is used, the router at each end of an intranet VPN connection may be called an *IPsec gateway*.

Two types of IPsec are used in VPNs: *L2TP/IPsec* and *IKEv2/IPsec*. Layer 2 Tunneling Protocol (L2TP)/IPsec is considered secure when AES is used for encryption but is less secure on networks that use preshared keys for authentication. Very secure connections are created when IPsec is combined with Internet Key Exchange version 2 (IKEv2) by leveraging PKI to check certificates and authenticate endpoints before VPN connections are established. PKI is described in Chapter 12. *IKEv2* works well on mobile devices whose users switch between cellular and Wi-Fi services but relies on AES or IPsec for encryption.

OpenVPN is one of the most common and widely used encryption protocols. It is supported on most routers, is typically their default VPN protocol, and works with most device operating systems. It is open source, highly configurable, works with both TCP and UDP, and has no known vulnerabilities. It is often considered the gold standard for VPN security.

Other popular VPN security protocols include *WireGuard* (very fast, very secure, and open source), *SoftEther* (very fast and very secure), and GRE. *Generic Routing Encapsulation (GRE)* is a tunneling protocol developed by Cisco Systems that can encapsulate and protect a wide variety of Network layer packets across virtual point-to-point links or point-to-multipoint links in IP networks. It is primarily used for transferring router table updates.

In sum, VPNs are popular because they are relatively inexpensive and enable public Internet infrastructure to be used to interconnect distributed business locations in business WANs. A variety of VPN protocols are used to create VPN tunnels over permanent or temporary point-to-point connections, and it is important for businesses to know their strengths and weaknesses. Additional discussion of VPN services is provided in Appendix 8-6.

8.5 WIRELESS WANs (WWANs) AND PRIVATE MOBILE NETWORKS

A **wireless WAN (WWAN)** is a network that uses mobile cellular network technologies, such as 4G, LTE, and 5G, to transfer data between devices over a wide area. It may leverage mobile network operator (MNO) infrastructure but can be a closed network that covers a large area and is built and utilized by a single business. *Low-power WANs (LPWANs)* are another type of WWAN. They connect and transfer small packets between geographically distributed things, often sensors, in the IoT and are included in Chapter 9's discussion of business and the IoT.

Private 5G RANs were introduced and briefly described in Chapter 7 as an alternative to Wi-Fi in business facilities. When a business chooses to use cellular infrastructure to interconnect private RANs at its geographically distributed locations, the private network may be a WWAN.

A **private mobile network** is a 5G or LTE network that is customized for a specific organization. Customization ensures that the network meets the organization's business needs and requirements, such as latency, mobility, QoS, and security. Privacy and security are especially important to businesses that choose to replace their WANs with WWANs.

Businesses have different implementation options for private mobile networks. For example, they can be owned/managed by the businesses, owned/managed by an MNO, or co-owned by the business and an MNO.

Private mobile networks utilize licensed or unlicensed spectrum. The 5G *New Radio Unlicensed (NR-U)* standard includes a standalone mode that eliminates dependency on licensed MNO spectrum. Private businesses can use it to deploy RANs, or, alternatively, managed service providers or network systems integrators can deploy them to provide customized solutions for their business clients. NR-U is being used by manufacturing to deploy Industry 4.0 applications with densely populated endpoints that require high-bandwidth, low-latency, reliable, and secure connections.

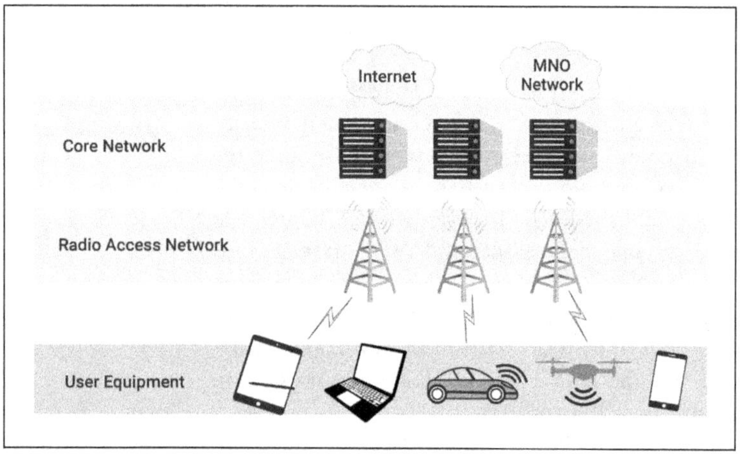

Figure 8-25: Three key elements of 5G networks.

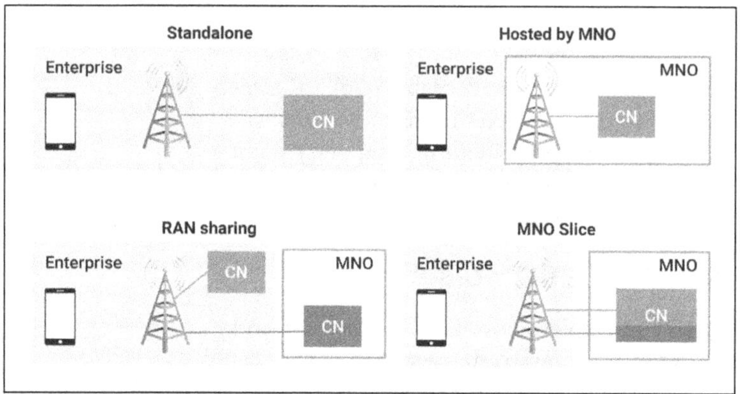

Figure 8-26: Deployment options for private mobile networks.

Regardless of the spectrum used, private 5G networks include three key elements (see Figure 8-25). The first is *user equipment (UE)*, the smartphones and other SIM card-equipped devices (factory equipment, IoT sensors, cameras, autonomous vehicles, etc.) that need to communicate with nearby RAN base stations.

The second is the RAN. Here, a *base station (BS)* contains antennas and other components used to transfer data between UE devices. The coverage area of a RAN base station is dependent on its antennas, hardware, and software capabilities. The collection of base stations in a business facility or campus forms the local RAN.

Data from UE is passed through the RAN to the *core network (CN)*, the third key element in Figure 8-25. The CN manages UE registration and movement; it enables network users or devices to communicate while they move around. Basically, the CN is the "brain" for the private mobile network.

As noted in Chapter 7, businesses can deploy private 5G networks in various ways. These range from completely standalone to RAN sharing to fully dependent on an MNO. These deployment options are illustrated in Figure 8-26.

Perhaps because RANs originated in the cellular services industry, private mobile networks are called *nonpublic networks (NPNs)*. Also, per standard definitions, there are two types of NPNs: standalone and public network integrated. A *standalone NPN (SNPN)* (or *independent private mobile network*) is not owned or operated by an MNO. It is separate from and does not rely on an MNO's public network. An SNPN may access an MNOs public network but is typically considered an untrusted network by the MNO.

A *public network integrated NPN* is deployed and managed with an MNO's help and support in one of three ways. Some MNOs use dedicated or virtual slices of their spectrum to create private 5G networks for business subscribers. The slice assigned to a business is physically or logically separated from those assigned to other businesses, and resources assigned to the private network are isolated from other slices and the MNO's public network. Physical separation is achieved by assigning a specific range of the MNO's spectrum to a business subscriber. These two approaches create private *network slice networks*.

The third approach is used to create a RAN sharing network. In a *RAN sharing network*, a local CN manages UE registration and movement, but the RAN and its spectrum are shared with the MNO's public network. The MNO handles wide area user and network control.

Further details about private RANs and WWANs are included in Appendix 8-7.

8.6 SOFTWARE-DEFINED WANs (SD-WANs)

SD-WANs are architected with cloud connectivity in mind, if not assumed. SD-WANs apply software-defined networking (SDN) concepts, introduced in Chapter 1, to WANs. SD-WAN technologies at WAN locations apply rules and policies to send traffic along the best paths to other locations.

Enterprise WAN architects consider many factors when determining how to interconnect different locations. Considerations may include risk/reward calculations when comparing very reliable but expensive MPLS services with less reliable but less expensive VPN services that leverage public Internet infrastructures. Network technology and PSN advances, such as Carrier Ethernet and SD-WANs, are other considerations.

A **software-defined wide area network (SD-WAN)** is a virtual WAN architecture that allows organizations to leverage a combination of transport services, including leased circuits, PSNs, and WWANs, to optimize access to WAN resources and the performance of mission-critical applications across business locations. The basic idea of an SD-WAN is illustrated in Figure 8-27.

SD-WANs may support a mixture of WAN connections and services. A business WAN may include last mile fiber, copper, or wireless connections to ISPs and carrier networks. It may also include 5G RANs, and PSN services such as Carrier Ethernet and MPLS.

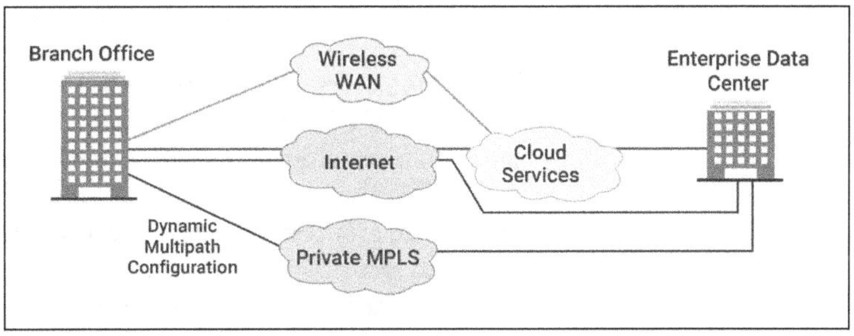

Figure 8-27: An SD-WAN enables a business to leverage and optimize the utilization of alternate connections between locations.

Dynamic path selection enables an SD-WAN to optimize application performance. When alternative transport paths between locations are available, the SD-WAN selects the path that optimizes application performance and changes to an alternate path or splits the application's data traffic between two paths if this improves application performance. The ability to simultaneously support and manage multiple paths through the WAN is called *dynamic multipath configuration*. In addition to optimizing application performance, it improves network resilience and load sharing.

An SD-WAN utilizes a centralized control function to direct data traffic across the WAN and to trusted cloud services. It strives to optimize the performance of applications and their users' experience. Like MPLS, SD-WANs are application-focused, but they are more inclusive than MPLS in that they support applications traditionally hosted on on-premises data centers or in private clouds as well as those hosted by software as a service (SaaS) providers or public clouds.

Basically, an SD-WAN provides application-aware routing across the WAN. Like MPLS, an organization's applications are categorized into classes, and each classification is associated with appropriate QoS and security priorities that align with business requirements. For both security and overall performance, applications can be assigned to different network segments. For example, IoT data traffic is often segregated from other WAN traffic in SD-WAN networks.

Often, SD-WANs are adopted by businesses that want to use lower cost connection services and commercially available Internet access to build high-performance WANs. Some businesses adopt SD-WANs to supplement or replace more expensive application-centric WAN services such as MPLS. These and other reasons why SD-WANs are attractive to today's businesses are identified in Appendix 8-8.

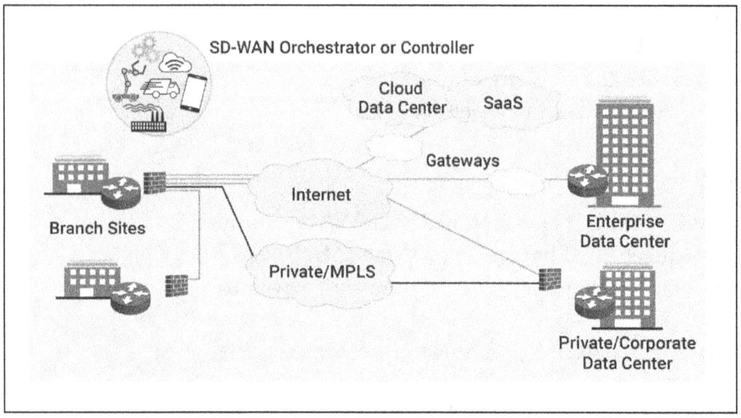

Figure 8-28: Key components of SD-WAN architectures.

An industry consortium of cloud, network, and technology providers, the *MEF Forum* provides guidance for the SD-WAN architecture. The MEF was originally the Metro Ethernet Forum and focused on Carrier Ethernet networks. Today, it has a much broader scope and includes SD-WANs.

The MEF identifies four key components of SD-WAN architecture: SD-WAN Edges, SD-WAN Gateways, SD-WAN Controllers, and SD-WAN Orchestrators. They are illustrated in Figure 8-28.

- An SD-WAN Edge is a physical device or virtual network software function located at an organization's different locations, data centers, and private and public cloud platforms. It defines the SD-WAN service.
- SD-WAN Gateways are devices that connect an SD-WAN to other networks or the Internet. They strive to shorten the distance (latencies) to cloud-based services or application users and to reduce service (application) interruptions.
- An SD-WAN Controller is a centralized management platform that enables network administrators to manage and monitor the entire SD-WAN infrastructure. It makes forwarding decisions for application traffic. As noted previously, like MPLS, applications are grouped into classes, called Application Flow Groups, that have different QoS and security priorities. The Controller applies the priorities to application packets and identifies the links via which they should be forwarded to destinations.
- An SD-WAN Orchestrator is a type of SD-WAN controller that provides additional functionality for managing and automating the deployment of SD-WAN devices. It is a cloud-based or on-premises tool that provides configuration, provisioning, and other functions while the SD-WAN operates. It strives to simplify the management of application traffic across the WAN.

As you can see, SD-WANs enable centralized monitoring and management of a WAN's circuits and edge devices. Having greater real-time visibility of end-to-end traffic flows helps network managers determine where changes are needed to facilitate traffic growth. SD-WANs can reduce WAN expenses by balancing network traffic over circuits with different costs and capacities. And their ability to segregate different types of traffic contributes to WAN security.

8.7 WAN SECURITY

Business WANs can span metropolitan areas, states, regions, or countries, and they may include a variety of wired and wireless connections between locations. Businesses typically do not own the circuits, networks, and services used to interconnect their different locations and do not control how they are deployed and secured by their owners.

Businesses typically include security in the due diligence they perform before signing contracts for new WAN services or renewing service contracts. However, their lack of control over ISP networks, the carrier network, and the public Internet typically causes them to focus on the security of the last mile circuits, customer premises equipment, and WAN components present at their locations.

Traditionally, much of the data traffic in a business WAN passed through a private centralized data center where security policies could be applied and enforced. Today, many of the applications and a lot of data have moved to the cloud, and centralized on-premises data centers have diminished in importance. Increased use of cloud applications and infrastructure is transforming business WAN implementations.

Connections to cloud services via the public Internet introduce new threats and vulnerabilities to business WANs. VPNs can help, but SD-WANs make more comprehensive contributions to WAN security. SD-WANs' central management of edge devices enables security policies to be consistently enforced in edge devices across locations. It provides a security overlay that minimizes the need for additional security mechanisms for different circuit or service types.

SD-WANs make liberal use of encryption and VPNs. Businesses no longer assume that carriers and other WAN service providers can guarantee security, so they routinely use encryption on all transport paths through their WANs.

8.7.1 WAN Security Threats and Issues

Common security threats and issues for WANs include security gaps, malware, network breaches, and application inefficiencies caused by security solutions. *Security gaps* can exist at the points where business data is handed off to an ISP, carrier network, ISP network, PSN, or cloud platform. Such points are targeted by attackers hoping to intercept unencrypted business data. WAN locations with media converters, for example, where wireless signals are converted to electronic or optical signals, can be security weak points, and since wireless signals are susceptible to eavesdropping, data transferred over wireless links should always be encrypted.

WANs can increase vulnerability to *malware*. WANs provide a wider attack surface than local networks, and attackers have more opportunities to introduce malware and facilitate its spread across network locations and devices.

Business WANs can attract *phishing* scams. Some attackers use wide-scale phishing schemes across locations to entice employees to give up their network login credentials via bogus validation requests.

Because of their geographic span, numerous edges, and various types of circuits and services, *network breaches* are a consistent threat to business WANs. Today, cloud services are important components of enterprise networks, and data transfers to/from cloud services must be secured. Increased use of WWANs and RANs also introduces new security challenges.

Another WAN security issue is *increased latencies for time-sensitive applications*. This results from deploying WAN security solutions that have a detrimental effect on application performance. Encryption and decryption can have noticeable and detrimental effects on time-sensitive applications, and higher latencies can result when more robust security mechanisms are deployed.

8.7.2 WAN Security Best Practices

Best practices for securing a WAN include *encryption*. It is especially important for data in transit between business locations, but encrypting data at rest is also important. Encryption has been frequently mentioned in previous chapters and is addressed most directly in Chapters 11 and 12.

Keeping software up-to-date and patched is another WAN security best practice. This is important for device operating systems, network operating systems, WAN-supported applications, antimalware software, and SD-WAN software.

Using network monitoring tools is a third WAN security best practice. It is especially important to track login attempt failures, requests to access network resources, and network traffic anomalies. Numerous tools exist for this, including firewalls, intrusion detection and intrusion protection systems, and network access control (NAC) tools.

An *intrusion detection system (IDS)* is a software application (or device) that monitors network traffic for suspicious activity and issues alerts when suspect activity is identified. An *intrusion prevention system (IPS)* acts in response to suspicious activity, such as blocking or dropping its associated traffic. *Network access control (NAC) tools* implement security policies when devices initially attempt to access the network. Device authentication and authorization controls are important aspects of NAC.

Security information and event management (SIEM) tools and secure access service edge (SASE) are also important aspects of WAN security. *Security information and event management (SIEM)* helps organizations recognize potential vulnerabilities and security threats before they disrupt business operations. SIEM uses AI (artificial intelligence) to detect network use behavior anomalies and to automate incident response processes.

Secure access service edge (SASE) combines SD-WAN and network security functions. It is a cloud service that delivers security controls to SD-WAN devices and edge locations. It ensures that all devices and endpoints are authenticated and assists SD-WAN in segmenting application traffic in separate virtual networks in ways that comply with data security mandates, such as those required by Sarbanes-Oxley, HIPAA, and other regulations.

The proliferation of RANs and mobile devices in enterprise networks has increased the importance of *enterprise mobility management (EMM)* and *unified endpoint management (UEM)*. UEM enables network administrators to deploy, secure, and manage network resources and applications on any device from a single console. It is considered an important step toward a comprehensive network management and security system that encompasses both wired and wireless networks.

Business WANs face a wide range of security threats and issues. WAN security best practices include various traditional safeguards as well as tools designed to consistently protect WAN resources across locations.

SUMMARY

A WAN is a geographically distributed telecommunications network that interconnects LANs at different locations. In the past, enterprise WANs were typically private networks with limited or no connections to the Internet. Today, business WANs have evolved to include remote users and cloud services that connect to the business network via the public Internet. RANs and cellular WWANs are other important parts of some business WANs.

Today's WAN architectures typically result from WAN aggregation, the process of consolidating the local networks at business locations into a single coherent telecommunications network. Historically, the first iterations of business WANs were created using leased point-to-point circuits to link business locations. They had identifiable topologies such as ring, star, and mesh.

Businesses continue to use dedicated copper circuits (T-carrier services) and fiber optic

(SONET) circuits to connect to ISPs, carrier networks, and PSNs. Terrestrial microwave, satellite microwave, and fixed wireless circuits are used in some WANs. Some businesses use MPLS, Carrier Ethernet, and VPN services to interconnect their different locations.

VPNs enable businesses to leverage public Internet infrastructure to interconnect locations and to enable their employees to connect to the corporate network from remote locations. Some businesses have embraced private mobile radio networks and cellular service-based WWANs. Some WWANs are private, independent, and separate from MNO public networks. Others are hosted by or shared with MNOs.

Many businesses have migrated to SD-WANs. SD-WANs are an approach to WAN aggregation that results in a virtual WAN architecture that leverages a combination of transport services, including dedicated circuits, packet-switched services, RANs, and broadband Internet access services. SD-WANs use an application-focused approach that strives to optimize application performance and securely connect users to applications and network resources. Application performance is optimized via application classes, QoS, and automated route selection. Dynamic multipath optimization features enable SD-WANs to be resilient, scalable, and self-healing.

SASE (secure access service edge) is used in conjunction with SD-WANs to improve WAN security. SASE is a cloud service that combines SD-WANs, firewalls, and other network security to securely connect and protect users and applications.

WANs have large attack surfaces and many potential vulnerabilities that attackers can exploit. Encryption is the most widely used WAN security mechanism. Firewalls, IPS, NAC, and SIEM tools and solutions are other aspects of WAN security best practices.

In Chapter 9, you will see that business WANs are also accommodating an increasing variety of IoT applications and services. They introduce a wide range of additional security challenges.

KEY TERMS

Channel Service Unit/Data Service Unit (CSU/DSU)
Common carriers
Communications satellite
Dedicated circuit
Packet-switched network (PSN)
Permanent virtual circuit (PVC)
Private mobile network
Software-defined wide area network (SD-WAN)
Wide area network (WAN)
WAN aggregation
WAN architecture
WAN topology
Wireless WAN (WWAN)

REVIEW QUESTIONS

1. What makes a WAN different from a CAN or a MAN? Why are business WANs usually depicted as clouds?
2. What are the advantages and downsides of business WANs?
3. Identify several factors contributing to the evolution of business WANs.
4. What are the differences between WAN architecture, WAN aggregation, and WAN topology?
5. Briefly describe the differences between the following WAN topologies: point-to-point, ring, hub-and-spoke, full mesh, and partial mesh. Identify the advantages and shortcomings of each topology.
6. Why do some businesses deploy dual-homed hub-and-spoke topologies?
7. What are common carriers? Briefly explain the meaning of each of the following: central office, customer premises equipment, local loop, and demarcation point.
8. Identify several organizations that define WAN standards and oversee their revisions. How do federal and state regulatory agencies affect WAN implementations?
9. What Data Link layer protocols are most common on point-to-point circuits? Briefly describe their differences.
10. What is Physical layer framing? Why is it used on some types of point-to-point circuits?
11. What is a dedicated circuit? Why is a dedicated circuit called a private line? What is a logical dedicated circuit?
12. What are T-carrier services? Identify examples of T-carrier services and circuits. What do they typically cost?

13. What is a CSU/DSU, and what communication functions does it perform?
14. What are SONET services? Identify examples of SONET services and circuits. What do OC-3 circuits typically cost?
15. What are terminal multiplexers, and what communication functions do they perform?
16. Identify and briefly describe examples of wireless point-to-point circuits used in some business WANs.
17. What is a PSN? Why are PSNs an attractive option for implementing business WANs?
18. What are the differences between connectionless and connection-oriented PSNs?
19. What is a PVC? Why are they popular among PSN business subscribers?
20. Briefly describe the roles of access links and PADs in PSNs.
21. What is MPLS? Briefly explain why MPLS has been a popular PSN option for businesses.
22. Briefly explain how application classes and labels are used in MPLS networks to support optimized application performance.
23. Briefly explain why some businesses have migrated from MPLS to Carrier Ethernet services or SD-WAN.
24. How do Carrier Ethernet networks differ from traditional carrier networks?
25. Briefly describe each of the following: UNI, EVC, E-line, EVPL, and E-LAN.
26. Briefly describe the differences between intranet, extranet, and remote access VPNs. What are dynamic multiple VPNs?
27. Identify examples of VPN security/encryption protocols.
28. What is a WWAN? What is a private mobile network? Briefly describe each of the following components of private mobile networks: UE, base station, RAN, and CN.
29. Briefly describe the differences between the following types of private mobile radio networks: (independent) standalone, network slices, and RAN sharing.
30. What is an SD-WAN? Briefly explain why SD-WANs are attractive to businesses.
31. Briefly describe each of the following SD-WAN components: edge, gateway, orchestrator, and controller.
32. Briefly explain why business WANs are challenging to secure and protect. Identify several WAN security threats and issues.
33. Identity examples of WAN security best practices and tools.

PROBLEMS AND EXERCISES

Exercise 8-1 Carrier Network Maps. Zayo (https://www.zayo.com/) is a carrier with an international customer base that has created extensive fiber optic WANs in North America, the EU, and elsewhere that are interconnected by subsea cables. Explore the Zayo website and its network maps (https://www.zayo.com/network/). Use screen captures or snips of Zayo's global core fiber, core wavelength, and dark fiber networks and the statistics associated with each network.

Include your screen captures/snips in a 3- to 5-page Word document that summarizes what you have learned about Zayo's carrier network through your exploration of the company's website. Cite the website and any other articles you find about Zayo as sources in a references section on the last page of your document.

Exercise 8-2 Georgia Southern University Dedicated Circuit Options. Georgia Southern University is considering investing in a backup dedicated circuit network to interconnect its three campuses (Statesboro, Savannah, and Hinesville). The network will have either a ring, hub-and-spoke, or full mesh topology. Although the three campuses differ in the sizes of their student populations, the IT Services department at the university has determined that a minimum connection speed of 50 Mbps is needed on the links connecting its campuses.

Use Visio or another network diagramming tool to create logical diagrams for each alternative topology. *Note*: The Statesboro campus would be the hub in the hub-and-spoke topology.

Identify feasible T-carrier and SONET dedicated circuit options for the university's dedicated circuit WAN and use information from the chapter to provide a cost estimate for the total monthly costs of each alternative topology.

Document your work in a 3- to 5-page Word document that concludes with a dedicated circuit network topology recommendation, identifies the type of circuit that should be used, and estimates the monthly cost of the network.

Exercise 8-3 Georgia Southern University PSN Options. Georgia Southern University has decided to investigate using a packet-switched service for backup connections among its three campuses (Statesboro, Savannah, and Hinesville). Although the three campuses differ in the sizes of their student populations, GSU's IT Services has determined that a minimum connection speed of 50 Mbps is needed at each location.

Use Visio or another network diagramming tool to create a logical diagram of a PSN connecting the three campuses. Be sure to include access links and PADs in the network diagram.

Because Ethernet is used at all three campuses, IT Services has decided to limit its packet-switching service options to Carrier Ethernet. Identify Ethernet services providers that serve southeast Georgia and their typical monthly charges for services with data rates of 50 Mbps or higher.

Document your work in a 3- to 5-page Word document that concludes with service provider recommendations and estimates for the monthly cost of the network.

Exercise 8-4 Do some research on business adoption of SD-WANs. Look for articles that focus on the rate of SD-WAN adoption, the types of businesses that are adopting SD-WANs, and the business factors that are driving adoption decisions. Summarize your findings in a 1000- to 1500-word document or five- to eight-slide PowerPoint presentation. Your paper or presentation should include tables or charts that visually summarize SD-WAN adoption rates and significant business drivers. It should also include a References page or slide that includes the titles and URLs for at least four sources. The source that you consider to be most informative should be highlighted.

CHAPTER REFERENCES

Antonenko, D. (2021). What Is a Wide Area Network? Understanding WANs. Business Tech Weekly. Retrieved from: https://www.businesstechweekly.com/operational-efficiency/computer-networking/wide-area-network-wan/

Aruba. (n.d.). SD-WAN Explained. Retrieved from: https://www.arubanetworks.com/faq/what-is-sd-wan/

bSimplify. (n.d.). T1 Lines—How Much Does a T1 Line Cost? Retrieved from: https://www.bsimplify.com/t1-lines-how-much-does-a-t1-line-cost/

Cato Networks. (n.d.). What Is SD-WAN? Retrieved from: https://www.catonetworks.com/sd-wan/

Cisco Networking Academy. (2017). WAN Concepts. In *Connecting Networks v6 Companion Guide*. Retrieved from: https://www.ciscopress.com/articles/article.asp?p=2832405&seqNum=4

Cloudflare. (n.d.). What Is an SD-WAN? Retrieved from: https://www.cloudflare.com/learning/network-layer/what-is-an-sd-wan/

Davis, D. (2009). 3 WAN Protocols You Should Know: HDLC, PPP, and Frame-Relay. Petri. Retrieved from: https://petri.com/csc_3_wan_protocols_you_should_know/

Dryjański, M. (2021). Private 5G Networks—Technology, Architecture, and Deployment. Rimedo Labs. Retrieved from: https://rimedolabs.com/blog/private-5g-networks-technology-architecture-and-deployment/

Editorial Today. (n.d.). Understanding the Differences in Cost Between T3/ DS3, OC3, FastE, and GigE. Retrieved from: https://www.streetdirectory.com/etoday/-ufopwc.html

Fortinet. (n.d.). What Is SD-WAN? Retrieved from: https://www.fortinet.com/resources/cyberglossary/sd-wan-explained

The Free Dictionary. (n.d.). Carrier Ethernet. Retrieved from: https://encyclopedia2.thefreedictionary.com/Metro+Ethernet+Forum

Fruhlinger, J. (2022). What Is MPLS, and Why Isn't It Dead Yet? *Network World*. Retrieved from: https://www.networkworld.com/article/2297171/network-security-mpls-explained.html

Hammad, M. (2020). Basic Frame Structure for HDLC. Geeks for Geeks. Retrieved from: https://www.geeksforgeeks.org/basic-frame-structure-of-hdlc/

Gokhankosem. (2019). WAN Topology Types. IPCisco. Retrieved from: https://ipcisco.com/wan-topology-types/

Huawei. (n.d.). Configuration Guide—MPLS. Retrieved from: https://support.huawei.com/enterprise/en/doc/EDOC1100301728/27fa7d9d

IBM. (n.d.). What Is SIEM? Retrieved from: https://www.ibm.com/topics/siem

IT ExamAnswers. (2020). CCNA 3 v7.0 Curriculum: Module 7—WAN Concepts. Retrieved from: https://itexamanswers.net/ccna-3-v7-0-curriculum-module-7-wan-concepts.html

McCauley, G. (2020). Dynamic Multipoint VPN (DMVPN). Field Engineer. Retrieved from: https://www.fieldengineer.com/blogs/dynamic-multipoint-vpn

Metaswitch. (n.d.). What Is 5G New Radio Unlicensed (NR-U)? Retrieved from: https://www.metaswitch.com/knowledge-center/reference/what-is-5g-new-radio-unlicensed-nr-u

MyWorkDrive. (n.d.). Total Cost of Ownership. Retrieved from: https://www.myworkdrive.com/vpn-alternative/software-costs/#:~:text=A%20business%20of%201000%20employees%20can%20expect%20to,procurement%2C%20basic%20setup%2C%20and%20deployment.%20Ongoing%20VPN%20Maintenance

Network Encyclopedia. (n.d.). Channel Service Unit/Data Service Unit (CSU/DSU). Retrieved from: https://networkencyclopedia.com/channel-service-unit-data-service-unit-csu-dsu/

PureVPN. (n.d.). Difference Between PPTP vs L2TP Protocols. Retrieved from: https://www.purevpn.com/blog/difference-between-pptp-and-l2tp-protocols/

Rehman, J. (2018). The Advantages and Disadvantages of Wide Area Network (WAN). IT Release. Retrieved from: https://www.itrelease.com/2018/07/advantages-and-disadvantages-of-wide-area-network-wan/

Teppo, P., & Norrman, K. (2020). Security in 5G RAN and Core Deployments. Ericsson. Retrieved from: https://www.ericsson.com/en/reports-and-papers/white-papers/security-in-5g-ran-and-core-deployments

TP-Link. (n.d.). Configuring VPN. Retrieved from: https://www.tp-link.com/us/configuration-guides/configuration_guide_for_vpn/?configurationId=2981#_idTextAnchor003

TutorialsPoint. (n.d.). What Are Terrestrial Microwaves in Computer Networks? Retrieved from: https://www.tutorialspoint.com/what-are-terrestrial-microwaves-in-computer-networks

Wachtel, B. (n.d.). All You Wanted to Know About T1 But Were Afraid to Ask. Data Comm for Business. Retrieved from: https://www.dcbnet.com/notes/9611t1.html

Witte, B. (2020). The Basics of 5G's Modulation, OFDM. 5G Technology World. Retrieved from: https://www.5gtechnologyworld.com/the-basics-of-5gs-modulation-ofdm/

MINICASE: CORE Credit Union—Accommodating an Expanding WAN

CORE Credit Union is headquartered in Statesboro, Georgia. It currently has about $150 million in assets and serves a growing customer base of approximately 15,000 members. It has four locations: two in Statesboro (Market District and Main Street); one in Brooklet, GA, a small town approximately 10 miles east of Statesboro; and one in the Savannah, GA, historic district as the result of a merger with Savannah Federal Credit Union. Its Market District Branch location (see Figure 8-29) serves as the credit union's headquarters. The Savannah office is approximately 55 miles from Statesboro. CORE will add a second location in the Savannah metropolitan area by the end of 2023 as the result of a merger with the Memorial Health Credit Union.

Like other banking institutions, CORE offers its members a wide range of deposit, checking, and lending products at its locations and online. Its online services are very popular. Its online banking system is feature rich, and its recently revamped website attracts more than 20,000 unique visits each month. In addition to the online banking system, CORE's members have access to the following:

- Electronic deposit capture (eliminates the need to present a physical check)
- ACH origination services (for transferring money)
- Online loan initiation (for completing loan applications)
- Shared branching (enables members of other credit unions to access their accounts through CORE's system)
- A nationwide ATM network (for accessing cash)
- Online membership (enables individuals to become members of the credit union without having to go to a branch office)

Several of these capabilities are facilitated by cloud infrastructure and cloud services. For example, CORE's website is hosted by a cloud services provider that also shares in website maintenance activities and the provision of web analytics.

The COVID-19 pandemic forced CORE to restrict access to tellers and loan officers at its branches for an extended period of time. Some branch locations temporarily closed in response to Covid infections of employees and quarantine requirements. As a result of the disruption to normal operations, CORE ramped up its use of electronic workflow and electronic signature systems that enabled required lending and banking documents to be electronically routed to employees and members for digital signatures. The expansion of the workflow and e-signa-

Figure 8-29: CORE Credit Union locations in 2023.

ture systems enabled the credit union to do what needed to be done for its members without requiring them to come to one of the branches. In short, the credit union and its members quickly got comfortable with greater volumes of electronic communications as a substitute for face-to-face interactions.

The credit union also pivoted to on-demand videoconferencing capabilities. This enabled employees to replace face-to-face interactions with members (and one another) with real-time screen-to-screen interactions. The credit union values being both a high-tech and high-touch (personal service oriented) institution, and the expanded videoconferencing capabilities enabled it to continue to do so during the pandemic.

Credit union management also ramped up videoconferencing to coordinate operations at the various branches. Being able to see and hear one another and work out management or member services issues in real time was especially important during the pandemic, but it has become part of CORE's standard operating procedures.

These capabilities ease the credit union's ability to add new locations to its WAN without having to bulk up its management staff. It also enables more complicated loans, like a mortgage, to be originated at any location with on-screen guidance from CORE's mortgage expert.

Federal and state regulations are obsessive about the security of bank and credit union computing systems. Data in transit must be encrypted. ATM transactions must use triple-DES or AES. Noncompliance with these regulations is not an option. Federal, state, and independent audits (exams) include annual reviews of the security provisions of contracts with all third-party service providers. And there are hard minimum requirements that each contract must include.

To protect the security of its systems, firewalls at each location are continuously monitored by a third-party business partner. An intrusion prevention system (IPS) is in place, and its attack signatures database is updated at least once daily to ensure that new tactics used by attackers are unlikely to result in network breaches. Network penetration tests are performed at regular intervals, and their results are used to shore up any weak points that are identified. Employees and managers are trained and regularly tested on phishing schemes, and cybersecurity educational materials are included on the credit union's website to help its members.

Credit union transactions are backed up to two different internal locations. They are also continuously backed up to a third-party data center several hundred miles away. This is done to protect against data loss and to ensure business continuity in the event of a disaster. Disaster tests (using simulated disasters) are conducted at regular intervals to ensure that managers and employees correctly implement required disaster recovery steps.

Recent federal, state, and independent auditors have focused more attention on the adequacy of CORE's WAN and its security. With growing use of electronic workflow, e-signature, and videoconferencing systems that span locations, auditors have begun to ask about CORE's plans to ensure continued operations in the event of link or hardware (e.g., router) failures at its different locations.

CORE values the input it receives from auditors, particularly about protecting the local networks at its branches and its WAN. With new locations to be added to the WAN by the end of 2023, the credit union is interested in identifying appropriate options for expanding electronic communications among its locations and with its members in ways that preserve its high-tech, high-touch interests while also preserving the privacy and security of its network.

Minicase Activities and Questions:

1. Use Visio or another network diagramming tool to create diagrams of CORE's current five-location WAN. Create logical diagrams for the following:
   - Ring topology
   - Hub-and-spoke topology (with the Market District branch [see Figure 8-29] as the hub)
   - Full mesh topology
   - PSN carrier network with PADs at each CORE Credit Union location
2. Provide total monthly cost estimates for each of the network options specified in Item 1 for each of the following types of connections:
   - T-3 lines
   - OC-3 lines
   - 10GbE
3. The federal, state, and independent auditors are primarily concerned with ensuring that the credit union has at least two distinct paths between each pair of locations. The current WAN already provides a path between each location. Given your calculations for Item 2, identify the network architecture (topology) you would recommend to CORE as a backup for its current WAN. Provide justification for your recommended backup
4. During the pandemic, remote access VPNs enabled CORE managers and some employees to work remotely from home. At one point, approximately 20 of the credit union's 40 employees were using VPNs to work remotely. The credit union's IT Services department thinks that CORE should consider investing in VPN routers at its branches with permanent virtual circuits between locations; a VPN hub gateway would be installed at its Main Street Branch location to serve the intranet and remote access VPNs. Develop a list of pros and cons for this possibility. Make and justify a recommendation for this proposed option.

5. A private radio network (WWAN) has been proposed as a WAN alternative for CORE. This could be a RAN sharing or virtual network slice arrangement with an MNO (probably Verizon). Develop a list of pros and cons for this alternative. Make and justify a recommendation for this proposed option.

6. With appropriate physical or virtual backup circuits in place, should CORE consider adopting SD-WAN? Develop a list of pros and cons for this possibility. Make and justify a recommendation for SD-WAN adoption.

Chapter 9

Enterprise Networks and the Internet of Things

LEARNING OBJECTIVES

After reading and studying this chapter, you should be able to:

- Briefly describe the Internet of Things (IoT) and its effects on businesses and enterprise networks.
- Identify examples of business processes and industries benefitting from IoT deployments.
- Briefly describe the IIoT, Industry 4.0, Warehouse 4.0, and the IoT's role in digital business and transformation.
- Describe the characteristics of IoT, IIoT, and M2M architectures and platforms.
- Briefly describe IoT sensors, actuators, and gateways.
- Identify communication/networking technologies and protocols used in IoT networks.
- Briefly describe edge computing and its roles in IoT networks.
- Briefly describe activities performed at the data accumulation, data aggregation, application, and collaboration and processes layers of the IoT reference model.
- Briefly explain why IoT devices, communication channels, and applications are common attack targets and how they may be exploited.
- Briefly describe how IoT devices, communication channels, and cloud services are typically secured and how SD-WAN can be used to protect IoT data and applications.

9.0 INTRODUCTION: Networks and the IoT

The **Internet of Things (IoT)** refers to the collective network of connected devices and technologies that facilitate device-to-cloud or device-to-device communication. The devices (things) are physical objects with embedded sensors, processing ability, software, and other technologies that enable them to connect and exchange data with other devices and systems via the Internet or other networks.

The IoT is one of the most important and disruptive technologies of the twenty-first century. It enables everyday objects to connect to the Internet and provides communication between them so they can indicate their status and changes in their surroundings. Smart appliances, smart homes, smart hospitals, and smart cities are IoT manifestations.

Through low-cost sensors and computing technologies, the IoT enables physical things to collect and share data with minimal human intervention. Cloud-based applications enable IoT devices to be monitored, and adjusted, with or without the intervention of mobile device users or digital system administrators. Device-to-cloud and device-to-device data transfers can be logged and analyzed by advanced analytics or Big Data processing platforms. IoT data is increasingly being used to train AI and machine learning algorithms and create autonomous processes and systems.

Businesses have not overlooked the IoT's potential as a game changer, and they are making changes to their networks to accommodate IoT connections and data transfers. IoT devices are used in all types of industries and consumer markets. In 2020, consumers accounted for about 60% of all IoT connections, and this percentage is expected to remain relatively stable through 2030. By then, consumers are expected to have about 17 billion IoT devices, and about 5 billion of those devices are expected to be in China.

Multiple industries already have more than 100 million connected IoT devices, including electrical utilities, water and waste management firms, retail and wholesale companies, transportation and warehouse companies, and government agencies. By 2030, several IoT application areas are expected to have more than a billion IoT-connected devices, including IT infrastructure, smart grid, asset monitoring/tracking, and autonomous vehicles (AVs). The total number of IoT devices across all industries in 2030 is expected to exceed 8 billion.

Statistica is one of the most respected sources that monitors IoT growth. Figure 9-1 summarizes the installed base of IoT devices from 2019 until now and identifies IoT's expected growth through 2030.

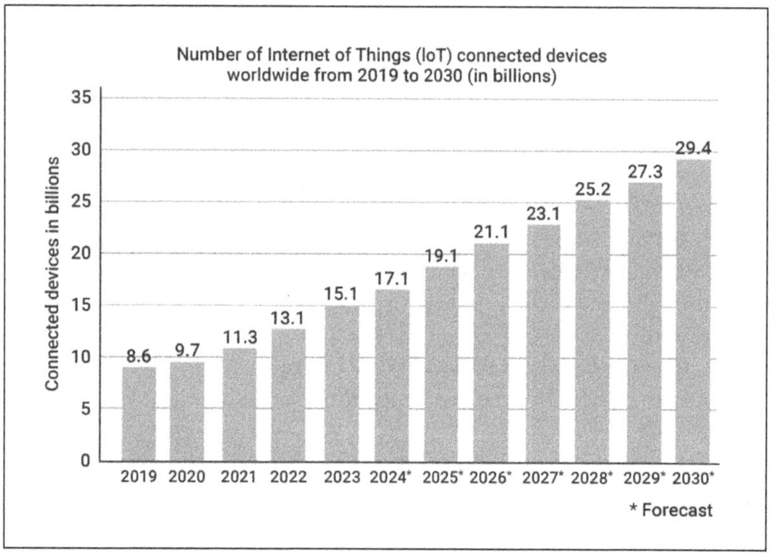

Figure 9-1: Real and anticipated IoT device connection growth from 2019 to 2030. Source: Statistica 2022

As Figure 9-1 illustrates, there are already many more IoT devices than assignable IPv4 addresses (which top out slightly above four billion). The use of private IPv4 addresses in residential Wi-Fi networks is insufficient to keep up; IoT growth is contributing to IPv6's growing prevalence and will continue to do so.

By 2025, more than 150,000 new devices are expected to connect to the IoT each minute—about 2500 per second. An increasing number of IoT devices are using cellular connections instead of Wi-Fi or Ethernet, and the number of cellular IoT connections is expected to surpass 3.5 billion by the end of 2023.

By 2030, experts expect IoT devices to generate more than 73 zettabytes of data. That is more than a 400% increase over the volume generated in 2019. Cloud storage enables IoT data to be inexpensively stored, accessed, and used for AI, machine learning, and other Big Data applications. IoT data is contributing to Big Data's continuous expansion and is fueling expanded use of AI.

The IoT concept has been around for a long time, but advances in several areas are facilitating IoT adoption and use:

- Low-cost and energy-efficient (low-power) sensor technologies.
- IoT-oriented network protocols that enable device-to-cloud or device-to-device data transfers.
- IoT-friendly networks. A low-power wide area network (LPWAN) is a wireless WAN that supports long-range, low bit rate communications between IoT devices, such as

battery-operated sensors. For various reasons, SD-WANs are also considered IoT-friendly.

- Cloud computing platforms that provide processing and storage infrastructure needed for IoT scalability and management.
- Analytics that enable insights into IoT data faster and more easily.
- Conversational AI and natural-language processing (NLP) that facilitate human-to-device communications. Alexa, Cortana, and Siri are examples of consumer-oriented personal digital assistants with conversational AI capabilities.
- Machine learning (ML) and AI algorithms that enable autonomous, self-managing, and ever smarter systems and processes.

As you make your way through this chapter, you will gain a better understanding of these developments and their importance. You also will gain a better understanding of the IoT's potential to benefit businesses and everyday life and how it is reshaping networks and communications.

This chapter primarily focuses on how the IoT is transforming businesses and enterprise networks, but its potential effects in other areas, including healthcare, transportation, and energy management, have the potential to be more far reaching.

Business networks and businesses themselves are evolving to accommodate the increasing prevalence of IoT applications, and the transformative effects are ongoing. This chapter will provide you with a better understanding of how IoT systems work and the technologies and platforms that support them. You will be introduced to some of the more important IoT communication protocols used in enterprise networks and some of the approaches used to address IoT security.

Hopefully, you may also gain some insights into why an understanding of distributed applications, cloud infrastructure, TCP/IP protocols, Wi-Fi networks, business WANs, and radio access networks (RANs) is needed to understand the IoT. As you read this chapter, you are likely to observe how many of the concepts discussed in previous chapters coalesce in the IoT.

9.1 THE IoT AND BUSINESSES

Many businesses have deployed IoT devices and systems to enhance existing processes, including manufacturing, supply chains, asset management, and employee health and safety (see Table 9-1). The IoT is also being used to improve warehouse and inventory management, IT and network management and security, customer service, and financial services. Often, existing business processes can be improved by the deployment of IoT devices without having to reengineer the processes.

Table 9-1: Examples of IoT business process enhancements.

IoT Improvement Target	Examples
Manufacturing processes	IoT sensors/devices can be deployed to monitor and analyze manufacturing equipment to ensure that it operates within required tolerances. Materials/products flowing through a manufacturing process can be monitored in real time to identify and address quality defects.
Supply chain coordination	The IoT enables materials/products in transit to be tracked by location and quality status. IoT-enabled fleet monitoring can increase efficiency and safety by dynamically rerouting vehicles.
Asset management	The health of IoT-equipped remote machines can be monitored, and changes can trigger preventive maintenance service calls.
Employee safety and health	IoT wearables and sensors can improve the safety and health of employees working in hazardous environments, such as mines, oil and gas fields, and chemical and power plants. Employees can be quickly notified of dangerous conditions or events/accidents that endanger them.

Table 9-2: Example of industries benefiting from IoT deployment.

Industry	IoT Benefits
Manufacturing	Manufacturers are using the IoT for production-line monitoring and proactive maintenance on equipment. IoT sensors can detect impending equipment failures that can compromise production output and alert production managers so that the equipment can be checked or removed from production for repair. This results in reduced operating costs and improved production equipment uptime and performance.
Automotive	The automotive industry is realizing significant benefits from IoT applications. In addition to using the IoT in vehicle production lines, sensors in existing vehicles can alert drivers to failures and provide failure details and recommendations. Basically, IoT applications are helping manufacturers, dealers, and owners to keep vehicles running and safe.
Transportation and Logistics	Transportation and logistical companies are benefiting from a variety of IoT applications. For example, IoT sensor data is being used to manage fleets of trucks, trains, and ships that carry products. Vehicles on the road are being rerouted based on weather conditions or redeployed to address vehicle or driver availability issues. Inventory carried in vehicles is being monitored by IoT sensors to track cargo compartment temperatures and humidity. This is especially important in vehicles that carry food, beverage items, flowers, pharmaceuticals, and other temperature-sensitive inventory whose quality is threatened by temperature or humidity levels outside specific ranges.
Retail	IoT applications enable retail companies to manage inventory, optimize supply chains, reduce operating expense, and improve customer experience. For example, "smart shelves" fitted with weight and other IoT sensors are being used to monitor inventory levels and trigger alerts when inventories are getting low. In-store beacons are being used by some retailers to push targeted offers and promotions to customers' smartphones based on their location in the store. This can create an engaging, but somewhat "creepy," customer experience.
Healthcare	IoT asset monitoring is an example of one of the many benefits that IoT applications are providing to healthcare firms. For example, in hospitals, IoT technologies are being used to inform nurses, orderlies, and doctors of the locations of available patient-assistance assets, such as wheelchairs. Numerous hospital assets can be similarly tracked to ensure proper usage and for financial accounting of the physical assets assigned to each department.

Several industries are especially well positioned to reap benefits from IoT advancements, including manufacturing, the automotive industry, transportation and logistics, retail, and healthcare. Some of the reasons why are identified in Table 9-2.

The IoT is also producing new business models and services. For example, the ability of cloud services to remotely monitor machines has enabled product-as-a-service business models, where customers pay to use a product instead of buying it.

For example, "connected cars" change the relationships between manufacturers, dealers, and car owners in the automobile industry. Traditionally, manufacturers and dealers have had an arms-length relationship with individual car buyers; now they can have a continuous relationship. Many car owners use connected car smartphone apps to start and preheat (or air condition) their cars, and in the future, vehicles may schedule their own service appointments. Connected cars also enable manufacturers to continuously upgrade their cars with new software that helps to prolong the quality, performance, and value of their products. Some manufacturers are exploring "transportation-as-a-service" usage fees for their vehicles to replace the need to buy or lease a car.

Businesses aren't the only beneficiaries of IoT advancements. In the public sector and other service-related environments, a wide range of advantages is being provided by the IoT. Government-owned utilities, for example, are using IoT-based applications in traffic control devices (e.g., stoplights) and to notify users of interruptions or outages for power, water, natural gas, or sewer services, and to quickly deploy resources to recover from them. Collectively, such applications improve efficiencies and help control/reduce expenses; hence, similar motivations drive both business and public sector IoT adoption.

Machine-to-machine (M2M) communication is being used in some industries to achieve wireless automation and control. M2M is a type of device-to-device communication. Traditionally, M2M applications have often required proprietary hardware, and devices used non-IP protocols to communicate. However, M2M communication between IoT devices often involves TCP/IP protocols, especially when cloud storage is used to log device-to-device interactions and to enable their analysis for actionable patterns. As a result, today, M2M is usually considered a subset of the IoT. When M2M communication is combined with cloud infrastructure, analytics, and ML, new levels of automation are enabled through what is often called the *Industrial IoT (IIoT)* or *Industry 4.0*.

9.1.1 The Industrial IoT

The **Industrial Internet of Things (IIoT)** refers to interconnected sensors, devices, networking infrastructure, and applications that work together to monitor, collect, and analyze data from industrial operations. An IIoT ecosystem includes connected IoT components (devices) that can sense, generate, communicate, and store data about themselves and their physical environments; networking/communications infrastructure; storage and preparation of IoT device data; analytics and applications that generate business information from IIoT data; and people whose decisions are informed by analyzed IIoT data.

Monitoring and analyzing IIoT data increases the visibility of industrial operations. It enhances troubleshooting and maintenance of industrial equipment and can increase efficiencies, reduce costs, improve safety, and bolster security. Applying advanced analytics to IIoT data positions manufacturers to do the following:

- Increase the productivity, uptime, and overall effectiveness of manufacturing equipment and facilities
- Improve the efficiencies of manufacturing processes and create end-to-end operational visibility
- Improve product quality
- Reduce operating costs
- Optimize production scheduling
- Accelerate innovation

According to the McKinsey Global Institute, given their current rate of adoption, IoT applications in manufacturing facilities have the potential to create as much as $3.7 trillion in value per year by 2025.

SCADA and the IIoT

In many manufacturing facilities, IIoT networks include traditional manufacturing systems such as SCADA. This is reflected in Figure 9-2.

Supervisory control and data acquisition (SCADA) is best described as a category of software applications for controlling industrial processes that uses real-time data to control industrial equipment and conditions. Traditionally, SCADA has been one of the most widely used industrial control systems. They have been in use since the 1960s, have demonstrated sufficient flexibility to manage most types of industrial processes, and have evolved in response to technological advances, including the Internet and cloud computing.

Like, IIoT systems and applications, SCADA systems include sensors and actuators. Sensors monitor/measure the status of industrial machines and devices, and actuators act like a switch, dial, or control valve that controls the machine or device. SCADA control units monitor and control them.

SCADA systems have two types of controllers: remote terminal units and programmable logic controllers. *Remote terminal units (RTUs)* interface with sensors to collect telemetry data, which

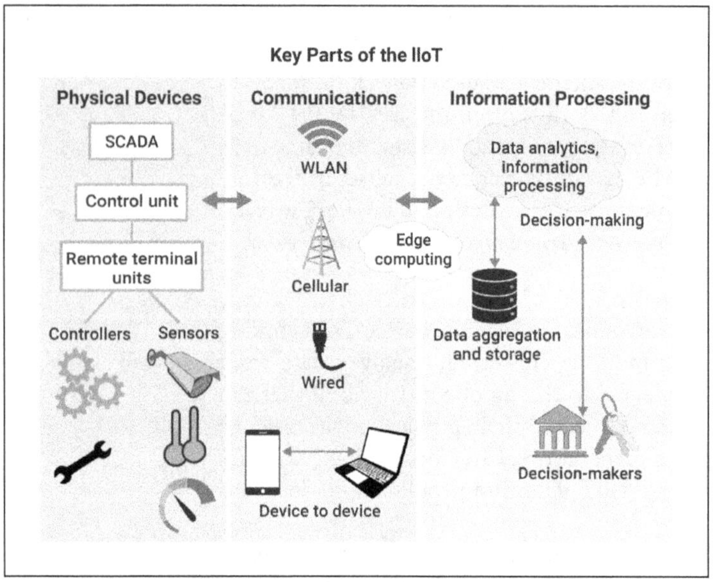

Figure 9-2: Key components in IIoT systems and applications.

is forwarded to the primary SCADA system for further action. *Programmable logic controllers (PLCs)* interface with actuators and are used to adjust/control industrial equipment and processes. Their programming logic reflects preestablished rules and standards for the processes. SCADA systems also include *supervisory computers* that oversee all industrial processes.

Although SCADA and the IIoT are considered to be similar and overlapping, there are some important differences. For example, SCADA vendors often pitch their products as more complete, monolithic systems that feature tight integration across levels and devices. In contrast, IIoT vendors focus their pitches on greater interoperability and more options for deploying devices and systems. Other differences are identified in Table 9-3.

Table 9-3: Some important differences between SCADA and the IIoT.

	SCADA	IIoT
Interoperability	Often uses proprietary communication protocols for controller components	Usually relies on TCP/IP protocols for interoperability
Sensors and Actuators	Typically uses wired connections to connect to controllers	Uses wireless connections more commonly than wired connections to controllers
Data Collection	Usually collected on premises directly from controllers	May be collected in cloud or on premises
Integration	Proprietary vendor lock-in may limit ability to integrate with devices or software from other vendors	Adherence to open standards facilitates integration of device and software from different vendors

Historical acceptance of SCADA systems has opened the door to the IIoT in many industries. Manufacturers who have experienced success or achieved comfort levels with SCADA are often more receptive to adopting and investing in IIoT systems and applications. However, some view the IIoT as a supplement to their SCADA systems and question what value it adds.

Like all IoT systems and applications, security is an important issue for SCADA and IIoT systems. All connected devices increase an IIoT network's attack surface, but attacks on operational devices that can disrupt industrial processes are especially concerning. Security is especially important in organizations that integrate SCADA and IIoT systems. SCADA systems are widely recognized as having exploitable security vulnerabilities, and their PLCs are a special focus of concern. If attackers succeed in breaching them, PLCs may be altered to shut down equipment or entire industrial processes. PLC programming can also be stolen and used to reverse engineer industrial processes.

Device-to-Device Communication

Broadly speaking, **machine-to-machine (M2M) communication** refers to any technology that enables networked devices to exchange information and perform actions without the manual assistance of humans. One of the primary objectives of M2M communication is to access sensor data and transmit it to a network. M2M communication allows devices and machines to pass small amounts of data or information directly to other devices and machines without having to use the Internet.

When machines communicate, they use a language known as *telemetry*. **Telemetry** involves the collection of measurements and other data at remote locations and their automatic transmission (typically wirelessly) to an IT system at a different location for monitoring and analysis.

Telemetry systems were once the province of scientists, government agencies, and other organizations that applied them in a variety of ways, including aerospace, agriculture, public utilities, and wildlife science. For example, wildlife scientists use telemetry to track the movements and habits of wild animals that have been tagged with radio transmitters.

Sensors in older telemetry systems were highly specialized and typically required strong power sources to transmit data. Today, most IoT sensors require low power and use batteries to prolong their useful life. And today's remote sensors have increased measurement sensitivity and reliability.

In industrial contexts, M2M communication can occur among machines, tools, sensors, and other devices; it involves direct data transfers and communication transactions between two devices. For example, a revolutions per minute (RPM) sensor measuring the spindle speed of a milling device that sends data to an upstream or downstream device in the manufacturing process so that it can make needed adjustments in its speed is using M2M communication.

Traditionally, centralized network architectures have been used in manufacturing settings to ensure that data that devices on the shop floor generate is channeled to the system (e.g., SCADA) that controls the entire manufacturing process. Now, wireless connectivity and wireless sensors that can send data wherever it is needed have reduced the importance of traditional central control systems. Work areas in factories may have decentralized, but preorchestrated, M2M communication.

Today, several advancements in industrial robotics, including robotic vision systems and ML, are enabling machines to autonomously make decisions about their next action. The action must conform to their installed programming rules, but these rules often include sufficient flexibility to accommodate communications from other devices. For example, a machine can be programmed to shift to a pause mode after completing an action to reduce energy use and check for M2M messages from other devices.

M2M communication is almost always wireless and typically involves specialized protocols. Several are identified and briefly described later in the chapter.

IIoT Application Areas Beyond Manufacturing

The IIoT is often considered a subset of the IoT in industrial sectors, but, as Figure 9-3 illustrates, manufacturing is just one of the IIoT application areas that are commonly identified. Collectively, these examples illustrate how the IoT can be used to achieve new levels of efficiency, innovation, cost savings, and digital connectedness:

- Smart cities
- Smart power grids
- Smart manufacturing
- Smart supply chains
- Smart logistics
- Smart warehouses
- Smart vehicles

Several important observations can be made about IIoT networks and application areas. First, IIoT networks need to be highly (ideally, continuously) available and reliable. Network reliability and sufficient bandwidth are needed to ensure that time-sensitive data can be transmitted without delay to the cloud and/or data centers.

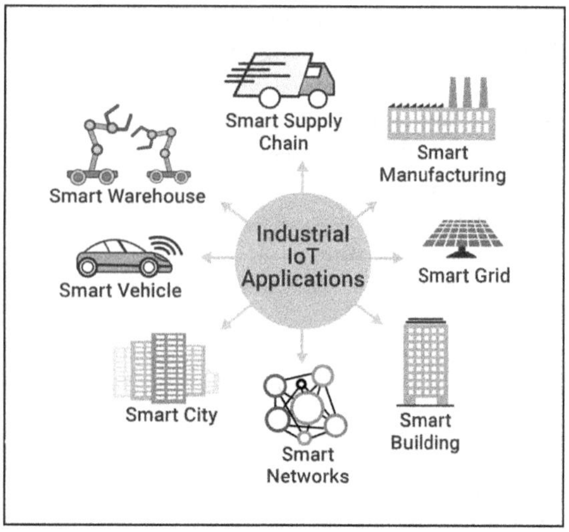

Figure 9-3: Examples of IIoT applications.

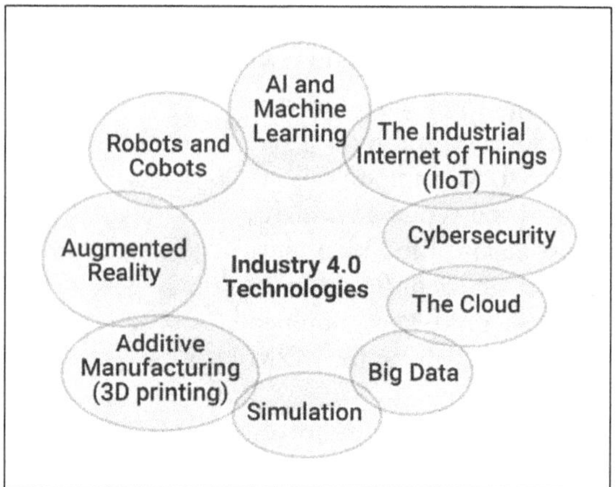

Figure 9-4: Some of the technologies and applications encompassed by Industry 4.0.

Second, IIoT device deployment and maintenance should be relatively effortless. Network controllers should automate and facilitate, not constrain, device deployment and maintenance. They should ensure the consistency of configurations and timely firmware updates even when IIoT devices are numerous and spread across a large geographical area. Controllers should also ensure that device performance conforms to expectations and should issue alerts when it does not.

Third, centralized visibility of device connectivity is important. This is needed to ensure that IIoT networks are performing correctly and to facilitate troubleshooting. Continuous tracking and monitoring of IIoT devices and assets helps ensure their availability and efficient performance. Such visibility facilitates the quick identification and resolution of performance problems and safety issues. For example, monitoring whether equipment is running too hot or if a control valve is not fully closed can enable corrective action before irreparable harm is done.

Fourth, businesses and other organizations are leveraging ML to analyze IIoT data. AI is being used to identify performance anomalies, send alerts to human operators, and, increasingly, to trigger proactive countermeasures or automated fixes. AI and ML are also important parts of Industry 4.0.

9.1.2 Industry 4.0

Industry 4.0 refers to the integration of intelligent digital technologies into manufacturing and industrial processes. These technologies include, but are not limited to, IIoT networks, AI, Big Data, robotics, and additive manufacturing (see Figure 9-4). Industry 4.0 is a new phase in the Industrial Revolution that facilitates smart manufacturing and the creation of intelligent factories focused on enhanced productivity, efficiency, flexibility, customization, and intelligent decision-making in manufacturing and supply chain operations.

Industry 4.0 assumes the presence of industrial robots and additive manufacturing (3D printing). It also assumes that Big Data and Big Data processing platforms are being used to identify patterns and correlations overlooked or missed in the past that may provide actionable insights for improving industrial processes and the products produced. And AI and ML are contributing to the development of autonomous, self-directing, self-healing industrial processes.

As you can see, the IIoT is one of many moving parts of Industry 4.0. IIoT networks are also increasingly prevalent in warehouses and supply chains, and they are an important aspect of Warehouse 4.0. Warehouse 4.0 is generally considered to be an important part of the supply chain aspect of Industry 4.0.

Warehouse 4.0

Warehouse 4.0 (W4.0) leverages the IoT, Big Data and data science, augmented reality, wearables, computer vision, artificial intelligence, sensors, collaborative robots (cobots), robots, and other technologies that enable warehouses to be "smart" components of integrated supply chains. An *integrated supply chain* is a holistic collection of processes (including raw materials procurement, production, quality control, packaging, and distribution) under the control of a single company or collection of partners. Integrated supply chains and W4.0 enable Industry 4.0 manufacturing facilities to achieve performance levels beyond what they can reach on their own.

W4.0 strives to facilitate materials management in warehouses, drive efficiencies, reduce costs, and improve overall warehouse management. As with Industry 4.0, multiple rapidly evolving and converging technologies are involved:

- Sensors that capture data about materials/products, storage locations, and warehouse processes. Temperature sensors and accelerometers are examples.
- Wireless communication technologies that transfer real-time data to enable agility and rapid adaptation to changes.
- Beacons (transmitters) placed on objects so they can be tracked. They usually transmit radio signals and are similar to beacon wearables used to track humans.
- RFID technologies. RFID tags affixed to products/materials can hold more data than barcodes and some QR codes. They are primarily used for inventory management and product location tracking. A typical reader can simultaneously scan up to 200 RFID tags.
- Integrated warehouse management platforms that process/analyze large volumes of data for real-time control, performance predictions, and informed decision-making.
- Autonomous guided vehicles (AGVs) for material handling and cargo transport. They may supplement or replace forklifts and can reduce material handling/transport time and cost. They also reduce risks associated with human effort in goods movement.
- Drones are increasingly being used in warehouses for safe and easy access to remote, hard-to-reach locations in the warehouse. To date, they primarily have been used for inventory tracking and are usually faster and more accurate than manual practices. They are typically equipped with cameras, sensors, RFID technology, or barcode scanners and are being used to locate items and perform inventory counts.
- Robots and cobots are automating warehouse "dirty work" such as unergonomic, heavy, repetitive, or dangerous material handling tasks. Cobots (collaborative robots) work collaboratively with employees and help them perform warehouse tasks such as lifting and moving (see Figure 9-5).
- Wearables, such as smart glasses, are being used to automate manual tasks and streamline workflows, such as receiving, putaway (placing goods in designated locations), and order picking. They are also being used for employee training and safety.

Collectively, these technologies reduce the costs of warehouse operations, increase inventory accuracy, decrease picking errors, improve information flows, and increase warehouse efficiency. Additional contributions of IoT systems and applications in warehouses are identified in Table 9-4.

It is not difficult to envision how the combination of Industry 4.0, Warehouse 4.0, and integrated supply chains can benefit businesses in the years ahead.

Figure 9-5: An example of robots and AVGs in a warehouse. Source: imagin-ima/iStock/ Stock photo ID:1313321187

Table 9-4: Examples of IoT-enabled improvement in warehouses.

Improvement Target	How IoT Contributes
Asset Tracking	IoT systems and applications are being used in warehouses to provide real-time data/information about materials locations, packing, and shipping.
Asset Management	IoT shelf sensors enable warehouses to better manage inventory. Out of stock notifications (from empty shelves) can trigger replenishment activities and can contribute to optimizing facility utilization. IoT technologies also enable the collection of asset location and condition data.
Inventory Optimization	IoT systems and applications are being used in warehouses to provide detailed data and analytics for planning and resource management. They help businesses forecast what is required to optimize inventory levels and warehouse space usage.
Predictive Maintenance	IoT sensors are being used to monitor warehouse equipment, machines, and their working condition. When sensor data is combined with ML algorithms, breakdowns of forklifts and other material handling equipment may be prevented. Maintenance costs and equipment downtime can be reduced.
Automation	IoT systems and applications can verify shipping and service tracking. This facilitates the monitoring of products and their movements within warehouses and can translate into significant labor savings.

9.1.3 Vehicle-to-Vehicle Communication

Vehicle-to-vehicle (V2V) communication is often described as an articulation of M2M communication that reflects the intersection of the IoT and *intelligent transportation system (ITS)* initiatives. ITS is a diverse and expanding subject area that overlaps with smart logistics, smart fleet management, connected cars, and smart cities.

Many businesses and industries have a keen interest in driverless (autonomous) vehicles, and V2V communication has a crucial role in making driverless vehicles a reality.

Vehicle-to-vehicle (V2V) communication enables vehicles to wirelessly exchange information about their speed, location, and direction. V2V technologies allow vehicles to broadcast and receive omnidirectional messages (up to 10 or more times per second), creating a 360-degree awareness of other vehicles in their proximities. This is illustrated in Figure 9-6.

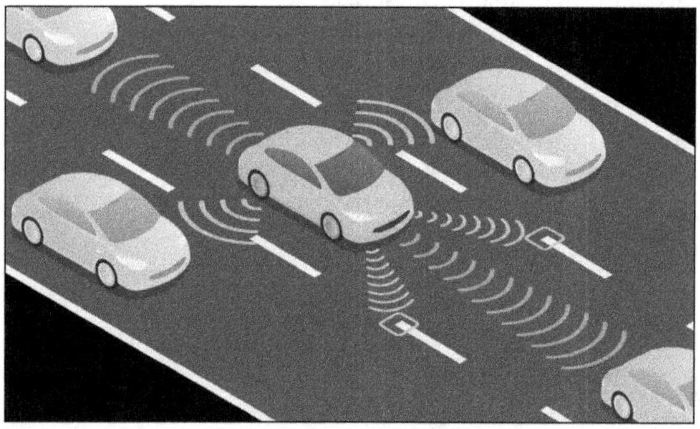

Figure 9-6: Very high level depiction of V2V communication.

Source: metamorks/istock/Stock illustration ID:685450008

Vehicles equipped with appropriate sensors, software, systems, and safety applications can use the messages from surrounding vehicles to determine potential collision threats as they develop in real time so that they can take actions needed to avoid crashes.

Some of the technologies needed for driverless vehicles are being used to warn/assist human drivers of real or potential on-the-road dangers. These technologies employ visual, tactile, audible, and electronic alerts (or combinations of alerts) to warn drivers of dangers (such as vehicles in blind spots or drifting into another lane). They are safety features that extend the radar and camera-based crash avoidance systems included in most newer vehicles.

Today, V2V communication is considered an important aspect of vehicle-to-everything (V2X) communication. **Vehicle-to-everything (V2X) communication** is communication between a vehicle and any entity that may affect or be affected by the vehicle. It includes *vehicle-to-infrastructure (V2I)*, *vehicle-to-network (V2N)*, and *vehicle-to-pedestrian (V2P)* communication (see Figure 9-7). V2X can also include *vehicle-to-device (V2D)* and/or *vehicle-to-barrier (V2B)* communication. The goals of V2X communication are road safety, traffic efficiency, and energy savings.

There is a lot involved with V2V and V2X communication and numerous issues and challenges that must be resolved to enable driverless trucks and vehicles to become standard features of smart supply chains, smart warehouses, and Industry 4.0. Several of these aspects are discussed in Appendix 9-1.

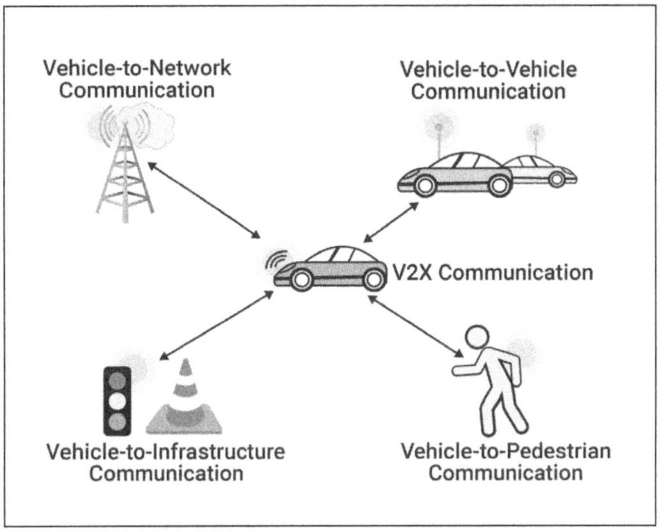

Figure 9-7: Some major aspects of V2X communications.

9.1.4 Other Applications

The breadth of the IoT's effect on business and society is not limited to the areas discussed in the previous sections. Certainly, the IoT is transforming factories, warehouses, and supply chains and is laying the foundation for driverless vehicles that communicate with one another, but it is also facilitating numerous types of innovation via digital twins and improvements in facility management and network operations. As a result, the IoT is contributing to the transition from *e-business* (using digital technologies to automate processes, improve efficiency, and reduce costs) to *digital business* (using technology to transform how businesses operate and deliver value to customers).

Digital Business Applications

Digital business is considered a step beyond e-business by enabling new business models and innovative applications of digital technologies. **Digital business** creates new business models and revenue streams from new combinations of people, technology, and business processes (see Figure 9-8). Like the IoT, digital business encompasses the convergence of digital and physical worlds, and digital businesses are leveraging technology to create new capabilities to support their core operations, new customer experiences, new levels of employee engagement, and new business models.

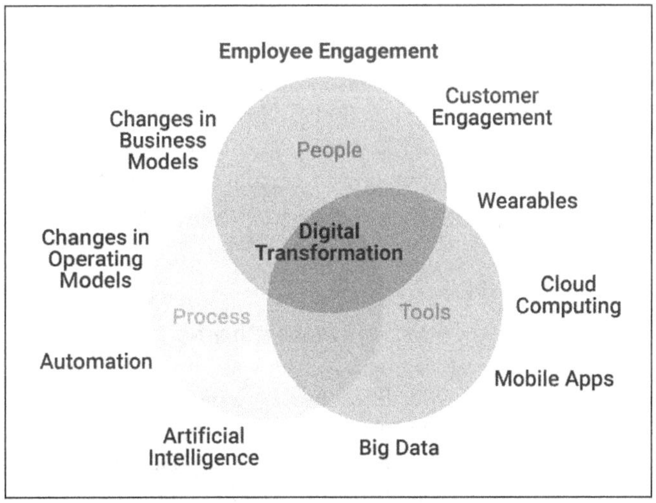

Figure 9-8: Aspects of digital transformation.

Digital business is considered an offshoot of **digital transformation**—the adoption and use of digital technologies to transform services or products and the replacement of manual processes with digital processes. It also involves replacing older digital technologies with newer ones. Basically, digital transformation is the integration of digital technology into all facets of business and fundamentally changing how businesses operate and deliver value to customers. It is associated with mind-sets and cultures that value continual experimentation with digital technologies and entrepreneurial thinking about how they can create new value streams. Digital twins are often identified as examples of how digital technologies can be used to improve products.

Digital Twins

A **digital twin** is a virtual representation of a physical object or process that serves as a real-time digital counterpart for the object or process. This often involves equipping objects with IoT sensors and

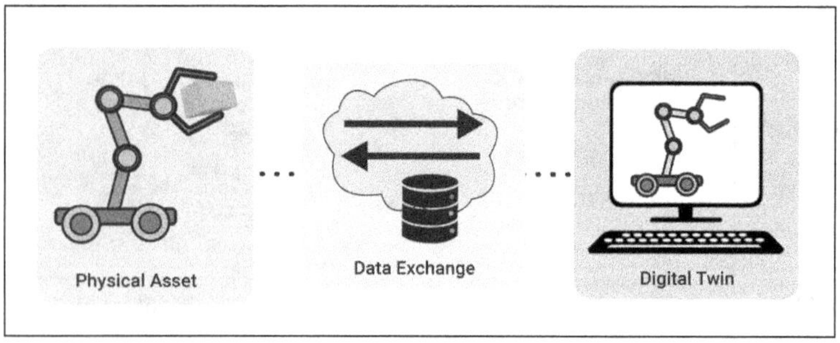

Figure 9-9: The digital twin concept. Source: elenabs/iStock/Stock illustration ID:1343498647

actuators and capturing data as they move or normally behave. Figure 9-9 provides a visual depiction of the digital twin concept.

Essentially, a digital twin is implemented as a software object (computer program) or model that mirrors the physical object or process. A digital twin can be used in simulations for learning/predicting how the object or process might perform in different conditions or to identify ways it might be improved.

For example, attaching sensors to a wind turbine to create a digital twin enables engineers to simulate the turbine's performance in various weather conditions, identify shortcomings in its current design, and generate the foundational data needed to create an improved turbine. Such examples demonstrate the potential of IoT sensors as innovation drivers.

Digital twins enable businesses to test or validate redesigned products or new products before they are manufactured. When virtual representations (twins) of a planned production process are created, engineers can identify potential bottlenecks or sources of process failures before actual production takes place.

Facility Management

IoT sensors and actuators are being deployed in business facilities to reduce electricity consumption and HVAC costs. There is little need to keep a room, hallway, factory, warehouse, or data center lit when humans are not present. Motion sensors can be used to instantly light such areas when humans enter unlit areas and to turn off the lights when human motion is no longer detected. IoT-enabled *building information management (BIM)* systems are increasingly being used to track and identify human movement patterns within facilities and to manage HVAC and energy consumption expenses.

Network Management

Some businesses are using IoT technologies to improve wireless communications within their facilities. For example, they are using IoT sensors to monitor and adjust Wi-Fi or RAN performance. These sensors monitor signal quality and identify needed *beamforming* adjustments to access point/base station antennas to steer radio signals in specific directions or when channel size adjustments would be beneficial. They can be used to identify and automatically adjust to signal interference. They are also being used to detect rogue access points and devices.

It is impossible to identify the full range of IoT applications in today's businesses. However, with a proven track record for producing beneficial results, it is easy to see why business adoption and use of IoT systems and applications is accelerating.

9.2 IoT ARCHITECTURES

The IoT and its applications have advanced rapidly, and it is widely recognized that while an IoT device operating by itself has limited value and usefulness, when it is interconnected with other IoT devices, its value and usefulness increases. This recognition spurred the development of IoT architectures to facilitate the creation of IoT device networks, such as the IIoT, and the realization of their potential benefits. Over time, IoT architectures have evolved to accommodate technological advancements and the development of supportive platforms for IoT networks.

9.2.1 IoT Architectures and Platforms

Online research on IoT architectures might cause you to think that there is little consensus about them. You would be likely to unearth a relatively simple, three-layer architecture, with perception, network, and application layers (see Figure 9-10), as well as IoT architectures with four, five, six, seven, or eight layers (see Figure 9-11).

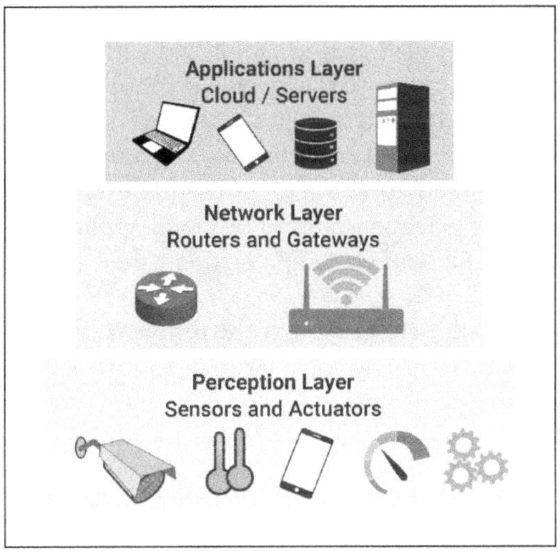

Figure 9-10: A conceptual depiction of an IoT three-layer architecture.

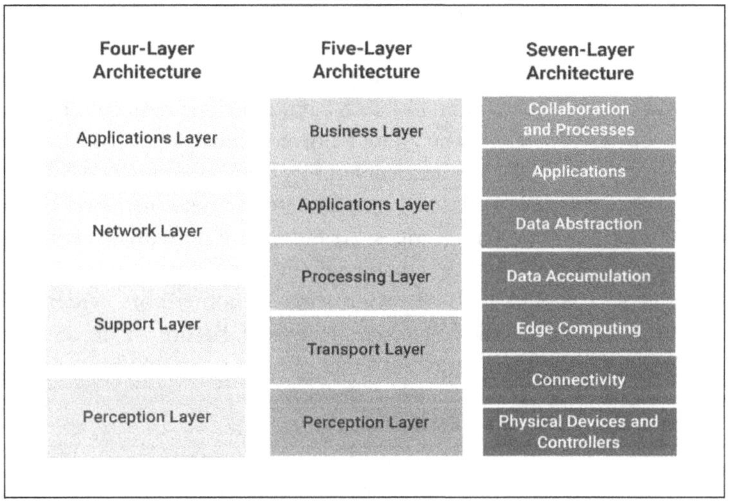

Figure 9-11: Four-, five-, and seven-layer IoT architectures.

Different numbers of layers across IoT architectures primarily result from evolving thinking about how to best structure the deployment of IoT network technologies to capitalize on their potential benefits. However, they are also the result of advances in the networking hardware and software in IoT networks, especially in IIoT networks, and the emergence of IoT platforms, which are software suites that facilitate IoT device management, connectivity and network management, data accumulation, data processing and analysis, application development, and IoT network security. IoT platforms are discussed more fully later in this chapter.

The seven-layer IoT architecture in Figure 9-11 is the IoT reference model developed by the IoT World Forum. The primary responsibilities/roles of each layer are briefly described in Table 9-5.

The seven-layer IoT reference model is used to structure the discussion of IoT technologies in section 9.3.

Table 9-5: Summary overview of the seven-layer IoT reference model.

Layer	Name	Primary Purpose
7	Collaboration and Processes	Involving people and business processes
6	Applications	Reporting, analytics, control
5	Data Abstraction	Data aggregation and access
4	Data Accumulation	Data storage
3	Edge Computing	Data element analysis and transformation
2	Connectivity	Communication and processing units
1	Physical Devices and Controllers	The "things" in the IoT

Before considering the IoT reference model layer-by-layer from the bottom up, it is valuable to point out some important patterns that should not be overlooked. First, like the OSI and TCP/IP models, supported IoT applications are located at/near the top, and much of the physical infrastructure is located at/closer to the bottom. Layer 2 in all models focuses on local network communications, and middle layers in all models involve communication and data transfers across networks.

Second, the IoT reference model's layers 3–6 are all data-related, and moving up layer-by-layer is consistent with the traditional data capture, storage, preparation/transformation, and data mining/analysis sequence associated with traditional business intelligence (BI) processes and applications. Today, like IoT data, most business data is accumulated and stored in cloud data centers, and this may facilitate being combined with IoT data and used in advanced analytics and ML applications.

Third, accelerating business adoption of IoT networks and applications is another example of how traditional enterprise network boundaries are being extended/blurred by cloud applications and services. As enterprise networks accommodate IoT networks and applications, they are also being transformed by them.

These patterns may become more evident when we take a closer look at the different layers of the IoT reference model. Before we do that, it is valuable to briefly consider IoT platforms, IIoT architectures and platforms, and M2M architectures and platforms.

IoT Platforms

An **IoT platform** is an on-premises software suite or a cloud that monitors, manages, and controls IoT networks and endpoints using applications. Usually, an IoT platform leverages scalable Web-based infrastructure to support both basic and advanced IoT systems and applications. It facilitates the development and support of business applications that provide digital interfaces to the physical world.

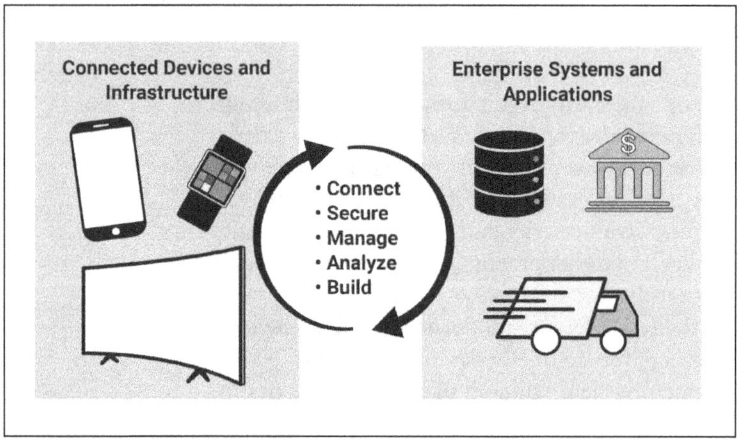

Figure 9-12: Common functions of IoT platforms.

IoT platforms facilitate device/endpoint management, connectivity and network management, data accumulation, data management, data processing and analysis, and application development (see Figure 9-12). Basically, IoT platforms include software that enables all layers of IoT architectures to work together to achieve business goals.

IoT platforms can also have important roles in securing IoT networks via access control, IoT system and application monitoring, event processing, component integration, and interface management. Additional description of IoT platforms is provided in Appendix 9-2.

9.2.2 IIoT Architecture and Platforms

Figure 9-13 is a depiction of the three-tier IIoT reference architecture developed by the Industrial IoT Consortium. At the edge tier, edge gateways collect data from the IoT devices in the proximity networks they serve. They pass device data to the platform tier for consolidation and processing, they also transfer control commands from the enterprise tier to the IoT devices in their proximity network.

The *platform tier* receives, processes, and forwards control commands from the enterprise tier to

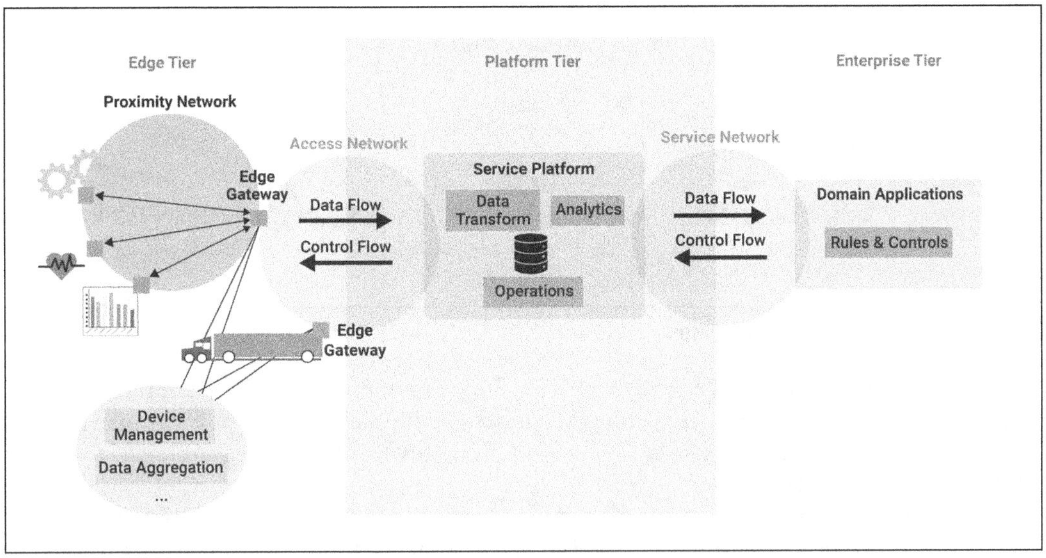

Figure 9-13: A depiction of the Industrial IoT Consortium's three-tier IIoT reference architecture.

the edge tier. It also consolidates, processes, and analyzes data flows from the edge tier, provides management functions for devices and other IIoT assets, and includes data query and analytics capabilities.

IIoT applications are located at *the enterprise tier*. This tier includes decision-support systems and application interfaces (such as dashboards) for end users and industrial operations specialists. It receives data from, and issues commands to, the edge and platform tiers.

One of the interesting things about this IIoT reference architecture is its platform layer. Generally speaking, an IIoT platform is a software suite or cloud service that facilitates connections between industrial processes and business information systems. It facilitates the development, monitoring, and maintenance of an organization's IIoT network and applications. Basically, IIoT platforms are tools for improving connectivity, control, and data analysis in industrial environments.

IIoT platforms include data accumulation, data management, data processing and analysis, and application development capabilities and facilitate the sharing of IIoT analytics with external stakeholders (e.g., business partners and regulators). They also enable IIoT data to be piped to BI dashboards, ERP systems, and other ESs used in manufacturing environments.

9.2.3 M2M Architectures and Platforms

Like IIoT architectures, M2M architectures usually have three tiers or domains: a device tier/domain, a network tier/domain, and an application tier/domain (see Figure 9-14). The device domain includes:

- M2M area networks that include the set of nearby IoT devices that engage in device-to-device communications
- M2M gateways that transfer device data to the network and application domains and transfer commands from M2M platforms and applications to devices in the M2M area networks

Several types of wireless communications and specialized protocols are used in the device domain. Some of them are discussed in further detail in Appendix 9-3.

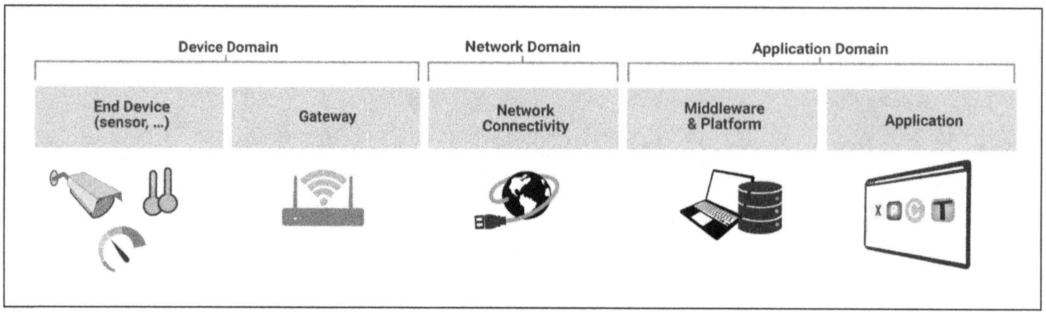

Figure 9-14: A three-tier M2M platform.

Like an IoT platform, an **M2M platform** is a software solution that sits between the device and application domains of M2M architectures and is designed to simplify and unify the management of M2M devices and applications. As Figure 9-14 illustrates, this typically is considered to be part of the application domain.

Typically, an M2M platform receives device data from M2M gateways and facilitates the accumulation, management, and formatting of data passed to applications and the processing of commands from applications to devices in M2M area networks. It also facilitates the management of device software (device driver) updates. Additional information about M2M platforms is provided in Appendix 9-3.

9.3 IoT TECHNOLOGIES

This section considers the technologies associated with each of the seven layers of the IoT reference model (see Table 9-5). It begins by looking at IoT components at the Physical Devices and Controllers layer.

9.3.1 Physical Devices and Controllers Layer

This layer consists of the "things" in the IoT. It includes physical devices and device controllers. It is a diverse array of things that vary in size, shape, and location. A thing can be as small as a silicon chip or the size of a large vehicle or piece of equipment. Things are endpoint devices that can generate data, send/receive information, perform analog-to-digital conversion, and act in response to commands received via the Internet or from other physical devices and controllers.

According to the Industrial IoT Consortium, IoT devices in IIoT networks should have several capabilities, including transducing, data, and interface capabilities. These capabilities are directly related to the device functionality and are illustrated in Figure 9-15.

An IoT device's transducing capabilities enable it to interact with the physical world. They provide connections between the device's digital and physical environments. A device's data capabilities (storage, processing, transfer) enable it to provide inputs into other IT systems, including IoT platforms and applications. Its interface capabilities enable it to interact with other IoT components (including networks and human users).

Supporting capabilities (see Figure 9-15) are indirectly involved in device functionality. They include monitoring, management, security, and orchestration capabilities. Latent capabilities are transducer, data, interface, or support capabilities that are not enabled and accessible outside the component. Some of them may provide "backdoors" to the other capabilities that can be enabled by trusted actors or exploited by bad actors with malicious intent, so awareness of the latent capabilities of components is an important part of IIoT network security management.

As noted in previous sections of the chapter, sensors and actuators are commonly identified as important technologies at the perception layer of IoT architectures.

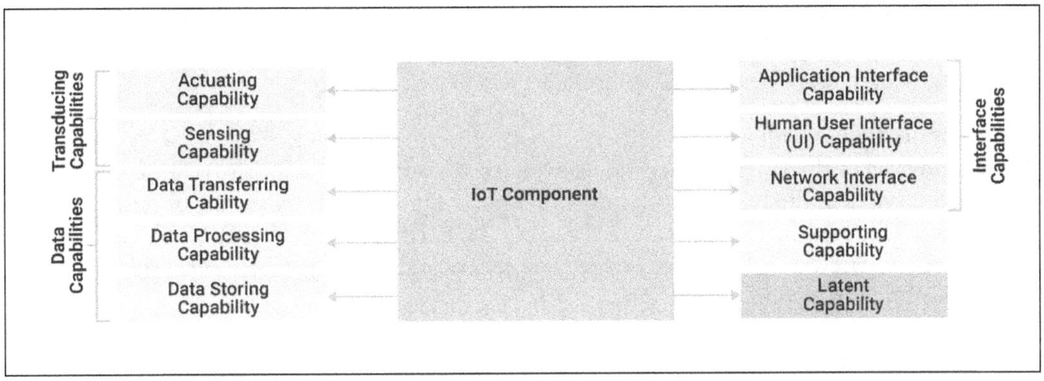

Figure 9-15: IoT component capabilities in IIoT networks.

In IoT contexts, a **sensor** is an electrical instrument that monitors and measures physical aspects of an environment. It provides an observation of an aspect of the physical world in the form of measurement data. The measurement data may be provided to other IoT components for processing and storage through the device's network interface. Sensing is a "read only" activity; it provides observations of a physical aspect of the environment without trying to change the environment.

In IIoT applications, sensors are used to monitor the health of equipment or the status of the environments in which they are located. A variety of sensors are used in IoT devices, including motion sensors, temperature sensors, humidity sensors, pressure sensors, proximity sensors, audio sensors, and optical sensors. Other types of sensing include computerized tomography (CT) scans (radiographic imaging) and spatial sensing (e.g., accelerometers, gyroscopes).

After IoT sensor data is translated into computer-readable (and manipulable) binary code, it can be transmitted across local, enterprise, and other communication networks to cloud services that alert IoT device owners/users (or others) of conditions that require their attention and possible intervention.

In an IoT device, an **actuator** receives electrical signals from an IoT controller and turns them into physical outputs or actions. Actuators make a change in the physical world based on inputs they receive from other IoT system components. Examples of actuating capabilities include activating heating coils to provide heating, locking/unlocking doors using electronic door locks, activating robotic movements, activating shutoff valves to close/open valves, performing remote controlled unmanned vehicle operations, and using pacemakers to control heart rates. Some actuators are programmable and can be coded to ensure that IoT devices take required actions.

Sensors and actuators often work in tandem but are essentially opposite devices. A sensor monitors conditions and notifies controllers or actuators when changes occur. An actuator receives signals and performs actions.

Numerous IIoT applications rely heavily on sensors and actuators. Sensors monitor processes and/or equipment and provide data on how it is functioning. Sensor data is transferred to IIoT platforms and is often stored in cloud data centers and used in applications that analyze the data to identify patterns, inefficiencies, and potentially beneficial adjustments. Sensors also are used to detect problems, malfunctions, and departures from normal operations. Actuators often perform mundane or routine actions but may sometimes make significant adjustments to equipment actions (such as robotic arm movement) to improve process efficiencies.

Some organizations leverage cloud-based *enterprise asset management (EAM)* software to analyze sensor and actuator data. EAM software is used to track sensor and actuator performance over time and to provide reports on costs, device and equipment histories, productivity, and ROI.

Sensors and actuators in consumer IoT devices and applications work in tandem to perform comparable roles. They also store sensor and actuator performance data and histories in the cloud and typically have user-friendly and informative dashboard interfaces.

9.3.2 Connectivity Layer

The second layer of the IoT reference model oversees all communications across devices, networks, and cloud services in the IoT network infrastructure. Connectivity between the physical layer and the cloud is achieved in two ways: directly using TCP/IP protocols (TCP, UDP, IP, Ethernet, Wi-Fi), or via gateways—hardware or software technologies that perform protocol conversion, encryption, and decryption for IoT data.

Several different networking technologies are commonly used for communications between physical layer devices and cloud services or gateways:

- Ethernet is typically used to connect fixed or stationary computer equipment or fixed IoT devices such as security and video equipment and permanently installed industrial equipment.
- Wi-Fi is a good fit for data-intensive IoT solutions that operate within a small area. This is arguably the most popular and versatile connection option.
- Near-field communication (NFC) enables simple and safe data sharing between two devices over very short distances, four inches (10 cm) or less.
- Bluetooth is widely used by wearables and mobile devices for short-range communications. To meet the needs of low-power IoT devices, the Bluetooth Low-Energy (BLE) standard was developed for small data transfers; regular Bluetooth is needed for large file transfers.
- Low-power wide area network (LPWAN) was created specifically for IoT devices. It provides long-range wireless connectivity for battery-powered low power consumption devices that are geographically distributed on a wide scale. LPWAN has been popular in smart city, building, and agriculture applications, where devices periodically send small amounts of data to controllers.
- Zigbee is a short-range, low-power option. It was created for home automation systems but has gained traction for medical, scientific, and industrial applications. An interesting thing about Zigbee is that it can handle up to 65,000 devices.
- Cellular networks offer reliable data transfer and nearly global coverage. Two cellular standards have been developed specifically for IoT things. Long Term Evolution for Machines (LTE-M) enables devices to communicate directly with the cloud and supports high-volume data exchanges. Narrowband IoT (NB-IoT) uses low-frequency channels to send small data packages.

Wi-Fi and Ethernet use TCP/IP Network (IP) and Transport layer protocols (TCP and UDP) to support device-to-cloud and device-to-device communications. NFC, Bluetooth Low Energy, LPWAN, and Zigbee rely on gateways that perform format and protocol conversions.

An **IoT gateway** enables a connection between IoT devices at the physical (perception) layer and device-to-cloud communication over the Internet or another communication network. Its general role is illustrated in Figure 9-16. As noted, an IoT gateway may perform protocol translation tasks. It may also be involved in IoT device filtering, aggregation, and local processing before the data is sent to cloud or local storage. Gateways may also be involved in controlling IoT devices autonomously, IoT device management, and device security.

Many IoT devices use batteries for power and strive to keep their power consumption low. Being configured to communicate directly or continuously with the Internet/cloud can mean a significant power drain. Communicating to the cloud via a gateway typically consumes less power.

As Figure 9-16 illustrates, an IoT gateway links IoT devices to the Internet/cloud or to private networks/WANs. It does so by converting IoT device data into formats needed to support a variety of specialized protocols used in IoT networks, such as the following:

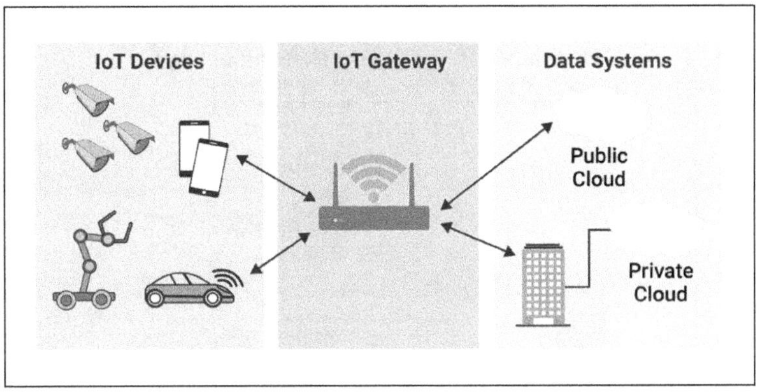

Figure 9-16: High-level depiction of the role of IoT gateways in IoT architectures.

- Advanced Message Queuing Protocol (AMQP), which is used for peer-to-peer data exchanges among servers
- Constrained Application Protocol (CoAP), which is used for communication that involves low-power and low-memory "constrained" devices, such as wireless sensors
- Data Distribution Service (DDS), which enables direct (M2M) connections between devices and between devices and applications
- Message Queue Telemetry Transport (MQTT), which provides centralized data collection from low-powered devices
- Network Time Protocol (NTP), which enables IoT devices with limited resources to obtain accurate clocks in real time
- Extensible Messaging and Presence Protocol (XMPP), which enables XML elements such as instant messages and presence information to be streamed over a network in close to real time

Several of these protocols and their use in device-to-device (M2M) communications are described in more detail in Appendix 9-3.

Figure 9-17 identifies several IoT system "helper" protocols in the TCP/IP protocol stack, including DTLS. Datagram Transport Layer Security (DTLS) is used to provide security for datagram-based applications that use UDP instead of TCP at the Transport layer. UDP's compactness makes it a good choice for securing IoT communications that involve low-power and low-resource devices; UDP datagrams are protected from eavesdropping, tampering, or message forgery. CoAP, for example, runs over UDP and is secured by DTLS.

Other IoT "helper" protocols shown in Figure 9-17 include:

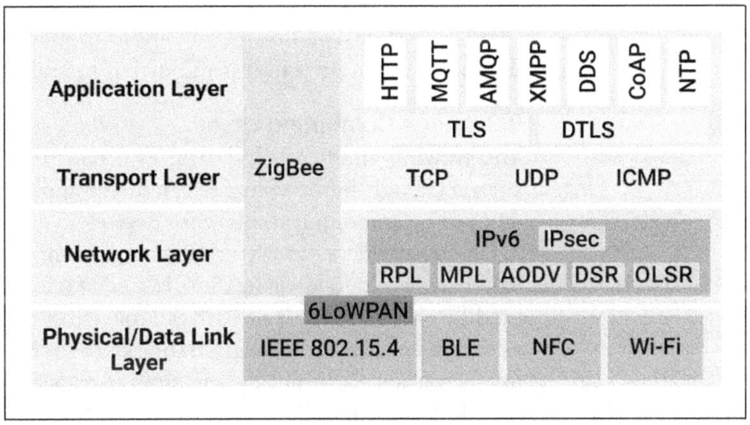

Figure 9-17: Protocols used to support IoT applications and how they map to TCP/IP layers.

- Routing Protocol for Low-Power and Lossy Networks (RPL), which is an IPv6 routing protocol standard for IoT developed by the Internet Engineering Task Force (IETF)
- Multicast Protocol for Low-Power and Lossy Networks (MPL), which is an IPv6 multicast forwarding protocol designed for communication in networks that include low-power devices
- Ad hoc On-Demand Distance Vector (AODV), which is a loop-free routing protocol for ad hoc networks that is designed for environments with mobile devices, such as M2M area networks

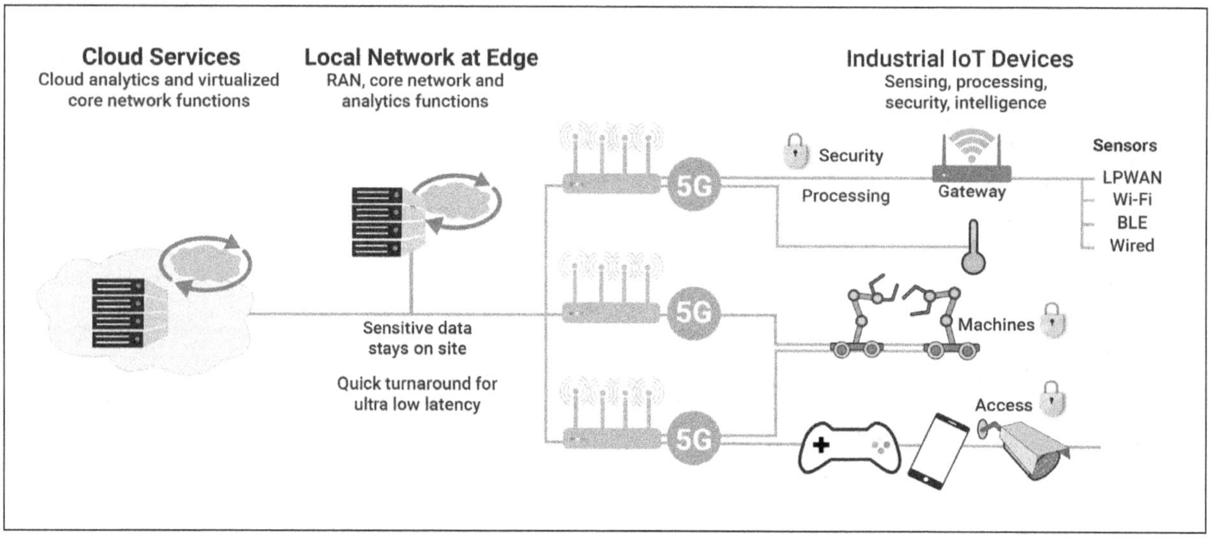

Figure 9-18: An example of a 5G-enabled IIoT architecture.

- Dynamic Source Routing (DSR), which is a routing protocol used in wireless mesh and ad hoc networks
- Optimized Link State Routing Protocol (OLSR), which is a link-state IP routing protocol optimized for mobile and other wireless ad hoc networks

In Figure 9-17, 6LoWPAN is shown at the border of the Network and Data Link layers. 6LoWPAN stands for *IPv6 over Low-power Wireless Personal Area Networks.* It is a standard protocol for IPv6 communication in wireless networks composed of low-power, short-range wireless devices, such as IoT sensors, and can be used to support M2M communication.

As noted in Chapter 7, private 5G RANs are increasingly being used for wireless communications in factories and warehouses, and 5G is widely considered to be an IIoT enabler. Figure 9-18 illustrates how 5G technologies and cellular systems can be deployed to support device-to-device and device-to-cloud communications in IIoT networks.

In sum, a wide variety of technologies are associated with the connectivity layer of the IoT reference model. Some of them have been described in previous chapters, but several, including IoT gateways and IoT-focused helper protocols, are specialized or unique. Their existence shows that IoT systems, platforms, and applications are evolving. Over time, some of them are likely to dominate, but at present it is important to realize how much variety currently exists.

9.3.3 Edge Computing Layer

The growing number of IoT devices is contributing to the growing volume of data traffic on the Internet. High traffic volumes can affect application latencies, especially when cloud servers are deluged by communications from devices.

Cloud providers can accommodate growing traffic, processing, and storage demands by adding load balancers and virtualization, but edge computing can also help. **Edge computing** is a distributed IT architecture that involves processing data at the periphery of a communications network as close as possible to the originating data source. It is sometimes considered a new paradigm that involves placing computing and storage resources at the edge of the Internet and close to sensors, IoT devices, or mobile devices.

The idea behind edge computing (which is sometimes called *fog computing*) is to process and store information as early as possible after it is generated and as close to its sources as possible.

It facilitates local analysis and transformation of high volumes of real-time data at the edge of networks. Doing this saves time and resources that would otherwise be needed to send all of the data to cloud services.

Edge computing occurs on gateways, local servers, or other edge devices in the local network. **Edge devices** have enough memory and processing power to collect, process, and use data from nearby data sources (in close to real time) with limited or no help from technologies in other parts of the network. The data that they handle can be decoded, filtered, and evaluated to determine if it needs further processing at higher levels in the IoT reference model; formatted for further processing; and redirected to additional destinations. For example, IoT gateways may send data to the cloud or a private centralized data center for storage or further processing, or to other edge devices for local processing. Generally, edge devices should have enough storage and computing power to process data and make decisions in milliseconds.

Several benefits can be realized when edge computing is used in an IoT network. For example, it enables the IoT system or application to react faster to changes or issues that require mitigation. The following are additional benefits:

- Faster response times and increased operational efficiency
- Improved network bandwidth from edge to cloud
- Rapid decision-making from the application's analytics, AI algorithms, and ML based on locally aggregated and processed data
- Continued offline system/application operation when connection to the Internet or another communications network is lost

Communication between edge devices and a cloud service may involve the transmission of a log of decisions made by the edge device to a data center for storage, processing, or Big Data analysis. Edge computing has become a standard practice in 5G networks that support IoT systems and applications, such as the one illustrated in Figure 9-18. Maximizing data storage, processing, and use at the edge of mobile networks saves time, conserves MNO bandwidth, and enables IoT systems/applications to react to device changes or commands from cloud services in close to real time.

9.3.4 Data Accumulation Layer

Activities associated with this layer are usually performed by IoT platforms. Data accumulation involves storing real-time data from edge and physical devices to meet the requirements of non-real-time applications. This layer serves as a transit hub between event-based data generation and data consumption by IoT applications.

Among other things, this layer defines whether data is relevant to the business requirements and where it should be placed. A wide range of storage solutions may be involved in data accumulation, from data lakes (introduced in Chapter 3) capable of holding unstructured data like images and video streams, to event stores and telemetry databases. The goal is to sort out a large amount of diverse data generated by IoT devices and ensure that it is stored in the most efficient or appropriate way.

High-volume data streams are often sent across IoT networks, and the data accumulation layer/stage ensures that incoming streams are directed to appropriate storage locations. Data comes in various forms (varieties), speeds (velocities), and sizes (volumes), and separating essential data (that needed for applications) from nonessential data in the data streams is a primary concern at this layer.

Unstructured data in raw form (such as photos, images, and video streams) can be enormous in volume, and efficiently separating what is essential from what is not is important for BI applications.

Pinpointing data for different data repositories is important at this layer. Some data may be accumulated for inclusion in data warehouses, NoSQL databases, or Hadoop clusters (described in Chapter 3) and used for near-term analysis and BI. Other data may be directed to data lakes for future analysis. Because of their scalability, cloud and enterprise data storage are commonly used for most of these data repositories.

9.3.5 Data Abstraction Layer

Like activities at the data accumulation layer, IoT platforms oversee data abstraction activities. At this layer/stage, data preparation is finalized to enable applications to use the data to generate insights. This layer also reformats data generated at the applications layer to ensure that it is sent to physical layer devices in a form that they can understand. Essentially, it prepares data for use by IoT applications and prepares data from applications for use by devices.

At the data abstraction layer, businesses begin to make sense of their accumulated IoT data and how it can be combined with other data for BI and other intelligence-focused applications. Relevant data from different sources is aggregated and prepared for at the Application layer. Data preparation may include normalization and integration. Extract, transform, load (ETL) processes may be applied to select data for inclusion in data warehouses and used in data mining BI applications. A business's data abstraction path might include:

- Combining relevant data from both IoT and non-IoT systems (e.g., CRM, ERP, and SRM)
- Reconciling multiple data formats
- Organizing data into appropriate schemas and flows for application layer analytics
- Expediting the transfer of high-priority data traffic or alarms
- Using data virtualization to make data accessible to applications from a single location
- Managing raw data in multiple forms for use in Big Data processing and analytics

Once data accumulation and abstraction are performed, it is easier for data analysts to leverage their business knowledge to productively use IoT data in BI applications. Together, the data accumulation and abstraction layers enable IoT platforms to separate networking and device details at the lower levels of the IoT reference models from the applications that use the data. These layers also enable application developers to focus on developing and refining applications that focus on performing business tasks without having to consider device or communication specifics at lower layers of the IoT reference model.

9.3.6 Applications Layer

At this layer, IoT data is analyzed by software to inform decision-making and provide answers to business questions. Hundreds of IoT applications have been developed. These vary in scope, complexity, and function. And, because of the IoT's rapid evolution, applications have been developed using different technologies and operating systems.

Examples of IoT applications include:

- Device monitoring and control systems
- Mobile apps for simple interactions with IoT devices/systems
- Cloud-based BI services
- Analytic solutions using ML

Today, many IoT platforms include application development and maintenance capabilities. They may include ready-to-use or easily customizable data mining, data visualization, and analytics tools. IoT applications developed outside of IoT platforms often have APIs to enable them to integrate with middleware (which is briefly described in Chapter 2).

So, application logic is executed at the application layer, often to gain business intelligence. Results of BI analytics and/or Big Data processing may be pushed to dashboards to enable process monitoring and optimization. Applications also enable IoT data to be used to fuel ML and AI applications.

IIoT applications are often used to improve/control manufacturing processes, warehouse operations, logistics, and supply chains. The application layer enables organizations to determine whether an IoT network's business requirements and goals are being realized.

9.3.7 Collaboration and Processes Layer

At this layer, application results are presented to users, business owners, and stakeholders. An application's results, and the information on which they are based, add value when they contribute to problem-solving and the achievement of business goals.

Decisions made at this level often involve multiple people leveraging the results of more than one application. This is what warrants it being considered a separate, higher stage than the application layer.

Information from different applications is often deliberatively and collaboratively evaluated by various stakeholders to identify opportunities to enhance efficiencies or productivity, improve existing processes, or introduce new processes. This layer involves human interaction with all layers of the IoT system, and it is here that the economic value of IoT data is determined or delivered.

One of the business challenges at this layer is to effectively leverage the growing volume and value of IoT data/information to promote business optimization and economic growth. It is here that an IoT system's potential to drive business performance or inform business planning and strategic decision-making is determined.

9.4 IoT SECURITY

On average, a newly connected IoT device is probed for security vulnerabilities or attacked within five minutes of being connected to a network. With accelerating IoT adoption and use, IoT networking is an important business issue, and businesses are coming to grips with IoT security to avoid having the IoT become an "Internet of Trouble."

9.4.1 IoT Network Security/Attack Concerns

Table 9-6 identifies three major IoT attack surfaces.

Table 9-6: Potential IoT attack surfaces and types of attacks.

IoT Attack Surface	Security/Attack Concerns
Devices	Devices are often the primary means by which attacks are initiated. IoT device vulnerabilities include their firmware, memory, physical interface, and cloud interface: • Attackers may take advantage of outdated components, unsecure update mechanisms, unsecure default settings, or latent component capabilities to compromise devices. • They may also attempt to add rogue IoT devices to an IoT network; this is called *malicious node injection*. • Attackers may alter compromised low-power devices to prevent them from going into a sleep mode after completing a task or transferring a sensor reading; such *sleep deprivation attacks* can deplete the device's battery and render it useless. • Because users usually trust IoT device alarms received on their mobile devices, attackers may trick users into giving up their login credentials via bogus alarms from compromised devices. This is a type of *social engineering* attack. • Compromised devices may also be used in *IoT ransomware attacks* that lock one or more IoT devices or use them in botnets that search for valid credentials in device firmware that can be used to install malware on devices in other networks.

Table 9-6, Continued.	
IoT Attack Surface	**Security/Attack Concerns**
Communication Channels	Attacks can involve an IoT network's communication channels and the other networks to which it connects. Protocols used to support device-to-device (M2M) and device-to-cloud communications may have exploitable security vulnerabilities that can be used to compromise IoT devices and applications. Some IoT systems/applications are vulnerable to device/user spoofing and denial-of-service (DoS) attacks: • Attackers that succeed in accessing an IoT network's security channels may be able to capture and analyze data generated by IoT devices or applications; these are called *traffic analysis attacks*. • RFID systems can be vulnerable to several different types of attacks, including *RFID cloning* (extracting data from a damaged RFID tag or replicating RFID tag data to create phony tags), *RFID spoofing* (impersonating an RFID tag on IoT network communication channels), *RFID skimming* (using phony RFID readers/transmitters to get RFID tags to give up their data), and *RF interference* (jamming RFID communication channels to prevent tags from communicating with readers/transmitters). • Compromised IoT gateways may be used in *sinkhole attacks* that attract traffic by advertising bogus router table updates; they may also be used in *router table poisoning* attacks that can disrupt an entire IoT network. • Compromised communication channels may be used in *side-channel* attacks aimed at exfiltrating encryption keys from IoT gateways or devices, or in other *cryptoanalysis attacks* aimed at exploitable weak points in encryption protocols.
Applications	Vulnerabilities in web applications and other applications that leverage IoT data can result in compromised systems. Web applications, for example, may be exploited to push malicious firmware updates or steal login credentials.

Additional consideration of IoT network security risks and threats is examined in Appendix 9-4.

9.4.2 Securing IoT Networks and Applications

Some IoT architecture models include a security layer that encompasses each of the other layers. This is included to reinforce the critical importance of security in IoT systems and applications. Often, the security layer focuses on hardening IoT systems against data breaches, malicious software, and hacking. Device, connection, and cloud security mechanisms are common parts of IoT infrastructure security:

- Device Security. Security for the IoT layers begins with IoT devices. Most IoT device manufacturers follow security guidelines for firmware installation and hardware integration in IoT systems. They typically integrate security features in both device hardware and firmware, including embedded Trusted Platform Module (TPM) chips with cryptographic keys for endpoint authentication and protection. These features also include a secure boot process to minimize the introduction of unauthorized or malicious code during that process, regular updates for security patches, and using metal shields to prevent physical access to the device.
- Connection Security. While transferring data across the IoT network, it should be encrypted from end to end. Device-to-device, device-to-network, device-to-cloud, network-to-network, and device-to-application communication should be encrypted. IoT-centric messaging protocols such as AMQP, DDS, and MQTT can be used with TLS and DTLS to ensure end-to-end data protection.
- Cloud Security. Cloud security is of paramount importance for IoT. Data at rest in cloud storage should be encrypted, especially sensitive data. Authorization and authentication mechanisms should be in place to limit access to IoT data and applications and to ensure that only authorized devices are allowed to connect to the cloud. Mechanisms for verifying new devices and connections should be deployed. IoT solutions from major cloud providers including AWS, Cisco, IBM, and Microsoft incorporate numerous security measures; access control, data encryption, and device authentication are standard features of their solutions.

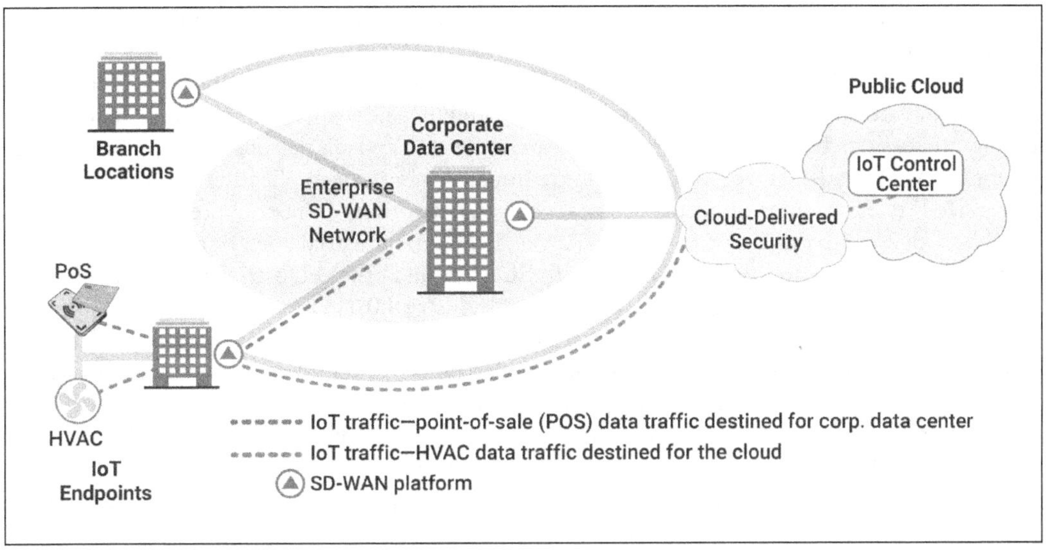

Figure 9-19: SD-WAN and IoT application security.

An obvious takeaway from Table 9-6 is that security should be an important consideration at all seven layers of the IoT reference model. Securing some layers while ignoring others leaves an IoT network with exploitable vulnerabilities. Table 9-6 also suggests that authentication is important for IoT application users, edge technologies, and IoT devices. User and device authentication is an important aspect of zero trust security, which is widely viewed as an IoT security best practice.

Many businesses with IoT deployments have adopted SD-WANs to segregate and secure the data flows generated and consumed by IoT devices, gateways, platforms, and applications. SD-WANs' software-based data traffic management is a good fit for IoT deployments because of its ability to scale network capacity and services in close to real time. It provides a flexible network architecture for connecting IoT devices to corporate and/or cloud data centers.

As noted in Chapter 8, SD-WANs are application-centric and strive to provide cost-effective connections that serve application requirements. SD-WANs can also contribute to IoT network and enterprise network security by segmenting IoT data traffic to go to specific connections, and by deploying predefined security policies and rules to network edges. Such policies/rules can be applied holistically across the network while also enabling customized security services at individual locations, or for certain types of devices, users, or data traffic. Hence, SD-WAN technology can improve the entire WAN while also securing IoT networks and applications at different locations.

Figure 9-19 illustrates how SD-WANs can isolate and manage IoT data flows for different types of IoT applications. Different security policies and rules may be associated with the different applications, and, if so, they can be enforced at SD-WAN edges and in IoT endpoints. As a result, it is not a coincidence that accelerating IoT deployment in businesses is associated with increased adoption and use of SD-WANs in enterprise networks.

As IoT systems in applications continue to proliferate and mature in enterprise networks, IoT security best practices will also evolve. Now, SD-WANs are poised to be an important part of IoT security in the years ahead.

SUMMARY

The Internet of Things (IoT) is rapidly growing and is expected to include more than 20 billion connected devices by 2026. Multiple industries have each deployed more than 100 million IoT devices, and several should exceed 1 billion deployed devices by 2030. Accelerating IoT growth contributes to rapidly increasing volumes of data traffic on the Internet and in enterprise networks and increasing use of cloud storage and services.

The IoT is enabling businesses to achieve new levels of efficiency, innovation, cost savings, and digital connectedness, and the range and variety of IoT business applications across industries is rapidly increasing. The IIoT, Industry 4.0, Warehouse 4.0, and digital business applications are examples. M2M and V2V communications are important in some application areas.

The IIoT refers to interconnected sensors, devices, networking infrastructure, and applications that work together to monitor, collect, and analyze data from industrial operations. Today, IIoT systems and applications are often integrated with SCADA and other industrial control systems that have been used in industrial settings for decades. In Industry 4.0, IIoT systems are converging with other technologies, including robots, additive manufacturing, Big Data processing, and AI/ML.

Warehouse 4.0 (W4.0) extends Industry 4.0 to warehouses and integrated supply chains. RFID technologies, robots and cobots, and IoT wearables are important W4.0 technologies.

Digital transformation is under way across industries, and digital business applications are creating novel business models and revenue streams from new combinations of people, things, technologies, and processes. Like the IoT, digital business represents a convergence of digital and physical worlds, and digital twins are an example.

Layered IoT architecture models provide guidance for deploying and managing IoT networks. Each model includes a physical layer that includes IoT devices and an application layer that includes applications that leverage IoT data to achieve business objectives. The seven-layer IoT Reference Model developed by the IoT World Forum has emerged as an important framework for IoT deployments via its incorporation of functions performed by IoT platforms.

IoT platforms are software suites or cloud services that facilitate the processing of IoT data and the development of IoT applications. They monitor and manage/control IoT devices and gateways via various applications.

In addition to TCP/IP protocols (TCP, UDP, IP, Wi-Fi, Ethernet), IoT networks include a wide range of other connections, including Bluetooth, LPWAN, NFC, Zigbee, and 5G, that support specialized device-to-device and device-to-network protocols (such as CoAP and MQTT) and IoT-oriented helper protocols. Edge computing technologies (e.g., IoT gateways) are also common.

IoT networks and applications are often targeted in cybersecurity attacks. Devices, communication channels, and applications/software are common IoT attack surfaces. Because a variety of attacks are associated with each area, security controls are important at all layers of IoT architectures. Zero-trust security mechanisms and SD-WANs are increasingly viewed as IoT security best practices.

KEY TERMS

Actuator
Digital business
Digital transformation
Digital twin
Edge computing
Edge devices
Industrial Internet of Things (IIoT)
Industry 4.0
Internet of Things (IoT)
IoT gateway
IoT platform
Machine-to-machine (M2M) communication
M2M platform
Sensor
Telemetry
Warehouse 4.0
Vehicle-to-everything (V2X) communication
Vehicle-to-vehicle (V2V) communication

REVIEW QUESTIONS

1. What is the IoT, and how is it influencing businesses and business networks?
2. What technologies are contributing to accelerating IoT adoption and use?
3. How are business processes being enhanced by IoT deployments? Provide examples.
4. Identify several industries that are benefiting from IoT deployments and examples of the benefits they are realizing.

5. What is the IIoT? Identify examples of how the IIoT enhances industrial operations.
6. What are SCADA systems? How are they like IIoT systems, and how are they different?
7. What is M2M communication? What is telemetry? Identify examples of M2M communication in industrial settings.
8. Identify several IIoT application areas outside of manufacturing that are likely to benefit from IoT deployments and advancements.
9. What is Industry 4.0? What technologies are converging in Industry 4.0, and what are the potential effects of this convergence?
10. What is Warehouse 4.0? What technologies are converging in Warehouse 4.0? What are the benefits of IoT deployments in warehouses?
11. What is V2V communications? What are the different aspects of V2X communications? How are V2V and V2X related to Warehouse 4.0 and Industry 4.0?
12. What is digital business? What is digital transformation? Why do businesses create digital twins?
13. How are IoT deployments enhancing facility and network management?
14. What are the characteristics of IoT architectures? What layers are included in the IoT World Forum's IoT reference model?
15. What are IoT platforms? What are the roles of IoT platforms in IoT architectures?
16. What layers/tiers are included in IIoT architectures? What are the characteristics and functions of IIoT platforms?
17. What layers/domains are included in M2M architectures? What roles/functions do M2M platforms perform in M2M architectures?
18. Briefly describe the differences between IoT component transducing, data, interface, supporting, and latent capabilities.
19. What is a sensor? What do sensors do? What happens to sensor data after it is collected?
20. What is an actuator? What do actuators do? What are examples of actuators?
21. Why is the connectivity layer important? Identify networking technologies commonly used for communications between physical devices, cloud services, and IoT gateways.
22. What are IoT gateways, and what functions do they perform?
23. Identify examples of specialized protocols used in IoT networks. Also identify examples of IoT network "helper" protocols.
24. What is edge computing, and how/why does it improve IoT network performance? What are the characteristics of edge devices, and what activities do they perform?
25. What activities are performed at the data accumulation layer? What activities are performed at the data aggregation layer?
26. What activities are performed at the application layer? Identify application development and maintenance capabilities typically included in IoT platforms.
27. What happens at the collaboration and processes layer? What challenges are associated with this layer?
28. Briefly explain why attackers target IoT devices. Identify examples of IoT device attacks.
29. Identify examples of attacks that involve compromised communication channels. Why may IoT application software be an attack target?
30. Describe how IoT device security is typically implemented. Identify examples of how IoT communication channels can be secured. What approaches are commonly used to protect IoT cloud data and services?
31. Briefly explain how SD-WANs contribute to IoT system/application performance and security.

PROBLEMS AND EXERCISES

Exercise 9-1 Describe the IoT system/application that has had the greatest influence on your life. Identify what you like about it and how it has affected you. Identify/describe changes that could be made to improve it or make it more useful. Identify an IoT system that you would like to have, and explain why it interests you.

Exercise 9-2 You have been tasked with designing an IoT wearable app that would:

- Sense when you are too impaired to drive
- Launch a ride sharing app (e.g., Uber/Lyft), notifying drivers of your location and your home address
- Use a digital wallet to pay the driver

Describe how the app would work and identify IoT devices and communication networks involved in supporting the app.

Exercise 9-3 The Waze app (from Waze.com) enables app users (Wazers) to report accidents, traffic jams, speed and police traps, and other traffic information to Waze servers, where the data is aggregated to update maps, recommended routes, likely travel times, and turn-by-turn directions, as well as provide real-time traffic alerts. Do some online research on Waze and answer the following questions:

- Are Wazer cell phones IoT devices? Why or why not?
- What communication networks are used to support Waze?
- Do active Wazers constitute an IoT network?

Exercise 9-4 After starting your vehicle, you establish a Bluetooth connection between your cell phone and the in-vehicle entertainment system, launch your Google Maps app, display the app on the entertainment system's display screen, and use the app to direct yourself to an out-of-town destination.

- Use Visio or another network diagramming tool to create a diagram of the connections being used to support the Google Maps app. It should include the in-vehicle entertainment system, the Bluetooth connection, your mobile device, your device's connection to your cellular provider's network, the cellular provider's connection to the Internet, and a Google Maps server.
- Explain how/why the displayed map changes in response to your changing location as you proceed along your route, using the components in your diagram to identify the device-to-device, device-to-cloud, and cloud-to-device data flows as they happen in real time.

Exercise 9-5 You have been tasked with designing a smart agriculture app that uses a moisture sensing system to monitor soil moisture and detect dry soil. The system/application should also activate a watering system when soil moisture is too low for an extended period of time, and the watering system should shut off when moisture levels return to acceptable levels. The system/application should be monitored and managed by a smartphone app. Design how the system would be implemented/deployed. Draw a sketch of the system and explain how it will work. Also draw a sketch of the smartphone display that monitors the system. Summarize your app in a PowerPoint presentation or 500- to 750-word report.

Exercise 9-6 You have been challenged to design a patrol robot to guard your residence whether you are at home or away. The patrol robot should be equipped with a night vision camera that can perform a 360-degree scan, and it should follow a predefined path (patrol route). When it detects human faces and movements, it will, at a minimum, send an alert and an image of the intruder to the application user. Draw a labeled sketch of your patrol robot. Briefly describe how it would work and the programming you would include to protect your residence.

Exercise 9-7 Do some online research on SCADA systems and their integration with the IIoT. Identify articles that describe SCADA systems, their components, and their protocols and how SCADA systems interface with other IIoT applications and systems. Also identify articles that focus on SCADA security vulnerabilities and remedies used to address them. Summarize what you learn in a PowerPoint presentation that includes at least seven slides and multiple images that bolster your research findings and observations. Your final slide should be a References slide that includes the titles and URLs of at least four online sources.

Exercise 9-8 Digital twins are examples of digital business applications. Suppose you had a digital twin of the Wi-Fi network in your residence that you could use to simulate its performance under different conditions. Identify and briefly describe the simulations and performance tests that you would run and briefly explain how you would use the results to improve your network.

Exercise 9-9 Artificial intelligence (AI) and the IoT are converging in Industry 4.0 and in other ways to improve IoT system/application performance. Do some online research on how AI and machine learning (ML) are being used to improve IoT systems/applications in businesses. Identify three business applications combining AI and the IoT that you consider to be especially impressive and describe them in a 500- to 1000-word report that provides a clear description of each application and explains why you are impressed by it.

CHAPTER REFERENCES

Adam, T., Kopp, S., Lang, S., & Winkelman, A. (2019). *V2x—An Important Building Block in Cooperative Intelligent Transport Systems (C-ITS)* [White paper]. Retrieved from: https://www.te.com/content/dam/te-com/documents/automotive/global/automotive-next-gen-mobility-v2x-09-2019-en.pdf

Ahn, N.-Y., & Lee, D. H. (2019). Physical Layer Security of Autonomous Driving: Secure Vehicle-to-Vehicle Communication in a Security Cluster. arXiv. Retrieved from: https://arxiv.org/ftp/arxiv/papers/1912/1912.06527.pdf

Alcatel-Lucent. (2022). The Internet of Things in the Enterprise. Retrieved from: https://www.al-enterprise.com/-/media/assets/internet/documents/iot-enterprise-solution-brief-en.pdf

Altexsoft. (2020). IoT Architecture: The Pathway from Physical Signals to Business Decisions. Retrieved from: https://www.altexsoft.com/blog/iot-architecture-layers-components/

Aronoff, A. (2016). Security in IoT Devices. Nautech. Retrieved from: https://nautechcorp.com/security-in-iot-devices/

AT&T Business. (n.d.). Four Reasons SD-WAN Is the Ideal Network Architecture for IoT Deployments. Retrieved from: https://www.business.att.com/resources/knowledge-center/how-sd-wan-can-improve-iot-functionality.html

AVSystem. (2021). LwM2M—Lightweight M2M Standard—Protocol and Its Benefits. Retrieved from: https://www.avsystem.com/blog/lightweight-m2m-lwm2m-overview/

Beaullan-Thong, Y. (2020). COVID-19 is Accelerating Digital Transformation in Accounting. Accsurant. Retrieved from: https://accsurant.com/covid-19-is-accelerating-digital-transformation-in-accounting/

Behara, G. K., & Naik, G. (2019). A Primer on Open Source IoT Middleware for the Integration of Enterprise Applications. *Open Source for You*. Retrieved from: https://www.opensourceforu.com/2019/10/a-primer-on-open-source-iot-middleware-for-the-integration-of-enterprise-applications/

Blackman, J. (2019). What's the Difference Between an IoT Sensor and an IoT Actuator? *RCR Wireless News*. Retrieved from: https://enterpriseiotinsights.com/20191107/channels/fundamentals/the-difference-between-an-iot-sensor-and-an-iot-actuator

Cisco Systems. (n.d.). The Role of IT in Industrial IoT. Retrieved from: https://www.cisco.com/c/en/us/solutions/internet-of-things/what-is-industrial-iot.html#~role-of-it

Cockerham, J. (2021). What's the Difference Between Sensors and Actuators? ManagerPlus. Retrieved from: https://managerplus.iofficecorp.com/blog/sensors-actuators

Crosby, T. (n.d.). How Machine-to-Machine Communication Works. Retrieved from: https://computer.howstuffworks.com/m2m-communication.htm

El Hakim, A. (2018). *Internet of Things (IoT) System Architecture and Technologies* [White paper]. Retrieved from: https://www.researchgate.net/publication/323525875_Internet_of_Things_IoT_System_Architecture_and_Technologies_White_Paper

Epicor. (n.d.). What Is Industry 4.0—The Industrial Internet of Things (IIoT)? Retrieved from: https://www.epicor.com/en/blog/learn/what-is-industry-4-0/#:~:text=Industry%204.0%20refers%20to%20a%20new%20phase%20in,on%20interconnectivity%2C%20automation%2C%20machine%20learning%2C%20and%20real-time%20data

Famark. (n.d.). Enterprise System and Internet of Things (IoT). Retrieved from: https://www.famark.com/IoT/enterprise-system-iot.htm

5GAA Automotive Association. (2017). *5GAA V2X Terms and Definitions*. Retrieved from: https://5gaa.org/wp-content/uploads/2017/08/5GAA-V2X-Terms-and-Definitions110917.pdf

Garcia, L. V. (2021). Warehouse 4.0. Today's Tech for Today's Problems. *SupplyChain*. Retrieved from: https://supplychaindigital.com/digital-supply-chain/warehouse-40-todays-tech-todays-problems

Harris, I. G. (2016). Social Engineering Attacks on the Internet of Things. *IEEE IoT Newsletter*. Retrieved from: https://iot.ieee.org/newsletter/september-2016/social-engineering-attacks-on-the-internet-of-things.html

IIoT World. (2020). Ten Benefits/Advantages of IIoT and Analytics for Manufacturers. Retrieved from: https://www.iiot-world.com/industrial-iot/connected-industry/ten-advantages-of-iiot-and-analytics-for-manufacturers/

Industry Week. (2020). Warehouse 4.0: Accelerate Your Digital Journey. Retrieved from: https://www.industryweek.com/sponsored/article/21146501/warehouse-40-accelerate-your-digital-journey

IoTDunia. (2022). What Is an IoT Platform? And What are the Key Components? Retrieved from: https://iotdunia.com/what-is-an-iot-platform/

i-Scoop. (n.d.). IoT Platforms–IoT Platform Definitions, Capabilities, Selection Advice and Market. Retrieved from: https://www.i-scoop.eu/internet-of-things-iot/iot-platform-market-2017-2025/

Jena, S. (2023). Internet of Things (IoT) Gateways. Geeks for Geeks. Retrieved from: https://www.geeksforgeeks.org/internet-of-things-iot-gateways/

Jovanovic, B. (2023). Internet of Things Statistics for 2023—Taking Things Apart. DataProt. Retrieved from: https://dataprot.net/statistics/iot-statistics/

Kim, E.-J., & Youm, S. (2013). Machine-to-Machine Platform Architecture for Horizontal Service Integration. *EURASIP Journal on Wireless Communications and Networking*, 2013, Article 79. https://doi.org/10.1186/1687-1499-2013-79

King, A. (2019). The Practical IoT: Network Planning and Designing. Corning. Retrieved from: https://www.corning.com/in-building-networks/worldwide/en/home/knowledge-center/practical-iot.html

Kumar, P. (2020). Everything About the Architecture of IoT Technology? BigForSure. Retrieved from: https://www.bigforsure.com/2022/01/architecture-of-IoT.html

La Rosa, A. (2021). LPWAN as a Communication Base for IoT. Pandora FMS. Retrieved from: https://pandorafms.com/blog/what-is-lpwan/

Loshin, P. (2021). SCADA (Supervisory Control and Data Acquisition). TechTarget. Retrieved from: https://www.techtarget.com/whatis/definition/SCADA-supervisory-control-and-data-acquisition

McClelland, C. (2019). Types of Network Connectivity for the Internet of Things (IoT)—A Simple Explanation. IoT for All. Retrieved from: https://www.iotforall.com/connecting-the-internet-of-things

Miao, L., Virtusio, J. J., & Hua, K.-L. (2021). PC5-Based Cellular-V2X Evolution and Deployment. *Sensors (Basel), 1*(3). Retrieved from: https://www.ncbi.nlm.nih.gov/pmc/articles/PMC7865993/

Mitrokotsa, A., Rieback, M. R., & Tanenbaum, A. S. (2009). Classifying RFID Attacks and Defenses. *Information Systems Frontiers, 12*, 491–505. Retrieved from: https://link.springer.com/article/10.1007/s10796-009-9210-z

Mujahid, M., & Safdar, G. A. (2021). 5G-Based V2V Broadcast Communications: A Security Perspective. *Array*. Vol. 11. Retrieved from: https://www.sciencedirect.com/science/article/pii/S2590005621000321

Oracle. (n.d.). What Is IoT? Retrieved from: https://www.oracle.com/internet-of-things/what-is-iot/

Red Hat. (2022). What Is IoT Edge Computing? Retrieved from: https://www.redhat.com/en/topics/edge-computing/iot-edge-computing-need-to-work-together

Rout, A. K. (n.d.). Internet of Things. Srinix College of Engineering. Retrieved from: https://srinix.org/lecture_notes/new/IO/IOT(MOD-2).pdf

Rullo, A., Bertino, E., & Saccà, D. (2018). PAST: Protocol-Adaptable Security Tool for Heterogeneous IoT Ecosystems. *2018 IEEE Conference on Dependable and Secure Computing*. Retrieved from: https://ieeexplore.ieee.org/abstract/document/8625143

Sahu, M. (2021). 5 Applications of IoT In Warehouse Management. Analytics Steps. Retrieved from: https://www.analyticssteps.com/blogs/5-applications-iot-warehouse-management

Simsek, G. (2018). Edge Computing and the Future of the Cloud. Software Engineering Daily. Retrieved from: https://softwareengineeringdaily.com/2018/09/14/edge-computing-and-the-future-of-the-cloud/

TE Connectivity. (n.d.). The Challenge of IoT: Engineering M2M Communications. Retrieved from: https://www.te.com/usa-en/trends/industry-4-digital-factory-production/integrating-m2m-communications-across-industries.html

Trend Micro. (2019). The IoT Attack Surface: Threats and Security Solutions. Retrieved from: https://www.trendmicro.com/vinfo/mx/security/news/internet-of-things/the-iot-attack-surface-threats-and-security-solutions

Trend Micro. (n.d.). What Is the Industrial Internet of Things (IIoT)? Retrieved from: https://www.trendmicro.com/vinfo/us/security/definition/industrial-internet-of-things-iiot

Turakhia, M. P., Estes III, N. A. M., Drew, B. J., Granger, C. B., Wang, P. J., Knight, B. P., & Page, R. L. (2012). Latency of ECG Displays of Hospital Telemetry Systems. *Circulation, 126*(13), 1665–1669. Retrieved from: https://www.ahajournals.org/doi/10.1161/cir.0b013e31826ae459

Zorkany, M. E., Yasser, A., Galal, A. I. (2020). Vehicle to Vehicle "V2V" Communication: Scope, Importance, Challenges, Research Directions and Future. *The Open Transportation Journal, 14*, 86–98. Retrieved from: https://opentransportationjournal.com/VOLUME/14/PAGE/86/

MINICASE: From the IoT to the Internet of Behaviors (IoB)

The Internet of Behaviors (IoB) refers to analysis and effective use of behavioral data gathered from IoT devices and other sources. This data is amassed through wearable IoT technologies, household IoT devices, individual online activities, and other sources to provide information about the behavior and interests of individuals. Basically, the IoB capitalizes on the IoT, analytics, and psychology to gain insights into human behaviors and what influences them.

Combining the IoT and the IoB makes it possible to track, gather, aggregate, and interpret massive amounts of data generated by online activities and personal behaviors, including social media actions and commercial transactions. It is not difficult for Big Tech to link an individual's mobile phone data with data from their laptop, voice assistant, smart home devices, or vehicle. This enables marketing research by Google, Facebook, or Amazon to be much more comprehensive and positions them to develop better algorithms for anticipating their customers' desires and behaviors. YouTube, for example, is tracking behavioral data and utilizing behavioral analytics to recommend videos and shows to individuals. The technologies that support Siri, Google Home, and Alexa also study and interpret their users' behavior data to work more efficiently.

In 2021, Gartner's strategic technology report identified the IoB as one of its top 10 trends because of its potential to drive significant value generation. According to Gartner, by 2023, 40% of the global population's activities will be tracked by the IoB. Gartner says the "IoB combines multiple sources of intelligence, such as commercial customer data, citizen data processed by public-sector and government agencies, social media, public domain deployments of facial recognition, and location tracking. From analysis of data in these myriad sources, it's possible to tag to an increasingly broad array of people's behavior as an 'event.'"

Basically, Gartner is saying that the IoB combines existing technologies such as location tracking, facial recognition, and Big Data to analyze human behavior and to connect the resulting data to specific behavioral events, such as purchases or device usage. Such *event tagging* involves labeling behavioral events with metadata to make them more searchable and understandable. The IoB uses event tagging to identify and categorize specific behaviors for further analysis and insights. Although this may be considered "creepy," it is increasingly being done behind the scenes.

In the United States, IoB methods are being used by businesses to prompt sales, increase revenues, and improve customer experience. In addition to facial recognition, biometric sensors are being used to measure various physical aspects of humans, including body temperature or moods. This information is then combined with other IoT device data and other data to influence human actions. A coffee chain, for example, is using the IoB to tailor beverage suggestions to patrons from data analysis results obtained from facial recognition devices that assess the individual customer's age, gender, and mood.

BMC, a software company, has developed a health app for smartphones that tracks diet, sleep patterns, heart rate, and blood sugar levels. The app can send alerts about adverse situations in the user's health and suggest behavioral modifications that may produce more favorable health outcomes.

Another software company, GBKSOFT, has carried out an IoB project to help golfers improve their skills with the help of wearable devices and a mobile app that tracks the golfer's current ball striking techniques, offers corrective feedback, and teaches new techniques. Using a handheld device connected to a mobile phone, each hit on the golf ball is recorded in the app and analyzed (for stroke force, angle, trajectory, etc.). This enables the golfer to see their mistakes and get visual recommendations for improving their swing and stroke.

In the automotive industry, large companies, such as Ford, have partnered with start-ups, including Argo AI, to design autonomous cars that can vary their driving behavior in different cities based on vehicle traffic volumes and different concentrations of scooters, bicycles, and pedestrians. Transportation companies, including Uber, are also moving toward the IoB by using IoT data on drivers, passenger locations, and preferences to reinvent their customer experience.

From a business perspective, the IoB has three primary advantages:

- Knowing the customer: By analyzing customers' data, a business can more accurately determine the demand for its products. For example, Researchers at Stanford and Cambridge created an algorithm that evaluates individuals' Facebook activity and "knows" individuals better than their families and friends do. Today's smartphones can track our online movements and geographic locations, unless we use permissions settings that prevent this. When we don't, businesses are positioned to know us better than anyone else and to use their knowledge to customize/personalize all parts of their advertising and marketing (such as product, price, channel, message, and timing) and track our responses to their activities.
- Marketing optimization: The IoB positions organizations to optimize their advertising and marketing campaigns. Traditionally, the success of a marketing/advertising campaign has been measured by views, clicks, shopping basket contents, and sales. With the IoB, businesses can also use behavioral and consumption data to judge the success of their campaigns. For example, a smartwatch vendor could look beyond sales numbers and use detailed usage data to understand how users interact with its newest smartwatch models. The insights it could gain could be used to better tailor its marketing and advertising efforts.
- Nudging opportunities: The IoB can be leveraged to improve consumer well-being. Many humans have self-control challenges. For example, individuals often prefer small short-term gains over larger long-term ones. As a result, many of us tend to eat more, drink more, study less, and spend more money than we intended. Hence, additional self-control mechanisms can be beneficial, and the IoB can deliver the nudge that many of us need. For example, it can be a personal coach that reminds us to stand up or exercise if we are stationary for long periods of time.

As Figure 9-20 illustrates, the IoB helps businesses and other organizations to move beyond data and information to knowledge and wisdom.

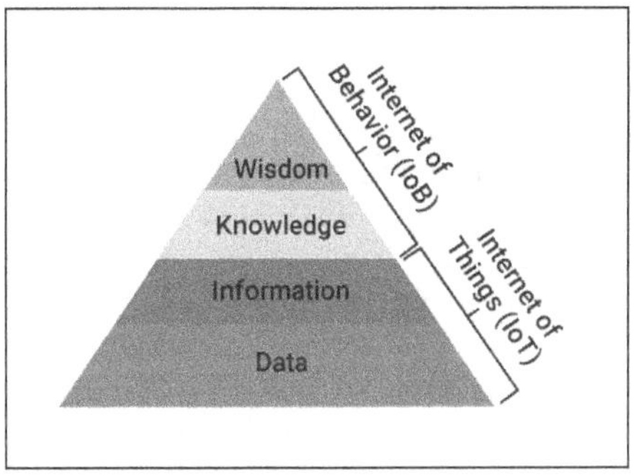

Figure 9-20: The IoB leverages IoT data and information to produce insights for influencing behavior.

One of the drivers of business adoption and use of the IoB is the assumption that by increasing service efficiency, consumer interactions with the company will increase and will provide more opportunities to know the customer, to optimize marketing/advertising, and to nudge. In short, a virtuous business cycle.

Should you (as consumers) be aware that businesses are using the IoB to close more sales, know where you are shopping, and analyze your buying habits on different platforms to better target their advertising or to send you real-time notifications to induce you to *not* purchase a competitor's product that you are just about to buy? This is just one of the many questions that should be confronted as the IoB continues to evolve.

Manipulation, privacy, and security issues must also be faced, including:

- Manipulation for profit: Consider a health-conscious individual who wants to be faithful to their diet. If this person has a healthy body, should they be manipulated by a healthcare provider using IoB data and an app to start a diet? People with above average concerns about their health might be induced to spend more on healthcare than they need to.
- Manipulation for control: Should governments or political parties be allowed to leverage IoB data and applications to manipulate citizens (e.g., during elections)? Purportedly, the People's Republic of China is planning to deploy IoB applications to induce specific behaviors in its citizens.

- Privacy concerns: Storing and analyzing Big Data that includes IoB data can be problematic because of the large volumes of private data. Use of private data is increasingly being regulated, but there is not a lot of clarity about who owns IoB data, what happens to it, who it gets sold to, and how it is used.
- Laws and regulations: Regulations lag technological development, especially for innovative technologies like the IoB. This means that consumers and healthcare patients need to be aware of the data being collected by the devices they are using and what is happening to their data after it is captured. Since standardization of data security measures at the state level is limited, regulatory and legal issues surrounding the IoB must be addressed.
- Threat of cyberattacks: The more we rely on IoT and other digital technologies for our daily tasks, the more vulnerable we become to cyberattacks. Despite a growing number of cybersecurity tools, IoT security schemes are limited, and both consumers and businesses need to consider the risks. Any business or organization that develops an IoB application should consider both cybersecurity and data privacy concerns from the outset.
- Convincing users to share data: Some people do not want to disclose their personal data. According to Deloitte, nearly 50% of drivers don't want to share their driving data (e.g., speed, average driving time, driving routes, etc.) or their online searches for "how to drive fast."

A wide range of private- and public-sector organizations are likely to be interested in using the IoB to effect or influence our behaviors. Psychologically, the IoB has the potential to go beyond operant conditioning (which focuses on rewards and punishments after a behavior) to other types of behavioral influence, such as adjusted information feeds. One should not overlook that value judgments will be applied to behavioral events to create desired behaviors.

With appropriate cybersecurity, data, privacy, and ethical protections, the IoB can be used to produce positive outcomes. IoB data, for example, may be used to help first responders to improve their behaviors in adverse or chaotic situations. It also has the potential to help soldiers gain an advantage over adversaries in firefights. One thing seems certain, for good or naught, we will be hearing and learning more about the IoB in the future.

Minicase Questions

1. Identify IoT devices and applications in and around where you live, provide examples of behavioral data that these devices could capture, and briefly describe how businesses might use such data to influence you.
2. Several examples of IoB applications are provided in the minicase. Design and briefly describe an IoB application that could be used to help someone be a more successful university student.
3. A medically focused research area is also called the IoB—the Internet of Bodies. Do some online research on the Internet of Bodies ecosystem and types of devices being used to collect personal health data, alter bodily functions, and treat illnesses. Summarize what you learn in two or three paragraphs.
4. Consider where you personally would draw the line that separates ethical from unethical IoB uses. Identify and briefly describe examples of IoB applications that you would include on the ethical side of the line. Also identify and briefly describe examples of IoB applications that would fall on the unethical side of the line.
5. What issues/concerns about the IoB would you add to those mentioned in the minicase? What else should we be concerned about as the IoB continues to emerge?

Minicase References

Dilmegani, C. (2023). Internet of Behaviors (IoB): Its Nature & Importance in 2022. AIMultiple. Retrieved from: https://research.aimultiple.com/internet-of-behaviors/

Javaid, M., Haleem, A., Singh, R. P., Rab, S., & Suman, R. (2021) Internet of Behaviours (IoB) and Its Role in Customer Services. *Sensors International, 2*. Retrieved from: https://www.sciencedirect.com/science/article/pii/S2666351121000437

Lawrence, S. S. (2022). Delving into the Implications of Internet of Behaviors. *Signal, 76*(9), 11. Retrieved from: Would you like to use this link? https://www.afcea.org/signal-media/presidents-commentary-delving-implications-internet-behaviors

Tech Funnel. (2021). What Is the Internet of Behaviors?—A Guide. Retrieved from: https://www.techfunnel.com/information-technology/internet-of-behaviors/

Underwood, K. (2022). Explainable AI Can Assist Internet of Behavior Efforts. *Signal, 76*(9), 13–16. Retrieved from: https://www.afcea.org/signal-media/cyber-edge/explainable-ai-can-assist-internet-behavior-efforts

Underwood, K. (2022). Internet of Behaviors' More Disturbing Trend. *Signal, 76*(9), 14–15. Retrieved from: https://www.afcea.org/signal-media/cyber-edge/internet-behaviors-more-disturbing-trend

Chapter 10

Enterprise Network Design and Management

LEARNING OBJECTIVES

After reading and studying this chapter, you should be able to:

- Briefly describe the characteristics of network life cycle models and their contributions to network design.
- Identify and briefly describe several enterprise network design project realities.
- Identify the characteristics of hierarchical architectures and the major components of enterprise architectures.
- Identify and briefly describe common business and technical requirements for network design projects.
- Identify and briefly describe examples of fundamental network design goals and how they may conflict.
- Identify and briefly describe several activities associated with each phase of the network design process and several network design best practices.
- Identify the major aspects of network management, the major components of network management architectures, and several types of network management architectures.
- Identify examples of data/information passed to network management systems (NMSs) by managed devices and the protocols used for device/NMS communication exchanges.
- Identify several examples of activities associated with each aspect of the FCAPS network management model.
- Explain how/why network auditing, software-defined networking (SDN), and unified endpoint management (UEM) are important to enterprise network management.

10.0 INTRODUCTION

Networks are critical to the success of both large and small businesses. They support applications and services, connect people, and provide access to the resources that keep businesses running. Over time, as they have adapted to new applications, technologies, and changes to day-to-day business operations, networks have become quite complex.

Today, the Internet-based economy makes it important for business networks to be available nearly 100% of the time. They need to detect and automatically react to security incidents and have the agility required to adjust to changing traffic loads to ensure that critical applications have consistent response times and performance levels.

Ongoing considerations for enterprise network design and management include:

- The need to support remote and mobile users
- An increasing need for network security and resilience
- Increased use of cloud storage and scalable cloud services
- The need to accommodate a variety of wireless connections, including 5G
- The need to leverage the capabilities of evolving Ethernet, Wi-Fi, and other standards
- Accelerating adoption and use of IoT systems and applications
- The convergence of Industry 4.0, Warehouse 4.0, and integrated supply chain technologies
- Increased use of SD-WANs and software-defined networking
- An increased need for manageable networks

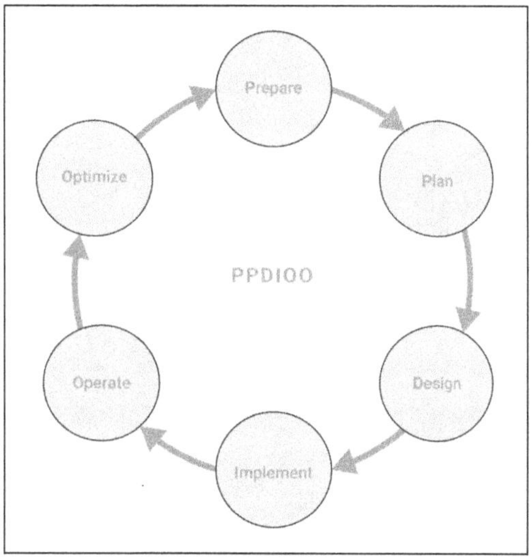

Figure 10-1: Cisco's PPDIOO network life cycle model.

These and other moving parts create numerous challenges for network designers and managers.

Network life cycle models help us appreciate how network design and management contribute to the broader lifespan of networks and their components. One of the best known network life cycle models is Cisco's Prepare, Plan, Design, Implement, Operate, Optimize (PPDIOO) model (see Figure 10-1). The PPDIOO is often described as a methodology that defines the continuous life cycle of services required for a network. The steps/phases of this model are briefly described in Table 10-1.

In addition to helping to organize network design and management activities, network life cycle models have other benefits. For example, they can contribute to lower cost of network ownership, increase network availability, facilitate access to applications and services, and improve business agility. Appendix 10-1 describes the connections among these benefits.

In short, numerous factors are contributing to the evolution of enterprise networks, and the PPDIOO and other network life cycle models are useful in helping network designers and managers to

Table 10-1: A summary overview of the phases of the PPDIOO network life cycle model.

Network Life Cycle Phase	Description
Prepare	High-level requirements and strategy are defined in this phase of the network life cycle. The organizational requirements for the network are identified, along with the organization's strategy for the network. A conceptual architecture and technologies that can best support the architecture may be identified. The prepare phase may also establish a financial justification for the network by creating and assessing the business case for the proposed architecture.
Plan	This phase identifies initial requirements for the network, which are usually focused on network goals, facilities, user needs, and so on. The plan phase involves characterizing network sites, assessing existing networks, and performing a gap analysis to determine whether the existing network infrastructure, sites, and operational environments can support the proposed network. A project plan is developed to help manage the tasks, responsibilities, critical milestones, and resources required to implement changes to the network. The project plan should align with the scope, cost, and resource parameters established during the prepare phase.
Design	During the design phase, information gathered from the previous two stages is used to create logical and detailed network designs. They should provide an adequately comprehensive and detailed design for the network that meets business and technical requirements. They also should incorporate specifications for supporting availability, security, scalability, performance, and other fundamental network requirements. The design specification provides guidance for implementation activities.

Table 10-1, Continued	
Network Life Cycle Phase	**Description**
Implement	This is when the work of configuring and deploying network infrastructure is performed. This phase usually includes testing to validate the network design and its configuration. A new network is built, or additional components are incorporated into an existing network, during this phase in accordance with design specifications. Typically, a goal of this phase is to integrate devices/infrastructure without disrupting the existing network or creating security vulnerabilities.
Operate	Operation is a final test of the appropriateness of the network design. In this phase, the network is placed in production. Monitoring is an important aspect of validating that the network is working as designed and can quickly detect and respond to issues when it isn't. The manageability of the network is realized during this phase. The operate phase involves maintaining the day-to-day health of the network while maintaining high availability and striving to minimize expenses. Fault detection, fault correction, and performance monitoring (which are important aspects of network management) provide the initial data for the optimization phase.
Optimize	This phase involves proactive network management that strives to identify and resolve issues before they affect the network or organization. Troubleshooting (reactive fault detection and correction) is needed when proactive management is unable to predict or mitigate network failures. In this phase, excessive network problems/errors or performance issues or the emergence of new applications/technologies to support organizational or technical requirements can trigger a network redesign and spawn another iteration of the network life cycle.

develop a longer view of what must change to improve the alignment of business requirements and enterprise networks.

10.1 NETWORK DESIGN REALITIES

Good networks don't just happen or miraculously appear. They result from hard work by network designers and technicians and other stakeholders who leverage network life cycle models and similar systematic processes for modifying existing networks. Identifying network solutions that best address business needs is common across the processes used, and common steps/phases in the processes include identifying network requirements, assessing the existing network, identifying needed changes, and crafting a plan for implementing the proposed solution.

Several important context factors/realities cannot be overlooked. First, businesses already have networks. This means that most network design efforts involve redesigning or tweaking an existing network rather than designing a new network from scratch.

Second, the network design process is usually progressive. New equipment and applications often coexist with older ones. Continuing to support legacy applications and equipment may result in a network design that is less than ideal but is often essential.

Third, businesses typically desire to leverage rather than replace existing wired and wireless infrastructure if that is possible. It can be expensive and time-consuming to replace existing cabling, even when structured cabling plans provide guidance for cable runs and types. As a result, companies often prefer to use existing cabling for as long as it is feasible to do so. Improving network performance in such instances may involve replacing switches, access points, routers, etc., to take advantage of evolving Ethernet and Wi-Fi standards and capabilities.

Fourth, while replacing existing infrastructure is not an issue when designing networks for new or completely renovated buildings, network personnel may have preferences for specific technologies based on prior network management and support experiences. Some organizations completely gut existing facilities when renovating, often leaving only the external walls. This creates network design opportunities like those for new construction and the potential to outfit the buildings with network infrastructure consistent with the latest standards. However, network personnel may instead prefer to deploy infrastructure that has worked well in the past.

Fifth, some businesses prefer to lease, rather than own, the network infrastructure that they use. In such instances, they often partner with third parties to deploy, maintain, and manage their LANs and CANs.

As noted in Chapter 8, businesses rarely own the circuits and services used to support their WANs. They have little or no input into how they are deployed and configured. Improving WAN performance, availability, and affordability may involve replacing/upgrading their connections to ISPs or carriers or switching from MPLS to Carrier Ethernet or VPNs.

To better control and manage their enterprise networks, many businesses are adopting SD-WANs. SDN and SD-WANs can improve application performance, network traffic management, and security and accommodate IoT systems and applications. Considerable due diligence and planning are needed for upgrading business WANs, but since network design practices focus on identifying business and technical requirements for redesigned or new networks, they can help identify WAN alternatives that best align with what the organization wants.

10.2 NETWORK AND ENTERPRISE ARCHITECTURES

The three-layer hierarchical model (core, distribution, access) and modular enterprise architectures provide important guidance in network (re)design. The three-layer hierarchical model was introduced in Chapter 6's discussion of backbone networks, and it provides insights into how networks can be designed for both flexibility and growth.

10.2.1 Hierarchical Network Architectures

Hierarchical networks have advantages over flat network designs. When LANs are combined by interconnecting or daisy-chaining Data Link layer (Layer 2) switches, large broadcast domains are created (see Figure 10-2). Flat networks have limited opportunities to filter undesirable traffic or to control broadcast traffic, and as more devices or applications are added, their response times and performance decline. By dividing a flat network into smaller, hierarchical blocks (see Figure 10-3), local traffic remains local, and traffic destined for other networks is moved to a higher layer. And network management is typically improved. Table 10-2 describes the different layers.

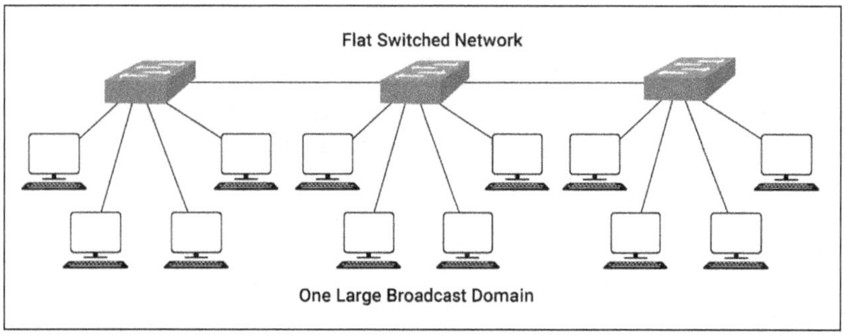

Figure 10-2: Example of a flat network design.

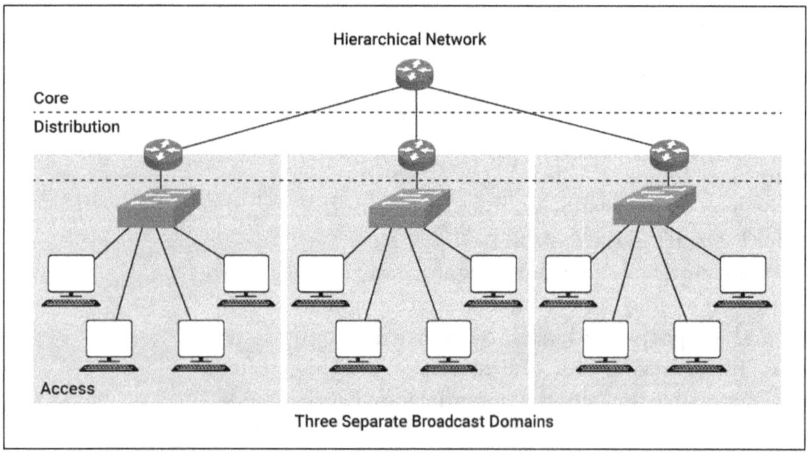

Figure 10-3: Example of a hierarchical network design.

Table 10-2: Design considerations for the three-layer hierarchical model.	
Layer	**Characteristics and Design Considerations**
Access	The access layer represents the edge of the network, where end user devices connect. Access layer devices and services are found in each building of a CAN, in the networks at each business location, and in data centers. User access to network resources is controlled at this layer. Network designers strive to facilitate the transfer of the data generated at this layer to other network segments or layers. If this layer is not properly designed, it can become saturated with data traffic and produce unacceptable performance levels for applications. The access layer primarily uses Data Link layer (Layer 2) switching technology to provide network access. Access is provided via wired infrastructure, wireless access points, or both. Since Ethernet over copper wiring has distance limitations and access points have transmission range limitations, a primary concern when designing access layer infrastructure is the physical location of the equipment.
Distribution	The distribution layer serves as the communication point between the core and access layer and is involved with traffic routing and filtering. It functions as a routing boundary between the access layer and the core layer and connects the core layer and local networks at different locations. This layer is built using Network layer (Layer 3) devices, such as routers or multilayer VLAN switches. These technologies are involved in: • Managing and filtering traffic flows • Routing among access layer VLANs • Implementing and enforcing access control policies • Summarizing routes advertised to core layer devices • Isolating the core from access layer failures or disruptions • Managing queues and prioritizing network traffic prior to transmission The distribution layer should be designed to complement the needs of the other two layers.
Core	In an enterprise network, the core layer may connect multiple locations and provide connectivity to a corporate data center or server farm. It may also include one or more links that support Internet, extranet, WAN, and VPN access. It is sometimes called the network backbone. It is responsible for quickly and reliably transporting large amounts of data. Designers strive to ensure that the core layer is designed for resilience and fault tolerance because all users can be affected by core layer failures. Avoiding unnecessary delays in network traffic is another design priority. Routers and switches at the core layer should provide high-speed connectivity.

10.2.2 Enterprise Architectures

Enterprise architectures (such as Figure 10-4) are often used to divide enterprise networks into modular areas/parts that identify where different functions are supported and how they are logically or physically connected. Because modular enterprise architectures were first introduced by Cisco, they are often called Cisco Enterprise Architectures.

Enterprise architectures enable designers to consider enterprise networks holistically, while also enabling them to concentrate on designing a single module and/or its connections to other modules. They can also help network managers troubleshoot network performance issues.

As Figure 10-4 illustrates, modular enterprise architectures have several areas, including enterprise campus, enterprise edge, service provider edge, and remote modules.

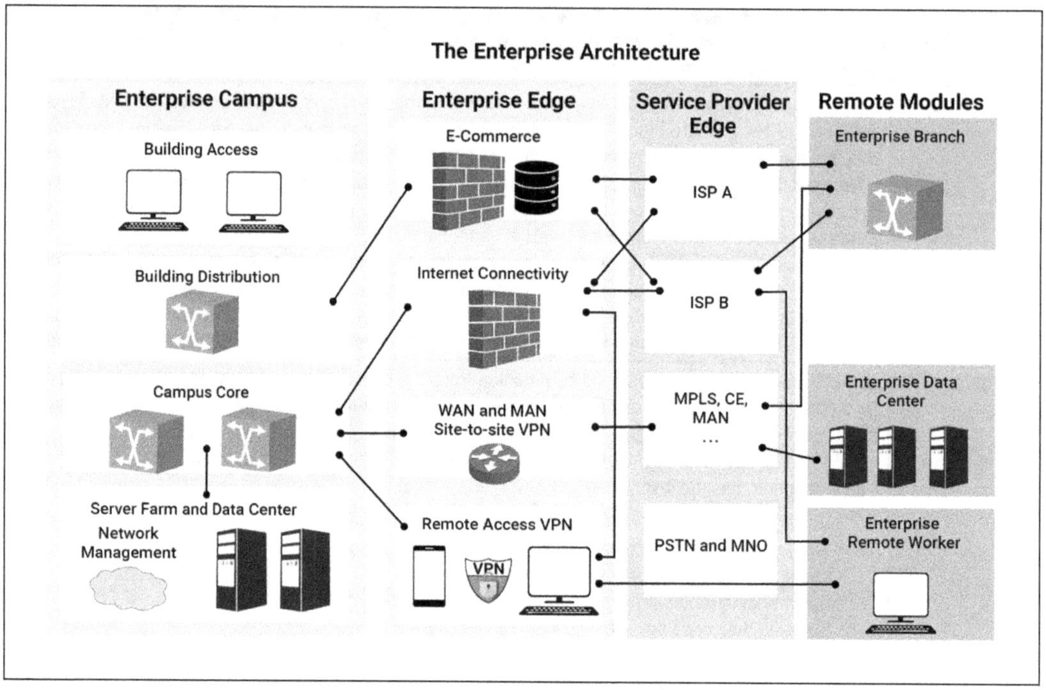

Figure 10-4: An example of a modular enterprise architecture.

Enterprise Campus Components

The *enterprise campus* module includes the network elements that local networks in a single campus or branch location require. It is here that building LANs, building distribution/backbone networks, and campus core/backbone networks are located.

In traditional enterprise networks, the enterprise campus also includes a private, corporate *data center* that traditionally serves on-site employees as well as those at branch locations or who work remotely. This placement is intended to protect server resources and provides reliable and redundant high-speed connectivity for internal services, such as email, application, printing, and DNS services. Traditionally, this data center has also housed network management services for the enterprise network, including monitoring, troubleshooting, and other common management activities.

The enterprise campus module usually has a resilient multilayer design to provide high availability. It usually has redundant hardware and links that are configured to automatically reroute traffic when link failures occur, as well as a variety of security protections to protect against and mitigate the effects of malware and other attacks.

Enterprise Edge Components

As shown in Figure 10-4, the *enterprise edge* module includes submodules that provide e-commerce services, Internet connectivity, remote and VPN access, and enterprise WAN connections, including site-to-site VPN connections:

- The e-commerce submodule enables enterprises to support e-commerce applications over the Internet. It typically has a high-availability design like that for the data center module in the enterprise campus. As noted in Chapter 2 (Section 2.5), an organization's web and public-facing e-commerce server is usually located in an enterprise network's public zone or demilitarized zone (DMZ) outside the firewalls that separate the Internet from the business's intranet or private corporate network. Other resources that may be included in the DMZ are identified in Chapter 11.

- The Internet submodule of the enterprise edge provides internal users with secure connectivity to Internet services, such as public servers, email, the DNS, cloud storage, and cloud services. Connectivity to one or several ISPs is also provided.
- The enterprise WAN submodule includes the various WAN technologies and carrier services used to interconnect the enterprise campus, branch offices, remote workers, and secondary data centers. As noted in Chapter 8, a wide range of circuits and services may be included in an enterprise WAN to interconnect an organization's various locations and resources. MPLS, T-carrier or SONET circuits, wireless and cellular circuits, intranet VPN gateways, and their supporting devices/technologies are examples.
- The remote access VPN submodule includes remote access termination services, such as authentication for remote users and sites. As noted in Chapter 8, remote access VPNs are typically used to support remote workers. Remote access servers, VPN gateways, firewalls, and authentication services may be included in this submodule.

Service Provider Edge Components

As noted in Chapter 8, enterprises use carriers or service providers (SPs) to link to other sites. As shown in Figure 10-4, the *service provider edge* module includes connections to ISPs, WAN services providers, and public mobile network operator (MNO) cellular and/or public switched telephone network (PSTN) services. It focuses on the logical and physical connections that provide connectivity among the enterprise campus, data centers, enterprise branch locations, and remote workers.

Overall, the SP provides the data, voice, and video services supported in the enterprise network and the collection of carrier circuits and services involved in delivering data, voice, and video services. The SP edge includes QoS and service level agreements (SLAs) with service providers. It also oversees VPN and WAN security at the demarcation points between carrier networks. Two ISPs are included in Figure 10-4 because multihomed connections to ISPs are considered best practices.

Remote Components

The *remote module* encompasses various enterprise network edge components that interconnect to the enterprise campus. This includes connectivity options for enterprise branch, enterprise teleworker, and enterprise data center submodules:

- The enterprise branch submodule includes business locations with employees that access resources at the enterprise campus. Remote sites often rely on the SP edge to provide services and connections. Traditionally, an enterprise branch connects to the enterprise campus site over private WAN links, but VPN services are increasingly used to provide logical connections that are private and secure.
- The remote worker submodule encompasses connections to the residential or telework center networks that enable employees to access resources across the enterprise network. Remote access VPNs are often used to support remote workers.
- The enterprise data center submodule is a separate data center designed with all or most of the functional options of the data center at the enterprise campus location. It is often configured to provide disaster recovery and business continuity services for the organization when the data center at the enterprise campus is unavailable. Having

redundant data centers in an enterprise network enables synchronous and/or asynchronous data replication as well as application replication. Such redundancy can also be leveraged for load balancing to maximize application performance and provides an opportunity for the enterprise to scale without having to make major changes to enterprise network infrastructure.

The modularity of enterprise architectures has several advantages for network designers. For example, boundaries between modules enable designers to see where network traffic originates and where it goes. The boundaries also make each module relatively independent and enable designers to focus on each individual area without having to consider the others. Modular enterprise architectures also facilitate enterprise network scalability and adaptability; often designers can add new modules (such as IoT and cloud services modules) without having to make major changes to the underlying network design.

Enterprise architecture frameworks can also be constraining. For example, the inclusion of a data center in the enterprise campus module may bias designers toward a hub-and-spoke topology. Also, it may be unclear where/how RANs should be incorporated, especially since they may be used as private, local networks and/or public communication services.

10.3 NETWORK DESIGN PROCESS

Both network life cycle models and enterprise architectures provide designers with important perspective and guidance as they work through the steps of (re)designing enterprise networks. While the specifics of the network design project will vary based on the size, scope, and complexity of the network, the process typically includes five steps, as discussed in this section.

10.3.1 Identify Requirements

The network design process begins with gathering information and developing clear business and technical requirements for the redesigned or new network. This step identifies goals/targets for the network and drives decisions made in subsequent steps. Both business and technical requirements for the network are identified during this step, and some overlap.

Business Requirements

Business requirements identify what the organization wants from the new or redesigned network. For example, the business may want to ensure seamless communication with a new branch office, improve customer experience, reduce costs, improve compliance with regulations, or create a network that better contributes to business continuity. Generally, business goals focus on how the network can help the business be more successful. Examples are included in Table 10-3.

Designers typically work closely with business executives and key stakeholders when identifying business requirements. They are the primary sources for how the network fits into the business and how it could be more valuable. They also improve designer awareness of budgetary and staffing constraints and how a failed network design project would affect the business.

A limited number of "must have" business requirements is typical. Examples include:

- The network should stay up all the time and should be able to handle failed links, equipment failures, and overloaded traffic conditions.
- The network should reliably deliver applications and services with reasonable response times.
- The network should be secure; it should protect data transmitted over it and data stored on connected devices.
- The network should be easy to modify to accommodate network traffic growth, new locations, and new applications.

Table 10-3: Examples of business goals for redesigned or new networks.	
Business Goal Examples	
Increase profitability	Reduce business operation costs
Increase market share	Improve employee productivity
Create new revenue streams	Shorten product development life cycles
Provide competitive advantages	Facilitate just-in-time manufacturing
Improve customer engagement	Facilitate stakeholder engagement (e.g., investors, suppliers, business partners)
Improve employee engagement	Improve collaboration and information access
Avoid business disruption from security breaches	Avoid business disruptions caused by natural or man-made disasters
Retire/replace outdated technologies	Reduce network costs
Source: Oppenheimer, P. (2010). *Top-Down Network Design* (3rd ed.). Cisco Press.	

- Network troubleshooting should be easy; finding and fixing a problem should not be time-consuming.

Technical Requirements

Designers typically work with network administrators and technical personnel to identify technical requirements for redesigned or new networks. Example technical requirements include bandwidth requirements, performance requirements, security requirements, protocols that must be supported, and uptime requirements. They typically identify technical performance measures that should be positively affected by the network.

Table 10-4 provides brief definitions for different aspects of bandwidth and performance details that may be used to determine technical requirements for a network. They are all considered contributing factors in network performance and demonstrate that an "improve network performance" goal for a network is not very technically precise about needed changes.

Table 10-4: Examples of network performance goals.	
Network Performance Goal	**Brief Definition**
Accuracy	The amount of useful traffic that is correctly transmitted relative to total traffic
Capacity (bandwidth)	The data-carrying capability of a network circuit or network; usually measured in bits per second (bps)
Delay (latency)	The time between a frame being ready for transmission and the delivery of the frame elsewhere in the network
Delay variation (jitter)	The amount of variation in average delay
Efficiency	The amount of effort required to produce a specific amount of throughput
Offered load	The sum of all data that network devices have ready to send at a specific time
Optimum utilization	The maximum average utilization before the network is saturated
Response time	The amount of time between a request for a network resource and the receipt of a response to the request
Throughput	The quantity of error-free data successfully transferred between devices per unit of time, usually per second
Utilization	The percent of total available capacity that is currently in use
Source: Oppenheimer, P. (2010). *Top-Down Network Design* (3rd ed.). Cisco Press.	

Fundamental Network Design Goals

Four goals are common to most network design projects: scalability, availability, security, and manageability. These *fundamental network design goals* are briefly described in Table 10-5.

Table 10-5: Four common network design goals.

Network Design Goal	Brief Description
Scalability	Scalable network designs can grow to include additional users, remote sites, and applications without affecting the level of service delivered to existing applications, users, and locations.
Availability	A network designed for availability delivers consistent, reliable performance, 24/7/365. The failure of a single link or piece of equipment should not have a significant effect on network performance.
Security	Security must be designed into the network during the network design process and not added later. The locations of firewalls and other security devices should be included in network designs.
Manageability	Network personnel must be able to support and manage the network. A network should be designed to be manageable. A network that is complex or difficult to maintain is unlikely to function efficiently or effectively.

Other technical and functional requirements identified as goals in many network design projects are sometimes also identified as fundamental network design goals, including usability, adaptability, affordability, and network performance. They are briefly described in Table 10-6.

Constraints also need to be considered when business and technical requirements for a network design project are identified. For example, the business may have a budgetary limit for the project or a requirement that the network continue to support legacy apps.

Table 10-6: Additional goals that are common to most network design projects.

Design Goal	Description
Usability	Usability focuses on how easy it is for users to access and use the network. Today, enterprise network users usually expect user-friendly interfaces and to be able to access the network anytime, anywhere, using any type of device.
Adaptability	Adaptability refers to a network's ability to adapt to new technologies, applications, and business practices. Designers should avoid including elements that would make it hard to accommodate new technologies or applications. Ideally, the network should be able to adapt to new devices, new protocols, new regulations/laws, new work habits and practices, changes to network traffic patterns or QoS requirements, the addition of new enterprise network locations, and myriad other changes.
Affordability	Most businesses want their networks to be affordable (*cost-effective*). When a network is affordable, it can carry high traffic volumes for relatively little cost. Low cost is a goal of many campus network design projects; for example, a low price per port goal may be specified for new switches in campus networks. Reducing WAN costs is another common goal; business migration from MPLS to Carrier Ethernet and SD-WAN adoption are examples. Reducing costs associated with network operations and management may also be a goal. Designers can facilitate such reductions by selecting equipment that is easy to configure, operate, and manage; a network design that is easy to understand or troubleshoot; and network applications and protocols that are easy to use and that enable users to support themselves to some extent.
Network Performance	Businesses are typically interested in improving network throughput, efficiency, and application response times. Determining/analyzing an organization's network performance goals is often closely tied to the analysis of the current network. When the existing network is assessed, the types of changes needed to meet performance goals become more apparent.

Network Design Trade-offs

After business goals and technical requirements for the network are identified, trade-offs must be confronted. For example, to achieve high availability, redundant links and equipment can be included in the network design. Doing so, however, drives up the cost of the redesigned or new network and may conflict with affordability goals. Recommending higher capacity WAN circuits or equipment that complies with current Ethernet and Wi-Fi standards can help achieve network performance goals, but these goals add costs that may conflict with affordability goals.

Security and affordability goals can also conflict. A frequently cited adage states that "a bulletproof network is never affordable, and an affordable network is never bulletproof." The point, of course, is that a compromise is needed to ensure that you have an acceptably secure network for a reasonable price.

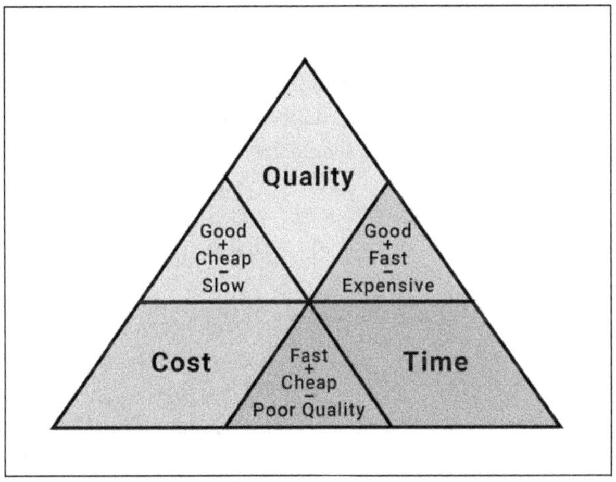

Figure 10-5: Trade-offs between good, fast, and cheap.

Another common network design adage is the "good, fast, cheap" rule, which states, "pick any two, because you can't have all three." This is illustrated in Figure 10-5. For network design, it works like this:

- If you want the network to be good and fast, it is not going to be cheap.
- If you want the network to be fast and cheap, it is not going to be good.
- If you want the network to be good and cheap, it is not going to be fast.

Security and performance can also be a trade-off. Encryption/de-encryption can slow an application's response time or have a detrimental effect on user experience. To improve their game playing experience, some gamers choose less secure encryption protocols over stronger ones that would provide better protection for their systems. Businesses, of course, typically do not give enterprise network users a choice when it comes to security, but business network designers know that more robust security often translates into reduced application performance.

Examples of other network design trade-offs are illustrated in Figure 10-6. Increased security, for example, has the potential to affect network availability. Users may not consider an application to be easily available if they must always provide login credentials to use it. And locking down network segments or the entire network in response to security breaches or the installation of security patches can reduce network uptime and availability. When stricter security requires more extensive (and expensive) monitoring, manageability may also suffer.

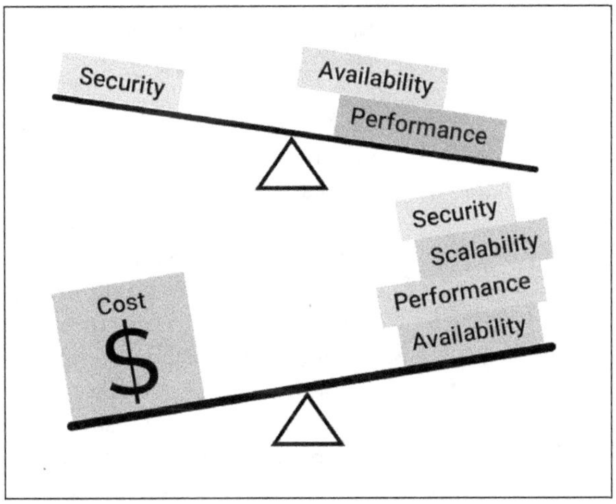

Figure 10-6: Examples of network design trade-offs.

There are many trade-offs between different network design goals that cannot be overlooked or downplayed. Designers should acknowledge them when making recommendations. Business and technical requirements for a redesigned or new network cannot be reconciled unless their trade-offs are confronted.

Prioritizing Network Design Goals

It is often helpful for designers to have business and network managers prioritize their requirements for the network. They can be asked to assign weights to the various design goals to identify the relative importance of each goal.

Consider the following ranking of network design goals:

Adaptability	25
Security	20
Availability	15
Performance	15
Manageability	10
Scalability	5
Usability	5
Affordability	5
Total (must sum to) 100	

This ranking of design priorities suggests that the business is primarily interested in its network being more adaptable and secure. It may have plans for deploying more IIoT systems and applications but wants them and the entire network to be secure. The rankings suggest that better uptime (availability), performance, and manageability are relatively important but not as important as adaptability and security. The low weights for scalability and usability may reflect that they are adequate in the current network and do not need to be significantly improved. The low weight for affordability may indicate that the organization is willing to make the investments needed to ensure adaptability, security, availability, and performance.

Confronting trade-offs and finalizing priorities can be more complex than described here, and an organization may have different goals for different parts of its enterprise network. For example, it may have higher weights for scalability and affordability for its service provider edge than for the overall network, and it may consider availability to be the highest ranked goal for its data centers. Nonetheless, identifying the relative importance of network design goals can help designers assess the current network.

10.3.2 Assess the Existing Network

Information about the existing network is gathered and analyzed during the second phase of the network design process. This enables designers to compare the functionality of the existing network with the goals for the new network. It helps designers determine whether existing equipment, infrastructure, and protocols can continue to be used and what needs to be added or replaced.

Except when designing networks for new or radically refurbished facilities, designers do not start with a clean slate. Instead, there is an existing network in place, and some parts of it are probably reusable. For example, if EIA/TIA-compliant structured cabling exists, it may be usable in the new network. However, if the existing cabling is an older generation, the existing cable infrastructure may be a design issue that must be confronted.

Whatever the state of the current network is, it's important to know before making design-specific recommendations. Assessing the existing network gives the designer a clearer picture of the enterprise architecture and its physical and logical topologies. It also provides a better understanding of the network's data traffic flows, performance, and security.

Some knowledge is gained by reviewing network diagrams, policies, network monitoring tool reports, and security tests/scans results. Baseline measures of network performance (e.g., throughput, utilization, and response times) are captured during this phase and are later used to ensure that the new network is meeting expectations.

Documenting Network Infrastructure

Enterprise networks are often too large and complex to capture in a single map/diagram. Some designers (and organizations) prefer to have a set of maps for each enterprise network location. Often a top-down set of diagrams is used to document an enterprise network, including:

- A map that illustrates the geographic locations of network sites
- A map that illustrates WAN connections among locations
- A map of BN and LAN connections among buildings on a campus
- Maps of network infrastructure on floors of buildings
- Maps that illustrate the locations of servers and server farms/data centers
- Maps of the locations of routers and switches
- Maps for the network management system at a location
- Maps of VLAN locations and reach
- Maps that illustrate significant concentrations of user devices
- Maps of IoT systems
- Maps for network services (e.g., DNS, DHCP, SMTP, VPN)

Ideally, the collection of diagrams accurately characterizes the network's infrastructure and provides designers with a clear picture of the network's logical and physical architectures.

Characterizing a network's logical architecture also involves identifying the logical addressing and naming schemes used in the network. The organization's current deployment of IP addresses and subnets may reveal opportunities to improve route summarization, routing, and VLAN performance within the network.

Opportunities to improve scalability and availability often become apparent when designers identify the wiring and media that are currently in place. Horizontal and vertical cable runs, and the placement of telecommunications and equipment rooms, can reveal the organization's engagement with structured cabling guidelines and readiness to support the newest generations of Ethernet and Wi-Fi.

Considering the network at the building level can reveal architectural constraints (or opportunities) that can affect the network, including HVAC systems, power, ventilation, electromagnetic interference, and space for cabling conduits, patch panels, and equipment racks. Wireless site surveys can also help designers get a better grasp of transmission ranges and potential wireless transmission issues, such as absorption, diffraction, refraction, and reflection.

Identifying Network Performance Baselines

Identifying baseline performance measures for the existing network is an important activity during this phase of the network design process. As Table 10-4 illustrates, numerous factors contribute to network performance, and baselines measures for most or all of these factors should be taken.

Developing an accurate baseline for network performance can be challenging. Ideally, data should be collected over multiple days to ensure baseline accuracy, but it is also important to identify appropriate times to collect the data. Collecting data during time periods with exceptionally low or high traffic volumes will not accurately reflect typical traffic loads, response times, error rates, or packet losses. Of course, if the goal is to improve performance during peak traffic loads, designers should focus on collecting baseline data during such time periods.

When measuring network utilization, it is usually best to collect data across different time intervals during a typical day. As noted in Table 10-4, **network utilization** is the proportion of the current traffic to the maximum amount of traffic that the network can handle; it indicates how much of the network's bandwidth is being consumed at that time. Here, the goal is to determine the times when the network is most and least busy. Taking multiple measures at different times of

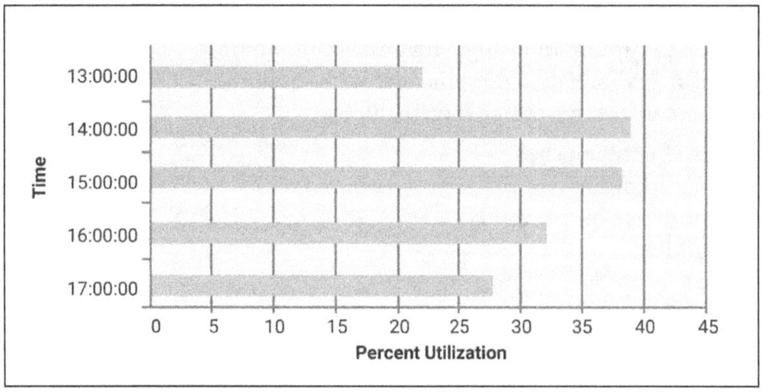

Figure 10-7: An example of a network utilization chart. Source: Oppenheimer, P. (2010). Top-Down Network Design (3rd ed.). Cisco Press

day enables designers to get a better understanding of average, normal, and peak traffic loads. Designers can get a more granular understanding of network utilization by collecting data on network utilization by protocol or application. Figure 10-7 provides an example of a network utilization chart.

Availability measures often drill down into MTBF, MTTR, and MTTD for the entire network and its major segments and components. These measurements are described in Table 10-7; they often document the network's recovery from actual failures.

These statistics position designers to recommend network components with higher MTBFs and lower MTTRs and MTTDs. They also are widely used network management measures.

Table 10-7: Examples of network availability measures.

Availability Measure	Definition
MTBF	**Mean time between failures (MTBF)** describes the expected time between two failures during normal operations. In networking, MTBF statistics may be collected for an entire network, network segments, and network equipment (e.g., routers).
MTTR	**Mean time to repair (MTTR)** measures the expected time it takes to get a failed network component (or network segment or entire network) running again.
MTTD	**Mean time to diagnose (MTTD)** measures the average amount of time it takes to diagnose the cause of a network (or network component) failure and to begin the process of restoring it to proper working order.

Characterizing Network Traffic

Characterizing network traffic involves examining traffic flow, traffic volume, and the behavior of protocols and applications. Collected information positions designers to identify logical and physical designs that can improve application performance.

Characterizing traffic flow considers sources of network traffic, where it goes, and the symmetry of data flows between sources and destinations. A simple method to characterize traffic flow is to measure the number of megabytes or kilobytes of data passed per second between senders and receivers. Protocol analyzers and other traffic flow monitoring tools can be used for this.

As noted in Chapter 2, client-server applications are usually bidirectional and asymmetric; most client requests are small, and server responses often transfer larger data volumes. Streaming applications are especially asymmetric, with very little data being required to initiate the streams, while the streams themselves are voluminous. Videoconferencing applications, such as Zoom meetings, are bidirectional and relatively symmetric for most participants but are slightly asymmetric for meeting hosts and presenters.

Understanding network traffic flows includes identifying the communities of users for applications. A *user community* is the set of employees who use a particular application or set of applications. It is also important to determine where user communities are concentrated, and the amount of bandwidth needed for adequate application performance in concentrated areas. Identifying where application data is stored is also part of traffic flow analysis.

Measuring traffic flows and volumes can help designers plan for network expansion and improvement. It also helps them identify design alternatives with few (or no) bottlenecks and sufficient capacity to meet business and technical goals.

Application and protocol usage patterns in the current network should be documented to determine the aggregated bandwidth that an application consumes. Such documentation may include the frequency of application sessions (e.g., per hour, per day), the length of each application session, and the number of simultaneous users of an application.

Traffic loads associated with application protocols (e.g., HTTPS) and service protocols (e.g., DNS) are usually assessed. The traffic loads caused by routing and error-recovery protocols (e.g., ARQ) are also typically measured, and QoS mechanisms and applications may be documented.

After the existing network is assessed and the network's business and technical requirements are reviewed, designers can begin designing and making recommendations for the new network.

10.3.3 Design the Network Topology

Once designers have determined the organization's requirements for the redesigned network and understand the existing network, they can begin mapping out the new network's functional components. This involves identifying physical and logical topologies for the new network.

Developing a physical topology design for the new network can involve:

- Determining where new cabling should be installed
- Identifying the number of required switch ports
- Identifying Wi-Fi access point locations
- Identifying locations for new components (e.g., RAN base stations, IoT gateways, security appliances)
- Identifying connection details for cloud services
- Determining equipment rack layouts
- Identifying cooling and power requirements

Logical topology design considerations include:

- IP addressing/subnetting
- VLANs
- Data flows
- Network protocols

At the end of this phase of the network design process, designers create a new set of physical and logical maps and plans for the proposed network.

As noted previously, three-layer hierarchical network architectures provide guidance for designing LANs and BNs at business locations and the WAN that connects them. Each layer includes technologies that contribute to data flows in the network and are physical design considerations:

- The core layer routes traffic between different geographical sites and is considered the network backbone. It is here where designers are most likely to recommend expensive high-throughput routers and switches that are interconnected by expensive, high-capacity fiber optic or wireless circuits.
- The distribution layer sits between the core and access layers, serves as a boundary between them, and implements policies to restrict/allow data flows between different subnets. Layer 3 (multilayer) switches, routers, fiber optic connections, and IoT gateways are technologies at this layer.
- The access layer provides network access to user devices, IoT devices, and servers. Wi-Fi access points, RAN base stations, Ethernet switches, and Ethernet cables are examples of access layer technologies.

Design considerations for each layer are described in Appendix 10-2.

It is important to note that designing network topology can be a top-down or bottom-up process. With a top-down approach, design activities focus first on the Application layer of the TCP/IP and OSI models and work down to the Physical layer. Bottom-up design is exactly the opposite.

Top-down is generally considered the better approach, especially since designers focus on applications and protocols that align with business and technical requirements for the network. However, a top-down approach is often more time-consuming than a bottom-up approach. Even though a bottom-up design process can be quicker, it can lose sight of applications that need to be supported and result in undesirable design trade-offs.

10.3.4 Select Hardware, Protocols, and Services

This step entails identifying hardware, software, protocols, and services for the network. Sometimes, this is done in conjunction with the previous step. However, all the previous steps provide guidance for this one. Collectively, they help designers understand what the network needs to do, what parts of the current network can continue to be used, what parts need to be replaced, and new equipment and capabilities that should be added. The goal of this phase is to make selections that best match the organization's performance, scalability, affordability, manageability, security, and other goals.

Choices are made regarding cabling, Data Link layer protocols, and networking hardware (such as switches, routers, and Wi-Fi access points). Selections for networks at the enterprise campus location are often made before choices are made for the business WAN. WAN technology and services choices should be based on the bandwidth and performance requirements of application traffic that flows from the enterprise campus to remote sites, remote workers, and cloud services, especially ES and other mission-critical data traffic.

Cabling is more of an implementation issue than a design issue. Enterprise networks need good (and documented) cabling infrastructure because, in many cases, the design for the new network must adapt to existing cabling. Other network components (such as switches and routers) generally have more limited lifetimes than cabling—often only a few years. Cabling infrastructure, however, is usually expected to last much longer, so organizations should carefully plan their cabling infrastructure and, ideally, should strive to make it "future proof." Structured cabling standards provide valuable guidance for cabling infrastructure.

Generally, designers should select equipment that conforms to the most recent standards for LANs. As noted in Chapters 6 and 7, Ethernet and Wi-Fi standards are amended every few years, and each new generation includes new capabilities, higher speeds, better performance, and better security. Typically, devices that comply with the latest standards are backward compatible with those of previous generations. Hence, designers can get away with recommending new-generation equipment for new LANs or network expansions, knowing it won't exclude older devices.

Replacing older generation LAN equipment can have a positive effect on network performance and security, even when existing cabling infrastructure is not changed. Adding new equipment often creates additional design opportunities. For example, new Ethernet switches routinely support PoE and VLANs. The PoE support enables designers to consider including devices in the network that can be powered by Ethernet cable instead of separate electrical wires. Most new switches are also manageable and can contribute to improving network manageability.

Numerous criteria may be considered when selecting network equipment, including number of ports, processing speed, throughput, amount of memory, latency introduced when the device relays data, media supported, ease of configuration, cost, MTBF and MTTR, traffic filtering and security measures, hot-swappable components, redundant power supplies, QoS support, and support for multicast applications. Additional selection criteria for routers may include support for IPv6, routing protocols supported, advanced queuing and optimization features, and support for encryption. The criteria that network designers use when selecting network components should, of course, align with the business goals and technical requirements for the network and the applications that will be supported. Additional network design and component selection considerations are outlined in Appendix 10-3.

10.3.5 Develop an Implementation Plan

After identifying hardware, protocols, and services for the network, implementation plans can be developed. Network implementation is often considered a project, and projects are typically best guided by project management guidelines (such as the Project Management Institute [PMI] Project Management Body of Knowledge [PMBOK]) and best practices.

Basically, this step entails creating a plan to acquire, deploy, configure, and test the network. In many cases (especially for larger networks or for network designs that include numerous changes to the existing network), this step may include small-scale test deployments to validate that the design works before large-scale deployments take place.

Appropriate project management practices and keeping stakeholders informed are key parts of this step. A network deployment typically involves numerous pieces that should be systematically and carefully combined. Hence, a network implementation plan should include project milestones, change management, and identifiable deliverables. In addition, since the network is likely to be managed by a different group of network personnel than those involved in designing the network, it is important to have a transition plan for monitoring and maintaining the network after it is implemented.

Detailed network implementation plans are most likely to result in successful implementations. Complex implementation steps often require the involvement and oversight of designers, but well-documented and detailed implementation instructions for less complex parts of the implementation may be carried out by other network personnel without designers' direct involvement. For larger projects, designers rarely perform the hands-on steps of deploying the new network. Instead, network operations and support personnel follow implementation plan details to deploy the network.

Designers must consider the possibility of deployment failures, even if pilot or network prototype tests are successful. This means that having well-defined tests for each step of the deployment are important, along with procedures for reverting to the existing network if significant problems are detected.

The implementation of a network design consists of several phases (install hardware, configure systems, launch into production, and so on). Each of these phases may include testing before moving on to the next. Each implementation phase typically consists of several steps, and, at a minimum, the documentation for each step should include:

- A description of the step
- References to design documents
- Sufficiently detailed implementation guidelines
- Sufficiently detailed roll-back guidelines in case of failure
- An estimated time for completing the implementation

Generally, poor implementation plans are likely to produce poor results. Today's enterprise networks are critical to business operations, and changes to their designs should be carefully planned and executed because every device removed from or added to the network can affect its performance.

10.4 NETWORK DESIGN BEST PRACTICES

Designers should document every step of the design process. Having a clear plan and a complete set of diagrams for the existing and new network helps ensure that designers do not miss anything and can contribute to successful implementation of the redesigned or new network. At a minimum, documentation should include:

- Business goals and constraints
- Technical requirements and constraints
- Existing network infrastructure details, including topology diagrams, performance metrics, routing protocols, and equipment lists
- New network details, including logical and physical topology diagrams, IP space allocation, routing protocols, and equipment lists
- An implementation plan detailing the steps for the installation of new infrastructure, services, and connections

It is considered best practice to lay out implementation steps in a tabular form to facilitate understanding by stakeholders and anyone involved in implementing the new network.

In addition to good documentation, other best practices are frequently identified. They are briefly described in Table 10-8.

As network life cycle models like PPDIOO demonstrate, after networks are designed and implemented, they are operated and optimized. These are important aspects of network management that help ensure that the network serves the needs of the organization and provides information for future network design decisions and projects.

Table 10-8: Examples of network design best practices.

Best Practice	Description
Anticipate the future	The demands being placed on enterprise networks are growing and changing. They should be able to scale in response to increases in the number of users and devices. Business networks should be able to adapt to new technologies and applications, such as the IoT and virtual reality. Scalability and adaptability should not be downplayed. Designers should strive to "future-proof" their designs. Designers should recommend designs with sufficient capacity to accommodate growth and new technologies. Making sure networks are sufficiently modular and flexible to accommodate expansion is important, even when there is uncertainty about future requirements.
Build in backup, failover, and resilience	No matter how well it is designed, a network faces the possibility of significantly diminished performance when one or more of its components fails. Even when on-premises business networks are working fine, ISPs and other service providers may experience outages that affect one or more parts of the network. Network design projects provide opportunities to include redundancies in networks that enable them to keep running when there are issues with one or more components. Redundancies can include alternate power sources, additional links and network paths, secondary ISP or service provider connections, standby/backup links to networking equipment, and readily available hot-swappable devices.
Embed security	No matter where security lands in the prioritized list of business and technical goals, security should be treated as a design priority to ensure that there are no gaps in the network's security posture. Being vigilant about identifying vulnerabilities in the existing network and ensuring that they are addressed in the new network is unlikely to be resisted by stakeholders—it is more likely to earn their respect and appreciation.
Standardize everything that can be standardized	Standardizing network infrastructure components facilitates troubleshooting, patching, maintenance, and management. Examples of things that should be standardized include hostnames (e.g., printer5.office2.lan3.building4), hardware models (e.g., access layer switches and access points), IP addressing, and security policy enforcement.

10.5 ENTERPRISE NETWORK MANAGEMENT

Improved manageability is a common network design goal. **Manageability** refers to the ability to monitor, configure, troubleshoot, and maintain a network of interconnect devices. The collective set of properties of a network or network component are what allow it to be managed.

Manageability is one of the most important aspects of network design. Adequate manageability and effective network management processes help an organization determine whether network design goals are being achieved and identify network parameters that should be adjusted when design goals are not being met.

Increasing network manageability can help improve the network's uptime. It can also reduce the network's total cost of ownership (TCO) over its lifespan and sometimes reduces the number of personnel required to monitor, troubleshoot, and maintain the network.

Network management (NM) is the process of administering, managing, and operating a network. It involves configuring, monitoring, and managing a network to ensure interconnectivity among devices and the people and applications they support. Network management processes help organizations assess network behavior and the effects of network upgrades.

Several types of network management can be identified, including reactive, proactive, and predictive. *Reactive network management* involves dealing with problems as they arise, without planning for the long run. It is often characterized as "firefighting."

In contrast, **proactive network management** involves assessing network performance during normal operations to identify potential problems before they arise, identify opportunities to optimize performance, and plan network upgrades.

Businesses that embrace proactive network management regularly collect statistics and conduct tests, such as response time tests, for ES and mission-critical applications. They use test results and statistics to identify performance and trends and the extent to which network design goals (availability, response times, utilization, throughput, etc.) are being achieved. Proactive network management is valuable but often requires more sophisticated network management tools than those required for reactive network management.

Predictive network management uses predictive analytics and automation to anticipate network problems before they cause downtime. This often relies on telemetry data, historical statistical data, and AI/ML models to predict network problems before they occur and to proactively reroute traffic and issue alerts to network engineers about impending outages. Long-term predictions enable network management teams to make advance preparations for upcoming conditions and to identify ways to make the network more resilient.

Network management is often viewed as a hierarchical collection of activities (see Figure 10-8). The different levels of the hierarchy are summarized in Table 10-9.

Business management is the level of the network management hierarchy that is most abstract, and the network element manage-

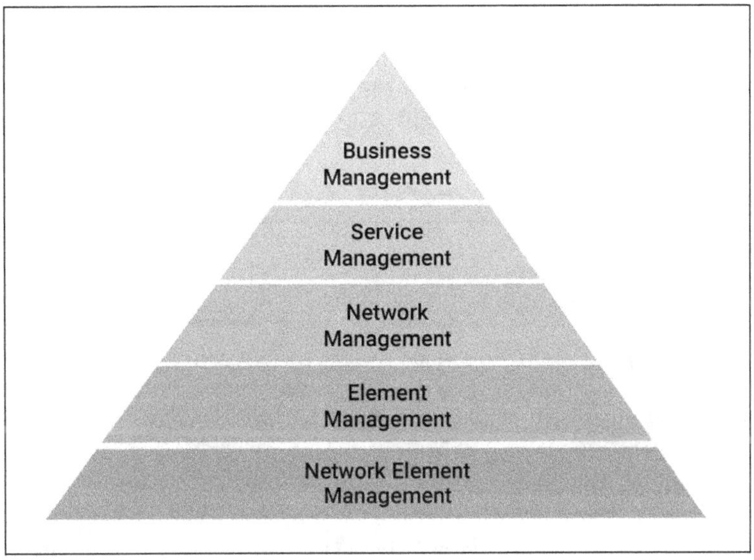

Figure 10-8: Network management hierarchy.

Table 10-9: Summary overview of activities associated with the different levels of the network management hierarchy.

Network Management Level	Description
Business Management	Business management involves managing a network's business aspects, such as network budgets, planning, resources, and service provider agreements.
Service Management	Service management focuses on the delivery of services to network users, for example, access layer bandwidth, data storage, and applications.
Network Management	Network management encompasses the management of all network devices across the entire network.
Element Management	Element management involves the management of collections of similar devices, for example, access layer switches, Wi-Fi access points, and routers.
Network Element Management	Network element management is the management of an individual network device, such as a single switch or router.

ment level is the most specific. Performance measures/statistics are used at the bottom three levels to make decisions and deploy changes. Management is applied in more abstract ways, often through policies, at the upper levels.

In short, many facets of network management are reflected in the tools and processes used to manage today's networks. Like networks, architectural concepts provide valuable perspective for considering the different aspects of network management.

10.5.1 Network Management Architectures

Network management architectures are models and frameworks used to manage and monitor computer networks. They are designed to provide a structured approach to network management and to enable network administrators to monitor network performance, identify issues, and troubleshoot problems.

Network Management Architecture Components

A generic network management architecture, such as that depicted in Figure 10-9, has three major components: managed devices, agents, and a network management system (NMS). These components are briefly described in Table 10-10. Network management protocols (protocols that facilitate information exchanges between the NMS and managed devices) are sometimes considered a fourth component of network architecture.

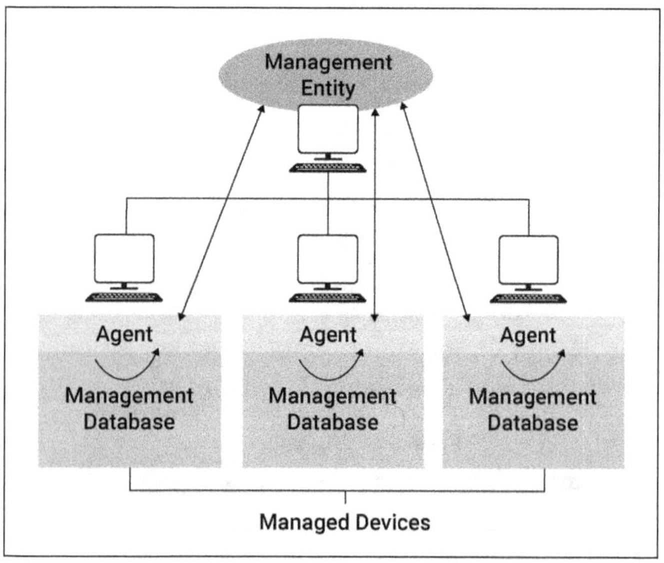

Figure 10-9: Network management architecture components.

From a network management architecture viewpoint, network management involves three basic functions: the transport of network management information from managed devices to NMSs, element management (the management of collections of similar network devices), and the management of individual managed devices. When these functions are adequately performed, they enable network managers to perform a variety of tasks, such as monitoring, configuring, troubleshooting, and planning.

Network devices (network elements) and their connections have characteristics that can be monitored and measured. These characteristics can be grouped into the three categories described in Table 10-11: end-to-end, per-link, and per-element. End-

Table 10-10: Key components of network management architectures.

Component	Description
Managed device	A managed device is a network node that collects network management data and stores it in a *management information base (MIB)*. Managed devices include routers, switches, servers, access points, IoT gateways, printers, and other important devices in network infrastructure. They are network elements in the network management hierarchy.
Agent	An agent is network management software installed on a managed device. An agent tracks local management information and uses a network management protocol, such as SNMP, to send management information to one or more network management systems (NMSs).
Network management system (NMS)	An NMS runs applications to display network management data and information, monitor and control managed devices, and communicate with agents. Powerful workstations with sophisticated graphics, storage, and processing capabilities may be used to support NMSs.

Table 10-11: Descriptions and examples of end-to-end, per-link, and per-element measures.

Type of Measure	Description	Examples
End-to-end	End-to-end measures include those that can be measured across network devices along the paths between senders and receivers. In some instances, they are applied to an entire network. Some organizations apply end-to-end measures to applications and protocols to track trends in their behavior on the network.	Examples of end-to-end measures include network availability (uptime) and various measures of network performance, such as capacity, delay, jitter, throughput, error rates, and utilization.
Per-link	Per-link measures are specific to the type of connection being monitored. They may be collected for individual links or combined to create end-to-end measures. Per-link measures for applications or protocols may be collected.	Examples of per-link measures include utilization, propagation delay, and errored frames.
Per-element	Per-element measures are specific to the type of network element being monitored. They may also be used to determine actual to maximum rates (the amount of the element's available capacity currently being used). Per-element measures for applications or protocols may also be collected.	Examples of per-element characteristics include filtering and forwarding rates (frames/packets per second) of switches, access points, routers, or firewalls, and router message queue length (which may be used to measure network congestion or saturation).

to-end and per-link/per-element measures are among the primary management information elements passed by agents in managed devices to NMSs.

Because these measures are transferred from managed network devices to NMSs by agents, it is important to consider the amount and nature of management traffic flows when making network decisions about the deployment of network architecture components. These considerations should drive decisions about whether network management traffic will be carried in-band or out-of-band, and whether a centralized, distributed, or hierarchical network management architecture will be deployed.

In-Band versus Out-of-Band Network Management

When network management traffic uses the same circuits as other network traffic, it is considered *in-band*. When different circuits are used to carry normal and network management traffic, the network management traffic is considered *out-of-band*. The advantages and disadvantages of the two types are identified in Table 10-12.

Some businesses strike a balance between in-band and out-of-band monitoring and management by creating a separate management out-of-band network that is used as a backup to in-band

Table 10-12: Characteristics, advantages, and disadvantages of in-band and out-of-band network management.

Type	Characteristics	Advantages	Disadvantages
In-band	In-band management occurs when network management traffic flows use the same network paths as the traffic flows of applications and their users.	Simplifies the network management architecture by not requiring separate paths or networks for network management.	Network management can be affected by problems/issues that affect other network traffic flows. Troubleshooting can be negatively affected when network management data flows are delayed or blocked by the same issues that affect other network traffic. Network management may not be available when it is most needed or when the network is under stress from traffic congestion; hardware, software, or link failures; or network security attacks.
Out-of-band	Network management data travels on different paths than user data. NMSs and agents are linked by circuits that are separate from those used for network user traffic. Out-of-band management is usually provided via a separate network.	This arrangement enables the NMS to continue to function during events that disable all or parts of the network that handles user data transfers. Network managers can continue to monitor parts of the network that are unreachable via the paths that carry user data. Having a separate network provides an opportunity to build in additional security mechanisms that make the NMS very difficult to attack.	This makes a network design more complex and expensive than one that relies on in-band monitoring and management.

management and is only used when the in-band network is down. The backup network may consist of inexpensive dial-up or VPN connections. Although this incurs additional costs, it enables network management functions to be performed when the user network is not available.

Centralized, Distributed, and Hierarchical Network Management Architectures

Another important consideration for network management architectures is whether a centralized, distributed, or hierarchical architecture will be used. In a *centralized network management architecture*, a single NMS manages the entire network (see Figure 10-10a). It is housed at a specific network location, which may be called a corporate *network operations center (NOC)*. Agents are distributed across devices at different network sites and send management data and information to the centralized NMS over in-band or out-of-band paths. In centralized architectures, network management data and information flows behave like the client-server flows described in Chapter 2.

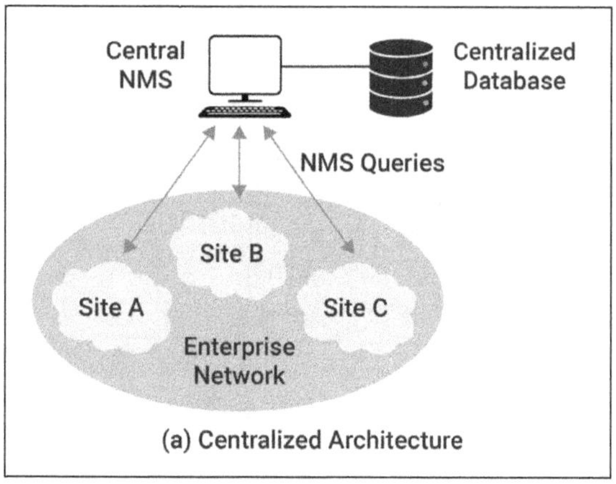

Figure 10-10a: An example of a centralized network management architecture.

An advantage of centralized network management is that only one NMS may be needed. This can reduce network management costs, but cost reduction depends on the NMS's range of management tools/applications. A disadvantage is that the sole NMS can be a single point of failure. Also, since multiple flows converge at the NMS, it may experience congestion that delays responses to network problems.

In *distributed network management architectures*, multiple NMSs provide localized network management at the network's different sites and essentially create multiple network management domains that are typically strategically located across the network. For example, in Figure 10-10b, each site in the enterprise network has its own local NMS that has a peer arrangement with other sites. NMS peers exchange management information about local link/element availability and performance that collectively provides an enterprise-wide view of the network.

An advantage of a distributed network management architecture is reduction of the volume of management information sent to a single network location. Another advantage comes from peer arrangements that enable peer NMSs to cover the loss of another peer. A disadvantage is higher network management costs from having and supporting multiple NMSs instead of just one.

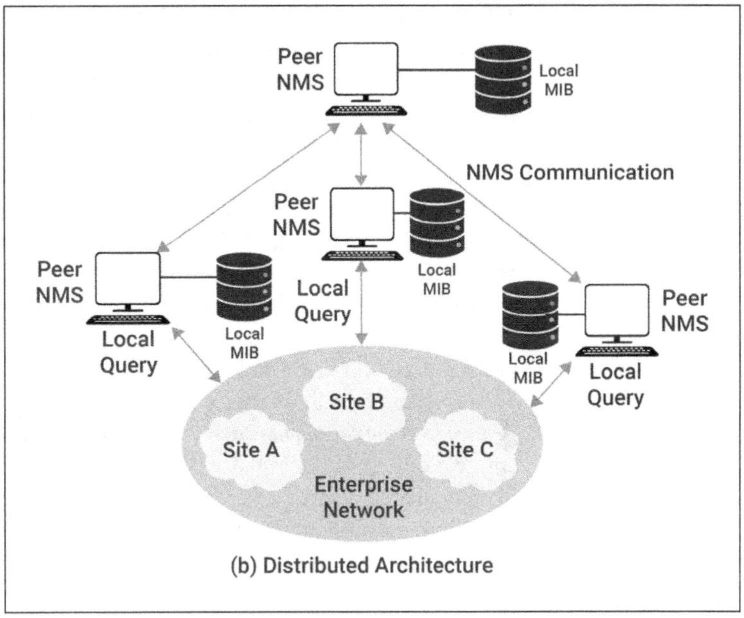

Figure 10-10b: An example of a distributed network management architecture.

Hierarchical network management architectures include distributed client NMSs that send management data and information to a centralized NMS. This is sometimes called a manager-of-managers (MoM) architecture, and the centralized NMS is sometimes called an *umbrella NMS*. Figure 10-10c depicts a hierarchical network management architecture for an enterprise network.

In hierarchical architectures, client NMSs filter management data from local network queries before sending it to the centralized NMS; this reduces the amount of management information that the central NMS might otherwise receive from the site. This configuration enables client NMSs to continue monitoring and data gathering activities when other parts of the network are failing. However, hierarchical architectures can be complex and hard to manage. They can also complicate security efforts.

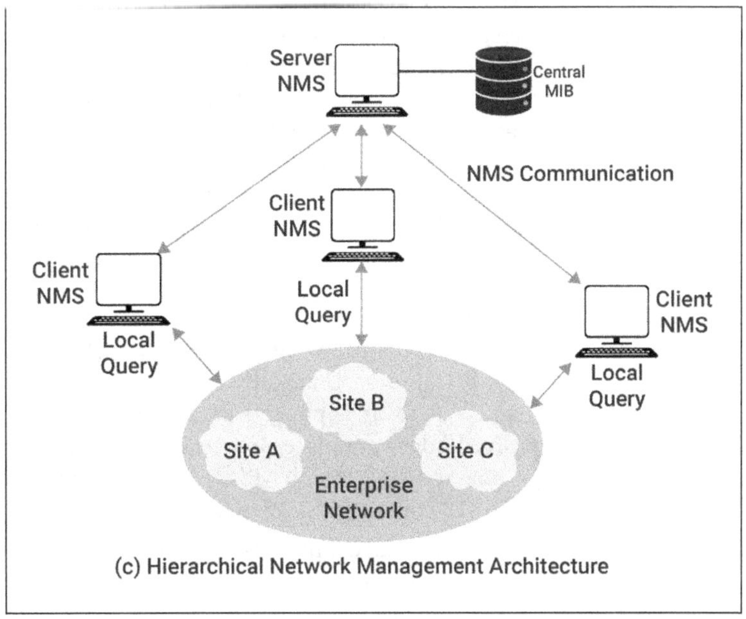

Figure 10-10c: An example of a hierarchical network management architecture.

Now that you have a better understanding of network management architectures, it is time to take a closer look at NMSs and network management protocols.

10.5.2 Network Management Systems (NMSs) and Network Management Protocols

A **network management system (NMS)** is an application or set of applications that is used to monitor, maintain, and optimize a network. It includes both hardware and software, but the term NMS typically refers to the software used to manage the network. An NMS allows an administrator to monitor all parts of the network (devices, servers, operations) from a central console in real time. And it can be used to optimize network performance and improve its security. An NMS can help avoid disruptions of network services, minimize errors, and maximize the availability of network resources.

As previously noted, NMSs collect data from network devices, such as switches, routers, and access points, and other devices connected to the network. They enable network administrators to monitor and control how the devices operate and interact with one another. Management data captured from devices is used to identify performance issues, accelerate troubleshooting, and monitor security. It is also used for proactive and predictive network management.

An NMS typically includes a network management station and network management software. A *network management station* is usually a server that runs one or more network management applications. It is equipped with sufficient processing capabilities to support the analysis of data from managed devices and reporting. The software on network management stations that is used to provision, monitor, maintain, and optimize the network is called **network management software**.

Network management systems can be expensive and can affect overall network performance by generating significant amounts of network monitoring data. Despite these drawbacks, businesses recognize the importance of NMSs, especially for proactive and predictive network management.

An NMS should include tools to quickly isolate, diagnose, and report network problems, and to facilitate quick resolution and recovery. Ideally, it should have sufficient intelligence to identify trends (for proactive network management), predict potential failures, and give network managers sufficient advanced warning so that they can act before network disruptions occur.

NMS tools and applications should have intuitive user interfaces and should react quickly to user input. The ability to easily create and maintain network management dashboards is usually highly desired. NMS tools that allow dynamic (re)configuration of devices should ideally enable changes to be made without having to reboot the device (and cause a temporary network service disruption). Network management software that supports dynamic configuration should require authentication to protect the network from attempts by unauthorized users to make changes.

SNMP and RMON

Simple Network Management Protocol (SNMP) is a protocol at the Application layer of the TCP/IP protocol stack that is used for monitoring and managing network devices in both LANs and WANs. It is popular because it is easy to install, configure, and use. When used sensibly, SNMP does not place an excessive traffic burden on a network.

In SNMP-based NMSs, managed devices are monitored and controlled using three basic SNMP commands: read, write, and trap.

- The read command is used by an NMS to monitor managed devices. This usually takes the form of an SNMP Get Request that is sent from the NMS to an agent to collect a management parameter.
- The write command is used by an NMS to control managed devices. This usually takes the form of an SNMP Set Request that is sent from the NMS to an agent to configure a parameter on the managed device.
- The trap command is used by managed devices to asynchronously report events to the NMS. This is sent autonomously (not in response to an NMS request) to the NMS to notify the NMS of an event.

SNMPv3 is the newest version of SNMP. SNMPv3 offers security features that SNMPv1 and SNMPv2 lacked. SNMPv3 includes authentication mechanisms to ensure that SNMP commands can only be sent/received by authenticated devices. Encryption is used to protect the payloads of the SNMPv3 messages, ensuring that the payloads cannot be read by unauthorized users. Encryption is especially for NMS applications that route SNMP messages over the Internet.

Remote monitoring (RMON) MIBs were developed in the early 1990s as an SNMP extension for monitoring Data Link and Physical layer per-link and per-element statistics in Ethernet networks. RMON agents are often called *RMON probes*.

The *RMON2* standard moves beyond per-link and per-element data to include end-to-end data for applications and services. For example, RMON2 includes Network, Transport, and Application layer traffic flow statistics, whereas RMON only provided Data Link and Physical layer statistics. RMON2 enables incoming and outgoing traffic for specific applications, such as email (SMTP) or HTTPS, to be measured, and RMON2 agents can provide information about the number of IP packets on device connections.

Today, SNMPv3 and RMON2 are supported in most managed devices and NMSs. However, SNMP-based network management is not the only game in town. Streaming telemetry offers an alternative. In *streaming telemetry*, the software agent in a network element enables it to stream data about the managed device's performance to the NMS in real time; the data does not have to first go to an MIB. Streaming telemetry has gained traction as a replacement for SNMP because it is efficient, scalable, and capable of producing more data points for tracking device performance that can be used for proactive or predictive network management. NETCONF/YANG (Network Configuration Protocol and the Yet Another Next Generation data modeling language) is a streaming telemetry standard that is supported in managed devices from multiple network infrastructure vendors.

Examples of SNMP-based NMS tools include SolarWinds, ManageEngine OpManager, and Progress WhatsUp Gold. Cloud-based network monitoring and management solutions have also gained considerable traction. For more information on NMSs and network management protocols, see Appendix 10-4.

10.5.3 Network Management Activities

The International Organization for Standardization (ISO) identifies five categories of network management tasks: Fault Management, Configuration Management, Accounting Management, Performance Management, and Security Management (FCAPS). The overall purpose and examples of associated activities of each category are briefly described in Table 10-13.

Table 10-13: ISO FCAPS network management task categories and related activities.

	Purpose	Related Activities
Fault Management	Avoid faults in the network and mitigate consequences when they occur.	Fault detection; diagnosis; isolation; correlation; aggregation; resolution
Configuration Management	Ensure that network equipment is properly configured to support network applications and users.	Update/upgrade network equipment; deploy software and software updates; monitor and modify device configurations
Accounting Management	Perform administrative tasks associated with the network and ensure that services and resources are fairly apportioned to applications and users.	Maintain equipment inventory list; generate network usage statistics; manage relationships with carriers and service providers
Performance Management	Improve overall network performance and the performance of applications that the network supports.	Monitor network equipment; monitor end-to-end, per-link, and per-element metrics; monitor quality of service; perform traffic engineering; maximize utilization
Security Management	Control access to network resources and keep them safe from malicious actions.	Access control; analyze incoming and outgoing traffic; enforce security policies; intrusion detection; intrusion prevention; encrypt sensitive data; respond to and recover from security breaches

The FCAPS model provides an overview of what network managers focus on and do. Each of these aspects of network management are briefly described in the following sections, and more fully in Appendix 10-5.

Fault Management

Fault management involves detecting, isolating, diagnosing, and fixing network problems. It also includes reporting problems to network managers and users, tracking trends in detected problems, and deploying workarounds until problems are corrected. Speedy problem identification and resolution help to minimize network downtime and unacceptable reductions in network performance.

Enterprise network users expect speedy and reliable resolution of network problems and to be provided with estimates of when the network will return to normal operations. Most organizations involve network users in fault management via trouble ticket systems.

A *trouble ticket system* is a software tool that tracks user reports of network problems and how the problems are resolved. A *trouble ticket* is created when a network user submits a help request to the problem tracking system. It is forwarded to an appropriate IT technician, who becomes responsible for addressing the user's issues Trouble ticket systems are common features of IT help desks in today's businesses.

Other fault management tools include monitoring tools and protocol analyzers. Monitoring tools often support SNMP and RMON.

Configuration Management

Configuration management involves the installation and modification of managed device configurations. It also involves keeping track of managed device configurations and defining/saving default configurations for use on similar network elements.

This information may be stored in network asset inventories that also include device specifics such as amount of RAM/cache/Flash memory, device interfaces, and connections. *Version logging* is also common; this involves keeping track of operating system versions on network devices and the versions of applications supported on the network.

Automated software distribution is used in many businesses to allocate software and software updates to network and user devices without user intervention. Software distribution tools also enable network administrators to monitor/supervise software usage and prohibit/block/remove the installation of unauthorized software and executable files.

Disk imaging and network backups are other common aspects of configuration management. *Disk imaging* copies or backs up a hard drive to a compressed file that can be stored on another device, in a network file system, or in the cloud. It enables the recovery of data stored when the image was made. A *network backup* copies data across all nodes and securely stores it. It also facilitates quick recovery from network crashes or failures.

Backing up device configurations is also common in enterprise networks. *Configuration backup* involves saving current device configuration specifics to a repository that includes incremental snapshots of the configurations. These backups are typically encrypted to ensure their security, and they can help networks recover from outages or security breaches.

Configuration management overlaps performance management by helping to ensure that managed devices are appropriately configured to support network applications and services. It also overlaps security management by ensuring that software updates and security patches are deployed to enterprise network devices.

Accounting Management

Accounting management involves aggregating network usage data and developing a comprehensive inventory of network assets. It tracks network utilization statistics, cloud service usage, data storage, and application usage overall and for various groups of network users. This information is used for capacity planning, network expansion plans, and proactive network management.

Network service providers leverage accounting management to be able to charge network users based on their usage. They may throttle network traffic for subscribers who exceed traffic flow volumes during a specified period of time. For example, mobile network operators (MNOs) may throttle connection speeds for individuals without unlimited voice or data plans, or levy surcharges when limits are exceeded.

User management is an important aspect of accounting management in enterprise networks. **User management** includes processes that network administrators use to manage user access to various network resources, such as applications, storage systems, intranets and extranets, and cloud services; it is a fundamental part of network security.

User management includes user account creation, maintenance, and deletion. It also includes the assignment of users to VLANs, single sign-on (SSO), and permissions management. Strict implementation of user access and identity verification is a core principle of zero trust security strategies.

Performance Management

According to the ISO's description of *performance management*, this category of network management processes focuses on measuring network behavior and effectiveness. It includes monitoring the behavior of network applications and processes, response times, and the reachability of network services and resources, and making/logging changes to network traffic routes. It helps organizations determine whether service level agreements (SLAs) are being met by carriers/providers, facilitates network optimization, and informs plans for network expansion.

Performance management also involves traffic engineering. *Traffic engineering (TE)* is concerned with optimizing the performance of a network and involves measuring, characterizing, modeling, and controlling network traffic flows to achieve specific performance objectives. TE sometimes involves forcing network traffic to take paths that are different from those chosen automatically by the routing protocol(s). SD-WANs, for example, support dynamic traffic routing.

TE may also involve *traffic shaping*, which limits the bandwidth that certain applications can consume to ensure adequate performance of critical applications. It may also involve *bandwidth (network) throttling*, which entails the intentional limitation of the connection speed of incoming/outgoing data from a specific network node or device. For example, an ISP or web server might intentionally slow Internet service to a specific client. This is a reactive mechanism to regulate network traffic and manage congestion, especially that being caused by specific devices or users.

Security Management

Security management in enterprise networks is multifaceted. It includes processes for authenticating devices, authorizing access to network resources, and controlling network access. It also involves the generation and distribution of encryption keys and using tools for analyzing router and switch configurations for compliance with security standards.

In FCAPS, security management is a network management function that focuses on protecting the network as a whole and its individual devices against intentional or accidental abuse, unauthorized access, and communication loss. It contributes to minimizing the potential for network disruption and other business continuity threats. Some of the more important aspects of security management are authentication, authorization, network segmentation, secure communications, and server hardening. They are briefly described in Table 10-14.

Table 10-14: Some of the major activities associated with FCAPS security management.

Security Management Function	Description
Authentication	Authentication is the process of identifying an individual user or device. Authentication ensures that the individual or device is who or what they claim to be. Typically, users are required to provide a valid username and password when logging into the network, but increasingly, additional identifiers, such as biometrics or multifactor authentication, are required. Device authentication is also common, and zero trust security requires authentication of all devices that use the network, no matter where they are located. Increasingly, continuous device authentication is used to require devices to re-authenticate after communication sessions are started.
Authorization	Authorization is the process that gives network users (and devices) access to network resources and services based on their identities. Granular privileges can be assigned on a per role or per user basis. Such privileges specify what the user is permitted to do on the network, what resources and services they can access, and what they are allowed to do with the resources they access. For example, one network user may be granted "read only" access to a database, which allows them to view database contents but not change them, while another network user with "update" privileges can see database contents and make changes to the database. Trusted network managers perform role creation, modification, and removal.
Network segmentation	Network segmentation involves splitting the network into logical domains and associating network objects (e.g., network elements, devices, links, subnets, VLANs, etc.) with specific network access domains (NADs). Network users and devices can be assigned to specific NADs to restrict their access and their views to the network objects in their NAD. Network segmentation is often used to ensure that IoT devices are assigned to NADs that are separate from those used to support network users.
Secure communication	*Secure communication* focuses on the end-to-end security of network communications. It strives to ensure that secure protocols are used and that the security features of communication protocols are enabled and appropriately configured. For example, network managers should verify that secure protocols are used for communications between the NMS and network elements. In SNMP-based NMSs, this may involve ensuring that SNMPv3 is used because of its superior security features.
Server hardening	Server hardening involves disabling or removing unnecessary services and software packages on a server, ensuring that encrypted passwords are used to access server resources, and performing server security scans and audits to identify vulnerabilities. Patch management for server operating systems is an aspect of server hardening.

Security management encompasses network intrusion prevention and detection, minimizing damage from data breaches and other attacks, and recovering from security breaches. It relies on the other aspects of network management for assistance in securing the network. Having backup out-of-band access to managed devices during attacks that disrupt the network can be beneficial.

An important but sometimes overlooked aspect of security management is the process used to collect, store, and examine security audits and the results of network security tests. Audit logs should document logins and logouts and attempts by network users to change their authorization levels. Network security scans and penetration tests yield valuable insights about potential vulnerabilities, and their results can be leveraged to strengthen network security.

10.6 NETWORK AUDITS

Network auditing is a process that involves gathering, analyzing, and studying data about a network. It is used to determine network health and the extent to which the network meets the organization's business and technical requirements for availability, performance, manageability, and security.

A network audit may be performed during the network design process to assess the existing network. It may also be performed after the deployment of a redesigned or new network to determine the achievement of design goals or to identify opportunities for optimization. Network auditing can provide insights into the effectiveness of network management/control practices or the network's compliance with internal policies or external regulations.

Because most businesses lack internal expertise, network audits are usually carried out by third-party companies or consultancies that specialize in network auditing and have personnel with requisite skills and experience.

Today, enterprise network audits primarily focus on network security and control. However, many also review the processes and measures that the organization uses to ensure the availability and performance of critical applications.

Network security audits typically focus on:

- Data security. This considers both data in motion and data at rest, access controls that restrict who can view the data, the inclusion of personal data in data repositories, and processes used to anonymize personal data.
- Access controls. This focuses on authentication protocols and procedures used to protect the network, how new devices are added to the network, access controls used for both wired and wireless connections, and the extent to which up-to-date authentication protocols are used.
- Physical security. This examines how physical access to the network is secured and where additional physical security controls should be used.
- Security and use policies. This should identify user password strength and password change policies, bring your own device (BYOD) policies, and how security policies are enforced.

In short, network audits involve collecting and analyzing large amounts of data about a network. Regular network audits should be viewed as an important part of network management. They help organizations identify opportunities to optimize the network and address security vulnerabilities before they become critical issues for the organization. For a more detailed examination of network audits, see Appendix 10-6.

10.7 SDN AND NETWORK MANAGEMENT

Software-defined networking (SDN) is an approach to networking that focuses on making a network more flexible and easier to manage; it increases a network's manageability. SDN architectures decouple network control and forwarding functions. Software-based controllers or application programming interfaces (APIs) communicate with network hardware infrastructure and direct traffic on a network.

The key difference between SDN and traditional networking is infrastructure: SDN is software based, while traditional networking is hardware based. In traditional networking, software in network routers and switches is used to determine/control the interface (port) on which a frame or packet should be forwarded; both forwarding decisions and transmissions occur at the device level. In SDN, forwarding decisions are made outside the devices that perform forwarding transmissions.

Basically, in SDN, the software used to forward traffic is decoupled from the hardware and moved to a *control plane*. Forwarding tables and forwarding table updates are maintained at the control plane instead of in the devices that forward data. In SDN architectures, the devices that perform forwarding transmissions are located at the *data plane* (see Figure 10-11)

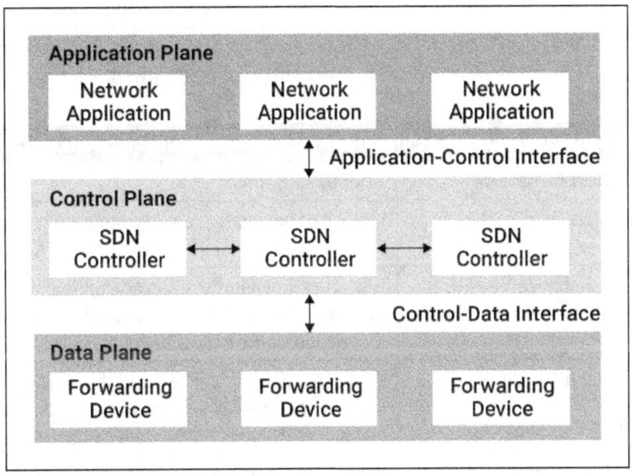

Figure 10-11: Software-defined networking (SDN) architecture.

Separating the control plane from the data plane enables network administrators to use SDN to centrally program and control the entire network; it is no longer necessary to rely on traditional distributed routing processes and protocols to provide end-to-end data transfers. This enables SDN to be application focused. SDN controllers ensure that application traffic is forwarded through the network in the manner needed to optimize application performance.

SDN architecture also includes an *application plane* that includes business applications supported on the network and networking applications such as load balancers, firewalls, and intrusion detection systems. Applications communicate with the control layer via APIs called *northbound APIs*. Communication between the control and data planes uses *southbound APIs*.

The control plane is considered the brain of SDN, and its intelligence is provided by centralized SDN controller software. Controller software resides on a server and manages network traffic policies and the flow of data traffic throughout the network. Routing protocols reside in SDN controllers, and the results of their work create and control forwarding tables that determine how packets are routed and frames are forwarded at the data plane.

The *OpenFlow (OF) protocol* is a networking protocol that is a standard in SDNs. This protocol defines the (southbound) communication between an SDN controller and forwarding devices at the data plane. It gives the controller access to the forwarding plane of the devices to manage and direct the flow of packets among them. OF is also used for monitoring switch and router port statistics in network management.

A number of SDN and SD-WAN models are advocated by SDN product vendors. Several of them are identified in Table 10-15.

SDN is widely considered a significant departure from traditional networking and network management for various reasons, some of which are identified in Table 10-16.

Table 10-15: Examples of SDN models advocated by SDN product vendors.

SDN/SD-WAN Model	Description
Open SDN	Open SDN uses open-source protocols to control the virtual and physical (data plane) devices responsible for routing/forwarding data packets/frames.
API SDN	API SDN uses southbound APIs to control the flow of data to and from each forwarding layer device.
Overlay Model SDN	Overlay Model SDN creates a virtual network above existing network infrastructure that provides tunnels (with channels) to data centers. The controller for the virtual network allocates bandwidth and assigns devices to each channel based on the needs of applications.
Hybrid Model SDN	Hybrid Model SDN combines SDN and traditional networking. It allows the optimal protocol to be assigned for each type of traffic on the network. This is often viewed as an intermediate step toward full-fledged adoption of SDN.

Table 10-16: Some of the differences between SDN and traditional networking and network management.

SDN Difference	Brief Description
Increased control and flexibility	Instead of having to manually program multiple devices at the data plane, network managers can control network traffic flow by programming a software-based controller.
Customizable network infrastructure	Network administrators can configure network services and allocate resources to make real-time changes to the network infrastructure. This enables them to optimize the flow of data through the network and prioritize applications that require more bandwidth availability.
Robust security	Because it delivers entire network visibility, SDN provides a holistic view of security threats. SDN enables network managers to quickly quarantine compromised devices to prevent them from infecting the rest of the network. However, because SDN relies on centralized controllers, securing the controllers becomes a crucial part of network security.
IoT security	With the proliferation of IoT and smart devices in businesses that connect to cloud services via the Internet, SDN enables network managers to create separate zones for IoT devices based on the different levels of security they require.

In short, SDN is much more flexible than traditional networking. It allows network administrators to centrally control the network, change configuration settings, provision resources, and increase network capacity without having to add more infrastructure. And, thanks to the ability to define pathways for different types of data, SDN can contribute to network security. Given these characteristics, it is not surprising that SDN is widely used in cloud data centers and most business WANs.

10.8 UNIFIED ENDPOINT MANAGEMENT (UEM)

Unified endpoint management (UEM) encompasses a set of technologies used to manage and secure a wide range of employee devices and device operating systems from a single network management console. UEM tools combine tools for managing and securing desktop PCs and laptops with enterprise mobility management (EMM) tools, including mobile device management (MDM) and mobile application management (MAM) tools. UEM strives to tie together all enterprise network endpoints and provide network managers with visibility into how corporate applications and data are supported on user devices.

EMM, MDM, and MAM were introduced in Chapter 2. EMM and some of its major components are described more fully in Appendix 10-7.

As Table 10-17 illustrates, EMM is often viewed as the evolutionary step after MDM, while UEM is considered the next generation beyond EMM. It also illustrates another network management theme and trend: central management of most or all facets of enterprise network infrastructure. This theme/trend is also evident in hierarchical MoM (manager-of-managers) network management architectures, SDN, and SD-WANs.

UEM platforms usually have extensive operating system support, including mobile (Android, iOS) and desktop OSs (Windows, macOS, ChromeOS). Linux is also supported in some UEM tools. Accelerating business deployment of IoT systems and applications is pressuring UEM software vendors to expand the device platforms they support. UEM platforms are usually available as SaaS, cloud-based tools.

Increasingly, UEM platforms are providing tighter integration with *unified endpoint security (UES)* systems that provide visibility into device security from a central network management console. UES coordinates detecting/addressing device vulnerabilities and managing security incidents.

Table 10-17: A high-level comparison of MDM, EMM, and UEM.

	Description	Characteristics
Mobile device management (MDM)	Tools that manage mobile devices and mobile users' data and provide basic mobile application controls	Enforces passcodes; installs applications; performs mobile device wipes; ensures compliance with corporate BYOD and corporate owned personally enabled (COPE) policies
Enterprise mobility management (EMM)	Tools that encompass MDM and provide more granular application controls	Enforces multifactor authentication; manages enterprise file sync and sharing; deploys web browser security settings to devices; applies conditional access policies
Unified endpoint management (UEM)	Tools that encompass EMM and enable full management of desktop computers, including their OSs, apps, and data	Applies EMM controls to PCs and desktops; enables desktops and mobile devices to be configured or updated at the same time; includes printer and IoT device management

SUMMARY

To realize their strategic and operational potential, business networks should be carefully planned, designed, operated, and managed to ensure that they meet business needs. Many businesses use network life cycle models, such as the PPDIOO and enterprise network architectures, to provide perspective and guidance for designing, deploying, and managing their networks.

Network availability (uptime), scalability, adaptability, security, and manageability are attributes that businesses commonly seek in their enterprise networks. They are reflected in business and technical requirements and design for redesigned or new networks. Network design goals may conflict, and trade-offs often must be confronted when network design goals are finalized. For example, an organization's desires to improve network performance and security may need to be balanced against the desire to make the network more affordable or manageable.

Careful and critical evaluation of the existing network is an important step in the network design process. It enables designers to determine the extent to which the existing network stacks up against the business and technical requirements for the new network to identify existing network components that can be used in the new one. Baseline measurements of various facets of network performance (capacity utilization, response times, availability, etc.) are taken for the existing network and are used to assess the performance of the redesigned or new network.

New equipment, software, and protocols are identified during the design and implementation phases of the network design process and the PPDIOO network life cycle. Network audits are commonly performed post-implementation to assess the extent to which network design goals are achieved.

Network design best practices include future-proofing the network; building backup, failover, and resilience into the network design; embedding security; and standardizing whatever can be standardized. Ensuring that the network complies with regulatory requirements, plans for cooling and electrical requirements, and plans for increased reliance on cloud infrastructure are other important network design considerations.

Network management is associated with the operate and optimize phases of the PPDIOO network life cycle, and NMSs are important network management tools. Managed devices, agents, and NMSs are the basic components of network management architectures. Agents in managed devices use network management protocols, such as SNMP, to communicate with the NMS. The communication may be in-band, out-of-band, or a combination of the two.

NMSs monitor and log end-to-end measures, such as availability, capacity, jitter, and response times for applications. They also monitor per-link measures (e.g., utilization, errored frames, propagation delay) for communication links and per-element measures (such as filtering and forwarding rates) for routers, switches, and other managed devices.

NMSs support all facets of network management specified in the OSI's FCAPS model. The five network management functions described by FCAPS are fault, configuration, accounting, performance, and security management. A variety of activities and tools are associated with each of these network management functions.

SDN is an important part of network management in many business WANs and data centers. SDN controllers make routing/forwarding decisions for routers and switches rather than having them made at the device level. Basically, SDN enables network managers to better manage and control application traffic.

UEM is also becoming an important part of network management. UEM is often considered a successor to MDM and EMM. UEM illustrates the increasing importance of mobile devices in enterprise networks and the desire to centrally provision, manage, secure, and control both mobile and nonmobile devices in enterprise networks.

Security is a central focus of network management and an important aspect of network design. Authentication, authorization, segmentation, secure communication, and server hardening are important aspects of security management.

KEY TERMS

Manageability
Mean time between failures (MTBF)
Mean time to diagnose (MTTD)
Mean time to repair (MTTR)
Network auditing
Network life cycle
Network management (NM)
Network management software
Network management system (NMS)
Network utilization
Predictive network management
Proactive network management
Software-defined networking (SDN)
Unified endpoint management (UEM)
User management

REVIEW QUESTIONS

1. Identify several ongoing enterprise network design and management issues/factors.
2. Identify and briefly describe each of the phases in the PPDIOO network life cycle model.
3. Briefly explain the value of network life cycle models in network design.
4. Identify several important network design context factors/realities.
5. Identify design considerations for each layer of hierarchical network architectures.
6. Identify the characteristics of enterprise network architectures.
7. Identify components/submodules of enterprise campus and enterprise edge modules in enterprise network architectures.
8. Identify components/submodules of the service provider edge and remote modules of enterprise network architectures.
9. Briefly explain how the modularity of enterprise network architectures helps network designers.
10. Identify common "must have" business requirements for redesigned or new networks. Identify other common business requirements.
11. Identify examples of technical requirements for redesigned or new networks.
12. Briefly describe each of the following aspects of network performance: accuracy, capacity, utilization, throughput, efficiency, latency, jitter, response time, and offered load.
13. Identify and briefly describe several fundamental network design goals.
14. Briefly describe each of the following network design goals: usability, adaptability, affordability, and network performance.
15. Identify and briefly describe several examples of trade-offs for network design goals.
16. Explain why prioritizing/ranking network design goals is helpful for designers.
17. Identify the activities that designers perform when they assess the existing network. Identify examples of opportunities and constraints that are revealed in the process.
18. Why do network designers take network performance baseline measurements? Identify some of the challenges associated with measuring network utilization.
19. Briefly explain how MTBF, MTTR, and MTTD statistics are related to network design and management.
20. How/why do network designers characterize network traffic?
21. What is involved with developing a physical design for a redesigned or new network? What is included in the logical design of a network?
22. Explain how designers select hardware, software, and protocols for a new network. Also explain why designers develop detailed implementation plans.
23. Identify and briefly describe several network design best practices. Also identify and briefly describe several network design considerations that should not be overlooked.
24. Briefly explain the difference between network manageability and network management. What are the differences between reactive, proactive, and predictive network management?
25. Identify and briefly describe each of the layers/levels of the network management hierarchy.
26. Briefly describe the role(s) of each of the following components of network management architectures: managed devices, agents, and the NMS.
27. Briefly describe each of the following: end-to-end measures, per-link measures, per-element measures, in-band management, and out-of-band management.
28. Briefly describe the differences between centralized, distributed, and hierarchical network management architectures.
29. Briefly describe the differences between network management stations, network management software, and network management protocols.
30. Identify and briefly describe the different categories of network management activities included in the FCAPS model.
31. Identify and briefly describe several common activities for each of the following aspects of network management: fault management, configuration management,

accounting management, performance management, and security management.

32. Briefly describe the characteristics and tools associated with each of the following aspects of network management: fault management, configuration management, accounting management, performance management, and security management.
33. What is network auditing? Why are network audits performed? What do network security audits typically focus on?
34. What is SDN, and how is it different from traditional networking? What is the OpenFlow protocol?
35. What is UEM, and what does it include? How is UEM different from MDM and EMM? What is UES?

PROBLEMS AND EXERCISES

Exercise 10-1 A business has finalized its ranking of network design goals and has established a weight for each goal in its finalized list:

Security	30
Availability	25
Adaptability	15
Scalability	10
Manageability	5
Performance	5
Affordability	5
Usability	5
Total	100

Given these rankings, explain what the organization is looking for in the network and how these priorities are likely to affect the technologies, software, and protocols selected for the new network. Identify some of the trade-offs among network design goals that the business seems willing to make.

Exercise 10-2 Georgia Southern University has three campuses: Statesboro, Savannah, and Hinesville. Most of the university's students (20,000) and employees (2,300) are located at the Statesboro campus. There are approximately 7000 students (and 175 employees) in Savannah and approximately 1000 students (and 31 employees) in Hinesville. The servers and storage that support the university's intranet are located on the Statesboro campus. All three campuses connect to the University System of Georgia's Peachnet WAN, which provides access to the Internet for all public universities in the state. Georgia Southern subscribes to several cloud services, including Google and AWS.

Using Cisco Enterprise Architectures (and Figure 10-4) for guidance, create a diagram/sketch for a modular network architecture for the university that a network designer could use. Your diagram/sketch should include enterprise campus, enterprise edge, service provider edge, and remote modules. You should identify and appropriately label submodules for each module to reflect specific locations and services.

Exercise 10-3 Figure 10-12 is a logical diagram for an existing network at a business location.

Modify (add links/devices to) the diagram to illustrate how the network could be redesigned to improve resilience, redundancy, and availability. Briefly describe what should be considered at each layer to improve the network's fault tolerance and performance.

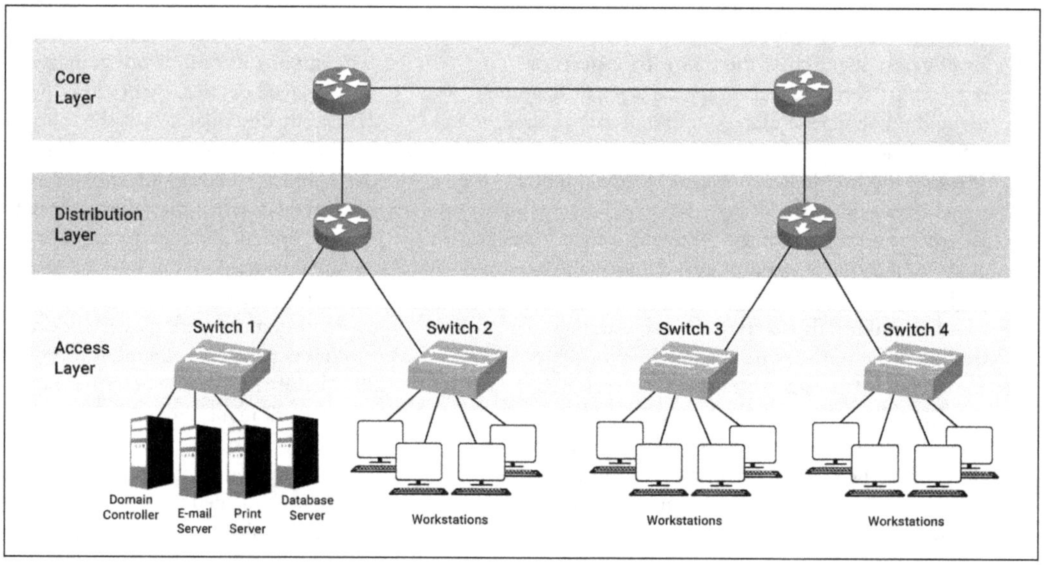

Figure 10-12: Logical diagram of a current network.

Exercise 10-4 Look for articles and other Internet resources (e.g., videos) on EMM, MDM, MAM, MIM (identity), MCM, and MIM (information) that summarize what each involves, and delineate their associated network management goals and tasks. Also look for online sources that address how traditional network management (FCAPS) activities and network management systems (NMS) have evolved to include EMM, MDM, MAM, MCM, and the like.

Develop a 10- to 12-slide PowerPoint presentation that addresses the following questions:

- What is EMM, and what are its major goals? What are its major components?
- What is MDM? Why is it important? What does it include?
- What is mobile identity management (MIM)? Why is it important? What does it include?
- What is MAM? Why is it important? What does it include?
- What is MCM? Why is it important? What does it include?
- What is mobile information management (MIM), and what does it include?
- What is mobile expense management (MEM)? What does it involve?
- How does UEM relate to FCAPS? *Note:* This should include a diagram/sketch that maps EMM subcomponents (MDM, MAM, MIM, etc.) to the OSI's FCAPS model.
- How does UEM extend EMM? What are the capabilities of UEM platforms?

Your presentation should include multiple relevant and informative embedded images (and/or tables), ideally one per slide.

The final slide of your presentation should be a References (or Sources) slide that includes the titles and URLs of at least four online articles that you consider to be particularly informative about EMM and its components.

Exercise 10-5 Given the information provided in Item 2 about Georgia Southern University, what type of network management architecture (centralized, distributed, hierarchical) would you recommend? Provide justification for your recommendation and describe the advantages of your recommended network management architecture for the university.

Exercise 10-6 Given the information provided in Item 2 about Georgia Southern University, use Visio or another network diagramming tool to illustrate how the university could deploy SDN. Determine where SDN controllers should be placed for centralized network management, and identify/label the devices that they would control. Provide justification for your recommendation and describe the advantages of SDN for the university.

CHAPTER REFERENCES

Bhoutkar, A. J. (n.d.). Software-Defined Networking. ATMECS Global. Retrieved from: https://www.atmecs.com/software-defined-networking/

Cisco Networking Academy. (2014). Hierarchical Network Design. In *Connecting Networks Companion Guide* (pp. 1–31). Cisco Press. Retrieved from: https://www.ciscopress.com/articles/article.asp?p=2202410&seqNum=6

Cisco Systems. (n.d.). What Is Network Management? Retrieved from: https://www.cisco.com/c/en/us/solutions/enterprise-networks/what-is-network-management.html

Finnegan, M. (2021). What Is UEM? Unified Endpoint Management Explained. *ComputerWorld.* Retrieved from: https://www.computerworld.com/article/3625231/what-is-uem-unified-endpoint-management-explained.html

Froom, R., Balaji, S., & Frahim, E. (2010). Analyzing the Cisco Enterprise Campus Architecture. In *Implementing Cisco IP Switched Networks (SWITCH) Foundation Learning Guide: Foundation learning for SWITCH 642-813* (pp. 1–43). Cisco Press. Retrieved from: https://www.ciscopress.com/articles/article.asp?p=1608131&seqNum=3#:~:text=PPDIOO%20is%20a%20Cisco%20methodology%20that%20defines%20the,identifying%20technologies%20that%20can%20best%20support%20the%20architecture

Kim, H., & Feamster, N. (2013). Improving Network Management with Software Defined Networking. *IEEE Communications Magazine, 51*(2), 114–119. Retrieved from: https://www.researchgate.net/publication/260514929_Improving_Network_Management_with_Software_Defined_Networking

McCabe, J. D. (2010). *Network Analysis, Architecture, and Design* (3rd ed.). Morgan Kaufmann.

MSP360. (n.d.). Network Audit Guide. Retrieved from: https://www.msp360.com/resources/blog/network-audit-guide/

Oppenheimer, P. (2012). *Top-Down Network Design* (3rd ed.). Cisco Press.

Petryschuk, S. (n.d.). Network Design and Best Practices. Auvik Networks. Retrieved from: https://www.auvik.com/franklyit/blog/network-design-best-practices/

Stewart III, K., & Adams, A. (n.d.). Chapter 1: Introducing Network Design Concepts. In *Designing and Supporting Computer Networks, CCNA Discovery Learning Guide.* PearsonHigherEd. Retrieved from: https://www.pearsonhighered.com/assets/samplechapter/1/5/8/7/1587132125.pdf

Swyx. (2020). Networking Essentials: Traffic Engineering. DEV. Retrieved from: https://dev.to/swyx/networking-essentials-traffic-engineering-13c4

VMware. (n.d.). What Is Software-Defined Networking (SDN)? Retrieved from: https://www.vmware.com/topics/glossary/content/software-defined-networking.html

MINICASE: NMS for New SSU Building

Review the information in the Chapter 6 and Chapter 7 Minicases. SSU plans to create a network management domain for the new wing of the building. It will be a new part of the university's distributed network management architecture.

The new network management domain will include a network management station that runs network management software that monitors and manages both the wired and wireless networks in the new wing. Managed devices (network elements) will include all switches, the Wi-Fi controller, the router, and all servers in the server room.

Task 1: Create an NMS Diagram

Use Visio or another diagramming tool to create a logical diagram of the NMS system. Your diagram should include the NMS station (console), all switches, all servers, the Wi-Fi controller, and the router. Every device in the diagram should be clearly labeled.

Task 2: Identify Network Management Measures

The university believes in proactive network management and wants to track both per-element and per-link measures for the wired and wireless networks in the new wing.

- What measures should the NMS track for the router?
- What measures should the NMS track for the backbone distribution switch?
- What measures should the NMS track for the server room switch?
- What measures should the NMS track for the Wi-Fi controller?

Initially, network managers plan to monitor the links from the building distribution switch to the Wi-Fi controller and server room switch. They also plan on monitoring the links from the server room switch to each of the servers.

- Is this enough? Why/why not? Which other links should be monitored? Why?
- What measures should be collected for the links?
- What version of RMON should be used? Why?

Task 3: Future-Proofing the New Networks

Network designers want to future-proof the wired and wireless networks in the new wing.

- Do some online research on future-proofing Ethernet LANs and BNs, and Wi-Fi networks. Summarize what you learn about future-proofing these types of local networks in a 150- to 300-word executive summary.
- Given what you have learned about future-proofing, make specific cabling recommendations for the links among the managed devices in the network management domain illustrated in your Task 1 diagram. Your cabling recommendations should reflect the current Ethernet standard and what is anticipated for the next generation. Ideally, the installed cable should enable SSU to migrate to next generation Ethernet without having to add new cabling.
- Also, leverage your future-proofing research to make specific recommendations about the filtering and forwarding capabilities of the switches and router in the building wing and redundant links among them to ensure availability and load balancing.
- SSU's long-range plans include migrating to SDN to help ensure adequate performance for applications used by SSU students and employees. To accommodate this migration, what features and capabilities should be included in switches and the router being installed in the new building wing?
- SSU network planners view 5G RANs as becoming an important part of the university's network infrastructure in the years ahead. What should the university be doing now to make this building wing (and future buildings) ready for a 5G future?

Bundle your work for Tasks 1, 2, and 3 in one or more document files, and follow your instructor's guidance for submitting your work.

Chapter 11

Enterprise Network Security

LEARNING OBJECTIVES

After reading and studying this chapter, you should be able to:

- Identify what enterprise network security encompasses and why it is challenging.
- Describe attack surfaces, vulnerabilities, common attacks, and attack responses.
- Identify enterprise network security goals.
- Identify the contents of network business continuity and disaster recovery plans.
- Briefly describe network threat analysis, risk management, security plans, policies, and procedures.
- Briefly describe network security architectures.
- Briefly describe the underlying assumptions of layered defenses and defense in depth (DiD).
- Identify examples of threats and security defenses for facilities that house network infrastructure.
- Identify and briefly describe security controls at the cloud layer of DiD.
- Identify network perimeter threats, defenses, and best practices.
- Identify internal network threats and security defenses.
- Briefly describe APTs and lateral movement and APT security tools/controls.
- Briefly describe encryption and cryptography.
- Briefly describe symmetric encryption algorithms, block ciphers, and stream ciphers.
- Briefly describe asymmetric encryption algorithms and public key infrastructure.

11.0 INTRODUCTION

Network security is a broad term that encompasses a wide range of goals, strategies, policies, architectures, technologies, devices, and processes. It is the set of rules, technologies, and technology configurations used to protect the integrity, confidentiality, and accessibility of an enterprise network. Every organization, regardless of size, industry, or infrastructure, requires network security solutions to protect it from the ever-growing array of cyberthreats.

Security is incredibly important in all parts of enterprise networks. Network administrators are constantly shoring up defenses against determined attackers and soliciting the help of employees via training and the enforcement of security policies.

Today's enterprise network architectures are complex, with many moving/evolving components, and they are confronted by an ever-changing threat environment, with attackers who persistently strive to find and exploit vulnerabilities. Malicious actors sell/buy/share known vulnerabilities on the dark web and are increasingly using AI to develop malware, hacking, and attack tools.

Enterprise network managers must be unceasingly vigilant in monitoring component security to quickly identify and respond to security breaches. They also need to be proactive in identifying network vulnerabilities and reducing the network attack surface. Many use cybersecurity companies for security audits, penetration tests, firewall monitoring, employee training, and other security services. Today, it is rare for businesses to rely solely on internal expertise to secure their networks.

Cybercriminals have various motivations for attacking enterprise networks. Some seek sensitive data for financial gain, others are political, industrial, or nation-state espionage operatives. Some attackers work alone, but many are members of cybercriminal collaborations. Cybercriminals are not the only perpetrators of network breaches, but their nefarious or malicious motives place them among the most worrisome categories of attackers.

Enterprise networks have a large attack surface with a broad range of vulnerabilities, and a broad array of defenses and tools are used to protect them. Even a few minutes of network disruption from a security breach can negatively affect business operations or damage a company's reputation. Successful attacks on corporate or government networks are major news stories, and their effects can take months or years to fully assess.

For example, the ransomware attack on the Colonial Pipeline on May 7, 2021, disrupted pipeline operations, caused temporary gasoline shortages in some parts of the United States and price increases nationwide. It was labeled a major cyberattack on American energy infrastructure and served as a wake-up call for addressing cybersecurity vulnerabilities in the energy sector.

Today, large and medium size businesses have staff members with cybersecurity expertise. However, such expertise continues to be expensive, despite increases in university-level education and industry cybersecurity training opportunities. Many smaller organizations lack the wherewithal for full-time cybersecurity employees and typically require their network administrators and IT support personnel to be knowledgeable about network security attacks and defenses. They also rely on companies in the cybersecurity industry to assist in securing their networks.

Over the past decade, most publicly traded corporations have added at least one cybersecurity expert to their board of directors. It is becoming rare for a corporate board to not include cybersecurity knowledge. Such high-level involvement in corporate governance illustrates the seriousness of enterprise network security in today's businesses.

It is impossible to provide a comprehensive summary of enterprise network security in the limited space of two textbook chapters. However, this and Chapter 12 strive to provide a reasonably sound foundation for further exploration of network security in information assurance and security courses or training.

This chapter considers network attack surfaces, common vulnerabilities, common attacks, and typical responses to attacks. It also considers layered defenses and how they are related to security goals, strategies, policies, procedures, practices, and technologies used to protect facilities, network perimeters, and internal networks from threats and attacks. Firewalls, intrusion detection and prevention systems, and encryption are among the more important network security controls described in this chapter. Chapter 12 considers technologies used to secure devices, applications, and data.

11.1 NETWORK ATTACK SURFACES AND VULNERABILITIES

Network vulnerabilities and network attack surfaces are closely intertwined, and this section discusses how and why they are related. This section also identifies some common vulnerabilities and several vulnerability controls used in today's businesses.

11.1.1 Network Attack Surfaces

Network attack surfaces refer to the potential vulnerabilities in a computer network that attackers can exploit to gain unauthorized access, steal data, or launch cyberattacks. An attack surface can

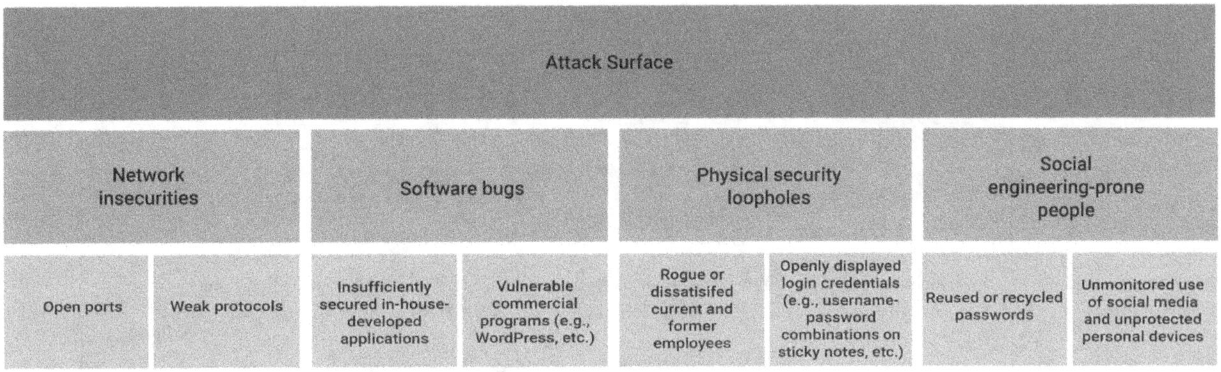

Figure 11-1: A network's attack surface is the totality of its vulnerabilities.

be divided into two categories: the *digital attack surface* and the *physical attack surface*. The digital attack surface includes all the hardware and software in an organization's network, including applications, program code, ports, websites, and servers. The physical attack surface includes all endpoint devices that an attacker can gain physical access to, including desktop computers, mobile devices, hard drives, and USB drives.

Basically, a network's *attack surface* is the entire external-facing area of the network. The attack surface contains all attack vectors (vulnerabilities) an attacker could use to access the network. Hence, a **network attack surface** is the totality of all vulnerabilities in connected hardware, software, and services that are accessible to unauthenticated or unauthorized users. This is illustrated in Figure 11-1.

The attack surface includes every point of network interaction. Hackers, industrial spies, and attackers use malware, ransomware, and advanced persistent threats (APTs) to target interaction points and known or potential vulnerabilities.

The external-facing areas of an enterprise network are usually what attackers exploit, through remote access and intrusion, but internal networks (such as Wi-Fi and Ethernet LANs) should also be considered parts of a network's attack surface. Tunneling technologies such as VPNs can also be vulnerabilities when they are configured to circumvent firewall filters, intrusion prevention, and other network access controls.

A network's attack surface can be reduced by closing unnecessary ports in firewalls, routers, and switches; restricting access to network resources to authenticated and authorized users and devices; and stringently controlling network access via tunneling.

Attackers often try to exploit multiple attack vectors to gain access to networks. This means that it is increasingly important for businesses to regularly perform comprehensive network security audits (see section 10.6 in Chapter 10) to ensure that firewalls, intrusion prevention systems, and breach detection systems (BDSs) are appropriately configured. Comprehensive security audits also provide valuable information for maintaining and enforcing security policies.

Often, it is also important to consider the attack surfaces of enterprise network components. Figure 11-2, for example, illustrates potential vulnerabilities (the attack surfaces) for IoT devices, platforms, and applications. Accelerating business adoption and use of IoT systems and applications makes it important to consider how each new device and application affects the enterprise network's attack surface.

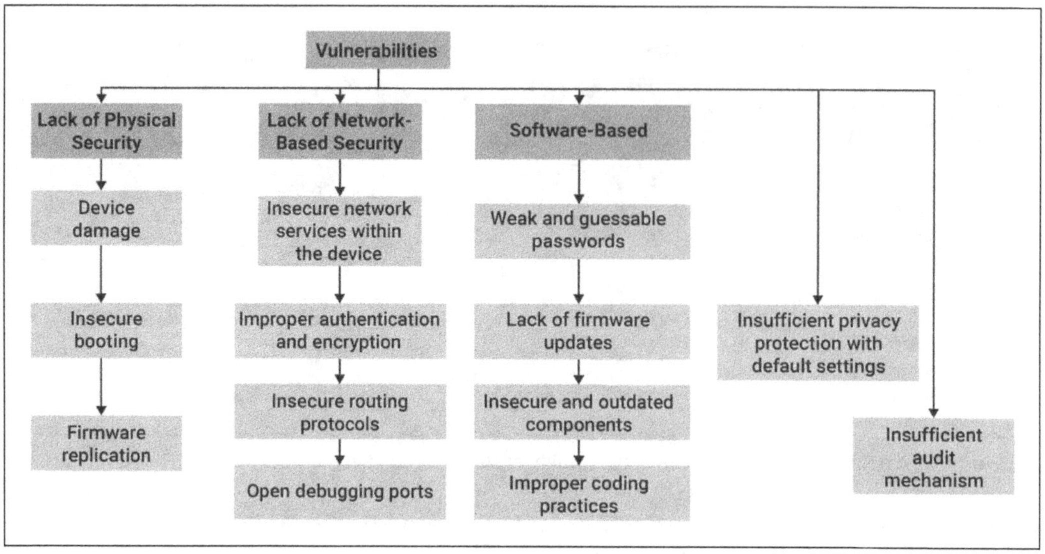

Figure 11-2: Vulnerabilities in the attack surface for an IoT system or application.

The desire for a comprehensive picture of a network's attack surface is a driver of the adoption of centralized network management tools like SD-WANs and UEM and their security capabilities.

11.1.2 Network Vulnerabilities

Enterprise networks are constantly evolving, including numerous rapidly changing components with the potential to expand a network's attack surface through the introduction of new vulnerabilities that put the network and its data at risk.

A **network vulnerability** is a weakness in a network system or its design that could be exploited by an attacker to access a network. A vulnerability is a potential *attack vector* if it is susceptible to a method or combination of methods that an attacker can use to infiltrate a network. Hence, it is important to identify vulnerabilities and methods for exploiting them.

Vulnerabilities that are common across businesses and other organizations include users who are susceptible to social engineering attacks (such as phishing), insufficient secured (unpatched) software, misconfigured firewalls, weak authentication controls, and insecure or unauthorized

Table 11-1: Common enterprise network vulnerabilities.

Vulnerability	Description
Weak passwords	Passwords that are shared, outdated, or insufficiently protected can facilitate network breaches. Most businesses have strong password requirements that enforce regular password changes.
Excess access privileges	Employees who can access systems or network resources they are not authorized to use or have access privileges that exceed those needed to perform their jobs put the network at risk. Poorly designed or executed authentication and authorization processes are often responsible for this issue. Many organizations have adopted *least privilege* policies to combat this vulnerability.
Unsecure backup methods	Backup methods without encryption can put enterprise network data at risk. Frequent backups with encryption and storing copies of backed-up data offsite contribute to data security.
Poor user tracking	Network use should be monitored to ensure that users are vigilant in contributing to network security rather than insecurity.
SNMP issues	SNMP-based NMSs should be configured to address known vulnerabilities in the protocol. For example, "public" SNMP community settings can make managed devices vulnerable to attackers.

Table 11-2: Examples of widely used vulnerability controls.

Vulnerability Control	Description
Prevention	Vulnerability prevention begins with configuration management. Configuration is the backbone of every device. Network administrators should periodically back up network configurations, monitor configuration changes, confirm appropriate configurations for new devices, and ensure that only authorized personnel make configuration changes. Persistent management of network device configurations can reduce security risks.
Patching	Vulnerability patching involves taking appropriate remediation steps after vulnerabilities are identified. Operating systems and software should be updated with security patches soon after they are available; hardware firmware should also be updated. Device configuration changes may be required, and more secure communication protocols may be needed.
Assessments/audits	Regular vulnerability assessments and audits are important parts of network security management. Security scans and penetration tests can help network managers identify common loopholes, devices that need configuration changes, outdated systems that should be upgraded or replaced, ports that need to be closed, and passwords that need to be changed. They also help ensure adherence to security policies and regulatory compliance.
Management	*Vulnerability management tools* automate many of the tasks associated with vulnerability assessment, patching, and prevention. They strive to reduce vulnerabilities, prevent future vulnerabilities, and make sure that all devices are appropriately monitored and configured.

devices. Vulnerabilities also include weaknesses present in network ports and services and poorly protected login credentials. Some vulnerabilities are flaws in hardware, software, or processes that have the potential to adversely affect network operations.

Vulnerabilities are often grouped into categories, such as hardware, software, firmware, and human (network user) vulnerabilities. No matter how they are categorized, awareness of vulnerabilities is important. Enterprise networks vary in complexity, and vulnerabilities vary in severity. Vulnerability awareness is an important outcome of network security audits and drives security policy updates and practices. Addressing vulnerabilities begins by knowing what they are.

Networks with outdated devices or devices near their end of service are often easier for attackers to exploit, and unpatched software can also put a network at risk. Examples of common vulnerabilities are identified in Table 11-1.

Businesses combat network vulnerabilities in various ways, including prevention, fixing, auditing, and utilizing vulnerability management tools. They are briefly described in Table 11-2.

11.2 COMMON ATTACKS AND ATTACK RESPONSES

11.2.1 Common Attacks

Numerous types of attacks are mentioned in the previous chapters to identify the parts of enterprise networks in which they are especially worrisome or problematic. Some types of attacks, including malware, phishing, man-in-the-middle, and denial of service attacks, are used to attack businesses across industries. These and other common attacks are summarized in Table 11-3; most of them are frequently referenced in this chapter and Chapter 12.

As noted in previous chapters, many other types of attacks on enterprise networks take place, and numerous prevention, detection, and mitigation mechanisms are deployed to provide some degree of protection. However, no matter how secure a network is, savvy attackers are ready to exploit whatever weaknesses there are.

In 2022, there were a record number of ransomware attacks, and such attacks are likely to continue in the immediate future. Social engineering (e.g., phishing) attacks continue to be popular, as are supply chain attacks, such as those used in the SolarWinds Orion platform and Colonial Pipeline attacks.

The cybercriminal ecosystem is both underground and elaborate. Cybercriminal gangs in the

Table 11-3: Common attacks on enterprise networks.	
Attack	**Summary Overview**
Malware	*Malware (malicious software)* includes viruses, worms, ransomware, and spyware. Often, attackers use malware to compromise user devices to help them to access or disrupt a network by exploiting network equipment vulnerabilities. Attackers often use social engineering attacks to tempt network users to click on a link or open an email attachment that installs the malware. Once installed, malware can: • Block access to key components of the network or the entire network (This is what ransomware does.) • Install additional harmful software • Covertly transmit stored data/information (This is what spyware does.) • Disrupt network components or make then inoperable
Phishing	*Phishing* is a type of social engineering that usually involves sending network users fraudulent communications, usually email, that appear to come from a reputable source, such as a company official or the organization's IT services. Typically, the goal of phishing is to steal sensitive data, such as login credentials or credit card information, or to install malware on the user's device. It is an increasingly common cyberthreat.
Man-in-the-middle	*Man-in-the-middle (MITM) attacks* are also known as eavesdropping attacks. They occur when attackers insert themselves into two-party communications. For example, attackers may use a rogue access point or hotspot that appears legitimate to intercept network users' communications and data transfers with the enterprise network. Once they have inserted themselves in communication transfers, attackers can filter and steal data. Two common points of entry for MITM attacks are: • Unsecure public Wi-Fi networks. Attackers can insert themselves between a user's device and the network to ensure that all the user's interactions with the network pass through the attacker. • Compromised devices. An MITM attacker who succeeds in breaching a user's device can install software that sends copies of all the device's communications to the attacker. Here, malware provides the vehicle for establishing and perpetrating the attack.
Denial-of-service	A *denial-of-service (DoS) attack* floods a network's systems, servers, or links with traffic to exhaust/overwhelm their resources and bandwidth. This renders them unable to fulfill legitimate requests for resources or services. Often, attackers use multiple compromised devices to launch DoS attacks. This is called a *distributed denial-of-service (DDoS)* attack.
Botnet	Some DDoS attacks are perpetrated by botnets. A *botnet* (robot network) is a large group of malware-infected devices that are remotely controlled. When the infected devices are used to launch large-scale attacks to disrupt services, to steal credentials to gain unauthorized access to critical systems, or to steal data/information, they are called *botnet attacks*. Malware turns compromised devices into "zombie bots" for the botnet controller and allows attackers to remotely control them. Botnets pose a significant risk to enterprise networks because they enable an attacker to use the compromised devices to perform multiple attack actions at the same time. Once infected, devices can also receive malware updates from the botnet controller that cause them to change their behaviors.
SQL injection	A Structured Query Language (SQL) injection attack occurs when an attacker inserts malicious code into a server that uses SQL to force it to reveal information it normally would not. Such attacks can take place when attackers submit malicious code in a vulnerable webserver's search box. Basically, a SQL injection attack consists of the insertion or "injection" of a SQL query via input data from a client of a client-server application. A successful SQL injection attack may cause the server to read/provide sensitive data from a database, modify database data (e.g., insert/update/delete data), execute administration operations on the database (such as shutting down the DBMS), or carry out other database/DBMS operations. SQL injection attacks enable attackers to spoof user identities, tamper with existing data, void transactions, change account balances, disclose/destroy all data in the database or make it unavailable, or become administrators of the server or database.
Zero-day	A zero-day exploit hits after a network vulnerability is announced/identified but before a patch or solution is implemented or installed. The disclosed vulnerability is targeted during this window of time. Constant awareness and monitoring are needed to identify zero-day threats and to detect zero-day exploit attempts. Applications, operating systems, and firmware may be vulnerable to zero-day exploits.
DNS tunneling	*DNS tunneling attacks* utilize the DNS protocol to communicate non-DNS traffic over port 53. Basically, DNS tunneling is a cyberattack method that encodes malware or other protocols in DNS queries and responses. It often includes data payloads that can be added to an attacked DNS server and used to control a remote server or application. For example, it may be used to send SNMP and other protocol traffic over DNS instead of TCP. There are legitimate reasons to utilize DNS tunneling; however, there are also malicious reasons, such as disguising outbound traffic from a malware-infected device on an internal network as DNS traffic to avoid detection by firewalls. When used maliciously, DNS requests are manipulated to exfiltrate data from a compromised device or system to the attacker's system. Attackers also can employ such requests to enable them to use DNS responses to communicate with compromised devices and systems.

same or different countries are partnering to share intelligence, research, and opportunities to breach networks. For example, the U.S. Department of Homeland Security (DHS) has evidence that Russian cybercrime groups are courting Chinese counterparts to scale up the capabilities of both groups. Also, amateur cybercriminals are collaborating with professional cybercrime syndicates on the dark web and encrypted websites. This means that sustained efforts to identify and exploit enterprise network vulnerabilities are not likely to lessen, and organizations must be geared up to respond.

11.2.2 Responding to Attacks

Businesses have plans and procedures for responding to cybersecurity attacks once they are detected. Because attackers are adept at hiding their activities and covering their tracks, attack detection is not necessarily easy.

According to IBM's *Cost of a Data Breach Report 2020*, on average, companies take 207 days to identify a data breach and another 73 days to contain it. Often, attackers can inflict a lot of damage before their attacks are detected and contained. The SolarWinds attack went undetected for more than nine months, affected the networks of hundreds of businesses and government agencies, and became a classic example of an advanced persistent threat (APT). You can learn more about it in Appendix 11-1.

When an attack is detected, the organization's plans and procedures for stopping attacks and mitigating their effects are triggered. The steps involved are described in Table 11-4.

Table 11-4: Business responses to cybersecurity attacks.

Response Step	Description
Mobilize the incidence response team	Mobilizing the cybersecurity response team is the first step in an organized response to a cyberattack. This should be a cross-disciplinary team that is trained in protecting the business from attacks and responding to them. Each member of the team has a predefined role and is trained in what they need to do when an attack occurs.
Identify the type of attack	To appropriately respond, the response team must identify the type of attack that is occurring. Once this is known, it can focus its attention on containing and recovering from the attack. Proper attack identification includes the extent of the attack, its likely source, and its probable effect.
Contain the breach	Once the type of attack is identified, it's important to determine and shut down all potential access corridors that attackers may be using. Most passive attacks strive to provide attackers with persistent backdoors into the network to enable them to continue to extract data over time. Whatever the type of attack, the response team should quickly strive to deny attackers access to the network and its affected systems by: • Disconnecting the affected network/system from the Internet • Disabling all remote access to the network • Rerouting network traffic • Changing all vulnerable passwords
Assess and repair damage	After the attack has been contained, the response team needs to determine which systems have been accessed, what data has been affected by the breach, which (if any) critical business functions have been compromised, and whether there are any unauthorized entry points. Systems/software may need to be reinstalled, damaged hardware may need to be repaired or replaced, and compromised data may need to be restored from backup copies.
Report the attack	Cybersecurity attacks should be reported to proper authorities, such as local law enforcement agencies and the FBI. Ideally, the attack should also be reported to the Secret Service's Electronic Crimes Task Force, the Internet Crime Complaint Center, and the Federal Trade Commission. Since most businesses have cybersecurity insurance, the insurance provider should also be promptly notified.
Communicate with stakeholders	Customers, business partners, investors, and other stakeholders should be notified about the attack in a timely manner, especially if their data has been affected by the incident. Organizations should be transparent and up-front about the attack to maintain stakeholder and the public's trust.
Learn from the experience	Businesses should critically evaluate the adequacy and effects of their responses to cybersecurity attacks. They need to be honest about what went according to plan, what did not, and what should be done differently in the future. Each attack incident and response should enable the organization to get smarter about its cybersecurity.

Security Information and Event Management (SIEM)

Across industries, businesses are increasingly adopting security information and event management (SIEM) technologies and solutions to help incident response teams identify and quickly respond to security breaches. These technologies support threat detection and security incident management through the collection and analysis of data about network security events.

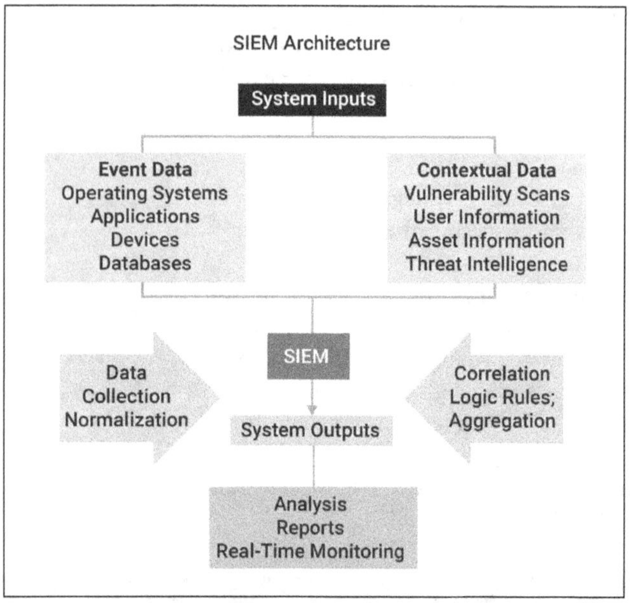

Figure 11-3: SIEM architecture and key capabilities.

The core capabilities of SIEM solutions include numerous log event collection and management tools and the ability to analyze log events and other data from multiple sources, including external threat intelligence sources, to support incident management, reporting, and dashboards. Figure 11-3 provides a high-level depiction of SIEM architecture.

A SIEM system enhances incident response management by enabling the incident response team to quickly discover suspicious activity, identify compromised devices/resources, and use automated tools to contain and combat attacks in progress. This shortens incident detection and containment time while also logging information that can be used to improve future responses. SIEM systems are further described in Appendix 11-2.

11.3 ENTERPRISE NETWORK SECURITY GOALS

An understanding of network vulnerabilities, attack surfaces, common types of attacks, and how organizations respond to attacks makes it easier to appreciate that securing an enterprise network includes protecting the availability, usability, integrity, and safety of network infrastructure, resources, services, and data. Network security also strives to prevent attackers from breaching the network and disrupting business operations.

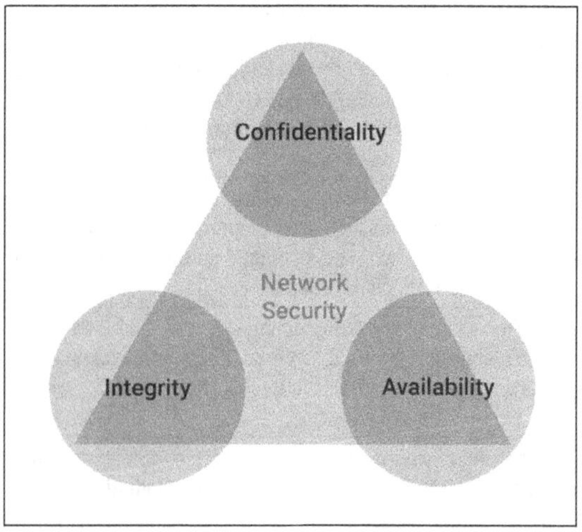

Figure 11-4: The CIA triad of network security.

11.3.1 The CIA Triad

Confidentiality, integrity, and availability are commonly identified as the three pillars of network security, and they are often represented as the CIA triad (see Figure 11-4). These pillars and nonrepudiation are described in Table 11-5.

The CIA triad identifies three crucial aspects of network, data, and information protection that provide guidance for establishing an organization's security strategies, policies, and practices. It enables an organization to use a three-pronged strategic approach to cybersecurity and to develop systematic and comprehensive approaches for managing cybersecurity risks.

The overarching network security goals in Table 11-5 concern data and information security. **Information security** refers to the preservation of data/information integrity and secrecy when data is stored or transmitted and protecting data against information security breaches. *Information security breaches* occur when data/

Table 11-5: Overarching network security goals.

Network Security Goal	Description
Confidentiality	This network security goal is to protect business data from unauthorized persons or devices. The confidentiality aspect of network security involves keeping data private. This may include restricting physical access to network infrastructure and devices and restricting logical access to stored data and network traffic. Firewalls, intrusion detection and prevention systems, and access control lists (ACLs) and processes contribute to confidentiality. Encrypted network traffic prevents data leakage when traffic is intercepted by an attacker.
Integrity	Networks have data in motion. Should an attacker succeed in gaining access to a network, they may be able to silently modify/tamper with data traffic and cause irreparable harm to people and organizations. Achieving this network security goal involves ensuring that the data is accurate and consistent, is reliable, and is not tampered with or intentionally or unintentionally changed by unauthorized persons. Data integrity can be compromised when data is uploaded to network storage devices and when it is stored in a database or another logical storage repository. Authenticating network users and devices contributes to integrity by verifying that data traffic originates from authorized sources.
Availability	This network security goal is to ensure that data, network resources, and network services are continuously available to legitimate users whenever they require them. For availability, the network must have properly functioning infrastructure, security controls, and communication channels. Critical systems and applications often require constant availability. Such systems must be resilient and have safeguards against power outages, hardware failures, communication link failures, cybersecurity attacks, and other events that might affect network availability. DoS and DDoS attacks are examples of attacks that affect network availability.
Nonrepudiation	Nonrepudiation is sometimes identified as a fourth pillar of network security. *Nonrepudiation* is a type of information assurance in which the sender of information is provided with proof of delivery and the recipient is provided with proof of the sender's identity, so neither can later deny having processed the information. Nonrepudiation provides evidence of data's origin, authenticity, and integrity. For networks, nonrepudiation often means that the sender and recipient of an encrypted message cannot deny the message's transmission. Important legal ramifications associated with nonrepudiation have resulted in increased use of digital signatures.

information is accessed by unauthorized individuals or parties and can result from intentional actions of hackers, intelligence agencies, cybercriminals, competitors, disgruntled employees, or others. They are often facilitated by weak security defenses or user carelessness.

11.3.2 Business Continuity and Risk Management

Business continuity refers to an organization's ability to maintain essential functions during and after a disaster. Since enterprise networks are crucial to business operations, natural or man-made disasters and other events that significantly affect network availability, including cybersecurity attacks, threaten business continuity. Hence, business continuity may be considered a network security goal.

Cybersecurity attacks are rarely overlooked in business continuity strategies and plans, and business continuity is an important aspect of IT management and governance, as are information security plans and practices. Today, any type of disruption that affects an organization's computing and network infrastructure is considered a cyber risk and is included in business continuity plans.

Business continuity planning (BCP) is the process of creating preventive and recovery systems to deal with disasters and other major business disruptions. BCP documents include a predetermined set of instructions or procedures that describe how business operations will be sustained during and after a significant disruption.

For networks, BCP includes specifying preventative and recovery mechanisms for natural and man-made disasters (e.g., fires, earthquakes, extreme weather events, warfare, sabotage, etc.) as well as electronic threats, including cyberattacks. For example, fire suppression systems may be deployed to prevent or minimize damage to physical network infrastructure, and backup power sources can be added to enable networks to operate during prolonged disruptions to primary power sources. Also, enterprise network data can be replicated in real time or near real time in the cloud to ensure that it is accessible if physical network infrastructure is affected by a disaster.

Businesses often invest considerable time and effort in the development of business continuity plans. Many also engage in disaster simulations to test the adequacy of their disaster recovery procedures and identify where adjustments are needed.

For networks, *disaster recovery (DR)* refers to how an organization would retrieve key data/information and restore important services after a disaster. Disaster recovery plans include policies and procedures used to get the affected parts of the network working again.

When disaster strikes or a major cybersecurity attack occurs, it is important to get the network and its important components back in operation as quickly as possible. Today, this usually involves restoring access to important databases. As a result, an organization's disaster recovery plan is likely to stipulate how often databases are backed up, where the backups are stored, and how to restore databases when major network disruptions occur.

Risk Management

The network-related contents of business continuity and disaster recovery plans are influenced by many inputs, including security audits, threat analyses, and risk assessment processes, that focus on both the risks of network assets being sabotaged, inappropriately accessed, or disrupted, and the consequences of risks. Hence, risk identification and management are important parts of network security management.

Network threat analysis is used to determine network components that need to be protected and the types of security threats they should be protected from. This is a standard part of network security audits and vulnerability assessments. A threat analysis identifies and evaluates security threats to important network assets. Examples of network assets and threats included in network threat analyses are identified in Table 11-6.

Table 11-6: Examples of assets and threats considered in network threat analysis.

Network Assets	Threats
• Servers	• Denial-of-service
• Network devices (e.g., routers, switches, etc.)	• Malware (viruses, worms, ransomware, spyware)
• Security devices/systems (e.g., firewalls, IDSs, IPSs)	• Physical damage
• User devices (PCs, laptops, tablets, smartphones)	• Theft of data, software, services, hardware
• Software (e.g., applications, operating systems)	• Corruption of data, software, services, hardware
• Network services	• Unauthorized access to data, software, services, or hardware
• Data (databases, stored data, archived data, data in transit)	• Unauthorized disclosure of data or information

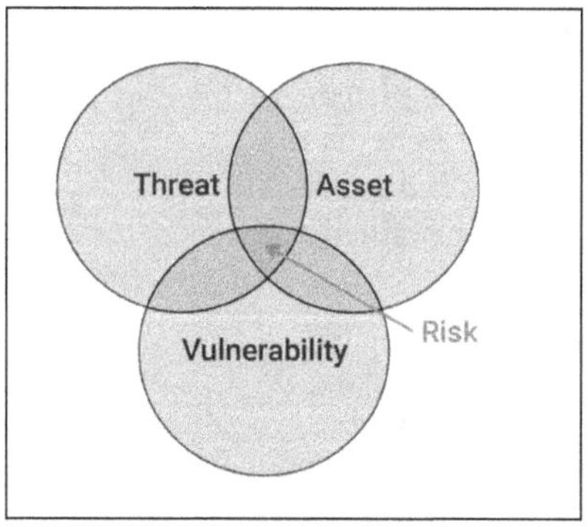

Figure 11-5: How risks are related to network assets, threats, and vulnerabilities.

Asset vulnerabilities, the probability of a potential threat affecting an asset, and the magnitude of the consequences (costs) of the asset being compromised are also considered in threat and risk analyses (see Figure 11-5).

Risk assessment also considers the danger associated with not taking action to protect a network asset. This considers the degree to which customer data is sensitive and the financial cost of someone accessing or changing data or stealing trade secrets. It also considers the financial costs associated with cybersecurity attacks that disrupt network operations and the ability of employees to do their jobs. Reputational damage can also be a consequence of a network security breach.

Risk values can be assigned to a network asset's potential threats. There are numerous ways to do this, but most boil down to considering the probability of the network security event and its associated costs: *Risk Value = Probability of Security Event x Cost of Security Event.*

As Figure 11-6 illustrates, threats with higher risk values are usually considered *critical risks*, while those with lower risk values are typically considered *low-level risks*. Obviously, organizations should devote more time, attention, and resources to protect against critical risks.

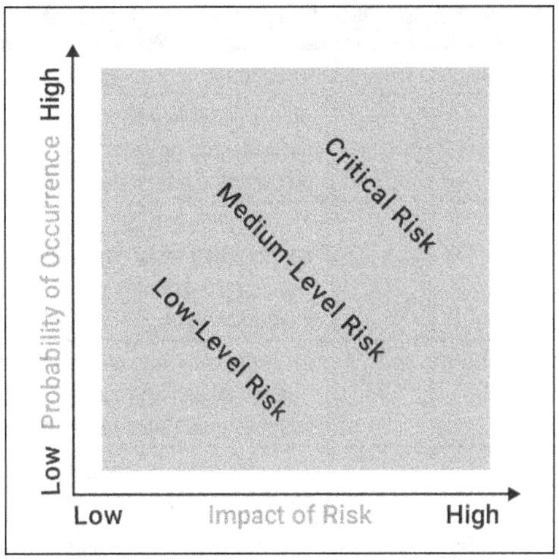

Figure 11-6: The severity of network risks is a function of security event occurrence and effect.

Identifying risks and their severity enables business to prioritize and deploy appropriate protections for network assets using security controls described in this chapter and Chapter 12. The path toward network security begins with awareness of what needs to be protected, and why, and such awareness facilitates systematic deployment of appropriate security mechanisms.

Despite being systematic attempts to identify and evaluate threats to network assets, threat analyses include some subjectivity. To minimize subjectivity, some businesses include representatives from various parts of the organization to ensure that different perspectives are considered.

Threat analysis results should be periodically reviewed to ensure that all network assets and potential threats are accounted for. As enterprise networks evolve, the mix of threats and their effects will change over time and new or additional security mechanisms will be needed to protect the network. For example, today's accelerating adoption and use of IoT systems and applications often translates into new vulnerabilities and an expanded attack surface that cannot be overlooked. The added risk involved should trigger additional rounds of network audits and threat analysis. Periodic reviews of network security plans, policies, and procedures should also be conducted.

11.4 SECURITY PLANS, POLICIES, AND PROCEDURES

A *security plan* is a high-level document that identifies what an organization intends to do to meet its network security requirements. It outlines the people, resources, time, and effort necessary to develop a security policy, and procedures for the technical implementation of it. An enterprise network security plan should be based on the network's business and technical requirements and network threat and risk analyses.

Network security plans typically reference the network's topology and major components. They commonly list major network services and resources and who provides, administers, and has access to them.

One of the most important aspects of an enterprise network security plan is the specification of the people and entities involved in network security implementation. This aspect of the plan should address whether specialized network security administrators will be used, how network users (e.g., managers and employees) will be involved in network security, and the type of training users will receive on security policies and procedures.

Today, network security plans strive to communicate the need for all employees to be involved. The plan should have the full support of corporate management and buy-in from networking personnel.

A *security policy* informs network users, managers, and technical personnel of their obligations for protecting network infrastructure and data. It is a formal statement that addresses rules for network, system, and information access and use. Security policies are developed to minimize exposure to security threats. They define/document how the network can be used with minimal

Table 11-7: Common aspects of network security policies.

Policy Area	Description
Access	An *access policy* defines access privileges and rights. It typically provides guidelines for connecting devices to the network, adding new software, and connecting to external networks and services. it may also specify how data is classified and how data access rights and privileges are determined for network users.
Accountability	An *accountability policy* defines the security responsibilities of network users, network managers, and network support personnel. The accountability policy should specify who is responsible for network security audits. It should also specify security incident handling guidelines that include what to do and who to contact when network security incidents occur.
Authentication	An *authentication policy* specifies how identities of network users are verified. This often includes a password policy that specifies minimum requirements for password strength and the frequency of password changes. It also typically includes guidelines for authenticating network users at remote locations.
Privacy	A *privacy policy* describes privacy expectations of network users regarding monitoring their behavior on the network, email, files, keystrokes, etc.
Technology Purchasing	*Technology purchasing guidelines* specify security and security configuration requirements for network devices and who can and cannot connect new devices to the network.

risk and how network user obligations can be met. Security policies are living documents; as businesses, enterprise networks, and security risks change, they should be updated.

The development of a security policy is the responsibility of network administrators and network security specialists. Some organizations get help from network security consultancies and security services firms. Implementation of security policies and procedures should be straightforward; they should clearly define areas of responsibility and be enforceable.

Examples of security policies and procedures include acceptable use statements, configuration modification policies, and security incident handling procedures. Business continuity and disaster recovery plans may be referenced. At a minimum, a network security policy should address access, accountability, authentication, and privacy, which are described in Table 11-7. Security policies may also include technology purchasing rules.

Enterprise network security policies may also address keeping anti-malware protection up to date, data backup policies, and requirements for monitoring Computer emergency response team (CERT) advisories and other reputable sources that monitor immediate threats or provide threat intelligence. CERT, formed in 1998 by the U.S. Defense Advanced Research Projects Agency, coordinates with Carnegie Mellon University's Software Engineering Institute (SEI) in researching and reporting on Internet-related security problems. SEI's CERT Coordination Center publishes security information and advisory bulletins via its website at https://www.kb.cert.org/vuls/.

Many organizations require employees to sign a statement that they have read, understood, and agree to comply with the policy and cybersecurity training requirements. Mandatory cybersecurity training is best practice; Figure 11-7 illustrates examples of common training course topics.

Security procedures implement security policies. They define login, configuration, security auditing, and security management requirements. Security procedures should be spelled out for network administrators, security administrators, and network users, and they should specify how security events should be handled.

Security procedures may be communicated to network users and operations personnel in self-paced training courses like those in Figure 11-7. Using cybersecurity training to inform users about what they should do and who they should contact when security events occur can help minimize the damage that may be caused.

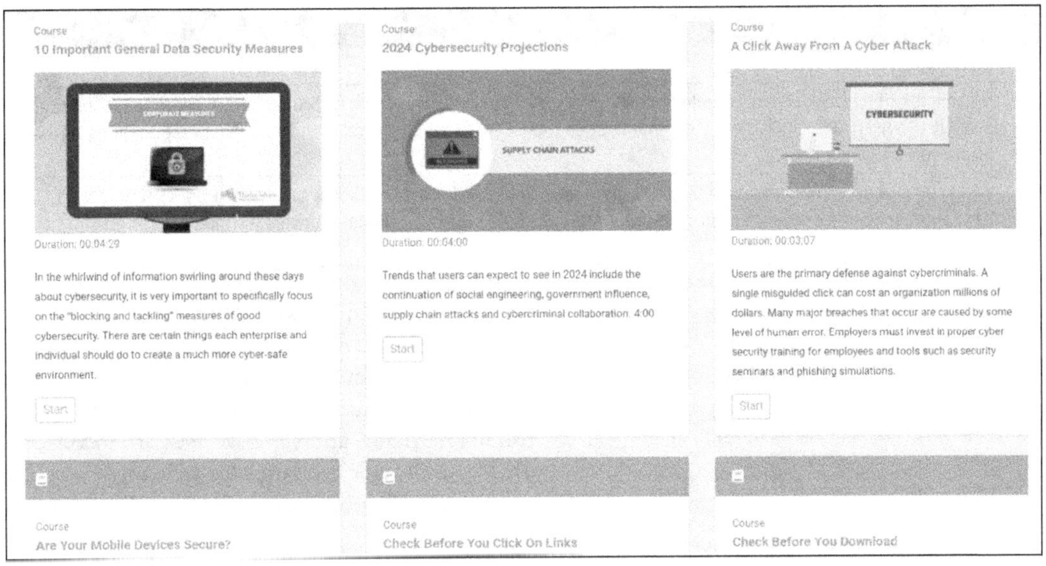

Figure 11-7: Examples of required cybersecurity courses for network users. Source: ThreatAdvice.com

11.5 ENTERPRISE NETWORK SECURITY ARCHITECTURES

Chapter 1 introduced Enterprise Architecture (EA) and its relationship to enterprise network architecture. EA contends that data, information, applications, and IT infrastructure, including business networks, should align with business goals and requirements.

Security architecture is an important part of EA that affects other EA domains. Like the other domains, it should align with the network's contributions to business strategy and roles in business operations. This alignment is illustrated in Figure 11-8.

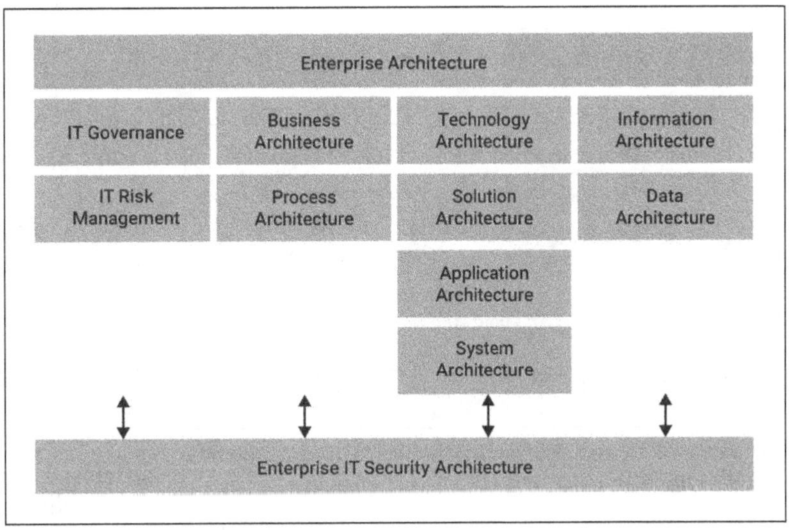

Figure 11-8: Enterprise IT security is an important part of Enterprise Architecture (EA).

The point, of course, is that today's businesses require a robust security architecture for protecting their data, information, and network assets. When security architectures are strengthened to address weaknesses, the risk of attackers succeeding in breaching the network and its computing systems is reduced.

11.5.1 Security Architectures

Network security architecture refers to the practice of designing networks to ensure the security of their infrastructure, applications, and data. A network security architecture includes both network and security elements (see Table 11-8) and provides guidance for protecting network assets against security threats.

Network security architectures are often developed and maintained by security architects. Security architects strive to develop an architecture that enables the organization to quickly identify and respond to network breaches.

Table 11-8: Examples of network and security elements in network security architectures.

Architectural Elements	Examples
Network Elements	Examples of *network elements* include network devices (servers, user devices, routers, etc.), communication protocols (DNS, HTTPS, IP, TCP, etc.), communication media (e.g., cabling, wireless), and network topologies (physical and logical).
Security Elements	Examples of *security elements* include security devices and software (e.g., firewalls, IDSs, IPSs, VPN gateways, etc.), secure communication protocols (e.g., IPsec, TLS, DTLS, etc.), and data privacy technologies (e.g., encryption and key management).

Well-designed network security architectures contribute to business continuity and resilience by providing protection against cyberattacks and infrastructure component failures. They can handle reasonable bursts or surges in network traffic while continuing to monitor the network for traffic anomalies and signs of network intrusions. They also provide guidance for structured security management processes, such as those identified in Appendix 11-3.

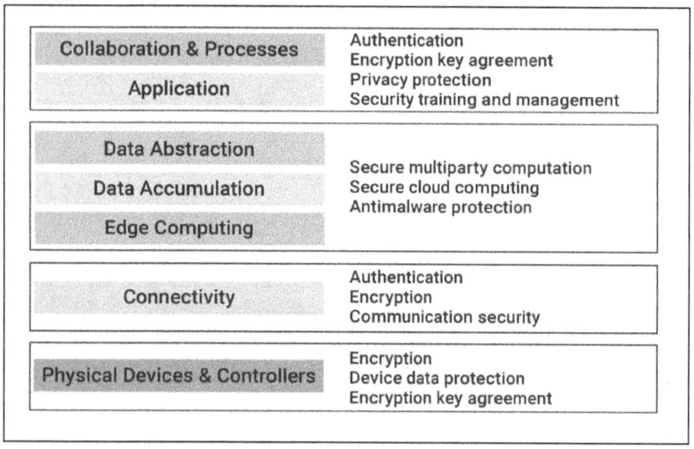

Figure 11-9: Example of a security architecture associated with an IoT architecture.

Layered security architectures often align with network architecture layers. Figure 11-9, for example, maps security requirements/elements to the different layers of IoT architecture.

Security elements/technologies can also be mapped to layers of the OSI and TCP/IP models. In Chapter 4, for example, security technologies at each layer of the TCP/IP model were introduced. And Figure 11-10 summarizes how some of the security protocols introduced in previous chapters map to layers of the TCP/IP model.

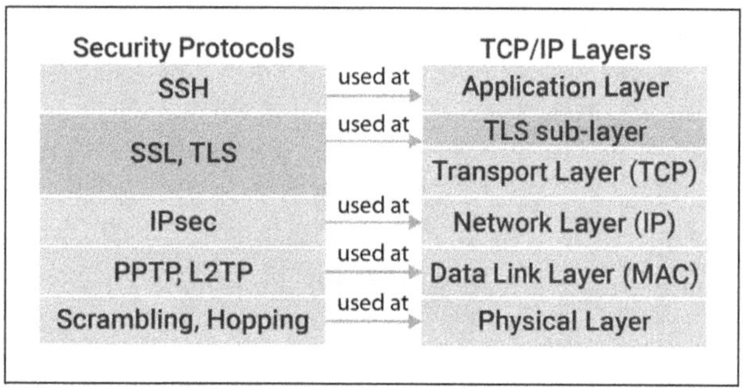

Figure 11-10: Examples of security protocols used at different layers of the TCP/IP model.

Security architects usually consider the security requirements of enterprise networks on a layer-by-layer and component-by-component basis. They consider what is already in place and what can be done to improve the security of each layer or component.

11.5.2 Zero Trust Architecture (ZTA)

Zero trust security is frequently mentioned in previous chapters. It represents a departure from traditional network security thinking by assuming that there is no traditional network edge and that no network users, devices, services, systems, and resources should be considered trustworthy. Anyone or anything that tries to access the enterprise network or any of its assets should be considered a threat until that person or thing is verified.

Zero trust is a security framework that requires all enterprise network users and devices, whether in or outside the organization's network, to be authenticated, authorized, and continuously validated for security posture before being granted access to, or allowed to continue to access, applications, data, services, or resources. The network is considered to have no traditional edge because an enterprise network's networks can be local, in the cloud, or both. Enterprise network resources can be anywhere, and workers may access the network from any location.

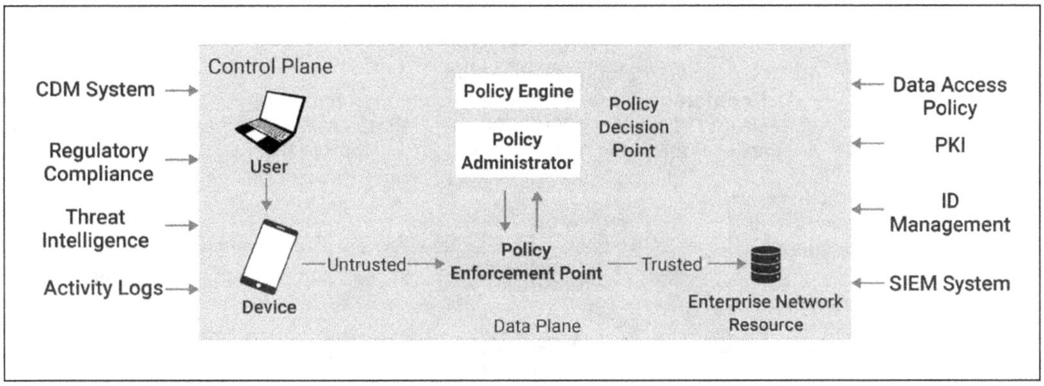

Figure 11-11: Some of the major components of zero trust security architectures.

In this security philosophy, any device, user, or application is considered unsafe and is not granted access to an enterprise network resource until it is verified as trustworthy. Independent authentication and verification are required for users and devices. And reauthentication and verification occur after access is granted. Continuous monitoring of network behavior occurs to detect anomalies.

The major components of zero trust security architectures are illustrated in Figure 11-11. ZTA includes a *control plane*, where zero trust policy decisions are made, and a *data plane*, where policies are enforced. Zero trust policies align with customer data management (CDM) requirements, industry regulations, and data access policies. Policy enforcement decisions are influenced by threat intelligence sources, user activity logs, SIEM tools, ID management practices, and public key infrastructure (PKI).

User and device behavior is assessed in real time to ensure compliance with security policies. Threat intelligence feeds from authenticated/verified external sources also contribute to zero trust policy enforcement. Multifactor authentication is typically required for network users, and network endpoints are continuously checked against device inventories and configuration databases, regardless of their locations in the network.

You will learn more about the security elements and processes used in zero trust security deployments in this chapter and Chapter 12. For now, it is important for you to understand that it is a security framework that aligns well with the evolving composition of today's enterprise networks.

11.5.3 Layered Security & Defense in Depth (DiD)

Layered security defenses are common in enterprise networks and are considered an effective way to protect network and IT assets. Layered defenses are a common response to threat analyses and are often addressed in security plans and policies. Layered defenses may be deployed to protect specific components and/or entire networks.

The use of layered defenses is based on two assumptions/ideas. The first is that reliance on any single defense for a network or network component is a flawed security strategy. Persistent attackers are likely to find a vulnerability to exploit and breach the system. Using a series of different defenses helps to cover weaknesses in the protective capabilities of any one of them. This is like both "a belt and suspenders"; if one breaks, the other keeps your pants up.

The second assumption/idea is that different types of security mechanisms have different capabilities, and each one helps to protect the network or component in ways that others do not. For example, firewalls, IDSs, and local storage encryption provide different types of protections and collectively offer greater protection beyond the capabilities of any one of them.

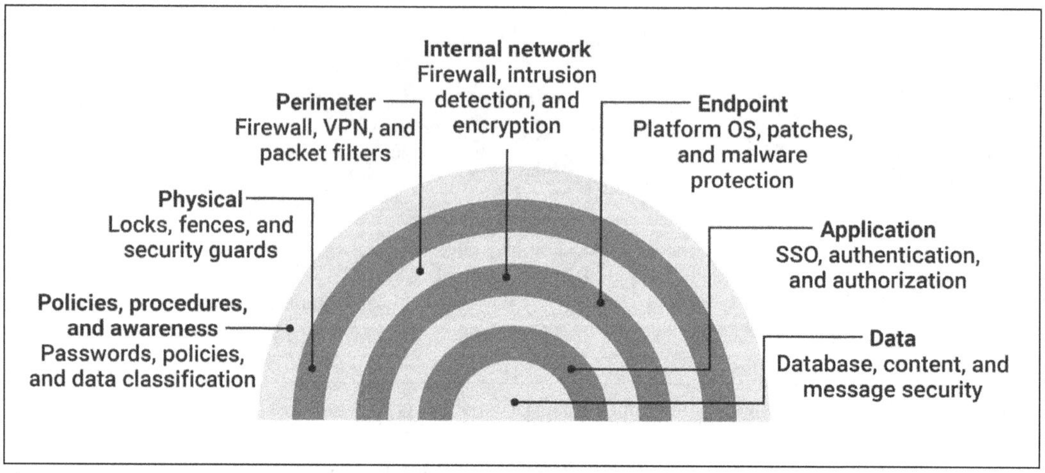

Figure 11-12: Layers and example defense mechanisms in the defense in depth model.

Layered security and defense in depth (DiD) are different concepts that overlap. Layered security practices combine two or more security mechanisms to address a specific security concern or to protect a specific IT asset. DiD, however, strives to address the full range of threats to an organization's network and computing infrastructure.

Traditionally, DiD has widened the scope of network security considerations and has encouraged flexible security policies and practices that enable evolving enterprise networks to add new defenses in response to threats. DiD is sometimes described as a security architecture or model, but there is no standard blueprint that has sufficient flexibility to provide guidance to different organizations with different needs.

Figure 11-12 depicts the different layers of a traditional DiD security architecture. In contrast to zero trust security, DiD reflects traditional thinking about what is in the network and what is external to the network. It also provides a vehicle for considering the relationship of security policies, procedures, and user training to layered defenses.

As 11-12 illustrates, security policies and procedures are found at the outermost layer of the DiD model. The DiD assumes that network infrastructure is in physical facilities that can be secured. It also assumes that defenses can be deployed at network edges, and in the internal network, they can be used to secure hosts (endpoint devices), applications, and data.

Data is located at the innermost layer of the DiD model. This makes sense because it is the ultimate target of most attackers, and forcing attackers to breach defenses at the other layers to reach the data can be a deterrent. Figure 11-12 identifies examples of defenses that can be deployed at the different layers of the DiD. Appendix 11-4 provides a more extensive introduction to the layers and their defenses.

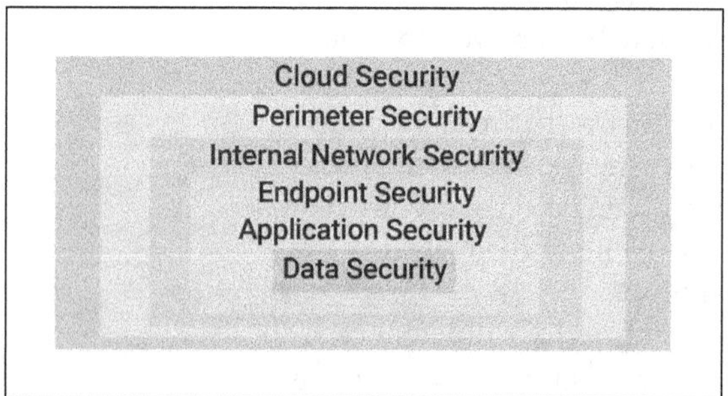

Figure 11-13: An example of a DiD extension to include cloud security.

Some DiD models include a cloud security layer that is outside the network perimeter (see Figure 11-13). This is reasonable because cloud services and infrastructure essentially extend the network beyond its traditional boundaries. This also makes sense because cloud services communicate with an organization's internal networks across traditional network perimeters.

The DiD model provides a convenient vehicle for structuring the remaining sections of this chapter and Chapter 12. Since security plans, policies, and procedures have already been addressed (in section 11.4), the rest of this chapter will describe some of the more important security mechanisms included at the physical, cloud, perimeter, and internal network layers of the DiD model.

11.6 PHYSICAL SECURITY

The physical layer of the DiD focuses on deterring or preventing intruders from gaining access to facilities that house enterprise network infrastructure. It also focuses on protecting network infrastructure from theft or damage.

Three categories of physical threats are typically identified: external, internal, and human threats. Examples of *external threats* include lightning, floods, earthquakes, tornadoes, hurricanes, wildfires, avalanches, and other forces that are largely outside the control of an organization. However, businesses are not entirely powerless against these forces and can take commonsense steps to protect network assets by placing them in relatively fireproof/fire retardant, windproof, and floodproof locations.

For example, since hurricane Katrina, server rooms in businesses in downtown New Orleans are typically located on windowless upper floors rather than in building basements or lower floors that might be flooded. Also, in the aftermath of hurricane Maria, data centers capable of surviving a class 5 hurricane have been built in Puerto Rico. Earthquake-proof data centers are common in Japan.

Internal threats include unstable power supplies, humidity in equipment rooms, and fire. Fire detection and suppression systems are common safeguards, and in data centers backup/standby HVAC units are typically available to take over when primary systems fail or undergo maintenance. Fire detection systems usually automatically contact 911 and fire departments.

Table 11-9: Examples of physical security control for data centers and network equipment facilities.

Facility Layer	Common Defenses
Facility perimeter	*Facility perimeter defenses* include fences, gates, lighting, locks, alarms, signs, dogs, security personnel, and surveillance systems. Climb-proof fencing may surround the facility, and there may be a limited number of gates for entering and exiting facility grounds. In war- or terrorist-prone locations, ram-proof barricades may be used to prevent vehicles from crashing through the fencing to gain access. Prickly or thorny vegetation may also be placed outside and inside fencing and barriers as an additional deterrent. Attempted intrusions typically trigger automatic contacts to police and 911 systems. Signs, such as "This area is protected by armed guards," "Beware of dogs," or "Surveillance cameras in use," can be used to deter would-be intruders. The grounds of facilities should be well lit at night to enable security personnel and equipment to quickly detect and respond to intrusions. Motion-detection systems for fencing, lighting, and alarm systems are increasingly common. Some, third-party security firms provide 24/7 drone monitoring of data centers and other business facilities.
Building exterior	*Building exterior defenses* include a limited number of entrances; strong, locked doors and windows; minimal use of ground-level windows; bullet- and explosive-resistant glass; continuously monitored and secured entrances; alarms; and surveillance. Door access controls (such as card keys and biometric readers) are common. Ample lighting should be provided for building exteriors, especially around entrances.
Building interior	*Building interior defenses* include safes and vaults, along with locked doors, desks, and files. Other safeguards include internal motion detection and alarm systems, lighting, mirrors (often placed at hallway corners to enable viewing of people in different halls), bolted-down equipment, security personnel, and interior surveillance systems. Door access controls and access logs, and employee movement monitoring systems, are also common. Some security experts recommend ensuring that there are no places in walls or ceilings in which intruders can hide; they also note that it is important to secure facility rooftops.
Computer room	To deter network asset theft, asset tagging, secure cabling systems, cabinet/server rack keys or controlled access systems, and GPS device location systems are widely used. Maintaining inventories of authorized and unauthorized devices is an aspect of network asset management and security. To deter network asset tampering, configuration change control mechanisms and physical device hardening (e.g., required biometric or MFA access) can be used. Secure configurations for network devices (servers, user devices, routers, switches) should be used, and only authorized personnel should be allowed to access devices in secured locations or make configuration changes.

Most data centers have redundant power grids with dual connections to devices. Usually, there are layers of backup power sources for the grids, including uninterruptible power supplies (UPSs), battery backup systems, backup generators, and redundant connections to electrical utilities. Increasingly, dedicated solar farms are also available to power data centers. Surge protectors for networking equipment are also common.

Human threats include theft, sabotage or vandalism, terrorist attacks, and intentional or accidental errors that disrupt network operations. Protecting against these threats begins by hardening facilities that house network infrastructure.

A variety of defenses are used to secure facilities and data centers. This includes protecting the perimeters of facilities, protecting building exteriors, and protecting the interiors of facilities and spaces where computing and network infrastructure is located Examples of defenses used at these facility layers are identified in Table 11-9.

Collectively, deploying layers of physical controls in and around data centers and network equipment facilities is consistent with DiD and layered security concepts. It may be impossible to fully secure a data center or enterprise network facility, but organizations can deploy layers of physical defenses to make it difficult to get in or avoid detection. To have confidence about physical defenses, it is important to conduct periodic physical penetration tests.

11.7 CLOUD SECURITY

The cloud is a logical extension of enterprise networks. For most businesses, it is no longer a question of whether cloud services and applications should be included in enterprise network architecture, but how much.

The addition of cloud services and applications to enterprise networks usually involves some degree of responsibility sharing for network security. In some cases, shared responsibility is mandated and must be documented. For example, the Federal Deposit Insurance Corporation (FDIC) and National Credit Union Administration (NCUA) require banks and credit unions to document how data and applications are secured by cloud and other third-party organizations that provide services. Examples of sharing relationships are identified in Appendix 11-5.

Since cloud providers own and manage their data centers, they are responsible for the physical security of their facilities. Many providers have redundant data centers that can take over in the event of a disaster or emergency. Most providers also have layered defenses to protect applications, services, and subscriber data that are consistent with DiD.

Most interactions between business networks and cloud services take place over the Internet; however, it is possible to use private WAN or RAN connections to cloud data centers. Many of the digital security controls associated with the cloud layer of the DiD are Internet-centric, including cloud firewalls, IAM, CASB, DLP, and CDP (see Table 11-10).

Table 11-10: Examples of security controls at the cloud layer of DiD.

Security Control	Description
Cloud firewalls	Cloud firewalls are software-based, cloud-deployed technologies designed to stop or mitigate unwanted access to private networks. They are sometimes called *firewall-as-a-service (FWaaS)*. Like a traditional firewall, cloud firewalls identify and block potentially malicious network traffic. They are typically stateful, managed network firewalls for private clouds and virtual private clouds (VPCs) that include intrusion detection and prevention services. They are sometimes considered perimeter defenses for a VPC or private cloud. Public cloud firewalls also exist; they are sometimes called *virtual firewalls* and have scalability and extensibility advantages over on-premises firewalls.
Identity and access management (IAM)	*Identity and access management (IAM)* security refers to technologies that manage digital identities and user access to data, systems, and resources. At the cloud layer, IAM is typically a web service that controls and secures access to cloud resources. It is used to control who is authenticated (signed in) to the cloud service and who is authorized (has permission) to use specific cloud resources. IAM security includes policies, procedures, and technologies designed to reduce a business's identity-related access risks.

Table 11-10, Continued.	
Security Control	**Description**
Cloud access security broker (CASB)	A cloud access security broker is software that sits between cloud applications and cloud service users. It monitors all user activity and interaction with the cloud service and enforces security policies, such as authentication, single sign on (SSO), authorization, credential mapping, device profiling, encryption, logging, alerting, and malware detection and prevention. In short, a CASB interjects a subscriber organization's security policies as employees access and use cloud-based resources.
Data loss prevention (DLP)	*Data loss prevention (DLP)* is a cybersecurity solution designed to detect and prevent data breaches. It strives to block the extraction of sensitive data from an organization's data repositories. Businesses deploy DLP solutions to comply with regulatory requirements and to shore up security defenses. With increased use of cloud storage to supplement or replace on-premises data storage, cloud-based DLP solutions have become common. DLP software detects potential data breaches and data exfiltration transmissions by monitoring the actions of network endpoints that access sensitive data. When suspicious activity is detected, the endpoints are blocked from transmitting data or accessing data at rest. A DLP solution typically combines several cybersecurity measures, such as firewalls, monitoring services, antivirus software, and endpoint protection tools. AI and machine learning (ML) are becoming more common in DLP solutions to detect anomalous activity and automate responses to suspected data breaches.
Cloud data privacy (CDP)	*Cloud data privacy (or cloud data protection)* (CDP) refers to the set of data storage and security measures designed to protect data residing in, moving in, or moving out of, a cloud environment. It includes the security of data both at rest and in motion. Cloud data protection solutions strive to keep the sensitive data intact, protected from security events, and safe from unauthorized access or distribution.

11.8 PERIMETER SECURITY

Perimeter security involves safeguarding the boundaries of a company's private network from intruders, hackers, attackers, and other unwanted entities. The provision of perimeter security involves threat recognition, perimeter surveillance, intrusion detection, analyzing network traffic for anomalous patterns, and quickly taking steps to minimize the effects of perimeter breaches.

A **network perimeter** is the physical and logical boundary between the private and locally managed side of a network and the public-facing side of the network. In today's enterprise networks, there may be many perimeters, including those that separate an organization's intranet from the public Internet, cloud services, and carrier networks, such as MNO, MPLS, and Carrier Ethernet networks. You may recall from Chapter 8 that *demarcation points* traditionally identify boundaries between a business's local networks and WAN service provider networks.

The concept of a network perimeter continues to have meaning for some network configurations, but in many of today's evolving enterprise networks, network administrators are realizing that "network perimeter" is a concept that is best treated abstractly. Network users are connecting to the enterprise network via both internal and external networks and are using a mix of wired and wireless connections to access network resources.

Data and applications that were once housed on servers owned, managed, and secured by the organization are increasingly being moved to the cloud to facilitate anytime, anywhere availability and access for any network user device. And web services often involve interactions outside of traditional trust boundaries.

In short, the increasing reliance of enterprise networks on interconnected ecosystems of online devices is challenging traditional notions of network perimeters. At the same time, it has elevated the importance of perimeter security and is expanding the range of defenses being deployed to protect enterprise networks against attacks and unauthorized access. The evolution of thinking about network perimeters, including zero trust security thinking, is helping network managers to focus on network vulnerabilities, network attack surfaces, and how to safeguard network assets and data from hackers, attackers, and other untrusted or malicious actors.

11.8.1 Perimeter Threats

In a network attack, attackers are focused on penetrating the enterprise network perimeter and gaining access to internal systems. They often use a combination of attacks, such as compromising endpoints, spreading malware, and exploiting software or device vulnerabilities, to help them breach perimeter defenses. Perimeters face numerous threats, including those identified in Table 11-11.

Table 11-11: Examples of common network perimeter threats.

Perimeter Threat	Description
Insider threats	*Insider threats* include *rogue/malicious employees* who attempt to sabotage or steal data, compromise or damage network infrastructure, perpetrate fraud, create/sell fictitious network login credentials, or carry out other nefarious activities. As insiders, they typically have little problem getting past physical security defenses and are considered valid network users permitted to enter the network via authorized access channels. Once inside, they may install *malware* or attempt to leverage their authorizations to perform activities they are not authorized to perform. Malicious insiders with specialized authorizations (e.g., configuration change or system administrator authorizations) are especially dangerous. In numerous insider attacks, rogue employees have used USB sticks to intentionally infect corporate networks. *Careless network users* who neglect to follow network security policies and procedures are also insider threats.
Outdated security software	*Outdated security software* in firewalls, routers, and other perimeter devices may also be considered an insider threat. Security software is often only as good as its most recent update, and network personnel who neglect to install the most recent updates and patches put perimeter security at risk.
Compromised user accounts	*Compromised user accounts/credentials* can be used by malicious actors to access the network. Unsuspecting or ill-trained network users may give up their login credentials in *phishing* or other *social engineering attacks*. If an attacker identifies a valid network user ID, they may use brute force *password attacks* to gain access to the network. Attackers who are successful in compromising network users with extensive privileges (e.g., network administrators) are especially dangerous.
Compromised mobile devices and applications	*Compromised mobile devices and applications* pose significant threats to network security. Most business applications on enterprise networks support some type of mobile access. As noted in Chapter 10, many businesses have embraced EMM and UEM to provide enhanced defenses against threats posed by mobile applications and devices.
Critical application integrations	*Critical application integrations* can pose perimeter security threats. Business processes are often executed across multiple interconnected, and integrated systems. In addition, mission-critical enterprise systems, such as ERP systems, are typically interconnected with other applications and organizations through interfaces that attackers may target.
Business partners and vendors	*Business partners and vendors with network access* can threaten network security. As noted in Chapter 5, businesses often create extranets that allow business partners, hardware/software vendors, or external contractors to have restricted access to an organization's intranet. For example, hardware/software vendors may be permitted to monitor their technologies within the enterprise network. If their connections are misconfigured or outdated, network security is at risk. Also, such arrangements provide additional sets of user credentials that attackers may compromise and use to gain access to the network.

DoS and DDoS attacks and *MITM attacks* are sometimes considered perimeter threats. As noted in section 11.2, some attackers build large botnets of compromised devices and use them to flood a network's perimeter devices (e.g., firewalls) or servers with bogus access or service requests. Doing this inhibits authorized users or devices from accessing the network and its resources. Also, if an MITM attack enables an attacker to obtain user login credentials, they may be able to access the network and elude other security defenses.

Given this hefty, but not exhaustive, list of network perimeter threats, it should come as no surprise that a wide range of perimeter security mechanisms exist to defend against them.

11.8.2 Perimeter Defenses

Perimeter defenses are deployed in perimeter technologies, both routine and specialized, to safeguard internal networks from attacks. Perimeter technologies include routers, firewalls, and secure web gateways.

In addition to performing routing functions, a router can be configured to perform basic checks on network activity, including ingress and egress packet filtering to identify malware and prevent it from reaching firewalls, switches, or other devices. Securing routers begins by disabling default settings for unused services that malicious actors seeking to gain access to the network can exploit.

A *firewall* is a device (or software) that enforces a set of prespecified rules about what traffic it will and will not allow through. Relative to a router, a firewall is typically configured to do a more thorough job of filtering incoming and outgoing traffic. Some firewalls do stateful packet inspection to identify anomalies in client-server connections and data exchanges.

Some firewalls, including *web application firewalls (WAFs)*, may be called *DDoS firewalls* because they use stateful packet filtering to identify and block some types of DDoS attacks. Because web servers are usually deployed in DMZs, WAFs can inhibit some DDoS attacks from overwhelming firewalls that protect internal networks.

A **secured web gateway (SWG)** is a perimeter security technology that prevents unsecured or malicious Internet traffic from entering an organization's internal network. It is deployed to prevent user devices and networking equipment from accessing or being infected by malicious websites and web traffic, Internet-borne malware, and other cyberthreats. It also is used to ensure regulatory compliance.

According to Gartner, an SWG should include malicious code detection, URL filtering, and Application layer controls for popular cloud apps like Microsoft 365. An SWG is configured to enforce granular use policies and to filter web and Internet traffic. Although SWGs and firewalls perform similar tasks, they are different. Most firewalls inspect incoming packets for known threats at the Network layer; SWGs operate at the Application layer.

DMZ Networks

DMZs were introduced in Chapter 2 as an enterprise network zone separating an organization's private network from the Internet. A **DMZ network** (or "demilitarized zone") functions as a subnetwork that contains an organization's exposed, outward-facing network services, such as web servers, email servers, and DNS servers. Isolating these services, servers, and resources in a DMZ enables them to be accessed via the Internet. They are also reachable from the internal network via a firewall that separates the internal network and the DMZ network.

From a cybersecurity perspective, a DMZ network is a perimeter network that protects an organization's internal network from untrusted traffic from the public Internet. It adds an extra layer of security to the internal network's perimeter.

As Figure 11-14 illustrates, a DMZ typically sits between the public Internet and corporate networks, ideally between two firewalls. It serves as a buffer between the Internet and an organization's private network. When properly configured, a DMZ makes it more difficult for an attacker to gain direct access to an organization's internal networks via the Internet, and if it is compromised, it alerts network administrators that an attack is under way.

Organizations required to comply with government regulations, such as the Health Insurance Portability and Accountability Act (HIPAA), may install a proxy server in the DMZ. A **proxy server** is a server application

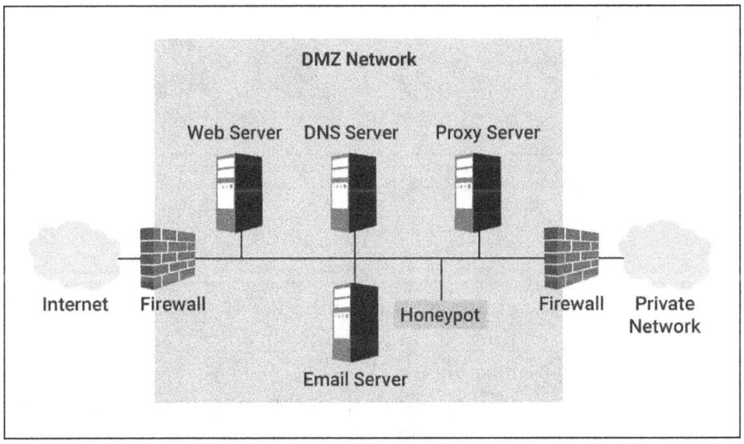

Figure 11-14: An example of a DMZ network.

that acts as an intermediary between clients and servers. Placing this function in a DMZ network enables the proxy server to handle client requests. It also enables user interactions with servers to be monitored and logged.

A proxy server is a dual-homed host with two network IP addresses. The address on the outbound side is the one the Internet sees; the other is what the internal network sees. Proxy server *Network Address Translation (NAT)* is described in Chapter 5.

As Figure 11-14 illustrates, email servers may be placed in DMZ networks because of their extensive interactions with both internal and external networks. This is one of multiple mechanisms used for email security. Several of them are identified in Appendix 11-6.

A DMZ may also include a honeypot. A **honeypot** is a fake attack target designed to lure attackers away from legitimate network assets and attack targets. It is like a baited trap for hackers and other attackers. Like hunting decoys, it mimics real targets, such as servers or databases. Security personnel are alerted when honeypots are accessed and often monitor honeypot intrusion attempts and behaviors to learn more about the hacking methods while also blocking access to legitimate targets.

Intrusion Detection and Prevention Systems

Intrusion detection systems (IDSs) and intrusion prevention systems (IPSs) are sometimes classified as network perimeter defenses and sometimes considered internal network defenses designed to limit attacker damage after perimeters are breached.

An **intrusion detection system (IDS)** functions as an alarm system that detects suspicious network activity and alerts security personnel that an attack may be under way. It may be a single device or a collection of activity sensors/monitors located at strategic points in the network. As Figure 11-15 illustrates, an IDS is typically deployed inside an organization's perimeter firewall to monitor suspect network behavior involving network equipment or assets.

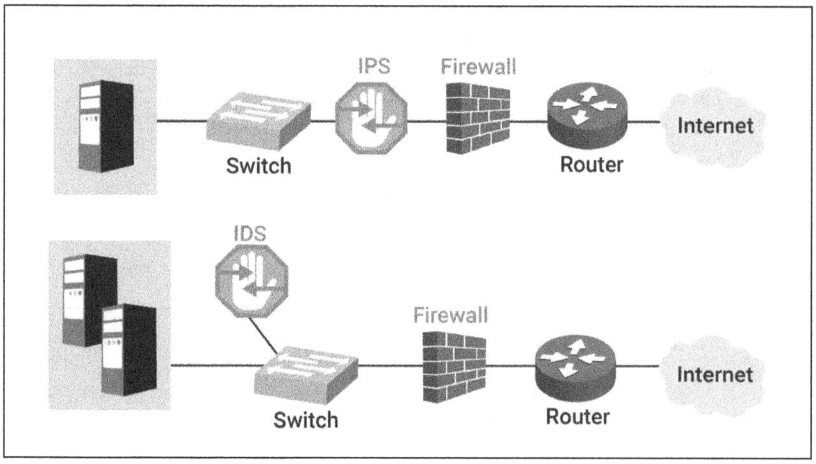

Figure 11-15: An example of IDS and IPS deployment in enterprise networks.

Like an IDS, an **intrusion prevention system (IPS)** performs intrusion detection, but it also takes action to block the attempted intrusion or otherwise remediate the security incident. When an IPS detects an intrusion, it automatically attempts to defend the network as it is alerting security personnel about the incident. It is configured to take immediate action without a network administrator's direct intervention.

Unified threat management systems are also used in enterprise networks. **Unified threat management (UTM) systems** combine the capabilities of IDS and IPS systems with network security functions in a single security device. UTM systems are sometimes called *UTM firewalls*, and they may perform numerous perimeter security functions, including firewall, antivirus, antispyware, antispam, VPN monitoring, and other functions (see Figure 11-16).

They use deep packet inspection to check for viruses, spam, malware, malicious attachments, trojans, and other threats. *Deep packet inspection (DPI)* does a complete evaluation of incoming and outgoing packets for known threats and compliance with defined security criteria. When issues are identified, information is blocked from being transmitted or received.

Secure access service edge (SASE) platforms combine remote access VPN and UTM capabilities. They are increasingly being used by organizations that house large volumes of data in the cloud and by those that have adopted SD-WANs. SASE systems are well suited for businesses with remote workers and cloud services that interact with corporate networks via the Internet.

It is important to note that many businesses contract with third-party network security companies for perimeter security solutions, such as firewall monitoring, IDS, IPS, and UTM. Companies such as Secureworks provide these and other security services for corporations and government agencies. The involvement of third-party security firms is more of a rule than an exception for today's enterprise networks.

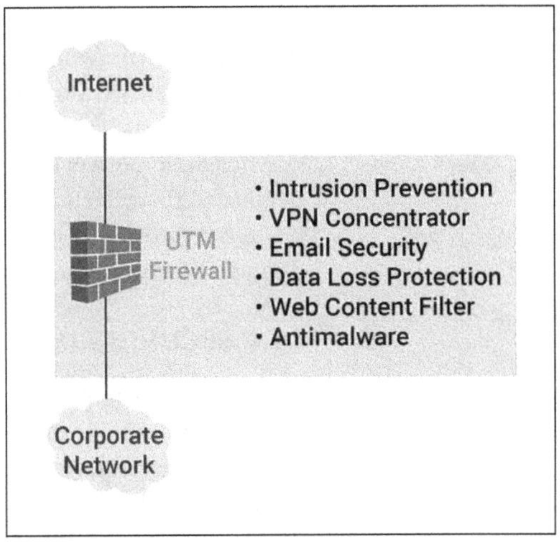

Figure 11-16: Examples of UTM system capabilities.

VPN Monitoring

VPNs are sometimes considered network perimeter protections, but are also sometimes identified as perimeter threats. Intranet, extranet, and remote access VPNs are illustrated and described in section 8.4.3 in Chapter 8. They enable branches, business partners, and remote workers to connect to private corporate networks from their locations via secure tunnels over the public Internet.

Some businesses have deployed UTM firewalls as endpoints for VPN connections. Their deep packet inspection capabilities enable incoming and outgoing traffic to be closely inspected for suspicious payloads and anomalous activity. This is important because should an attacker succeed in compromising VPN user credentials, they may be able to tunnel through firewalls and other perimeter defenses to gain access to the private network and exfiltrate data using man-in-the-middle or other types of attacks. In short, because VPNs provide direct routes to an enterprise network, they need to be monitored and secured.

11.8.3 Perimeter Security Best Practices

Given the variety of perimeter security threats and controls and their importance, it should come as no surprise that there are best practices for perimeter security. Some commonly identified best practices include strong authentication, mobile and IoT device hardening, embedded security services, and security intelligence collection (see Table 11-12).

Table 11-12: Examples of perimeter security best practices.

Best Practice	Description
Strong authentication	*Strong authentication* includes two- and multifactor authentication. It enables organizations to allow controlled access to enterprise networks and network assets. It provides extra layers of security for logins and helps security personnel detect attempted intrusions before damage is done.
Mobile and IoT device hardening	*Hardening of mobile and IoT devices* that connect to the enterprise network facilitates the enforcement of security requirements that determine who can access enterprise network assets and the circumstances under which they can be accessed.
Embedded security	*Embedded security services* in devices and applications help protect devices and systems from security exploits. They are considered best practices for banking ATM devices and devices in automated manufacturing systems, such as ICS, SCADA, and IIoT. Security features embedded in IIoT devices and applications include antivirus protection, encryption, and whitelisting.
Security intelligence gathering and distribution	*Collecting security intelligence* directly from cloud applications and their hosts is considered a best practice. It enables threat intelligence to be shared with subscribers and their perimeter security solutions and helps organizations contextualize their information about potential and real security incidents and how they should respond.

Zero trust security is causing some rethinking about enterprise network boundaries. Devices inside private network perimeters are no longer considered more trustworthy than those outside the perimeter. While this has generated some "perimeterless" and "no perimeter" thinking among security experts, the use of traditional perimeter defenses is not going away.

Enterprise network security personnel devote considerable attention to perimeter security, but despite their diligence and best efforts, determined attackers continue to find ways to penetrate private networks. With this in mind, DiD identifies internal network safeguards to minimize the damage that attackers can cause.

11.9 SECURING INTERNAL NETWORKS

Gaining access to private, internal networks is an objective of most attackers, no matter what their motivations and intentions. When attackers succeed in thwarting perimeter defenses, they are in a better position to exfiltrate data or carry out other attacks. When malicious actors acquire valid login credentials from compromised devices or phishing-prone employees, they can access the internal network and the assets that the user is authorized to use.

This makes it important to consider the security of internal networks from the perspective of insiders who have legitimate access to systems, applications, and assets in the private network. By masquerading as valid insiders, attackers can do significant damage.

Insider security incidents are common and costly. As reported in the *Verizon Business 2020 Data Breach Investigations Report*, insiders are involved in 22% of all security incidents, and the percentage of insider security incidents is increasing. The Ponemon Institute's *2020 Cost of Insider Threats Global Report* indicates that the overall costs of insider threats are also rising.

Insider threats include malicious threats that come from people with insider knowledge and access to an organization's data, systems, or security practices. Insiders may be current employees, former employees, business partners, or contractors with login credentials for internal networks. Examples of insider threats include:

- Fraud—for example, when an insider steals, modifies, or deletes data for deceptive or illegal purposes
- Sabotage—for example, when an insider uses their legitimate access to damage or destroy network systems or data
- Espionage/spying—for example, when an insider uses the internal network to monitor business operations or steal company data or information for someone else
- Intellectual property theft—for example, when an insider steals an organization's patents, inventions, designs, etc., for a competitor or to sell to others

Some organizations use *internal vulnerability scans* to assess insider threats. Such scans examine network security from the perspective of an insider or valid user of systems and network assets.

Advanced persistent threats (APTs) are considered major internal threats. APTs are attacks that go undetected for prolonged periods of time. When threat actors can avoid detection and retain network access for a protracted time, data theft may not occur until weeks or months after the original network breach.

Enterprise networks' wireless networks may be susceptible to eavesdropping, rogue access points, and other security threats that may be viewed as vulnerabilities that deserve special attention.

11.9.1 Internal Network Security Controls

Security controls for internal networks include MFA, authentication logs, session monitoring/recording, IDS and IPS, network segmentation, least privilege access, and endpoint privilege man-

Table 11-13: Examples of internal network security controls.	
Internal Control	**Description**
Multifactor authentication (MFA)	*MFA* can be used to provide an additional layer of security for insider access to important network assets, including databases and critical applications. Ideally, these assets should require at least one identity verification mechanism that is different from those used to access the internal network.
Authentication logs	*Authentication logs* record and display information about authentication events that occur when network users attempt to access network assets protected by authentication access controls. They can identify suspicious activity on the internal network such as brute force attacks on network assets.
Session monitoring and recording	*Session monitoring and recording tools* enable network administrators or security officers to monitor critical assets, such as databases, servers, and internetworking devices. They enable session and user activities to be monitored and recorded in real time. They are used for identifying and terminating anomalous sessions in real time. Session recording playbacks are useful for forensic analysis of security incidents. Session monitoring and recording is considered an important aspect of *privileged access management (PAM)* and security.
IDS and IPS	*IDS and IPS systems* can be deployed as collections of activity sensors/monitors located at strategic points in internal networks. Such deployments enable them to be used to detect lateral movement and APTs.
Network segmentation	*Network segmentation* (*network segregation*) is a *lateral movement control*. Splitting the internal network into segments can make it more difficult for attackers to reach their ultimate targets if their initial points of entry do not provide them with direct paths to reaching the target. Network segmentation is based on the idea that systems and data that do not need to communicate or interact with each other should be placed in different segments, and that users should only be able to access segments required to perform their jobs. Attackers that succeed in breaching one segment should not be able to access others.
Least privilege access	The principle of *least privilege* is another lateral movement control. *Least privilege access* refers to situations where users and accounts have the minimum amount of access needed for their organizational roles. They should not have more rights to a network asset than the bare minimum they need. Least access privileges can be extended to network administrators. There can be tiers of administrative accounts and strict limits on the number of highly privileged accounts. If an attacker compromises a lower privilege administrative account, there are limits on what they can do. Ideally, accounts with full privilege across an enterprise network (such as a domain admin, global admin, or cloud admin account) should not be used except to implement major network design changes.
Endpoint privilege management	The principle of least privilege can also be applied to network assets. High-risk devices, services, and applications should be identified during access privilege planning and implementation. *Endpoint privilege management* governs access privileges to network endpoints and ensures that admin privileges are not excessively distributed among network users. It prevents users from exploiting functions that are beyond those needed to perform their jobs and helps to thwart attacker attempts to elevate the privileges of compromised accounts.

agement. These controls are described in Table 11-13. As Appendix 11-7 explains, change management can also be an important internal network control. Lateral movement monitoring and control and encryption are other important internal network security controls.

Lateral Movement Monitoring and Control

Lateral movement refers to techniques used by attackers after gaining access to an internal network to move deeper into a network to find sensitive data or other high-value assets. This often involves using various tools to increase access privileges after entering the network. Often, attackers impersonate legitimate users, obtain additional credentials, escalate privileges, and move through multiple systems in the network until their final targets are reached.

Because lateral movement of threat actors may resemble normal network user behavior, it can be very challenging to detect. Real-time monitoring and behavioral analysis tools are helpful in detecting lateral movement and APTs. They are described in Table 11-14.

Table 11-14: Examples of lateral movement and APT defenses.

Lateral Movement/ APT Tool	Description
Real-time monitoring and alerting	*Real-time monitoring and alerting* involves collecting and correlating data across the network to provide real-time alerting of suspicious activity that should be investigated. By aggregating and correlating alerts, these tools help security personnel identify and observe the progression of a threat act in real time and view successive activities that suggest an APT.
Behavioral analysis	*Behavioral analysis* includes capabilities to identify significant deviations from the normal behavior of network users and entities. *User and entity behavior analysis (UEBA)* solutions often leverage machine learning (ML) to determine both the baseline (normal) behavior of each user and entity and the degree to which any activity deviates from that baseline. Understanding and contextualizing deviations helps alert security personnel to suspicious activity.

11.9.2 Encryption

Encryption is pervasive in enterprise networks to protect data in motion and data at rest. A wide range of encryption protocols were introduced and discussed at varying levels of detail in previous chapters to provide a sense of where and how they are used. In this chapter, we will take a closer look at some of the fundamental concepts of encryption on which the various protocols are based.

Encryption refers to the process of disguising data or information to hide its true meaning from anyone not authorized to see it. Today, sophisticated mathematical algorithms are used to encode the data into an unintelligible form, but in earlier times, encryption was often less complex. However, throughout history, encryption has deterred unwarranted use of information by making it time-consuming or costly to decipher encrypted messages.

The science of encrypting and decrypting information is called *cryptography*. *Decryption* is the process of translating encrypted information back to its original form. In computing, unencrypted data is *plaintext* (cleartext) and encrypted data is *ciphertext*. These cryptography fundamentals are illustrated in Figure 11-17 and are described more fully in Appendix 11-8.

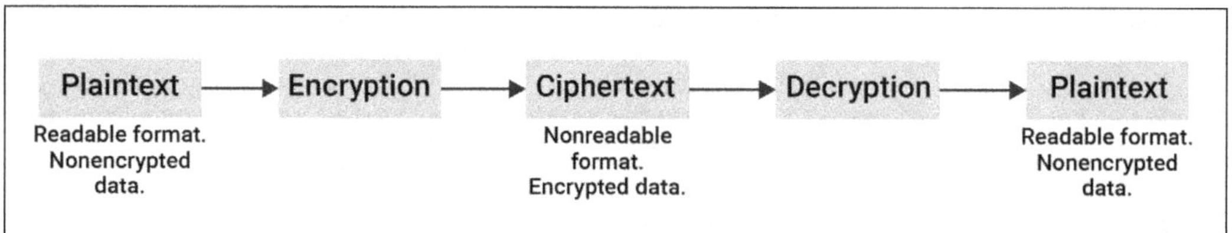

Figure 11-17: Cryptography fundamentals.

Ciphertext appears unintelligible to interceptors, such as network intruders, and converting ciphertext back to plaintext can be a time-consuming and laborious process for those who intercept encrypted messages and do not know the encryption algorithm and key.

All encryption algorithms involve substituting one thing for another. Today's encryption algorithms use advanced mathematics to encrypt and decrypt data, which makes the ciphertext very challenging for interceptors to decipher.

Symmetric Encryption

Two major types of encryption algorithms are used in today's enterprise networks: symmetric and asymmetric. **Symmetric encryption algorithms** use the same key (cipher) to encrypt and decrypt the plaintext message. This key is sometimes called a *shared key* because it is known and used by both the sender and receiver of a message. The sender uses the key to encrypt the plaintext, and

Figure 11-18: Symmetric encryption.

the receiver uses the same key to decrypt the ciphertext and convert it back to plaintext (see Figure 11-18). Because both sender and receiver are responsible for keeping the shared key secret, symmetric encryption is often called *secret key encryption.*

Block and Stream Ciphers

Block ciphers and stream ciphers are two different methods of encrypting data with symmetric encryption algorithms. They differ in whether they encrypt plaintext data in chunks (blocks) or bit-by-bit:

- A block cipher breaks plaintext messages into fixed-size blocks before converting them into ciphertext using a key.
- A stream cipher breaks a plaintext message into single bits (or bytes), which are converted individually into ciphertext using key bits (or bytes).

For a simple analogy to understand the differences, imagine that you are encrypting this textbook. You could encrypt the book one page at a time (block cipher) or one letter at a time (stream cipher). Both processes, of course, are more complicated than this analogy, but it gives you the basic idea of how they differ. The basic differences between them are illustrated in Figure 11-19.

Block ciphers are used in many of the cryptographic processes and technologies employed in today's enterprise networks. Examples of block ciphers are identified in Table 11-15. Today, strong encryption typically means key lengths of 192 bits or more.

Unlike block ciphers, which require the formation of blocks prior to encryption, *stream ciphers* encrypt data in long streams. This is done by adding an encryption key bit to each plaintext bit to create the ciphertext bit. Basically, this means one bit of plaintext data is processed at a time instead of waiting for a data block to form. The process is reversed at the other end to

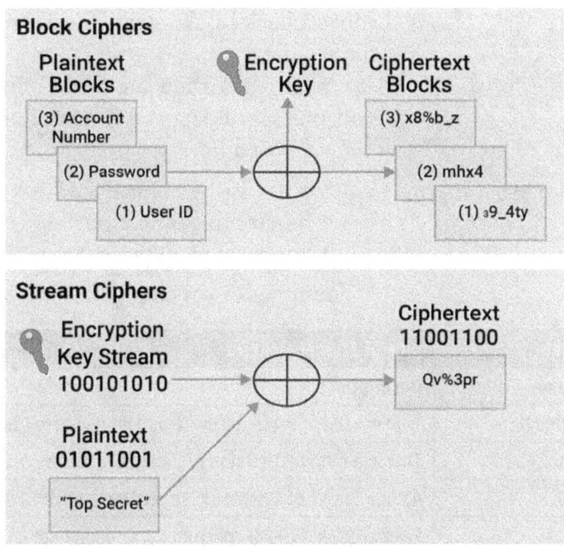

Figure 11-19: Key differences between block and stream ciphers.

Table 11-15: Examples of symmetric block ciphers.	
Name	**Description**
Data Encryption Standard (DES)	The DES was an early block cipher and standard for nonclassified government data. It used 64-bit blocks and 56-bit keys. At one time, it was the go-to, symmetric key algorithm for encrypting data, but it has been superseded by the Advanced Encryption Standard (AES).
Triple DES	*Triple DES (a.k.a 3DES or TDEA)* was derived from DES. Introduced in 1998, the algorithm was primarily adopted in banks and other financial firms to encrypt data in motion and data at rest. Like DES, it has fallen out of favor because of the rise of more secure algorithms such as AES. It is scheduled to be officially retired in 2023 but is likely to be used after that date. 3DES applies three different DES keys to plaintext when it is encrypted.
Advanced Encryption Standard (AES)	AES is a symmetric block cipher used by the U.S. government to protect classified information and is also widely used by other organizations. It is used in current Wi-Fi generations. The AES algorithm (the Rijndael algorithm) is a symmetric block cipher algorithm that breaks plaintext data into 128-bit blocks and encrypts them using 128-, 192-, and 256-bit keys. Once the blocks are encrypted, they are joined together to form the ciphertext.
RC5	RC5 is a symmetric-key block cipher notable for its simplicity. It was designed by Ronald Rivest and stands for "Rivest Cipher" or "Ron's Code." RC5 has a variable block size (32, 64, or 128 bits). It also has a variable key size (0 to 2040 bits) and a variable number of encryption rounds. The original suggested parameter choices were 64-bit blocks, 128-bit keys, and 12 rounds.
Blowfish	Blowfish is a symmetric-key block cipher that is included in numerous encryption products. It has a 64-bit block size and a variable key length from 32 to 448 bits. It is a 16-round encryption cipher.
Twofish	Twofish has a block size of 128 bits and accepts a key of any length up to 256 bits. Twofish is efficient on both 32-bit and 8-bit CPUs, such as those in smart cards, and embedded chips in hardware. It is flexible and can be used for applications where keys are changed frequently or where there is little or no available RAM and ROM.

convert back to plaintext. The encryption key bit is subtracted from the ciphertext bit to produce the plaintext bit.

Stream algorithms are faster and more efficient than block ciphers because they're encrypting only one bit of data at a time rather than entire blocks, and they are less mathematically complex. They are used in:

- SSL/TLS connections
- Bluetooth connections
- Some cellular connections

Examples of stream ciphers are identified in Table 11-16.

Table 11-16: Examples of stream ciphers.	
Name	**Description**
Salsa20	This is used in some software and hardware IoT implementations.
ChaCha20	This is a modified version of Salsa20; it is supported in TLS 1.3.
A5	*A5* is a family of symmetric stream ciphers used in Global System for Mobile (GSM) cellular networks.
RC4	*Rivest Cipher 4 (RC4)* encrypts data one byte at a time. RC4 has been used in SSL and TLS protocols. While known for ease of use and performance speed, known security flaws have reduced its usage despite variants that have been developed to increase its security.

Symmetric Key Management

One of the main challenges of symmetric cryptography is securely sharing the key. Key agreement protocols, key encapsulation mechanisms, and out-of-band sharing procedures are discussed in Appendix 11-8 as symmetric key management strategies.

Session keys are symmetric encryption keys. A *session key* is randomly generated to ensure the security of a single communications session between a sender or receiver. Subsequent communication sessions between the same devices use different session keys. In TLS, the client and the server generate session keys during the TLS handshake prior to any data exchange. The official RFC for TLS does not refer to these keys as "session keys," but functionally that is what they are. Tokens used for digital wallet transactions are also session keys.

Asymmetric Encryption

Asymmetric encryption algorithms use different keys for encryption and decryption. The keys are mathematically related, but the key used to decrypt ciphertext is not the key used to encrypt the plaintext. As Figure 11-20a shows, the key used to encrypt plaintext can be called the encryption key and the one used to convert ciphertext back to plaintext can be called the decryption key. When a sender uses an asymmetric encryption key to convert plaintext to ciphertext, it is unable to decrypt it using the encryption key. Only the decryption key can convert the ciphertext back to its original form.

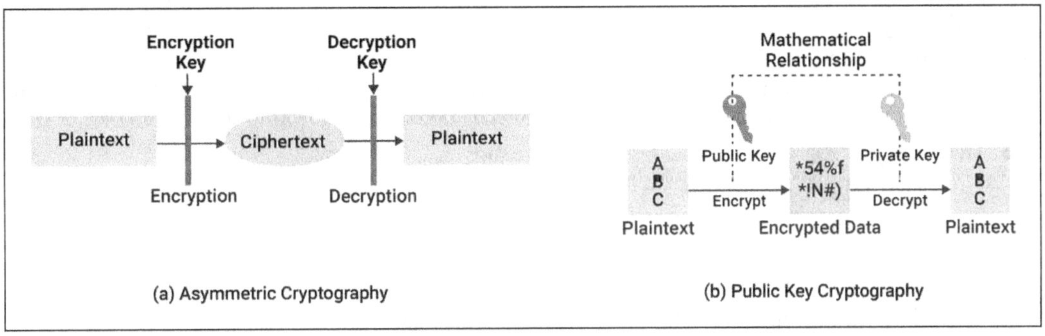

Figure 11-20: In asymmetric and public key cryptography, different keys are used for encryption and decryption.

Asymmetric encryption uses one-way mathematical functions to encrypt plaintext. A one-way function is a function where computation in one direction is straightforward but computation in the reverse direction is far more difficult. There is a symmetry in computational effort required to perform the function evaluation and to reverse it. One-way functions are the mathematical foundations of public key cryptography.

In *public key cryptography*, one of the keys is made public (is accessible) and is called the *public key*. The other key is kept secret and is called the *private key* (see Figure 11-20b). The private key is known to only one entity in the message exchange, the receiver or the sender, depending on the type of asymmetric encryption that is used. Typically, these keys are 512, 1024, or 2048 bits in length.

Most commonly, the public key is used to encrypt the message, and the private key is used for decryption. This requires the sender to look up the recipient's public key in a repository and to apply it to the plaintext message to encrypt it. When the encrypted message is received, the recipient uses their private key to decrypt the message. This process is illustrated in Figure 11-21.

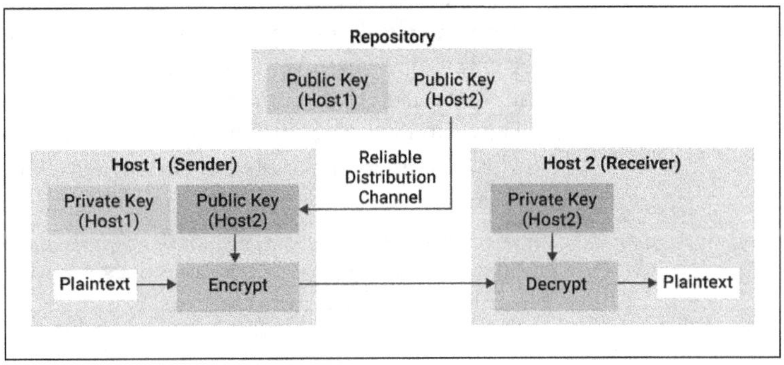

Figure 11-21: Public key encryption process.

A second type of asymmetric encryption uses a sender's private key to encrypt the plaintext and the sender's public key to decrypt the

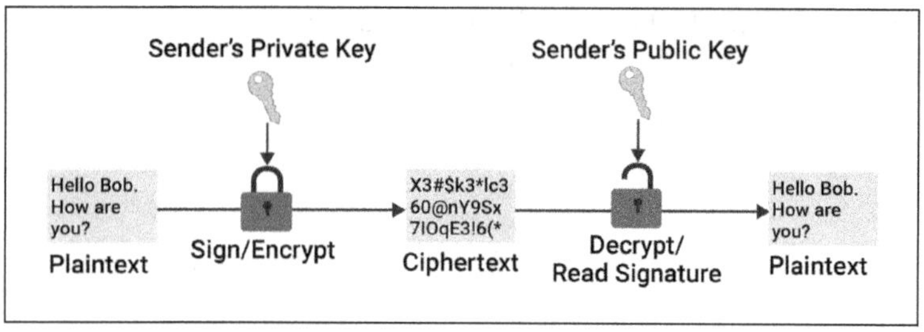

Figure 11-22: Digital signature encryption.

ciphertext (see Figure 11-22). This is called *digital signature encryption* because the sender essentially "signs" the message when they use their private key to encrypt the plaintext. The recipient of the message obtains the sender's public key from the key repository and uses it to decrypt the message. Because the sender's public key enables the recipient to decrypt the ciphertext, it authenticates the holder of the private key as the sender.

Asymmetric Key Management

Asymmetric key management alleviates some of the issues associated with symmetric key management. Because pairs of encryption keys are used, it is no longer necessary for endpoints to keep a shared encryption key secret. However, asymmetric encryption still requires safeguarding the secrecy of private keys.

As Figure 11-21 illustrates, public keys are publicized in public key repositories. Because anyone can post a public key on the Internet, there is no guarantee that the public key is associated with the listed entity unless additional safeguards are used.

Asymmetric key administration includes:

- Key pair creation
- Public key distribution
- Key storage, safeguards, and restoration
- Standards and policies for changing and renewing keys

Public key infrastructure (PKI) is an important part of asymmetric key management. **Public key infrastructure (PKI)** refers to tools used to create and manage public keys to ensure that they are trustworthy.

PKI implements two technologies: certificates and keys. Certificates enable Internet users to verify the identity of organizations or people they want to communicate with. Certificates are issued by a **certificate authority (CA)**, a trusted organization that can vouch for the authenticity of the organization or person. Verisign is a CA. An entity's public and private keys are issued when it registers with the CA. PKI certificates are stored in a certificate database on a server hosted by the CA.

PKI certificates are not issued indefinitely. They must be periodically renewed. You have probably encountered warning messages from a CA indicating that an entity's certificate could not be validated. PKI certificates are used in HTTPS, SSL, IPsec, and PGP (see Appendix 11-8).

Internet Key Exchange (IKE) is a widely used key management protocol standard for exchanging encryption keys over unsecured connections. In IKE, the encryption process is negotiated by endpoints using PKI infrastructure. Each endpoint generates a random key and sends it to the other endpoint using PKI infrastructure. The two keys are combined to produce the symmetric key used to encrypt subsequent message exchanges between the two endpoints.

Poor PKI execution and unsecured digital identities pose serious security risks. For example, attackers/intruders may attempt to use an expired certificate to masquerade as a valid certificate holder. Key management best practices are identified by NIST and federal regulators to protect the integrity of PKI infrastructure.

SUMMARY

Ongoing changes to enterprise networks introduce vulnerabilities and expand the networks' attack surfaces. Vulnerability audits/scans and vulnerability prevention, patching, and management help thwart attackers seeking to exploit vulnerabilities and access network resources.

Malware, zero-day exploits, and social engineering attacks are common. Other common attacks include botnet, DDoS, DNS tunneling, SQL injection, and MITM attacks. Businesses have cybersecurity incident response teams trained to rapidly respond to attacks and mitigate their damage. Adoption and use of SIEM technologies for threat detection and security incident management are increasing.

Confidentiality, integrity, and availability are pillars of network security. Business continuity is another important goal. Business continuity and disaster recovery plans result from threat analyses and risk management processes. Risk management uses the results of threat analyses and the consequences of compromised network assets to determine network security improvement priorities, as well as security plans, policies, procedures, and architectures.

Network security architecture serves as the foundation of an organization's defenses against security threats. Well-designed network security architectures contribute to business resiliency (and continuity) against cyberattacks and network infrastructure component failures. ZTA is a good fit to the makeup of today's enterprise network.

Layered security defenses are widely perceived as an effective way to protect enterprise networks and their assets. DiD provides guidance for layering defenses. Threats, vulnerabilities, and security controls are identified for each DiD layer. This chapter focuses on describing major concerns and safeguards used at the physical, cloud, perimeter, and internal network layers.

In the DiD model, policies, procedures, and network user security awareness and training are found at the outermost layer, and data, the target of most attacks, is the innermost layer. Physical, cloud, perimeter, internal network, host/endpoint, and application layers are between the outermost and innermost layers.

Facility perimeter defenses, building exterior defenses, and building interior defenses are examples of security mechanisms used at the physical layer. Cloud firewalls, IAM, and CASB are examples of cloud layer defenses.

Zero trust security is challenging traditional notions of network perimeters; however, considerable attention is still devoted to securing enterprise network perimeters. DMZ networks, honeypots, IDS, IPS, UTM, SASE, and VPN monitoring are examples of perimeter defenses.

Lateral movement and APTs are major concerns when attackers succeed in breaching perimeter defenses. Lateral movement controls include real-time monitoring and alerting systems, user behavior analysis, network segmentation, and least access privileges.

Encryption is used in enterprise networks to protect data in motion and data at rest. Two major types of encryption algorithms are used: symmetric and asymmetric. Symmetric encryption algorithms, such as AES, use the same key to encrypt and decrypt messages. Keeping shared keys secret is an important aspect of symmetric key management.

Asymmetric encryption uses a pair of mathematically related keys for encryption and decryption. One of these keys is publicly available, while the other is not. Public key encryption is widely used, and it leverages PKI and CAs.

KEY TERMS

Asymmetric encryption algorithms
Business continuity
Certificate authority (CA)
DMZ network
Encryption
Honeypot
Information security
Internet Key Exchange (IKE)
Intrusion detection system (IDS)
Intrusion prevention system (IPS)
Lateral movement
Network attack surface
Network perimeter
Network vulnerability
Proxy server
Public key infrastructure (PKI)
Secure access service edge (SASE)
Secured web gateway (SWG)
Symmetric encryption algorithms
Unified threat management (UTM) systems

REVIEW QUESTIONS

1. What is network security? What factors make it challenging to keep enterprise networks secure?
2. What is an attack surface? What are network vulnerabilities, and when are they attack vectors?
3. Identify examples of common enterprise network vulnerabilities. Also, identify several widely used vulnerability controls.
4. Identify attacks that are common across industries and businesses. Also, identify recent trends for attacks and attackers.
5. How do businesses respond when attacks are detected?
6. What capabilities do SIEM solutions have, and how do they help incident response teams?
7. Identify and briefly describe the three pillars of network security. Why is nonrepudiation often considered to be another primary network security goal?
8. What is information security? What are information security breaches?
9. What is business continuity? What is typically included in network business continuity and network disaster recovery plans?
10. What does network threat analysis involve? What are risk values? What are the differences between low-level and critical risks? Why should threat analysis results be periodically reviewed?
11. What are the differences between security plans, policies, and procedures? What areas are typically addressed in network security policies? How are cybersecurity training requirements related to security plans, policies, and procedures?
12. What is network security architecture? What are examples of network elements included in security architectures? What are examples of security elements included in security architectures? How are security architectures related to business continuity and resilience?
13. Briefly explain the underlying philosophy and assumptions of zero trust security and how they differ from traditional network security thinking. Identify the major components of zero trust security architectures.
14. What assumptions underlie the use of layered defenses for networks or network components?
15. Identify the different layers in DiD. Why is data the innermost layer of DiD?
16. Identify examples of external, internal, and human threats to the physical security of facilities that house networking and computing infrastructure. Also, identify examples of facility perimeter, building exterior, building interior, and computer room security controls.
17. Briefly describe how cloud firewalls, IAM, CASB, DLP, and CDP contribute to securing the cloud layer of the DiD.
18. What is a network perimeter? What does perimeter security involve? How/why has traditional thinking about network perimeters evolved?
19. Identify examples of network perimeter threats. Also, identify examples of perimeter defenses.
20. What are DMZ networks, what do they include, and how do they contribute to perimeter security?
21. Briefly describe the differences among IDS, IPS, UTM, SASE, and VPN monitoring.
22. Identify and briefly describe several examples of perimeter security best practices.
23. What are examples of insider threats? Why is it important to consider internal network threats from the perspective of an insider? What are APTs?
24. Identify and briefly describe examples of internal network security controls.
25. What is lateral movement? Identify and briefly describe examples of lateral movement monitoring and APT defenses.
26. What is encryption? What is cryptography? What are the characteristics of symmetric encryption algorithms?
27. How do block ciphers differ from stream ciphers? Identify examples of each type. What are session keys?
28. What are the characteristics of asymmetric encryption

algorithms? Why are two keys needed? How does public key encryption differ from digital signature encryption?

29. What does asymmetric key administration involve? What is PKI? What is a CA, and what is its role in PKI? What is IKE?

PROBLEMS AND EXERCISES

Exercise 11-1 Many of the threats to enterprise networks are also threats to personal computing devices. For example, you may be targeted in a phishing attack by intruders who want to install malware (e.g., viruses and ransomware) and/or compromise your device for botnet attacks on other networks. Also, if you have important files stored on your device, a hard drive failure could make them inaccessible. Your life could also be affected if your device was stolen. Given these everyday realities, do an abbreviated threat analysis for a personal device such as a laptop.

- Identify at least five major threats, existing safeguards to protect your device from the threats, and additional security controls that could be added to provide further protection or to mitigate attack damage. Consider using the table below to organize this information.
- Consider how you would arrange current and additional security mechanisms for your personal device in a layered manner, such as defense in depth (DiD). Identify the layer at which the security mechanism is used (e.g., physical, perimeter) and briefly describe how it deters intruders from reaching the next layer.

Exercise 11-2 You have been hired as a security analyst by a start-up that creates, hosts, and maintains websites for clients. The company's 15 web developers generate an average of 250 Gigabytes of content per person every month, and most of this is shared with clients over the Internet before being added to their websites. As the company's client base continues to grow, so does its processing and storage requirements and its reliance on cloud services. The company's founders want to ensure that adequate security controls are in place for the cloud layer of DiD.

- Identify and briefly explain what the company should know about the physical security of the cloud data centers that it uses to host its clients' websites and storage. Ideally, what physical security controls should be in place?
- Identify and briefly describe the digital security controls that should be in place at the cloud layer of DiD to ensure that the company's clients' websites and storage are adequately protected.
- The company's founders have asked you whether remote access VPNs should be used for communicating with clients. Would you recommend them? Why or why not?

Exercise 11-3 After taking a computer networking course at your university, you have grown more concerned about securing the Wi-Fi network in your residence. Review the section of Chapter 7 that focuses on Wi-Fi security and use it to identify potential threats and the security mechanisms that could or should be used to protect your Wi-Fi network from potential intruders/attackers. Consider how these security mechanisms could be arranged in layers (e.g., perimeter, internal network, endpoint/device) to deter attackers/intruders from reaching deeper layers.

Exercise 11-4 Authy (from Authy.com) is a free app for mobile devices, laptops, and desktops that provides two-factor authentication. Many popular websites use Authy to authenticate visitors. It is also being increasingly adopted by individuals to protect their personal devices and their online interactions with Internet sites. Do some online research on Authy and compose a brief report on how it works and how it can be used to protect businesses and individuals from security breaches. Summarize the results of your research in a 150- to 300-word report.

Exercise 11-5 CORE Credit Union has two branches in Statesboro, Georgia; two branches in Savannah, Georgia; and a branch in Brooklet, Georgia. It has 46 employees across these different locations and uses extensive electronic communication between its locations and to communicate with its members. The NCUA requires credit unions to document how data and applications are secured by cloud and other third-party organizations that provide them with services (e.g., online banking, bill pay, credit card transaction processing, remote deposit capture, ATMs, cloud storage, firewall monitoring, etc.). There is much that

Threat	Existing Safeguards	Additional Security Controls

needs to be protected, and employees are the first line of defense. If you were responsible for overseeing security training for new employees, what topics would you include in their training? Develop a list of at least 10 required security topics that should be included in the training program and briefly describe why each topic is important.

Exercise 11-6 Do some online research on Pretty Good Privacy (PGP). Develop a 300- to 500-word report on PGP, what it is used for, and how it works. Your report should also describe how/where you can acquire PGP tools, how you generate public-private key pairs, and how/where you can share your public key to enable others to send you encrypted messages that only you can decrypt.

CHAPTER REFERENCES

Barracuda. (n.d.). Network Perimeter. Retrieved from: https://www.barracuda.com/glossary/network-perimeter

Baykara, S. (2020). Encryption Key Management Essentials. PCI DSS Guide. Retrieved from: https://www.pcidssguide.com/encryption-key-management-essentials/

Check Point Software Technologies. (n.d.). Network Security Architecture. Retrieved from: https://www.checkpoint.com/cyber-hub/network-security/what-is-network-security/network-security-architecture/

Cisco Systems. (n.d.). What Is a Cyberattack? Retrieved from: https://www.cisco.com/c/en/us/products/security/common-cyberattacks.html

Crane, C. (2021). Block Cipher vs Stream Cipher: What They Are & How They Work. Hashed Out. Retrieved from: https://www.thesslstore.com/blog/block-cipher-vs-stream-cipher/

Crowdstrike. (2023). Advanced Persistent Threat (APT). Retrieved from: https://www.crowdstrike.com/cybersecurity-101/advanced-persistent-threat-apt/

Cyber Security Memo. (2019). Layered Security Architecture—Cybersecurity Technology with NIST Cybersecurity Framework. Retrieved from: http://blog.51sec.org/2019/05/cyber-security-architecture-with-nist.html

Cynet. (n.d.). Network Attacks and Network Security Threats. Retrieved from: https://www.cynet.com/network-attacks/network-attacks-and-network-security-threats/

Fortinet. (n.d.). What Is Email Security? Retrieved from: https://www.fortinet.com/resources/cyberglossary/email-security

Fortinet. (n.d.). What Is Public Key Infrastructure (PKI)? Retrieved from: https://www.fortinet.com/resources/cyberglossary/public-key-infrastructure

Fulber-Garcia, V. (2023). How to Share a Key in Symmetric Cryptography? Baeldung. Retrieved from: https://www.baeldung.com/cs/symmetric-cryptography

Gillis, A. S., & Rosencrance, L. (n.d.). Security Information and Event Management (SIEM). TechTarget. Retrieved from: https://www.techtarget.com/searchsecurity/definition/security-information-and-event-management-SIEM

Hubbard, B. (2022). Defining Your IT Network Security Perimeter. InvGate. Retrieved from: https://blog.invgate.com/defining-your-it-security-perimeter

IBM. (2020). *Cost of a Data Breach Report 2020*. Retrieved from: https://www.ibm.com/security/digital-assets/cost-data-breach-report/1Cost%20of%20a%20Data%20Breach%20Report%202020.pdf

Imprivata. (2021). Defining the Different Types of Insider Threats. Retrieved from: https://www.imprivata.com/blog/defining-different-types-insider-threats

ManageEngine. (n.d.). Network Vulnerabilities. Retrieved from: https://www.manageengine.com/network-configuration-manager/network-vulnerabilities.html

Mukhadin, B. (2023). What Is Defense in Depth? Strategy for Cybersecurity. Wallarm. Retrieved from: https://www.wallarm.com/what/defense-in-depth-concept

Perez-Etchegoyen, J. P. (2020). 8 Reasons Perimeter Security Alone Won't Protect Your Crown Jewels. Dark Reading. Retrieved from: https://www.darkreading.com/cloud/8-reasons-perimeter-security-alone-won-t-protect-your-crown-jewels

Petcu, A. G. (2022). 10 Common Network Vulnerabilities and How to Prevent Them. Heimdal. Retrieved from: https://heimdalsecurity.com/blog/common-network-vulnerabilities/

Shea, S. (n.d.). Cryptography Basics: Symmetric Key Encryption Algorithms. TechTarget. Retrieved from: https://www.techtarget.com/searchsecurity/feature/Cryptography-basics-Symmetric-key-encryption-algorithms

Tutorials Point. (n.d.). Network Security—Overview. Retrieved from: https://www.tutorialspoint.com/network_security/network_security_overview.htm#:~:text=The%20primary%20goal%20of%20network,business%20data%20from%20unauthorized%20persons

Zscaler. (2022). What Is a Secure Web Gateway? Retrieved from: https://www.zscaler.com/resources/security-terms-glossary/what-is-secure-web-gateway

MINICASE: Securing SSU's New Building Wing

Review the information in the Chapter 6, Chapter 7, and Chapter 10 Minicases. The new building wing will add new assets to the university's network as well as additional vulnerabilities and an expanded attack plane. As a result, SSU needs plans for securing the building wing and its network infrastructure.

The new building wing and new network management domain (described in the Chapter 10 Minicase) come with an educational opportunity that computing degree programs (CS, IT, and IS) at the university would like to leverage. The administrators of these degree programs would like to increase the visibility of the network management console and server room equipment to provide students with a clearer picture of network management dashboards and server room layouts. They argue that the area around the server room in the new building wing can be used as a "teaching, observation, and learning" space that enables students to witness the deployment of course concepts in real life. They suggest that this might help attract students to the university and their degree programs.

The building plan alterations that these administrators are advocating include removing the storage room next to the server room in the original plans for the building wing (illustrated in the Chapter 6 Minicase) and replacing it with a hallway. Another hallway from the server room entrance to the foot of the stairwell could be added by eliminating the Lab Assistants' office and replacing it with one of the restrooms. Making this change would also enable each of the restrooms to be slightly larger than is currently planned.

Creating hallways on either side of the server room entrance and adding see-through glass on the interior walls of the server room would enable students and building visitors to see the network management console and the cabinets where servers and storage equipment are located. See-through glass on the equipment cabinets would enable students and visitors to observe the servers, storage equipment, switches, routers, and security appliances that they contain. Students and visitors would also have multiple viewing angles for observing server room patch panels; patch cables; cable bundles from labs, offices, and classrooms; and cabling conduit. Adding a supersize display screen for the network management console would enable students in networking courses to witness what is included on network management dashboards.

In a nutshell, the changes to the planned layout of the new wing being advocated by the computing degree program administrators involve transforming an otherwise nondescript (and boring) server room into a showcase and teaching/learning space. The proposed changes have met little resistance from university officials and building architects but have raised several security concerns and questions about how to best leverage the changes for educational purposes.

Securing the Building

Like other buildings on the SSU campus, the new building wing will be locked and secured weeknights after classes end. It also will be locked and secured on weekends outside some limited hours for students to use the labs on Saturdays (from 10:00 a.m. to 4:00 p.m.) and Sunday's (from 2:00 p.m. until 8:00 p.m.) for general purpose computing. These labs also will be available for students to use for general purpose computing during normal operating hours when they are not scheduled for a class. SSU is a public university that strives to have an open and inviting campus but has several facility and building exterior security controls, including ample lighting on walkways, emergency phone kiosks, and campus police patrols.

Several physical security features are planned for the new building wing. Door alarms—loud ones—will be installed on all classroom, lab, and office doors in the building wing to deter entry attempts during the hours when the building is locked and secured. Card access readers will be installed for the doors at the building entrance, server room, labs, and faculty offices to enable faculty members, maintenance workers, campus police, and other authorized personnel to access the building and authorized rooms after hours. Each card access attempt will be electronically logged, and any attempts to use force to enter the room will trigger door alarms and notifications to the campus police.

Like the planned alterations for the server room, the hallway walls of the labs will have see-through glass to enable people in the hallways to see whether there is a class in session or if seats are available for general purpose computing when they are not being used for classes. The long interior wall for Lab C from the building entrance to the stairway will also have see-through glass.

Security cameras will be placed in all hallways and rooms, except faculty offices and rest rooms. They will connect to a PoE switch in the server room via Ethernet cable. If the glassed-in server room becomes a reality, a security server, console, and supersize display screen may be added to enable students to see how real-time video surveillance systems work.

Task 1: Identify Additional Physical Security Controls

Review section 11.6 and its discussion of physical security threats and controls. Identify several additional building exterior, building interior, and computer room security controls that should be considered for the new building wing. Briefly justify each recommended addition by explaining how it would enhance the security of the building and its contents. Consider using something like the following tables to summarize your recommendations, replacing the examples provided. Strive to include at least three entries in each table.

Building Exterior Defense	Justification/Explanation
Motion-activated floodlights near entrance	

Building Interior Defense	Justification/Explanation
Biometric scanners for server room access	

Computer Room Defense	Justification/Explanation
Cabinet access controls	

Also answer the following questions:

1. Should a video surveillance server and display screen be added? If so, should it be visible to people in the interior hallways? Why or why not?
2. In response to the proposed alterations to the building plans, SSU's CIO is recommending the placement of battery backup equipment (and batteries) in the section of the server room next to the staircase. The CIO also recommends adding UPS equipment and fire suppression devices to the server room "to let students and visitors know what they look like and how they are deployed." Are these good suggestions? Why or why not?
3. The IT manager who oversees network security for the university worries that the proposed changes will add new vulnerabilities that will expand the network's attack surface. He composed a memo stating "Making it possible for people outside the server room to record real-time videos of network management and security displays on their smartphones is asking for trouble. The videos can fall into the wrong hands and be used to identify potential attack vectors. And letting people record the layouts of our labs through glass walls may give them better ideas about how to steal the expensive display systems in the labs, which have been targeted/stolen in the past." Are these concerns justified? Why or why not?

Securing the Perimeter of the Building Network

As noted in the Chapter 6 and 7 Minicases, much of the network infrastructure for the Ethernet and Wi-Fi networks will be in the building wing's server room, including Ethernet switches, the Wi-Fi controller, the servers, and the router that connects the building to the campus backbone network. Having so much networking equipment in a single location is one of the primary reasons why physical security defenses are needed for the building wing and server room.

Both degree program and network administrators advocate adding perimeter security appliances to the equipment cabinets in the server room "for educational purposes." Proposals have been floated for a DMZ network and adding IDS and IPS appliances or UTM appliances with large and easily read labels to the equipment cabinets.

Task 2: Create a Diagram to Conceptually Illustrate the Proposed DMZ Network and Perimeter Defenses

Using the information from section 11.8.2, and the Chapter 6, Chapter 7, and Chapter 10 Minicases, use MS Visio or another network diagramming tool to create a diagram of the proposed DMZ. Assume that each server would be placed in the DMZ. A firewall would separate the DMZ and the Ethernet network; a second firewall would separate the DMZ and the Wi-Fi network. A UTM firewall would be placed between the building router and the "internal" campus network. The building distribution switch, server room switch, and Wi-Fi controller would have IPS protection.

Task 3: Security Recommendations for the Wi-Fi Network in the Building Wing

It is standard practice at SSU to have both "guest" and "authorized" access to the Wi-Fi networks in its facilities. Visitors and other guests are allowed to use the "guest" network to access the Internet, while authorized users (those with valid credentials for logging on to mySSU, the university's intranet) can connect to the authorized Wi-Fi network.

1. Is the use of "guest" and "authorized" Wi-Fi networks an example of network segmentation? Why or why not?

2. Review Wi-Fi security threats and security controls in Chapter 7. Use the information to develop a list of Wi-Fi network threats that SSU should be aware of. Also develop a list of security controls that you recommend for protecting the Wi-Fi network in the building wing and provide brief justification for each control. Consider using a table such as the following to summarize your threat and recommended security control lists, including or replacing the example provided.

Wi-Fi Network Threats	Recommended Security Controls	Justification/ Explanation
Rogue access points		

Task 4: Recommendations for Secure Communications

The university's network security policy dictates that login credentials be encrypted during login and secure protocols be used for client device/server communications. It also requires that anyone with access to the university's intranet complete security training programs that include modules on phishing, the university's strong password requirements, and its acceptable use policies.

Increased use of personal mobile devices, (laptops, tablets, smartphones, etc.) to connect to university Wi-Fi networks has elevated the importance of two- and multifactor authentication for users and devices that log in to the university's intranet.

1. To protect against lateral movement and APTs, the university is considering implementing user and entity behavioral analysis (UEBA) tools to detect unusual

behavior patterns. Should this be done? Why or why not? How do you think students would react to the university's monitoring of their online behaviors?

2. Many universities use Duo for two-factor authentication at login. Briefly describe how Duo works, and briefly explain why you would or would not recommend that the university use it.

Task 5: Defense in Depth Considerations

Step back and consider your work and recommendations for additional security mechanisms for Tasks 1–4. IT Services at SSU values defense in depth (DiD) security and maps its security defenses to DiD layers. Identify what you consider to be the two most important security mechanisms that SSU should add to its current and planned security controls for the physical, perimeter, and internal network layers. They should be additional defenses that the university is not planning to install. Provide justification/explanation for each of your recommendations, and briefly explain how each mechanism would improve security. Consider summarizing your recommendations and justification using a table like the following.

DiD Layer	Two Recommended Additions	Justification/Explanation for Each Addition
Physical	1. 2.	1. 2.
Perimeter	1. 2.	1. 2.
Network	1. 2.	1. 2.

Package and submit your work on Tasks 1–5 per the instructions provided by your instructor.

Chapter 12

Protecting Endpoints, Applications, and Data

LEARNING OBJECTIVES

After reading and studying this chapter, you should be able to:

- Identify examples of network endpoints.
- Identify and briefly describe several malware and other endpoint threats.
- Identify and briefly describe endpoint security defenses.
- Identify endpoint security best practices.
- Identify examples of application controls.
- Briefly describe characteristics of enterprise system (ES) applications that make them complex and challenging to secure.
- Identify and briefly describe common ES applications and ES security controls.
- Identify secure coding techniques and best practices.
- Briefly describe sensitive data and why data controls are at the innermost layer of DiD.
- Identify examples of technical and nontechnical data threats.
- Identify the differences between data exfiltration, data modification, data destruction, and data in use (DIU) attacks.
- Identify and briefly describe examples of data security defenses.

12.0 INTRODUCTION

Enterprise network security is an important topic in each of the previous chapters. That is rightly so because no part of an enterprise network is immune from security threats. And as enterprise networks continue to evolve, their defenses are also evolving.

Chapter 11 focused on several overriding security topics, including common network vulnerabilities and attacks, security goals, threat and risk assessment processes, security plans, policies and procedures, security architectures, and layered defenses. It also described security issues and defenses for the physical, cloud, perimeter, and internal network layers of DiD.

This chapter will complete the "tour" of DiD by considering security issues, threats, and controls at the endpoint, application, and data layers (see Figure 12-1). Relative to previous chapters, Chapter 12 provides an expanded perspective on security for enterprise network devices (endpoints), applications, and data. Providing a broader context for appreciating the contributions of endpoint, application, and data security controls beyond the contextualized discussion provided in previous chapters is one of this chapter's primary goals.

Increasingly, employees are using mobile devices to interact with ESs and the other applications that enterprise networks support. Mobile and IoT devices have broadened network administrators' perspectives about network endpoints and how they should be secured. They blur traditional

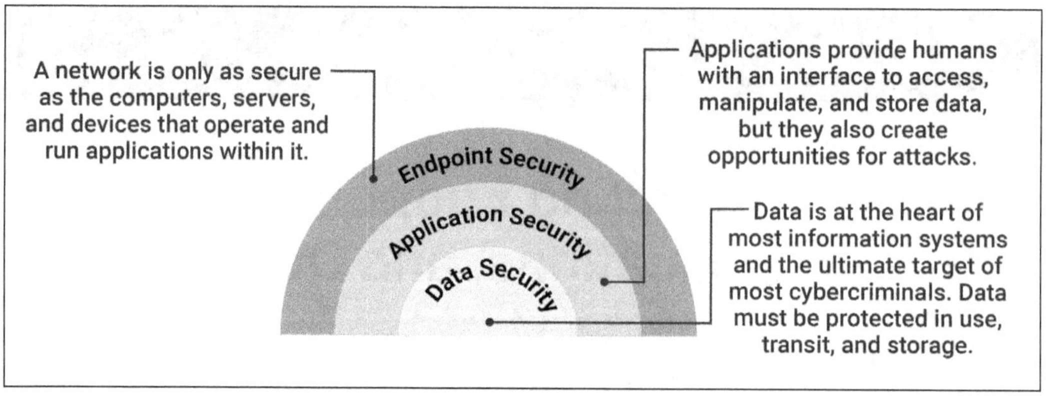

Figure 12-1: This chapter focuses on the endpoint, application, and data security layers of DiD.

lines between devices and applications and do not conform as neatly as other network devices to traditional models of layered security.

ERP, CRM, and other ESs are mission-critical applications in many businesses. They support core business processes and are essential to business operations and competitiveness. They are "crown jewels" among the more important network assets. As crucial applications, ESs' data traffic is considered high priority, and enterprise networks are configured accordingly. Special attention is also devoted to ESs' security, and specialized security mechanisms are often used to protect them.

Data, especially sensitive data, is typically the ultimate target of attackers. The value of data in the eyes of attackers emphasizes the need to ensure that it is adequately protected. Data is purposely located at the innermost layer of DiD, with defenses at each of the other layers contributing in part to its protection. Requiring attackers to thwart defenses at other DiD layers before they can get to the data they seek is a sensical security strategy.

In Chapter 11, encryption is discussed in the context of protecting data in motion. Encryption is also used at the data layer to protect data at rest and is one of numerous controls that can be used to secure stored data. Increasing use of cloud storage makes it essential for businesses to know how data at rest is protected in cloud provider data centers.

This chapter serves as a suitable ending for this book's discussion of enterprise networks. It serves as a reminder that enterprise networks exist to support business applications. It also is a reminder that data in all its various forms is the lifeblood of today's businesses, no matter where it is stored or processed and how it is transmitted. Enterprise networks, the applications they support, and their data continue to evolve, and so must the security controls used to protect them.

12.1 SECURING NETWORK ENDPOINTS

Earlier renditions of DiD refer to the endpoint layer as the *host* or *platform* layer, and some continue to do so. The term *host* continues to be used for originators and destinations in TCP/IP and client-server communications.

Traditionally, hosts (both clients and servers) were usually located in the same network, such as a private LAN or WAN, with a distinct perimeter that separated it from other networks. Hence, for DiD, hosts were devices connected to an organization's internal network and were placed between the internal network and application layers of DiD endpoints for the network's client-server applications. One of the most important aspects of a host's security posture was ensuring that its operating system (platform) was patched and up to date.

Platform continues to be used as a reference to a computer's OS and the processor on which it runs. The combination of software (the OS) and hardware (the processor) provides the "platform" for running applications. So, essentially, using "platform" instead of "host" provides slightly greater technical detail about the software used in client-server and other distributed applications.

The OS that a device uses is typically dependent on the type of processor installed in the device. Differences between the processors used in servers, laptops and desktops, and mobile devices are part of why they have different operating systems. Operating systems evolve in response to evolving processors to take advantage of new processor features and capabilities. This is one reason why an operating system is identified by its generation—for example, Windows 11 or iOS 17.

Windows Server and Linux are examples of widely used server operating systems. Linux is one of many Unix-like operating systems in use today. MacOS is another Unix-like operating system; like Windows, ChromeOS, and Linux, it is used on laptops and desktops. Android and iOS are widely used operating systems for smartphones and tablets.

As network device users know, OS and security patch updates occur with great regularity, and users may have some control in scheduling the installation of updates. Given the many types of devices connected to today's enterprise networks, keeping their operating systems updated and patched is an important part of network security. The wide array of devices and operating systems is also a reason why "host" and "platform" have given way to "endpoint" in recent renditions of DiD.

In this chapter, an **endpoint** is any physical device connected to, or that communicates with, an enterprise network. This definition is consistent with the notion that endpoints are originators or final destinations of data traffic. However, there are other views of what an endpoint is and is not.

Sometimes, *endpoint* is used to distinguish between user devices and servers and networking equipment. Here, user devices and servers are endpoints, and networking equipment is used to relay data between them. Such distinctions are consistent with traditional differences between data terminal equipment (DTE) and data communication equipment (DCE).

Less inclusive views include the notion that endpoints are "remote" or "mobile" computing devices that communicate back and forth with the networks to which they connect but are located outside the private network's perimeter. An alternative view is that an endpoint is a LAN- or WAN-connected device that is inside the network's perimeter.

Application- and protocol-centric descriptions of endpoints also exist; they include API endpoints and TCP/IP endpoints. For TCP/IP client-server applications, an endpoint is a "socket," or a combination of an IP address and a port number in a TCP connection (see Figure 12-2).

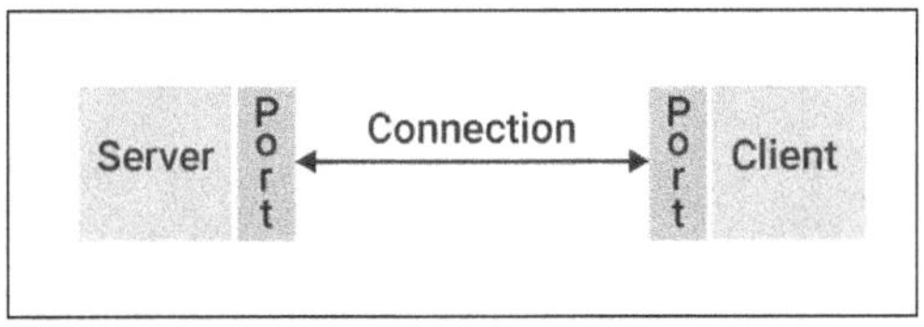

Figure 12-2: TCP/IP sockets (IP address and port number combinations) may be called endpoints.

Such views of endpoints should not be summarily dismissed because they are software-centric or only apply to specific applications or connections. For example, as noted in Chapter 10, northbound and southbound APIs are components in some SDN architectures to address both software-to-software communications between the SDN control plane and applications and software-to-device communications between the control plane and network elements (routers and switches). Also, Chapter 9 noted that in IoT architectures, APIs are used for communications between IoT platforms and applications and for IoT platform to IoT gateway communications. Communication occurs, and physical devices are involved, but the communication may be considered software-to-software instead of device-to-device.

This chapter's inclusive definition of an endpoint means that servers, desktops, laptops, tablets, and smartphones are endpoints. However, network printers, fax machines, cameras, smartwatches, health/fitness trackers, navigation systems, and any other types of devices that can connect to a network can also be considered endpoints. Over time, the list of endpoints continues to grow as we add smart appliances, IoT and IIoT devices, bank ATMs, RFID readers, and wireless point-of-sale (POS) devices. Devices that remote workers use when they connect to corporate networks (e.g., printers and personal laptops) are also considered to be enterprise network endpoints.

Widescale use of mobile and wearable devices, COVID-19 pandemic-inspired increases in remote work, and cloud computing are among the factors that have pushed us toward a more inclusive view of network endpoints. The growing list of endpoints is also blurring traditional network perimeters.

Infrastructure devices used to run or secure a network are not always considered endpoints, including access points, firewalls, load balancers, routers, switches, Wi-Fi controllers, and VPN gateways. However, since attackers may target or exploit them, they are considered endpoints in some security solutions.

12.1.1 Endpoint Threats

An important takeaway from previous chapters is that any device that an employee uses to connect to a business network is a potential risk to network security. This is also true for every connected IoT device. Given the sheer number and variety of endpoints, it is not surprising that they are common targets of attackers.

As noted in Chapter 11, if an intruder succeeds in gaining access to the corporate network by compromising a user device, they may be able to move laterally through the network to access high-value network assets or steal intellectual property or sensitive data. Attackers often install malware on compromised devices to enable them to assume control over the devices for use in DoS attacks or other attacks.

Malware

Malware, both known and unknown, is the most frequently acknowledged endpoint threat. This is illustrated in Figure 12-3. According to Verizon's *2022 Data Breach Investigations Report*, approximately 30% of data breaches were the result of malware being installed on endpoints.

As noted in previous chapters, numerous malware types are concerning for businesses, including adware, ransomware, spyware, worms, and viruses. And, as Figure 12-3 illustrates, there are several

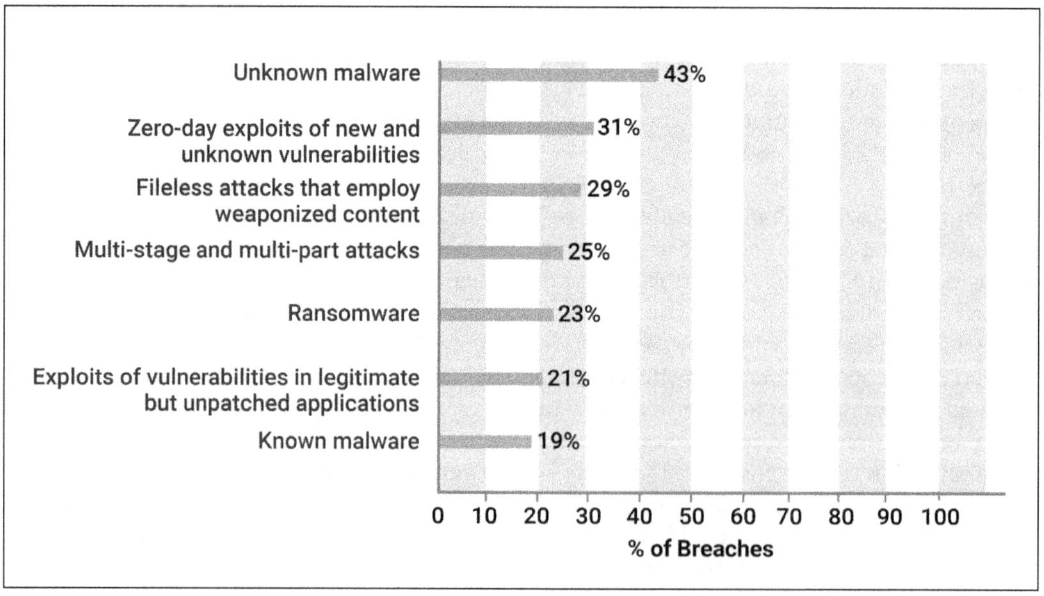

Figure 12-3: Relative frequencies of common endpoint security threats. Source: Help Net Security (https://www.helpnetsecurity.com)

Table 12-1: Known and unknown malware differences.	
	Description
Known malware	Known malware includes viruses, worms, adware, and ransomware that have been previously identified by cybersecurity experts. In response, antivirus and other security solution vendors create defensive anti-malware signatures for detecting and preventing the malware from being installed on network endpoints.
Unknown malware	Unknown malware represents new threats that are not yet known to the cybersecurity community. As never-before-seen malware, unknown malware is extremely difficult to detect and prevent. Attackers can make slight alterations to known malware (creating mutations or variants), or they may develop new types (families) of malware to compromise endpoints. Most variants are designed to bypass current existing signature controls, evade known malware defenses, or create new opportunities for cyberattacks. Because they don't match known malware signatures in anti-malware databases, anti-malware software in firewalls or endpoints is unable to detect them.

categories of malware that are identified as endpoint threats, including known malware, unknown malware, fileless malware, and ransomware. The differences between known and unknown malware are briefly described in Table 12-1.

Anti-malware databases are continuously being updated as new attack signatures are identified. The number of attack signatures is growing rapidly, at a rate that often overwhelms the ability of antivirus and other anti-malware solutions to find them and include them in their databases. On some days, the number of new signatures being added to the databases exceeds 500,000. Anti-malware signature databases often include more than a trillion signatures. Such growth makes it important to update anti-malware software at least once a day.

Phishing and other social engineering attacks are widely used by attackers to install malware on user devices. Today, most phishing and email-oriented attacks are *automated malware attacks* that involve multiple threat actors. Botnet operators usually want to compile as large a set of compromised devices as possible and don't care about who is victimized. Devices that are easiest to attack and compromise, typically user devices, are the usual targets of automated attacks; servers and other endpoints that are more difficult to crack are skipped. Their goals are to find as many vulnerable endpoints as possible so that they can build a sizeable botnet (often thousands of computers) to control and use in DDoS and other types of attacks.

Zero-Day Malware

When new malware is detected, there is a time lag before its signature is available in anti-malware databases. During this time lag, attackers have an opportunity to install the new malware on network endpoints. When attackers infect software or devices with unknown malware, the malware may be called *zero-day malware*.

Zero-day vulnerabilities are endpoint threats. A **zero-day vulnerability** is a device or software security flaw that has not been discovered or disclosed by vendors or developers. It can also be a vulnerability that has been disclosed but not yet patched.

"Zero-day" is used to describe these vulnerabilities because the vendor or developer has been aware of the vulnerability for zero days and has not fixed it. Such vulnerabilities are security risks until a patch is issued and installed on the affected endpoints.

Device vendors and software developers constantly look for vulnerabilities that need to be fixed. The fixes are software or firmware patches. When malicious actors spot vulnerabilities before vendors/developers do, they can write and deploy code (called *exploit code*) to turn the vulnerabilities into attack vectors. When attackers are successful, it is called a *zero-day exploit*.

Zero-day vulnerabilities can be alarming or devastating when cybercriminals exploit them. For example, if attackers succeed in installing ransomware during the time lag, an enterprise network may be brought to its knees. However, zero-day malware attacks are a relatively small fraction of all malware attacks.

Fileless Malware

Fileless malware uses legitimate tools built into a device, application, or system to execute a cyberattack. Usually, fileless malware uses legitimate programs to infect the device. Unlike most malware, fileless malware does not require the installation of code on the target. By not relying on files and not leaving a "footprint," fileless malware is hard to detect and remove.

Fileless malware has been considered a mainstream type of attack for less than a decade. The 2016 hack of the Democratic National Committee and the Equifax breach involved fileless malware. Similar attack methods used in other attacks (e.g., Frodo, Number of the Beast, and The Dark Avenger) are now considered early examples of fileless malware.

While not a virus, fileless malware works like viruses that operate in memory. Fileless malware is not installed on an endpoint or stored in a file, it goes straight into memory (RAM), and its malicious content never touches the device's hard drive or storage.

Like other malware attacks, fileless malware attacks often use attachments in phishing emails or other social engineering attacks to compromise endpoints. However, in fileless malware attack scenarios, the attacker usually does not have to figure out how to get the malicious code by antivirus or other malware defenses that might detect it. By having the code go straight to memory and execute there, the attacker has an alternative path to access the network and move laterally or gain access rights to valuable assets or data.

Claims that fileless malware is undetectable are not literally true, but it often is undetectable by antivirus and traditional endpoint security defenses. The Ponemon Institute contends that fileless attacks are 10 times more likely to be successful than file-based attacks.

Ransomware

A ransomware attack is a malware attack that enables an attacker to seize a device's data or folders, or the device itself, until a ransom fee is paid. Ransomware attacks exploit open security vulnerabilities or infect a device or network via a phishing attack or malicious website. The malware may lock the user out of the device or encrypt files on the device until a payment is made to restore access to the device or its files.

This type of attack usually exploits software vulnerabilities to infect and hijack the victim's device (computer, smartphone, wearable, POS terminal) or other type of endpoint. The attack can target an individual, an organization, a network of organizations, or a data center.

Ransomware attackers use a variety of malware distribution techniques including, infected email attachments, links to infected websites, drive-by downloads, malicious pop-ups, social media, malvertising, infected programs, infected USB sticks, and self-propagation. Ransomware infections often involve a downloadable PDF file, DOC file, or XLS file.

When the ransomware code is activated, it takes control of the device and attacks files, folders, or the entire device. It scans and maps the target file types and determines their respective locations on the local device or network. Individual files or folders on a device or network of computers may be encrypted. Device users lose their admin rights and can no longer access certain files or the entire device.

After being activated, the ransomware notifies the victim and demands a ransom to unlock the device/data and remove the ransomware. If the victim fails to pay the ransom by a specified deadline, the attacker may initiate the process of corrupting, terminating, or deleting the targeted data files.

Other Malware Threats

Malvertising, drive-by downloads, rogue USBs, and macro and script attacks also pose threats to endpoints. They are described in Table 12-2.

Table 12-2: Additional types of malware threats to endpoints.	
Type of Attack	**Description**
Malware ads (malvertising)	Malvertising uses malware-laden legitimate-looking advertisements to infect endpoints with user interaction. The malware is embedded in the main scripts of web pages, which enables them to run and automatically install malware without being clicked by users. They can spread across reputable websites or social media before being identified as malware ads and removed. Victims of malware ads have included popular sites like Spotify, *The New York Times*, and the London Stock Exchange.
Drive-by downloads	Like phishing, these attacks try to trick device users into clicking a malicious link or downloading malware. Fake system alerts, bogus antivirus notifications, and deceptive installation agreements that differ from the application that the user wants to download are examples of drive-by downloads. The types of malicious code installed when these attacks are successful include ransomware, Trojan backdoors, and keyloggers that record keystrokes.
Rogue USB drives	Some attackers leave malware-infected USB drives in employee parking lots. Should an employee find one and think that it was dropped by a fellow employee, they may infect a network endpoint by accessing it to identify its owner.
Macro and script attacks	For a macro attack, the malicious actor uses a macro language, such as those used by spreadsheet, word processing, and database apps, to create a virus. This disguises the virus as an innocent-looking Excel or Word file. A script attack involves malware-infected sites or browser-based apps. When a user views the infected site or uses the app, malicious code executes in the user's browser without their knowledge. Both attacks are designed to compromise the endpoint. A macro attack usually automatically downloads malware; a script attack may gain control of the device's webcam or microphone, or steal session cookies that can be used to spoof the user on other websites.

Additional Endpoint Threats

Network endpoints are also vulnerable to *human error*, *insider threats* (such as those described in Chapter 11), and *misuse of legitimate applications*. If phishing or other social engineering attacks succeed in acquiring valid login credentials, attackers can use the compromised credentials to access the enterprise network and potentially its valuable data and assets.

Theft is also an endpoint threat, particularly for mobile devices. Many individuals use external or built-in fingerprint scanners (see Figure 12-4a) to protect their laptops, and touchpoint or touchscreen fingerprint readers (Figure 12-4b) to protect their tablets and smartphones, from being misused if they are stolen, lost, or misplaced.

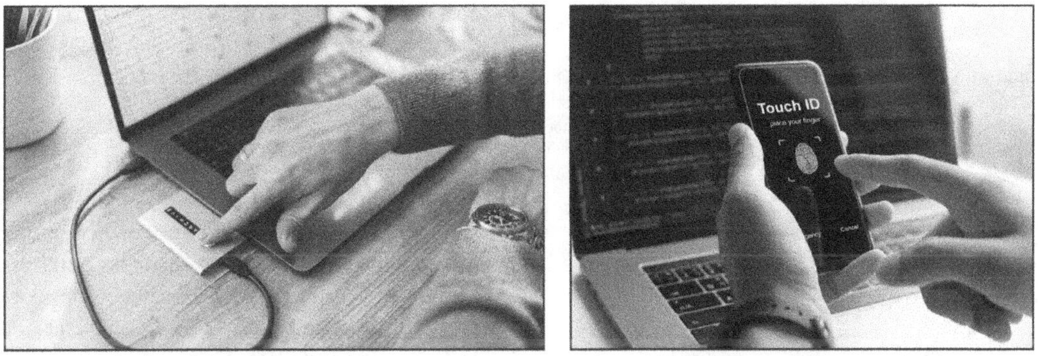

(a) Laptop Fingerprint Reader (b) Touchscreen Fingerprint Reader

Figure 12-4: Examples of laptop and touchscreen fingerprint readers. **Source (a)**: iStock/martin-dm/ Stock photo ID:1310614298; **Source (b)**: iStock/Tippapatt/ Stock photo ID:1345666333

As noted in Chapters 2 and 10, businesses that issue mobile devices to employees or allow their employees to use personal mobile devices to access corporate networks typically lock and wipe mobile devices that are stolen, lost, or misplaced. Such practices as using device tracking tools and geofencing are consistent with EMM and UEM recommendations.

12.1.2 Combating Endpoint Threats

Because botnet attacks on network endpoints are automated, it is important to reduce endpoints' and the enterprise network's vulnerabilities. Given the wide range of endpoint threats, it is impossible to block all attacks, but identifying and eliminating as many vulnerabilities as possible makes the network harder to attack and can encourage botnet operators to move on to easier targets.

Botnet attacks often focus on relatively few known vulnerabilities. If these vulnerabilities are identified and plugged, say by installing the latest patch or tightening the security of web applications, the bot is likely to move on to other targets rather than work harder to compromise the endpoint. This means that *vulnerability assessment* and *patch management* are important endpoint security defenses.

Vulnerability Assessment and Management (VAM)

Vulnerability assessment and management (VAM) has traditionally been a key aspect of endpoint security. Vulnerability assessment tools scan network endpoints and devices on a frequent and regular basis. This is different from penetration tests, which are usually performed just once or twice a year. VAM tools assess vulnerabilities on a weekly (or more frequent) or monthly basis; this enables vulnerabilities to be identified and addressed more rapidly.

As you probably know, Microsoft alone discloses boatloads of vulnerabilities in its operating systems and applications every month, and many pose serious security risks. And with many organizations deploying new IoT systems and applications at accelerating rates, new vulnerabilities are being introduced on a recurring basis.

When frequent vulnerability scans are combined with basic malware detection and blocking and the installation of software/firmware updates/patches when they become available, the chances of an endpoint being compromised or becoming part of a botnet are minimized. While none of these defenses provides adequate protection by itself, their combined use can sufficiently harden endpoints to encourage botnet operators to move on to weaker targets. In short, being proactive and running periodic vulnerability scans can help prevent endpoints from being exploited by attackers.

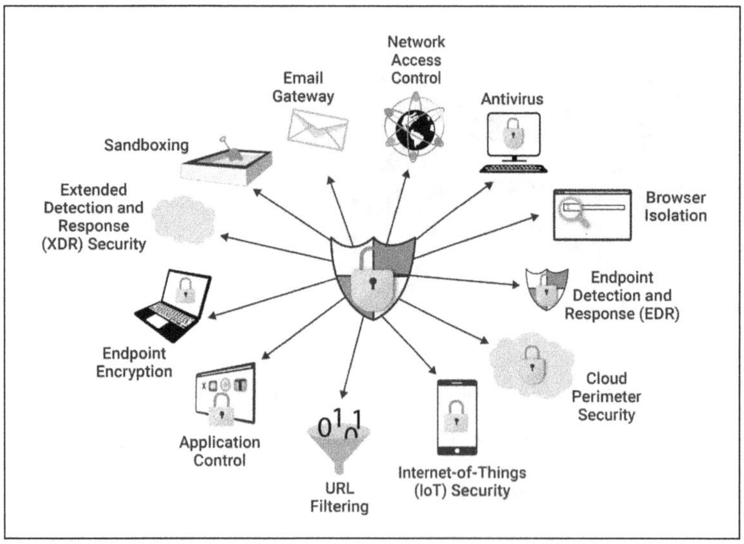

Figure 12-5: Examples of endpoint security defenses.

Browser Isolation, Sandboxing, and Application Control

Figure 12-5 illustrates some of the other major types of endpoint security defenses. Some of them (e.g., email gateways, network access control, antivirus, cloud perimeter and IoT security, and URL filtering) are described in Chapters 9 and 11, and some of them apply to more than endpoints. Others focus more directly on protecting endpoints, including browser isolation and sandboxing.

Browser isolation keeps network user browsing activity secure by separating the process of loading web pages from the process of displaying web pages on user device screens. Such separation prevents potentially malicious web page code from running on a user's device and infecting it with malware. Isolating browsing activity in a remote virtual environment helps to ensure that malicious web content does not reach the endpoint or corporate network. Browser isolation is often part of zero trust security.

In cybersecurity, **sandboxing** involves running code in a safe, isolated environment on a network that mimics the corporate network. This enables the code to be observed and analyzed before it is allowed to run on an endpoint. Like browser isolation, sandboxing is designed to prevent threats from compromising endpoints or getting to a business's internal network. It is frequently used to inspect untrusted or untested code. By running and inspecting the code in an isolated (or test) environment (a "sandbox"), it is possible to learn how it works and what effects it might have on endpoints or the network.

Application control is also used to protect endpoints from potentially harmful code. Basically, an **application control** blocks or restricts unauthorized applications from executing at all or from executing in ways that put data at risk. The main objective of application control is to help ensure the privacy and security of data used by or transmitted between applications. Most application control solutions include whitelisting and blacklisting capabilities to identify which applications to trust and allow to execute and which to block.

Application control and endpoint security have become entwined via the addition of IoT and IIoT systems to enterprise networks. When attackers exploit IoT vulnerabilities, it may be possible for them to issue control commands to sensors, actuators, SCADA process controllers, or devices in industrial control systems. The importance of application controls and their relationship to endpoint security should become clearer in section 12.2.

Endpoint Encryption

Endpoint encryption uses encryption to protect data at network endpoints to ensure that only authorized personnel can access the data. *Endpoint encryption software* is used to monitor endpoints, encrypt/decrypt endpoint data, manage encryption keys, and enforce security policies.

Endpoint encryption uses two deployment strategies: full-disk (drive) encryption and file encryption. *Drive encryption* secures the device from attackers and authenticates network users prior to allowing access to data stored on the drive. *File encryption* protects specific files on the endpoint, such as configuration files. Some endpoint encryption solutions support endpoint encryption agents on disk or USB drives that communicate with endpoint encryption servers and databases to ensure that security policies are enforced.

Endpoint Protection Platform (EPP) and Endpoint Detection and Response (EDR)

An **endpoint protection platform (EPP)** is an integrated suite of endpoint protection technologies (such as antivirus, data encryption, data loss prevention, and intrusion prevention) that detect and stop a variety of endpoint threats. EPP tools typically support data sharing among the endpoint protection technologies. An EPP includes multiple integrated detection and remediation technologies that provide anti-malware signature scanning, browser security, and credential threat monitoring.

Most EPP tools also include rollback remediation to restore compromised devices to their states prior to infection. An EPP requires continuous access to real-time threat data and threat intelligence from both internal and external sources to enable detection and blocking of zero-day attacks. As EPP tools evolve, EDR and DLP capabilities are increasingly being added. An abbreviated comparison of EPP and endpoint detection and response (EDR) is provided in Table 12-3.

Table 12-3: Some of the differences between EPP and EDR.	
Endpoint Protection Platform (EPP)	**Endpoint Detection and Response (EDR)**
Prevents malware and malicious script execution	Continuous real-time monitoring
Detects memory exploitation	Advanced cyberthreat detection
Detects unsecure network connections	Forensics (threat hunting)
Controls device access	Automated incident response

Endpoint detection and response (EDR) (a.k.a. *endpoint detection and threat response [EDTR]*) is an EPP-like endpoint security solution that continuously monitors endpoints to detect and respond to cyberthreats like ransomware and malware. Unlike EPP, EDR tools monitor endpoints and record endpoint event information in a central database for further analysis, forensic investigation, threat detection, alerting, and reporting. A software agent installed on the endpoint enables security monitoring and event reporting. Ongoing monitoring and threat detection are facilitated by analytic tools that identify, respond to, and deflect endpoint threats and attacks.

By recording the activities and events taking place on endpoints, EDR tools provide security teams with sufficient endpoint visibility to identify security incidents that might otherwise remain invisible. In addition to advanced threat detection, investigation, and response capabilities, EDR tools include suspicious activity validation, threat hunting, and malicious activity detection and containment capabilities.

Extended Detection and Response (XDR)

Extended detection and response (XDR) is more comprehensive and sophisticated than EDR, extending EDR capabilities to other security control points, including email, servers, clouds, and external networks. Extended visibility and collecting data across domains facilitate faster threat detection and remediation. Figure 12-6 provides a conceptual depiction of XDR.

Fundamentally, XDR is a consolidation of tools and data that enable it to provide security monitoring and incident response management across an enterprise network. Because XDR has access to data collected across enterprise network components, it can help security teams identify and contain threats, including those associated with lateral movement, anomalous connections,

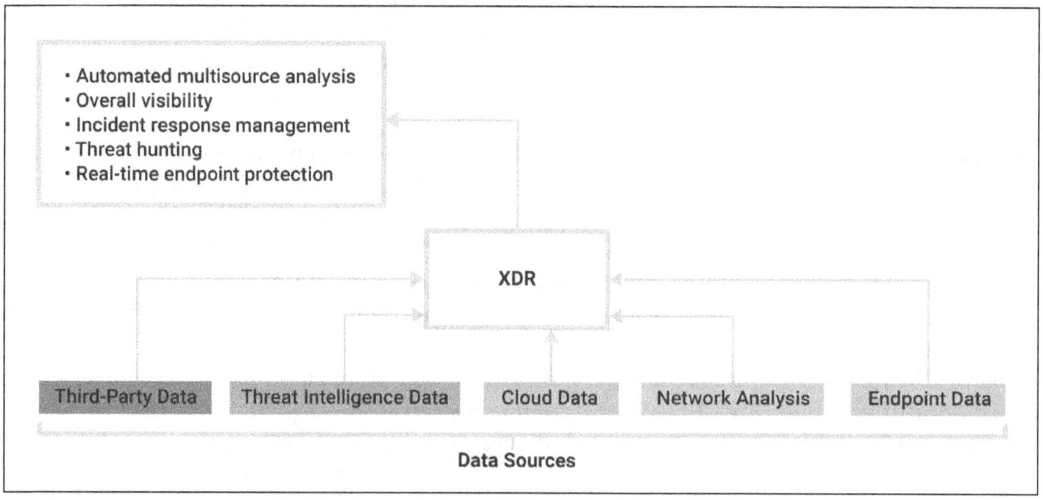

Figure 12-6: A conceptual depiction of XDR capabilities.

rogue beacons, and data exfiltration attempts. Like EDR, XDR responds to threats by containing and removing them.

XDR is frequently compared to SIEM, but there are differences. Both pull and analyze data from multiple sources to detect and respond to threats. However, XDR typically collects more granular data and provides very detailed information about activity taking place in endpoint, network, cloud, and user devices. SIEM serves as a broader threat and operational risk platform for an organization, while XDR provides a platform for deeper and narrower threat detection and response.

Host-Based IDS and IPS

A **host-based IDS (HIDS)** tracks changes made to system configurations, registry settings, and log and content files and generates alerts when anomalous or unauthorized activity is identified. Because the purpose of HIDSs is to identify suspicious activity, not prevent it, they are often used in conjunction with IPSs. Figure 12-7 provides an example of how a HIDS might be deployed in distributed HIDS and IPS security strategies.

As noted in Chapter 10, MDM, EMM, and UEM can also be viewed as endpoint security controls. They enable operating system updates and security patches to be pushed out to mobile devices and other endpoints and provide mechanisms for quickly remediating missing or infected devices. User education and cybersecurity training are also important aspects of endpoint security.

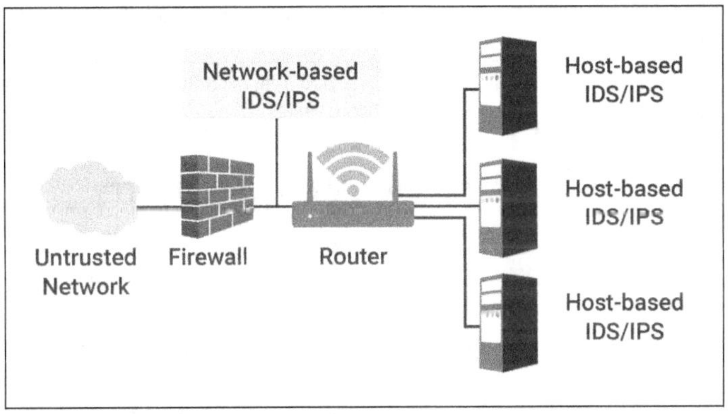

Figure 12-7: Host-based IDSs (HIDSs) are often deployed in distributed IDS solutions.

12.1.3 Endpoint Security Best Practices

Endpoint security is an important aspect of the overall security of enterprise networks. Over time, numerous endpoint security best practices have been specified. Some of these practices are identified and briefly summarized in Table 12-4.

Additional endpoint security best practices are likely to be identified in the years ahead, but this list provides a sense of what businesses should be doing to ensure that endpoints are not weaknesses in overall network security.

Table 12-4: Examples of endpoint security best practices.

Best Practice	Brief Description
User training	Educate/train users to recognize telltale signs of phishing and social engineering attacks. Employees should be aware of how to protect the devices they use to perform their jobs.
Require strong passwords	Make longer and more complex passwords mandatory for everyone, require periodic password changes, and ban the reuse/recycling of old passwords.
Track/monitor all endpoints	Identify, track, and monitor all devices connected to the network. This includes maintaining a list of all endpoints and keeping it up to date. It also involves ensuring that every device has appropriate safeguards and the latest patches.
Keep endpoints and configuration files encrypted	Encrypt the endpoint's disk or memory so that it remains inaccessible if it is lost, stolen, or transferred to another device. Practice *endpoint hardening* to limit access to the device's configuration settings.
Enforce least privilege access	Enforce *least privilege access* to limit access and device privileges. "Non-administrator" should be the access default, unless administrator rights are truly needed. To prevent unauthorized executable code from being loaded onto devices, regular users should not have administrator rights.

Table 12-4, Continued.	
Best Practice	**Brief Description**
Continuous endpoint scan	Run continuous endpoint scans to keep track of every connected device in real time. This should include constant endpoint location awareness, especially for mobile assets, like smartphones and laptops, that are vulnerable to loss or theft.
Remediate missing devices	Quickly remediate lost, stolen, or missing devices to ensure that they cannot be used for nefarious purposes.
Automate patching	Implement *automated patching* instead of relying on users. This should also apply to third-party patches.
MFA	Require multifactor authentication (MFA) to access endpoints.
Granular application control	Implement *granular application control* to restrict unauthorized application execution that poses risks.
Network segmentation	Practice network segmentation to reduce lateral movement options if the endpoint is compromised.
Regulate USB ports	Regulate USB port access to ensure that malware is not installed via rogue USB drives.
Isolate/remove infected endpoints	Quickly isolate or remove infected endpoints to minimize the potential for malware to spread to other endpoints.
Zero trust	Employ a zero trust security approach for all endpoints by requiring them to authenticate when requesting access to network assets.

12.2 APPLICATION SECURITY

Layered defenses and/or DiD are often needed to protect enterprise network applications. Although secure coding practices exist, developers do not always use them to ensure that their code has few vulnerabilities. This inconsistency enables attackers to exploit or compromise applications to capture or exfiltrate sensitive data.

As Target learned in December 2013, it is not always necessary for attackers to breach corporate databases to obtain sensitive data about shoppers. Sometimes all they need to do is compromise applications that process data.

After gaining access to Target's network via a contractor's compromised credentials, attackers were able to modify the code used to process credit and debit card payments at the point-of-sale. The modified POS code caused the data for each credit/debit card swipe to be transmitted to the attackers. Sensitive data for 110 million shoppers was stolen as the POS application executed during the busy holiday shopping season.

12.2.1 Application Types

Some application security technologies compare actual network traffic flow to normal communication patterns. If actual traffic flows differ from normal patterns, anomalous or suspicious activity may be indicated. Traffic flow patterns can also be used to whitelist or blacklist applications or identify applications that should be closely monitored.

With respect to network traffic, there are different ways to classify applications. For example, applications may be categorized by degree of security risk, the network resources they use, or their type or purpose.

Security risk levels may be assigned to enterprise network applications to reflect their respective security risks. For example, applications that create, store, or transfer sensitive data may be classified as high-risk applications because of the nature of their associated data traffic. Since the risk of data exfiltration is high for such applications, securing them is essential and should take precedence over the security of other applications. Assessing the vulnerabilities of high-risk applications is an important first step in securing them.

Resource usage can be another important criterion for classifying applications. Some applications are more demanding on networks than others and consume greater volumes of network bandwidth. Videoconferencing applications and collaboration platforms such as Microsoft Teams or Slack are examples of bandwidth-hogging applications. They generate significant volumes of network traffic and often require oversize network resources to run properly.

Classifying applications by their type or purpose is also valuable. For businesses, applications that support core business processes, such as ERP and other enterprise systems, are likely to be considered critical systems whose traffic flows should be prioritized, managed, and secured.

12.2.2 Application Control

Application control is a fundamental aspect of application security in enterprise networks. It helps ensure that harmful or malicious code is not executed on network devices and that only nonmalicious applications are allowed to enter an enterprise network or its endpoints. An overarching purpose of application control is to secure the data that is utilized by or transmitted between network applications.

As noted previously, application control uses whitelisting and blacklisting to authorize or block/restrict, respectively, the execution of applications or files. *Whitelisting* will allow some programs to run but block all others without explicit permission from administrators. *Blacklisting* will block specific programs but allow all others to run.

After authorized network applications are categorized and prioritized, several security-oriented application controls may be used. Some seek to ensure that only authorized users are allowed to run the application; others are designed to ensure that data that the application processes comes from the correct sources and has not been tampered with. For users, three application control functions are pertinent: identification, authentication, and authorization. They are briefly described in Table 12-5.

Data handling application control functions include completeness checks, validity checks, input controls, and forensic controls. They are briefly described in Table 12-6. Zero trust controls may also be used to ensure that access to sensitive data is restricted to authenticated users, devices, or applications.

Because application control also focuses on application traffic flows, departures from normal network routing or use of security protocols may indicate anomalous or suspicious application behavior. Application-specific security policies can be applied to block, restrict, or permit certain types of application traffic. At more granular levels, such controls can examine an application's inputs and outputs based on PKI certificates, CA, and encryption algorithms.

Table 12-5: Examples of application control applied to users.

Application User Control	Description
Identification	Identification controls help ensure the accuracy and uniqueness of the account credentials of application users.
Authentication	Authentication controls help verify the authenticity of application users. Zero trust mechanisms may be used to ensure that only authenticated users and devices are allowed to run the application.
Authorization	Authorization controls certify that only approved (authorized) users with appropriate rights are allowed to use the application.

Table 12-6: Examples of data handling application controls.

Data Handling Control	Description
Completeness checks	Completeness checks confirm that the data being processed is complete and completely processed from start to finish. Data records should not be lost or fragmented in transit.
Validity checks	Validity checks ensure that the application processes only valid data inputs.
Input controls	Input controls guarantee the integrity of the application's data feeds.
Forensic controls	Forensic controls check the data for mathematical and/or scientific correctness.

Application control can provide an organization with visibility into incoming and outgoing application traffic. This is useful for prioritizing application traffic flows and network resource utilization. When used in conjunction with least privilege access, it can help ensure that employees only have access to applications at levels required to do their jobs.

12.2.3 ES Application Complexities

Because they support and integrate core business processes (such as procurement, production, and fulfillment processes), enterprise system (ES) applications are typically considered mission-critical applications.

ERP, SCM, and CRM systems were introduced in Chapter 2. Because they store and process much of a business's most valuable and sensitive data, ES applications are security risks. Security risks are amplified by the fact that most ES applications are boundary-spanning and complex, and because they interact with other crucial applications. ESs are high-priority applications that warrant and receive special attention and specialized security technologies.

This section considers ES applications in more detail to provide a clearer picture of how/why they are complex and why they can be challenging to secure. Section 12.2.4 focuses on ES threats and some of the common approaches used to protect against them.

As noted, ESs have three-tier software architectures (see Figure 12-8) that align well with two- or multi-tier client server architectures and networks.

Users interact with the ES software at the presentation tier using a variety of devices, including desktops, smartphones, tablets, and laptops. Graphical user interfaces (such as SAP GUI and SAP Fiori®) are available for a variety of devices, and ES software vendors such as SAP and Oracle have established app stores to facilitate the download and installation of user interfaces.

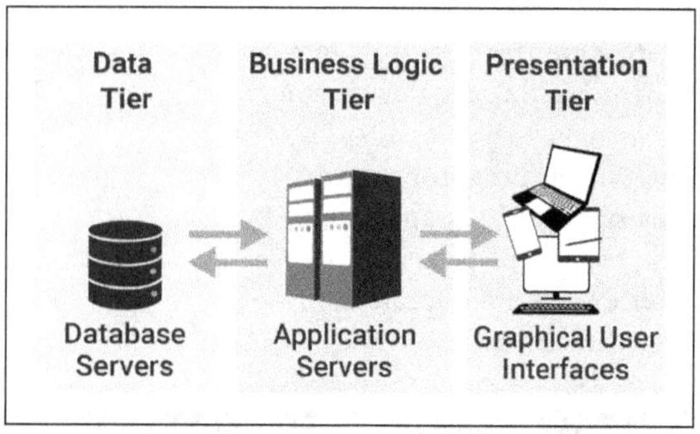

Figure 12-8: A conceptual depiction of ES software architecture.

Data processing occurs at the business logic tier and is performed by application servers. User interactions with ES software often involve retrieving data from the ES database, inputting new data, and generating new data that is saved in the database.

For example, to create a purchase order, master data about the supplier and the materials being ordered is retrieved from the database to facilitate purchase order creation. Often, the user may only need to input order quantities and need-by delivery dates to complete the purchase order. Each new purchase order is saved to the ES database for future review and use. It is also transmitted to the supplier.

ES databases include various types of master data (including data about materials, products, employees, suppliers, and customers), transaction data (e.g., data from daily operations such as customer orders, purchase orders, and production orders), and organizational data (e.g., data about organizational units and facilities). The variety, volume, and importance of data in ES databases and their central roles in business operations mean they must be secured.

Tiered ES software architectures provide flexibility for ES deployment by a business. For example, an organization could choose to maintain the privacy and security of these mission-critical applications by including all three tiers inside corporate network perimeters or via the use of a private cloud.

However, the three tiers also facilitate application deployment across business locations or data centers. For example, application servers could be placed in a private data center or private cloud, and database servers could be placed in cloud data centers. The deployment choices that are made will affect how the applications are secured.

Because ES applications store and generate huge volumes of data, many businesses are leveraging cloud infrastructure for their storage and processing needs. As noted in Chapter 2, such arrangements enable businesses to take advantage of the scalability of cloud services. When more processing or storage capacity is required, it is there, often on demand. As a result, ES deployments such as that in Figure 12-9 are common, and cloud security mechanisms help to secure them.

Fully hosted ES SaaS solutions are an option for today's businesses. However, many businesses choose IaaS for the cloud infrastructure they need to deploy their ES software.

Most ES applications are interorganizational. They cross organizational (and private network) boundaries and interact with computing systems in the networks of business partners.

Interorganizational connections, such as those illustrated in Figure 12-10, facilitate an organization's procurement (materials acquisition) and fulfillment (sales and distribution) processes. From a security perspective, however, such connections expand an enterprise network's attack surface through the addition of vulnerabilities in the networks of business partners, even if communications between the networks are encrypted.

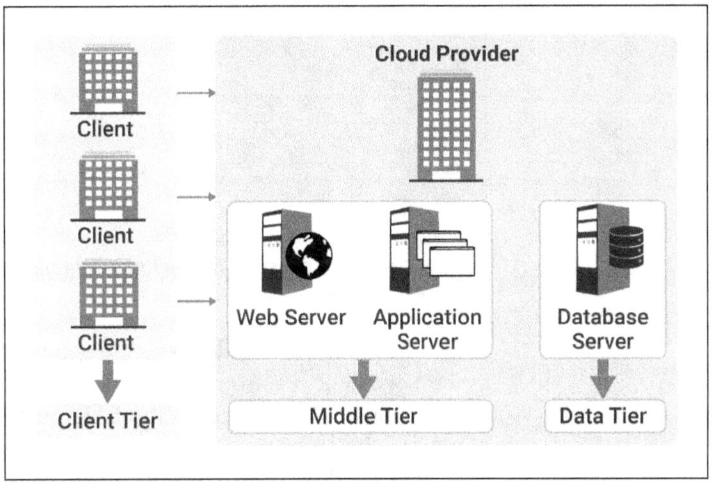

Figure 12-9: Cloud services are commonly used for ES deployment in today's businesses.

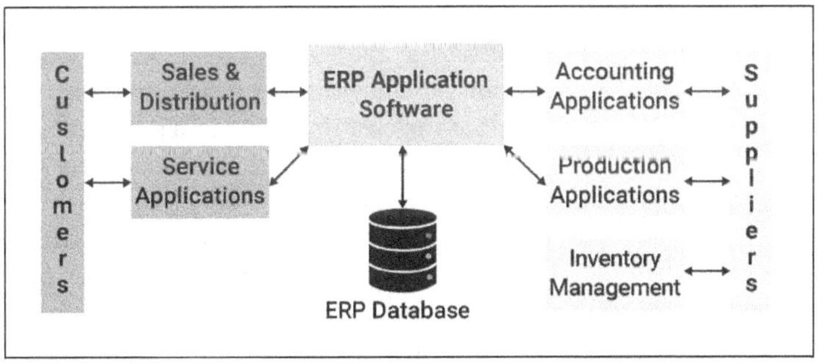

Figure 12-10: ERP and other ES applications are typically boundary-spanning via electronic links to vendors (suppliers) and customers.

Connections such as those in Figure 12-10 are often enabled by electronic data interchange (EDI) software used to exchange standard business documents, such as purchase orders and invoices, between the business partners.

EDI was introduced in Chapter 2, and a high-level depiction of the EDI document exchange process between a supplier and a customer is provided in Figure 12-11.

Here, both the supplier and customer EDI systems handle the conversion of internal document formats to one of the standardized EDI document formats. The EDI systems also route documents to/from the ERP systems and other document-producing applications. For example,

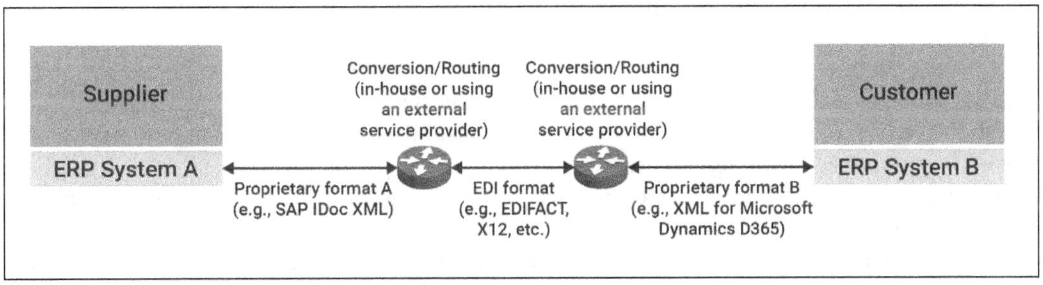

Figure 12-11: A high-level depiction of an EDI document exchange between business partners.

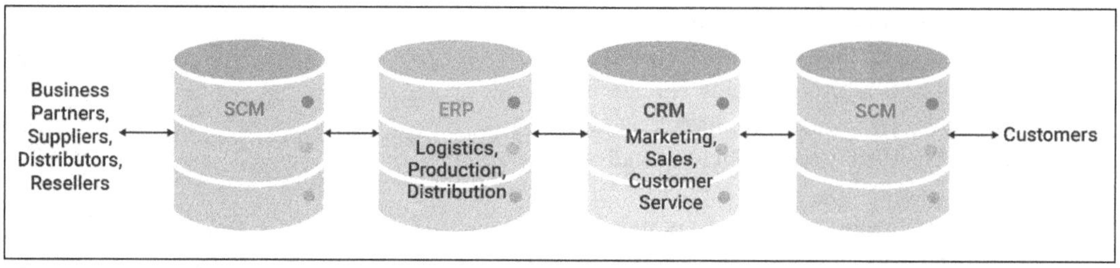

Figure 12-12: Businesses with multiple enterprise systems usually integrate them to take advantage of the strongest capabilities of each system.

when the customer's ERP system generates a purchase order, it is passed to the customer's EDI system, where it is converted into a standardized EDI purchase order document and transmitted to the supplier. Upon receipt, the EDI purchase order document would be converted again, this time into the purchase order document format used in the supplier's network, and routed to the supplier's ERP system so the customer order could be fulfilled. Subsequently, the supplier's ERP system would create an invoice document, pass it to the supplier's EDI system for conversion into a standard EDI invoice document, and transmit it to the buyer.

EDI is also used to support *vendor managed inventory (VMI)* arrangements between suppliers (vendors) and customers. In VMI, contractual arrangements are made between a vendor and customer to allow the vendor to monitor customer inventory levels and create purchase orders on behalf of the customer when its supplies run short and need to be replenished.

Additional complexity in a business's ES landscape is created when it chooses to integrate different ESs. A business may use multiple ESs to support its processes, including SCM, CRM, and ERP systems (see Figure 12-12). The systems may be different products from the same ES software vendor, such as SAP or Oracle, or different products from different vendors. Salesforce, one of the most widely used CRM systems, is a fully hosted SaaS service that is often integrated with ERP and SCM systems.

When two or more ESs are integrated, decisions must be made about which ES is responsible for performing specific tasks in a business process. Frequently, a business process task (or the entire process) can be performed by either of the two ESs being integrated. For example, when a CRM system and an ERP system are integrated, either system could be used to create a sales quotation for a customer or to receive a purchase order from a buyer. For efficiency, it does not make sense to require both systems to perform the same task, so the business is faced with choosing which system to use.

Figure 12-13 illustrates some of the overlapping tasks that CRM and ERP systems perform. Because a CRM system is more externally focused on customers than an ERP system, it may make more sense to use it as more of a front-office system to record interactions with customers and receive purchase (sales) orders from customers, while relying on the ERP system for back-office activities, such as managing product inventories, picking/packing/shipping products, and accounting.

However, because both systems have a database, data captured or generated by one of the two systems about a specific purchase order must also be reflected in the other. Also, if master data for a new customer is captured by the CRM system, it must be added to the customer master data in the ERP system. In short, although using the two systems to perform the tasks that each one does best makes sense, the need for them to share data cannot be ignored. And data exchanges between the two ESs must be secure.

ES applications are usually centerpieces of business computing infrastructures. Other important applications, such as warehouse management systems (WMSs), e-commerce, and point-of-sale

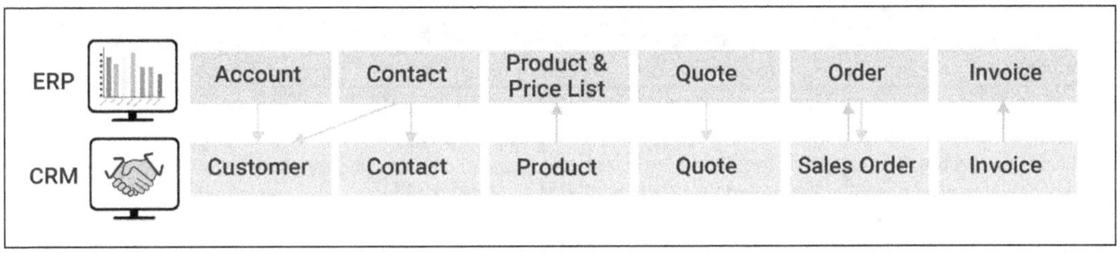

Figure 12-13: An example of overlapping tasks and data for ERP and CRM systems.

(POS) systems, usually interface and share data with enterprise systems. Increasingly, IIoT systems are also being integrated with ERP and other enterprise systems. The fabric of interconnections and interactions among these systems increases their security challenges.

Organizations running mission-critical applications typically have multiple firewalls deployed across the network. They protect the infrastructure and provide a basic level of security for all applications. However, ESs and other mission-critical applications are often so complex that specialized processes and technologies are needed to adequately protect them.

12.2.4 ES Application Threats and Defenses

Variations in ES deployment, the interorganizational nature of ES applications, and the integration of different types of enterprise systems create security challenges. As mentioned earlier, ES applications are often considered to be enterprise network "crown jewels." Increasing use of cloud infrastructure in ES deployments increases the exposure of these crown jewels to the world outside the organization. Today, most ESs are mobile-enabled applications, and many are deployed in integrated multi-cloud environments and accessed via untrusted networks, including the public Internet.

ES Threats

Considering their current deployment realities, ES and other business applications face numerous threats. Some of the most common threats are identified and briefly described in Table 12-7.

Table 12-7: Examples of ES application security threats.

ES Threat	Description
Insider threats	Because ES applications are mission-critical and are often used enterprise-wide, they are typically accessed and used by a wide range of employees. This means that ESs are susceptible to insider threats (described in Chapter 11) and malicious employees. Users are authorized to use the ES application to perform specific tasks. In the absence of appropriate controls, users may try to escalate their access/use privileges to perform tasks or access resources for which they are not authorized. These risks are more significant for ES users with specialized authorizations, such as developers and system administrators. Adopting and enforcing least access privilege policies is one way to combat insider threats.
Compromised accounts or credentials	Single sign-on (SSO) mechanisms are often used to authenticate ES users. If an attacker succeeds in stealing or compromising the credentials of an ES user, they can access the ES application and leverage the privileges associated with the user's credentials. If attackers compromise the credentials of users with extensive privileges, such as developers or system admins, their ability to escalate their attack on the ES system is facilitated. Least access privileges can combat this, but distributed IDSs/IPSs and lateral movement controls are also important.
Business partner and vendor access	Businesses often provide VPN connections to enable business partners, vendors, and external consultants or contractors to access ES applications. Also, the mission-critical nature of ES applications usually requires them to be constantly accessible by ES vendors for technical support or to enable them to monitor the status of the technologies that support applications. Such external accessibility presents potential vulnerabilities and risks that should be monitored. Outsiders with access privileges should be authenticated prior to being granted access to the ES.

Table 12-7, Continued.	
ES Threat	**Description**
Mobile-enabled apps	Most ES applications support mobile access. SAP's Fiori® interface is an example of the company's attempt to make its applications mobile-friendly. Mobile enablement, however, can expand an application's attack surface to include the mobile devices on which it runs. If the mobile device is lost, stolen, misplaced, or compromised, unauthorized access to the application may be possible. To combat this, MDM and EMM security procedures should include the ability to track, isolate, lock, and wipe devices used to access ES applications; they should also include the ability to push OS, application, and security updates to the devices.
Internet-facing applications	Because many ES applications are interorganizational, mission-critical, and increasingly reliant on cloud infrastructure, their attack surfaces and associated security risks can be greater than those of other applications. As they become increasingly Internet-facing, attackers are viewing ESs as potential entry points to enterprise networks. In 2016, the United States Computer Emergency Readiness Team (US-CERT) began issuing alerts about cyberattacks on SAP applications, and it has since issued critical vulnerability alerts for different parts of SAP software architecture.

ES Security Controls

Firewalls are typically liberally deployed to protect ES applications from malware and malicious intrusion. Also, ES data passed between business partners or integrated ES applications is usually encrypted. However, with increasing ES application reliance on cloud infrastructure, cloud security mechanisms are common. Security controls used at the perimeter, internal network, and endpoint layers of DiD also have roles in ES application security.

Specialized technologies, such as SAProuter and SNC, that understand how ES applications interact with other networks and applications are used to provide additional ES defenses. Role- and attribute-based access controls are also common.

SAProuter and Secure Network Communications (SNC)

SAProuter is an application that enables access to SAP applications in private business networks via the Internet or other untrusted networks. It is usually installed in a firewall on the edge of the corporate network and serves as a proxy for network connections between SAP systems in different businesses (see Figure 12-14) or between an SAP system and an external network.

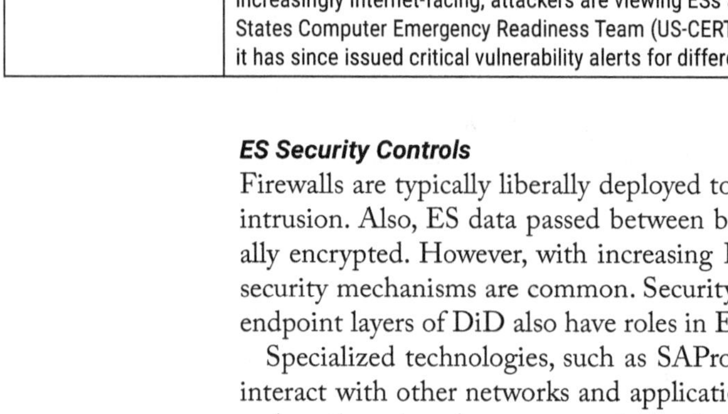

Figure 12-14: A high-level depiction of SAProuter.

Basically, SAProuter functions as an extra firewall in an existing firewall that has a router port that serves as a gateway through which connections to the firewall-protected SAP system can be opened. Allowed connections are specified in a *route permission table.*

Some businesses include SAProuter in DMZ networks to enable authorized business partners to connect to the SAP systems in their private networks (see Figure 12-15). SAP Web Dispatcher may also be placed in an organization's DMZ network. *SAP Web Dispatcher* serves as an entry point for HTTPS requests to SAP servers in the private network. As a software switch, it can accept or reject connections. When connections are accepted, it can function as a load balancer that distributes the requests to the organization's SAP servers.

SAP's *Secure Network Communications (SNC)* provides application-level, end-to-end security between two SNC-enabled communication partners. SNC is a software layer in the SAP software architecture that provides secure communications between two SNC-protected SAP system components, such as an SAPGUI client and an SAP application server. SNC can be used to authenticate the identities of communication partners, detect changes to data passed between communication endpoints, and encrypt messages exchanged between the two endpoints.

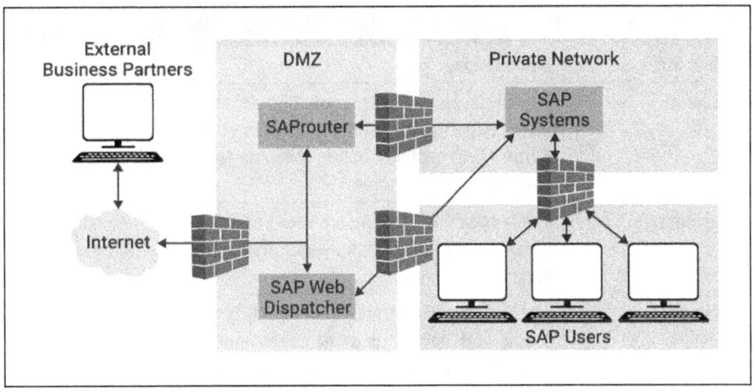

Figure 12-15: Businesses may locate SAProuter in DMZ networks to facilitate connections with business partners.

SAProuter, SAP Web Dispatcher, and SNC are examples of security elements in SAP system architectures that contribute to the integrity of SAP ES applications. Similar security defenses are included in ES products from other vendors. Regardless of the vendor, like other applications, these applications need to be secured. If they are misconfigured, outdated, or unpatched, they can be exploitable vulnerabilities.

Role- and Attribute-Based Access Controls

As noted in Chapter 11, identity and access management (IAM) is a security defense in most business networks. IAM strives to ensure that only authorized people and devices are permitted to access specific applications and data.

Many IAM systems use a method called role-based access control (RBAC) to assign user permissions to applications and other network resources in a manner that aligns with the organization's structure and the user's responsibilities. Most large businesses use RBAC to assign varying levels of access to their employees based on their job responsibilities. It is designed to protect sensitive data and ensure employees can only access information and perform actions required to do their jobs.

Basically, **role-based access control (RBAC)** is a method of restricting network access based on the roles of individual users within an enterprise. It can restrict a network user's actions and access to data using criteria such as business unit or department, position (job title), and authority level. For example, RBAC can be configured to enable HR employees to view employee records but restrict them from viewing customer data. It might also be used to allow an HR manager to modify or delete employee records, while a lower level HR specialist would only be able to view them.

With RBAC, each individual user is assigned one or more roles, and privileges are assigned to each role. Role categories, such as employee, contractor, business partner, etc., can be specified, with each specified role within those categories having predefined permissions. When an individual's functions or responsibilities change (for example, from being promoted or transferred), that person is assigned a new role in the RBAC system.

In RBAC, a "role" is a collection of user permissions. In a typical organization, functions and activities associated with roles (such as HR specialist) don't change as frequently as the identities of the individuals who serve in those roles. Permissions enable access to objects (e.g., network data or resources) and the ability to perform specific actions (e.g., read, modify, create, delete). Within RBAC, there are both permission and role hierarchies (see Figure 12-16).

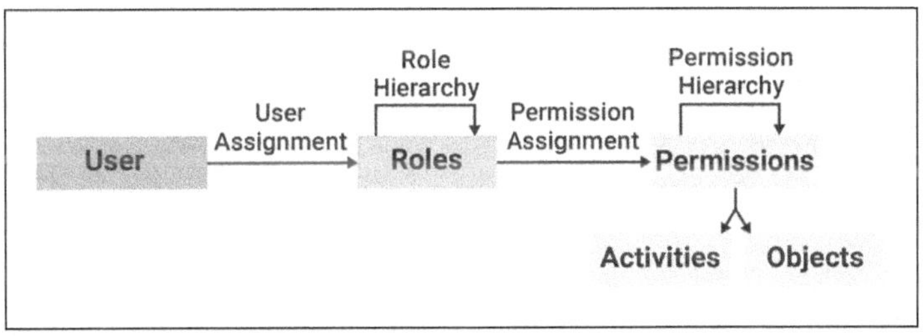

Figure 12-16: A high-level depiction of role-based access control (RBAC).

Table 12-8: ABAC elements.

Attribute	Description
Subject	The *subject* is the user requesting access to a resource. Subject attributes include user ID, job titles or roles, group memberships, departmental and organizational memberships, management levels, security clearances, and other identifying criteria. Some ABAC systems obtain this data from an HR system or directory, while others collect subject attributes from authentication tokens during login.
Resource	The *resource* is the network asset or object (such as an application, server, file, or API) that the subject wants to access. Resource attributes include identifying characteristics such as file creation date, file owner, file name, file type, and data sensitivity.
Action	The *action* is what the user (subject) is trying to do with the resource. Common action attributes include "read," "write," "edit," "copy," and "delete." In some cases, multiple attributes may describe an action. For example, an online banking action might have the characteristics "action type = transfer" and "amount = $200."
Environment	The *environment* is the broader context of the access request. Environmental attributes address contextual factors like location, time of day, subject's device, communication protocol, and encryption strength. Contextual attributes can also include preestablished risk signals, such as authentication strength and the subject's normal behavior patterns.

ES applications often combine RBAC with attribute-based access control (ABAC). **Attribute-based access control (ABAC)** is an authorization process that evaluates attributes (characteristics) of user attempts to access network resources instead of solely relying on roles. It is designed to protect objects such as data, network equipment, and other network resources from unauthorized users and actions. Users or actions are unauthorized when they lack characteristics that are "approved" by the organization's security policies.

Setting up and maintaining ABAC is more complex than RBAC but provides more granular security for network resources. With ABAC, access decisions are based on the attributes of the subject, resource, action, and environment involved in an access event. They are briefly described in Table 12-8.

Figure 12-17 provides an example of how ABAC might be applied to a particular user who wants to access sensitive data.

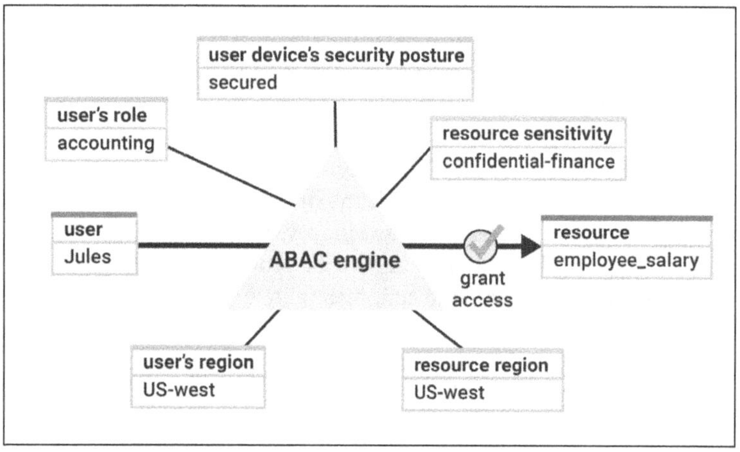

Figure 12-17: An example of attribute-based access control (ABAC).

SAP access controls use RBAC as the foundation of their access policies. However, they also use ABAC to control user access to data and transactions by considering the context of the access attempt (who, what, where, when, and how) before allowing or denying access. Combining RBAC and ABAC is illustrated in Figure 12-18.

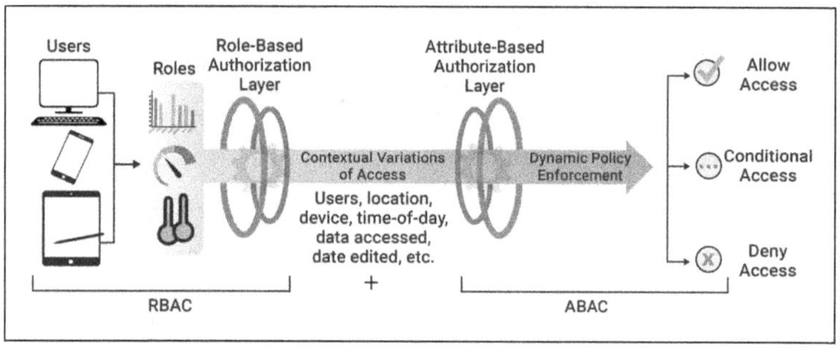

Figure 12-18: SAP access controls combine RBAC and ABAC.

If RBAC and ABAC remind you of elements and processes in zero trust security, that is because they should. Zero trust policy engines typically apply role- and attribute-based factors to users and devices before concluding that they can be trusted and allowed to access a network resource, such as an application or database.

12.2.5 Secure Coding Practices

The functions that software performs can typically be coded in different ways with varying levels of efficiency and complexity. Some coding practices are more secure than others. For example, secure coding practices typically mandate a "default deny" approach to application access. This involves including code that denies access to sensitive data and resources unless a user or device can verify that they are authorized to access the data or resources.

Software developers are increasingly expected to follow secure coding practices to reduce the chances of application vulnerabilities that hackers can exploit. Secure coding standards govern the coding practices, techniques, and decisions that developers make while building software. They are designed to help developers write code in ways that minimize security vulnerabilities; they encourage software engineers and developers to write safe program code.

Several secure coding standards and coding security guides are widely used. They include the *Open Web Application Security Project (OWASP) Secure Coding Practices* and the *Software Engineering Institute and Computer Emergency Response Team (SEI CERT) Coding Standards.*

OWASP monitors and lists common software vulnerabilities to make sure software engineers and developers are aware of the vulnerabilities malicious actors are trying to exploit. Their common vulnerabilities list is periodically updated. Table 12-9 summarizes the OWASP 2021 common vulnerabilities list.

OWASP's secure coding guidelines strive to assist software engineers and developers in adhering to secure coding practices. They are arranged in sections, with specific guidelines identified in each section. Table 12-9 identifies the major sections of OWASP's secure coding guidelines.

Specific recommendations are made in each section to ensure that software engineers and developers have detailed guidance for securing applications. Table 12-10 illustrates checklist items for secure communications from the Sensitive Information Storage or Transmission section of the OWASP secure coding guidelines.

OWASP secure coding practices focus on input validation, authentication, authorization, communication session management, the transmission and storage of sensitive data, configuration management, database security, file management, and memory management (to protect against fileless malware). This can be observed in Table 12-11.

Table 12-9: The 2021 OWASP lists of common software vulnerabilities and securing coding practices sections.

Common Software Vulnerabilities	Secure Coding Guidelines Sections
Broken access control	Data Validation
Cryptographic failures	Authentication and Password Management
Injection	Authorization and Access Management
Insecure design	Session Management
Security misconfiguration	Sensitive Information Storage or Transmission
Vulnerable outdated components	System Configuration Management
Identification and authentication failures	General Coding Practices
Software and data integrity failures	Database Security
Security logging and monitoring failures	File Management
Server-side request forgery	Memory Management

Table 12-10: Communication security checklist items for securing web applications.
Communication Security Checklist
Implement encryption for the transmission of all sensitive information. This should include TLS for protecting the connection and may be supplemented by discrete encryption of sensitive files or non-HTTPS-based connections.
TLS certificates should be valid and have the correct domain name, not be expired, and be installed with intermediate certificates when required.
Failed TLS connections should not fall back to an insecure connection.
Utilize TLS connections for all content requiring authenticated access and for all other sensitive information.
Utilize TLS connections to external systems that involve sensitive information or functions.
Utilize a single standard TLS implementation that is configured appropriately.
Specify character encodings for all connections.
Source: OWASP

Table 12-11: Examples of OWASP secure coding practices.

Secure coding technique	Description
Input validation	Applications should properly validate input and only accept input from known and trusted sources. Input that cannot be validated or that comes from sources that cannot be authenticated or trusted should not be processed.
Error handling	Applications should include appropriate error handling routines. Error messages should not cause detailed system information to be revealed. Error handling mechanisms should not impair security mechanisms, crash the system, or deny service.
Authentication and authorization	Application users and the developers/coders that modify an application should invariably be authenticated and verified as having appropriate rights to use or modify the application. Multifactor authentication should be used.
Access control	Access to applications should be based on role, affiliation, or membership, rather than individual credentials, whenever possible. Role-based access is especially important for ES applications. Access decisions for both developers and users should be biased toward permission rather than exclusion. Users and developers should only be assigned the access privileges they legitimately need based on the "principle of least privilege."
Encryption	Inputs and outputs of applications that maintain, process, transmit, or store sensitive data should be encrypted. Whenever possible, secure communication protocols (e.g., HTTPS) and communication channels (e.g., VPNs) should be used for data in motion (DIM). Also, encrypt data at rest (DAR).
Communication session management	Session tokens should be used for client-server communications, and new tokens should be required for each session. Only use HTTPS for session token communication, and do not include session identifiers in URLs.
Logging	Whenever possible, ensure that application use is logged. Maintain logs for all user accesses, including time of access and access duration. Leverage log files to identify anomalous use.
Code management	Implement and maintain application change management processes, including version control processes, that document application modifications. Include comments in the program code to document all changes and (re)design decisions.
Vulnerability management	Patch applications and/or application components for known security vulnerabilities as soon as the vulnerabilities are discovered. Test all patches/updates to ensure that they do not adversely affect application functionality.
Quality assurance	Utilize quality assurance techniques (such as source code audits, application scanning and auditing, and penetration testing) to identify and eliminate vulnerabilities prior to placing application code changes in production.
Application and web firewalls	Use application and web application firewalls. *Application firewalls* use predefined policies and rules to monitor and block suspicious incoming requests or systems calls. *Web application firewalls (WAFs)* are application firewalls that protect web apps by filtering, monitoring, and blocking any malicious HTTP/HTTPS traffic sent to the application; they also prevent unauthorized data from exiting the app.
Runtime monitoring	Monitoring applications while they are executing can alert security personnel to anomalous behavior of the software and/or anomalous application use by users. When anomalous behavior is detected, the application should be isolated or quarantined before other applications are affected. Service- and/or microservice-level runtime monitoring also should be used.

Table 12-12: Examples of secure coding best practices.	
Best Practice	**Description**
Security by design	Security by design means that application security is a priority throughout the software engineering/development process. The code that is developed should be analyzed, tested, and modified throughout the software development life cycle to minimize vulnerabilities and potential costs associated with insecure application code.
Password management	Passwords continue to be the most widely used security credential, even though they are often weak points in software systems. OWASP and SEI CERT secure coding practices include requirements for sufficient password length and complexity to withstand common attacks. MFA authentication and storing passwords as cryptographic hashes are also recommended.
"Default deny"	Access to secure data should only be permitted to users who need it, and their privileges should be limited. Access should be denied to any user or device that cannot be authenticated or demonstrate authorization. All requests for sensitive information should be checked to verify that the request is from an authorized user.
Error handling and logging	Software errors are often indicative of bugs, and bugs can cause vulnerabilities. Error handling strives to catch errors in the application code before they result in software failures. Error logs help developers to diagnose and fix what is causing errors and help software engineers and developers to comply with secure coding standards. Documenting and logging all failures, exceptions, and errors should be implemented on trusted compilers and systems.
System configuration	This involves ensuring that the application does not include unnecessary components and that necessary components are updated with current versions and patches. Outdated software is a major source of application vulnerabilities. Ensuring that updates and security patches are installed in a timely manner is an important part of secure coding practices.
Threat modeling	Threat modeling includes documenting, identifying, addressing, and validating application threats. This should be done throughout the software development life cycle, especially during testing and after the code is placed in the production environment. New threats continually emerge, and the vulnerability of applications should be continually assessed.
Cryptographic practices	Encrypting data in transit and at rest with strong cryptographic algorithms and following secure key management best practices contributes to the security of application code in the event of a security breach.
Input validation	This involves identifying and validating all data inputs and sources, especially those from untrusted networks, such as the Internet.
Sanitizing outputs	Application outputs, especially those sent to client devices, should be "clean" and devoid of malware. Applications should not contribute to the spread of malicious code. Data sent from one software system to another should be clean and encrypted while in transit.
Defense in depth	Layered defenses for applications help to protect them from malicious actors. Application layer firewalls and stateful packet inspection can help secure distributed client-server applications. Secure communication protocols can help ensure that messages and data exchanged between devices are protected. MFA and other authorization and access controls can provide additional layers of application security.

The SEI CERT Coding Standards complement the OWASP guidelines. Like the OWASP guidelines, the SEI CERT secure coding practices incorporate and build on the fundamental application controls identified in Tables 12-5 and 12-6. Considering both sets of recommendations enables several secure coding best practices to be identified (see Table 12-12).

Secure software is valuable because it is likely to continue to operate normally even when subject to malicious attacks. It contributes to network availability and business continuity by minimizing the chances of supported applications causing network disruptions. Cybersecurity experts estimate that approximately 90% of software security problems are caused by coding flaws or errors. Minimizing coding errors and software deficiencies that cause exploitable vulnerabilities makes sense.

Data validation and handling is an important aspect of secure coding practices. The data layer of DiD encompasses a wide range of data defenses beyond the data protections provided at the other layers.

12.3 DATA SECURITY

Data, especially sensitive data, is typically the ultimate target of enterprise network attacks. **Sensitive data** is confidential information that must be kept safe and out of reach from anyone who does not have permission to access it. Sensitive data includes private information that should be protected from third-party access. It is data that must be protected from unauthorized access to safeguard the privacy or security of an individual or organization. Unauthorized sensitive data exposure can result in financial losses, compromised security, loss of privacy, or diminished competitive advantage.

Extra security should be provided for sensitive data, and this is one of the reasons why data security defenses are located at the innermost layer of DiD. The rationale is easy to understand—require attackers to penetrate multiple layers of security defenses before they can get to valuable business data. If attackers succeed in reaching this DiD level, they are likely to encounter other data defenses, especially for sensitive data.

12.3.1 Data Threats

There are various ways to classify threats and vulnerabilities to enterprise network data, including those identified in Table 12-13.

Data threats may also be classified as technical or nontechnical. Examples of technical data threats are identified in Table 12-14. Table 12-15 identifies examples of nontechnical data threats.

Table 12-13: Data threat categories.

Threat Category	Description
Hardware vulnerabilities	This includes unencrypted data or unprotected storage hardware. Today, hardware vendors routinely deploy digital certificates and managed PKI to protect hardware devices. MDM, EMM, and UEM security mechanisms are also used to protect mobile devices and other network endpoints.
Software threats	Applications and device operating systems have numerous vulnerabilities that require continual assessment and robust patch management practices. The complexity of enterprise systems and other critical applications and systems warrants special attention. Secure coding practices should be required.
Network risks	Unencrypted data transfers between enterprise network components should be rarely or never allowed. Secure communication protocols should be used for all internal and external data transfers. Regular vulnerability scanning should be used to identify and address known vulnerabilities.
Cyberattacks	Exploitation of hardware, software, or network vulnerabilities can expose data and open the door to cybercrime and disruptions to business operations. Unmonitored systems with known security vulnerabilities are prime targets for attackers. Those that use weak encryption keys or outdated ciphers, and those with expired certificates, are especially vulnerable.

Table 12-14: Examples of technical data threats.

Data Threat	Description
Hacking	Hacking refers to unauthorized access to a computer or a network. It is a multi-billion-dollar industry for cybercriminals that incentivizes them to extract data for monetary or political gains. Hackers use a variety of ways to gain access to networks or computers. Some are straightforward, such as guessing a user's passwords, while others are more intricate, such as altering the system's security settings or configuration.
Cracking	Cracking involves the reverse engineering of software, passwords, or encryption to provide unauthorized access to systems or sensitive information. It is considered a form of hacking.
Malware	Malware, especially that used to steal, exfiltrate data, or gain access to a computer system or network to destroy, modify, or compromise data and information, is a significant risk.
Misuse	Employees may take advantage of entrusted resources or privileges for malicious or unintended purposes. Included in this category is abuse of administrative privileges and attempts to access and use nonauthorized network assets. These actions may or may not be driven by malicious intent but pose data risks in either case.

Table 12-14, Continued.

Data Threat	Description
Errors	Errors in device configurations or software code can enable unauthorized data access by cybercriminals. Software errors may be due to faulty programming or nonadherence to secure coding practices. Device hardening can help secure a device even when its configuration is faulty.
Data leakage	Data leakage may result from unintended or unauthorized electronic or physical transmission of data or information between enterprise network components or from within a company data source to an external destination or recipient. There can be big problems when leaked data gets in the wrong hands.
Cloud computing	Lax access controls or storing sensitive data in an unencrypted form can make data stored in the cloud vulnerable to improper disclosure. With the growing reliance on cloud infrastructure, especially for data storage, this should not happen.
Mobile devices	Mobile devices that carry or have access to sensitive data can be lost, misplaced, or stolen. This has the potential to cause corporate data to fall into the wrong hands. MDM, EMM, and UEM security should include the ability to wipe or lock mobile devices that employees use to perform their jobs.
Availability attacks	Availability attacks designed to extort or damage businesses threaten the availability and use of corporate data. Websites and other online assets should be protected from DoS and other availability attacks.
APTs	The goal of most APTs is to access corporate data. Lateral movement controls can help protect data from APTs.
Third parties	Cybercriminals may use third-party and service provider login credentials or networks as an initial access point into a company's network. Acquisition of a contractor's login credentials enabled the exfiltration of the payment card data of Target customers in 2013.
Ransomware attacks	Ransomware attacks target corporate or personal data. The malware can prevent authorized users from accessing files, applications, or networks and demand a ransom payment for restored access. They can cause costly disruptions to business operations and the loss of critical data or information. Ransomware can encrypt files and folders on local drives, attached drives, and even virtual drives. Users are often unaware of ransomware infections until they cannot access data or they see messages that demand ransom payments.

Table 12-15: Examples of nontechnical data threats.

Data Threat	Description
Physical threats	These include theft, tampering, snooping, sabotage, and vandalism that lead to modification, destruction, or loss of data or information.
Environmental threats	Natural events such as tornadoes, power loss, fires, and floods pose hazards to the facilities that house data assets. Terrorist attacks and man-made catastrophes also pose threats to business data.
Insider threats	Employees, contractors, or business partners can engage in espionage, fraud, theft of intellectual property, or attempts to steal, modify, or destroy data.
Social media	Employees may fall victim to scams or reveal data and information that should not be made public on social media.
Social engineering	Attackers may trick authorized users into revealing their login or account credentials.
Dumpster diving	Improper disposal of storage media that holds sensitive data can lead to leakage of sensitive data and information. Businesses should have appropriate procedures for disposing of storage media used to store sensitive data and information to ensure that it does not fall into the wrong hands.

Data Theft and Exfiltration

Data theft can be defined as the act of stealing data and information stored in corporate databases, devices, and servers. It is a significant risk for businesses of all sizes, and the threat can originate both outside and inside an organization.

Data exfiltration (also known as *data extrusion*, *data exportation*, or *data leakage*) is the unauthorized removal or movement of any data from a device or network. This includes unauthorized copying, transfer, or exportation of data. Data exfiltration is usually considered to be a type of data theft. It may be the result of a person manually accessing a computer or network, but today it is more commonly an automated process caused by a malware infection.

Passwords and login credentials, bank account or payment card information, personal identity information (such as Social Security numbers and healthcare records), and other types of sensitive data are common targets of data exfiltration.

Data exfiltration attempts can be challenging to detect because they often resemble ordinary network activity, such as accessing accounts within a network or copying and uploading data to an external source. The 2013 data breach at Target that exposed credit and debit card information for millions of customers is usually considered an example of data exfiltration.

Data Modification and Destruction Attacks

Data modification and data destruction attacks are other threats to enterprise network data. A **data modification attack** is a type of attack in which the perpetrator edits or changes data in a database or computer system to gain unauthorized access or to manipulate data.

Data destruction attacks involve the intentional destruction of data to paralyze business operations. When they are successful, data destruction is likely to render stored data unrecoverable by forensic techniques through overwriting the files or data on storage media.

In 2012, the world's largest oil producer, the Saudi company Aramco, was forced to shut down operations following a devastating virus infection that erased data from tens of thousands of network devices; nearly 75% of its devices were affected. The virus (worm) was traced to a rogue employee who uploaded the malware from a USB drive.

Data in Use Threats

Data in use (DIU), or in memory, may include sensitive data, such as digital certificates, encryption keys, intellectual property (e.g., design data or trade secrets), and personally identifiable information (PII). Hence, if attackers succeed in accessing or compromising DIU, they may be positioned to steal, modify, or destroy sensitive data or information.

In some instances, compromising DIU can help attackers decrypt encrypted data at rest (DAR) or data in motion (DIM). For example, an attacker with access to a server's RAM may be able to parse that memory to find the encryption key for DAR and subsequently use it to decrypt encrypted DAR. Cold boot attacks, malicious hardware devices, rootkits, and bootkits are examples of DIU threats. They are described in Table 12-16.

Positive uses of rootkits should not be overlooked. For example, rootkits are frequently used to enforce digital rights management (DRM) and to prevent copying, modifying, and distributing digital content, such as movies, music, games, and software. Rootkits may also be used to enhance system security by using them to monitor system activity and detect attacks. Rootkits can also

Table 12-16: Examples of data in use (DIU) threats.

Data in Use Attack	Description
Cold boot attack	A *cold boot attack* is a type of attack in which the power supply to a computer is cycled off and on without letting the operating system shut down properly. Dynamic RAM (DRAM) is widely used in today's computers; it is a type of random-access semiconductor memory that stores data bits in memory cells. DRAM cells can retain data, but they must be periodically repowered or rewritten to do so. This property makes it possible for the system to withstand brief power outages without losing DIU. However, this also makes it possible for attackers to steal sensitive DIU, such as encryption keys, because to perform encryption, a software program must first load the encryption key(s) in the computer system's main memory. An attacker with physical access to a running computer typically executes a cold boot attack by cold booting the machine. This is done by cycling the power supply to a computer off and on, without letting the operating system shut down properly, and subsequently booting a lightweight operating system from a USB or removable disk and dumping the contents of memory to a file. Once the attacker has a copy of the computer's memory, they can analyze the dumped data to find encryption keys and other sensitive data.
Malicious hardware devices	*Malicious hardware devices* include CPUs in computing devices (e.g., servers, desktops, laptops, tablets, smartphones) with built-in backdoors that enable attackers to access the CPU. They also enable malware to be loaded that enables access to DIU.

Table 12-16, Continued.	
Data in Use Attack	**Description**
Rootkits	*Rootkits* are malicious software that gives attackers full administrator rights on the computer being attacked. A rootkit creates a backdoor that enable hackers to log in and gain full access to the computer system. Initially, rootkits were developed as legitimate software. Operating system developers included rootkits to provide backdoor access to OS software to fix software issues. Now rootkits are primarily used for illicit purposes. Attackers may plant a rootkit in fake software to gain access to the OS. Alternatively, they may directly attack the OS and install a rootkit after gaining access to the administrator account. The primary goal of the attacker is to gain access to the system without being detected. Gaining full access rights means that attackers can change the device's anti-malware software to ensure that users are not alerted to the rootkit's presence or the presence of other malware, such as spyware or keyloggers.
Bootkits	*Bootkits* are an advanced form of rootkit. They seek to infect the master boot record (MBR) or volume boot record (VBR) or boot sector of the disk that holds the OS to enable a rootkit to be installed on the device before the operating system boots. Because it operates at the kernel level of the OS, a bootkit can be used to find encryption keys stored in the computer's memory that can be used to gain access to encrypted DAR.

provide anti-theft protection by providing backdoor access that device owners can use to access, locate, and wipe data and information if the device is stolen, lost, or misplaced.

12.3.2 Data Security Defenses

As noted in Chapter 11, encryption is widely used to protect data in motion (DIM). Encryption is also used to protect data at rest (DAR). Today, businesses, government agencies, and other institutions are increasing their efforts to protect data in use (DIU) to prevent theft of encryption keys.

Securing Data in Use

Storing encryption keys in CPU registers and enclaves, rather than RAM, is a mechanism used to prevent attackers from exploiting DIU. Storing encryption keys in CPU registers does not protect all DIU, but it does protect servers and other computers against cold boot attacks. When a CPU loses power, the contents of its registers are lost. Hence, by holding encryption keys in registers rather than in memory (DRAM), the keys are better protected.

Enclaves enable data in RAM to be secured by encryption while making the enclave data available as plaintext when it is moved to the CPU and/or CPU cache. Usually, enclave data is encrypted by a key known by a specific CPU to ensure that only that CPU can decrypt the data. This key is sometimes called the *sealing key*. Enclave data capabilities are available in newer generations of CPUs.

Secure Disposal of Storage Technologies

Data destruction by nefarious actors is a data threat. However, it can also be used to safely dispose of storage media that have been used to store sensitive data. Performing safe data destruction can thwart efforts to steal data by dumpster divers. Safe disposal of storage media is called data erasure.

Data erasure (which is also referred to as *data clearing*, *data destruction*, or *data wiping*) is a software-based method of overwriting all electronic data on a hard disk drive or other digital media. It performs an irreversible process that uses zeros and ones to overwrite data on all storage sectors of the device. The goal of data erasure is to destroy data stored on the medium and to make it impossible to recover the original contents.

The procedure makes it impossible to recover data using data recovery software or services. Hence, when an organization plans to replace, sell, donate, or recycle storage devices, data erasure can avoid potential data breaches should the devices reach the hands of threat actors. The process enables the medium to be safely reused or disposed of without revealing its original storage contents or leaking the data that it previously held.

Enterprise Data Rights Management (EDRM)

Data rights management (DRM) technologies focus on controlling the use of digital content. These technologies were originally invented by publishers to protect copyrights for digital media, such as audio, video, and proprietary software. Today, they also are used in conjunction with access controls and data classification to protect enterprise network data, and DRM is considered an additional layer of protection in a DiD architecture to protect DAR, DIM, and DIU.

Rights management technologies use identity, context, and content attributes to control file/document access and use across server and endpoint applications to ensure that they comply with centrally managed security policies. DRM enables organizations (or content owners) to:

- Restrict or prevent users from editing, saving, printing, sharing, or forwarding files, documents, or other digital content
- Disallow users from capturing screenshots or screen grabs of documents, files, or other digital content
- Set an expiration date on a document or media, after which the user will no longer be able to access it
- Restrict access by IP addresses, locations, or devices
- Watermark artworks, documents, and other content to establish ownership and identity

There are two main categories of DRM:

- Consumer DRM focuses on controlling the copying, use (execution), and alteration of media, such as audio, video, e-books, and software.
- Enterprise DRM (EDRM) focuses on protecting enterprise network assets, such as email, documents, and files, by enforcing usage rights policies.

EDRM technology has been around for a while, but its adoption and use surged during the COVID-19 pandemic. EDRM is often considered a combination of IAM and encryption. EDRM-protected content is encrypted, and permissions and privileges (e.g., view, edit, download, save, print, share, forward) are specified for different user groups and users.

User authentication is required to access EDRM-protected documents, files, and content. EDRM provides more robust security and access control than traditional application-oriented IAM mechanisms by ensuring that content is secured independently of application, device, or access location.

EDRM is typically used to protect highly sensitive business documents and emails exchanged or accessed by multiple parties. Commercially sensitive documents, such as product design documents, financial reports, customer information, board of directors memos, and merger and acquisition (M&A) plans, are examples of content protected by EDRM.

In EDRM, a content owner is identified who is empowered to revoke or change access rights or set the expiration date for content sensitivity and/or when access rights can be relaxed or removed. Granular protection is possible and can range from protecting an entire folder or document library to a single file or a specific (e.g., confidential) part of a document or file.

Data Security Controls

Data stored in databases is considered *data at rest (DAR)*. As detailed in Figure 12-19, numerous controls exist for databases and the facilities in which they are housed. They include physical access controls for data centers and data equipment cabinets, such as the controls described in Chapter 11.

Data and Database Access Controls

Authentication, authorization, and other database access controls are used to protect databases (see Figure 12-19). As noted in section 12.2.4, *role-based access control (RBAC)* and *attribute-based access control (ABAC)* are commonly used to protect ES databases. They are also used to protect other databases that include PII, sensitive data, and data that is crucial for business operations.

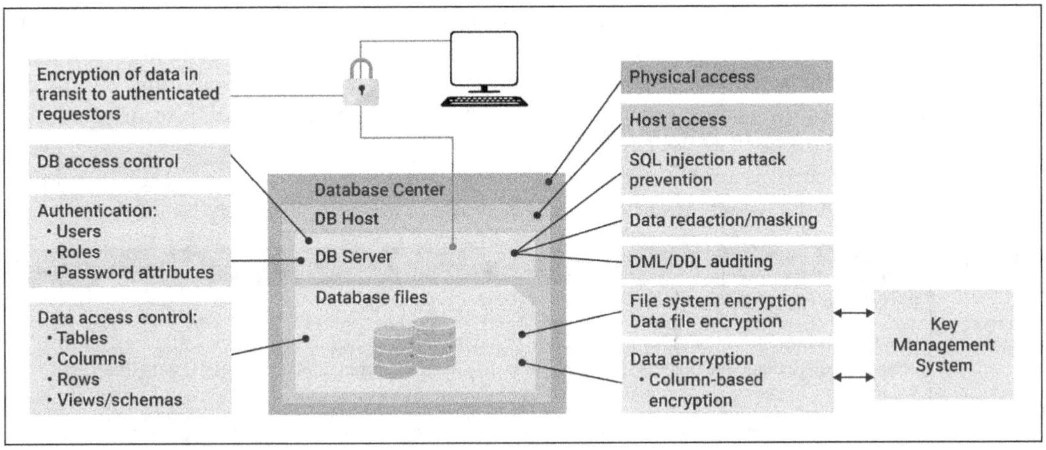

Figure 12-19: Examples of database and data center controls.

Database management systems (DBMSs) also include access controls. **Database access control** (*DB access control*) restricts database access to authorized user groups and individuals. Such restrictions are controlled by database administrators (DBAs) and are deployed to minimize the likelihood of data breaches.

Database access control involves creating user accounts with varying levels of access and use privileges. It also involves controlling the database/DBMS login process to ensure that only authorized users have access to sensitive information. The DBMS can be configured to keep track of all operations performed by individual users while they are logged into the database.

DBAs can create different schemas (logical representations of parts of the database), and users may only be allowed to log into one or a limited range of schemas. This, of course, is designed to limit not only what users see but what they can do. Schemas can be limited to specific database tables and/or to specific attributes (columns) and rows (records) within tables.

Database login processes mirror those used for network access. Database users are usually required to provide a user ID and password to log into the database. Users' authorizations, privileges, and schemas are coupled to the login credentials that they provide.

Authentication is used to verify user identity when someone logs into the database. This is designed to ensure that the user logging in has the rights/privileges to perform specific database activities.

Most users have a limit to their database privileges, and such privileges can be controlled at granular levels. For example, a user may be able to view (read) specific data in specific tables but may not have privileges/rights to modify (update), delete, print, copy, share, or add data to the database.

Data Masking and Redaction

Data masking can be used to protect sensitive data. **Data masking** secures the data by removing sensitive data (e.g., specific attributes in relational database tables) and replacing it with a "mask" that is similar in structure and format but has a different value. This enables the masked data to be used in training or testing without revealing sensitive data to trainees or testers. This is different from column-based encryption, which changes the sensitive data to ciphertext that is unreadable without the decryption key.

Column-based security was one of the first methods to protect sensitive data and ensure that it was not exposed to database users without required privileges. Column-based encryption can be used for data redaction, but other approaches may also be used.

Data redaction is a data masking technique that enables data owners to mask (redact) data by removing or substituting all or part of the field (column) value in a table row. Data redactions are widely used to protect sensitive PII such as Social Security or account numbers.

Redaction typically ensures that user queries return a column value that substitutes/masks the real value of the sensitive attribute. This may involve redacting the entire column and replacing it with a constant. Doing so ensures that a query returns the proper number of columns, but instead of real values, each column value is a constant. For example, to redact a Social Security number (SSN), the result might be "999.99.999" or "###.##.####."

Column-based security is often implemented using data definition language (DDL) and data control language (DCL), which are briefly described in Table 12-17.

Table 12-17: Languages used to implement column-based database security.

Language	Description and Examples
Data definition language (DDL)	DDL is used to create and modify the structure of a database and includes commands that are used to create or delete database objects. Some of the widely used DDL commands are Alter, Create, Drop, and Truncate.
Data control language (DCL)	DCL is used to create roles, permissions, and referential integrity among database tables. It is also used to control access to a database and to secure it. For example, it includes commands such as Grant and Revoke, which are used to allow or restrict access to a database.

Data manipulation language (DML) is another important language used with relational databases. It is used to retrieve, store, modify, delete, insert, and update data in a database. It includes commands, such as Insert, Update, Select, and Delete, that are used to manipulate the data stored in a database.

Because the use of DCL, DDL, and DML has significant effects on database structure, access, content, and use, auditing how these languages are used is an important part of database security. For example, DML auditing enables data owners to audit database reads, updates, inserts, and delete operations, and the results of such audits can help identify malicious activities. DDL audit triggers can be configured to audit all changes to database schema and report the exact changes that were made, when they were made, and which database user made them.

Preventing SQL Injection Attacks

Structured Query Language (SQL) is the most widely used language for relational databases. It is a broad language that includes DML, DDL, and DCL components. SQL is also considered a *data query language (DQL)* and is widely used for database queries. A *query* is a request for data or information from a database table or combination of tables.

Because SQL is used to formulate queries and is supported across a wide range of database products, web and database server SQL injection attacks are potential database threats. According to OWASP, an *SQL injection attack* consists of the insertion or "injection" of an SQL query via input data sent from a client to a web or database server.

When successful, an SQL injection can allow the attacker to read sensitive data or modify the database data (using Insert/Update/Delete commands). Attackers may also succeed in executing administration operations on the database, such as shutting down the DBMS or recovering file contents.

Preventive measures for SQL injection attacks include:

- Limiting the types of queries that users can perform to parameterized queries
- Using only stored procedures for applications (A stored procedure is defined and stored in the database and is called from the application.)
- Using allow-list input validation, and "escaping" all user-supplied input by not allowing user-supplied input to be executed

For example, parameterized queries created by database developers are saved to the database and are available to users to query the database. They restrict the input that users can provide as well as the results that the queries return. Stored procedures also restrict what database users can do and what data they can retrieve.

Data Encryption and Hashing

DAR can also be encrypted, and key management systems can be used to protect encryption keys. Both symmetric and asymmetric encryption may be used for DAR. For sensitive data, encryption should be required instead of optional. This may be done on a wholesale basis, such as encrypting entire drives, files, or databases, but encryption may also be used selectively.

As noted in Figure 12-19, column-based encryption may be used to protect database contents. **Column-based encryption** is a database encryption method that enables data owners to select specific information (attributes) for encryption rather than encrypting an entire database, file, or drive. Since not all attributes (columns) in relational database tables include sensitive data, encrypting specific attributes (columns) can help ensure that truly sensitive data is protected.

Hashing is often used to protect database or network login credentials. **Hashing** involves the use of algorithms that transform an input string into another string, called a *hash value*, that is usually shorter than the original and is ciphertext.

Because the hash value is usually a concentrated summary of the original data, it produces results that are like data compression results. (Data compression is described in Chapter 3.) While hashing is not compression, it can take a larger amount of data and shrink it into a more compact form.

Because hash values are the result of mathematical transformation of original data, hashing is often considered a type of encryption. As Figure 12-20 illustrates, hash codes transform plaintext into hashed text, and that can be considered a type of ciphertext.

If a hacker breaches a database and finds hashed text instead of plaintext login credentials, the hashed text is useless to them unless they have a key to decipher it. SHA-1, SHA-2, and MD5 are popular cryptographic hashes. SHA-2 is shown in Figure 12-20.

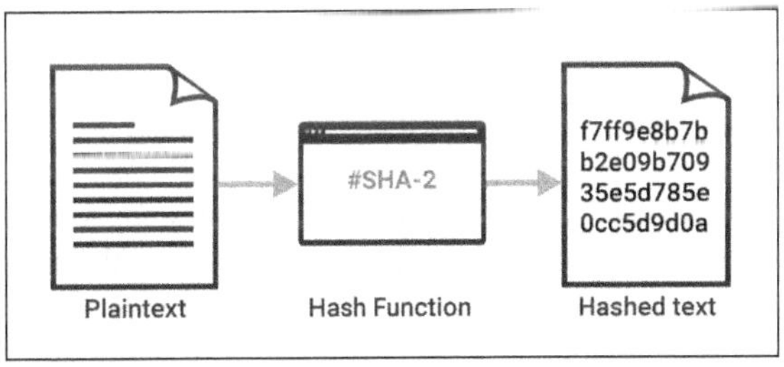

Figure 12-20: A conceptual depiction of hashing.

A good hash function is a unidirectional process that uses a one-way hashing algorithm. Like the one-way functions described in Chapter 11, a hashing algorithm creates hash values that cannot be converted back to the original plaintext using the same algorithm.

In cybersecurity, hash functions are used to create hash values where there is no intention of converting them back to the original plaintext. Figure 12-21 provides an example of how this might be used in a database or network login process.

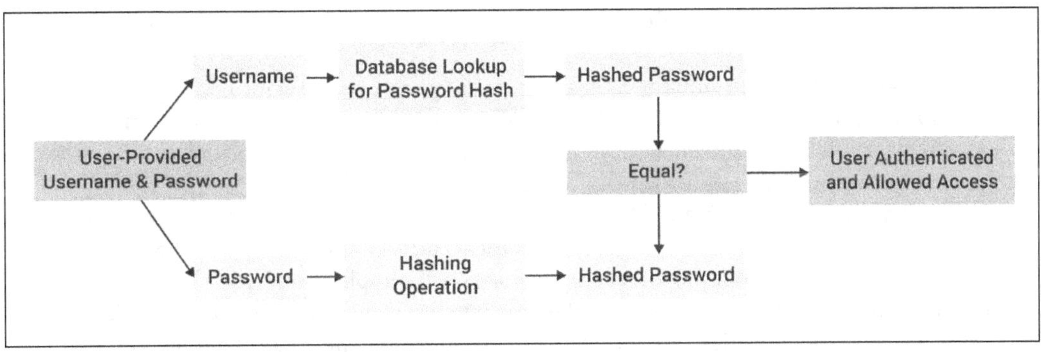

Figure 12-21: Example of how hashing can be used for database or network login and access.

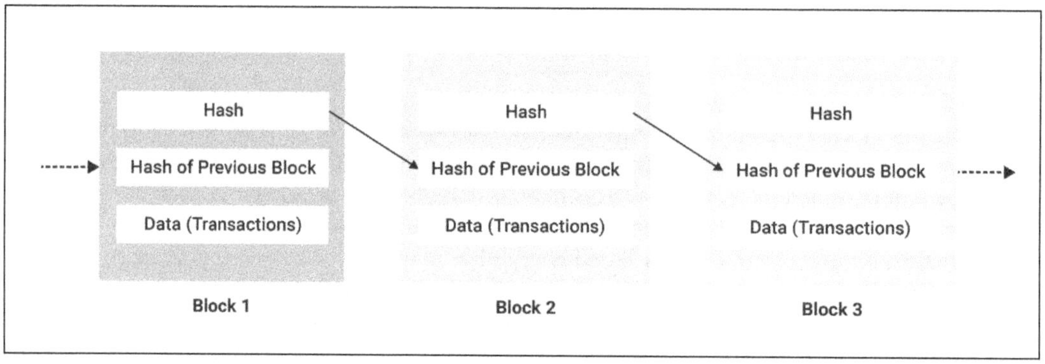

Figure 12-22: Conceptual depiction of how hashing is used to protect data integrity in a blockchain.

In this figure, a user's current password is stored in a database table as a hash value; the user's username (user ID) can be stored in the same table. When the user logs into the database or network, the hashing algorithm used to create the hashed password is applied to the user's password input. If the hash function returns the same result as the hashed password in the database, the user's identity is authenticated, and the user is allowed to access the database or network and exercise their authorized privileges.

As noted in Chapter 3, hashing is also used to protect blockchain databases. In a blockchain, each block of transactions data is hashed and includes a hash of the previous block. This is illustrated in Figure 12-22.

Basically, the hashed values serve as the links between blocks and chain each block to its predecessor and successor in the block sequence. Any changes to data in a block would result in a different hash value for the block and would require each subsequent block to be rehashed. This also means that any attempts to alter data in a block would be visible to all devices in the distributed blockchain network. Hence, attackers, even sophisticated ones, are virtually guaranteed to be detected.

A wide range of defenses can be used at the data layer to make it difficult for attackers to perpetrate malicious activities, even if they succeed in circumventing security controls at all other DiD layers. While data is the usual target of attackers, a wide range of controls are available at the innermost layer of DiD to protect against data exfiltration, modification, or destruction.

SUMMARY

Three layers of DiD have traditionally been considered inside the network perimeter: the endpoint, application, and data layers. The endpoint (host or platform) includes a wide range of devices. Keeping the operating systems and software installed on endpoints patched and up to date continues to be an important aspect of endpoint security to counter malware, zero-day exploits, and other endpoint threats.

Malware, both known and unknown, is a significant threat to network endpoints that comes in various forms, including zero-day malware, fileless malware, and ransomware. Human errors, insider threats, application misuse, and theft are other threats. Browser isolation and sandboxing can be used to prevent malicious code from being executed on endpoints. VAM, EPP, EDR, XDR, endpoint encryption, and HIDS are other endpoint security defenses. Application control also contributes to protecting endpoints. Numerous endpoint security best practices have been identified.

Application controls are examples of security defenses at the application layer of DiD. They include whitelisting authorized applications and blacklisting potentially harmful program code. Application user controls (e.g., identification, authentication, authorization) and data handling controls (e.g., completeness, validity, input, forensic) are examples of fundamental application controls.

A wide range of applications are supported on enterprise networks, and they are often classified in terms of their business importance, network resource usage, and security risks. ES applications are among the applications that are considered mission-critical. Because they are interorganizational, are complex, generate large volumes of data, and are supported by cloud infrastructure, network managers are especially attuned to their security.

SAProuter, SAP Web Dispatcher, and SNC are examples of specialized security technologies for ES applications. RBAC, ABAC, and IAM are widely used, and sometimes combined, to limit ES access and use to authorized users.

Cybersecurity experts estimate that approximately 90% of software security problems are caused by coding errors. Secure coding practices exist and are being more widely used to protect ES and other applications.

OWASP and SEI CERT monitor common software vulnerabilities to ensure software engineers and developers are aware of software flaws that attackers can exploit. They also identify secure coding guidelines, checklists, and best practices to help programmers develop/maintain secure software that is likely to continue to operate normally even when subject to malicious attacks.

Because data, especially sensitive data, is the ultimate target of most attackers, the innermost layer of DiD focuses on data security. The numerous existing data threats include hardware vulnerabilities, software threats, network risks, and cybersecurity attacks. Data threats can be either technical (e.g., hacking, cracking, misuse, and malware) or nontechnical (e.g., physical and environmental). Data theft (exfiltration), data modification, data destruction, and DIU attacks (e.g., cold boot, rootkit, and bootkit attacks) are other data threats.

Storing encryption keys in CPU registers, rather than memory, and enclaves provides protection against DIU attacks. Safely disposing of storage equipment and implementing EDRM are examples of DiD data layer security practices. Data and database access controls, data masking and redaction, and SQL injection prevention mechanisms are widely used to protect enterprise network data. Encrypting data at rest is common, and in some cases, column-based encryption is used to protect sensitive data in database tables. Hashing is commonly used to protect database and network login credentials. Hashing is also used to secure transaction blocks in blockchain databases.

KEY TERMS

Attribute-based access control (ABAC)
Column-based encryption
Database access control
Data destruction attacks
Data exfiltration
Data masking
Data modification attack
Data redaction
Data theft
Endpoint
Endpoint detection and response (EDR)
Extended detection and response (XDR)
Endpoint encryption
Endpoint protection platform (EPP)
Fileless malware
Hashing
Host-based IDS (HIDS)
Ransomware attack
Role-based access control
Sandboxing
Sensitive data
Zero-day vulnerability

REVIEW QUESTIONS

1. The endpoint layer of DiD was once called the host or platform layer. Briefly explain why this layer is now usually called the endpoint layer.
2. Identify examples of network endpoints.
3. Why is malware considered an endpoint threat? What are the differences between known and unknown malware? What are automated malware attacks?
4. What is a zero-day vulnerability? What is a zero-day exploit? What is zero-day malware?
5. What are fileless malware attacks? What are ransomware attacks? Identify examples of other malware threats.
6. Identify and briefly describe security mechanisms used to address endpoints that are stolen, lost, or misplaced.
7. What is VAM? What is endpoint encryption? Briefly explain the role of each of these tools in endpoint security.
8. Briefly explain how browser isolation, sandboxing, and application control contribute to endpoint security.
9. Briefly describe each of the following and its role in endpoint security: EPP, EDR, XDR, and HIDS.
10. Identify examples of endpoint security best practices.
11. Why are enterprise network applications categorized

or prioritized in terms of security risk, resource usage, and application type or purpose?

12. How does application whitelisting differ from blacklisting? Identify several application controls. Also identify several data handling application controls.
13. Identify several characteristics of ES applications that make them complex and challenging to secure.
14. Identify examples of ES application security threats.
15. Briefly describe SAProuter, SAP Web Dispatcher, and SNC and how they contribute to the security of SAP ES applications.
16. Briefly describe the characteristics of RBAC. Also describe the characteristics of ABAC. How are they used in SAP ES security?
17. Briefly explain why businesses are adopting secure coding practices such as those included in OWASP and SEI CERT guidelines.
18. Identify examples of secure coding techniques/practices specified by OWASP.
19. Identify examples of SEI CERT secure coding best practices.
20. What is sensitive data? Why are data and data defenses located at the innermost layer of DiD?
21. Identify examples of data threat categories, technical data threats, and nontechnical data threats.
22. What is data theft? What is data exfiltration? What are the differences between data modification attacks and data destruction attacks?
23. Why is DIU a security risk? Identify examples of DIU attacks. Also identify how DIU can be secured.
24. How does data erasure contribute to safe storage media disposal?
25. What is EDRM? How is it used to protect/secure important/sensitive enterprise data?
26. What are database access controls? How are they deployed and used to protect databases?
27. What is column-based security? What are the differences between data redaction and column-based encryption?
28. How can DML, DDL, and DCL auditing contribute to database security?
29. What are SQL injection attacks? Identify mechanisms used to prevent SQL injection attacks.
30. What is hashing? Briefly explain how hashing is used to protect database or network login credentials and to authenticate database users. Also, briefly explain how hash codes are used to secure blockchains.

PROBLEMS AND EXERCISES

Exercise 12-1 Do some online research on cybersecurity certifications. Identify several cybersecurity certifications that business organizations value and are not too far out of reach for recent university graduates. Describe how each certification can be earned and identify organizations that provide training and/or preparation for certification exams. Identify topics covered in certification training/prep programs and program costs. Summarize your research results in an 8- to 10-slide PowerPoint presentation or a 3- to 5-page Word document.

Exercise 12-2 Do some online research on ethical hacking. Identify examples of ethical hacking. Should vulnerability scanning/assessment be considered a type of ethical hacking? Why or why not? Summarize the results of your research in a 500- to 750-word Word document.

Exercise 12-3 A friend has contacted you for recommendations of endpoint, application, and data security mechanisms for her e-commerce start-up. She wants to ensure that there is adequate protection at each DiD layer for her online company but does not want to get bogged down with security defenses that are overly complicated and could delay the launch of the e-commerce website. Assume you are limited to recommending just two defenses at each layer. Identify the security defenses you would recommend for each layer and provide compelling justification for why each defense should be deployed. Summarize your recommendations in a 5- to 7-slide PowerPoint presentation or a 500- to 1000-word Word document.

Exercise 12-4 Do some research on how to encrypt the hard drive on either a Windows or MacOS laptop. Identify step-by-step instructions, illustrated with screen captures/snips, to describe how users can encrypt the hard drive on their laptop. Summarize the hard drive encryption process in a PowerPoint presentation or Word document.

Exercise 12-5 Do some research on how to encrypt and decrypt individual files on either a Windows or MacOS laptop. Specify the step-by-step instructions that must be followed to encrypt a file, illustrating the steps using a series of screen captures or snips. Also provide step-by-step instructions illustrated with screen shots or snips for decrypting an encrypted file. Summarize the individual file encryption and decryption processes in a PowerPoint presentation or Word file.

Exercise 12-6 Do some research on recent ransomware attacks that have caused significant disruptions to businesses or other organizations. Focus on three recent attacks and identify the victims, suspected perpetrators, suspected causes of the malware infections, and effects of the attacks on the operations of the victimized organizations. Also identify how the organizations recovered from the attacks and the steps they are taking to avoid/prevent future ransomware attacks. Summarize your results in an 8- to 12-slide PowerPoint presentation.

CHAPTER REFERENCES

Aarness, A. (2021). What Is Endpoint Security? How Endpoint Protection Works. CrowdStrike. Retrieved from: https://www.crowdstrike.com/cybersecurity-101/endpoint-security/

Casey, K. (2022). What Is Attribute-Based Access Control (ABAC)? Okta. Retrieved from: https://www.okta.com/blog/2020/09/attribute-based-access-control-abac/

Cloudflare. (n.d.). What Is Browser Isolation? Retrieved from: https://www.cloudflare.com/learning/access-management/what-is-browser-isolation/

Deloitte. (n.d.). Towards Data-Centric Security: Enterprise Digital Rights Management (EDRM). Retrieved from: https://www2.deloitte.com/ch/en/pages/risk/articles/enterprise-digital-rights-management.html

Digicert. (2014). Enterprise Defense from Security Threats, Cyber Attacks, and Data Leakage. Retrieved from: https://www.digicert.com/blog/enterprise-defense-vulnerabilities-cyber-attacks-data-breaches#:~:text=4%20Key%20Areas%20for%20Enterprise%20Data%20Vulnerability%201,susceptible%20to%20vulnerabilities.%20...%204%20Cyber%20Attacks%20

Fortinet. (n.d.). What Is Endpoint Security? How Does It Work? Retrieved from: https://www.fortinet.com/resources/cyberglossary/what-is-endpoint-security

Foster, S. (2020). Security Standards: What Are Securing Coding Standards? Perforce. Retrieved from: https://www.perforce.com/blog/qac/secure-coding-standards

Help Net Security. (2017). Top Threats Impacting Endpoint Security Decisions. Retrieved from: https://www.helpnetsecurity.com/2017/10/27/endpoint-security-decisions/

Hollister, A. (2021). Similarities and Differences Between XDR and SIEM. *Forbes*. Retrieved from: https://www.forbes.com/sites/forbestechcouncil/2021/03/31/similarities-and-differences-between-xdr-and-siem/?sh=5b67602779c1

Imperva. (n.d.). Role-Based Access Control (RBAC). Retrieved from: https://www.imperva.com/learn/data-security/role-based-access-control-rbac/

Kanade, V. (2022). What Is Endpoint Encryption? Definition, Architecture, and Best Practices. Spiceworks. Retrieved from: https://www.spiceworks.com/it-security/network-security/articles/what-is-endpoint-encryption/#:~:text=Endpoint%20encryption%20refers%20to%20data,access%20only%20for%20authorized%20users.

Kanade, V. (2022). What Is Ransomware? Definition, Types, Examples, and Best Practices for Prevention, and Removal. Spiceworks. Retrieved from: https://www.spiceworks.com/it-security/vulnerability-management/articles/what-is-a-ransomware-attack/

Miller, B. (2022). What Is Data Exfiltration? Definition, How to Prevent It & More. Code42. Retrieved from: https://www.code42.com/blog/data-exfiltration/

Perez-Etchegoyen, J. P. (2020). 8 Reasons Perimeter Security Alone Won't Protect Your Crown Jewels. Dark Reading. Retrieved from: https://www.darkreading.com/cloud/8-reasons-perimeter-security-alone-won-t-protect-your-crown-jewels

Polston, V. (2019). What Is Rootkit? MalwareFox. Retrieved from: https://www.malwarefox.com/rootkit/

Popa, M. (2023). Application Control 101: Definition, Features, Benefits, and Best Practices. Heimdal. Retrieved from: https://heimdalsecurity.com/blog/application-control/

SailPoint Technologies. (n.d.). Role-Based Access Control (RBAC) Retrieved from: https://www.sailpoint.com/identity-library/what-is-role-based-access-control/?campaignid=11540240355&adgroupid=107757757170&keyword=&device=c&network=g&utm_source=google&utm_medium=cpc&utm_content=ams-bofu-all&gclid=EAIaIQobChMI0aWz9eet-gIVXhbUAR1hgwKvEAMYASAAEgL0vfD_BwE

Society Insurance. (n.d.). Common Data Threats and Vulnerabilities. Retrieved from: https://societyinsurance.com/blog/common-data-threats-and-vulnerabilities/

Trellix. (n.d.). What Is Endpoint Security? Retrieved from: https://www.trellix.com/en-us/security-awareness/endpoint/what-is-endpoint-security.html

Trellix. (n.d.). What Is Fileless Malware? Retrieved from: https://www.trellix.com/en-us/security-awareness/ransomware/what-is-fileless-malware.html

Verizon. (2022). *2022 Data Breach Investigations Report*. Retrieved from: https://www.verizon.com/business/resources/reports/dbir/

MINICASE: The 2022 Uber Hack and Market-Driven Data Insecurity

Uber was hacked in September 2022. The purported attacker, a teenager, was arrested in London not long after the security breach. The attacker is suspected of using the corporate password of an Uber contractor to breach the tech company's enterprise network. The contractor's credentials enabled the attacker to access several of Uber's internal systems, including internal Slack messages, the dashboard that the company's security researchers use to report bugs and vulnerabilities, and a finance tool for invoices.

Although Uber said that it did not find evidence that user data was compromised by the security incident, the breach nonetheless was an embarrassment for the company, which was often identified as one of the leading big tech companies. More details about the incident are likely to be revealed in expected lawsuits spawned by the breach.

Litigation against the company may be brought by the Federal Trade Commission (FTC) or other government agencies. Class-action lawsuits by customers or shareholders are likely. The lawsuits are likely to focus on the proximate causes of the hack rather than more fundamental questions about why most companies, even Big Tech companies, are susceptible to security breaches.

Like it or not, current economic and political forces incentivize companies to skimp on network security. This puts both personal data and national security at risk. If market incentives do not change, there is little hope of companies ramping up the security of their networks.

High-tech start-up companies often cut corners, which appears to make business sense. In the early days after launch, start-ups are usually focused on building a customer base and growing quickly enough to stay in business when venture capital runs out. Anything not considered essential to business operations and growth is left for later.

Too often, this includes security practices and the creation of a security-focused culture. Money is spent on speed and features rather than security because being underfunded or underfeatured is considered worse than being insecure. The start-up mind-set is often this: security can be improved later, but only if necessary.

To survive and be considered a success, it is important for a start-up to scale to accommodate customers or users. It is also important to improve performance and reliability, especially when high-profile customers demand it. The business focuses on enabling its systems to scale to accommodate hundreds or thousands of employees because it believes it must look and act like an established company. If quick-and-dirty systems built to launch the business still work, and if customers/users don't know what's going on behind the scenes, where is the need to change? Employees are expected/trusted not to spill the beans or to act like chefs who are told to stay in the kitchen.

So, start-ups often lack incentives to upgrade security. Security, after all, is expensive, and it would be time-consuming and costly to rebuild everything from the ground up to ensure security.

This start-up mind-set is not limited to start-ups. Even established companies may think that there is no payoff for investing in security. For example, when Elon Musk was acquiring Twitter to rebrand it as X, former Twitter security chief Peiter Zatko became a whistleblower and accused Twitter of skimping on security.

Basically, both large and small companies fail to sufficiently invest in security because the market doesn't reward them for doing so. This makes it easier for hackers to find network vulnerabilities to exploit and sometimes enables them to access just about anything in the internal network.

Some companies do manage to change their security narrative. Microsoft did so after a now-famous memo from Bill Gates. And Google made its shift to a more robust security culture after being hacked by Chinese attackers in 2010.

The lack of economic and political incentives has profound implications for the security of the vast array of data that different companies have aggregated about the movements and habits of individuals. There are also national security implications. We know that countries are persistently striving to steal as much data as possible to serve their own purposes. China, for example, is especially keen on using its resources to collect data on American citizens and businesses. State-sponsored Chinese hackers are believed to be behind theft of the personal data of U.S. government employees in the U.S. Office of Personnel Management in 2015. They were especially interested in data about individuals with security clearances.

Chinese hackers suspected of working on behalf of China's civilian spy agency were also purportedly responsible for the 2018 theft of data for 500 million guests of the Marriott hotel chain. They are also suspected of stealing data of about 80 million individuals covered by health insurance from Anthem.

In every instance, the victimized organizations could have done a better job protecting data, but the market does not reward companies for robust security. Frequently, it is not easy or feasible for customers to abandon companies with poor security practices because the companies build "digital moats" to lock in users.

If customers don't/can't leave and stock prices recover quickly after security breaches are publicized, there are few incentives to change. According to some economists, this is a classic market failure, where a powerful few can take advantage of the many without fear of reprisal. It is a situation that only government regulation may be able to fix, and where only political will and muscle can make that happen.

Compelling arguments can be made for strong regulations that force organizations to use good security practices. The focus must be on robust and resilient security for the data entrusted to companies by customers, users, and employees.

Government regulation does not need to focus on security lapses like Uber's, which enabled attackers to steal the source code for its phone apps or the internal Slack channel used by employees. Instead, regulations should come down hard on the kind of security flaws that enable attackers to steal data about the rides taken by its 100-million-plus users, especially since this data can reveal unflattering details about rider behaviors or expose them to blackmail or social ridicule.

Start-ups are likely to howl that such regulation will stifle innovation. However, good security isn't incompatible with agility, features, or time to market. Worries that any regulation will somehow quell innovation are overblown.

A smart regulatory regime for security can take a page from successful industry regulations, such as those for banking and financial services, that do not give companies the option to underinvest in security. Also, regulatory requirements can be tailored to the size of the organization, just as small community banks don't have to follow the same level of regulation as a large national bank. Similarly, the preflight security checklist for a single-engine two-seat Cessna is less extensive than that for a jumbo jet.

For tech companies, there is no reason for a small start-up with few customers to be asked to follow the same rules as an Uber or a Twitter. But, as a company becomes larger and more successful, its security requirements should increase because the potential effect of insecurity increases.

In 2020, Russian hackers breached SolarWinds, an Internet infrastructure company. SolarWinds followed the usual trajectory from tech start-up to established company, and the SolarWinds hack was a national security disaster.

The hackers succeeded in accessing the networks of more 18,000 SolarWinds customers, including the Department of Homeland Security, the State Department, and other government agencies. They were able to access the networks of government contractors, IT companies, nuclear research labs, and nongovernmental agencies around the world.

The presence of attackers went undetected for months, and the incident became a poster child for APTs. The market bears responsibility for rewarding poor security practices in the name of short-term profits at SolarWinds and other companies. If the government mandated different practices for its contractors and service providers, things might have turned out differently.

Perhaps the United States is headed in a better direction. In September 2022, at a U.S. Senate Judiciary Committee hearing on "Protecting Americans' Private Information from Hostile Foreign Powers," compelling arguments were made that personal data privacy and security is a matter of national security. While government regulation of data security isn't a panacea, it may serve to align corporate incentives with broader societal goals by making our data safer from hackers and foreign governments.

Minicase Questions

1. Hacker "gangs" and collaboration are becoming more common. Do some research on hacker gangs and collaborative hacking and identify some of the groups that are involved in these endeavors. Also identify examples of their successful hacks.
2. Like the 2013 Target hack, the September 2022 Uber attack involved a hacker who purportedly used the login credentials of a contractor to gain access to the network. Given the different types of security defenses described in this chapter and Chapter 11, what steps could Uber (and Target) have taken to protect business partners' login credentials from being used in this way?
3. Uber's launch was in March 2009, and Twitter started in 2006. Neither can be labeled an immature start-up, and both make billions of dollars from the data they collect on their users. Both, however, have also been criticized for neglecting the security of their networks. One might argue that they value the money they can make from user data more than they value the security of that data. Is this a business failure, a market failure, or a failure of something else altogether? Explain your answer.
4. As noted in the minicase, customers and users are often reluctant or unable to abandon companies with poor data security practices, and when customers don't defect, the companies' lax security is not punished. What steps do you think customers, employees, and stockholders should take to force companies to adopt more robust security practices?
5. The SolarWinds hack is an example of an attack on a private company that had major national security repercussions. Do some research and identify several examples of other attacks on businesses that have posed national security threats. For each security breach, identify the attacker(s), the type of attack, attack impacts, and lessons learned.
6. Government regulation often emerges in response to market failures. Has the time come for the government to regulate data security? Why or why not? Provide compelling arguments for your observations.
7. If you were a federal bureaucrat in charge of developing data security regulations for smaller e-commerce companies, what would be the first five regulations that you would put on the list? Justify each of your listed regulations.

Minicase Reference

Schneier, B. (2022, September 26). The Uber Hack Exposes More Than Failed Data Security. *The New York Times.* Retrieved from: https://www.nytimes.com/2022/09/26/opinion/uber-hack-data.html?searchResultPosition=1

Index

Page numbers in this index greater than 424 reference material in the appendices, which are not included in the print edition. The appendices can be accessed at https://www.prospectpressvt.com/textbooks/case-enterprise-networks

www.ingramcontent.com/pod-product-compliance
Lightning Source LLC
LaVergne TN
LVHW080120011026
849160LV00013B/1139